Ethical Marxism

Series: Creative Marxism
Series Editor: Bill Martin

Volume 1: *Ethical Marxism: The Categorical Imperative of Liberation* by Bill Martin

Volume 2: *Marxism and the Call of the Future: Conversations on Ethics, History, and Politics* by Bob Avakian and Bill Martin

Other books by Bill Martin

SOCIAL THEORY:
Matrix and line: Derrida and the possibilities of postmodern social theory
Politics in the impasse: Explorations in postsecular social theory
Humanism and its aftermath: The shared fate of deconstruction and politics
The radical project: Sartrean investigations
Marxism and the call of the future: Conversations on ethics, history, and politics (with Bob Avakian)

MUSIC:
Music of Yes: Structure and vision in progressive rock
Listening to the future: The time of progressive rock, 1968–1978
Avant rock: Experimental music from the Beatles to Björk

Ethical Marxism

*The Categorical Imperative
of Liberation*

BILL MARTIN

OPEN COURT
Chicago and La Salle, Illinois

Volume 1 in the series Creative Marxism

To order books from Open Court, call 1-800-815-2280 or visit
www.opencourtbooks.com.

Open Court Publishing Company is a division of Carus Publishing Company.

Library of Congress Cataloging-in-Publication Data

Martin, Bill, 1956-
    Ethical marxism : the categorical imperative of liberation / Bill Martin.
        p. cm. — (Creative marxism ; v. 1)
    Summary: "Argues for a revised Marxism that takes ethics rather than
political economy and scientific investigation as its core"—Provided by publisher.
    Includes bibliographical references and index.
    ISBN-13: 978-0-8126-9650-9 (trade paper : alk. paper)
    ISBN-10: 0-8126-9650-6 (trade paper : alk. paper)
    1. Ethics. 2. Political ethics. 3. Economics—Moral and ethical aspects.
4. Socialism. 5. Communism. I. Title.
BJ37.M285 2008
171'.7—dc22
                                                                    2007048667

In Memoriam
Jacques Derrida 1930–2004
teacher and friend

Contents

Preface and Acknowledgments

In many ways this book brings together thoughts that have been percolating in my mind and life for decades. This is my attempt to bring them into systematic focus. Much of my life and thinking comes out of a radical sense of Christianity set against the background of the late 1960s (and in particular all that is invoked, politically and culturally, by simply using the expression—which is more than a year—"1968"). However, I am also fond of saying that, at least for some of us, "the sixties" seems both like yesterday and yet also like a million years ago—so near and so far. And for all that there might still be some energy from the sixties that could still be harnessed and directed toward changing the world of the present, it is also the case that we are in a different time now and we have to take stock of this. We who believe that the present world system is both deeply unjust and ultimately unsustainable (either of itself or, what is more important, of life on our planet) are in the difficult position of needing to learn from and build on the past and yet to apply those lessons to a social system that has as a key imperative to erase history and memory. Some of this goes to what my friend and fellow social theorist, Raymond Lotta, calls "the learning curve of the revolution," but it also goes to the qualitative leaps that capitalism has made especially in the twentieth century, and even in the last few decades.

Radicalized Christianity in the context and shadow of 1968 points toward an engagement with Marx and Marxism, perhaps just as anyone who is seriously committed, and not merely academically committed, to Kant's ethical philosophy is going to have to come to grips with the systemic dimensions of the situations in which this commitment really means something. Indeed, when Alasdair MacIntyre, who as a young person was something of a Marxist, proposes to address contemporary society through the "teleological arguments of an updated Thomistic Aristotelianism," well, that is still one way of describing a certain Marxist project, in my view.

(Right-wing critics of MacIntyre sniff this out readily enough.) But my point is not that all roads lead to Marx. If anything, my argument will be that there is a road toward which Marx stands in an ambiguous and difficult relation; this relation needs to be clarified, and through this process we will find a different sense of what Marxism could be and needs to be. Toward the end of the nineteenth century there was discussion in some circles of "Kantian ethical socialism," especially around the German-Jewish philosopher Herman Cohen. The title of the present book plays on that idea. This book is not meant as an exhaustive "Kant-Marx dialogue," not even remotely, but certainly the possibility of such a dialogue hovers over every page. The larger aim is a contention over what ought to be at the heart of Marxism, and why this matters for how we understand the past and for what we ought to try to do about the present and future.

There is in a sense a "companion" text to the present one, which appears in the same series (Creative Marxism, from Open Court). The book is a series of dialogues with the Maoist leader and theoretician, Bob Avakian—titled, *Marxism and the Call of the Future: Conversations on Ethics, History, and Politics*. The relationship between Marxism and ethics, especially in a Kantian sense, was a constant theme in the conversations. As Avakian characterized the dynamic of our discussion, I was looking for more ethics in his materialism, and he was looking for more materialism in my ethics. Significantly, the other poles of the dynamic are what might be called "science," on the one hand, and "religion," on the other—or what I have chosen to call the "religious perspective." Note that I am using this latter term in a special way. By "religious perspective" I mean the kind of vision that is absolutely necessary for the transformation of society and yet is underdetermined by systematic study of the "social evidence." In terms of modalities, the vision is necessary for the possibility of transformation, but the vision does not represent the necessity of the transformation itself. This characterization I see as a departure from Marx, so it may be said that "Ethical Marxism" is in the range of what can be called "postnecessitarian" and "postinevitablist" Marxisms. On the point about ethics and materialism, I would say it is unlikely that Avakian and I completely agree, and yet our discussion was, I think, politically and philosophically fruitful. I think that we do agree on necessity and its aftermath, so to speak, though perhaps we disagree on what it means to take the full measure of contingency. These questions return throughout the present book. This book and the book of dialogues with Bob Avakian are each meant to stand on their own, but I believe they can be productively read together as well.

The "ethical thread" of Marxism needs to be brought to the fore, and to be seen as the heart of Marxism, *so that* Marxism can do a better job of playing its role in the liberation of humanity and the creation of a global community of mutual flourishing. This book represents an attempt at such a deconstruction and desedimentation.

* * * * *

For sharing their thoughts with me through the process of writing this book, I especially want to thank Bob Avakian, Scott Bontz, Stan Cox, Andrew Cutrofello, David Detmer, Patricia Huntington, Eleanor Kaufman, Raymond Lotta, Martin Matustik, Patrick Murray, Jean Schuler, and Caroline Williams. Although this book emerged from thoughts that have been with me for many years, the specific circumstance that caused me actually to start writing was an assignment from Jennifer Mensch and I thank her for that. My colleagues in our superb Philosophy Department at DePaul University are a constant inspiration, and I thank the starry heavens above, as well as the moral law within, for the privilege of being in their midst. I would especially like to thank three of my senior colleagues, Peg Birmingham, Rick Lee, and Michael Naas, for many excellent conversations on Marxism, ethics, violence, and deconstruction.

Kerri Mommer, my friend and editor at Open Court, has traveled a sometimes very difficult road with me these past several years both on the present project and with *Marxism and the Call of the Future*. All gratitude and respect to you, Kerri, for your patience and forbearance. Thanks as well to Cindy Pineo and David Ramsay Steele at the venerable institution that is Open Court.

All of the arguments in this book, as well as all of the travails in writing it, have been shared with my wonderful life companion, Kathleen League, an incisive thinker who has helped me to improve the thoughts presented here. The chapter on Marxism and the animal question is especially dedicated to my dear Bascenji.

Jacques Derrida was an extraordinarily kind and generous man, and one of the great thinkers of the twentieth century—in a way both avant-garde and yet very classical. I was very fortunate to have known Professor Derrida, and to have studied his work, and even to have studied with him a little. Jacques helped me tremendously at key junctures in my professional and philosophical life, for which I will always remain grateful. Even more I will remain grateful that he stood for many good things; in this book I am trying to carry forward some of those things. The world needs him, and I miss him very much. I will continue to study his work, and I will continue to do what I can to help his work make a difference in the world.

Introduction

Not Simply One Adjective
among Others

Ethical Marxism is a philosophical theory of justice that attempts to show us clearly that we need to overturn the existing society and create new forms of society that are transitional to the global community of mutual flourishing. This theory has its utopian side, but it is not exactly utopian, because it aims to incorporate scientific and political economic investigation to help us understand where the openings are. The theory aims to subordinate strategic thinking to the ethical perspective, but not to eliminate strategic thinking, because to do so would render the ethical dimension into a mere formalism and therefore not capable of helping us do the overwhelmingly ethical things that need to be done.

One of Malcolm Bradbury's pithy academic fictions has the superb title, *Eating People Is Wrong*. As if anyone needed to be told, right? To leap from the (intentionally) ridiculous to the sublime, when the subject of ethics began to go through a revival in Anglo-American analytic philosophy, one argument that was raised, in an Aristotelian vein, was that there are basic ethical questions about which nothing can be said, and that it would itself be a violation of ethics to presume to give an "explanation" as to why it is wrong to do certain things. First of all this is in fact a matter of *situations*, and the insight is that the violation occurs even in the idea that certain situations might become questions, brought into the discursive realm. One example that was raised was the situation where a Nazi death-camp operative is tearing a child away from its mother's arms in order to kill the child by throwing it into an oven. It offends the very idea of the ethical to presume that the Nazi operative might be given an explanation that demonstrates why his action is "wrong." As they say in some circles of analytic philosophy, it does seem there is a powerful "intuition" there. (The cornerstone of this Aristotelian-ethical turn in analytic philosophy is the 1958 essay by G. E. M. Anscombe, "Modern Moral Philosophy.") Richard T. De George provides a similar example in a discussion of the ethics of

capitalism. (Professor De George is one of the founders of the field of business ethics.) He takes up Marx's term, "wage slavery," and asks whether
capitalism can indeed be regarded as a form of slavery. (See *Business Ethics*,
111–32.) As for the ethics of chattel slavery itself, what needs to be discussed? If we know anything at all, surely we *know* that slavery is wrong—
right?

And yet there were Nazis who took babies from their mothers' arms
and threw them into ovens. In my own work I have tried to cultivate (what
I hope is) a healthy skepticism about ethical arguments that hinge on
Hitler and the Nazis to motivate them. These sorts of arguments especially
seem to emanate from the United Kingdom, for reasons that are entirely
understandable, but that also have deep limitations, especially where anything *systemic* or political (in the larger sense of the overall shape of society, of the polis) is concerned. But let us dwell for a moment on what
seems to be the one, perhaps undeniable, strength of arguments of this
sort.

Did the Nazis who exterminated Jews and many others, who committed genocide—did they act because of "reasons"? Did the international
slave trade kidnap hundreds of thousands of people from Africa and press
them into slavery in the Americas because of "reasons"? Are these reasons
that can be answered by other reasons? Doesn't Anscombe have a point in
arguing that this scene could only be considered one of polite disputation
at the expense of giving great offense to the victims?

Marx attempts to give an account of why, to use completely inadequate
language, *bad things* happen. It is a *systemic* account, but ethics (questions
of ethics, the kind of discourse one finds around such questions) seems to
be no part of it. Marx's account explains why "bad things" (horrible
things, though perhaps not *evil* things) happen only insomuch as it
explains why anything and everything happens in society. In fact, however,
there are at least indicators of an implicit ethical terminology in much of
Marx's writing. Many commentators have discussed this, to be sure.
Perhaps one way into the question that has not been tried thus far in the
literature is simply to ask whether it is possible to use a term such as
"exploitation" in a way that factors out all judgment of value and renders
it a purely "scientific" category. (In *Marxism, Morality, and Social Justice*,
R. G. Peffer goes some distance down this road, and makes a convincing
argument for the normative value of the concept of human dignity
throughout Marx's work; see esp. 118–23 and 137–65. I take heart at the
fact that Marx's work is permeated with moral concepts, as Peffer demonstrates overwhelmingly, but my worry here is also the embarrassment that
Marx clearly feels toward such concepts, and the pernicious effect this
rejection of explicitly ethical discourse has had on Marxism in the context
of revolutionary practice.) A more general approach to such a question

would take issue with the "fact/value distinction." Donald Davidson, for instance, has shown that, although there are terms that are more directly "evaluative," there is also an undercurrent of evaluation in all language, and there is no clear line to be drawn between the part of language that concerns "fact" and that part which concerns "value." The critique of this distinction could be said to follow up W. V. Quine's challenge to the analytic/synthetic distinction, and Davidson's challenge to Quine's own "scheme/content" distinction, which Davidson calls a "third dogma of empiricism." Readers familiar with Davidson's work know that these arguments do not lead, for him, to subjectivism, skepticism, or relativism—on the contrary, Davidson argues that the distinctions themselves are "invitations" to subjectivism and the rest.

A more narrowly focused approach to the particularities of exploitation would be to argue that Marx's economic-systemic account is adequate but missing one crucial ingredient. Marx argues that the "dirty little secret" of capitalist exploitation is that the capitalist pays for labor power in the same way that he pays for all other inputs to production: at the "going rate," which is to say the market price. However, all of the other inputs, Marx argues, can only generate as much exchange value for the capitalist as was put into them by a labor process, while the "living labor" of living people can generate more. In paying wages, the capitalist pays for the regeneration of living labor, but he skims off the value (generated by the labor process) that goes beyond what is necessary for paying for the inputs to production. This is what the capitalist calls profit and Marx calls "surplus value." Thus far "Marx 101," and the point is not that there are not many nuances in this process—having to do with the ever-more far-flung nature of the process (into colonialism and imperialism), the class, race, and gender differences inherited from precapitalist formations, the relationship between city and countryside, episodes of "primitive capitalist accumulation" (plunder outright), skilled and unskilled labor, new technologies, and so on—but instead that Marx has explained a general mechanism that describes the general situation as regards those who own and control the means of production and those who only have their labor power to sell. Part of the genius of Marx's conception is that it places main emphasis on this mechanism, which is social and economic, and not first of all something that issues from the intention to exploit people.

I said that this conception is "adequate, but. . . ." I mean "adequate" in a philosophical sense—in other words, this conception is not "merely adequate," but is rather essentially correct and very insightful in its orientation toward the systemic dimension. What is the missing ingredient? To put it crudely but directly, capital is a process of generating surplus value, which means that actual, living and breathing (if sometimes barely) people are *squeezed*, and this squeezing is *wrong*, morally wrong. The people who do the squeezing are also wrong, or at least they are doing something that is wrong, and they ought to be stopped from doing it.

Marx does get around to saying these kinds of things, in so many words, but hardly ever directly, and in some sense the present book revolves around the meaning of this reticence or avoidance, and the meaning and value of, and need for, its overcoming. For Marx, it is not that the mechanism of exploitation *ought* to be stopped, but instead that the mechanism *will* be stopped because there is a wrench in the works—a fundamental contradiction—that is generated by the mechanism itself. In other words, Marx aims for, or presumes to aim for, a purely immanent critique of capitalism. An "Ethical Marxism" would say that "capitalism is based upon exploitation, *and* exploitation is wrong." Marx saw the addition of the moral claim as, at best, pointless, and, at worst, a distraction, an opening to the unnecessary notions of intentionality and responsibility (unnecessary in the sense that Occam's razor would eliminate them as not needed in an adequate account of the phenomenon), and perhaps even an opening to troubling issues of transcendence and something that looks too much like theology. So, again, this book is about how the ethical point, or what I sometimes call the "ethical moment," is indeed needed, and along with it intentionality and responsibility (and agency) and even a discourse that partakes of aspects of transcendence and theology. *Needed*: to understand the world, to change the world, to understand the world *in order to* change it. But these fundamentally Kantian points do not amount to a cancellation of Marx's systemic account, but rather a reorientation and, I argue, a strengthening of that account. By "strengthening" is meant the same thing as with "needed": neither simply as an academic exercise, nor even as an attempt to achieve greater philosophical adequacy under the Marxist paradigm (not that this is not important), but ultimately to help Marxism become a more powerful instrument for guiding humanity in going from an unjust and unsustainable world to a global community of mutual flourishing.

Arguments about ethics are always underdetermined; the gap between *is* and *ought* is never fully closed, never fully systematized. This aporia is intrinsic to what ethics is (or aims to be), and there is no ethics without this aporia: otherwise, people would be acting out of systemic imperatives that allow no space for actual "response-ability," there is no *person* who is responding to a situation that requires an ethical response. In absence of persons who are able to think about right and wrong, a situation will not receive an ethical response—we do not expect such a response from stones, trees, ants, or salamanders (though, in fact, they generally do the right thing!–more often than humans do). This is why we hold (human) parents responsible for the actions of their young children and owners responsible for the actions (which, strictly speaking, are not "actions" in the intentional sense) of their bulldogs. For ethical action a leap is required. It could even be said that ethics is not only about the other, the fundamental regard for the other as Kant conceived it, but also about *distance*. Kant was attempting to grapple with this issue, though not always thematized as such, in some of the "post-Critical" essays that deal with both geographical and temporal distances (for example, "Perpetual Peace," "Idea for a Universal History," "The End of All Things"). The ethical and political implications of these distances are raised especially well in the literary genre of science fiction, for example, in the interaction between "rational beings" from different planets, where the material bases of their different forms of life are not materially connected.

On the other hand, underdetermination (of the other, distance, meaning, or what-have-you) does not cancel the need for *Wissenschaft*—that bothersome German concept by which Marx meant either "science" or "systematicity." Let us just say for the moment that the critique of *scientism* (the philosophical, not "scientific," view that only questions that are answerable—in principle—through scientific investigation are "real" questions) does not lead to the conclusion that we do not need all of the science we can get our hands on. I argue in this book that Marxism needs to resituate the ethical moment at its core, and to assimilate its scientific work, especially work in political economy, to that core. One aspect of this argument is to demonstrate that, in actual revolutionary practice, this resituation is at least implicit in the orientation of the revolutionaries. Again, however, the argument is not that we do not need all of the systematic political economy we can get our hands on. Indeed, there are several areas in which political economy needs to make crucial breakthroughs, but where one can perhaps only see the urgency of the need from an ethical perspective. There needs to be a deepening of the political economy of imperialism and of the transition from colonialism to imperialism. The urgency of this undertaking is seen not only in the need to understand the factors that have led to the present (and developing) global situation, but also—and I would say centrally—from the ethical thematics of loss, tragedy, memory, and redemption that must guide the creation of a new society that truly "transcends the narrow horizon of bourgeois right" (to quote Marx's memorable phrase from *Critique of the Gotha Programme*).

The flip side of this coin—and it is important that the emerging world configuration be seen as such (even if perhaps not only as such, and certainly not as necessarily or predictably as such)—is the need for a deepening of the political economy of new technologies, especially technologies that employ computers and cybernetics, as well as something closely related to these new technologies, what I call, following Fredric Jameson, "postmodern capitalism." Among the elements that Jameson identifies with the emerging postmodern culture of the last few decades are (what he calls) the "loss of affect," the increasing difficulty of "cognitive mapping" (whereby a person locates her- or himself in historical, economic, or even geographic matrices—or, in this case, fails to accomplish such location), the completion of a process of modernization of the arts (whereby the arts are brought fully into the machine age), and the qualitative effects on consciousness wrought by several generations of settling into "consumer society" in the United States and other "advanced capitalist" countries.

Taken together, these two, interrelated aspects of the two sides of contemporary capitalism are the new economies of exploitation and false consciousness, with the latter becoming something like "commodity *hyper*-fetishism." This is why the notion of the "flip side of the coin" is crucial, because the new economic forms remain extensions of the material base created by colonialism and imperialism, even if these extensions have now taken some qualitatively new forms—because, in part, these forms themselves play the role of obscuring (as with commodity fetishism in its more classical form) the value creation process. In postmodern capitalism, however, the big capitalists themselves bring about this obscurantism more consciously (a point which goes to ethical questions). Today's capitalist (I mean one of the "top capitalists," a member of the grand bourgeoisie) does not simply tootle down to the labor market, feeling fine that he is paying for labor power the same way he is paying for every other input to production, in Marx's famous scene where "Moneybags must be so lucky." Even this "classical, industrial capitalist" of Marx's time had a "dirty little secret"—but the workings of the market in the case where a small class owned the means of production and most others only owned their ability to work ("labor power") did well enough to obscure the creation of value through a socialized labor process. The exception, where the reality of actual social relations begins to be apparent on a broad scale, is what Marx called a "crisis of overproduction." Part of what is needed today in political economy, however, is a deeper understanding of the way that this crisis has been sublimated, transmuted, and transferred into what was already in Marx's time a global economy of colonialism and (emergent) imperialism (in part 2 I will discuss in more detail the specific, technical sense in which I am using this term), as well as into categories of race, gender, sexuality, nationality, and others that have gotten in the way of what might be called the universalism of the ethical mission of working people. Even in Marx's day these sublimations, transmutations, and transferences were increasingly the result not only of the "normal workings" of the labor process under conditions of commodity production (in other words, Marx's great discovery that, fundamentally, there is commodity fetishism because there is commodity production—this point goes to the essence of Marx's materialism), but also of ways in which commodity fetishism took on a life of its own, or, as I like to put it, capitalism went into the consciousness business. In other words, if there is the danger to capitalism that working people might achieve a consciousness of the way things really work (that, to use terms to which we will return a little further on, there is not a "level playing field" for the supposed competition in which "we all" are engaged, supposedly to make a place for ourselves in the world), then capitalism had better go into the business of creating whatever forms of consciousness will best undermine—perhaps simply through mindless distraction—proletarian consciousness.

(These class categories will need sorting—for instance, "working people," "working class," and "proletariat" do not absolutely or necessarily refer to the same class. If this is the case, then certainly we have to recognize the complexity of the question. Class is problematized by other considerations, too, of course.)

There is a gap, therefore, already theorized by Marx and even more so by Lenin, whereby even the working class must make a leap beyond bourgeois consciousness. The present book is motivated by two concerns: (1) that this gap can only be bridged by "the ethical"; (2) that this gap, which already existed in Marx's day because of both the problem of false consciousness and the previously mentioned sublimations, has grown even "larger," indeed, "qualitatively larger," in the period between Marx's time and our own. (Indeed, the gap threatens to swallow up any historical sense of what "our own time" might mean.) Thus the crucial role of the ethical moment is qualitatively heightened, and Marx's tendency to negate that role is itself even more in need of negation.

Allow me to back up for a moment and make three simple points. This book is meant primarily as a contribution to the radical project, the project of understanding and transforming our world, and not first of all as an analysis and critique of capitalism. And yet the two projects are necessarily related, and, it ought to be stated clearly, *dialectically* related. We need no reductive sense of the dialectic to establish this point. All that is being claimed here is that, without an understanding (a systematic and even "scientific" understanding) of the real contours of the world system—as an imperialist order that is turning, in significant respects, "postmodern"— our talk of ethics will be no more than what Marx feared, mere bourgeois moralizing. In considering Kant's ethical philosophy, a great deal hinges on grasping the actuality of the *situation*, the *context* of ethical decision. This attempt to grasp the situation faces two dangers: that, on the one side, the ethical becomes merely "situational," and thereby devoid of its categorical force, or, on the other side, so "universal" that the ethical is rendered, as Hegel said in his critique of Kant (and which Marx and Engels repeated), "an empty formalism." This first point will require a good deal more elaboration in subsequent chapters to establish.

My other two points are simply comments about how crazy capitalism is in our day. (The reader will perhaps forgive me for taking a gratuitous pot shot or two.) For sure, there will be more to say about the basic problems of capitalism by and by. It would not be a bad idea for someone to write a book under the title, "Arguments for Capitalism, and Why They Fail Miserably," simply taking up attempts to create intellectual foundations for capitalism as offered by Milton Friedman, Ayn Rand, and perhaps even some proposals for "radical capitalism" from the libertarian camp, and even some proposals for "market socialism." This is not that book. (John Roemer does a superb job on Milton Friedman in *Free to Lose*.) Still, it will not hurt to say a couple of things about capitalism at the outset, the one having more to do with "classical" capitalism and its transformation into imperialism, the other to do with some of the more recent, "postmodern" developments. Both of these points, I think, are perfectly obvious and non-controversial.

First, it seems perfectly reasonable to argue that the concept of "competition," so valued by advocates of capitalism, is philosophically insepara-ble from the notion of the "level playing field." That is, to truly hold to the former means also holding to the latter. That this is not the case in practice tells us something about the concept of competition as held by advocates of capitalism. (Indeed, the argument is a simple instantiation of *modus tolens*.) Either competition is a "false concept" (a kind of lie or even self-deception, in other words) or it is somehow held in place by an even "deeper" concept, something other than the level playing field. Holding to this last concept for the moment, surely it is reasonable to think that a "fair competition" would not start out with one side holding all the marbles.

Analogies to games and sporting contests are attractive here. Chess players come to the game with different abilities, but even a grandmaster is not going to win if she only has her king and a pawn against a relative beginner who has the full set of pieces. The same could be said of a sport-ing contest in which one team has only a third as many players as the other team. (There is also the question of an "inheritance of ability," the institu-tions in which some receive more training, encouragement, and sense of entitlement than others.) There is the ability that one has "earned," through hard work and training (though Marx shows that this ability is itself a social product, built up through a labor process—as in the case of the transition from unskilled to skilled labor, and even in the way that it would be almost impossible to define truly "unskilled" labor), and surely one ought to be able to bring this ability to the playing field. But, as is said in sports, the situation of "no contest" is not a true competition.

Other than purely partisan fans of one team or another, no one else wants to watch a competition where one side is dealt a crushing defeat. In sports, such a situation could arise in a "fair" way, or relatively fair—at least we might not be talking about a "contest" in which the deck is stacked from the start. (The draft process in many sports exists precisely to address lopsidedness.) In capitalist "competition," however, the terms of play are fundamentally skewed. It is true that even capitalist societies have institutions of "fair" economic competition, such as the Securities and Exchange Commission in the United States, or the World Trade Organization (which is rightly seen as one of the leading organs of the more recent form of "globalization"). But these are *class* institutions. Economic entities operating within these institutions play fair or not—indeed, they often get up to dirty tricks, and the largest of these entities are sometimes able to dictate the rules as they go along—but this is not the fundamental divide around which the term "competition," as understood by capitalists, operates. American-style football, to return to the analogy, requires a good deal of equipment—indeed, as much as I personally like football, I have to recognize how quintessentially and problematically "American" it is in its conspicuous consumption and its division of labor (a division so deep that, if a player from one position, the place-kicker for instance, were suddenly required to substitute for, say, the running back, the result could conceivably be fatal). Imagine a "competition" in football where one team has all of its protective pads, helmets, and so on, while the other team has shown up dressed to play what the rest of the world calls football (namely, soccer). Oh well, you may not have the equipment to play American-style football, but let the slaughter, er, I mean "game," begin!

Clearly, if we are not talking about a level playing field, then we are not talking about real competition, but instead about something else whereby the powerful take from the weak. Working people, broadly, do not own the means of production, which, in the world of the last two centuries, are increasingly concentrated in fewer and fewer hands. These working people are, roughly speaking, in the situation of being required to show up at the (American-style) football competition with only their (Third-World style) soccer outfits. Some other justification might be offered for the set-up, something about rising tides that lift all boats, but then, "fairness" is not a part of this equation, and the "rising tide" position is not an "argument," per se, but instead an empirical claim that can be tested. The context of this test itself is a bone of contention. I would argue that the context has to be the entire planet and at least several decades of world history, not some momentary "economic miracle" in Brazil or Thailand.

Marx's thesis is that capitalism leads by and by to progressive immiseration. If anything, his context for making this argument was not nearly large enough, for in his time he was mainly looking at contention between the proletariat and the bourgeoisies of Western European countries, and not in the way that the entire globe was being shaped into a capitalist world-system by colonialism and imperialism. Nor did he have to consider the scale of environmental destruction that we are now aware of, a destruction that is severe to the point that it is not inconceivable that the global ecosystem has already been dealt some potentially fatal blows. Nor did he consider the immense machinery of cruelty that is the system of "carnivorism" (meat-eating), which has developed through many qualitative leaps since Marx's day. This cruelty is an issue in and of itself, as I will argue in part 3. There are also ecological and health issues connected to carnivorism. Marx probably could not have imagined a world that is increasingly filled with excrement, in which the methane gas of cows is a significant contributor to global warming, cows and pigs are fed the diseased remains of other cows and pigs, and one part of the world is dying from not enough to eat and the other from too much to eat (this itself is a significant testament to the lopsidedness of the imperialist world system). Marx did not consider, nor could he have considered, the possibility of a world held hostage for decades by superpowers who played games of Mutually-Assured Destruction.

The *argument* behind the "rising tide" claim is utilitarian. Although one aspect of the present book is to criticize those versions of Marxism that, in one way or another, embrace a kind of utilitarianism (though sometimes in a "cosmic" way, a coin whose two sides are utilitarianism and theodicy—more on this in part 1), surely there is something to be said for a social set-up where the lot of the great majority is on the upswing, and in a sustainable way. (Proponents of this "rising tide" utilitarianism must have some interesting arguments about what rate of failure is acceptable; if five percent are losers in this game, is that acceptable? how about twenty-five percent? and so on. Asking "acceptable to whom?" opens up the question even further.) This, however, would not be a conversation about basic fairness (which is *fine*, on some level, but do not claim that it is), and, in any case, the rising tide claim does not test true for any significant length of time (surely the minimum ought to be a generation—nineteen or twenty years), when placed in global perspective. Certainly the period from 1945 until about 1972 (and the beginning of "stagflation") was a boom time for white people in the United States; examine, however, the larger national and global demographics of this boom, and you will see my point.

There is also the libertarian-capitalist argument that we do not have "real competition," in a marketplace where trade is fair, because there is interference from the state. It is interesting that most libertarians of this sort do not call for the major corporations to be dismantled, presumably because this would require even more interference from the state, and thereby give more power to the state. That is not an illegitimate worry, I think. The conception of the state held by libertarians is problematic, however, and here again some lessons from Marx 101 would be helpful: the state is not a "neutral" institution that, by and by, is hijacked by those with power and property. Instead, those very people formed the modern bour-geois state precisely to look after and extend their power and property. All right, everyone knows this. However, to be fair to the libertarians, what I think is really driving their notion of the market is the particular hierarchy of their political conceptions: competition is dear, but private property and ownership are dearer. This is taken to insane lengths in the philosophy of Ayn Rand, where ownership means the right to dispose of one's property in any way that one wishes, even if that means destroying said property. Capitalism at present is doing a fine job of both monetizing every last bit of earthly existence (how far off is the day when you will wake up and ask your partner for a kiss, only to be told that the person across the hall is will-ing to pay nine dollars for one?) and disposing of it as well. The biggest undercutters of market competition are themselves the biggest players in the market; this is a contradiction that is basic to capitalism itself, and the role of the state in this is simply an extension of the way that capitalism works. Now, I myself neither believe in competition as a way of *basically* organizing a large economy, nor in some sanctity of property and owner-ship. Ownership will trump competition in such a way that talk of fairness in this context is at best silly. One proof of this (here is my little pot shot, but surely I am being more than fair), is that outstanding proponents of bootstrap competition such as George W. Bush are barely qualified to be ditch diggers, and would not get very far in any real, fair competition.

Well. We could say a good deal more about the "market" and fairness, and I will, by and by. A term was slipped into the discourse just now, "a *large* economy." The term "market" originates in not large economies, and not industrial economies, but instead in village and agriculturally based economies. In the village farming economy, one farmer may be proud of having grown larger yams than the other farmers, but does not thereby hold the power of life and death over them, or put them out of the activ-ity of farming, perhaps by outsourcing their jobs to some distant land. "Your yams are smaller, so now you must starve!" Stuff like this happens in the real world of modern capitalism all the time. But then, that quaint term, "marketplace," is nowadays a misnomer, as commodity production progressively eliminates both the sense of place and actual places them-selves (as we move even further into the McWorld), and the "global mar-ket" is, taken altogether, not a "place." These issues are pursued in part 3. One might want to offer a justification of this global capitalist system in terms of the rising tide or the supposed sanctity of private property (though both fail, and we should note that Ayn Rand's understanding of property is a far stretch from John Locke's or Thomas Jefferson's; at the same time, while it might be easy for us supposedly more sophisticated intellectuals to scoff at Rand, I would say that her views do speak to a cer-tain, perhaps pathological, insecurity that is widespread—perhaps among intellectuals as much as elsewhere), but let us not presume to talk in this context of fairness or the good or what is right. While there are, I think, certain limitations to the term "fairness" just as there are to certain interpretations of "justice" (if all it means is something like "adjustment," which can therefore also mean *vengeance*—Jacques Derrida takes up this question in *Specters of Marx*, 23–29), and even if, therefore, I would tend to be critical of the proceduralist/"political, not metaphysical" deployment of the term by Jürgen Habermas and John Rawls, it is very important to be able to say when a system should have no part in being able to claim that it is fair.

My second point also has to do with the way concepts become distorted in economies that are tremendously far-flung. The term "post-industrial" has been bandied about for some years now, and perhaps it arose at about the same time people started talking about "multinational" or "transnational" corporations. All of these terms speak to what might be called a paradox of placelessness. In the capitals of postmodern capitalism, which are (in a real sense that has real consequences) "consumer cultures," there obviously must be a great deal of stuff out there to consume. That stuff is made in a process, involving both the traditional inputs to production and some significant new ones, and that process occurs *somewhere*, if not so often anymore where people in the urban centers are able to see it on an everyday or firsthand basis. "Stuff"—where does it come from, and how is it made? The process is now so complex and far-flung (even the tables and chairs that populated analytic ontology in the classical period from Russell to Quine, one would be very hard-pressed to say what many of them are made of, some *synthetic* something-or-other, and where all of the materials that go into making all of the other materials, come from—but it all shows up at Wal-Mart or Target or Ikea eventually), it takes commodity fetishism into a whole other level, perhaps a level beyond alienation, forgetting, and false consciousness. And yet there is a somewhere, *probably in China* (in *Did Somebody Say Totalitarianism?*, Slavoj Žižek writes that, ironically, China is now truly the "working-class country"), where stuff is made, or at least assembled.

Meanwhile, giant corporations and other large entities of capital remain rooted in modern nation-states at least to the extent that, when force is required to protect and extend their property (or the social, legal, and ownership relations upon which this property is established), it is the armies and police of their "base nations" that do the enforcing. While it is true that capital now flows globally in ways and at speeds hitherto unimagined, the rootedness of capital in particular nation-states does not depend on some emotional attachment such as patriotic loyalty. The big capitalists of the United States, for instance, "love America," because, after all, it is *their* country, with their armed forces and their police (including the alphabet soup of secret police organizations, with their secret budgets and sources of funding) to enforce the basic social set-up in which they are the ruling class. That any of them would, under the right conditions, "sell out" the people of their country (something that, in actuality, these capitalists do every day) simply goes to what Marx and Engels said in the *Communist Manifesto* about all traditional and affective relationships having been replaced with the cash nexus. In part 2 I take up the question of patriotism and what it might mean to love and be loyal to "one's country," weighing this against what can be called an ethic of internationalism.

Perhaps, then, it is more correct to say that the pole of placelessness in the contemporary paradox of place is balanced not only by the reality of actual places where production, including industrial production in a more or less classical sense, is situated, but also by those places where the elements of force are based, the spaces they transverse, and the places, again, where this force makes itself felt. This is an enormously complicated picture, requiring extensive cartography and perhaps even a bit of remote sensing; part of what holds this picture together, at least ideologically, is its very complexity—who can challenge this set-up when it is close to impossible to wrap one's mind around it? Fredric Jameson calls this the "cognitive mapping" problem. Behind the complexity, or underlying it and permeating it, are not *arguments*, whether these be about fairness, rising tides, or property rights, but instead enforcement—violence. With all of the new expressions that capitalism has taken in the twentieth century, and all of the transmogrifications of recent decades, there is still the underlying current of reification and the disposal of people. There is still the concentration of wealth and ownership of the means of production in relatively few hands. There is still socialized production and privatized accumulation. Indeed, twentieth-century imperialism was the greatest machine for disposing of people that the world has ever seen.

From a Kantian perspective, violence is *the* crucial ethical question, because nothing instrumentalizes people (or other creatures that have feelings, for that matter) like violence. However, if systemic reification—capitalism—stands condemned for its systemic violence, what about counterviolence, one form of which is the revolutionary seizure of power by the proletariat and "the people" (I do not mean this sarcastically, but instead only to refer to the need to grapple with the complexity of class structure in the contemporary world)? How would we square this counterviolence with Kant's universalist critique of instrumentalization? Is the dialectic of "unethical capitalism" and "Ethical Marxism" given, by the brutal terms of the reality it must confront, to a narrow reductivism, whereby counterviolence—by which I mean simply "fighting back"—is condemned to be merely reactive? Such reactivity has certainly been seen when the revolution has come to power, and though some of it may be justified, or at least understandable, surely the narrow dialectic of mere violence/counterviolence cannot lead to the radical state of human emancipation that Kant calls "perpetual peace"—even if Kant's conception itself needs deepening, in light of both the limitations of his universalism (the Eurocentrism and androcentrism of which, significantly, carries over into Marx to some extent) and the limitations of his sense of systemic violence. I take up these questions in the section on Maoism (in part 3), since it is the Maoists, almost alone among those calling themselves Marxists these days, who still talk about a violent revolution to overthrow the capitalist ruling classes, and who adhere to the ethic of internationalism—even while not always understanding this "ethic" as such.

Incidentally, the Marxism 101 lesson on the state is not all there is to be said on the issues that are raised by libertarians (whether of the middle-class "shopkeeper mentality" variety or the more anarchist sort). There are real problems with large social institutions, whether they are states, corporations (a significant number of which have operations that are bigger than those of many states), or feudal fiefdoms, for that matter: big institutions are alienating. Even when such institutions have a supposedly "popular" cast to them, their largeness (sometimes their far-flung giganticism) can by itself lead to reification, the violence of abstraction. This is where the agrarian communitarian critique of modern society, as proposed by figures such as Wendell Berry, Wes Jackson, and Thomas Jefferson, for that matter, gets its ethical force. (Figures ranging from Simone Weil to E. F. Schumacher make parallel arguments about big institutions.) Given that, on a Marxist reading, the essence of the state is violence (the rule, by force when necessary, of one class over others), it is necessary to understand that one dimension of the question of violence is indeed this issue of big institutions.

My references to figures outside of the Marxist tradition (for instance, Wendell Berry, Jacques Derrida, Donald Davidson, Simone Weil) as well as to diverse figures within that tradition (for example, Sartre, Adorno) should demonstrate that I am not interested in recreating orthodoxy. My sense of the radical project is broad and open, perhaps even "ecumenical." Elsewhere I have written of "endlessly-adjectival Marxism" and of the "team concept" (that, for example, I want to be able to have both Sartre and Adorno on my "team"—the "Go Reds, Beat State!" team—even if their conceptions differ profoundly on many points). However, I do not take "ethical" to be simply one modifier among others. Instead, I am reaching for a conception that is at work in actual revolutionary processes, and that would play an even greater role in human emancipation and critical emancipatory theory if it were clarified and embraced for what it is.

At the outset of this discussion I made some oblique references to one of the most horrible spasms of violence in history, and certainly one of the defining episodes of the twentieth century, the Holocaust. When I say "one of the most . . .", let me add that I recognize the *singularity* of the Holocaust even if the question of its "uniqueness" is open to further debate. For a Marxist, some of the most important events of the twentieth century would include the Bolshevik Revolution, the Chinese Revolution, and of course the major moments in the unfolding of these revolutions, and the year 1968, when the whole world was rocking. As a Marxist, I am often caught short by very "American" views of the twentieth century in which these events seem to hardly figure at all. (There is a "European" variation on this theme in which the Chinese Revolution does not seem to figure very much.) When Sartre wrote, not long after the end of the Second World War (in his *Notebooks for an Ethics*), that "history is in danger of dying in the world of nonhistory," even then he was probably not yet anticipating the utterly trivializing "culture" of celebrity and contrived "events" that we have seen in recent years (though, surely, Theodor Adorno, with his analysis of the culture industry, and Guy Debord, with his concept of the "society of the spectacle," did significantly anticipate this culture).

Now, after the experiences of the Soviet and Chinese Revolutions, and their reversals into new forms of capitalism (a story that will have to be told elsewhere), it would be difficult to reinstate a vision of linear human progress. It would be more than difficult, it would be wrong; and it would not only be "factually" wrong, it would be wrong ethically. It is ethically wrong to glide blithely by historical episodes that not only do not indicate that humanity is progressing toward some better future, but that also seem instead to tell us that there is no "lower limit" on the horrors of which humanity is capable. Marxism, in at least some of its forms, can be rightly accused of this blitheness. In the first part I attribute this to a kind of theodicy that Marxism inherits from Christianity (or at least from a certain strain in Christian thought and attitudes that is found in both the mainstream and fundamentalist varieties of Christianity—and perhaps significantly more in Protestantism than Catholicism). It was against this theodicy that Adorno made his famous remark, "the whole is the false." I argue that, if Marxism is going to be able to take both history and ethics seriously, it has to "cough up" this element of theodicy, and embrace more deeply the question of what it would mean for human lives to matter. The same goes for Christianity. This speaks to a fundamental contradiction. I like to call this one of Christianity's fundamental embarrassments—in both mainstream and fundamentalist quarters—which can be summed up quite easily: if the message of Jesus of Nazareth was really about a kind of ontological bridging between infinite, omnipotent Being, and finite creatures such as ourselves who are in a fundamental (and inherited) state of alienation, and if this bridging can be accomplished by the simple *decision to accept* that the bridging is accomplished by the execution of Jesus and his

amazing magic trick (though actually no big deal for an omnipotent god)
of coming back from the dead (given a special definition of "death," of
course, in which one is still living in some other part of reality) three days
later, then why did Jesus bother with all of his other teachings, the ones
that seem to relate to ethical and political questions?

A Christianity for which these ethical-political teachings are taken to
heart would also have to be one that coughs up the sort of theodicy that
cancels any meaning to history. We have seen numerous forms of
Christianity that have attempted just this excision, almost all of them
highly politicized, and there is something to be learned from these
attempts. The question is also important if it can be argued, as I think it
can, that Kant was aiming for a certain philosophical formalization of at
least one compelling interpretation of Christianity. (Many thinkers, from
Hermann Cohen to Steven Schwarzschild, have argued that this was a very
"Jewish" interpretation.) Really, though, I am concerned with the other
side of this coin, or the mirror image of this problem of theodicy and its
excision, which is the fact that both Marxism and Christianity have had
rather blithe responses to certain horrible episodes in history, and on this
point the Holocaust can be called "singular" (if not only on this point, of
course). Indeed, not to overstate the point, but it seems that both
Christianity and Marxism have been singularly blithe about the Holocaust.

There is a kind of equivalence between God and History at the point
when everything is simply an instantiation of the cosmic plan (it all works
out in the end), and when you throw what seems to be a kind of systemic
anti-Semitism into the mix—well, there is a great deal to be said about this
that cannot be said here, but the main point is that the formulation of an
"Ethical Marxism" requires getting beyond the *impasse* of theodicy. After
all, to resort to parallel issues in Christianity, a Christianity of theodicy
ought to be perfectly at home with a postmodern capitalism where humanity is so reified that nothing matters whatsoever (other than perhaps the
"active acceptance" of belief in one's perfect and infinite passivity).

One has to be careful, very careful, in using the Holocaust as mere
"example." Especially in this postmodern world of nonhistory, the dangers
of trivialization are greater than ever. Just as the ethical is not one adjective
among others, the Holocaust is not just one bad thing among others, even
apart from debates about the "uniqueness" of the Nazi genocide, or
debates about the uses to which the Holocaust has been put (some of
which also play the role of trivializing the genocide). So, when I use the
Holocaust as an acute example of the sort of phenomena that an Ethical
Marxism ought to be able to respond to, I realize that I am treading on
dangerous ground. The idea of an Ethical Marxism, where elements of
Kant's path of thinking are brought together with Marx's, is to show the
following. The Nazi genocide was the expression of a social system, and yet

there were elements of the genocide that were not simply expressions of the workings, in any straightforward, "mechanical" sense, of a social system. These elements were also expressions of cultural currents and undercurrents. Regarding these currents we could say that ideology (in this case the ideology of anti-Semitism) played a relatively autonomous role, which is to say that there is at least a relative degree of systematicity to ideology itself. Furthermore, the people who carried out this genocide, on different levels of the murderous apparatus, were themselves expressions of a system (or overlapping set of systems), they were the "living representatives" of a set of social relations that, while they perhaps cannot be completely characterized by analysis of the mechanisms of capital, neither can they be understood apart from capital's logic of self-expanding value. Lastly, however, the people who carried out the genocide, and the people who helped with it, and the people who were complicit with it, and the people who acquiesced in it, and the people who could have done something and instead did nothing, these people are all *personally* responsible—if perhaps in varying degrees—for their actions and for their inactions.

If all of these things are true, the question becomes one of how all of them can be true *together*. Where does ethical responsibility fit into history and social systems, and where do history and social systems fit into ethical responsibility? These are more important questions than fretting over the extent of the complicities that are created by events such as the Holocaust, or New World slavery, where the implications for personal responsibility are far-reaching. And there is an even more important question than the more philosophical question of the relationship between ethics and history. For, suppose that for practical purposes we say that it will take us some time to specify how this relationship works, and it may even be that there are riddles and enigmas and even aporias within this relationship that, let us just say, may not be worked out anytime soon. There are those who would argue that the project of understanding the Final Solution as an historical phenomena, as Arno J. Mayer does in *Why Did the Heavens Not Darken?*, is fundamentally misguided, as it is does not give proper respect to the *unspeakable* character of something that refuses to be brought under categories such as "event" and "phenomena." While I would argue, instead, that, if we are serious about saying "never again," then we had better grapple with the systemic structures in which the Holocaust occurred, *even if* there is also an aporeatic element that absolutely must be respected, still, there remains the problem that, to fully "explain" this horrible thing in purely structural terms will result once again in a kind of theodicy. Space must be maintained for the gaps, for the aporias—and then it becomes a difficult philosophical problem that is also an ethical problem, How do we understand the space around the space? How do we understand where the line is, exactly? There is an even more important question than these philosophical questions, as important as they are. I am simply going to assume that history (and social systems) and ethical responsibility are in a fundamental kind of relationship, and will instead ask after the implications of this relationship for understanding and redeeming the world.

Actually, that's a little too straightforward, because the character of the history-ethics relationship makes a difference in how we understand the implications of the relationship. The simple way of putting this would be that what has happened in the past bears on our responsibilities in the present. It may be that what has happened in the past means that different people have different responsibilities in the present—something that may be hard to grasp from one kind of Kantian perspective. What then, is the specifically Kantian perspective of my argument, and, in light of this perspective, and of the aforementioned "ecumenical" approach, why say that the project of this book is "Marxist"? Allow me to conclude this introductory chapter with a few remarks on these issues, all of which will be dealt with in more detail in the rest of the book.

There are readings of Kant's ethical philosophy, and possibly of his philosophy as a whole, that do in fact succumb to the "empty formalism" charge. The problem comes down to the status of the "situation" in Kant's ethical philosophy, as well as the situatedness of Kant himself and his philosophy itself. While this is not a book about the "Kant-Marx encounter" (I will refer to a number of books from this encounter in the course of my argument, as well as books that have aimed to reinstate the question of ethics in places where it has not been welcome, such as Marxism and analytic philosophy), and I do not attempt to develop here a full-scale interpretation of Kant's philosophy, still, I take a number of positions within Kant's philosophy that ought to be set out explicitly. At the same time, in this project (and in my work generally) I rely on a number of figures whose basic philosophical impulses I would call "Kantian," especially Donald Davidson, Jean-Paul Sartre, and Jacques Derrida (and even John Rawls and Jürgen Habermas here and there). Furthermore, I am aiming for an intermotivation of themes from Marx and Kant, as opposed to original scholarship in either figure. Thus, for my purposes, it works quite well to quote Marx (and occasionally Engels) from the *Marx-Engels Reader* (second edition) edited by Robert C. Tucker, abbreviated hereafter as "MER."

The "empty formalism" charge is most often directed at the categorical imperative; at the same time, the categorical imperative is, so to speak, the beating heart of Kant's ethical philosophy. So, let us start there. After all, I am interested in a Marxism that takes seriously the *reality* of principles, and the question arises concerning what sort of reality this is. Surely there is no Marxism without a philosophical commitment to materialism?

Defining the "reality" of materialism also is not so simple a project, however. We can make a promising beginning, however, by taking a Davidsonian approach to the role of ideas in a materialist theory of human action, even while, at the same time, avoiding a reductivism into which Marxism all too often falls (or rushes). If there is an idea that is indispensable for closing the gap in an explanation of action, then that is enough for saying that the idea is a part of our material world. Indeed, there is a concept that, for Davidson, is indispensable in defining what it is that qualifies at least a certain kind of human behavior as falling under the category of action, namely, *intention*.

A reductivist Marxism attempts to eliminate such notions as quickly, and sometimes as brutally, as possible. In analytic philosophy, the name for such a reductivist program is "eliminative materialism." There have been many attempts in the history of philosophy to deal with the materiality of the human mind, given that it appears there is a problem with seeing human thinking in terms of strict causation. Davidson, in a series of remarkable essays ("Mental Events," "Psychology as Philosophy," and "The Material Mind"), develops the problem:

> Mental events such as perceivings, rememberings, decisions, and actions resist capture in the nomological net of physical theory. How can this fact be reconciled with the causal role of mental events in the physical world? Reconciling freedom with causal determinism is a special case of the problem if we suppose that causal determinism entails capture in, and freedom requires escape from, the nomological net. But the broader issue can remain alive even for someone who believes a correct analysis of free action reveals no conflict with determinism. *Autonomy* (freedom, self-rule) may or may not clash with determinism: *anomaly* (failure to fall under a law) is, it would seem, another matter. ("Mental Events," 208)

What is the meaning of being able to thematize issues of right and wrong in this material world? After all, if the material world is one of strict causality, of absolutely lawful motion as described in the physics of medium-sized objects such as bugs, trees, mountains, people, and planets, then ethical considerations are simply epiphenomenal. (It has been hypothesized, by Roger Penrose and others, that quantum physics plays a role in the functioning of the human brain, but let us leave this fascinating question for another day.) Davidson makes an argument for both the materiality (and therefore the causal dependence, as he puts it) and the anomalousness, of mental events—he says that both are "undeniable facts." The problem is to see how these are undeniable facts *together*, and without turning to either philosophical dualism or idealism.

Davidson is avowedly in sympathy with Kant's formulation of the problem:

It is as impossible for the subtlest philosophy as for the commonest reasoning to argue freedom away. Philosophy must therefore assume that no true contradiction will be found between freedom and natural necessity in the same human actions, for it cannot give up the idea of nature any more than that of freedom. Hence even if we should never be able to conceive how freedom is possible, at least this apparent contradiction must be convincingly eradicated. For if the thought of freedom contradicts itself or nature . . . it would have to be surrendered in competition with natural necessity. ("Mental Events," 208; quoting Kant, *Fundamental Principles of the Metaphysics of Morals*, trans. T. K. Abbott, 75–76)

My point in setting up this problem is that much in the history of Marxism has indeed surrendered not only freedom, but also ethical reasoning (and therefore political reasoning, any real reasoning about justice and the polis, or about the possibility of a just polis, as opposed to mere instrumental thinking about social arrangements), responsibility, meaning, and what might be called "the matter of mattering," to "natural necessity." There seems to be a tremendous, often overwhelming tendency for materialism, even Marxist, dialectical materialism, to become mechanical—and mechanical materialism is remarkably, uncannily similar to transcendental theodicy when it comes to "factoring out" meaning, responsibility, and the rest—in other words, humanity.

Davidson's solution is anomalous monism. Many materialist and "physicalist" philosophers find the solution wanting. It has significant affinities with some of the distinctions in Wittgenstein's early philosophy (for example, the idea that logical form cannot itself be displayed, and the distinction between saying and showing) and with what Fred Dallmayr calls Heidegger's "ontology of freedom." There is inspiration from Kant in all of these ideas, and the inspiration is against a reductive materialism. One way out of the anomaly is to argue or demonstrate that human consciousness (or whatever kinds of consciousness there are) is not such a big deal. The Kantian suspicion is that this is also to say that humanity is not such a big deal. However, the truth and the material force of the anomaly (even while recognizing that Davidson did not tend to speak this way) is humanity itself, even while humanity is not apart from the natural world. The question for my inquiry, then, is how Davidson's two "undeniable facts" can not only stand together, but also stand with the Marxist project of human emancipation and what I call "the social future."

There are analytic philosophers for whom human consciousness is not such a big deal. These folks generally take it that Davidson's anomaly is something about the brain that is not yet understood by neuroscience, whereas Davidson's aim is not to discourage physical investigation of the physics of the human brain, but instead to make *qualitative* distinctions regarding human thinking and activity that are not reducible to mere quantities. There was a moment some years ago, when I was studying Davidson's philosophy in graduate school, and I happened to hear an interview with a major proponent of "neurophilosophy." She explained how, when neurophilosophy is fully worked-out, we will be able to "fix" people who have psychological problems. At that moment I realized that anomalous monism had its ethical and political import.

Heidegger too, especially in his later philosophy and, for example, in his "Letter on Humanism," could be said to have thought that human consciousness, and indeed humanity itself, was no big deal. In some respects surely this is true. Marx was a strong advocate of Darwin (though not of "social Darwinism," and it is one of the strange yet significant aspects of our ideologically topsy-turvy times that many right-wingers and fundamentalist Christians advocate social Darwinism but oppose Darwin and evolution), and Darwin tells us that consciousness is simply a survival trait in humans the same way tremendous speed is for leopards and jaguars. Nietzsche reminds us that our pretentious notions of the good, the true, and the beautiful will most likely be gone long before the stars start to wink out, and that even the stars are not eternal ("On Truth and Lie in an Extra-Moral Sense"). Quite possibly, indeed, most likely, this is true. Even Mao Zedong, who often talked about how the people can move mountains, and about how "nothing in this world is impossible, if we dare to scale the heights," also said that, if a large meteor hit the earth and wiped out all human life, that would be a major event for the solar system, but a relatively insignificant event for the galaxy. I suppose that depends on what "the galaxy," as a frame of reference, really comes to—it may be that life, and especially self-conscious life, is very rare in the galaxy. Then again, if that is the case, then it could turn out that no one will mark our passing, and that also goes to the issue of the frame of reference. But what this ought to give us pause to consider is the fragility of our human situation, the fragility of goodness (as Martha Nussbaum put it), and how the *finite* meanings that we finite humans might create are not only a matter of an ontology, but also a struggle.

This struggle is seen in Kant's attempt not only to specify the meaning of freedom and responsibility, but also to capture the difficulty of getting these ideas to make sense in this phenomenal world, this world of natural necessity, and this social world of finite human beings. In a sense this is a hope against hope. But it is a hope that can play a role in transforming the world—a belief in the possibility of doing the right thing that enables the actual attempt to do the right thing. What is the basis for such a belief, against what can appear to be overwhelming odds? How could one doubt that Kant's work as an astronomer influenced his sense of the human struggle—especially when he referred to the two things that held him in awe: the starry heavens above and the moral law within? This

struggle is reminiscent of Socrates's attempt to answer Thrasymachus—
and it is significant that Socrates continues the attempt long after
Thrasymachus, supremely self-satisfied, pleased with his own view that justice is only power, that might makes right, that power is also the power to
define, has walked away from the discussion, not really giving a damn. It is
not only about defining intention (which is not easy, either), it is also about
the struggle to form intentions, for there to be *real* human action (in
Davidson's sense, as opposed to the simple *event* of the movement of a
human body where the cause of movement is not a reason—it is a matter
of two different vocabularies of description, and perhaps one can see the
distinction most clearly in legal reasoning), in other words real *praxis*. The
philosophical problematics of praxis in the modern world come from Kant,
and it is up to any Marxism that hopes to engage in and encourage praxis,
and to not simply be an empty formalism of theodicy-like thinking to come
to grips with this Kantian framework. At the heart of this framework, and
holding it together, is ethics, the fundamental regard for the other, for trying to do right by the other.

This struggle to form intentions also goes to Mao's response to Engels
on the question of necessity. I do not accept the now common claim that
Engels is responsible for all that is reductivist in classical Marxism (that's a
little too neat, and it lets Marx off the hook too easily), but certainly he
had a very strong reductivist streak. Following Hegel, Engels said that freedom is the recognition of necessity. Mao responded that freedom is the
recognition and *transformation* of necessity. In a parallel gesture, not only
Kantian but also Cartesian in form, Sartre stakes a claim for what *matters
to us*—it may not matter to the Milky Way galaxy whether our little species
continues on our little planet (though perhaps the point is that it neither
matters nor does it not matter—we will return to this odd question in part
1), but it matters to us, and that is the mattering that matters. Indeed, neither is the sort of meaning that relies on the logos or transcendental (signified) available to us, as Derrida and Davidson each in their own way
demonstrated (as did Nietzsche, Wittgenstein, and Quine, for that matter—the difference with Derrida being that he aimed for the next step in
the investigation, to "materialize the signifier," as he put it), but, were an
omnipotent, omniscient god to open the heavens and do whatever it takes
to show us such cosmic meaning, this would be an obliteration of our finite
meaning and therefore any meaning for us. Better, in all humility, to follow Moses and show *this* god our backside, at least for now and the fore-
seeable future.

From another angle, without intentions, we are in the "matrix" (I am
referring to the film)—and contemplating this fact shows why a materialist
interpretation of Kant, which is part of what we see in philosophers of
Kantian inspiration such as Sartre, Habermas, Derrida, and Davidson, is

both possible and necessary; this encounter also broadens and deepens our materialism. Kant is not Berkeley; however, the seeming coherence of Berkeley's vision (of a purified empiricism that only requires God's coordinating work and not the existence of material objects) is also what allows Marxism to so often fall into reductivism—if everything is ultimately mechanical causality (or everything in our social world, at least, and our world of medium-sized objects) then, again, intentions, meaning, responsibility, caring, freedom, and concern and hope for the possibility of human flourishing are epiphenomenal at best.

It is because these things are not merely epiphenomenal, but instead *real, really potential and potentially real,* or things that *really* can be hoped for (which is not to accept any "political realism," in fact it turns out to be on the contrary), that these Kantian impulses surface again and again—and not just because of some class-based resistance to accepting that Marx has surpassed and therefore canceled all previous philosophies. These impulses arise again and again in figures in the Western philosophical tradition who are also influenced by Marx, as well as in the practice and thinking of leaders of actual revolutions such as Lenin and Mao. These impulses arise again and again because Marxism, despite the philosophical claim that being determines consciousness, also has to find ways that consciousness can play a transformative role, and this means the struggle to form an intention. What is the beginning of intention, and therefore the beginning of praxis, except the impulse to respond to the other, to do right by the other, to do what we can to make a better world, to do what we can to bring about a global community of mutual flourishing, and to know that to talk about right and wrong, we need to talk about right and wrong, not first of all our "interests" or pleasures?

Perhaps what I just said also makes a statement on the "adjectival" question? Will this be more Marxist Kantianism than Kantian Marxism? It would be easy to say it does not particularly matter, at least as a practical question. In some sense this is true, in that the adjectival question will ultimately be resolved in practice, not through a "merely academic" comparison of philosophical systems. But I think this also goes to the question of what Marxism is. More orthodox Marxists have long referred to "revisionism." Indeed, this term was used by Engels to refer to Eduard Bernstein's "evolutionary socialism." Actually, Kant's philosophy was in the middle of that controversy. On the one hand, Bernstein wanted to join the Kantian ethical socialists in rejecting violence. On the other hand, Bernstein advocated what was called an "automatic Marxism," wherein capitalism would peacefully grow into socialism, and social struggle and upheaval would not be necessary. It should go without saying that the "automatic" part of this is hardly Kantian. The question of violence is very important, and the fact that I have saved discussion of it until the final section of part 3 should not mislead anyone, as I want to take up this question in the context of discussing actual revolutionary movements. However, let it be said here that *nothing* that happens in an imperialist society is *not* predicated on violence. In any case, "revisionism" is a term that could be applied to formulations of Marxism that in some important or essential aspect do not seem really to be Marxism anymore.

We have Marx's own perspective on this question to contend with as well, which is captured nicely by Derrida. Referring to statements made by Marx and Engels about the "aging" of their work, and the "intrinsically irreducible historicity" of the authors and their writing, Derrida asks,

> What other thinker has ever issued a warning in such explicit fashion? Who has ever called for the *transformation* to come of his own theses? Not only in view of some progressive enrichment of knowledge, which would change nothing in the order of a system, but so as to take account there, another account, the effects of rupture and restructuration? And so as to incorporate in advance, beyond any possible programming, the unpredictability of new knowledge, new techniques, and new political givens? (*Specters of Marx*, 13)

To put it bluntly, Marx even invites us to "pitch overboard" any part of his theorizing that no longer helps us to explain the world and to show where we need to work to change the world. This retheorizing of Marxism has to occur precisely in that context, however, in the effort to bring about a fundamentally better world. It is well known that Marx once said, in response to some French erstwhile followers who thought they were themselves Marxists, "I am not a Marxist." But actually, this is not so well known anymore—what is well known is that any number of intellectuals whom *no one* would ever have suspected of being Marxists are quoting Marx on this point (and few others), and now some of their epigones are quoting these intellectuals. There is no shortage of people, including some intellectuals, who are either reactionary or ignorant or both who would gladly pitch over all of Marx's theoretical work (without reading it first, of course), and, even more, the revolutionary spirit that motivated that work.

With my "ecumenical" and some would say "eclectic" standpoint, it would seem that my "lines of demarcation," to use one of Lenin's favorite expressions, are fairly far apart—and so the question arises, Where does one draw the line? The question might be reformulated this way: Can the line be drawn such that this conversation with Kantian themes is possible, without losing the core "motivating revolutionary spirit" of Marx's work? In *Specters of Marx*, Derrida says that there is one thing that he will never let go of in Marx, what he calls the "emancipatory promise" of Marx. Quite right. Derrida develops the problematic of the promise, and my sense of this is that it is a Kantian sort of idea, or that it at least makes sense in terms of certain themes from Kant (again, I would say certain Jewish messianic themes), even if these themes are not developed precisely as Kant might have developed them. Derrida says more than this, much more, for instance:

> It will always be a fault not to read and reread and discuss Marx—which is to say also a few others—and to go beyond scholarly "reading" or "discussion." It will be more and more a fault, a failing of theoretical, philosophical, political responsibility. When the dogma machine and the "Marxist" ideological apparatuses (States, parties, cells, unions, and other places of doctrinal production) are in the process of disappearing, we no longer have any excuse, only alibis, for turning away from this responsibility. There will be no future without this. (*Specters of Marx*, 13)

However, one could have a commitment to these sorts of things, and even to what Derrida calls "new, effective means of organization" (which gets into the "party" question, which is also taken up in the final section of part 3), and yet still have a Marxism that is lacking in certain essentials. After all, Marxism is not the only revolutionary theory or approach to organizing practice, and, in the present context, we might wonder why, if a certain "return to Kant" or "reactivation of Kantian themes" is warranted, we would then need Marx or Marxism at all.

It is a part of the present project to argue that some of the Kantian themes that need reactivation are in fact there in Marx, from the latter's own categorical imperative to the idea of self-activity that runs throughout Marx's work. But the heart of the issue for this return to Kant and for "the ethical" is something that Marx saw quite well (even if he did not draw the conclusions from this insight that I want to draw here): "the ethical" does not have, by itself, what it takes to be ethical. This theme will be developed much further, but allow me to set it out at this juncture in light of the following example. Ronald Aronson published a very interesting book in 1995, in the aftermath of the dissolution of the Soviet Union, with the title *After Marxism*. The book argued that many aspects of Marx's philosophical-political project turned out to be wrong, or not necessarily wrong but all the same played out, or, at worst, inviting of disaster. The particulars here can be debated, of course, but for the record let me say that I don't think it is very productive in the face of this kind of critique to just "dig in" and hold one's (ostensibly Marxist) ground. Aronson's project is not one of despair either and his aim is to reconceptualize radical theory, radical hope, and radical activism after Marxism. Significantly, the two final chapters of the book deal with the idea that "We Should Be Talking about Right and Wrong" (the title of the chapter), and a reconceptualization of utopian socialism (with the help, significantly, of Herbert Marcuse and

Ernst Bloch). One of the final sections of the book is called, "A Five-Hundred Year Perspective." Now, in fact, Mao Zedong also talked about this 500-year perspective, and there is undoubtedly a utopian aspect to this, or at least one that goes to a kind of commitment, one I would call fundamentally ethical, that outruns notions of "interest" considerably. I pursue all of these subjects extensively in the rest of this book. My short answer to Professor Aronson is that we do indeed need to be talking about right and wrong, and we do indeed need to bring forward and reconceptualize and reintegrate aspects of utopian socialism (and what might be called utopian communitarianism), but that to do this and to make these things a real force in the world, we also need something like Marxism.

Perhaps it is because I find most of the basic Marxist thematics still quite useful, and indeed I do not think society can be understood apart from these thematics (even if, as Derrida says, there are "also a few others"), that this "something like Marxism" is still what I would just call Marxism. By these thematics I mean the mode, forces, and relations of production, labor power and its exploitation, classes and class struggle, the state and state power as representing a class and a class-based set of social relations, social relations more generally as interrelated with the mode and relations of production (even if not in a simple, *one-to-one* way), the commodity as the "cellular form" of capital, capital as a set of social relations as opposed to simply wealth or the privatized ownership of the means of production, the commodification of labor power, commodity fetishism, false consciousness and the critique of ideology, the dominant ideology thesis, and on and on. If it can be established that Kant's three formulations of the categorical imperative are extended, in some sense *fulfilled*, by Marx's "fourth formulation," the "*categorical imperative to overthrow all those conditions* in which humanity is abased, enslaved, abandoned, contemptible" (MER, 60, italics in original), then it is also our Kantian, ethical duty to apply systematic analysis to these "conditions." The ethical cannot be ethical except in the trivial sense if we do not do what we can to understand systemic exploitation, oppression, domination, repression, and violence.

If it is necessary from Kant's perspective to deal with a certain wall, in order that we may do right by people, or do right period, because the wall stands in the way of doing right, then from Marx's perspective we will also need to study the *composition* of this wall. In studying this composition we will see if the answer to the ethical demand is to climb over the wall, drill a hole in it, or, if necessary, knock it down. We need the "science of the wall," in other words, a theory of society, and I cannot see letting go of most of the tools that Marx gave us here, even if we need a few others too. One of these tools I did not mention in the earlier list is an historical materialist perspective—that social relations can be studied systematically, even if they are not subject to absolutely strict causality and even if a great deal of contingency is involved in history (for that matter, I follow Sartre in thinking that existence itself is contingent, and that we must "think" this contingency), and that we need this study if we are to see where the openings might occur to new and better forms of social organization. We are motivated to undertake these investigations, in a broadly Marxist spirit and with the Marxist aim of doing what we can to bring about radical, substantive change, by the ethical demand, "the call of the future." Surely Immanuel Kant was a kindred spirit with one of those in his own future, Karl Marx, when he not only expressed concern for "the most distant future generations," in his great essay, "Idea for a Universal History, From a Cosmopolitan Point of View," but also attempted to grapple with the difficult issue of what material basis—as he put it, a science of history that would be akin to Newton's laws of motion—can be found to ground this concern.

In some sense, my *only* argument in this book is that *the concern itself is the ground* of the "science," of the systematic theorizing. That is the essence of Ethical Marxism.

One would already be on the road to Ethical Marxism if one took historical materialism to be prior to dialectical materialism (rather than the other way around, as Marx took it and Marxist orthodoxies take it).

In *Specters of Marx*, Derrida argues "a promise has to promise to be kept." In a sense that is a Kantian response to the charge of "empty formalism" often directed at Kant. Because *praxis* is an issue of central importance to the project of Ethical Marxism, I am going to discuss not only Kant and Western philosophers inspired by broadly Kantian impulses, problems, and themes, but also the history of Marxist and socialist revolution, from the Paris Commune to the Cultural Revolution in China and beyond. Some theorists reject Marx because they believe it is no longer possible to believe in history (Aronson is in this group, but hardly alone there), and some others at least reject what appears to be a teleological "History" in Marx. For my part, I reject teleology when it comes to the idea of something foreordained or what amounts to theodicy. Indeed, I will argue that anything that smacks of theodicy is not only unscientific, but, even more, morally wrong. Indeed, it is evil. However, I accept a certain Aristotelian teleology that grapples with the promise of humanity (and even the promise of our once and hopefully future beautiful world), even if in a history that is yet unwritten. And I believe in the idea of a learning curve of revolution, and I do not think we will get anywhere in changing society if we do not build on (though certainly in a critical way) the struggles of the past.

In part 1 of this book I consider the relationship between Marxism on the one side, and "traditional" discourses, in the Western philosophical canon, of good and evil and right and wrong.

In part 2 I consider the discourses of good and evil and right and wrong in terms of the way that economy and society are organized globally. Lenin's term for this form of organization is "imperialism," by which he meant capitalism as a global mode of production. I attempt to explain and develop this idea, and to apply it especially to historical atrocity; in particular I discuss what the United States did to the people of Vietnam. I argue that imperialism, especially, demonstrates a certain gap in the world that cannot be entirely addressed by political economy or a purely "scientific" theory of society (which, purportedly, Marxism is), and that there is an irreducible role for ethics, or what I variously call "the ethical," "the ethical relation," and so on. It is important to sort out these terms; however, in this book, at least, I am more interested in getting the ethical question on the "table" of Marxism, so to speak.

In part 2 and in the first section of part 3 I use what might seem an odd locution when I refer to imperialism as a "question" and to "the animal question." Certainly we know this way of talking from Marx and Sartre, both of whom authored texts under the title, "The Jewish Question." Still, one might want to ask exactly what imperialism and perhaps even more "the animal" are as "questions." My intention is to highlight the idea that these matters ought to be the subjects of interrogation. As concerns imperialism, my aim is to bring this matter directly into the foreground.

In the third part of this book I will turn to some specific practical questions, in a way that might be unusual, controversial, and provocative as regards the kinds of discussions that usually take place in Marxist discourse. For instance, I raise the "animal question" as an example of where great and horrendous wrongs are done, but where Marxism (if not always Marx*ists*, but even so) has almost always turned a deaf ear. The question of place is hardly thematized in most Marxist discourse, especially as it relates to questions of the land and agriculture. The irony is that Marx, perhaps more than any other philosopher, cements a certain understanding of the whole earth as a place. However, one might say that Marx gives us Earth, but not the earth. The animal question and the place question are each significant in their own right. Each has a significant ethical dimension, and I will even argue that the animal question is the paradigm of ethical questions. Methodologically, then, we might learn much from Marxism's resistance to these questions. Lastly, in part 3, I will explore some issues in the international communist movement, Mao's revolutionary theory and practice, the subsequent development of Maoism, and the role that this form of deeply committed, anti-imperialist and internationalist theory and activism might play in giving rise to the next synthesis of Marxism that is necessary for changing this world.

The conclusion aims to be a substantive chapter in its own right, dealing with the ethical in the matrix of meaning and mortality (questions that are foreshadowed significantly in the other parts of the book). I attempt to develop the notions of "ongoingness" and the future as the background for ethical questions, and I extend some feelers from Ethical Marxism toward a kind of "religious perspective." I believe there are some truths in what I call the "religious perspective," and in various religious traditions, that do not depend on the existence of the god of classical Western monotheistic theology. This brings us once again into conversation with the claims of science and the problem of truth. As a matter of methodology, and of ontology and epistemology, my hope is that ethics can be understood as substantial and real, even if it is not clear yet, and perhaps may never be clear, how the reality of ethics squares with the picture of reality that science gives us. In the book as a whole I argue repeatedly that we cannot let go of this latter picture either. On the other hand, perhaps there is a sense in which I would want to claim that a person who does not know that certain things are simply wrong cannot really know anything else, either. Well, that is probably bending the stick back too far the other way. Most scientists, of course, are not "moral idiots." However, there does not seem to be anything in science itself that prevents moral idiocy, and perhaps there is something in science as it is often conceived that opens the door to such idiocy and repugnance. This is where the difference between a Marxist, "objectivist" tendency toward correspondence theory in epistemology comes up against a more Kantian, intersubjective perspective. This question arises in many different contexts throughout this book; in the conclusion I return to this question in asking about the relationship between the first and second formulations of the categorical imperative, and the third formulation. I argue that Kant captures what is a valid insight from certain religious traditions, regarding the relationship between the present and past, on the one side, and the possibility of a redeemed future, on the other.

Speaking of "validity," however—my *only* coherent argument in this book is the "ethical basis" argument, the argument that the concern for what is right has to motivate the systematic investigation into what is true. Even this argument is proposed in some sense as a hypothesis about what is needed if we are to transform the world. Everything else here is even more hypothetical, if that is an expression, and does not claim to reach the level of integration that would form a philosophical system. Indeed, in using terms such as "thematics" (perhaps especially this term), I am occasionally playing a bit loose with ideas taken from Kant, Marx, and numerous others. I own up to this, and my intention is not contempt or condescension toward more detailed and exacting scholarship in the history of philosophy. One of the contradictions I live with here is that between a Kantian perspective and the rethought tradition of Aristotle and Aquinas that one finds especially in the work of Alasdair MacIntyre, which is pretty good stuff. I want some of that stuff, and, for that matter, I am interested in a Marxism that does a far better job of inheriting philosophical traditions than declaring them over and done with and best gotten rid of. A few of the incoherencies, if not outright contradictions, between an Aristotelian and a Kantian approach to finding an "ethical heart" to pump blood to Marxism's scientific brain will be discussed in the first chapter. This is also to some extent a conflict between ethical-political universalism and radical communitarianism. In other work I have tried (and will try) to address this conflict on different levels; here I mostly live with it for the sake of doing some philosophical open-heart surgery. Well, this is a bit of an exaggeration; there are lots of arguments here, some of them even well formulated in and of themselves, and there are also numerous projects for further research and struggle. There are at least fragments of a "system" here, or at least a perspective, the further forging of which will take place in both theoretical and practical arenas.

Humanity has to find a way to live up to its promise, it has to find a way to be responsible to its promise, or else the human world, at least, will come to an end. On this point Kant and Marx are inseparable.

Marxism and the Language of Good and Evil, or, Theodicy and the Iron Law of Wages

The Language of Good and Evil

Should we not only be talking about right and wrong, but also good and evil?

"Evil" is a word that has dubious status in social theory. We could take this fact as a cue to move in one direction or another, but which one? Perhaps it would be better to stay away from social theory, and instead stay with philosophy or even theology, even while focusing on the political components of these disciplines. This temptation is not without substance. After all, if all that social theory can do is describe or contextualize, without any normative force, then what good is it when it comes to understanding some of the unbelievably terrible things that have occurred in human history? But there are good arguments to the effect that, as soon as we are dealing with meaning, we are in the sphere of evaluation—and, since people cannot avoid dealing with meaning, neither can values ever be factored out of any human activity. However, there is also a problem with going completely philosophical or theological on this question, namely that "evil" tends to assume the character of a force or substance outside of materiality and the fabric of social relations. There are strong trends in both Western and non-Western societies, especially associated with gnosticism, neo-Platonism, most versions of Christianity, and Buddhism, that associate materiality itself with evil. Versions of Christianity and Buddhism that accept this view are committed to the idea that, essentially, nothing good can happen in this world (except through divine intervention—which Buddhism rules out). No social theory is possible from such a perspective—all that could be done would be to catalogue human decline or forms of illusion. And yet social theory is needed as the glue that makes our talk of right and wrong and our aspirations for a radically better society something more than mere moralizing or fantasizing. Therefore, the other direction is here recommended: to establish the place of the concept of evil in social theory. This in turn will help us think about how the term can function appropriately in philosophy.

Surely the philosophical discourse on evil, from Plato to Arendt and beyond, is close to exhaustion by now. Not surprisingly, the same might be said about the discourse of the good. Some of the exhaustion comes from the postmodern machinery of the endless trivialization of everything. On this point, Arendt's thesis about the banality of evil is far truer now than when it was first set out. When it comes to the philosophically more difficult and nuanced levels of the question, such as the conflict concerning radical evil and evil as privation—well, as they say, there are substantive arguments on both sides. But perhaps we can come at the problem from a different angle and, if not arrive at a definitive set of answers, at least generate some insights that might advance the discussion. This particular look at evil, therefore, will be both marginal to and parasitic upon what has been set down canonically in philosophy. We might talk about a kind of work that could be called philosophically motivated social theory. Surely Habermas is the exemplar here. In such work, one might rightly be skeptical of philosophical "ideas" that do not fit in somewhere with a theory of society, because through such skepticism social theory is less likely to come unstuck from a materialist foundation. However, what separates a thinker such as Habermas (whom I take as exemplary while not agreeing with him on many things) from either reductivist Marxism or positivistic social science is the rejection of a "materialism" of "brute stuff," where humans are simply one form of causally determined "material." Language, meaning, and subjectivity are peculiar "things," and strange motions are generated as a result of their existence. Not to be glib, but all of the canonical figures recognize this in one way or another, though perhaps it is only with Leibniz and Rousseau, and then Wittgenstein and Heidegger, that language comes fully to the fore as a pressing concern. It is no longer acceptable to work in social theory without giving some account of these enigmatic phenomena.

Descriptions and Norms

A social-theoretical approach to the concept of evil must be careful, then, about coming too close to the logical positivism from the 1920s and '30s. Furthermore, Marx could be said to have taken a positivist approach to this particular question: terms of ethical evaluation—not only evil, but also justice, good, and so on—were for him not especially helpful, and indeed got in the way of understanding the workings of history and society. As with the positivists, for Marx a "scientific" theory of society and history would be purely descriptive, not normative. The proletariat and oppressed people generally are in the happy position, in Marx's view, that historical development is ultimately on their side—and thus they can be partisans for truth on a purely scientific basis, without the need for a normative dimension.

Is a perspective such as this undermined if history seems to go very wrong? Well, it doesn't help. But then, as Sartre established in works such as "Materialism and Revolution" (1946) and *Search for a Method* (1960), if history is nothing other than what is already "in the cards" (to use one of his expressions from the former work), then it would be hard to call it "history" in any sense that involves real human beings. Indeed, it might be interesting to go back into the debate, around the later 1950s and into the 1960s, between existentialism and structuralism, from the standpoint of recognizing evil as at least some kind of reality. How can one recognize this reality if there is not a substantive sense in which subjectivity and intentionality are not also real things—even if they are constituted, have a material basis, exist as nodal points within overarching structures, and so on? Subjectivity and intentionality may not be "essential" or ontologically irreducible from some (utterly inaccessible) perspective of "ultimate reality," but they are ineliminable "for us." And, at least from the perspective of the *pour soi*, I can recognize some things as aiming toward the good, some things as against the good, and I can try to aim for the good myself, and, in the absence of this striving, I may very well be complicit in the structures and human actions that undermine the good. Indeed, I not only can do these things, I *must* do them, I have no other choice than to choose—in fact, I *am* my choices. This is the Sartrean perspective as I understand it, and I tend to see it as situated in the Kantian universe of discourse.

Structures and History

There is an odd passage in Derrida's book, *Of Grammatology*, that (to my knowledge) has not been placed under the microscope of analysis. (Admittedly, the passage is made even stranger when the context for it is eliminated.)

> Our question is therefore no longer only "how to reconcile Rousseau and Marx" but also: "Is it sufficient to speak of superstructure and to denounce in an hypothesis an exploitation of man by man in order to confer a Marxian pertinence upon this hypothesis?" A question that has meaning only through implying an original rigor in Marxist criticism and distinguishing it from all other criticism of suffering, of violence, of exploitation, etc.; for example, from Buddhist criticism. Our question clearly has no meaning at the point where one can say "between Marxist criticism . . . and Buddhist criticism . . . there is neither opposition nor contradiction." (120, ellipses in original)

Derrida is quoting from *Tristes Tropiques*, where Claude Lévi-Strauss argues that Buddhism and Marxism both aim at a kind of liberation, and therefore are not in conflict. Occasionally the thought occurs to me that, if we were to all become contemplative Buddhists, not focused on the material things of this world, then the problems of exploitation and class struggle would be immediately solved. But there would still be the problem of production, if humanity were to be understood as an ongoing concern, and Buddhism does not appear to have anything to say on this problem. In Buddhism, history is primarily illusion and error, and though it could perhaps be considered the process by which one comes to enlightenment, as well, or at least the context, there is nothing in Buddhism that allows us to focus on the particularities of history. We might even go so far as to say that, in Buddhism, it is history itself that is evil, and the point of enlightenment is to "rise above" this evil, to become "light" by throwing off the burden of historicality. Then one can see that this evil, like history, never really existed in the first place.

The full context needs to be developed, but one reading of the passage from Derrida is as a criticism of and resistance to the synchronic perspective taken up by structuralism—in other words, the point where Buddhism and Marxism can come together is one where the diachronic perspective has been factored out. This is thumbnail "continental philosophy," but we might say that, for Sartre, the answer to this misstep into purely analytical reason is to reassert the primacy of subjectivity, while for Derrida it is to turn to the primacy of writing and textuality (even to the point where there is a sense in which writing precedes speech—which is itself a response to Sartrean subjectivity). This reading is only a partial gloss, however, as it is the work of deconstruction to question all that claims "primacy."

Consider the affinity of Heidegger with Buddhism (or Asian thought more generally). Whatever might be profound or useful in the Heideggerian notion of "historicity," it does not seem to help very much in the understanding of history. The problem parallels that of Being and being, the famous ontological/ontic distinction—the focus on the former seems to lead to a philosophy where the latter does not especially matter. And, if we little beings do not matter, what is the point of talking about good and evil in the first place? Good and evil there may be, but the conflict is played out on a cosmic plane that is qualitatively beyond the ken of mere, mortal human beings (hence the interest in Heidegger from certain precincts of Christianity). Tom Rockmore sets out the problem in very pointed terms. He invokes what many take to be *the* example of evil in modernity, and the example that disturbs both ahistorical historicity (not that Heidegger seemed especially disturbed by it personally) and any historical teleology that sees history as the uninterrupted march toward redemption.

> Heidegger's critique of modernity is not only compatible with but in fact necessarily leads to Holocaust relativism. Whatever the merits of this critique, it clearly does not allow for distinctions to be drawn between different events in the modern period that fall under the same heading. If all modern events are explicable in terms of the fall away from being, if they are all the same in that crucial respect, then obviously the Holocaust and all other events lose their historical specificity. . . . From the Heideggerian angle of vision, it is not possible to pick out the Holocaust as a particular event unlike others in the modern period. From Heidegger's exalted perspective, all modern events are like all other modern events. ("Heidegger and Holocaust Revisionism," 117)

It seems to me that, instead of this cosmic or purely transcendent perspective, a social-theoretical perspective would have to be concerned with the idea that it is *only in history* that anything good or evil happens. That phrase, "only in history," should be read three times over, with the emphasis shifting among each of its constituent words.

History and Theodicy

Perhaps there is a theology where God is indeed in history, or is at least historical and material—embodied—in some sense, and clearly Judaism and Christianity have leanings in this direction. To put this in the standard language of philosophy of religion, this would be a "compatibilism" where humanity and human agency matters fully; perhaps it would be a theology in which it can truly be said that "God so loves the world." Personally, I think this would have to be a theology where there would even have to be a physics of it, and in which the future sometimes extends a hand back to us, helping us out in ways that could not be expected or understood in purely teleological terms—in other words, eschatological intervention. In my view, the person who has the deepest grasp of this sort of theology is Orson Scott Card, the novelist who is also a devoted Latter-day Saint (Mormon)—a good (and readily accessible) example would be his novel *Pastwatch: The Redemption of Christopher Columbus.*

But if the evil that happens in history does not rise to the level of concern in Heidegger's philosophy, what worries me more is that historical evil is not accorded the status of reality (a reality, some kind of reality) in Hegel or Marx, either.

Here is the paradox, or at least the intractable irony. On the one hand, Marx sets aside evil as a useful concept in his theory of society, in large part because he takes it to be a concept with too many theological overtones. But on the other hand, we supposedly do not have to worry about evil because everything works out in the end, and this happens inevitably, because of the way that historical laws work—some of which Marx even calls "iron laws." The irony, which may even rise to the level of paradox, is that this sort of contrast and working out of history has been given the name "theodicy." The problem that Sartre attempted to confront, in setting up existentialism as a "parasitic" but necessary addition to Marxism, is the way that "real, sensuous human beings" (to use Marx's language from the "Theses on Feuerbach") drop out of the picture in any theory, even an historical materialist theory, that takes history as working out according to strict laws.

Hazel Barnes provides a helpful gloss on one of the key arguments from Sartre's 1946 essay, "Materialism and Revolution": "No objective state of the world can by itself evoke a revolution" (670). This claim may be taken as asserting the role that consciousness plays in social change. Not to detract from that crucial point, but there is something else here as well, something in the Kantian frame that bears on the question of good and evil. On the assumption that, in the case that a social system is unjust, a revolution to address this injustice through the overturning of the existing system and the attempt to create a better one is a good thing, the Kantian-Sartrean argument is that it is only with the intent to do something good that something good might be done. A corollary of this thesis is, If people are not trying (intending) to create a good society, then they won't.

Now, claims such as these have not typically been a part of the discourse or practice of Marxism. Indeed, as has been much remarked upon, Marx is not even likely to employ the discourse of justice, much less that of good and evil. A social system must be superseded if it has shown itself no longer capable of advancing production (generating advances and revolutions in technology is one way to put it); the fundamental problem with capitalism is that it becomes increasingly inefficient and unsustainable—"justice" and other "ethical" issues are secondary in this scheme, even epiphenomenal.

Production and the Need for Social Theory

And yet Marx is continually cited here because his work has to remain the touchstone for systematic social theory in our era, the era of capitalism and imperialism. This does not mean that he is the only figure to learn from, by any means, but a systematic social theory has to deal with Marx, whether going with him or against him. To put it in a formula, this means a primary focus on the question of production: How is it that societies sustain themselves, from day to day and over longer periods of time? What are the ways in which society is organized to sustain itself? What are its social relations? What tools do people have to work with? I think it is possible to focus on the question of production, or what some call "social reproduction," without falling into a reductive "productivism"—which might otherwise be expressed in the words "man does indeed live by bread alone." Despite this possibility, the history of Marxism is the story of repeated and significant falls into reductivism. Lenin called this fall "economism," and his critique of this reductivism might help us understand what role the concept of evil could play in social theory. Notably, for Arendt, communication rather than production is the key to society; for her, however, production is set aside in the realm that she calls "the social," it does not rise to the level of "the political," and thus political theory need not much concern itself with production. It would be interesting to explore how her famous argument about the banality of evil is connected to this division of spheres. To return to Marx for a moment, the dilemma is that setting aside concepts such as good and evil from social theory lands us in the same sort of theodicy (even if a secular one) that trafficking with the fully "transcendental" or theological concepts does.

However, one of the great breakthroughs in Marx's philosophy is the way that it contextualizes the subjectivities of members of particular social classes. Although the individual capitalist—the individual owner of the means of production—is quite likely to be a morally suspect person, given the realities of production in the industrial and imperialist world—Marx saw that the factors that lead the capitalist to make this or that decision are "structural," rather than first of all "moral." Given that, for Marx, the essence of capitalism is the commodification of labor power, the most basic point where this distinction applies is in the hiring of workers by the capitalist. For the capitalist, in Marx's view, there does not need to be any intention to exploit—and I take it that an intention to exploit another human being would surely be a good case of something we would call evil, unjust, wrong.

The capitalist, in order to run his enterprise, purchases factors of production, which include the materials that make up the plant, the materials for producing whatever it is the plant makes, and the labor power necessary for production. For these factors of production, the capitalist pays the going market price—and, in Marx's view, the capitalist can do this without the intention to exploit, dominate, reify, or even commodify any person qua person. In a wonderful little book with the superb title, *Moneybags Must Be So Lucky* (the expression comes from *Capital*, vol. 1, ch. 6: "The Buying and Selling of Labour-Power"), Robert Paul Wolff sets out the problem Marx faced—that, whereas the arenas of the church and the state were not surprisingly shrouded in mystifications, in the marketplace everything looks straightforward and above board. Wolff writes that, before Marx, the concept of mystification "had never systematically been applied to the field of political economy" (38). Religion and, therefore, philosophy, Wolff writes, were "dramatically demystified" by efforts that began with Kant's critique of the claims of rational theology (in *Religion within the Bounds of Reason Alone*, a book that did cause Kant a little trouble with the emperor). The transcendental patina was "washed clean" from the political realm by the French Revolution: "When the head of Europe's most glorious king fell into a basket and the heavens did not open, the aura of monarchy was forever dissipated" (39–40). Recall that, in his early work, Marx was especially concerned with the mystifications of church and state—the same text in which Marx gives us a "fourth formulation" of the categorical imperative begins, famously, with the claim that "the criticism of religion is the premise of all criticism." I will return to what appeared to be a shift in Marx's work away from this idea, especially because there are many Marxists who seem to hold tenaciously to a kind of antireligion perspective that, in its dogmatism, looks suspiciously like a mere "flipped-over" religiosity.

Mystification

There are many things to be said about this, but one thing that Wolff makes clear is that it is in some sense not so bad to find mystification in the church, when the church would itself claim to be dealing in mysteries. The special problem that Marx faces is that the economic arena presents itself as a sphere where mystification is neither needed nor present. Significantly, Wolff draws a comparison between the marketplace and Plato's allegory of the cave.

> In his youth, Marx was much concerned with the mystifications of church and state. However, when he turned to the third great realm—the economic—he encountered a special problem, reminiscent of that with which Socrates had wrestled. For the economy did not seem to call for demystification. Mysteries there might be in the throne room or the sacristy, but what mysteries could lurk in the marketplace? There all was plain as day. Men came to trade, to bargain, to advance their individual interest as shrewdly as they might. They wore everyday clothes, not ritual garments tricked out with precious gems in iconic patterns. They spoke the demotic tongue, priding themselves on being simple, straightforward, no-nonsense men.
>
> The political economists who recorded and anatomized the doings of the marketplace reflected this simplicity, this absence of pendulous transcendent significance, of shadow and echo. Adam Smith and David Ricardo, James Mill and Jeremy Bentham, John Stuart Mill, all wrote a transparent, serviceable prose—clear, efficient, devoid of the metaphor and metaphysics that clouded the great rationalizations of church and state. Land, labor, and capital. Equals exchanged for equals in a sunlit market where every interaction was a contract, every contract a quid pro quo and the law enforced all contracts with blind impartiality. The English had no head for theological subtleties, and *their* Reformation, unlike Germany's, had arisen more from the concerns of the flesh than those of the spirit. Their brutal truncation of monarchy had been softened by the compromises of the Glorious Revolution. Where better than in England to observe the plain dealings of the market, free of the lingering wisps of religion or monarchy?
>
> Or so it seemed. For Marx was persuaded that the market was more deeply mystified than ever the altar or the throne had been. The market was a strange and ghostly place, inhabited by things that behaved like people, and people who were treated, and came to see themselves, as things. (40–41)

Everything seems to make so much sense in the marketplace—"you pays your money and you takes your chances." Certainly, there is "something about England," or many things; undoubtedly its being part of an island is one thing that makes it an intensive laboratory for studying the rise of capitalism—and much else (everything from Druids, Celtic Christianity, Blake and Shelley, the international slave trade, dark Satanic mills, to the Beatles and King Crimson). Significantly, I think, this land of utilitarianism has never been able to sustain noneconomistic forms of Marxism—indeed, the main trends there, the Communist Party of Great Britain and the neo-Trotskyist Socialist Workers Party, along with numerous other Trotskyist factions, are not only economistic, but indeed are avowedly and proudly so.

The ghostliness of the marketplace was concealed by what Marx calls the "dirty little secret of capitalist exploitation": while all of the factors of production other than labor-power are themselves the product of labor, labor itself is able to create more value than is needed for its own sustenance. (In the case of "natural" inputs, such as water, air, dirt, etc., a labor process is involved in making them available for the capitalist mode of production—which gets into Marx's distinction between "use value" and "exchange value," and his argument is that the application of labor-power is the basis for the latter.) The market price of the bricks that the capitalist needs to build his factory will hover around the cost of the labor required to produce the bricks. Marx argues that the same thing goes for the laborer him- or herself, and this is the key point. In other words, the price that the capitalist will pay in the marketplace for the use of labor-power for however many hours, days, or years the labor-power is needed, will be the cost of the labor that it takes to sustain that laborer—and, again, the point is that labor-power is able to produce more value than what is represented in this cost. This production above and beyond what is necessary to sustain the laborer is what Marx calls "surplus value." Under the capitalist form of production, this capacity of labor to produce more than what is necessary to sustain the laborer is the basis of exploitation—the laborers, as a class, do not have returned to them what they have produced.

Embarrassment of the Ethical

All right, this bit of Marxism 101 is well known to any political theorist or philosopher who has bothered to do her or his homework, but what does it have to do with the problem of evil? Well, Marx is very Biblical, we might say, in that the pursuit of money is the root of all exploitation by the capitalist—or, as Marx liked to put it, "Accumulate, accumulate, accumulate!—that is Moses and the Prophets to the capitalist." For Marx, capitalism has a role to play that is historically "progressive"—but it is here that you see the divide between ethics and politics in his argument, such that the former has to simply drop out of consideration, because to raise ethical questions here is a an embarrassment, even grotesque. (Returning to remarks made in the introduction, it is interesting how much this embarrassment resembles what I called one of the main embarrassments of Christianity—drawing from the teachings of Jesus and the early Christian movement an ontology and theodicy, and thereby cancelling the ethical-political thrust of the "good news." What this means is that the "good news" is that this mere, mortal, human life does not matter.) The divide is this: certain currents of history can be politically "progressive" and yet ethically "reactionary" (to borrow that term from the political side) at one and the same time. One sees this divide at work especially in Marx's view of colonialism—indeed, he scoffed at those who raised questions about the ethics of England's role in India, even arguing that the former was "the unconscious tool of history . . . sweeping aside [India's] backwardness and repressive social order" (see Harry Van der Linden, *Kantian Ethics and Socialism*, 262–63, as well as my essay, "Ethics and the force of history: three possibilities in Kantian political philosophy," in *Politics in the impasse*). My point is that, even if Marx had been right about the role of Western colonialism in precapitalist societies (which is highly questionable, to say the least), there is still a problem with the way that the divide between ethics and politics opens up in his work.

Divide between Ethics and Politics

This divide can be characterized in at least two ways that bring out the need for radical social theory not to part with either ethics or the question of evil. Remember that my purpose here is to see if there is a social-theoretical basis for talking about evil; if there is, I will take this as having shown that there is a basis in other discourses—including philosophy and even theology—for such talk. Perhaps strangely, but surely not insignificantly, to proceed this way parallels Plato's methodology in the *Republic*: going from the polis to the soul, so to speak. Well, Plato was a good Marxist on this point: evil is first of all in social systems, and from there it gets into our souls. This is a something to keep in mind when we turn to the problem of social systems that are global, but that create both global divisions (and bifurcations) and deep complicities that result in what I would call widespread and deep "moral rot."

First, we might consider the argument that, even if capitalism is in some sense "historically progressive," it also represents something of a cul-de-sac. (One of the arguments in social theory that I have pursued for some time now is that this cul-de-sac can be seen in the fundamental *impasse* of contemporary capitalist societies.) While capital is tremendously productive and is better at sheer accumulation than any other form of society before it—reasons, Marx and Engels said in the *Manifesto*, that the bourgeoisie is the most revolutionary ruling class in history, and their argument is that capitalism, in boosting productive capacity to the point where abundance is possible, sets the stage for the sharing of that abundance—it is also the case that, historically, no other social form has accumulation for its own sake as its *raison d'être*. I know that many Marxists would disagree with me, but I would argue that even cultures that have as their driving motivation something that is completely illusory—serving the sun god or something on that order (not that I am absolutely sure that the sun god is illusory!)—are better than "cultures" that have no other aim, in the end, than to just pile up junk. (The scare quotes around "cultures" have to do with the way that the telos of mere accumulation progressively leads to the junkification of culture, especially through its homogenization in the form of purified "product.") To have a society that is made to exist for the purpose of mere accumulation—and that primarily for the ruling class, and to the point where the sustainability of the human species and the whole planet is increasingly at stake—well, in my opinion, that is wrong, it is garbage, it is a load of whatever expletive you would like to place here, and, most of all, it is *evil*.

The second approach to answering the question of what ethics might mean to social theory is as follows. We need one more bit of Marxism 101 to complete the picture. Marx argues that it is precisely capitalism's tremendous productive capacity that is its own undoing (see *Capital*, vol. 1, sec. 3, in MER, 422–28). Marx's argument is that the exploitation of labor-power ultimately backfires, and this has to do with the conversion of "living labor" into "dead labor" in the labor process under capital. "Dead labor" is Marx's term for what happens when the work done by workers becomes commodified (it is through this process that what Marx called "commodity fetishism" arises), and, as supposedly "finished products" that appear to exist as self-standing entities, are allowed to circulate in the same market which determined the price that the capitalist paid for labor-power, the commodities come to stand over and against the workers who produced them. The first form in which this alienation is manifest is in what Marx calls the "crisis of overproduction." The worker is capable of producing more than is necessary for his or her own sustenance; the capitalist only returns to the worker what is required for the maintenance of the worker during the time that the worker is needed by the capitalist (apart from which the worker can go to hell for all the capitalist cares—in other words, starve), and expropriates the rest as his "reward" (i.e., profit) for having set up the venture in the first place. (This ought to lead us toward a fundamentally ethical question, namely, How can it be justified to have a form of society where a minority are in the position to "offer" employment—that is, the means to sustain life—while the majority must continually seek it?) The problem comes when overproduction leads to its necessary twin, under capitalism that is (under some other form of society overproduction would not in and of itself be a problem, this would just be called "saving up for a rainy day"), namely, the crisis of underconsumption. Capitalism produces more than can be sold at a profit, therefore workers are laid off, therefore masses of people do not have the income to purchase products, and from there you get the downward spiral into general social crisis and attendant social unrest. Here we see another form of the cul-de-sac, in fact perhaps the most dramatic form: capitalism is the only social form wherein people can be starving even while there is no shortage of food; indeed there is an overabundance of food, and people starve *precisely because* of this overabundance. Is this not evil? Indeed, is this not something like the very paradigm of evil?

So, Marx's argument is that capitalism has within it basic tendencies to crisis; crises—in the form of depressions or wars (the two being fundamentally connected)—are not things that swoop down upon capitalism from the outside.

However, my point in this thumbnail sketch of the crisis of overproduction, and the way that I ended the sketch by talking about evil, is to demonstrate the problem of the divide between ethics and politics (or history) in Marx.

Ethics and Contradiction

We can say two different things about the picture outlined above: (1) the system ultimately breaks down of its own accord, and therefore will *have* to be replaced; (2) the system is fundamentally unjust, and therefore *ought* to be replaced. The first is something like an economic imperative, while the second is definitely an ethical imperative. What is the relationship between the two? Simply put, there are two main differences between the two imperatives. The first difference is that the economic imperative does not rely primarily on the role of intention and consciousness in the transformation of society. The system breaks down because of its structure, and it is only secondarily that people then have to decide what to do about this and then to try and do something. Another way to put this, in Marx's general philosophical scheme, is that "being determines consciousness"—in his view, the alternative is philosophical idealism. (We see here, too, some of the thematics at work in the structuralist response to Sartrean existential Marxism, with the latter's emphasis on subjectivity and consciousness, contrasted with Althusser's formula, "history is a process without a subject.") The second difference is just the other side of the first, namely that, from what is generally accepted as an historical-materialist conception, the ethical imperative by itself or "in the first instance" just does not have the necessary purchase on lived realities to bring about the transformation of society. This is the great irony, and Marx is right to make something of it, that ethical judgment, per se, does not have enough grip on people and the lives they lead to push them to do what would be an overwhelmingly ethical thing, to overturn unjust systems and systems of injustice. *Ethics does not have what it takes to be ethical.*

It ought to be noted, even if only incidentally, that the "early Marx" did more often couch his views in ethical terms. The most striking example, which bears repetition and further consideration, is found in the "Contribution to the Critique of Hegel's Philosophy of Right: Introduction," where Marx writes of the "categorical imperative to overturn all of those social institutions in which humanity is debased." The "later Marx," while he could still rail in the voice of a prophet against injustice, framed his arguments almost exclusively in the terms of political economy (all the while employing a powerful literary style, which is a matter of some ethical significance—it could be argued that there is a surplus of ethical feeling that cannot be entirely contained in the language of structure). Again, one might say that Marx went in this direction out of a recognition that ethics alone cannot accomplish the ethical.

Immanence and Utilitarianism

By "ethics" here is meant ethics in the sense argued for by Kant: doing what is right out of a regard for the other, for what can be understood as universal, and for the reason that it is right, and not for some other reason. By "ethics," I do not mean any version of utilitarianism. This issue must be raised because, in rejecting ethical discourse, Marxism can appear to be a more thoroughly socialized and class-oriented version of utilitarianism, and all of the problems of expediency that are often raised of the latter ("what if the present happiness of the majority consists in oppressing a minority?") come to attach themselves to Marxism with even greater force in the case where state power is held (or even in person-to-person relationships within Marxist organizations). It is worth mentioning in the present context that an important problem as regards utilitarian tendencies in Marxism is that Marxist revolutionaries will almost "naturally" tend to be "ethical Marxists" before the revolution, whereas after the seizure of state power there is a "natural" pull toward calculation, instrumentalism, and utilitarianism (as well as other alienating practices and alienated sensibilities that tend to spring from or accompany *large* institutions of whatever kind—this issue is explored most directly in the second and third sections of part 3). The *Kantian* argument about intention is that these tendencies need to be thematized and grappled with in their own right, so that the "natural" pull toward an ethical discourse can be understood as substantive, not merely an instrument to be used to appeal to the masses until the actual revolution renders it inexpedient and therefore unnecessary.

"Rational choice" theories, incidentally, are in my view to be understood under the category of utilitarianism, and this includes the attempt to ally such theories with Marxism—Jon Elster's *Making Sense of Marx* being the most systematically developed. However, as I said in the introduction, there is certainly room for further discussion here, especially concerning what counts as "reason" and "rational." Certainly, in attempting a more straightforwardly methodological-individualist interpretation of Marx, Elster (and John Roemer, among others) brings clarity to what Marx meant, going back to the Theses on Feuerbach, by arguing that classes and societies are *aggregate* structures, not some sort of "collective overmind." An interesting line of inquiry could be seen in the fact that Elster was a student of Louis Althusser, and the latter declared that his aim, more than being a "structuralist," was to be a consistent follower of Spinoza—and certainly it can be said that both Althusser's structuralist Marxism and Elster's analytical Marxism are attempts to create Marxisms of pure (and purified) immanence. They are trying to get all of the *German metaphysical* stuff out of Marx. They not only want to get Hegel out of Marx, but also Kant. For, it can be said that, even if it is the case that the discourse of ethics (and even of the political or of the just polis) is a subordinate track in Marx, at times barely there and at times merely epiphenomenal or merely "rhetorical," at least that track is there. It might be argued that, had Marx lived another ten or fifty years, he still would not have tried to "purify" his analysis such that this track would have or could have been dispensed with. But the rational-choice Marxists have indeed dispensed with this track (and conceivably the structuralists have as well).

Passion and Prophecy

The subtitle of Wolff's *Moneybags Must Be So Lucky* is "On the Literary Structure of *Capital*." The conclusion to this lovely little book is remarkable altogether, especially Wolff's claim that the "ironic authorial voice" is integral to Marx's project in *Capital*. It might similarly be claimed that the *prophetic* voice is, at least at times and in significant moments, integral to his project in works on either side of the "epistemological break" as the

Economic and Philosophic Manuscripts of 1844, The German Ideology, The Civil War in France, and *Critique of the Gotha Programme.* This is a subject for much further discussion, but clearly irony and prophetic passion are mere distractions from the standpoint of analytical Marxism. The problem is that the analytical Marxists might be able to convince Marx himself that they are right, whereas my view is that not only was Marx right in incorporating these voices and that these voices are integral to the project of human emancipation, but that it would help to make Marx even "more right" about this. Still, the difference points to a fascinating historical debate within Marxism, between the side that (at least mostly) says *viva* to the inheritance of German Idealism in Marx's thought, and the side that simply or mostly sees this inheritance as a burden and an unnecessary chunk of "clutter." (Apparently Richard Wagner once attempted to explain his music theories to Hector Berlioz, and the latter replied that, "In France we call that indigestion.") Of course, we do have the words of the Marx of *Capital* as regards Hegel and the fashion then-current of treating the latter as a "dead dog": "I therefore openly avowed myself the pupil of that mighty thinker." At the least, though, we can learn from thinkers such as Elster and Althusser what the significance might be of purifying Marx of seemingly epiphenomenal and even ephemeral notions such as consciousness, intention, ethics, and the good. We may also get a better sense of why some argue that even Kantian arguments are not going to be sufficient for shoring up the "second track" in Marx—which they argue, and I am arguing, ought instead to be the "first track"—and that, instead, we need Aristotle and Aquinas. For the moment, however, let us rejoin the "Kant track."

With his three formulations of the categorical imperative, Kant recognized the unity and interpenetration of the personal, interpersonal, and political in ethics, and Marx could be said to have extended this unity to the historical and economic with his "fourth formulation." But then the argument could be made that, with his supposed "break" (the famous "epistemological break" that Althusser argued for), Marx took his recognition concerning the shortcomings of ethics to the point where it was no longer a matter of filling out the categorical imperative, but instead of kicking away that discourse altogether, in a way not unrelated to Hegel's claim that Kant's ethics is an empty formalism.

One way to characterize this transition in Marx (which has traditionally been characterized as the transition from the "humanist" and "philosophical" Marx to the "communist" and "scientific" Marx) is that Marx went from recognizing the irony of ethical discourse—that it needs help, that ideals have to confront materiality and the modes of actual human ("sensuous") existence—to rejecting this discourse and indeed sneering and scoffing at it.

Mere Moralizing

Now, it needs to be added that a good deal of Marx's scoffing was aimed at what can be rightly called "bourgeois moralizers," those purveyors of "values" whose main purpose is to just keep people, especially the working masses, in line. We know these purveyors today, in the form of figures such as William Bennett. (On "The Reality Beneath William Bennett's 'Virtues'," see Bob Avakian, *Preaching from a Pulpit of Bones*, 7–26.) A more difficult case is the contempt in which Marx held people who spoke against the mistreatment of animals (antivivisectionists and members of the SPCA—Society for the Prevention of Cruelty to Animals). On this score, it might be said, Marx remained a "humanist" to the end of his days, in that narrow sense of humanism that is highly problematic. One still hears expressions of this from Marxists, often in the form of the statement, "It is people I care about." Besides the simple stupidity of this, as if the horrible treatment of animals that is an integral part of sitting down at the dinner table in most households was at the same time an expression of "care" about our fellow human beings, it is also a fundamental indicator on the status of ethical discourse. It might even be argued that scoffing at ethical discourse and scoffing at concern for the treatment of animals are deeply related—or, understood from another angle, the "animal question" might be one of the touchstones for the very possibility of ethics. (My colleague Peter Steeves has made some powerful arguments to this effect, arguments that played a role in enabling me to see the importance of this question— hence the long first section of part 3.) As much as ruling-class figures such as Bennett deserve every bit of scorn that might be heaped upon them, what happens when this scorn is spread out more generally—what might be called a general disgust at people who "talk that way"—to the very pro- ject of ethics? I would say that a bad thing happens, the sort of thing that allows evil to do its dirty deeds. If this is the case, then there ought to be an argument for the material role that the ethical, and the discourse of the good, needs to play in creating a better society. In other words, if eco- nomics, politics, and history also cannot do what they were supposed to do, then we had better reconsider the materiality of the ethical—which also means grappling with the materiality of evil.

As hinted earlier, the way that Marx sometimes wrote (like one of those old Israelite prophets), perhaps apart from his expressed content, could be understood as an implicit recognition of an "ethical gap" in arguments that attempt to remain within what is taken to be a purely immanentist frame- work of politics, history, and, ultimately, the unfolding of modes of produc- tion, and that, therefore, eschew any supposedly transcendental effort such as represented by ethical discourse. If anything, this gap has opened up fur- ther, or at least has made itself more manifest, in the decades since Marx. I would even go so far as to argue that not only can the discourse of the ethical no longer be excluded from the (supposedly) immanent matrix of history, politics, and economics, but that, indeed, the ethical has an absolutely crucial and irrefutable role to play. There are gaps in the world, and there are gaps in whatever telos might be constructed on the basis of history and economics alone, and only the intervention of the ethical can begin to bridge these gaps. (The use of the term "intervention" here is meant to coincide with Derrida's arguments, in *Specters of Marx*, about the eschatological and the "weak messianic force.") If this is the case, then, arguments about immanence and transcendence aside—in other words, regardless of the "real" meaning of the term—we have to recognize that ethics is real and has a claim on the real. And the same goes for the language of good and evil.

I have always liked Malcolm X's statement, regarding the situation of Black people in the United States, "We didn't land on Plymouth Rock, Plymouth Rock landed on us." This is an excellent concentration of what happens in the twists and turns of history, where the process—if that is what it is—can never be considered a simple progress toward enlightenment. In the largest social terms, we might give five names to the historical gap, the gap that only ethics can address, the gap that is filled by evil when it is not understood for what it is—a moment of invisibility in the forward "progress" of history. The five names are: colonialism, imperialism, slavery, genocide, and Holocaust.

This is not the place to enter into a thorough analysis of the imperialist mode of production, though such an analysis is sorely needed by radical social theory and activism. However, without denying forms of evil that existed before and apart from the emergence of the modern West, I think it is right to say that all of the "large" forms of evil that exist in the modern world arise from the juggernaut of reification that is capitalism, which has displaced itself upon the whole world in the form of the imperialist system, the imperialist mode of production. To wax biblical again, we are seeing the effects of usury extended on a world scale, and what happens is that humanity, and indeed all of earthly creation, is reduced to the level of the "mere thing," to be used up and thrown away. Nothing has any value, and therefore the discourse of values has no place; ethics and the bottom line do not go together. But if the ethical has no place in the worlds of capitalism and imperialism, then it will have to come from somewhere else; it will have to intervene.

"Marx Forgot" Human Nature

It is a commonplace to hear about what Marx "forgot" or what Marx did not see. Often, when these locutions are used, the speaker is referring to something that Marx in fact analyzes at length. (The one we hear most often is that "Marx forgot about human nature," though the kinds of people who say this almost always have themselves "forgotten" to do any thinking on the subject, and simply give us the old bit that human beings are essentially greedy and acquisitive. Whether Marx has a view of human nature that leans more toward Aristotle's essentialism, as Scott Meikle argues, or toward Sartre's radical anti-essentialism is an interesting debate, and one we will return to in a moment—but it is not a debate that is addressed by the legions of "Marx-forgot"-sayers.) Supposedly something that has been forgotten by anyone who invokes Marx's critique of capitalism in the twentieth century is that there are plenty of workers who live above the level of mere subsistence, and thus it would appear that the "iron law of wages" is no longer operative. But this is merely a first-world perspective and needs to be understood as such. When capitalism becomes a fully global mode of production, it undergoes qualitative transformations. Lenin argued that a handful of countries find themselves in the position of bourgeois ruling classes in relation to the rest of the world, while the majority of countries are more in the position of the proletariat. As local economies are undermined in the Third World, and are forced (very often through direct military and police intervention) to participate in a global "free market" that is controlled (and to a large extent coordinated and planned) by finance capitalists in the imperialist capitals, the iron law of wages asserts itself most aggressively. A global *lopsidedness* emerges such that a sector of "bourgeoisified" workers in the first world are able to have middle-class incomes and standards of living, while many in the Third World live *below* the level of mere subsistence, and thus their lives are indeed solitary, poor, nasty, brutish, and short.

Intentionality

Thus the dirty little secret of capitalist exploitation rules the world, and it does this with a systematicity—the logic of the commodity—that makes it appear as though no one is intending that anything bad or evil happen to anyone. And what is evil if there is not intention? In some sense the whole point of Western theological scenarios is to show that there is an intentionality to evil, that evil occurs when there is an active and intentional rebellion against the good, against God. If evil is instead simply the result of the way that certain social structures work, then why invoke either the languages of theology or subjectivity/intentionality?

It has been noted by philosophers such as Michel Foucault that the languages of theology and subjectivity are linked in important ways. Foucault argued that the "death of God" needed to be followed by the "death of man," at least in the sense of "man" as some sort of unified subjectivity and as the basis for humanism as it has been understood since the time of Descartes. What if, in the wake of this wave of critique (from Nietzsche to Foucault) that has supposedly washed away the outline of the human face from the beach that is the indifferent cosmos (these are all Foucault's metaphors), the subject makes something of a comeback? Does this open the door to some sort of theological comeback as well? Perhaps this is not a pressing issue in the case of discussing ethics per se, but certainly there is no getting around the theological overtones in considering the question of evil.

Of course, clearly there is intentionality in imperialism, just as there is intentionality in slavery, colonialism, genocide, and the Holocaust. Slave ships do not get from one continent to another by themselves. Death camps do not set themselves up. Napalm and Agent Orange do not arise "naturally." The economic planning mechanisms of finance capital, seen in such institutions as the World Bank, the International Monetary Fund, and the "G20" (or whatever the number is now), are run by people who expend enormous effort attempting to see that their intentions are realized. Perhaps one of the best and most concentrated examples of this is the formula that was proposed by Lawrence Summers—former president of the World Bank, a member of the Clinton Administration, and former president of Harvard University—for the purposes of determining the value of a human life. The occasion for this formula was a World Bank austerity program for several sub-Saharan African countries; the program included a provision for these countries to accept garbage from the United States and Western Europe, which would then be placed in giant landfills and mounds in these Third World countries. Such mounds are filled with carcinogenic materials, and one form of cancer that is endemic near these mounds is prostate cancer. However, men are generally not at risk for prostate cancer until they are in their fifties and sixties, and the average longevity of men in the countries in question was only about that long. Therefore, men exposed to these carcinogens were not likely to live long enough for prostate cancer to kill them. Summers captured this scenario in a formula: expected wages times expected number of years in the workforce equals the *value* of a person's life. The acceptance of toxic landfills by the African countries was expected to generate some wages for workers, so, on average, according to the formula, the aggregate "value" of human life would increase in these countries. The possibility that the landfills would lower that value is taken account of by incorporating expected life span into the formula. (Many readers will already be familiar with the Summers memo of Dec. 12, 1991, and it is easy to find; see, for example, Jim Vallette, International Trade Information Service, May 13, 1999.)

A formula such as this strikes me again as both evil and a paradigm of evil, because it makes mere things out of human beings; it purely instrumentalizes human life. We can say at least two things about the formula, at least in terms of questions already raised. First, the formula is expressive of a structure, an economic structure that has a financial structure at its core. Formulas such as this one function throughout the structure, even if the Summers formula is especially clear in its instrumentalizing brutality. But the additional thing that can be said in terms of structure is that this formula is expressive of the iron law of wages. For it is integral to this law that the wage that is paid to the worker will hover around the cost (the market price) of replacing the ability to work for as long as the capitalist requires that labor-power—and, when that labor-power is no longer required, the personification of that labor power, namely, the individual worker, can be left to his or her own devices, left to beg or die or some damn thing in which the capitalist has no interest, in other words. In imperialism, such a formula is enforced by a system of sugar-coated bullets in the first world and real bullets in the Third World. Now this system has reached a point where it is willing to write off an entire sub-continent, as in the case of sub-Saharan Africa and the AIDS crisis.

Commodification

There is a thread that runs from the first forms of the division of labor, especially the division between mental and manual labor, and from the first production of commodities, to the international and ever-more-globalized system of production that exists today, and it is a systemic thread. There is a connection between the first forms of class society and the far-flung class system that exists today. So, to again wax "biblical-Marxist," the fall of humanity into class society is a fall that continues to deepen today. This fall crosses a threshold when labor power itself is commodified—that's when capitalism emerges. When this commodification is employed most efficiently, in the system of industrial production, the juggernaut of reification is unleashed on an increasingly global scale, and it makes its way into every nook and cranny of human life. As Marx and Engels wrote so stirringly in the Communist Manifesto,

> The bourgeoisie, wherever it has got the upper hand, has put an end to all feudal, patriarchal, idyllic relations. [It should be noted here that what Marx and Engels mean by "patriarchal relations" is something on the order of kinship relations in which social roles are defined; clearly, capitalism has not gotten rid of patriarchy-indeed, it has made great use of it; but, for that matter, it has not gotten rid of, but instead incorporated, aspects of feudal aristocracy as well.] It has pitilessly torn asunder the motley feudal ties that bound man to his "nat-

ural superiors," and has left no other bond among people than naked self-inter-
est, than a callous cash nexus. . . . In one word, for exploitation, veiled by religious and political illusions, it has substituted naked, shameless, direct, brutal
exploitation.

   The bourgeoisie has stripped of its halo every occupation hitherto honored
and looked up to with reverent awe. It has converted the physician, the lawyer,
the priest, the poet, the man of science, into its paid wage-laborers.

   The bourgeoisie has torn away from the family its sentimental veil, and has
reduced the family relation to a mere money relation. (MER, 475–76)

What we find here is the conflation of a structure and an intentionality. But
first of all this is the intentionality of a class, the bourgeoisie—which is
itself a structure. Which is the prior "agency," the structures of capital, or
the intentionalities of the capitalists?

   For Marx, it is clearly the structures, and in *Capital* vol. 1, especially,
he provides a detailed argument for this. It is only within the structures of
capital, Marx argues, that people can function *as* capitalists (or as proletarians in the modern sense, for that matter). This point can be demonstrated
in many ways, but a simple way to see it is that, without a financial system
and set of increasingly global structures, a money economy would have no
purchase on the lives of people—because, in a society where the main form
of production is agricultural self-sufficiency, money is just pieces of colored
paper. There is nowhere where these pieces of paper have come to structure ways of life that has not been accompanied by physical force and violence. Novels such as Chinua Achebe's *Things Fall Apart* and Alice
Walker's *The Color Purple*, in showing how village economies in Africa are
supplanted by the money economies of globetrotting corporations,
demonstrate the point about violence as well or better than any theoretical work. Decisions about the unknown modes of life in such far-flung
parts of the world as Zaire or Malaysia or Mississippi are made in offices in
New York and London and Paris and Berlin—*unknown*, because who
really cares? We aren't interested in what was there, only in the profits to
be abstracted from what we will put in place.

Subjectivity and Responsibility

However, there remains the second and "secondary-but-crucial" point to
be made on this question of structures and subjects. Even if the "primary"
source of the instrumentalization and reification of human beings and
indeed of everything else under the sun, and even the sun itself, is indeed
a social structure (or set of interlocking structures), and even if we might
therefore speak first of all of "systems of evil," still, as has already been
emphasized, there are decisions being made by some people and not

others, and there is a place for intentionality in all of this. In some sense the project of Sartre's *Critique of Dialectical Reason* was to work out the relationship between subjects and structures. Contrary to much opinion on this question that has been influenced by structuralism (Althusser and Lévi-Strauss, specifically), Sartre's aim is not to say "three cheers for the subject," but it is perhaps to claim the space for one cheer. One could even understand the project of the *Critique* as exploring what Marx meant when he spoke of humanity becoming the subject rather than the object of history. It is integral to Marx's framework, after all, that there is a basic relationship between the exploitation and reification of the much greater part of humanity, on the one side, and the fact that the decision-making process regarding the means for humanity to collectively sustain itself (which is the larger conception of "production" at work in Marx's thought, a conception quite beyond the caricature of "productivism" that he is often charged with but that some dogmatic Marxists do indeed fall into—and this larger sense of production is then also understood as the material basis for human flourishing) is skewed toward a tiny minority in the capitalist and imperialist mode of production. Sartre's argument is that the members of this minority, the individual capitalists, are responsible for their decisions. If there are structural factors driving the capitalist that are outside of intention, namely profit, the callous cash nexus, the iron law of wages, ultimately the logic of commodity production, why then would we call the capitalist him- or herself evil? Precisely because—and I think this is an essentially Kantian argument—these factors are both ultimately outside of intention and because these factors are intentionally *allowed* to hold sway over the much greater part of humanity.

The real sense of "allowed" here is that these factors are brutally enforced, ultimately through the political power that flows from the barrel of a gun (or cluster bomb, land mine, nuclear weapon, or anything else that is in the immense arsenal of the imperialists), and, again, all of this requires a great deal of intentionality. In the dirty work that imperialism does there are direct lines that can be drawn from the "sins of omission" to the "sins of commission." Indeed, the basic contradiction of capital in stark form can be seen here. Even while the ideologists of capital claim that "economic planning does not work," imperialism requires ever more planning on a scale that even Marx probably could not have imagined. Apparently it is possible to plan for the subjugation of humankind, even if this requires the coordination of resources representing trillions of dollars, but as for the basic material needs of human beings, well, no, that is beyond the pale—this is where we need the free market, you see, so that people can make their "own choices" about homelessness, disease, malnutrition, and starvation, or having things fall on them from the sky.

Iron Law of Wages

Marx was right to invoke iron—a metaphor with ancient roots—in writing of the logic of the wage system and where it leads. For the system of exploitation of labor power, which is the fully ramified logic of commodity production, turns the hearts of men and women to iron—how could it not? When the essence of crossing the threshold into the commodification of labor power itself is the turning of human beings into one lot of material resources among others, then evil on a scale hitherto unseen becomes possible. It isn't that there was never any evil before capitalism, but rather that what it was that made a person's heart turn to iron in precapitalist societies took a qualitative leap with the commodification of labor power. (More on the "what it was" and the reason it is appropriate to call it "evil" in a moment.) It is in this context, incidentally, that we might revisit Heidegger's formula, "mechanized agriculture equals mechanized death." To the extent that we can isolate the formula from the circumstances in which he uttered it (in the famous *Der Spiegel* interview that he would only allow to be published after his death), Heidegger is on to something fundamental here. There is something about an agriculturally based society that keeps people sane, and there is something about mechanization and industrialization (and perhaps the most significant threshold is when "agriculture" is industrialized and globalized) that destroys human sanity. Although the point has been made many times, it bears repeating here: what made the Holocaust unique was not that it was an incident of genocide, but rather that it was genocide on the industrial model. (A thorough and important exploration of these issues is found in Michael Zimmerman, *Heidegger's Confrontation with Modernity: Technology, Politics, Art.*) Not to detract from the historical specificities of the Holocaust, but it can also be understood as what happens when a whole population is understood as mere things that no longer have any use. Here we see a connection between the always interrelated histories of colonialism and imperialism.

Perhaps we finally have to come around to a question that would seem to have an obvious answer. (This is the "what it was" question.) That is: Why is the instrumentalizing and reification of human beings "evil"? What makes it the antithesis of good? What is this term, "good," all about? What *is* good? The answer would seem to be obvious because the idea that to treat persons as things is evil runs deep in most cultures. The Old Testament injunction against usury already conveys the perception that a money-dominated economy will result in the instrumentalization of persons. The Golden Rule has a background assumption that no one wants to be treated like a mere thing. The second formulation of the categorical imperative enjoins us to treat persons as ends and never as means only. The tradition in ethics that includes Aristotle and Kant could be summarized as always urging us to consider these questions. Even if such questions cannot be considered without trafficking in philosophical idealism, transcendental principles, and even theological concepts (I am not convinced of this, but even if . . .), there is a material difference between cultures where such questions circulate and those cultures that have set aside the discourse of the good, or have fully privatized it, taken it out of the public sphere. Although there are much earlier anticipations in Western philosophy, Thomas Hobbes initiates the systematic inquiry into the possibility of a discourse of politics where the question of what is good need play no role—and this discourse continues through the work of Adam Smith and, it needs to be said, Karl Marx. Some notion of justice is always lurking somewhere in the writings of these philosophers, but perhaps mainly as an embarrassment.

Eliminating Hypotheses

There had to have been a cultural shift that allowed the possibility of eliminating consideration of the good from political theory, on the basis of arguments ranging from ontological to anthropological. But this shift even goes beyond LaPlace's famous rejoinder regarding the absence of God from one of his scientific treatises: "Sir, I have no need of that hypothesis." No, it is not enough simply to drop the terminology of the good from theoretical pursuits—instead, this sort of talk should be actively disparaged, sneered at, even, or taken as the subject of a good laugh, or the province of the naïve, uneducated, or hopelessly nostalgic.

By way of theological interjection, I have wondered in recent years, and this wonder has been inspired by incidents of what appears to be radical evil, if it is wrong for an historical materialist such as myself to feel nostalgia for a loving god who could save us—or, at least, save some people and other creatures who have been subjected to the worst things that humans have come up with. It isn't that I can bring myself to believe in the god of classical Christian theism (which is not the theism of the early Christians, I think, but instead of the Catholic philosophical tradition from Augustine forward). Indeed, one of the two reasons that I cannot believe in this omnipotent and omnibenevolent god is that his existence is incompatible with the existence of radical evil in our human world, and I find the standard arguments for compatibility (free will, final harmony, or some "logic" that is beyond our kin) wanting and/or insulting. The other reason goes directly to what is called compatibilism, namely the compatibility of omnipotence with human agency—I don't think this one works either. But when I think about the people in Argentina who were "disappeared" during military rule (the "Dirty War," 1976–1983), some of whom were taken up in airplanes high over the ocean and dropped, I can't help but wish there was someone to catch them, to catch them in the air and to take them to a place of safety, of salvation. Wishing will not make this so, but is it wrong to have such a desire? Does feeling such "nostalgia for God" instead weaken our human sense of what other human beings have done to these poor souls? Part of what motivates the feeling/wish is the desire that there be something for these people, that their lives not suddenly come to nothing.

Well, these ruminations could be extended significantly, and one direction they might take is an encounter with Walter Benjamin's argument about anamnestic solidarity and what might be called a redemptive Marxism. (A very good discussion of Benjamin's argument is found in Helmut Peukert, *Science, Action, and Fundamental Theology*, 206–10.) This discussion would also benefit from working through what Derrida says in *Specters of Marx* about the notion of justice as mere "adjustment." Socrates has a thing or two to say on this question in the first book of the *Republic*. It seems just as hard to believe in "the good" as it is to believe in God. It is very difficult to believe that "some good may come of this"— which is, in some sense, the very definition of radical evil. Radical evil is evil that is so horrendous that, no matter what happens subsequently, there is at least some significant part of it that cannot be saved, redeemed, or "made good." To recognize radical evil is to recognize the possibility of real loss, where there is no possibility of recovery. Meanwhile, if we strain toward some sense of the good, we cannot do this without the recognition of evil as well.

"Beyond Being"

Are good and evil therefore bound together, conceptually? The suspicion of this relationship goes back at least to Plato, for whom the good is "beyond being," while evil is beneath being—in other words, each is apart from being. The suspicion has deeper roots still, in Judaism, captured well in William Blake's famous line, "Did he who made the lamb make thee?" Did he who made the lamb also make the serpent? (In Blake it is a tiger, but the point is that the same creative force produced the one who will comfort and clothe you and the one who will rip your flesh apart.) Should we then speak of "good/evil"? I am taking a cue here from Derrida's book, *The Gift of Death*, where he argues that it is right to speak of "life/death"—in part because a significant aspect of what it means to be alive is that one is the sort of creature who can die. (Obviously Derrida is developing themes from Heidegger: Dasein is the sort of being for whom death is an issue, therefore there is no moment of life for the human that is not marked by mortality.)

Perhaps these ruminations, though they are inconclusive and nonsystematic, are still enough to point us toward the prior questions, namely: How do we know what is evil and what is good, such that we can say that the global effects of the logic of the commodity and the iron law of wages (which is an effect of labor-power having been commodified) are evil and are set against the good? Let us here finally appeal to Aristotle. The question as regards Aristotle's conception of *eudaimonia* is whether some of the more troubling aspects of his essentialism can be avoided. In the *Politics*, Aristotle makes a crucial distinction between maintaining a household and the mere "getting of money," and the way that the latter can be at odds with the former. The maintenance of the household—the term for which, *oikonomia*, is also the root of our modern word, economics—is a sure guide to *eudaimonia*, while the mere getting of money, when taken as an end-in-itself, is something like the opposite, it is the road to ruin. The translations of *eudamonia* are various, one of the more popular being "happiness." This is not a bad translation, as long as one keeps in mind that, for Plato and Aristotle, there is a fundamental connection between happiness and virtue, such that only the virtuous person can be truly happy. Kant, as the reader undoubtedly knows, was very skeptical about happiness as a guide in ethics, so much so that he argued that it should play no role (except as something about which to maintain a rigorous skepticism) in ethical considerations. But the worlds in which Aristotle and Kant formulated their ethical philosophies were radically different, perhaps most of all precisely on the question of economy in the largest sense. This is again a point about colonialism and imperialism: although Kant did not use these terms, he was still arguably the first systematic philosopher of international relations, and a good argument could be made that he was attempting to formulate an ethics for a world in which social relations are increasingly far-flung. In this ever-more globalized world, happiness as a guide just will not cut it.

The argument could be extended to show that people who find themselves in the far-flung and ever-more quickly paced world increasingly find it very difficult, perhaps even impossible, to get in touch with whatever used to be deep down in a person's being that allowed them to experience the happiness of living a virtuous life. Indeed, this inner core, if it ever existed, might be numbered among the casualties of commodification. I sometimes call this core the "human reserve." I don't know that this reserve ever existed, and certainly everything is set against it in our postmodern capitalist world, but one might look for it in any- and everything in a culture that has not yet been fully determined by commodification and reification. This is the distinction that Jürgen Habermas makes between what he calls the "lifeworld" and the "system," for instance. In other words, there might be a way to speak of the human reserve in a nonessentialist way.

Flourishment

In that light we might consider another translation of *eudaimonia*: "flourishment." This term is helpful because it can be used in a nonessentialist way and because of the fundamental connection that Aristotle demonstrates among the notions of the good person, the good life, and the good society. The nonessentialism holds because, even if flourishment might be understood in different ways in different times or places, or even if it is barely understood at all, we humans are good at recognizing what is *not* flourishment, and in knowing that we need something else—at least some of the time we are good at this. Perhaps it is this capacity that is the locus of the human reserve. The systematic articulation of why a certain personal, interpersonal, social, political, or cultural arrangement is not conducive to flourishment will remain to be developed, as long as we only have this bare feeling or reaction, but it is from this feeling that normative social theory develops. And it is from understanding the interrelatedness of the "three goods" (person, life, society) that the *social* in social theory proceeds.

The distinction between "household" and "money" economies was already a good distance along the path that led to Marx's distinction between use value and exchange value. Although some argue (some more affirmatively and others critically) that Marx's distinction also partakes of an Aristotelian essentialism, I tend to think that it could instead be set out as a regulative ideal, without the essentialism. But what is more intractable in Aristotle is his essentialism as regards women and the so-called "natural slave." Recall that Plato does not include slaves among the classes of the *Republic*. His communalistic polity consists in three social groupings: the philosophers, also called the guardians, who govern; the auxiliaries, who maintain order and defend the city-state; and the working people, most of whom will be engaged in agriculture, animal husbandry, and crafts. This division of labor is deemed sufficient for the sustenance of a virtuous society, and the communalism is reinforced by the stricture that there should be no material advantage to being guardians or philosophers—and, indeed, they live in austerity.

One thing that is interesting about this arrangement is that functions such as these must exist in a socialist society (by which I mean a postcapitalist society that is transitional toward communism—a society that progressively breaks with the logic of the commodity, progressively breaks down the division of labor, and stands on the side of the basic masses internationally), but without the recursion or reification of these functions into a rigid or supposedly "natural" class structure. Plato himself does not argue that the classes in the ideal society are "natural" (in the *Republic*, that is; the *Laws* is another story—but it is generally argued that *Laws* represents something more "feasible" and less ideal). Indeed, he does not even accept, at least among the philosophers, what might be taken as the most "natural" division of labor of all, that between women and men. In the first systematic treatise on Marxism and "the woman question," *The Origin of the Family, Private Property, and the State*, Frederick Engels argues that the very first divisions of society into classes were based on this "natural" difference. Engels goes so far as to say that the emergence of class society was at the same time "the world-historic subjugation of women as a class." And yet, in the Marxist scheme, the emergence of class society can be interpreted as an "advance" for humankind.

Such an interpretation, which we can safely call the "productivist" version of Marxism, is exemplary of what happens in social theories that eschew normativity. (Much more will be said on these issues in part 3, sec. 1.) This example is important for at least two major reasons. The first is that "women hold up half the sky," so it is incumbent upon us to ask whether the forms of flourishment available to them are "naturally" of a lesser type than those available to men. The second reason has to do with this idea of an historical "advance." It isn't that Marx and Engels claim that the emergence of social classes is an "ethical" advance. In fact, the division of society into classes is, in a very biblical sense, a "fall." To take the point even further, we not only see a bifurcation in the emergence of classes, such that economics, history, and politics "advances" through more efficient and effective modes of production, while possibilities for cruelty and reification increase, such that we might see the history of class society as one long ethical decline. Marx and Engels accept this. But they take the further step of then dismissing the discourse of ethics altogether. Again, and on a generous reading, it might be granted that there are at least a few good reasons for this dismissal, the most important of which have already been mentioned: the inability of ethical discourse to go very far (or perhaps to go any distance at all) toward accomplishing the ethical, and the hijacking of this discourse by pompous moralists who are in reality nothing more than apologists for oppression, domination, and hierarchy.

Perhaps, however, another direction is possible, one that still holds central the basic Marxist argument about production, but that also appeals to a normative sense of the possibilities for human flourishing (which, in Aristotle's scheme, and mine, is interconnected with a more general co-flourishing of all creation). But before we attempt to articulate this other direction, we need to come to terms with Plato's lie and Aristotle's essentialism. In Plato's ideal city it is recognized, at least by the philosophers, that no division of labor is simply "natural," and that only certain functions are necessary to a well-ordered society. Rather than argue that social classes are a product of nature, the philosophers propagate a myth, the famous myth of the metals. In other words, they tell people that their social position is a matter of nature, when in fact the philosophers know that this is not true, and they do this for the sake of good order, at the expense of doing what philosophers ought to do, which is to tell the truth. Indeed, Book 1 of *Republic*, especially the argument between Socrates and Thrasymachus, is the model of the idea of philosophy as speaking truth to power.

Division of Labor and Social Participation

What Plato seemingly does not consider is the idea of making all of the necessary functions in society (they might simply be called production, defense, and leadership) thoroughly participatory, such that there is no need for a basic division of labor. Was this because the development of the mode of production was not yet at a level where such an idea could be conceived? That is a Marxist proposal, at any rate. I cannot entirely accept this particular Marxist proposal, precisely because Plato knows that the leaders, even being philosophers and even in a supposedly ideal society, will have to lie to the *hoi polloi* about why there are social classes and therefore why there is a division of labor, especially between mental and manual work. But there is something to the Marxist idea, in that a greater level of productivity, made possible by developments in technology, would seemingly do more to give the lie to the "need" for a class whose main function is to accumulate wealth. From this standpoint, Plato is simply offering apologetics for the ruling class—but I don't think that argument holds up. For one thing, at least in the ideal conception, the class of philosophers does not accumulate wealth—indeed, in the *de jure* sense they have no possessions, and even in the *de facto* sense they have to be the sorts of people who only require the bare minimum of creature comforts. They sound like good Bolsheviks to me! More importantly, Plato's conception (and Aristotle's too) is of a collectivity that is conscious of itself as such and is formulated under some conception of the good.

Collectivity

By contrast, what is remarkable about capitalism, especially as bourgeois classes settle into state power, is that it organizes collectivities beyond anything that could have been imagined in precapitalist times, and yet it avows to an ideology of anticollectivity. No form of society was ever more collectively organized in actual content, and no form of society was ever more avowedly anticollective in ideology. The parallel here is to what was said about economic planning—one historical irony being that a postcapitalist society might actually need less planning than has been attained now by the imperialist global order. The parallel is filled out by the fact that global, imperialist collectivity is what Simone Weil perceptively called a "blind collectivity" (which is a pointed way of making Marx's point that, even while capitalists attempt to secure their fate through planning and monopoly, capital itself remains anarchic), and imperialist planning is not for the sake of sustainability and meeting the basic material needs of humanity, but instead for the sake of the cash nexus taken as an end in itself. Capitalism and imperialism need legitimating ideologies, too, up to a point—beyond which they simply depend on overwhelming imbalances of power—and we might ask whether there is some basic relationship between Plato's supposedly "noble lie" regarding class division in his time, and the clearly ignoble lies told today by imperialism (using terms such as "free trade," "open markets," and "democracy"). After all, Athens, the so-called "cradle of democracy," was in fact a slave society, where the rights of citizenship extended to about fifteen percent of the population. Where did *Republic* truly stand in this society? Was it a critical theory that put the existing society to shame, or was it legitimating ideology that, in the end, demonstrated that class division is necessary for the well-ordered society?

Gold is a fluid, pliable metal, and in the famous myth it is gold that philosophers are made of. Meanwhile, the common people, who do not possess the mental grace to become dialecticians, are made of the baser metals, especially iron.

Aristotle's Legacy

Aristotle's legacy is similarly divided. He gives us the basic distinctions that allow us to critique the logic of the commodity, as do the Bible writers with their claims about usury, captivity, and community. Between Aristotle and the biblical prophets and messiahs (Jesus was not the only one called messiah in the Bible, Moses and David were also), this strain of Western thought remains strong through the time of Thomas Aquinas (who gives us a version of the labor theory of value, and who is writing at a time when "money money"—wealth based on early mercantile capitalism rather than on something recognizable as work—is starting to play a major role in economy and society) and into the commonwealth ideals of John Locke and Thomas Jefferson. But Aristotle also resolves the difficulty that Plato has (namely, that the latter needs to tell a lie in order to justify the existence of social classes) by arguing instead that class division, and indeed divisions among genders and peoples, are *natural* divisions. Furthermore, these divisions are the basis for a natural hierarchy among persons. In both

Plato and Aristotle, there is the argument that, if each person does not fulfill his or her assigned role, there will be unhappiness in the person and there will be general unhappiness because society will not be well ordered. Each and every thing has a natural level, and every thing must seek that level; any thing that is out of place will experience disequilibrium; in humans, this leads to discontent and unhappiness. How can any particular person flourish if he or she is not in the proper setting for doing so?

Well, we can obviously go on at even much greater length with criticisms and contextualizations of Plato and Aristotle, and with comparative perspectives on *Republic* and *Politics*, but we now have enough to generate a definition. Evil occurs when possibilities for flourishment are cut off through the efforts of some human agency, either by direct intention, or by the machinations of some social structure.

"Radical evil" is partly a question of scale, and partly a question of forms of destruction that are in principle irredeemable. The Holocaust is again the example on both counts, and, on the second, the point is that even a "divine plan" cannot make moral sense of the Shoah, and neither can an appeal to historical teleology.

Again there is a need to resist mere theodicy or historical teleology—or, at least, to see that they come to the same thing and that this same thing is inimical to there being real ethical questions in a strong sense, as well as to there being any real point to talking about good and evil. We encounter once more the cosmic irony: even though the language of good and evil cannot help but have theological overtones, if the God of classical theology exists (omnipotent, etc.), then "good and evil" (or "good/evil") is just one of his cosmic games, and we finite humans are just toy figures in the cosmic sandbox.

Theodicy and the Strange

Chess sometimes provides useful examples for philosophy (Wittgenstein appealed to chess analogies quite often, for example), and Gadamer supplies one such example that bears on the question of theodicy and intentionality. (Unfortunately, I do not at present know the original source of this passage, as I found it presented as the epigraph for a book of poems by David Solway, *Chess Pieces*. Apparently the passage is not found in *Truth and Method*, despite the fact that Gadamer discusses the concept of "play" extensively in that book. However, Solway has recently come clean as the perpetrator of a literary hoax—it turns out that he was the inventor of an obscure Greek poet, supposedly also a longshoreman, whose works, in fact authored by Solway, have been highly acclaimed and even considered for the Nobel Prize in Literature. So, who knows?)

This idea recalls what we said about the *atopon*, the strange, for in it we have "seen through" something that appeared old and unintelligible: we have brought it into our linguistic world. To use the analogy of chess, everything is "solved," resembling a difficult chess problem where only the definitive solution makes understandable (and then right down to the last piece) the necessity of a previously absurd position.

This is a very nice statement of theodicy—the previously absurd position (which might also correlate to moves that had appeared to be blunders) turns out to have made perfect sense, in twenty-twenty hindsight. Of course, if the game is not won after all, then the blunders stand as such. But this does not seem an entirely adequate analysis—or, at least, this analysis shows the shortcomings of theodicy—because the moves only "make sense" if the strategy of which they are a part results in a win. Could there not be correct moves (what chess players call "accurate" moves), even brilliant moves (with one or two exclamation marks after them), that still do not result in a win? You did the right thing (made the right moves), so you won—you won, so you must have done the right thing: isn't a facile equation such as this exemplary of a very thin pragmatism, of a sort that could never capture any deep truth of the world (or of chess, for that matter)?

The Human Project

Marx was rather fond of Aristotle, calling him the greatest mind of antiquity. The concept from Aristotle that is often associated with Marx, especially the early Marx, is "species being." One debate on Marx's philosophy has concerned whether this is another bit of essentialism, and then the question is whether or not this essentialism is to be embraced or deconstructed. If the concept of species being is essentialist, it partakes of the same essentialism as the use value/exchange value distinction. The debate can be sidestepped entirely, however, by partaking of a little Kantian "formalism"—of the sort where calling it "empty" (as Hegel did) is actually no criticism. Part of what it means to be a human being, as Sartre argued, is to have a project, to project oneself into the future. One might even say that what humans can do, what is peculiar to their Dasein, is to connect past, present, and future. Our responsibilities to the future are also responsibilities for the past, because it is a necessity of the existence of the human past that there be a human future. What is the "human project," in the largest sense? The Aristotelian answer would be that it is to create possibilities for human flourishment. We can say two seemingly contradictory things about this project, which might also be called the fundamental responsibility: it is substantive, even if in a purely "formal" sense, and yet, perhaps in accordance with its "merely formal" structure, it is also *empty*; flourishment is a placeholder. In different epochs, different cultures, different modes of production, there are different ideals of flourishment. These ideals have always been marked by the limitations of their historical contexts (and by their strengths, too)—how could things be otherwise? Kant's universalism, for example, what it means to be an "end" in his philosophy, is marked by the usual limitations of his period regarding what it means to be human. Science fiction is one of the best mirrors of the limitations of "universalism." This point is, by now, more than obvious, and has been restated repeatedly and systematically in recent years. The argument that discourses of universalism are often used to oppress people still depends for its force on the ethical norm that people should *not* be oppressed. It makes a material difference in the world if people have some sense—however vague, unconscious, poorly grasped—that human flourishment is possible, and evil is that which, as a result of human actions, blocks or destroys the pathways toward this possibility.

Meaningless Existence

What is different about capitalism in this scheme of things is that it works to short-circuit possibilities of collective human flourishment by generating an ever-greater cynicism about the regulative ideal of flourishment itself. This passage into what I would call the "purely secular" or perhaps the "hypersecular" has real, material effects, and is, arguably, the greatest evil of all. Without the ideal of flourishment, without any real sense in which we can talk about good and evil, and try to advance the former and resist the latter, in other words, in a purely secular and disenchanted world where human beings are just so many things that bump into each other and bounce around, and, to be crude about it, in a world where "shit happens," the Henry Fordist–nightmare comes fully true: history is bunk; it's just one damn thing after another. In a striking passage from his book, *The Seeds of Time*, Fredric Jameson calls such a state of the world "absolute violence":

> Parmenidean stasis [changeless Being-in-itself, to which Jameson is comparing the postmodern resistance to history] . . . to be sure knows at least one irrevocable event, namely death and the passage of the generations. . . . But death itself . . . is inescapable and [has been rendered] meaningless, since any historical framework that would serve to interpret and position individual deaths (at least for their survivors) has been destroyed. A kind of absolute violence, then, the abstraction of violent death, is something like the dialectical correlative to this world without time or history. (19)

When the previously fragmented and not yet fully ramified system of com-modity production makes the leap to an ever-more pervasive capitalism, by making the leap to the commodification of labor and putting into place institutions that violently enforce the iron law of wages (the State, in the European sense of the term), this is at the same time a banishment of the good and any ideal of flourishment.

Either sincerely or as mere "lip service," theorists such as Adam Smith offer a justification for what I would call this essential leap into the secular, arguing that, while the common good should not be the guiding principle of the newly emerging economy, the happy news is that good effects are produced as a by-product. It is easy to see, again, why Robert Paul Wolff raised the question, "what mysteries could lurk in the marketplace?" The irony is that, in some sense, Marx is working out of a similar scheme—what leads to socialism and communism is not first of all the human desire for a conscious collectivity, or any normative sense of the commonwealth, but instead the material workings of the mechanisms of class struggle and the mode of production. Although Adam Smith could perhaps be character-ized first of all as a moral philosopher, having written the important book, *Theory of Moral Sentiments*, the core of his work that Marx built on was political economy. To make political economy rather than philosophy the core of a political theory is a displacement similar to what we spoke of ear-lier in terms of the shortcomings of ethics. If ethics cannot do what it needs to do, by not only being descriptive, but by helping people to treat each other better, then we had better look elsewhere for help in creating a better society. It isn't that Marx was wrong to look for the mechanisms that reify persons and beat people down and destroy the earth, but that might also, out of their own internal contradictions, generate possibilities for a better world. To think that we could make sense of this world and of the possibilities for a better one and indeed of the possibility of saving this world—all of this without Marx, is a dangerous form of foolishness. But the problem is in thinking that in laying the mechanisms bare and show-ing their contradictions, all sense of normativity can be dispensed with.

"Utopian" and "Scientific"

It has become commonplace, within Marxism, to take most anything that is problematic in Marx and lay the blame on Engels. I do not accept this perspective, nor do I want to disavow the many important analyses that Engels provided. It is often the case, however, that the more worrisome tendencies in Marx become more acute in Engels's work, and a significant case of this is the distinction between "utopian" and "scientific" socialism. The distinction crystalizes and hardens the setting aside of hope and idealism; the distinction sets the stage for the forms of Marxism that inevitably become reductivistic, mechanistic, dogmatic, and cold-hearted. In contrast to this, there is a subterranean tradition of Marxism that attempts to restore hope and normativity to the more "systematic" (or "scientific") project. Among the representatives of this trend are Benjamin, Bloch, and Derrida. As a theoretical issue that has practical consequences, the question is one of taking the parts of radical social theory, including political economy, that need at times to be coldly analytical, and wrapping them in the warmer blankets of human striving toward the good society.

In Adam Smith's political economy, the last thing that is needed in the direction of a society is good will—or, at least, it is certainly not anywhere near being the first thing. To believe in such a thing, European humanity has to be a good distance down the road of secularism: to take as normative that other persons are to be treated as things among other things, to be treated merely as the "material reserve" (to use Heidegger's insightful term), to make any sense that "we are all God's children" a merely "private affair," a sentiment only applicable on Sunday morning, if then—all of this is part and parcel of a world where normativity is progressively banished and even derided. The invisible hand will take care of whatever good is to be found in this world—but, again, for Adam Smith, the happy news is that it will turn out that there is plenty of good to be passed around, at least in terms of material well-being. Arguments of a utilitarian sort make much of their supposedly straightforwardly empirical basis. Empirical arguments have to submit to empirical confirmation or disconfirmation. Smith's argument for the invisible hand is of the form, "the rising tide lifts all boats." It turns out, empirically, that the rising tide does *not* lift all boats, even if capitalism in its industrial stage seems to create more "wealth" than had ever existed before. To say that, in absolute terms, there is enough wealth around to create, on average, a decent standard of living for everyone, does not address the point that an average can be made up of people living in luxury at one end, and people who are starving or dying from polluted water, at the other.

However, quite apart from the empirical disconfirmation of arguments supporting the wonders and freedoms that capitalism will supposedly bring to humanity, there is a deeper point to be made about normativity. If, as Kant argued, there is nothing that is truly good in the world apart from the good will, then a world that banishes normativity will, by and by, have nothing good in it. Perhaps it will have nothing "evil" in it, either, insomuch as it will have become a world of billiard balls and other objects bumping into each other—a world of Parmenidean stasis or changeless Being, which calls to mind Herbert Marcuse's statement (from *One-Dimensional Man*) about capitalism's having generated an exceedingly dynamic society in which, in fact, nothing really happens. But this form of passage "beyond good and evil," at least, is what I am calling the absolute evil of our secular times—and it is an opening toward the possibility of doing *absolutely anything* to other human beings, other animals, and the rest of creation. What the displacement of philosophy by political economy obscures is that the passage beyond this pure secularization of society requires the passage to a postsecular understanding of the world, and ultimately a postsecular society.

Marginalization of the Good

The mechanisms of reification, the most severe of which is the iron law of wages, insure that the discourse of the good is increasingly marginalized. When the iron law of wages begins to work on a global scale, people in the rich, colonialist, and imperialist countries are able to ignore the immiseration that occurs at great distances from them. Indeed, the moral rot that sets in because of imperialism allows people to ignore immiseration that is right around them—given that there are very few first-world countries that do not have large chunks of the Third World within them—or else people feel simply powerless to do anything about "the way things are." The world settles into the idea that there is nothing other than the invisible hand, there is nothing other than mechanism, and all that one can do is to endure this experience, whether one has lots of distractions (material goods, such as plasma TVs, sports cars, boats or jet-skis, etc.) or is living in a shanty.

Kant was prescient in recognizing that ethical theory had to come to terms with an increasingly far-flung and commercial world. As Sankar Muthu writes in a truly important book, *Enlightenment against Empire*, in a chapter titled "Kant's Anti-Imperialism,"

> Kant recognized that the ongoing, often antagonistic relationships among diverse peoples constituted the global political reality of his day, one that demanded, in his view, not only a conjectural history of their earlier development as he had earlier provided, but also an ethical and political analysis. His concept of cosmopolitan right . . . is meant precisely to offer a critique of empire. (187)

It might even be said that ethical distance is what Kant's philosophy is all about, and that he was attempting to take account of the role that geographical and cultural distance plays in the problem of conceiving what is right. Hobbesian alternatives to Kant (which again can include rational choice theories, for instance the work of David Gauthier) might be understood as recognitions of a distance that individuals cannot really do anything about. Either I take the core of moral theory to be the treatment of the other as an end-in-herself or -himself, or I simply take it as *realpolitik* that I find myself in the midst of a war of all against all, and the only sense in which I can treat even myself as an end is purely biological. This would be a narrow and mechanistic "biology," at that.

The Good Society

I contend that Marxism and radical social theory generally needs to be restitched into the tradition of the good society, otherwise these theories and the practices based in them will be purely reactive, and some invisible hand or other (what Sartre calls the "practico-inert") will continue to exercise its force. Although I tend to think that the saying that "all that is needed for evil to triumph is for good men to do nothing" is part of the arsenal of bourgeois moralizing, there is something to it. What happens in the world of immense structures of reification—systems of evil—is that evil triumphs because people are rendered into things. The structures are immense, therefore the forces that are brought against the possibilities for human flourishment are also immense, and, from time to time, these structures give rise to a spasm of "antiflourishment" that can properly be called "radical evil."

Wolff's argument at the very end of *Moneybags Must Be So Lucky* is that

> Precisely because Marx's vision of capitalist society requires for its expression an ironic authorial voice, *Capital* is not, in the modern acceptation, a scientific work. Its insights and revelations are imperfectly rendered by a textbook redaction of the theory of surplus value or the thesis of the tendency of the rate of profit to fall. Like a great novel, a great work of social theory is an inherently perspectival rendering of an authorial vision. Its truth as well as its power resides at least in part in the ironic implication of its author in the mystifications and injustices that it exposes.
>
> It is for this reason that we continue to read *Capital* more than a century after its publication. And it is for this reason, as well, that we who aspire to follow Marx's path must struggle to find for ourselves a voice in which to speak of the inversions, the mystifications, the *verrucktheit* [craziness, insanity], of our own age. (82)

There is an interesting question here regarding what might be called the *modalities* of truth, or perhaps the *tonalities* of truth. The very idea of an "iron law" partakes of both scientific and, in its ancient tropological traces, theological modalities. It is the latter that is suspect within the "modern acceptation" of scientific inquiry. That which requires more "at the one end" than is, strictly speaking, grounded in empirical science, demands more "at the other end" as well—neither what people do that is evil nor what they may try to do for the good is entirely within the realm of scientific confirmation/disconfirmation. The same is the case for Kant's categorical imperative—to say that it exists in the very logic of reality is a bit of an overstep, to say the least. Philosophically, it is a matter of "reaching"; it is a matter of striving and struggle. Not just philosophically: practically, even more so practically. Like revolution, the ethical is never finished—as Kant said, the tasks it sets are infinite.

However, perhaps I disagree with Wolff's conclusion a little bit, though this may be a matter of semantics. Much of what Marx set out in *Capital* has not been disconfirmed, in my view, but instead has to be recast in the light of the development of capitalism into a fully global mode of production, a development that continues to this day and that has generated even newer forms of inversion, mystification, and *verruckheit* since Wolff's book was published in 1988. I would recast Wolff's conclusion slightly and ask, What is it in the prophetic and ironic tonalities that themselves bring forth the *truth* in Marx's systematic exposition? What is it in these tonalities that make this overall truth complete or at least something that strives toward completion—not as a philosophical system, but as a theoretical guide to social transformation? What is it about the slippage of modalities, from the scientific (where the standard can never be metaphysical certainty) to the self-consciously value-laden modes of poetic and prophetic discourse (where there is at least a kind of certainty that this evil must be stopped and overcome) that itself motivates, philosophically, the systematic project of Marx?

In *After Marxism*, Ronald Aronson argues similarly to Wolff, that Marxism never was the science that it claimed to be, and he draws the conclusion that we ought to let go of the Marxism that was never really what Marx thought it was in the first place. In response to this position I want to conclude part 1 with a few final remarks.

From Positivism to Hope

Most likely, not much more argument is needed against a "Marxism" that still clings to a positivist conception of "science." Even apart from whether Marxism could be "scientific" (indeed, in its more rigidified versions of dialectical materialism, simply another name for science itself) in some nonpositivistic sense, all we will ever get from positivistic Marxism from now on is reductivism and dogma, and that will not help us change the world. Indeed, this reductivism itself reflects the overwhelming machinery of capital, which already does a fine job of reducing all qualities to quantity.

As a matter of methodology, we can make an analytical distinction in Marx between the parts that can be set out more systematically, and in that sense are *Wissenschaftliche*, and those parts that go to the aforementioned tonalities and modalities. To make these distinctions is not a new idea; indeed, what Aronson calls for is not at all new either, but instead a reminder of some arguments that go back to even the time of Marx and certainly to the Kantian ethical socialists at the end of the nineteenth century. Instead, what Aronson is doing is *timely*, and in that sense interesting and valuable. (It should go without saying that the accounts in the book of Aronson's trajectory through the New Left are valuable.) In particular, the timeliness of Aronson's project has to do with the collapse of the Soviet Union and the Soviet Bloc. A good many people take this collapse to have made a significant statement about Marxism—but what is perhaps surprising is that many of these people are on the political Left. The collapse is significant, but for two reasons especially, reasons that do not seem to me to affect the need for "something like Marxism." First, the collapse marked the end of a trajectory in which two nuclear powers, imperialist powers with global reach, were on a collision course that could have led to the end of humanity. The terms of things were clearer back then, in the Cold War, because of the dramatic dichotomy operating on a global scale, but there were points when humanity was quite likely only "a minute away from midnight." Second, the collapse opened the door to the present trajectory, in which the United States is attempting to forge its empire (to both shore it up and extend it) on an historically unprecedented scale, and within an imperialist world-system that is at present "monopolar" (as opposed to the dipolarity of the years of U.S./Soviet contention). No one can say where this trajectory will lead, but it is not overreaching to say that things look very bad. Aronson argues that our new response needs to rely on both ethical discourse and on the rekindling of utopian discourse and aspirations, and I do not disagree with him. (It should be added that *After Marxism* was published in 1995. Some elements of the post–September 11, 2001 trajectory will be addressed in the conclusion.) Does it, however, cancel what ought to be at least conditional autonomy for these realms of ethics and hope to also talk, or attempt to talk, in a systematic way about the social mechanisms at work that both enable evil and dystopia and that may, in their fundamental contradictions, create openings to organizing society in a fundamentally better way?

In his concluding chapter, "Sources of Hope," Aronson speaks of the possibility of a certain "integration," and this speaks to the questions of "science" and systematicity.

> Immanuel Kant thought that all of reason's concerns are embraced by three questions: What can I know; what should I do; and what may I hope. Integrated into a single project, these are precisely the questions that have been addressed by the critique of radical hope that I present in this book. In exploring how we

radicals should think about ourselves after Marxism, I have been suggesting what we can know, how we should act, and what we can hope. In a sense, hope is the central issue throughout this discussion, framing every page. (279)

We will turn to one of Aronson's specific ideas about what we can know shortly. Before that, there are three points I want to make in response to what can be taken as a concluding methodological summation. First, it seems to me that Aronson is largely right in his characterization of what the radical project is: it is to explore the questions that Kant raises, in theory and activism, and, again in theory and activism, to explore the possibility of the integration of these questions into a single project.

Second, it is an interesting question how to proceed with Kant's own integration of the three questions into a single project. The claim that the ethical question is the integrating element is not especially controversial. Aronson shifts the focus to hope. This is a valid and worthwhile proposal, I think, especially if seen in the context of what might be called "materialized" Kantian epistemologies, such as those found in the work of William James and Jean-Paul Sartre (in addition to the figures Aronson cites the most in the chapter, Herbert Marcuse and Ernst Bloch), where the structure of belief itself is inextricably linked to commitment, the future, and the idea of a project (where humanity is pro-jected into the future). An immediate integration suggests itself in that surely there is an ethics of hope, just as there is to the dream. Marx spoke to this point in 1844, but in a way that, at least some would say, clearly suggests he was not yet a "Marxist":

> the world has long been dreaming of something that it can acquire if only it becomes conscious of it. It will transpire that it is not a matter of drawing a great dividing line between past and future, but of carrying out the thoughts of the past. And finally, it will transpire that humankind begins no *new* work, but consciously accomplishes its old work. ("For a Ruthless Criticism of Everything Existing," MER, 15)

Later, after he created "scientific Marxism," Marx spoke quite differently, as we see in this famous passage from *The Eighteenth Brumaire of Louis Bonaparte*:

> The social revolution of the nineteenth century cannot draw its poetry from the past, but only from the future. It cannot begin with itself, before it has stripped off all superstition in regard to the past. Earlier revolutions required world-historical recollections in order to drug themselves concerning their own content. In order to arrive at its content, the revolution of the nineteenth century must let the dead bury their dead. There the phrase went beyond the content; here the content goes beyond the phrase. (MER, 597)

Take Kant's three questions, these two passages from Marx, and the methodological proposal (as I am reading it, at any rate) from Aronson, and there is a book in itself. We could add to this mix, as well, an idea that hovers over Aronson's project, namely, that what Marx said of the revolution of the nineteenth century shows clearly that the present period is much different.

The Epistemology of Hope

It is pretty clear, and yet not absolutely certain. As a guide to the creation of a Marxist "science" based in Kant's three questions, it can be readily asserted that Marx's focus is epistemology. That is the "first track," and, to return to language employed previously, ethics and hope are set aside to the second track at best. If being "after Marxism" means displacing this first track from its privileged position, then certainly the arguments presented in this book are just as much "after Marxism" as are Ronald Aronson's. However, there is too much of Marx's "knowledge" that I still accept, and too much of the methodology that Marx used to get his "knowledge" that I still accept, for me to give up on the Marxist project. The dissolution of the Soviet Bloc, for instance, and the subsequent trajectory of the imperialist world-system, which is the proximate cause of what Aronson calls "a period of mourning" for "the end of Marxism," needs itself to be understood through the categories and forms of analysis that Marx left to us. The phenomena themselves will force these terms on us, even if not only these terms and even if not always these terms in the way that Marx understood them. To attempt an analysis of the imperialist system without these terms will just lead to a reinvention of the wheel. So what I propose instead is a reorientation of Marx, a different integration of Kant's three questions that comes closer to the way Kant and certain more recent figures such as Adorno, Marcuse, Sartre, and Derrida, see things. And yet I recognize how close this reorientation is, at least in some respects, to the project that Aronson is outlining in *After Marxism*, at least methodologically, and certainly more orthodox Marxists will see the idea of "Ethical Marxism" as being more "after" than "Marxism."

However, and this is the third point, there is at least a difference on a purely political level, a difference that might be read back into what might at first appear to be only a slight difference in methodology—namely, that the orientation for which Aronson hopes to create a post-Marxist foundation is reformist and social-democratic, whereas the orientation for which I hope to create a revitalized Marxist foundation aims to be revolutionary and communist.

Why Call It "Marxism"?

Even if on a fairly superficial level, the association with the term
"Marxism" is related to this difference. What does it matter what "it" is
called? Well, the difference is in what "it" is. "Ethical Marxism," as I conceive it, still holds on to a certain methodology and categories of analysis, even if also arguing that whatever "science" there is to be had must
ultimately receive its orientation from an ethical perspective. Kant, James,
and Sartre (among others, of course) understand belief and knowledge
this way, as not disinterested, as involving commitment and an orientation toward the future. In the last twelve years or so of his life James was
involved in attempting to understand—and fight—the emergence of
American imperialism. Undoubtedly, James had his political limitations,
and at the same time he was tracking the emergence of imperialism in the
same timeframe as when Marx and Engels were somewhat ambivalent
about what they understood to be colonialist ventures. Without removing the edge from what ought to be a sharp critique of Marx's and
Engels's Eurocentrism, to be fair it can also be added that the world was
in a period of rapid change in the last decades of the nineteenth century
and the first decade of the twentieth. New configurations were emerging
on a global scale—precisely what Lenin was coming to understand as
imperialism, in the technical sense, the qualitative changes that come
about when capitalism operates as a fully global mode of production, and
not just on a country-by-country basis or as a matter of plunder by colonialist powers. (Again, more on this in the next chapter.) Significantly,
James argues that there is a connection between the "violence of abstraction" which he associates with German Idealism and America's having
entered into an age of "abstractionism and the mass" (Cotkin, 155). Not
to trivialize, but imperialism, especially understood in Lenin's sense, is a
tough nut to crack.

   Imperialism is not itself the ethical stumbling block of Marxism, but it
is very close to this stumbling block. There is a basic component of Marx's
conception that runs up against the questions of hope and ethics, and that
component is Marx's conception of *interest*. We will pick up this thread in
part 2. The question for a hypothetical "Ethical Marxism" is whether one
can address the problem of "interest," as one way of conceiving human
motivation, and either excise the conception or at least radically reconfigure it, and at the end of the process still have something that ought to be
called "Marxism." Another way to put this is to ask if what I have said thus
far about right and wrong, good and evil, and maintaining an orientation
toward the future in the form of an epistemology of hope can be *taken to
heart* within a framework that remains recognizably Marxist. Can this be
done? Should this be done?

In answer to the first question, this project can be carried through if there is the possibility of at least a minimal systematic integration of Kantian themes of ethics and hope with at least a large part of Marx's theoretical and methodological (historical, philosophical, political economic, sociological, cultural) apparatus.

In answer to the second question, this project *ought* to be carried through if there is a pressing need for it, a need directly related to the future of humanity and the possibility of creating a global community of mutual flourishing.

Unforgivable Napalm: Imperialism Is the Ethical Question of Our Time

Looking West to East

If you ever have the good fortune to visit San Francisco, take a walk up Telegraph Hill and you will see a curious sight. Standing at the top of the hill is a statue of a man in a confident stance, looking out over the Pacific Ocean. When I first took the climb, in the summer of 1990, approaching the sculpture from behind, I had no idea who I would find, who would be represented. None of the guesses I made as I approached were correct.

Christopher Columbus.

Christopher Columbus, having made it from the "West Indies" to the Pacific coast, carried upon the wings of manifest destiny, now looks even further west, to the Hawaiian Islands, to the Samoan Islands, to the Philippines, so far west that he finally sees the East, and he looks to Japan, and finally he looks to the "main prize," China.

However, this statue, assuming that it has no greater powers of actual eyesight than a real, flesh-and-blood Columbus would, is not able to look directly upon these prizes of colonialism and imperialism. In fact, what is directly in the line of view of this statue is an island rather closer to the State of California . . . an infamous island—Alcatraz.

Now, in fact, this statue has only been in place since 1957. ("Columbus Day" itself dates from 1910, when it was declared by President Taft.) Although the commissioning and placement of this statue was supposedly meant as an expression of Italian-American pride, the positioning of the statue makes an imperialist statement. This is the case regardless of what anyone intends; however, the people who decided to put the statue at the top of Telegraph Hill (and in front of Coit Tower, a WPA building that contains social-realist murals depicting working-class readers reading such authors as Marx and Lenin), or at least some of them, surely knew what they were doing.

Why Do Bad Things Happen?

The large-scale, terrible things that happen in the world and that have been happening for some time now all go back in one way or another to the imperialist system. To stop these terrible things from happening, we have to change this system, get beyond it, and create a new social system, a new set of social relations. Ultimately, this has to happen on a global scale, or else the brutal system of exploitation, domination, and reification will destroy our planet. Nothing could be clearer and indeed this is clear to many people, and, even if it is not clear to some, most people are not unaware of systemic problems in general, and have some sense that things are not right. But most people in the world are caught in a web of powerlessness (or the overwhelming feeling of this, at least) or complicity, and there is a spectrum here that runs from the imperialist hyperpower at the complicitous end of things to the Third World at the other end.

Certain effects of imperialism are completely visible to anyone who has eyes to see, even to the point that one is almost struck dumb by the power of a set of interlocking dominant ideologies that allow the better-off citizens of imperialist countries to not see the evil that is perpetrated in their name, and often with their active participation on various levels. One of the reasons why I argue that imperialism is *the* ethical question of our time is that, despite the fact that it seems dramatically simple and straightforward to make a case against imperialism on ethical grounds, this case seems to go nowhere for tens of millions of people in an imperialist country such as the United States. Grasping why this is the case, as a matter of not only ethics, but also epistemology, requires bringing the methodology and categories of Marxism into the picture. In part 1 of this book I argued that the great irony is that ethics does not have what it takes to be ethical. Now, it can be argued that ethics, in order to be true to itself, has to go in pursuit of whatever it takes, which may run the gamut from epistemology to revolutionary military strategy. But "ethics," as some abstract conception, does not go in pursuit of anything, instead *people* do—or they do not, for various reasons that we will discuss in what follows. These reasons have to do with the powerlessness and complicity.

Empathy

Is there some "natural connection" between seeing bad things and wanting to do something to help make things better, some natural, human bond of empathy? Despite the fact that this may seem like a hopelessly naïve question, surely there is something to the fact that many people are willing to help when presented with a person in need right in front of them. This empathy seems even to transcend political differences. In a society such as the United States, where there is an entrenched racist system, "racial" difference remains a barrier even in the "immediate" case. In crowded urban environments, too, what Georg Simmel called the "blasé attitude" affects our ability to respond to so many people with basic needs, especially when we are approached repeatedly and seemingly from all sides. Here, too, people find themselves up against the "systemic," the poverty and abjection caused by a social system the parameters of which are epistemically difficult to grasp—and, once grasped (or even glimpsed), even much more difficult to do anything about.

And yet empathy is everywhere; it is not so very rare. Even the big city, in a social system where everything is aimed at pressing the advantage, where even the most good-willed person would not last very long without at least some sense of wariness, has not yet squeezed every last bit of empathy out of people. When I first moved to Chicago, I was a bit overwhelmed by this dense, yet sprawling, urban environment. Although I had grown up in fairly large cities, they were quite different, and in any case, we had lived in the suburbs. One day, feeling somewhat disoriented by a new job and environs, and miserable from the cold, I was making my way down a snow- and ice-covered sidewalk. Even on a warm and sunny day I am quite capable of tripping or slipping and falling down, something I do two or three times a year, thanks to general clumsiness, the mental wanderings typical of those in my profession, and a pair of trick ankles. This particular winter day was just made for a fall, and indeed I began to slip and go down. A hand reached out and grasped me firmly enough to keep me from falling; it was the hand of an African-American man. I was most appreciative for the assist and also for the fact that this man helped me feel that my new world was not so completely cold after all.

Since the summer of 1998, I have divided my life between Chicago and a small city (population 48,000) in the middle of Kansas. When I am in Kansas, I take lots of long bike rides in the countryside. I occasionally have a breakdown a good many miles from home, and when this happens I simply walk along the side of the road and hold out my thumb. I have never waited more than five minutes for a ride, and the person who picks me up takes me right to my house. Sometimes a riding partner has gone on ahead to get their vehicle to come back for me, so I do not put out my thumb, but still people stop to see if I need a ride. I never get into a political conversation with whoever picks me up, but it is a safe bet that most, if not absolutely all, of those who give me a ride have political views that are very different from mine. On this "personal" level people are quite willing to approach one another with good will, friendliness, empathy, and a desire to help someone when it seems possible to do so. I suppose that it is the word "possible" in this last sentence that makes all the difference. One measure of possibility is that, while I do not hesitate to issue an open-ended call for help in the form of putting my thumb out on the roads of rural Kansas, I do not do this if I have a bike breakdown in the Chicago area. Not only would I be wary of what could come of such a request in that area, but also I fully understand why a driver in that locale would be quite wary of answering this request. What is much harder is understanding that the fundamental issues are not primarily psychological, but rather social-systemic.

Definite Social Relations

All I mean by this last point is that we humans live in societies, and every society is set up in a certain way. Everyone knows this, of course, and yet this remains somehow an elusive truth. As Marx said in *The German Ideology*, people everywhere have had to enter into definite social relations and a definite way of producing that which is needed to carry on with life. By "definite" is not meant predetermined by some transcendent scheme. Instead think of a trip to a destination where there is a choice of roads on which to travel. The traveler may go on this road or that road, but she will definitely go on one of them. In the case of the form of production and social relations in general, we make our way in the world, but, as Marx said, we do not do this "just as we please." We have to work with an "inheritance"—an inherited division of labor, inherited "roads" to our goals. For sure, we can struggle against these inherited pathways, and sometimes we have no choice but to engage in such a struggle, but our struggle will be *unrealistic and we will fail* unless we understand the existing pathways for what they are. We will fail *because* our struggle is unrealistic, if we do not understand at least the broad contours and indeed many of the particulars of the "such and such a way" that society is set up. However, there is a tendency, as Marx also argued in *The German Ideology* and elsewhere instead to see social structures and social relations and "the production of life" as "natural." (The reader is most likely quite familiar with these themes, but for a refresher, see *The German Ideology*, in MER, 149–57.) If that is the limit of understanding what is going on in society, however, the tendency will be to see the difference in my bicycle-breakdown situations in urban and rural settings as mainly psychological. Even if it is recognized that there are good reasons for people to be "less helpful" in metropolitan urban settings, however, what is really needed is not to remain at the level of the psychological, but instead to grapple with the underlying systemic factors. For instance, in the rural setting, people may feel more able to relate to others "as people," because, for one thing, there are far fewer of them. This may have something to do with the possibility of "eye-level" relationships, but it is not the same thing as the Sartrean ideal of reciprocity in relationships. (Though I would happily reciprocate for the help the person has given me on the rural highway, I have yet to encounter the situation where there was even the least expectation of that.) Ethics, the ethical relationship, seems to encounter greater problems the greater the distance there is to be bridged among people (and of course these distances are even greater between human beings and nonhuman animals and the rest of the "nonhuman world"). That is one axis, an axis of distances and gaps that have to be bridged. The other axis of "ethical difficulty" is the problem of grasping the way that these distances are shaped and even produced by the social system.

There is a relationship between epistemology and ethical regard, perhaps better conceived as a relationship between the constellation of knowledge and understanding on the one side (though perhaps there can be "knowledge," but not *understanding*, without empathy?), and caring, concern, the desire to help, and the actual attempt to help, on the other. There are those who would care, if they "knew," but they do not know. There are also those who, seemingly, do not care even though they do "know." This is a philosophical problem as old as Plato, to be sure. It is an even much more difficult problem in our day, as the distances and gaps in this world are greater and bigger. It is also a philosophical problem in our contemporary world that goes to the fact that, in hoping to show that caring and concern need to be understood as deeper than knowledge, and are in fact the basis for the pursuit of knowledge, some have looked to Aristotle, and others to Kant. We will return to this issue.

Vietnam

In these days of a triumphant, capitalist America that has no past, except with regard to offenses supposedly done to it (themselves not marked by memory, as with the famous "Why do they hate us?" nonquestion), it ought to be said repeatedly, with the force of an ethical imperative: *Vietnam, Vietnam, Vietnam.* To put it bluntly: What did the people of Vietnam ever do to the people of the United States?

What did the people of Vietnam ever do to deserve the terror rained upon them by the United States?

Or, to put this even more directly: The people of Vietnam *never* did *anything* to deserve the treatment they received at the hands of the United States.

That is the sum total of the ethical case as regards the issues between the United States and Vietnam. Let us be clear about this, and in that light let us recognize the "justifications" that are offered in response to the first two questions for what they are: not anything having to do with ethics, except in the negative sense of a cancellation of ethics, a response that aims to negate the ethical response.

The world of capitalism is completely upside-down as regards the ethical response; it is, to quote the title of a well-known film, a "say anything" world. Thus the justifications offered for what was done to the people of Vietnam range from "geo-political" considerations having to do with the machinations of a competing imperialist power (the Soviet Union) to the idea that the Vietnamese people are Buddhists and therefore believe in reincarnation (and therefore do not care about dying). Underneath these "nonethical" and indeed antiethical "justifications" is racism (for example, anti-Asian racial slurs, which are still heard today) and the assertion of the supreme right of the United States to determine the fate of the world— something heard even more today in terms of doctrines of preemption and conditional sovereignty. There is a Marxist analysis that tells us what likely *will* happen, given the way that capitalism, colonialism, and imperialism work, regardless of what would be right and what *ought* to happen. We cannot ignore this analysis—we will not find the openings for what *ought* to happen without engaging with a materialist analysis of social causes and effects, causes and effects that go, *ultimately*, to the mode of production, even if Louis Althussser was also right to argue that "the lonely hour of the economy never arrives," in the sense of an "unalloyed truth" of the system that can be seen in its bare-bones essentials. And yet, even though things never become so clear, analytically or empirically, we can still speak *this* unalloyed truth with certainty, with the force of modality: The people of Vietnam never did anything to deserve the treatment they received from the United States.

Memory

At a time when Americans are suffering from something that goes beyond memory loss, when memories are apparently never formed in the first place, a time when Americans can ask, seemingly without the least compunction or self-consciousness, "Why do they hate us?" this sentence ought to be repeated as a mantra: *The people of Vietnam never did anything to deserve the treatment they received from the United States.*

As the Vietnam War recedes into the past, Americans will ask more and more, What does this have to do with me? A very "American" question, really, even if it is a question heard elsewhere too (for instance in the U.K., in relation to immigration from the former colonies that are now part of a supposed "commonwealth"). The most "postmodern" American sense of the question was captured well by the character Richard Fish, from the *Ally McBeal* show, who, *immediately* upon offending another person would say, "bygones!" The offender is already "over" the offense, so let's move on! Recall, too, the theme song from the first Clinton administration, Fleetwood Mac's "Don't Stop Thinking about Tomorrow"—"yesterday's gone, yesterday's gone!" History is rather thin on the ground. This thin, very thin, sense of history comes together nicely with advanced capitalism, even if there was no grand teleological scheme to the march of modes of production that put these elements together. Then again, the thin, nearly nonexistent, sense of history (perhaps it should be called the "nonsense" of history, but the semantics of that expression go too far in giving in to the problem itself) that is almost synonymous with "America" (especially in the eyes of the rest of the world), works *so well* with contemporary capitalism that, at the very least, one can say that the antihistory and antimemory elements are strong enablers of this capitalism.

Indeed, Americans will *not* ask more and more, "What does this have to do with me?"

Trajectories of Capital

Capitalist systems have, within themselves, no natural limits to how far they will go with schemes of exploitation. In capitalism, to use Heideggerian language, the whole world is set "ready-to-hand," the whole world is "resources," the "standing reserve." Marx, in my view, is at times deficient on the question of culture, in the sense that "culture" for Marx is simply a superstructural expression of an economic base. In many societies, however, capitalism has developed not only "organically," as was more the case with continental Western Europe and England (which gave, in the latter case, a trio of ingenious Scots—David Hume, David Ricardo, and Adam Smith— a privileged view of the development), but instead has been "implanted" from elsewhere. Even in the case of England, which was for Marx the classical laboratory, there were many points where the earlier culture was an impediment to the development of capitalism. Marx examined very carefully and thoughtfully the ways in which emergent capital encountered and overcame the earlier culture and economic formation—first and foremost through the driving of the peasants off of the land and into urban factories, their replacement on the land with sheep, the invention of the cotton gin by Eli Whitney, and the situatedness of these developments within an international frame of the slave trade, the production of cotton in the American South, advanced weaving techniques (the moving loom inspired Charles Babbage's notion of the calculating engine—an earlier form of the computer), and colonialism in India. A line can be traced from the "cell form" of capital—the commodity—to this global system, but it is not a line that can be predicted in advance. Instead, capital must work through existing cultures, or around them, and sometimes in contradiction with them. If imperialism is now creating a world of even greater homogeny (and it is), it is doing this through the broad destruction of cultures and their replacement with a bland and pointless, if often buzzing, "McWorld." (One of the best depictions of what such a world might look like when the present forces of globalization have done their work is William Gibson's *Neuromancer*—but, more and more, *Neuromancer* is now.) If what remains of historic cultures are, among other things, repositories of history and memory (not always in written documents or even in oral practices, but often in practices and rituals), then the *activation* of history and memory becomes a practice of resistance to globalizing McWorld-ization.

In actual fact, Marx did think that capital has "natural limits," or at least limits as natural as anything can have—for Marx, everything in the world works through a logic of internal contradictions and external conditions, and nothing lasts forever. However, my point is that there is no limit to what capitalists will do in the pursuit of their capitalist interests, and by this I mean that there are no *moral* limits. If there are elements of any given culture that stand in the way of more efficient and profitable exploitation, then these elements must be overcome. What cultural conservatives who support free-market capitalism (or something they perceive as such) have the greatest difficulty recognizing is that anything that can be deemed valuable within the price structure of the market can also be deemed less valuable or even worthless, especially if land or resources can be used more profitably. The greatest works and monuments of Western culture, to say nothing of non-Western cultures, are readily thrown on the trash heap when another way to make a buck is found. The clique within the ruling class that is setting the terms for American imperialism as of this writing, namely those around George W. Bush, are a perfect example of what Daniel Bell referred to several decades ago as the "cultural contradictions of capitalism"—indeed, Bush is in some sense the "outcome" and perfect representative of these contradictions: a quasi-literate president with no recognizable "culture" whatsoever. Of course it is all too easy to take potshots at such an individual; the more important point is to see both the underlying workings of the social structure and the way that certain individuals are positioned to act as proud representatives of this structure (in the case of G. W. Bush by representing, championing, and validating ignorance). Undoubtedly Marx was right to be completely skeptical about representatives of a capitalist system undertaking to lecture the masses on the question of "virtue." There can be no virtue in a system that is premised upon the commodification of everything, where each and every thing is reduced to its price, to its equivalent quantification, and indeed to its mere "thing-ness."

The Fall

The experience and premises of this reduction are deep in human history and prehistory. The stories of a human fall capture something very essential, and these stories are widespread and go far beyond Western monotheism. How is it that the first "objectifications" emerged, such that human beings felt themselves to be fundamentally alienated from the rest of "our" planet and the rest of "our" cosmos, and ultimately alienated from each other? This "fall" is something more than the struggle for survival; it is an antagonistic mindset about the world, nonhuman animals and nature, and about other people. Certainly it is a matter of material circumstances and the need for food, shelter, and clothing, but it is also a matter of recognition, of who and what counts as a subject of moral concern. My own view of this (developed in the first section of part 3) is that myths of a human fall point to a time when humans first began to eat nonhuman animals on a regular basis. This most likely occurred out of physical necessity, during the last ice age (starting roughly thirty-five thousand years ago). Note, for instance, that in the biblical account of the Garden of Eden, there is no mention of carnivorism—God gives various plants, most notably the fruit of various trees, to Adam and Eve for their sustenance, and he also gives to them the right to name the animals. Furthermore, Adam and Eve appear to be in a harmonious and nonantagonistic relationship with the animals and to engage in discourse with them (including a certain reptile who presents his own arguments about this seeming utopia). Of course, one does not have to accept the idea that there was a golden age when lions and lambs lay together in order to imagine a passage from vegetarianism to carnivorism, and to imagine that this passage involves a need for myth structures that explain how creatures with their own lives, life cycles, feelings, and forms of flourishing can come to be viewed as mere objects of consumption.

In *The Origin of the Family, Private Property, and the State*, Engels argued that the emergence of class society was at the same time "the world-historic defeat of women as a class." Luce Irigaray and other philosophers have argued that, if the commodity is the "cellular form" of capitalism, then the domination of women is the cellular form of the commodity. Certainly control over the means of reproduction is intimately related to the control of the means of production in general, and this former domination requires means of control that are intimate indeed. Commodification and objectification arise together and go hand-in-hand. Imperialism is commodification as a global process, and this process works through massive objectifications, massive reifications, with consequences that are almost unimaginably brutal. Almost unimaginable, and yet someone, some group of people, had to imagine substances such as napalm and Agent Orange, and they had to imagine the consequences of using such substances—but this "imagination" (truly, these examples are an insult to the word) is of a "chemical," not moral, sort.

Historical Debt

However, my worry, and the reason I have undertaken to formulate "Ethical Marxism," is that there are lines in Marx's thought, and certainly in the thought of a number of important Marxist thinkers and political leaders since Marx's time, that simply lead to what might be called the "higher objectification." As a matter of epistemology, I think that we can have reality, and that we do not have to give in to a broad relativism (as opposed to the more legitimate scope of cultural difference and indeterminacy and underdetermination), without "objective reality," the worry, again, being that objectivism and objectification are closely linked. This "higher objectification" is seen most clearly around the questions of colonialism and imperialism. I will return to this issue and develop it at length, but simply as foreshadowing of this development it can be said that, even while imperialism itself must negate any sense of history in which, for example, the United States, to some extent with the broad complicity of many of its people, committed a horrendous wrong against the people of Vietnam (a wrong that is ongoing and continuing, in the historical and moral sense, and even in the "chemical" sense—for instance, there are still high rates of cancer in Vietnam associated with the widespread use of defoliants such as Agent Orange), it is not clear that Marx's conception has much room, either, for the idea of an historical and ethical *debt*. History for Marx is not imbued with any "world spirit," it is simply an unfolding according to a certain general logic of commodities and modes of production (made up of forces and relations of production that can, under certain circumstances and after the completion of certain circuits of development, come into contradiction with one another, ultimately giving rise to new modes of production). For Marx, history is what it is and there is no point in crying over spilt milk. At least that is one side of Marx. The argument of this book is that either there is another side of Marx that can be developed from within Marx's own language and premises, or there is another side of radical social struggle and theory that needs to find a way to integrate itself into Marxism—at any rate, there is another side, the ethical side. But let us stay for the moment with the question of imperialism.

The crimes of colonialism and imperialism are many, and go far beyond what was done to the people of Vietnam, and indeed far beyond what the United States has done to the world. Certainly there is a prima facie case for focusing on the United States, as it has been the most powerful and most dangerous imperialist power since the conclusion of the Second World War, and it is now embarked upon an unprecedented project of global domination and reconfiguration. There is also the matter of responsibility; people everywhere ought to oppose all imperialism, which means both the global-imperialist system as well as the particular machinations of imperialist countries. People in particular imperialist countries have special responsibilities. It is fine and good that people in France, for instance, oppose and fight U.S. imperialism, but they need to fight French imperialism too, which has its own horrible legacy. The fact that the United States used the contention among European imperialists (and Japan) to greatly expand its own empire does not cancel the historical and ethical debts incurred by these imperialists, and of course these imperialists continue to dominate and exploit. However, people in the United States arguably have the greatest responsibility to address the imperialist system, and yet it is part of the very working of this system that it is in the imperialist hyperpower that this responsibility is recognized the least. In fact, it can be said that this responsibility is not only not recognized, but also actively negated on the ideological plane by the workings of both jingoistic patriotism and (perhaps even more, at least until September 11, 2001, but still quite significantly) a pervasive culture of cynicism and of powerful and immense distractions. At the same time, it can be argued that this negation of history and the ethical dimension is in fact a perverse kind of recognition. It is a bit like the person who declares passionately a "love for animals" while ordering veal in a restaurant—it would be hard to make the case that this person loved that particular animal, and surely the contradiction between the declaration and the action is itself a perverse recognition of a fundamental connection. The misogynist who protests that he "loves women" is using a similar logic.

Cynicism and Complicity

Even though the crimes of colonialism and imperialism extend far beyond the case of Vietnam, the proposed mantra "Vietnam, Vietnam, Vietnam" stands, I would argue, as a significant reminder, at this historical juncture, of a great and horrible wrong that was done to a people, without any ethical justification or provocation of any kind. Certainly it is significant that, with the Gulf of Tonkin resolution, the U.S. Congress and the Johnson administration felt it had to concoct a justification for increased involvement. As the reader undoubtedly knows, what was concocted was an "incident." An entire study might be written on the idea of the "incident" in the history of imperialism, the "offense" that justifies an intervention that grows to large proportions. In the transition of the United States from some relatively limited colonialist ventures to full-blown imperialism, there is a string of such incidents and offenses, beginning with the supposed sinking of the battleship *Maine* in Havana Harbor in 1898. Well, the battleship did indeed sink, but the explanation of this has never been clear. That the justifications for intervention are often paper thin, even if they are actually true (which for the most part they are not), speaks to the moral rot of imperialism. People get into the habit, or they are ideologically trained in the habit, of believing the self-serving tales of the ruling class. This could only go so far in the case where the ruling class has done a good job of creating popular identification with imperialist interests, in other words complicity.

A great deal of the political maneuvering by the ruling elites in the United States since the late 1970s has been oriented toward dealing with the problem of Vietnam: how to justify large-scale foreign interventions once again, and how to prepare ordinary people to accept once again the idea that these interventions may involve significant numbers of deaths and serious injuries. Unfortunately, many Americans are fine with the idea that interventions will involve death and destruction to a supposed "enemy," to the extent that they are even aware of these things. That is part of the moral rot of imperialism also: the lives of most people in the world do not count for much, and most Americans cannot tell you much or anything about the places where these interventions occur. However, if there are significant American casualties, suddenly there is interest—understandably, and yet we see here also the limitations of a framework that is motivated primarily by the category of interest.

The Vietnam War is in the relatively recent past, and therefore there is a greater possibility of reminding people of it, of "reactivating" it as a moral question. Tell us, please, what did the people of Vietnam ever do to the people of the United States? After Vietnam and up until the Iraq War the United States had not only not been willing to risk significant numbers of American casualties, it had not even been willing to use the term "war" to name its interventions. The exception was the first Gulf War, and one of the extraordinary facts of that intervention is that American troops stationed on the borders of Iraq and making ground and air incursions into Iraq were, on the whole, safer than if they had remained on bases in the United States. In other words, there would have been more casualties from accidents on American bases than there were in this actual "war," which was more in the character of a high-tech massacre. One reason that the Vietnam War stands the chance of being reactivated as a moral problem is that there are still many Vietnam veterans among us in the United States, and they are indeed among us as a problem. Nothing could be clearer than that there is a strong basis for Vietnam vets to despise the social system that sent them to the other side of the world to kill people who had never done anything to the people of the United States, and therefore to experience the moral trauma that such an unjust crusade entailed. It was not hippies and war protesters who sent these people to Vietnam, in batallions that disproportionately represented the working class and ethnic minorities.

Since the U.S. withdrawal from Vietnam in 1975, however, the imperialist social system has worked overtime to divert the hatred that these veterans naturally want to feel toward something and someone, even to somehow make it appear as if the Vietnamese people had been the aggressors and the war protestors the ones who had really put the American soldiers in harm's way (and conveniently forgetting that many Vietnam vets returned to the United States and became war protestors themselves). This diversion and reversal is typical of the imperialist system, and indeed these maneuvers are part of a comprehensive theodicy in which America and Americans are supremely good (we are also supremely innocent and have nothing to do with the terrible things going on elsewhere, we only get involved to try to help), and whoever does not carry out the will of America is evil. Such a political theology is absolutely necessary in the case that one would have to recognize otherwise that purely geo-strategic cal-culations of power and profit have no room for ethical discourse—it must be that Americans are good in some sense that is "beyond" ordinary con-siderations, just as a certain version of the Christian god remains good despite being vengeful, jealous, capricious and arbitrary, murderous, and even genocidal. When things get "theological" in this way, there is no questioning actions and policies and interventions and the make-up of political structures and institutions in ethical terms. In theological terms, napalm is a species of divine damnation; as to why many people in Vietnam (and elsewhere in southeast Asia) were horribly burned, tortured, and killed by it, the ways of God are mysterious.

And yet many of the Vietnam veterans are torn apart precisely by eth-ical questions, and their trauma is exacerbated by the fact that the very *social system* that required them to torture, kill, and die in Vietnam was all too ready to abandon them upon their return. By the late 1970s it became clear that this meant there would be, at the least, tens of thousands of vet-erans wandering the streets with very serious psychological problems (including high levels of drug addiction). The social system that created this situation had no interest in addressing the problem directly—after all, the problem was that the United States waged an unjust war upon a peo-ple who had never done anything to the people of the United States. Imperialism does not exist to critically interrogate itself, after all. Instead there began an ideological campaign that continues to this day, to divert the anger, resentment, and trauma of the veterans, or, in the fine American tradition, to tell these people that their problems are of their own creation. It would be hard to say that this campaign (which includes such cultural phenomena of not only resentment but also of "re-masculinization," as with the *Rambo* films) has not been very successful, when its crowning achievement is a president who is representing an attempt to reforge American empire on an unprecedented level, who has done a fine job of mobilizing military and popular sentiment against anyone who questions the warmongering aims of the United States, and who himself went to great lengths to avoid going to Vietnam. As has been said, George W. Bush gives a bad name to the term "draft dodger" (as did Sylvester Stallone— "Rambo"—who spent his draft-eligible years in Sweden). This, however, is not only hypocrisy: George W. Bush belongs to a different class of people, the class that orders the wars, not the class that fights, kills, and dies in them. What is especially sad and troublesome, and of course this has been the case for a long time, is that broad masses of people come to identify with this class—and therefore there are broad masses who identify with the ruling class *against* those who would question this social set-up.

Turning Point

Vietnam remains to be rethematized in another sense, namely, that it was the turning point for many people. For many millions of people in the United States, Vietnam seemed to speak the truth of the system—as indeed it did. Vietnam affected several generations and, as political signifier, continues to affect new generations, even if in subtle ways. One possible negative consequence of the war is suggested by the fairly long list of serial killers who are Vietnam veterans. The list as it existed in the early 1970s is given in a riveting scene in Stanley Kubrick's *Full Metal Jacket*, where a Marine drill sargent is gloating over the shooting skills of such murderers as the veteran who killed sixteen people (wounding another thirty-one) from the bell tower in the middle of campus at the University of Texas at Austin. More recently, it was only briefly mentioned that the prime suspect in the "BTK killer" case in the Wichita area is a Vietnam vet. "BTK" stands for "bind, torture, kill," skills that could have been acquired in the U.S. Army or in the Marine Corps. The culture of dehumanization that prepared young men to fight in Vietnam—a culture for which presidential candidate John Kerry was pilloried for reminding us of it, a culture that is well depicted in *Full Metal Jacket*—also dehumanizes those who are sent to fight, and God knows what will come back to U.S. society from the Iraq War. (The account by Evan Wright, *Generation Kill*, paints a frightening picture of the current state of military culture.) The point is *absolutely not* that many Vietnam vets returned to the United States to become serial killers. Of course they did not. On the other hand, it is clear than many thousands did return scarred and traumatized, and they remain so. The point, rather, is that there is a social system that underlies such trajectories and traumas, a social system that drives these things. Many who came of age during the Vietnam War, or who were already of age, saw this, they saw the truth of the system revealed in scorched earth, Agent Orange, napalm, the Strategic Hamlet Program (destroying a village in order to "save" it), systemic rape and the creation of semi-official "long-houses" of prostitution, and the massive use of hard drugs, marijuana, and alcohol that American soldiers needed in order to cope with the endeavor they were involved in. The enormous irony is that their shame was even more the shame of ordinary Americans who went along with this, and those who did what they could to stop it took the only moral high ground. The war was unjust, as imperialist wars always are. The people who fought in the war did an unjust thing, but it can also be said that many were simply doing what they thought they were supposed to be doing. Many of them learned otherwise in the war itself; they were taught an ethical lesson by a people who refused to submit, despite everything that was thrown at them. (More bombs and incendiary devices were dropped on Vietnam, a country of forests and rice paddies roughly the size of Italy, than were used by all parties in all of Europe during the Second World War.) This ethical lesson was largely lost on the Americans who "support[ed] our troops," the people who blamed everything on flower-power and Black militants and bra-burners, and that lesson has been by now thoroughly "disappeared."

Disappearing of Memory

Is the ethical lesson completely lost? *Has* every moral trace of it disappeared? The imperialist social system, in the form of its ideological operatives, so fervently wishes and works for this absolute disappearance and for an absolute and complete reversal of the turning point that many people experienced as a result of Vietnam, that this absolute forgetting has become integral to the present functioning of capitalism. (I would say this absolute forgetting is especially integral to "postmodern capitalism." That the absolute forgetting is so agitated by any reminder of the horror that it takes, ultimately, to keep this empire at the top of the imperialist heap, shows, *I hope*, that the forgetting and reversal are not so absolute. (Again, the case of John Kerry's congressional testimony against the Vietnam War, film of which was shown in the 2004 presidential campaign, is an excellent example of how the system *freaks out* when this still-open wound is displayed. It is an especially excellent example because Kerry ran on a platform of being able to do a "better job" of imperialist warmongering.) To use the language of Derrida's *Specters of Marx*, there are ghosts, and these ghosts call us to responsibility. To recognize the ghost, to learn to speak with and live with the ghost, is what Derrida calls "hauntology" (the neologism is a play on "ontology"—in French, the difference can only be seen in the written word rather than the spoken word). Ethical Marxism aims to be a hauntology, and it is in this idea in *Specters* that Marx and Kant can be seen to come together.

"What does Vietnam have to do with me?" The same can be said of other horrors that mainstream America is at pains to deny, especially slavery and the genocide of Native Americans. How can "I" (whoever "I" happen to be) have these debts placed upon me? For that matter we might return to ancient discussions about what harm is done to the dead. Athens in the time of Socrates was an extremely litigious society. An argument was raised to the effect that the relatives of persons who were accidentally or unjustly killed deserved no compensation; only the dead person him- or herself deserved such compensation, but in this case there is also no compensation to be paid, as the dead person does not exist, and one does not pay compensation to a "person" who does not exist. Colonialism and imperialism have this sense of their victims, though not of members of colonialist and imperialist ruling classes themselves, or of their property. (The Opium Wars are a good example of this double-standard, to which we will return.) The larger point is that imperialism creates a basic bifurcation in the world. On either side of this bifurcation there are institutions that people inhabit and that form and inform persons.

It is in this context that imperialism creates and consists in basic social divisions that pose an ethical question in light of which many other discussions of ethics, especially in a purely academic frame, are almost laughable in their naïveté. Instead of simply dismissing these other "ethical questions" altogether, we need to situate them within the larger framework of social relations and the ethical issues and imperatives that are found there. One obvious way to see this is in the dehumanizing imperatives that are operative in the imperialist social organization of the world, and in more direct forms of imperialist domination and invasion. Even in these days of more politically correct reporting on imperialist invasions, we can still see the basic bifurcation at work. During the Vietnam War (and the Korean War, for that matter—and we still have to keep in mind that in neither case were the invaded peoples even afforded the dignity of being presented with an outright declaration of war by the U.S. Congress), it was typical to hear anti-Asian racist language even in official political and military circles, and the idea that the Vietnamese (and other southeast Asian) people are subhuman or a lesser type of human was not far from being an official norm. (The history of how this racism was made to backfire on the imperialist invaders is itself significant, given the ethnic disproportionalities in the invading force.) In the Iraq War, given both the history of imperialism since the Vietnam War, and the global-hegemonic scale on which the United States hopes to operate in the initial years and decades of the twenty-first century, there has been something of an official retreat from more overtly racist and ethnocentric rhetoric. (This is not without exception, and in the ranks of the military itself racist slurs against Arabs are common.) This retreat is also strategically predicated on the fact that the United States is a diverse, multi-ethnic society, where official racism and (white, especially northern European) ethnocentrism, while still the order of the day in terms of how the society is structured and ruled, cannot be expressed so overtly. And yet, as with Vietnam, while we hear on a daily basis the casualty figures for American military personnel, we are kept in the dark about deaths and serious injuries among the invaded population.

Indeed, it has been the officially stated view from the U.S. Government (specifically from the departments of State and Defense) that the number of Iraqi casualties are of little concern.

Bygones

On this score, two further factors are important in order to understand the Iraq War (and to understand the "other war," in Afghanistan, that is taking place simultaneously, and the other invasions that are likely to take place in the coming years). The first has to do with the ambiguity of the term "casualty" in recent years. In purely military terms, a "casualty" is someone who can no longer play a role on the field of battle, for whatever reason. Injured soldiers in past wars (fought by whatever country), if they could no longer fight, were considered casualties. It might be said that such soldiers were "as good as dead," from a purely military standpoint (this is a callous perspective, and what is even more callous is that such soldiers are even worse than dead, to the extent that living personnel must now deal with these injured fighters). Now it is more common to use the term "casualty" to refer to combat deaths. This is helpful to the powers-that-be, given the composition of its fighting forces primarily through an economic draft (and what has been called the "backdoor draft" in the case of reserve and National Guard forces pressed into full-time duty on foreign soil, the sort of duty that George W. Bush expressly refused), as it allows them to underrepresent the large number of soldiers who have been seriously injured. The second factor is the expanded role for so-called civilian contractors. In many cases there is no difference between these "contractors" and outright mercenaries. Besides the fact that these factors signify difficulties that the United States must face in its present drive to extend and reconfigure its global hegemony, they are also indicative of the different levels of bifurcation that occur in a world operating within the imperialist system.

To apply the "bygones" standard to the victims of colonialism and imperialism, and for that matter to apply the notions of debt and reparations, involves us in questions of human incarnation, of "people-hood" and familial relations, and therefore even of the especially difficult issue of "blood relations." Here let us return to Kant's perspective, and also to why the Aristotelian and neo-Aristotelian perspectives do not go far enough (though they are helpful to a point and clearly figure into the perspective developed here). The cruelty done to our species, and to other creatures on our planet, and to the planet itself, comes back around and will continue to come around, possibly to the point of our ultimate demise. But this does not necessarily happen on an individual basis, and it is not first of all a matter of virtue and happiness at the level of the individual. In Claude Lanzmann's film about the Holocaust, *Shoah*, a train engineer reminisces happily about the days of shuttling Jews to Auschwitz. The Aristotelian discourse thematizing the question of whether or not this man was "truly happy" just does not cut it, for reasons both obvious and not obvious. What is obvious is that the enormity of what was going on with the Holocaust is not addressed by these questions of virtue and happiness, and indeed the Holocaust is trivialized by this approach. This is a case where the knee-jerk reaction to this application of Aristotelian categories is justified: *Who cares* whether this train driver was "truly" happy at the time when he was a participant in the Nazi genocide or at the time of his own death? The part of the issue that is not so obvious, and that is difficult to thematize in any case, is the question of the social system: that we human beings live in social relations, working within the context of forces of production, and being formed within social institutions. These things make up a "social system," but a social system is always a very complicated thing, even in societies that are much "simpler" than an advanced capitalist society. Even to use the phrase "mode of production," which I would argue is still essential to understanding any society, is to invoke a set of relationships that is terrifically complex and that involves not only class—itself not a simple concept—but also relationships shaped by gender, sexuality, the constellation of concepts involving race, ethnicity, nationality, peoplehood, and color, types and levels of technology, the relationship to nonhuman species, and the relationship to the Earth and even to the cosmos. These relationships form us and make us what we are, and Kant's argument is that the norm for how we work through these relationships is the idea of the "kingdom of ends." We cannot work through these relationships under this norm without addressing systemic factors; in the modern world this becomes increasingly difficult to do. Complexity becomes a problem in and of itself, and one of its effects is to leave even people of good will feeling powerless and in a state of anomie.

Universality and Complexity

Even the most straightforward issues in Kant's ethical philosophy are affected by this complexity. It is more than obvious that imperialist invasions and occupations do not treat dominated peoples as "persons," and "counting as a person" is central to Kant's perspective. But the obvious thing turns out not to be that straightforward in this world of complexity and capitalist and imperialist bifurcations. "I want to count as a person." Kant shows us the intersubjective basis for this demand. One essential dimension of "counting as a person" is to be treated as an end and not merely as a means to an end. Marx added to this "formal" demand (I do not follow Marx and Engels in calling it "merely formal") the substantive issues that have to be addressed if a person has any *real* hope of counting as an end, that is, basic material needs that must be met if a person is to hold body and soul together. Kant was already beginning to see that these issues in the modern world are primarily systemic, though he did not go as far in this as Hegel and Marx, who were able to witness the unfolding of industrial capitalism and to see the way that it relies on not only a division of labor and proletarianization that certainly treats people as means (and avowedly so in the utilitarian justification for capitalism given by Adam Smith, where it is taken as a fine thing that the worker does not have to know the end to which she or he works, as long as the invisible hand coordinates the process), but also impoverishment, unemployment, and (what Marx called) "primitive accumulation."

Primitive accumulation is Marx's name for the ways in which capitalists create their initial fortunes, through processes that are themselves outside of the wealth-generation processes of capitalism. Among these ways are slavery, colonialism, and dirty tricks and thievery, as in the case of John D. Rockefeller's sabotage of rail lines in order to gain the upper hand in the oil market. In the present period, certain manipulations within finance capital, for example, those associated with figures such as Donald Trump and Michael Milliken especially during the Reagan era, and with the "FIRE" economy in New York City—Finance, Insurance, and Real Estate—bear some resemblance to primitive accumulation, even as they are also representative of capitalism in its purest form: money that is about money that is about money, with the connection to some *object* that is actually the result of a process of production being extraordinarily tenuous.

The norms by which Hegel and Marx criticized this emerging process come from Aristotle and Kant, even if they are often recognized (especially by Marx) only in the breach, as it were, or backhandedly. It is certainly the case, however, that these norms are easily lost in the "object world" (a world where everything is quantified and reduced to the status of an object of monetary equivalence) of capital, and certainly Marx loses these norms at times. Indeed, the key area where Marx loses these norms of flourishing, "end-being" (to give the idea a Heideggerian spin, but also to play on what might be a valid translation of "Dasein"—at least in a Sartrean frame) and the realm of ends, and personhood, is precisely on the matter of colonialism, and this loss carries over into the emergence of imperialism as a world system. The imperialist world, especially, which might finally be called the world of "world history" that Marx saw emerging in his time (and certainly he recognized that it is a world emerging in and through the most grotesque brutality), is not only almost unfathomably complex, but there are levels and breaks within this complexity. What does it mean that

"I want to count as a person" in a world where many thousands die each day, and many millions suffer, from causes and problems that are completely preventable, from causes that are systemic, and where the social system that produces these causes also produces a standard of living that enables a relative few to read Kant and wonder about personhood?

"End-being"

It is a Kantian insight, captured especially in the second formulation of the categorical imperative, that a person cannot promote the dignity and "end-being" of others by denying that dignity and end-being (with the Sartrean spin this could be called the quality of being *pour soi*, of experiencing a "for-itself-ness") in him- or herself. The personhood of the Vietnamese subject of American imperial aggression will not be affirmed through my own denial of personhood. (Giving one's life in the struggle against the oppressor is another thing altogether, though cases such as those of Simone Weil and of the Vietnamese Buddhist monks who engaged in self-immolation bear further study.) Indeed, I can only affirm the personhood of the Vietnamese in the same movement as affirming my own personhood. However, on the "substantive" points that Marx raised, there is a sharp conflict. The person who benefits materially, even if only in the relative terms of "crumbs from the feast table," from this imperialist aggression and domination, has been brought into a complicity with the imperialist system. It is against this situation of complicity that some efforts that are aimed at reform *purely within the terms of the existing system* need to be understood.

Reform

There are reforms that have been granted as a concession to radical struggle; many reforms in the areas of civil rights and gender equality (and the right to abortion) are of this sort. Unfortunately, people can become accustomed to the idea that the system can grant such reforms, and therefore they become convinced that the best thing to do is to work within the system. In moving in this reformist direction, people lose sight both of the overall nature of the social system, as well as the struggle that won these reforms in the first place. Having been won over to working purely within the terms of the system, their reformism becomes both a support and a legitimating factor for the system, and in this way the material aspect of counting as a person in an imperialist country is set against the personhood of people who are subjects of imperialist aggression and domination.

Certainly many reform efforts are well intentioned, and indeed many things that might be understood as reforms ought to be supported. Reproductive autonomy is one of these reforms. Clearly the U.S. imperialist system can allow for this autonomy in some sense, or else there never would have been the decision for abortion rights in *Roe v. Wade* to begin with. On the other hand, as abortion rights began to get chipped away in subsequent decades, the temptation to accept the terms that the system itself hands down is both a denial of the struggle in the streets that forced a legal concession *and* one of the roads that will lead to the eventual overturning of abortion rights.

For reformism generally, we might at least attempt to make a distinction between reform efforts that address something basic in the system, that "touch a nerve," so to speak, and efforts that are more on the order of making a relatively "livable" situation more livable. Wage struggles in the relatively well paid parts of the working class in the United States are not insignificant and, of course, a lowering of wages (perhaps by their not being raised to keep up with inflation and increased costs of living) for these workers will not lead to a wage increase for, say, workers in the athletic shoe industry in Vietnam and elsewhere in southeast Asia. Here we can see where there is already a materiality to Kant's second formulation: material self-denial of basic needs for myself does not lead to the provision of these needs for the subject of domination. Self-denial may, *in certain circumstances*, create a powerful example, but it also may be only a path toward a sense of self-righteousness, as well as a way of simply removing oneself from the actual struggle to create a more just world. Here again we have to think about Kant within the context of the actual material world, where the formation of an intention is a struggle, not a mere armchair activity. Intentionality as "merely formal" would take us down the path of mere "good feeling" about our moral sentiments, and yet Kant is clearly not on the side of much good feeling in this world where there are many basic questions of justice to be addressed. Indeed, for Kant, this is where Aristotle's focus on virtue is just not "big enough" or "solid enough" for the complex world of far-flung social systems. Consider the issues of international relations that Kant takes up in "Perpetual Peace," for instance— what does individual virtue have to do with the world he is attempting to address? If we all lived in self-sustaining village economies—and perhaps we should, but we do not—then the relationship between virtue and flourishing could come more to the fore.

Needs

However, again there is a systemic complexity; self-denial with regard to basic needs is one thing, recognizing that even the term "basic needs" is at least somewhat relative. Higher levels of imperialist comfort and ostentatiousness are something else. To take a pop culture example, "living well" (materially) in an imperialist country, especially in the imperialist hyperpower, is a bit like living in the Tony Soprano household—you know these nice things have a suspicious source, but you try to not look too deeply into the question. The analogy is appropriate: the "geo-political" justification for the invasion of Vietnam, and all of the terrible things that followed upon the invasion, works according to a *gangster logic*, not a moral logic. There can be no justification according to a moral logic, for the fact is that the people of Vietnam never did anything to the people of the United States. Three million people (to count only the deaths, and even then only the deaths at the time and not those whose deaths are still caused by what was done to Vietnam during the war) in southeast Asia were simply "collateral damage" in a geo-political struggle between two contending empires (the United States and the "Western bloc" on the one side, and the Soviet Union and its bloc on the other) whose message to the world was that the only choice was between who would dominate, and even that choice would not be made by the subjects of domination.

It is worth noting that the common devolution of politics into a gangster logic is at least a big part of the reasoning behind Emmanuel Levinas's conceptual separation of ethics and politics; the latter, in his view, always comes ultimately to a state of war. Not to elide differences between Levinas and Kant, but Levinas's separation is certainly in the vein of Kant's skepticism about, for instance, the idea of waging war for the sake of achieving a substantial and ongoing peace. Such issues have to be addressed if "Ethical Marxism" is to be more than a self-contradictory and fatally compromised construct.

In this larger context, then (and to complete a thought), one should not go overboard in estimating the "social justice" content or the "political struggle" content of the wage struggles of better-off workers in the first world. Certainly, however, this arena, of what Lenin called the "labor aristocracy," and the better-off workers of imperialist countries who have developed some longstanding material and ideological attachments to the system (Nixon's construction workers who beat up anti-war protestors would be the paradigm), is being transformed in the era of globalization. The present tendencies toward homogenization (represented by trade agreements such as NAFTA, as well as the post–Cold War wave of outsourcing) make the concepts of historical and ethical "debt" even more difficult.

What's In It for Me?

Imperialist aggression and domination function on a global scale; it is not simply a matter of what the United States (or France, for that matter) "got out of" the imperialist war in Vietnam. The whole language of "what did we get out of that war?" is not only so completely alien from any ethical reasoning as to be the complete antithesis of anything that can be called ethics, but also it serves to constitute a "we" in such as way as to legitimate dehumanization.

This is where we see that imperialism functions on two levels, one predicated upon the other. There are imperialist "acts" of aggression, domination, and exploitation. Indeed, Lenin and Sartre referred to the imperialist process of value extraction in the Third World as "superexploitation." Exploitation in the classical capitalist economies is at least aimed at preserving the working class, or most of it, over some period of time, since the capitalist classes need the working class to persist in a state of submission, but not so downtrodden that they cannot actually work. In the colonies and neo-colonies foreign imperialist-capitalists view the people in the same way they view the natural resources they are aiming to exploit—in other words, as expendable. Certainly, all people, as persons, and as individuals, are expendable from the standpoint of the object-world of capital. (This even goes for members of the bourgeoisie; any one of them "as one" is expendable in the interests of the class, and, for that matter, the very ground we stand upon is expendable in the pursuit of profit, up to and including the whole earth.) The capitalist process of value creation is no respecter of persons; all are subject to the violence of abstract calculation. When we resist this violence, it is on good Kantian grounds: "these are *people* we are talking about here," "it is wrong to treat a person that way," "no one ought to be treated that way." Imperialism is founded upon quantitative distinctions that become qualitative: a bifurcation of the world into a relative handful of powers that dominate and super-exploit the rest. This is the systemic level of the functioning of imperialism, where imperialism is not simply the actions of imperialist countries, but is instead a global mode of production. The resistance to the violence of the actions has to lead, ultimately, to an overturning of the actual system of production (taken broadly to mean not simply the narrow sphere of "points of production," or even "economics," but the larger culture as well); short of this, the system continually regroups and initiates further actions of domination and the rest.

Given that superexploitation in the Third World is even qualitatively more distant from capitalism's proclaimed meritocracy than is exploitation in the advanced-capitalist countries (and certainly recognizing that there are significant bits of the Third World *in* the first world, even to the point that, for example, the proletariat in Germany is largely Turkish), it could be argued that capitalism from the start and at every point until this day has never even come close to living up to its own principles of bourgeois economics, as it has always depended on large infusions from endeavors of primitive accumulation. It is no exaggeration, either, to say that labor conditions in many Third World settings approximate slavery and that the difference from slavery is merely formal and nominal.

A Kantian critique of capitalism gets off the ground quite easily: a person cannot be allowed to starve if there is food to be had. Could anyone imagine Kant accepting the idea that people should starve in the case that there is food but there is an inability on the part of some people to pay for the food? Actually, it is hard to imagine *anyone* accepting this idea before the development of industrial capitalism, and this is where certain recastings of Aristotle become a bit dangerous, because they cannot help but get intermixed with Calvinist notions of "virtue" and the idea that one's lot in life is what one deserves, because one's lot in life issues from the will of God. (My aim, on the contrary, would be to expand this argument beyond the place where Kant left it and say that it is wrong to treat in a cruel manner any creature who can experience cruelty. But I take this expansion to be in a Kantian spirit.) Could one imagine Kant accepting the idea that the "reason" to let the person without any money for food starve is because "that is the way the system works"?

The Way Things Work

For Marx, it might be said that "that is the way the system works" is indeed the "reason" why this poor person *will* starve. This is a "reason" for Kant, too, but not, certainly, a justification. The reason is actually a "cause," one that is outside of reason because it is outside of ethical intention. Marx and Adam Smith agree on this. Smith thinks it is fine, because the emergent capitalist system of wealth creation will make for a rising tide that lifts all boats. This is a utilitarian and empirical hypothesis that, it turns out, fails to live up to even its own standards. (These are standards that Kant would not accept as having anything to do with ethics, in any case.) The utilitarian standard can only be applied as a broad aggregation: many boats do not rise, they sink, and if the meaning is instead that, "in the long run and ultimately," all of the boats will rise, or many more boats will rise than would have been the case in some other socio-economic scenario, then one would want to ask how long this will actually take, how much suffering and destruction has been caused in a "shorter run" that has gone on for more than two-hundred years since the publication of *An Enquiry Concerning the Wealth of Nations,* and how much time do humanity and the earth really have to keep trying to make things work this way. To be fair, Smith's perspective was bound up with real hope for the potential of capitalism to create abundance and to provide what might be called a "rising minimal standard" of human livelihood. The Owl of Minerva takes flight at dusk, and Smith was grappling with emergent industrial capitalism in its dawn (though also at a time when William Blake was already writing of "dark Satanic mills"). Marx too, living in a time before atomic physics and genetics, underestimated the world-destructive potential of capital, though this hardly stands as an exoneration of capitalism ("Marx was wrong about us!—We're vastly worse than he ever could have imagined!"). Like Smith and the other originators of modern political economy (David Ricardo, David Hume), Marx aimed to be "scientific," and not "normative." It might even be said that Marx aimed to be scientific *as opposed to* normative. The "out" for him, however, the reason why Marx seemingly cannot be accused of just saying to the starving person "that's the way it is," is that "the way the system works" will supposedly lead to its own undoing and its transformation into a different system, one where there will not be the systemic violence of starvation, exploitation, super-exploitation, domination, and the rest. Because of its productive capacity and because of the contradictions of this very productive capacity (in short, crises of overproduction that provoke crises of underconsumption that provoke a "shortage," for the capitalist, of profit, which then leads to unemployment, immiseration, and death from the inability to meet basic needs, and the attempt by capitalist powers to militarily draw new lines on the global map—that is, war), capitalism itself creates the conditions where another world appears both possible and necessary.

Modalities

However, to speak of what is *both* possible and necessary is to pass over too quickly the gap that exists between these modalities, and indeed the gaps that exist within each. My argument is that at least some part of each of these gaps is "normative." This is to say that there are gaps in Marx's analysis that can only be addressed in irreducibly normative terms. Marx appeared to have thought, in a vein that I would identify as utilitarian and "calculative" within the terms of the object-world of capitalism, that these gaps would take care of themselves in relatively short order, as capital was reaching the limits of its potential. These gaps would not be a matter of many more generations, and so the final resolution of capital's contradictions would be part of a struggle that is present to people or at least in the living memory of people. People would be in motion against capital, transforming society, and that is the main thing, that motion itself would address the ethical gaps. Marx was right that this struggle to transform society is indeed the main thing; indeed, it is the thing without which philosophical discourse about the ethical or ethical gaps is, to be blunt, just whistlin' Dixie. But even on this main point, Marx was not entirely right, and the gap in his own theoretical project is significant. When I say "Marx appeared to have thought," I mean that Marx did not feel compelled to go very far in addressing the ethical gaps that, in his view, would take care of themselves in deeds rather than words. Add to this two further lacunae: (1) that which might conceivably have taken care of itself in proletarian struggles in the advanced capitalist countries of Marx's day would certainly not have been taken care of in the global terms in which colonialism had been operating for centuries at that point; (2) the ethical gaps that might have taken care of themselves in a more immediate timeframe have instead festered and undergone significant transformations in the span of decades and generations that has passed since Marx breathed his last.

Normativity

Regarding the first of these lacunae, it is significant that Marx could not or would not marshal the philosophical resources, fundamentally Kantian, that would show the necessity of a normative humanism—in other words, and to be simplistic and direct about it, the capacity to say of people in Asia and Africa and Latin America that, "these are people too," and not to just talk about the way the capitalist system works and that this systemic working would lead to things working out by and by. (See the eerie parallel to Adam Smith here?) Colonialism is based upon economic factors, of course, and perhaps it is based upon these factors first and most of all. But colonialism is also predicated upon a philosophical and ideological legitimation of dehumanization. Significantly, this dehumanization works through phases of feminization, infantilization, and animalization. The acceptance that people in the colonies (and people outside of Europe or "European civilizations") are less than "fully human" is based in philosophical and ideological premises—indeed, premises to which even the great Immanuel Kant was susceptible.

It is not that Marx did nothing but give explanations (that look too much like justifications) for colonialism in terms of political economy; he did in fact speak against colonialism as well, sometimes on grounds that are broadly humanistic and even Kantian. However, in seeing the question of colonialism as, at best, secondary or epiphenomenal to the "main struggle" (between the capitalist classes and the proletariat of the capitalist countries, especially those of Western Europe), and where the resolution of colonialism would itself be an epiphenomenon of the resolution of this main struggle, Marx accepted, even if in the breach, the division in humanity that colonialism fashions into an economic and cultural system of exploitation and domination. It seems likely that the bogus "scientific" ideology of "race" played its role in this acceptance, and it has to be said that Kant's "universal humanism" came under the sway of this ideology as well. (See Emmanuel Chukwudi Eze, *Achieving Our Humanity*, 97–106, for a detailed examination of Kant's role in developing this ideology.) The difference is that Kant was attentive to the philosophical resources for rejecting colonialism's divisions, even if he did not always take the full measure of these resources. Marx, meanwhile, was skeptical of these (or any) philosophical arguments, because he increasingly saw philosophy as impotent in the face of "the way things are"—in 1837, at the age of nineteen, Marx is writing to his father to explain his conversion to Hegelianism; approximately eight years later he is complaining that "the philosophers have *merely* explained the world. . . ."

Even from a purely practical standpoint, however, I would say that the world has paid a price for this unwillingness to deal with certain philosophical questions in a philosophical way. The great irony of this failure is that, when Marxist philosophy reemerges, either in the writings of Lenin or Mao (who, as Lenin wrote, are philosophical revolutionaries rather than revolutionary philosophers), or in the work of Western European figures from Lukacs and Adorno to Sartre, Althusser, and Habermas (and including figures such as Derrida who wrote, in *Specters of Marx*, of "this radicalization of Marxism called deconstruction"), it deals everywhere with broadly Kantian themes and problems.

Regarding the second lacuna, capitalism itself has festered and undergone qualitative transformations, and it has become a global mode of production. In so becoming, the greatest ethical gaps have been created, gaps that are rarely recognized as such. In the name of the people of the United States, and its and their global interests, three million people in Vietnam and southeast Asia were killed, many of them in horrifyingly brutal ways, many of them children or babies. An imperialist world is one where America thinks it can just walk away from that, and where its people largely do not care about this "bygone" past, or they do not know about it, or they do not care to know about it. For the most part they don't give a damn. Vietnam is in the past, and the past, for many Americans, is always another country.

("The past is another country" is one of my favorite sayings, one that is especially applicable to the "blank slate" ideology of America and to the postmodern turn in capitalism.)

Making Imperialism Personal

This is to make the ethical question of imperialism sound very personal. Let us consider, as best we can, the question from the perspective of people dominated and oppressed by imperialism. Whether or not such a per-

spective would lead to the severity of Sartre's claims in his preface to
Fanon's *The Wretched of the Earth* (referring here to the part that connects
anticolonial violence to identity formation on the part of the colonized),
surely it would not be unexpected that a Vietnamese person whose village
had been consumed in napalm fire, this jellied gasoline product of an
American corporation, dropped from an American helicopter flown by a
U.S. Army pilot, would harbor personal feelings toward the American people and the American system. What sort of reasons could be given for why
these people should not take the matter "personally"? What could someone from the imperialist dominating power say to someone dominated by
such a power? "Don't take it personally—it is really a systemic issue? Your
children have been killed, your village has been burned down, your brothers and sisters have been horribly scarred with napalm, the agricultural
basis on which you sustain yourself has been destroyed, and everyone in
your country will be at risk for cancer and other diseases because your land
and water have been poisoned with chemical defoliants that were designed
in American laboratories to kill the botanical life of your country and, even
more to the point, the people who lived around and under the trees—but
do not take this personally, it is really for systemic reasons, for geo-political reasons." "Oh, it's cool, those guys dropping the napalm on me don't
really *mean* it, not toward me personally, they're just doing their jobs."

One often finds that people who are under U.S. domination are extraordinarily generous, they are willing to make a distinction between the
U.S. government and its military, on the one hand, and something called
the "American people," on the other. Certainly there are many in the
United States who do not benefit very much from imperialist ventures or
the imperialist system; not everyone in the U.S. is a privileged child of
Tony Soprano. However, the greater part of the U.S. population does
benefit from these ventures, and even more so from the global position of
the United States within the imperialist system. An analogy could be made
to certain entitlements of race and gender that white people and males (in
the U.S. at any rate) do not have to actively pursue, and toward which
many white males may be ideologically opposed (on some level or
another), but that all the same provide advantages to individuals of the
favored race and/or gender.

Apparently not being Vietnamese meant that what the United States
did to the people of Vietnam did not matter that much as an ethical question to many people in mainstream America. What happened was the
expression and outcome of a social system, and those most to blame and
qualitatively more to blame, if that makes any sense, were those more
directly involved in making the strategic decisions for this social system,
and those who have the greatest material stake in having this basic social
form and not some other (in other words, the imperialist ruling class). And

yet, even though the United States ultimately lost the war in Vietnam (after which, unfortunately, the Vietnamese revolution was stillborn, as it was assimilated to the Soviet bloc), this particular effort and the overall effort of American imperialism sustains both a generally and a relatively high standard of living for many millions of Americans, not only the many strata of the middle classes, but even a substantial (though arguably shrinking) part of the working class—and *we*, my friends, are the material beneficiaries of this horrible crime that was committed and that has now been shoved deep down the memory hole.

Part of what I am saying here is that this is a matter of personal responsibility, and this goes for the author of these words as well—the material culture and institutions that now give me the opportunity to write these words are also the product of the imperialist system. It is certainly the case, as well, that opportunities such as this also arise from countercurrents within the system and perhaps even, to speak in Derridean terms, currents set against the system "from a certain outside." In *Specters of Marx*, Derrida writes of listening to, speaking with, and learning to live with ghosts, and that this is the essence of responsibility. Here I have tried to speak about the specter of Vietnam, or of the Vietnam War, even if I cannot yet begin to speak with this ghost, and even if "living with" this ghost is neither only nor ultimately a matter of purely personal responsibility but instead of changing society, changing the system and the institutions that for "geo-political" reasons would murder and torture millions on the other side of the world. But this is "my" responsibility also.

What is the relationship between intention and this complicity? Either out in the countryside, in the amber waves of grain, or in the buzz of the metropolis, people do not seem to be going about their business with the intention of hurting anyone. Certainly there is a point to saying that "it is not *our* system, it was not part of our intention to be a part of a system that systematically exploits, oppresses, dominates, and murders." Especially in times when imperialism is acting with overt belligerence (as it is at the time of this writing), it is important that citizens of the imperialist superpower at least speak up. Part of what people need to speak up about, however, is the systemic nature of imperialist acts, the rootedness of these acts in social structures and institutions.

Global Divisions

As for the geo-political nature of imperialism, at the point when imperialism emerges as a global system, around the end of the nineteenth century, there are really two kinds of bifurcations or basic divisions in the world. One of these is between the advanced capitalist countries, on the one side, and what emerges as the Third World, on the other. The other division is among the imperialist countries themselves. In the twentieth century this bifurcation tended to lead to the division of the world into two competing blocs, each made up of dominant imperial powers, their imperialist allies, and the Third World countries under their domination. To be sure, this division of the world into blocs and spheres of influence (in fact, spheres of dominance) piggybacked upon colonialism. (Part of the transition from colonialism to imperialism involved creating neo-colonial relationships, with the more direct governance of Third World countries being taken over by "indigenous," comprador classes. The term "indigenous" is placed in scare quotes because there are many examples where the class divides are racialized. This is especially the case in Latin America, with the ruling classes composed of "white" men of European heritage—not only Spanish or Portuguese, but even German or Dutch in some cases—or even Japanese in the case of Peru—and the working class and peasantry being of more properly "indigenous" descent.) Consider the division of Latin America into Spanish and Portuguese spheres, and then the U.S. effort, throughout much of the nineteenth and twentieth centuries, to claim the entire Western Hemisphere as its own. Included in this claim is the extraordinarily insulting and racist idea that South America, Central America, and Mexico are the United States's "backyard." The point of political economy that I am driving toward, however, is that the emergence of imperialism as a world-system heralds the opening of a period when the relative handful of imperialist powers are compelled to view every part of the world in terms of competitive advantage and opportunity cost.

Logic of M-C-M-prime

This compulsion is not first of all a matter of intention, but instead there emerges what might be called a political economy of intentions, in which intentions are organized in the service of self-expanding value—Marx's famous formula, M-C-M′ (money, commodities, and, if all goes well for the capitalist, more money). And yet it cannot be said that "they know not what they do." The Pentagon knows very well what it is doing when it asks scientists to develop a substance such as napalm, and the Pentagon knows very well what it is doing when it orders that this substance be dropped on innocent people in the countryside of Vietnam. The ruling class and its administrative apparatus, its state and its military, may be acting in the service of the compulsions of capital—indeed, they *are* acting in this service— but they are also *intentionally* doing things that are as wrong as wrong can be. The geo-political imperatives of this need—a need that is in fact a "true need," within the terms of the capitalist system of production—to produce an ever-larger pile of money (with never any end in sight, never any point where there is "enough") are always dressed up in terms of "values," not only "democracy" ("saving the world for . . .") or "civilization" or the elimination of tyranny or terrorism or some supposed threat to the "free world," but even the defeat of imperialist domination and capitalist exploitation themselves, terms taken up by the Soviet Union when it passed from being a (terrifically flawed, to be sure) socialist country to being a capitalist country that called itself socialist. (All of this adds another layer of complication, as does the question of world divisions in the case that there actually are socialist countries in the world; I will return to these issues in part 3, sec. 3.)

The Global March

Let us be clear and call these proclamations of value what they are: lies, garbage, deliberate ideological obfuscations, bullshit. The execrable nature of these proclaimed "values" is revealed in the learning curve the capitalist classes pursued in their formulation. In the transition to imperialism, political and military leaders of the colonialist and emerging-imperialist powers said many interesting things, and it is significant how large a role was played by open, officially sanctioned racism. For instance, we have the following from influential Massachusetts senator Henry Cabot Lodge:

> In the interests of our commerce . . . we should build the Nicaragua canal, and for the protection of that canal and for the sake of our commercial supremacy in the Pacific we should control the Hawaiian islands and maintain our influence in Samoa. . . . and when the Nicaraguan canal is built, the island of Cuba . . . will become a necessity. . . . The great nations are rapidly absorbing for their future expansion and their present defense *all the waste places of the earth*. It is a movement which makes for civilization and the *advancement of the race*. As one of the great nations of the world the United States must not fall out of the line of march. (Zinn, 292; my emphasis)

These words were not written in some secret document for the eyes of the ruling or administrative class only, but were instead published in a magazine article. The "commercial supremacy" of those who were in a position to engage in large-scale, international commerce (what they like to call "trade," so that it sounds like children playing with marbles) is nicely mixed here with the interests and advancement of "the" race. In order to remain in the small group of "great nations" (and indeed, for the United States to finally take its place among the great nations), the United States must pursue the game of comparative advantage, and suddenly the uncivilized, "waste places" become very important.

A good deal of the U.S. empire was acquired through seizing or pick-
ing up the pieces of empire that the other "great nations" (principally
England, France, Spain, Portugal, the Netherlands, Belgium, and Japan)
lost in their own inter-imperialist conflicts. The greatest part of the U.S.
empire was acquired from England, which, in the nineteenth century, was
the predominant colonialist power, ruling an enormous part of the world.
In this respect, consider the case of Cuba. As Howard Zinn wrote in his
absolutely indispensable *A People's History of the United States* (in the chapter titled, "The Empire and the People"), the administration of President
Grover Cleveland

> said a Cuban victory [in its independence struggle against Spain] might lead to
> "the establishment of a white and black republic," since Cuba had a mixture of
> the two races. And the black republic might be dominant. This idea was
> expressed in 1896 in an article in *The Saturday Review* by a young and eloquent
> imperialist, whose mother was American and whose father was English—
> Winston Churchill. He wrote that while Spanish rule was bad and the rebels
> had the support of the people, it would be better for Spain to keep control: "A
> grave danger represents itself. Two-fifths of the insurgents in the field are
> negroes. These men . . . would, in the event of success, demand a predominant
> share in the government of the country . . . the result being, after years of fight-
> ing, another black republic." (Zinn, 296)

The reference is to Haiti; in the spring of 2004, France and the United
States colluded to have the elected president of Haiti, Jean-Bertrand
Aristide, kidnapped and removed to the Central African Republic.
Significantly, as Zinn reports, the Spanish ambassador to the United States
at that time also used the threat of a "black republic" as a reason why the
U.S. should not attempt to wrench Cuba away from Spain: "In this revolution, the negro element has the most important part. Not only the principal leaders are colored men, but at least eight-tenths of their supporters.
. . . and the result of the war, if the Island can be declared independent,
will be a secession of the black element and a black Republic" (Zinn, 296).
In every imperialist venture and every justification for imperialism, one sees
this mixture, the inherently unsatisfiable drive for "commercial supremacy"
mixed with ideologies of racial supremacy and racial superiority. Indeed, as
I said before, today it is hardly different, even if some terms are now less
deployable in official discourse (while still serving their purpose in all of
their openly racist ugliness at other levels of the process). Given the central
role that domination of the Middle East, especially the oil-producing
regions of it, plays in the imperialist process of organizing (brutally and
chaotically, to be sure) the world today, let us look to Winston Churchill
once again for a perspective on what it means to press the advantage of a
"great power." "I do not understand this squeamishness about the use of
gas [to put down an Arab nationalist insurgency in Iraq, in 1920]. I am

strongly in favor of using poison gas against uncivilized tribes" (Everest, 42). In the case of largely desert lands where the main objective of the imperialists is to secure oil, we should not mince words: Churchill was perfectly comfortable with genocide in the name of "civilization." After the First World War, the horror of poison gas was quite clear. Underneath the rhetoric about terrorism and weapons of mass destruction, and even underneath the rhetoric of tyranny, democracy, and civilization, there is a line to be drawn from Churchill's openly racist and genocidal perspective to the current attempts by the United States to "secure" the Middle East. In a moment I will present some of the broad details of the global march of imperialism, especially British and American imperialism.

Race Ideology

We are entitled to ask which comes first, race ideology or the drive for economic supremacy. Certainly, forms of race ideology have been around for thousands of years, even simply in that the name many ancient peoples had for themselves meant something like "the people," while others were "not the people" or were "barbarians" (people who spoke nonsense— "bar, bar, bar . . ."). However, the meaning of this ideology (which is extraordinarily complicated and, again, involves the *constellation* of concepts of race, ethnicity, peoplehood, nationality, color, and language groups) was transformed and assimilated into a different, global process in the rise of European colonialism and then again when imperialism arose to lay claim to all of the "waste places" of the earth. This does not mean that Churchill, Lodge, and others were only "opportunistically" racist—most likely they were racists to the core. Racist race ideology (leaving aside for the moment the difficult question of whether there is any other kind) fits colonialist and imperialist ventures to a *T*, but it certainly has its own dynamic as well. And yet it is one thing to regard people in distant lands as uncivilized, heathen, unwashed, and so on, and still another thing to undertake long-distance, brutal ventures to "civilize," "save," and purify these people. It is another thing to force millions of people into wage and money economies and to undermine their village economies for this purpose, as every high school or college student who has read Chinua Achebe's *Things Fall Apart* or Alice Walker's *The Color Purple* can readily see.

Excellent Capitalist Thinking

As a matter of political economy, the dynamic of this brutality is impersonal. For the imperialist ruling classes and their political, administrative, cultural, and military operatives and advocates, there is no great difference between whatever it is that is "uncivilized" about, say, the Arabs, than there is about, say, East Asians. Indeed, there is little sense that there are diverse Islamic cultures, except perhaps if such knowledge is useful for strategic purposes (for example, to set Sunni and Shi'a at odds). It is not an exaggeration to say that most people in the United States, from the ruling class or otherwise, who today support the invasion of Afghanistan, did not know yesterday the difference between Afghanistan and banana-stand—and neither could they tell you today much of anything about the history and culture of the place. Most could not tell you much about the difference between Iran and Iraq, other than that one ends with an *n* and the other with a *q*. Either one is fine for invading, if that is what is needed. (Nor could most even tell you about the war that the United States encouraged Iraq, led by Saddam Hussein, to wage against Iran from 1980 to 1988, at tremendous human and material cost to both countries, and where Iraq, aided by the United States and its allies, built a comprehensive "arms industry capable of turning out everything from light arms to Scud missiles and chemical weapons"—and it used all of these, including chemical weapons, against Iranians and Kurds; see Everest, 119–21.) The point, however, is that this ignorance (apart from purely strategic or tactical considerations) of the degree of "civilization" or lack thereof of the peoples of the waste lands of the earth is in fact *excellent capitalist thinking* and *excellent imperialist thinking*. As Marx showed very well in *Capital* and elsewhere—in the process not telling the capitalists anything that they did not already know—the capitalist is fundamentally indifferent to what particular commodity is produced, whether this be apples or oranges or automobiles or Agent Orange. The point is not what "C" is produced, the point is that "M-prime" is generated at the conclusion of any given circuit of production. (Indeed, this is the true "end," in the Aristotelian sense of *telos*, of the production process under capitalism, not the object that is created through the application of labor power to materials that came, at some point, from the earth.) A capitalist who aims to produce, say, cars or electric guitars, *only because* he happens to be "into" cars or electric guitars, will not remain a capitalist for very long.

The logic of M-C-M′ does not have any use for anyone who gets too hung up on the value of a particular object or kind of object that is something other than its price. Recall Ayn Rand's archetypal capitalist in *The Fountainhead*, the architect Howard Roark. At one point in the story, facing challenges from an inferior architect regarding Roarke's innovative designs, Roarke declares that he does not build in order to have clients, he has clients in order to build. No real capitalist could operate this way, and in fact Roarke is not a real capitalist. (In Rand's other big novel, *Atlas Shrugged*, philosopher John Galt leads a strike by the "greatest minds" in the world—the "greatest" chemist, the "greatest" composer, and so on. With these minds on strike, the world trembles, unable to function without them. Meanwhile, the great minds sequester themselves in Galt's Gulch, where, significantly, they seem to form a communal society. For some further reflections on Rand, see Martin 2003.) The Japanese real estate market in the 1980s supplies a wonderful example of how value and price get mixed up in capitalist societies. In Japan, real estate is heavily regulated. This proved to be a problem for Japanese markets during the economic boom—the so-called "bubble economy" of the 1980s. The term "bubble economy" has been applied in other areas in more recent years, most notably to the "dot-com" economy of the late 1990s. Significantly, the term "bubble economy" reflects the fact that even enthusiastic capitalists themselves recognize the precariousness of such an economy. The idea is to get while the getting is good, then get out of the market in time to insure that it is merely the ordinary working people who are hurt by the inevitable crash. The way around real estate regulation in Japan was to work deals where buyers bought a package deal of a building and a painting. Buyers were allowed to pay whatever they could afford for the painting, and thus the prices of many minor masterpieces were unnaturally inflated. When the bubble burst and the real estate market crashed, the bottom also fell out of the international art market for a time. (See Yoko Shibata, "The Art of a Failed Economy.")

To return to the idea of "excellent capitalist thinking," which is purely strategic (at best), the person in this example who is interested in acquiring a building and therefore enters a bidding process, is not actually concerned about which painting by which (generally European) minor master is used to displace the regulation of the real estate market. The painting is no more than a means to an end, and the same can be said for the commodities created in the capitalist production process. The capitalist, *qua capitalist*, cannot afford to care about which particular commodities are produced by his enterprise (except, again, in a purely strategic sense—for example, in determining which markets to enter). Just to take a simple example, sometime around 1990, the last schools that taught people how to repair manual and electric typewriters closed. There are still bureaucracies in some Third World countries that use manual typewriters, and this will probably remain the case for some time to come, but these typewriters will have to be patched together, and parts for them will have to be taken from other old typewriters. Now, suppose there were a capitalist who just loved those old manual Royal typewriters because "they were so beautiful, yet utilitarian, and they remind us of a bygone era," etc. Well, any capitalists who pursued such sentimentality very far would lose their shirts, except perhaps in the case of a retro market where sentimentality itself is highly marketable. In this case, however, the motivation for getting into the market (and using advertising to sell the appeal of "the way things used to be in the good old days") is not itself sentimentality (or some other "merely aesthetic" value or concern for craft), but instead once again the M-prime that the capitalist hopes for after producing the C.

What Is Imperialism?

Imperialism is capitalism as a global mode of production. Marxist political economist Raymond Lotta has this to say about the broad contours of this development:

> By the last third of the nineteenth century, Western European feudalism had been overcome and capitalism was spreading its reach to the farthest stretches of unconquered land in the world. In great measure because of this, the system could develop relatively peacefully at home (although not without breaks in growth). Indeed, this stabilization of capitalism was linked precisely with the savagery of its expansion into regions it newly or more thoroughly penetrated. At the close of the nineteenth century, what has come to be known as the Third World was transformed from a subsidiary market and outlet for capital of the advanced countries into an indispensable component of their prosperity. Internationalization of investment of productive capital transformed the world market. On a political level, Great Britain's military, colonial, and economic preeminence was challenged by rival empire-builders. Free trade was being eclipsed by an aggressive and bellicose protectionism. A veritable paroxysm of colonial conquests culminated in the complete partition of the world among the great powers. The great powers had imposed their power over every corner of the globe. Lenin summarized the leap that had occurred: "On the threshold of the twentieth century we see the formation of a new type of monopoly: firstly, monopolist capitalist combines in all capitalistically developed countries; secondly, the monopolist position of a few very rich countries, in which the accumulation of capital has reached gigantic proportions." [*Imperialism*, in *Lenin Collected Works*, v. 22, 241]
>
> This emergence of monopoly, inward and outward, as it were, at a deeper level expressed [the] "narrowing circle" to which Engels referred. Capitalism was pressing against the limits of private ownership and facing ever more formidable barriers in the international arena. The compelling force of anarchy had propelled socialization of the productive forces to a whole new level of domestic concentration and centralization. This same compelling force pushed these powers outward, where they collided with the less powerful, old-style colonial powers, let loose their cannon on nascent national movements, and lashed out at each other. [In a footnote, Lotta adds that "The Anglo-Boer and Spanish-American Wars and the subsequent Russo-Japanese War of the late nineteenth and early twentieth centuries were the first significant imperialist conflicts.] The contours of modern capitalism could be discerned: capitalism was in violent transition to something higher.

> The emergence of imperialism, then, was nothing less than the fundamental development of capitalism into a separate and distinct phase. (*America in Decline*, 72–73)

With the development of imperialism, there is a sense in which blocs of capital constituted as a set of imperialist nation-states behave somewhat like corporations. (This analogy has its limits but will serve well enough for the point I am driving toward here.) In "excellent capitalist thinking," the capitalist owner, firm, or corporation is interested first of all in pursuing surplus value, not in which particular commodity is produced. In "excellent imperialist thinking," the imperialist country is interested first of all in dominating other countries for their material resources, cheap labor, and markets, in the pursuit of the generation of surplus value through super-exploitation, and not in what the culture or history of this or that country is. Again, these things may be taken into account for strategic purposes. For instance, the CIA depends on certain universities to train people in languages that are not commonly taught at most universities. In Soviet times, there were a handful of universities and colleges that received CIA and Department of Defense funding to offer courses in languages spoken in the regions on the southern border of the Soviet Union. (More recently, as one might expect, it is the languages of the Muslim countries that are of strategic interest to the intelligence and defense establishments.) The imperialists might be interested in the difference between Sunni and Shi'a Islam, for instance, in terms of the kinds of resistance to domination that might be encountered. As the reader undoubtedly knows, anthropology, as an academic discipline, has at times been enlisted in this effort—or at least certain anthropologists have. The question of "culture" for imperialism is no more than this: What are the *best ways* to exploit, to dominate, to control?

And thus the road to Vietnam—nothing "personal" was meant.

Marx spoke of "the violence of abstraction." In a similar vein, we might speak of the brutality of market equality. In the case of imperialist ventures, there is a "market equality" of countries, peoples, and cultures who are potential targets of invasion, occupation, and domination: what matters is the cash nexus—how much money is to be made from any given venture? Of course, imperialism is sometimes not so crude. There is no way to exactly quantify what will be gained from invading Vietnam or Afghanistan or Iraq (or Panama or Granada or Haiti or the halls of Montezuma or the shores of Tripoli); indeed, the benefit is ultimately in the global standing that an imperialist power achieves, including the standing that is achieved by repeatedly showing the world what an imperialist power is willing to do to assert its dominance. No imperialist power has asserted itself as effectively as the United States, with its unsurpassed arsenal of *world-destroying* nuclear weapons and its many threats to use them—in every decade since these weapons were used in Japan.

Global standing is the best way for the imperialists to secure surplus value, however, and there are legions of accountants, at various levels, keeping track of the actual money that is brought in. As Lotta argues, super-exploitation in the Third World allows for the relatively peaceful operation of capitalism within the imperialist countries themselves—up to a point. Within any given global configuration, there is a limit to what can be squeezed out of the labor process both within the imperialist countries and the countries dominated by imperialism. This is the case for two inter-related reasons. First, every advanced capitalist country has to face the problem of the overproductivity of capital; because commodities are produced first of all with profit in mind, there comes a point where the "invisible hand," not being primarily concerned with whether people will be able to absorb (buy) everything that is produced, is faced with a pile of goods that cannot be sold. It is at this point that capital goes on strike and the spiral of layoffs, unemployment, underconsumption, impoverishment, and civil discontent and unrest is set in motion. Second, just as firms compete for "market share" in any given area of production (apples, oranges, Agent Orange, or what-have-you), imperialist powers compete for every nook and cranny of the world, "culminat[ing] in the complete partition of the world by and among the great powers" (Lotta, 73). Firms in capitalism cannot simply be satisfied with their existing portion of market share; classical economics already teaches us that, if there is profit to be taken, then new firms will enter the market. Thus the capitalist (or capitalist firm) must continually seek out new opportunities, and every opportunity passed up is what classical economics (what Marx called "bourgeois political economy") counts as an "opportunity cost." It is sometimes difficult for people to understand, either in considering classical microeconomics (what is also called "price theory"), or in Marx's arguments about bourgeois political economy, that an "opportunity cost" is a *real* cost—a firm that passes up opportunities will eventually go out of business.

Opportunity Cost

I will give a simple example. In the 1970s and 1980s, a few scrappy fellows in northern California got the idea of returning to "fat tire" bicycles for adults, to ride on trails and dirt and roads that are not in the best of shape. These bikes morphed, over the course of a few years, into what we now call the "mountain bike," and one of these original fat tire enthusiasts, Gary Fisher, built a company around this new kind of bike. Other companies arose, some becoming bigger than others. Indeed, the most successful of these, Trek, bought out Gary Fisher Bicycles in 1994. However, the most famous American bicycle company, Schwinn, which has made some great bikes for more than a century, was slow to get in on this trend. Obviously, the people running the company did not see how important mountain bikes would become in the overall bicycle market, and one can easily imagine that they thought, at least in the early years, that mountain bikes were merely a passing fad. Schwinn failed to take advantage of an opportunity, and the opportunity cost that they have paid, the result of this miscalculation, is that Schwinn repeatedly went into bankruptcy and was sold several times over, and today is mainly a brand name for bikes that are mass produced in China (along with everything else) and sold in discount stores such as Wal-Mart and Target. The opportunity cost is that, effectively, Schwinn does not exist as the company that it once was.

To shift to an obviously far more brutal arena (though mass production of cheap commodities in Third World countries is no walk in the park), Vietnam presented an opportunity for imperialism. In the 1950s, France, having been substantially weakened as an imperial power, was losing its grip on Vietnam. From an imperialist, geo-strategic standpoint—and obviously not any kind of ethical standpoint—some power was going to step in and pick up this part of the "imperialist market" in Third World countries. As the still-rising imperialist power in the world, and as the great power that was least "injured" (as such, as a power capable of operating globally) in the Second World War, the United States was in a position to pick up Vietnam, and the United States had to consider the opportunity cost of not adding Vietnam to the list of countries under its domination. In the early stages of intervention, the rhetoric of "commercial supremacy" as justification for invasion was heard straightforwardly: President Eisenhower explained that Vietnam was a major source for tungsten and tin. However, precisely because of the wave of anticolonialist struggles that took place in the aftermath of the Second World War (and with the Chinese Revolution of 1949 presenting a powerful and influential example), the blatant rhetoric of conquest that had previously sufficed as imperialist justification was no longer sufficient. Undoubtedly, in the United States, the rise of the post-WWII Civil Rights Movement also contributed to the delegitimation of this rhetoric, the establishment purveyors of which had rarely bothered to conceal their racism up until that time. Suddenly new attempts at justification had to come to the fore, and first among these were the Cold War rhetorics of the "domino theory" and the need to halt the spread of communism.

Soviet Union

Indeed, there was one bit of truth in this view. The United States, in the period from the end of the nineteenth century until the aftermath of

WWII, had emerged as the leading power involved in carving up the world, but there was always competition. For a brief period after the Second World War there was even a "socialist camp," of the Soviet Union and China, and countries of Eastern Europe. This was a camp riddled with contradictions, many of them emanating from Stalin's leadership of the Soviet Union and the International Communist Movement. I will discuss this question further in part 3, but we can enumerate some of these contradictions and problems here, simply to present a schematization of the world as it emerged from WWII—I will attempt to go from the obvious to the less obvious: (1) Stalin's authoritarian model of socialism, and the fact that a deep-seated, siege mentality played a role in shaping that model; (2) the fact that the Chinese Revolution came to power largely despite Stalin and the Comintern; (3) the fact that Stalin tended to compromise with the Western powers at every turn, the most spectacular example of which was the undermining of the revolution in Spain; (4) the fact that the great "prize" won by the Soviet Union, besides of course not being defeated by Germany, was the addition of the Eastern European countries to the "socialist camp," except that these countries were never socialist, because there were never socialist revolutions in these countries. (On this point, the more difficult cases of Albania and Yugoslavia will have to be set aside for another day's discussion.) This last point brings us full circle, for it was part of Stalin's authoritarian model that "where the Red Army goes, it installs the Soviet social system." This was Stalin's conception of how the Eastern European countries "became socialist."

At the very least, whatever existed of socialism in the Soviet Union and Eastern Europe (in the Warsaw Pact) was in a deep, deep muddle. The leaders of the Communist Party of the Soviet Union after Stalin's death "resolved" this muddle, by restoring capitalism. Being a "great power," with global reach as well as a good deal of prestige after having defeated Germany, this new form of state capitalism that continued to call itself "socialist" ("the better to deceive you with, my dear") came into the world as an imperialist empire, and it quickly reoriented its economic, political, and military apparatuses toward global, imperialist contention. The one bit of truth to the American view about the domino theory and the need to halt the spread of communism was that the premise of the Cold War was that two powers would contend over every part of the world and indeed over the fate of the world as a whole. (At the same time, the Soviet effort in the Third World was one thing, and the indigenous basis for revolution in these countries was another thing altogether, even if the former attempted to subsume the latter under its purview.) But to talk of a geo-political contention, where every other part of the globe is going to be under the domination of one superpower or the other, and that even includes the possibility of "winning" by destroying all of humanity, has nothing to do with what is right.

"Geo-politics"

What geo-political calculations have to do with instead are the essentially capitalist compulsions that imperialist nation-states are subject to, where the entire rest of the world (including whatever other imperialist countries there are, as well as "their" imperial possessions at any given time) has to be understood as a set of potential opportunities and a set of potential opportunity costs. In the case of imperialist countries, capital circulates internally and internationally; in both cases, internal and external, the capital of a particular national ruling class comes up against the capital of other imperialist ruling classes—these different circuits of capital bump into each other and jostle around. (Automobile manufacturing in the United States is a helpful example here. In many ways, all that is meant by an "American car" is that it was assembled in the geographical United States, or at least the final assembly occurs there. But now other cars are also assembled in the United States, especially "Japanese" cars, Toyota, Honda, Nissan, and Mitsubishi all have plants here. Even Chrysler, formerly one of the "Big 3" American car manufacturers, was acquired in a hostile takeover—which was presented to the public as a merger—in the 1990s by the German corporation, Daimler-Benz.) These circuits of capital, which exist for the production of profit, can reach their limits both "internally" and "externally" (domestically and globally), and these two different levels interact with one another. To be direct about it, the basis of value-creation under capitalism is the exploitation of labor-power, and if capital can no longer squeeze value out of people in some of the places where it operates, it will have to squeeze even more out of people in other places. Extraction of value from the Third World has tended, for the first century of imperialism at any rate, to be both far more brutal (again, often under conditions that approximate slavery, and that piggyback on colonial practices such as cutting off the hands of uncooperative subjects), and far less efficient. When capital reaches what Marx called the "limits of accumulation" under existing circuits, it has to reconfigure the ways in which it pursues profit, and it does this in a world where other units of capital, either at the level of the individual capitalist, or the capitalist firm, or the imperialist nation-state, all must seek out every opportunity, and each must do whatever is necessary to avoid paying opportunity costs.

Capital continually divides and redivides the world, and when all of the interrelating circuits of capital are pressed up against each other, this redivision can take the form of war, and even of world war. In the pursuit of this redivision, there is no moral limit to the forms of military technology that will be applied. In this respect it can be said that napalm and Agent Orange and eight-thousand pound conventional bombs (so called "bunker busters," dropped from planes or launched from ships) and nuclear bombs are not simply *neutral* artifacts of technology, but instead are indeed *con-centrated expressions* of the social systems that deploy them. I will return to this point.

It can be added that these dynamics of capital, of which I have only provided a thumbnail sketch (and without any claim of originality), are no great secret—indeed, these dynamics were very openly displayed in the first five decades of imperialism, and even now they are not at all hard to see. In the case of early imperialism, just review not only what Henry Cabot Lodge said, but also the way he said it—for the sake of commercial supremacy, let's cut a canal right across Nicaragua (this ended up being the "Panama" canal, but Panama itself was created by ripping off a piece of Colombia), then we're going to need Cuba, and then we'll head out across the Pacific and just take as much of it as we can. Statements such as this (which I am paraphrasing a bit here, but without exaggerating in any way), and statements about "access" to "cheap" labor and materials were not at all unusual or outrageous in the first decades of imperialism. It was only when former colonies and neo-colonies began to stand up for themselves, in a way that the imperialist powers could not so easily put down, that the rhetoric shifted *somewhat* in the direction of something that was supposed to be taken for the value categories of political modernity. But even then, in imperialism's second half-century and beyond, there is still plenty of talk of access to materials and labor, and one does not have to look very far to find accounting and dollar amounts (this is regular fare in publications such as the *Wall Street Journal* or *Business Week*). To take the most obvi-ous example in recent years: the invasions of Iraq in 1991 and 2003 were not only about oil, they were about larger geo-political problems in the imperialist system, but the American domination of Iraq is not *not* about oil, either, and this is no secret. An imperialist economy that runs on fossil fuels will have to try to control the sources of those fuels, and the machi-nations that occur around the attempt to secure and control the sources of oil have global ramifications. Such machinations have as much to do with the other imperialist countries in the world as they do with Iraq itself, and indeed the upshot once again is that geo-political considerations are set against any kind of ethical thinking, for the fact is that it is also the case that the people of Iraq never did anything to deserve the treatment they have received from the United States.

To understand the way things are in the world, to understand imperi-alism as a system, is absolutely necessary if there is to be any chance of defeating imperialism (which means not only its economic structure, but ultimately its whole culture and the way that human beings have been shaped as subjects of imperialism—on either side of the imperialist bifurca-tion of dominator and dominated) and creating an alternative. However, this alternative also has to be conceptualized in itself, it cannot be merely a "reaction formation." In a completely Kantian formulation, Marx said that humanity must become the subject of history instead of merely history's object. The closed dialectic of the reaction formation will not simply deliver humanity into the space of emancipation—and this is the case by definition. (On this point, see Roger Gottlieb, *History and Subjectivity*, esp. 16.) In other words, critical consciousness, philosophy, the imagination (not only the moral imagination, but the aesthetic imagination as well), intentionality, and ethical thinking have crucial roles to play. I would add to this list the idea of redemption (and what Adorno called the attempt to see the world from the standpoint of redemption). To encounter such an idea involves working out the large and difficult question of the relationship of the ethical and what I am choosing to call a "religious" perspective. (I will return to this topic in the conclusion.) We can see the broad contours of the relationship in Kant's three fundamental questions: What can human beings know? What ought we to do? For what may we hope?

Reaction Formation

Although to talk about Stalin and the Soviet Union during the period of his leadership seems very backward-looking and perhaps even completely irrelevant these days, one thing that we can learn from this period is what socialism looks like as a "reaction formation" (or concatenation of such formations). We can see this on numerous fronts, from the military structure that the Soviet Union learned too well from the Germans, to the acquisition of nuclear weapons in the late-1940s. This last in itself is a difficult question. Before dropping atomic bombs on Hiroshima and Nagasaki, President Harry Truman informed Stalin that the United States had developed "a new weapon of unusual destructive force" (this is from the "terse" account in Truman's memoirs, as quoted in *The Decision to Use the Atomic Bomb* by Gar Alperovitz, 386). Truman had the impression that Stalin did not know what Truman was talking about, and the exchange, at the Potsdam Conference on July 24, 1945, was very brief and "casual." The United States and Great Britain had asked that the Soviet Union enter the war against Japan three months after the surrender of Germany. When Stalin informed the other allies that the Soviet Union was prepared to enter the war in the Pacific a month ahead of schedule, Truman urged that research and testing of the atomic bomb be speeded up. Clearly, the United States aimed to defeat Japan before the U.S.S.R. could enter the Pacific theater, and thereby prevent the Soviet Union from participating in surrender negotiations with Japan. (Alperovitz's book is a substantial and fascinating account on all aspects of the questions just raised, and many others; for the "timetable" issues, as they relate to Stalin, see 375–89.)

One often hears persons of a right-wing persuasion presenting Stalin's seeming ignorance of the real destructive power of the atomic bomb as though this is mainly a comment on Stalin's lack of mental acuity. Somehow it is not an issue that the United States was about to unleash a weapon that could destroy people and places on a scale never before seen, and that the United States was soon (less than a month later) going to actually use this weapon to obliterate two large, industrial cities. Stalin could not see what a horrible thing the United States was about to do, so let's talk about how dumb Stalin was! (By the same token, Marx did not foresee that the capitalist powers would become such that, in the pursuit of their aims, they were willing to destroy the whole planet—"if necessary." Old dumb Marx!) More recent accounts of Stalin and Potsdam that are based on archival material that has become available since the dissolution of the Soviet Union are clear on the fact that Stalin had known for some time that the United States was developing a new kind of weapon, and the U.S.S.R. had initiated its own version of the Manhattan Project in 1942. (See Volkogonov, 498, and Montefiore, 491–501. It is also true that the Soviet Union's work on the atomic bomb was slow, not very advanced, and depended upon the findings of spies placed in the United States.) Whether Stalin, or anyone, including the scientists and politicians in the United States who were developing and preparing to use the bomb, fully understood the ramifications of this new weapon is highly doubtful. The problem of the reaction formation is that of avoiding a deadly, closed dialectic where the supposed alternative to capitalism and imperialism comes to increasingly mirror those very social forms, for the not inconsiderable reason that there are times when fire has to be fought with fire. Simon Sebag Montefiore wrote a book about Stalin that has as its basic aim to demonstrate the "nature of evil" (*Stalin: Court of the Red Tsar*, 2004), and yet here is Montefiore's account of a meeting held with top Soviet leaders right after the Potsdam Conference:

> [Stalin] then convened a meeting with Molotov and Gromyko at which he announced: "Our allies have told us that the U.S.A. has a new weapon. I spoke with our physicist Kurchatov as soon as Truman told me. The real question is should some countries which have the Bomb simply compete with one another or . . . should they seek a solution that would mean prohibition of its production and use?" He realized that America and Britain "are hoping we won't be able to develop the Bomb ourselves for some time . . ." and "want to force us to accept their plans. Well that's not going to happen." He cursed them in what Gromyko called "ripe language," then asked the diplomat if the Allies were satisfied with all the agreements. (Montefiore, 500)

The Soviet Union developed its own atomic bomb because the United States had already developed the bomb, and yet even this was not a simple political question from Stalin's perspective.

However, under real, world-historical pressures, the Soviet Union did indeed develop nuclear weapons, and the question that was ultimately swept under the carpet is that no weapon or military strategy is politically neutral. The weapons that a polity develops represent the social relations of that polity, broadly speaking, roughly in the same way that, as Karl von Clausewitz said, "War is a continuation of politics by other means." Acquiring the atomic bomb was not the final nail in the coffin of what was already a tremendously flawed form of socialism, but it was another step in the direction of the restoration of capitalism in a polity that too often fell into the trap of being a reaction formation—under circumstances of embattlement suffered by no other modern state, and under leadership that was very often deeply dogmatic and reductivistic.

Justice as Adjustment

The point of this seeming digression in the present context is that a supposedly "purely scientific," descriptive theory of "the way things are," or "the laws of motion" of particular social formations, can easily fall into one of two traps, which are mirror images of one another: either the trap of "the real is the rational," or that of the reaction formation. In either case, the furthest one can go on value questions within such frameworks is "justice" as "adjustment," bringing things back into a supposed equilibrium. Leave aside for now the shortcomings of this model for a socialist polity. After capitalism was restored in the Soviet Union, an imperialist competition for world domination started between the two nuclear superpowers. "Equilibrium" in the context of global-imperialist bifurcation means "adjustment" to one bloc or the other.

Given that no ethical justification can be given for what the United States did to the people of Vietnam, all we can look for is some other sort of explanation. The other sorts of explanations that can be given are "geopolitical" or "systemic." With regard to ethics, if what was done to the people of Vietnam is the expression or "outcome" of a particular social system, then we who care about ethical questions have an obligation to do something, whatever is necessary, to address this system.

The ethical dilemma for those who would fight for a different future (and again a reason to study the Soviet experience, from Lenin to Stalin and after) is one of not falling into a philosophical idealism that, in practice, does not actually challenge the existing order of things, on the one hand, and, on the other, also does not fall into a reductive materialism of "justice" as mere adjustment.

In the Soviet Union when it was socialist, many things were done that reflected a more capitalist way of doing things, and these things prepared the ground for the restoration of capitalism. The acquisition of atomic weapons by itself did not signal the triumph of capitalism in the Soviet Union, but it did signal a perspective on war that was very much capitalist, as these are purely offensive weapons—indeed, they are instruments of mass murder and potential destruction of all of humanity and most of our other fellow creatures. It is significant, that when the Soviet Union first developed its own atomic bombs, it was clearly not with the intention of entering into an arms race. Furthermore, when China acquired nuclear weapons (when it was a socialist country, unlike now), the aim was not to create an enormous arsenal of atom bombs, such as the United States began to develop fairly quickly, but instead to have only a few of these weapons, in case there was a need for a counterthreat. Again, one can readily see the global situation that led to Marxist political leaders, such as Mao and the revolutionary communists in China, thinking in this way. In this period, in the 1950s and 1960s, the United States made nuclear threats on a regular basis. Within two years of the countrywide seizure of power by Mao and the communists in 1949, the United States was fighting a war on China's border, and threatening to use nuclear weapons. In the early 1960s, leading American politicians such as Barry Goldwater were proposing that the Vietnam War be resolved by dropping a hydrogen bomb on Hanoi (the northern capital). Indeed, although the Chinese Revolution went forward despite Stalin, the existence of the Soviet Union as a socialist state in 1949, as a counterbalance to the United States, is very likely what kept the U. S. from exercising its "nuclear option" on Beijing.

Nevertheless, it was a mistake (or worse), for socialist states to get involved with nuclear weapons—even if this was in some sense understandable, and even if this can perhaps only be seen in twenty-twenty hindsight. Indeed, the problem is that the need for an "equal and opposite force" to oppose an imperialist, nuclear power that was all too ready to grab everything that it could in the aftermath of WWII, is all too understandable—but the ethical response has to exceed what is "all too understandable" and which therefore only requires reaction and not what Kant understood to be autonomous action, which is human action that has its basis in the formation of intention. Now, Montefiore's quotation from Stalin ("The real question is . . .") demonstrates that there was some consciousness on this point, and it could even be said that it was precisely because there were key ways in which Stalin did continue to try to thematize doing things differently than capitalist and imperialist countries did them that the Soviet Union under his leadership was still socialist, despite everything. To say the least, it was not a socialism that good-willed people would ever want to recreate in the world again, and yet we had better learn some lessons from this problem of the reaction formation, and my argument here is that these need to be lessons about "the ethical."

"Good Business"

Now, let us return to the issue of Vietnam. "Socialist nukes" are a mistake. But they are a mistake precisely because nuclear weapons for capitalist powers are *not* a mistake. For the United States nuclear weapons have not been a mistake, they have been a part of "good business," the business that has created a high standard of living for many in the United States, and that has created tremendous and justified fear in the rest of the world. They are a result of the system of capitalist commodity production having become global, having become imperialism and imperialist. Within this system, intentions are formed, nonautonomous and anti-ethical intentions. One is tempted to say that these are *evil* intentions. (In that respect I will say something that may seem very personal, but that goes to the point I raised a good while back, about what Vietnam meant for the generations who were politically aware in the 1960s and in the aftermath of "the sixties." For me, napalm was *it*, to learn of what napalm actually is and how it was used and *that* it was used extensively in Vietnam—well, I won't say that this immediately made me a Marxist or an anti-imperialist activist, but it set me on the road to wanting to understand what sort of people—and, later, what sort of social system—could create and use such a thing, and to wanting to know what could be done to stop it.) Napalm is more than just another weapon of war to be used to stop an opponent; it has elements of torture and psychological torment *intentionally* built into it. People—*scientists*, no less— had to devise the formula for this stuff, as fire from the sky, intended to burn people horribly, ending either in death or painful, grotesque disfigurement, as emblems of what happens to the people of countries that resist the United States, even if they are just going about their everyday lives.

Napalm Is the System

This blood (this cruelty, this murder and torture) does not simply wash out of the American imperialist social system; napalm *is* the American imperialist social system.

How could this blood get washed out, when it is not even acknowledged? There is not even a beginning here, nor could there be, because of the very nature of the imperialist system.

Perhaps this last statement will be controversial, for even the last part of it contains at least three ideas: that imperialism is a system, that it has a basic nature, and that napalm is an expression of this nature. This view might be contrasted with that of Richard Rorty, for example, who put forth the idea that the reason the "North Atlantic democracies" are wealthy is "luck," and that the Vietnam War was an "atrocity of which Americans must always be ashamed" (a position that, to be sure, goes far beyond what is recognized in either official circles or in the mainstream of American political discourse), but not something "systemic" (see *Achieving Our Country*, 56). There are many aspects of his philosophy that I either admire or at least find to be a valuable provocation. Surely, however, it is not "luck" that has brought the United States and other imperialist powers cheap materials and cheap labor and "open doors" to markets from all around the world.

Rorty resists the idea of a social system, I think the very idea seems too deterministic to him. Marx argued that it is capitalism that brings forth capitalists, not the other way around—capitalists are the "living representatives" of capitalist social relations. When Henry Cabot Lodge set out his imperialist shopping list of what would "become a necessity" for the United States (from the canal across Central America, to Cuba, to the Hawaiian islands, to Samoa, and beyond, to all the "waste places of the earth"), he was not merely speaking as some acquisitive, money-grabbing jerk. Lodge was representing the interests of a capitalist class that was ready to get into the global hunt for labor, materials, and markets with other advanced-capitalist classes, and that had no choice but to pursue these things or to pay the opportunity cost otherwise. The choices they made, including the "atrocities" they engaged in along the way, were in the context of the compulsions of capital, compulsions that are, in broad outline, indeed determined—in the sense that capital is determined to expand, and any particular unit or bloc of capital will either expand and absorb other units, or it will contract and be absorbed. Within this matrix, people make choices about things to do to further the expansive logic of capital, and among these things are both "common, everyday" forms of exploitation that are nevertheless very ugly, as well as things that are horrible beyond words, such as the formulation, production, and use of napalm. An argument might be made that a substance such as napalm (and all that goes into its actual use) is a contingent rather than necessary expression of the system. What does it say about this "atrocity of which Americans *must* always be ashamed" (my emphasis, and referring to the Vietnam War as a whole), however, when memory of this atrocity is systemically suppressed, such that it only bubbles up at the margins of society, in terms of traumatized individuals (and even then only in terms of the trauma that was caused to individual *Americans*)? Being ashamed might be at least the beginning of an ethical response, of an acceptance of responsibility—but the fact is that the social system can in no way allow such a response. To understand why this is the case, and to formulate the alternative, we need a perspective that integrates the systemic and the notion of the ethical response—a perspective that is generated by the intermotivation of Marxist and Kantian themes.

Dehumanization in War

Consider again the issue of dehumanization in war. It is commonplace to say that the enemy must be dehumanized in order for "us" to accept killing him or her. This is often said as if it is just a matter of the orderly, businesslike waging of war—again, "nothing personal." Then it is said that "our" soldiers have to be dehumanized, too, so that they can do what needs to be done. Both of these points are quite right, when understood within the context of imperialist warfare (and the colonialist military operations that lay the ground for such warfare). But it is also the case that imperialism's soldiers have to be dehumanized, rendered into "killing machines," so that they will not ask troubling questions, such as "Why are we fighting these people?" (On this point, see Jeff Tietz, "The Killing Factory"; I will return to this question in the conclusion.) The Vietnam War did more than previous wars to place this issue in the forefront, because U.S. soldiers could not help but wonder what Vietnam ever did to the United States (or to anyone) to deserve the extraordinary amount of firepower that was thrown at it. In this context race became a very important issue, given the disproportionate percentages of African-Americans, Chicanos and other Latinos, and even Native Americans, in the U.S. Army who were sent mainly as enlisted personnel (while the officer corps was overwhelmingly white) to fight the Vietnamese. U.S. imperialism has spent the decades since the Vietnam War trying to learn the lessons of that experience, from an imperialist perspective. For instance, since Vietnam, the U.S. has been much more careful in setting out the *casus belli* in any military conflict, and even if these justifications are often paper-thin, there is still the sense that more is needed than simply that some Third World country has something that we want. Since the collapse of the Soviet Union, of course, there has been a mad scramble to portray some group of countries as a power bloc that is some kind of new "evil empire," against which the United States can and should "fight the good fight," and this role appears to have fallen upon the Muslim world. It just so happens that a preponderance of industrial capitalism's most precious resource is to be found in parts of that world, so this works out nicely as a "clash of civilizations," or, even better, the new scene where there is civilizing work to be done.

Imperialism is a mode of production; it represents a qualitative development within capitalism, when capitalist social relations become globally dominant. Within this perspective on imperialism as a system, which operates according to root compulsions in a broadly law-like way (even if always in a world of many contingencies and, of course, countervailing forces—either of the different imperialist powers, or real, revolutionary resistance), it is also the case that imperialism is the "global march" of a handful of imperialist powers. It is important that we have some sense of the history of this "march," so that the systemic forces of imperialism are also understood as the actions of real people who are either working (fighting, terrorizing, or, what seems so innocent, "directing," "managing," etc.) to extend domination, or are resisting this domination. Recall that I opened part 2 with the image of the statue of Christopher Columbus on Telegraph Hill in San Francisco, looking so far to the west that he is looking to the Far East, especially to what I called the "main prize," China.

Opium and the Open Door

One of the more egregious examples of imperialist interests having asserted themselves in the Third World was the so-called "Open Door" policy directed toward China and Asia in general. Other "great powers" had gone to tremendous lengths in the nineteenth century to open Chinese markets, with the British taking the lead. The Manchu Dynasty was only interested in selling, not buying foreign products (China already being the "Middle Kingdom"), and therefore required payment in cash. The British were not happy with this arrangement, and proposed to start paying the Chinese in a different "currency"—opium. Though the Manchus had eliminated the sale and use of opium in 1729, the British, extending their empire through and beyond India, reintroduced opium in 1781. By 1838, China was importing over five million pounds of opium a year, *which represented fifty-seven percent of China's total imports.* By the late 1830s, the Chinese imperial government finally acted against the opium trade; roughly two and a half million pounds of opium were seized and destroyed. This the British imperialists did not like, and thus they declared war on China—to defend British "interests." The British won the war and imposed a humiliating treaty; included among the provisions was the surrender of Hong Kong. (In other words, the British acquired Hong Kong in a drug deal.) The Chinese were forced to pay for both the opium and the (first) opium war. Two years later, in 1844, the United States was able to impose a treaty on China that included the right to freely navigate all Chinese rivers. (I based this thumbnail sketch on the narrative in *Red Star over China* by Edgar Snow.) This "right" was claimed not only for the sake of commerce, but also so that

Christian missionaries could save heathen souls. As so often in Western history, the hangmen and the priests worked hand in hand. By the time of the 1949 revolution, ninety million Chinese were addicted to opium.

The British came to China by way of decades of plunder in India; at the end of the nineteenth century the United States was ready for a much bigger piece of the action in the Pacific, in China, and in Asia generally, and the Americans took it in the form of Hawaii and the Philippines. The British plunder of India and then China in the late eighteenth and the nineteenth centuries was typical of colonialism; by the time of the American seizure of the Philippines, the whole world was increasingly bound by a single mode of production and on a trajectory that continues to this day.

Civilizing Mission

The very last years of the nineteenth century saw America on the march—from Cuba to Puerto Rico to Hawaii to Guam to the Philippines. Cuba was "liberated" from Spain in an actual war—and notice that the name of this war, the Spanish-American War, doesn't bother to actually mention that what the war was about was which country would dominate Cuba. This speaks to the way that a world that is dominated by a handful of imperialist powers is not, and cannot be, a "democratic" world; indeed, a world dominated by imperialism is an undemocratic and antidemocratic world, and the overall political configuration of the world has implications for what counts as democracy in the imperialist countries themselves. Puerto Rico, Guam, and the Philippines were not first of all taken as prizes in a war with Spain, but instead bought for the price of twenty million dollars. The people of these island nations of course had nothing to say about this. In the U.S. itself these conquests were presented as divine ordinations, as part of a civilizing and Christianizing mission. As President William McKinley said of the people of these islands, "we could not leave them to themselves—they were unfit for self-government—and they would soon have anarchy and misrule. . . . there was nothing left for us to do but to take them all and to educate the Filipinos, and uplift and civilize and Christianize them, and by God's grace do the very best we could by them, as our fellow men for whom Christ also died" (quoted in Howard Zinn, *A People's History of the United States*, 305–6). McKinley claimed, to a group of visiting ministers, that these colonial-imperial acquisitions were inspired by a vision from God; as Howard Zinn notes, "The Filipinos did not get the same message from God" (306).

My aim here is not to give a detailed account or theory of imperialism. Every reader of this book will almost certainly already know something of the history of plunder by the great powers, including the United States. Furthermore, most readers will know that the imperialist trajectory of the United States, which really gets going in 1898, is a trajectory toward global hegemony that has as key turning points the two world wars of the twentieth century, the direct neo-colonial wars in Korea and southeast Asia, the Cold War, and now the post–Cold War period, and the post-9/11 period, when the U.S. is attempting to establish a truly unprecedented hegemony. My aim here is instead to show the rootedness of the present form of capitalism (and of what appears more recently to be an emerging form of fascism) in the trajectory of imperialism, and then to reiterate the point that this trajectory, while *driven* (or perhaps "powered" would be a better term) by the expand-or-die compulsions of capital, is also *guided* by the ruling class (or, to be clear, a different ruling class for each nationally based bloc of capital—more on this in a moment). The U.S. ruling class, and its top layer of administrative, managerial, and political operatives, make strategic decisions about how best to pursue profit and profitability. Internationally, "open door" policies aim to open up and expand markets. This activity probably sounds nice and fine to people who have done well enough in the "market" in the United States, because the international dimensions of this activity are both obscured and ignored—better not to think too hard about where all this cheap stuff comes from. Willful ignorance is an ideological pillar of imperialism; it is the cognitive basis for complaints about "foreign aid" and supposedly sincere questions along the lines of "Why do they hate us?"

"The Market"

To reiterate and expand upon a point made earlier: the word "market" itself is deceptive. Even though Marx called the commodity the "cellular form" of capital, barter in the village center has only the most tenuous connection to the pursuit of wealth through modern colonialism and the pursuit of markets and consumers through imperialism. Village trade can be pleasant and friendly, eye-level, and not determinative of whether one lives or dies. The aim of village trade, unlike capitalist competition, is not to undermine the viability of others who live in the village. This remained true, to some extent, even in the farming communities of the rural United States up through the 1950s; Wendell Berry notes the transition, in *The Unsettling of America*, from mutual support among farmers to the point where the goal became to acquire neighboring farms. Even now, riding my bicycle out among the vast grain fields of central Kansas, it is easy for me to see how the systemic perspective can slip away: What do these amber waves have to do with anything global, much less *imperialist*? And yet the connections can be traced without much difficulty, even if these connections are not always in the forefront of the minds of people who live and work in such an area. Rest assured that those closer to the actual mechanisms of commodity trading are very clear on the global connections. The transition to "competitive agriculture" has occurred completely at the point where the agricultural economy becomes thoroughly *monetized*, a money economy rather than a mostly self-supporting and bartering economy. On a global scale, this is also the transition—an expansionist economy needs a stable international monetary system, and the trade in money itself (arbitrage, a mind-boggling dimension of international finance capitalism) becomes a central feature of the global economy. In the village, just to complete the picture, someone who defrauds or even opportunistically takes advantage of his or her neighbors will not get away with this for very long. Global "trade" is just the opposite. Even to the extent that "opening up the markets" of the Third World may have brought some rise in the living standards of some (and claims for this are always overplayed), this was done through the implementation of suffering on a vast and absolutely unjustifiable scale. Although my aim here, again, is not to provide a history of imperialism, let us stay one more moment with the scene of the founding of U.S. imperialism, for this is the initiation of a trajectory that runs from the Philippines to the threat of global nuclear destruction to napalm to the occupation of Iraq and the torture at Abu Ghraib. This founding scene is extraordinarily ugly; it was to be exceeded by scenes of even greater ugliness and evil. These scenes are connected, by the compulsions of capital, by the guidance of the U.S. ruling class, and by the complicity and "cheerleading" support of significant parts of the population of the United States (the same dynamic is operative in other imperialist countries as well).

The March of Imperialism

Rereading *A People's History* is an especially good idea in this time of postmodern capitalism. The shattering of historical consciousness is integral to the functioning of the system; it leads to such perverse (but systemically necessary) consequences as people asking, "Why do they hate us?"—an *absolutely, fantastically* bizarre question for anyone with the least sense of history. Such a question could only be asked in a country that surely must appear to the rest of the world to be made up of outright morons. I'm not claiming that the United States is made up of morons, but what reason could we give to people in other countries not to think this? They wouldn't be right *exactly* (the U.S. is not "made up of" morons, but it's not like there is a great shortage of morons, either, or at least willful *dupes*), but neither would it be an *unreasonable* thing for many people around the world to think. The following passages are from chapter 12, "The Empire and the People."

> A *Washington Post* editorial on the eve of the Spanish-American War: "A new consciousness seems to have come upon us—the consciousness of strength— and with it a new appetite, the yearning to show our strength. . . .Ambition, interest, land hunger, pride, *the mere joy of fighting* [my italics—BM], whatever it may be, we are animated by a new sensation. We are face to face with a strange destiny. The taste of Empire is in the mouth of the people even as the taste of blood in the jungle. . . ."
>
>   Was that taste in the mouth of the people through some instinctive lust for aggression or some urgent self-interest? Or was it a taste (if indeed it existed) created, encouraged, advertised, and exaggerated by the millionaire press, the military, the government, the eager-to-please scholars of the time? Political scientist John Burgess of Columbia University said the Teutonic and Anglo-Saxon races were "particularly endowed with the capacity for establishing national states . . . they are entrusted . . . with the mission of conducting the political civilization of the modern world." (Zinn, 292)

(Thus begins the inglorious legitimating mission of what at that time was a fairly new academic discipline, political science, especially as practiced in the Ivy League schools and institutions such as the University of Chicago and Stanford. For the past twenty years or so one outcome of this mission has been that particular breed of social-science animal known as the "terrorism expert.")

> Several years before his election to the presidency, William McKinley said: "We want a foreign market for our surplus products." Senator Albert Beveridge of Indiana in early 1897 declared: "American factories are making more than the American people can use; American soil is producing more than they can consume. Fate has written our policy for us; the trade of the world must and shall be ours." (Zinn, 292)

(The state of affairs that Beveridge describes is what Marx called a crisis of overproduction, something endemic to the capitalist economic and social form. Note that Beveridge does not say that American *workers* are doing the "making," but instead somehow it is the *factories* creating overproduction. But he was right: it is indeed the *fate* of the capitalist factory system to overproduce, precisely because it is not organized according to what people can use, but instead according to what surplus value the owners of the means of production can appropriate. Are there many scenarios where Marx's categories apply more clearly than this one, even in the way that these emergent imperialists are themselves describing?)

The Department of State explained in 1898: "It seems to be conceded that every year we shall be confronted with an increasing surplus of manufactured goods for sale in foreign markets if American operatives and artisans are to be kept employed the year around. The enlargement of foreign consumption of the products of our mills and workshops has, therefore, become a serious problem of statesmanship as well as of commerce." (Zinn, 292)

(Only in capitalism does it cause a crisis if there is a surplus—only in capitalism can people go hungry because there is *too much* bread. Does this state of affairs not seem completely *irrational* and *completely unethical*? The mind has to enter into wild gyrations to justify this state of affairs. This irrationality, which Marx analyzed in minute detail, was exposed publicly and dramatically in the Haymarket rebellion of May 1885. Note the proximity to the conscious yet "fated" fashioning of imperialism. As overproduction widens the class divide, and visibly demonstrates the irrationality of capitalism—Haymarket itself was sparked off by labor agitators who pointed out the contradiction of hunger in the midst of grocery stores full of food—the rhetoric used to justify the system becomes increasingly irrational and even downright crazy. But the imperialists made an end-run around the stark contradictions, employing not only the idea of the civilizing mission, but also a rhetoric of race that was inherited from modern Europe—indeed, a rhetoric that in significant ways forged and was stamped into the identity of modern Europe, and was now being employed similarly in the case of white Americans. From a larger perspective—namely, the rest of the world, against which the United States has now set itself in an open-ended war—all of this still appears completely irrational and insane; but the imperialist cast of mind, which has, at least on the level of historical intertwining, racism in its core, can also become second nature to citizens of imperialist countries, to some extent even of all classes and colors of people. This cast of mind, also ensconced as a sense of global entitlement, perhaps even as the "mere joy of fighting"—truly a sick notion—may become so deeply rooted as to no longer be understood in terms of political legitimation. In any case, this is the dynamic that is unleashed at the end of the nineteenth century.)

These expansionist military men and politicians were in touch with one another. One of Theodore Roosevelt's biographers tells us: "By 1890, [Massachusetts Senator Henry Cabot] Lodge, Roosevelt, and [Captain A. T.] Mahan [U.S. Navy, "a popular propagandist for expansion"] had begun exchanging views," and that they tried to get Mahan off sea duty "so that he could continue full-time his propaganda for expansion." Roosevelt once sent Henry Cabot Lodge a copy of a poem by Rudyard Kipling, saying it was "poor poetry, but good sense from the expansionist standpoint." (Zinn, 292–93)

(Incidentally, this same Theodore Roosevelt, of "Rough Rider" fame, is G. W. Bush's declared role model among former U.S. presidents.)

> When the United States did not annex Hawaii in 1893 after some Americans (the combined missionary and pineapple interests of the Dole family) set up their own government, Roosevelt calls this hesitancy "a crime against white civilization." And he told the Naval War College: "All the great masterful races have been fighting races. . . . No triumph of peace is quite so great as the supreme triumph of war."
>
> Roosevelt was contemptuous of races and nations he considered inferior. When a mob in New Orleans lynched a number of Italian immigrants, Roosevelt thought the United States should offer the Italian government some remuneration, but privately he wrote his sister that he thought the lynching was "rather a good thing" and told her he had said as much at a dinner with "various dago diplomats . . . all wrought up by the lynching." (Zinn, 293)

(Here one might reflect on the limitations of our "multicultural" society—which has its definite strengths as well—and trace a line from this obnoxious attitude of white supremacy demonstrated by Theodore Roosevelt to the blue-blood, Ivy League pedigree of George H. W. Bush. In one of the presidential debates in 1988, the elder Bush referred to the Greek heritage of the Democratic candidate, Michael Dukakis, saying the latter was certainly right to be proud of "his people." The insinuation was that there are the "ethnic Americans" and there are the "real Americans," white people whose lineage goes back to northern Europe. As on numerous other points, the Democratic candidate, as with the Democratic Party more generally, being a part of the imperialist political compact, could not summon the wherewithal to give this racist garbage the response it deserved.)

> William James, the philosopher, who became one of the leading anti-imperialists of his time, wrote about Roosevelt that he "gushes over war as the ideal condition of human society, for the manly strenuousness which it involves, and treats peace as a condition of blubberlike and swollen ignobility, fit only for huckstering weaklings, dwelling in gray twilight and heedless of the higher life. . . ." (Zinn, 293)

(We will come back to William James. Let us now go to some specifics of the imperialist subjugation of the Philippines. Zinn's narrative is rejoined at the point where he is describing the differing perspectives on the divine mission of the American imperialists.)

> The Filipinos did not get the same message from God. In February 1899, they rose in revolt against American rule, as they had rebelled several times against the Spanish. Emilio Aguinaldo, a Filipino leader, who had earlier been brought back from China by U.S. warships to lead soldiers against Spain, now became

leader of the *insurrection* fighting the United States. He proposed Filipino independence within a U.S. protectorate, but this was rejected.

It took the United States three years to crush the rebellion, using seventy thousand troops. . . . It was a harsh war. For the Filipinos the death rate was enormous from battle casualties and from disease.

The taste of empire was on the lips of politicians and business interests throughout the country now. Racism, paternalism, and talk of money mingled with talk of destiny and civilization. In the senate, Albert Beveridge spoke, January 9, 1900, for the dominant economic and political interests of the country: "Mr. President, the times call for candor. The Philippines are ours forever. . . . And just beyond the Philippines are China's illimitable markets. We will not retreat from either. . . . We will not renounce our part in the mission of our race, trustee, under God, of the civilization of the world. ...

The Pacific is our ocean. . . . Where shall we turn for consumers of our surplus? Geography answers the question. China is our natural customer. . . . The Philippines give us a base at the door of all the East. . . .

It has been charged that our conduct of the war has been cruel. Senators, it has been the reverse. . . . Senators must remember that we are not dealing with Americans or Europeans. We are dealing with Orientals."

The fighting with the rebels began, McKinley said, when the insurgents attacked American forces. But later, American soldiers testified that the United States had fired the first shot. After the war, an army officer speaking in Boston's Faneuil Hall said his colonel had given him orders to provoke a conflict with the insurgents.

In February 1899, a banquet took place in Boston to celebrate the Senate's ratification of the peace treaty with Spain. President McKinley himself had been invited by the wealthy textile manufacturer W. B. Plunkett to speak. It was the biggest banquet in the nation's history: two thousand diners, four thousand waiters. McKinley said that "no imperial designs lurk in the American mind," and at the same banquet, to the same diners, his Postmaster General, Charles Emory Smith, said that "what we want is a market for our surplus."

William James, the Harvard philosopher, wrote a letter to the Boston *Transcript* about "the cold pot grease of McKinley's cant at the recent Boston banquet" and said the Philippine operation "reeked of the infernal adroitness of the great department store, which has reached perfect expertness in the art of killing silently, and with no public squalling or commotion, the neighboring small concerns."

James was part of a movement of prominent American businessmen, politicians, and intellectuals who formed the Anti-Imperialist League in 1898 and carried on a long campaign to educate the American public about the horrors of the Philippine war and the evils of imperialism. It was an odd group. . . . Whatever their differences on other matters, they would all agree with William James's angry statement: "God damn the U.S. for its vile conduct in the Philippine Isles."

The Anti-Imperialist League published the letters of soldiers doing duty in the Philippines. A captain from Kansas wrote: "Caloocan was supposed to contain 17,000 inhabitants. The Twentieth Kansas swept through it, and now

Caloocan contains not one living native." A private from the same outfit said
he had "with my own hand set fire to over fifty houses of Filippinos after the
victory at Caloocan. Women and children were wounded by our fire."

A volunteer from the state of Washington wrote: "Our fighting blood was
up, and we all wanted to kill 'niggers.' . . . This shooting human beings beats
rabbit hunting all to pieces. (Zinn, 306–7)

Consider how this initial imperial venture hovers over the invasions and
occupations in Afghanistan and Iraq that are taking place at the time of this
writing.

Zinn goes on to point out this same period was "a time of intense
racism in the United States" (307). "In the years between 1889 and 1903,
on the average, every week, two Negroes were lynched by mobs—hanged,
burned, mutilated" (308). Colonialism and imperialism forge an intertwining of race and class, the legacy of which is absolutely and completely
with us today.

Taking Possession of the World

To highlight a few salient points, first, it is clear from the statements of
Senator Beveridge and others that the United States was coming to view
much of the world as its legitimate possession—"The Pacific is our ocean."
Second, while the purpose of invading the Philippines was ambitious
enough (involving as it did the aim of gaining control of the natural
resources there—in Beveridge's speech he says the "wood of the
Philippines can supply the furniture of the world for a century to come"
[306]), it is also clear that the "main prize" was China. China would do
for the emergent U.S. empire what India did for the British.

Third, however, herein lies a difficulty, for indeed there are other imperial powers in the world, and in the march to dominate what was then
emerging as the Third World, U.S. imperialism ran into not only the resistance of the "natives," but also the ambitions of other imperialist powers.
In this case, these other powers included not only the United Kingdom,
but also Japan. A line could be drawn, then, from this march across the
Pacific, ultimately to China, and the Japanese attack on Pearl Harbor.
There are periods in the history of imperial plunder, by the "great powers,"
when there is enough to go around and the different imperialist nations—
or, more accurately, the different ruling classes of these nation-states—*col-
lude* in plunder (and exploitation, domination, torture, and so on) rather
than *collide*. (This occurs at the beginning of a circuit of accumulation.)
But capitalism is insatiable; there is no point when it gets enough. A hungry stomach can eventually be filled, but not so with the banks of the capitalists. Therefore inter-imperialist collusion will always turn into collision

by and by; some "incident" will be determined by one ruling class or another as the "final straw," and in this way one or another ruling class will seize the initiative, take advantage of *its* "Pearl Harbor," and take the fundamental hostility that exists between competing blocs of capital to the level of outright war. Here there are no "natural limits" either: whatever gets the job done, whether it be napalm, massacres of people living in villages in the Philippines or Vietnam, or nuclear weapons, will be employed. There is no "morality" in any of this. Let us be clear: the capitalist ruling classes of the world are compelled by the logic of their exploitative system; at the same time, they are the biggest scumbags in the history of the world, and therefore the ruling class of the United States, being the most powerful ruling class in the world, leads the pack. But imperialism creates complicities, too, and this leads to moral rot in the imperialist countries, and this moral rot itself becomes a part of the imperialist system—this is the case even if, in some circumstances, this rot also can be a problem for the system itself.

We might also pause for reflection over the question of what it meant, when Mao and the Communist Party of China came to power in 1949, that the conversation in the United States within elite political and diplomatic circles—but broadcast without compunction, without a moment's worth of moral hesitation, to the rest of America and the world, that the essential question was "Who lost China?" The Pacific is our ocean, China is ours to lose, and ultimately there is only one sovereign nation, the United States, the sovereignty of all other nations being conditional.

Sovereignty and "Us"

The "we" that is constituted by such formulations of what is "ours" is primarily the U.S. ruling class, which deliberates through various procedures (some quite "public," but not in a way that reflects a vibrant, participatory public sphere, and others far from public view or scrutiny) and formulates its global strategies; but an additional "we" is forged through a fairly broad complicity with imperialist aims—and it is this complicity that also plays an essential role in the shift toward fascism. To put it bluntly, there comes a time when imperialism needs its cheerleaders and its appreciative audience for these cheerleaders, and its thugs who will deal with those who are not cheering at the right time, or loudly enough. This time comes when the circuits of capital are up against limits—the logic of expand-or-die has to either break through or go into decline. It may be that this logic is now working on a whole different basis, with the unprecedented scale of American power, global position, and global ambition. If moral rot and outright thuggery are substantial bases for the imperialist system and impe-

rialist ambitions, however, then it is also the case that the *ethical* critique
of imperialism assumes a heightened role.

It is in this context that the United States has, since September 11,
2001, set out the doctrine of "conditional sovereignty" in explicit form, as
an aspect of public policy. Certainly this doctrine is implicit in the global
comportment of every imperialist power: there is no sovereignty for non-
imperialist countries, and even the sovereignty of other imperialist powers
is a matter of putting up with their spheres of influence until the time
comes when something must be done about this. Marx did not write in the
language of national sovereignty, perhaps for the very reason that such a
thing is an obvious fiction in a world of expand-or-die capitalist powers,
but it might be said that, in his theory, the only real sovereignty would be
one that is rooted in the popular will of the working people, and this sovereignty cannot ultimately be a matter of national boundaries. Certainly
the notion of a general will is a theme that both Kant and Marx take up
from Rousseau. In *The Politics of Autonomy: A Kantian Reading of
Rousseau's Social Contract*, Andrew Levine claims that Feuerbach and the
early Marx are "the best disciples of Rousseau after Kant" (26–27). The
pursuit of this line of thought will help us to frame the ethical problem of
imperialism, and also to make the transition toward the discussion of a
Marxism that more fully recognizes both the reality of ethics and the reality of the ethical problem of imperialism.

> For Rousseau, the *de jure* state requires legitimating myths and an elaborate
> state system of public education and civil religion to enforce the reign of these
> myths. In this respect, Rousseau stands in the venerable Platonic tradition of
> the "golden lie." To form the sovereign, Rousseau tells us, is to transform
> opinion, to develop a consciousness of social solidarity.
>
> To do so, it is of course necessary to intervene directly on the level of opin-
> ion; but this action will not be sufficient. Ultimately, "consciousness arises out
> of life" (in Marx's words). For a collection of individuals to become a commu-
> nity with a single will, aiming (successfully) at a general interest, *there must be
> a general interest to be discovered*. And this supposes an integrated society, where
> divisions pose no threat to the generality of the will.
>
> What renders this view of society fanciful or utopian is, above all, the divi-
> sion of society into classes. For the theory to become fully *practical*, class divi-
> sions must be taken into account and treated (that is, transformed) accordingly.
>
> For this reason, it is not enough just to intervene on the level of opinion.
> Indeed, this is the reason why interventions on the level of opinion are doomed
> to fail, unless the golden lie is somehow made true; for what divides society
> thereby divides opinion also, at least tendentially. Rousseau's proposals for pub-
> lic education and civil religion can counteract this tendency only to a certain
> point. Even the assault on opinion requires an assault on what divides opinion,
> the division of society into classes.

> This assault constitutes the endpoint of Rousseau's practical argument. It will be remembered that Rousseau assimilates class interests to private interests, effectively denying in this way the very existence of social classes and their interests. However, social classes do exist. (187–88)

A very quick gloss on this passage (which Levine himself presents in so many words) is that real social solidarity cannot be predicated on myths of commonality propagated by a state (which will rely, in the end, on force for this propagation) but instead must be based on actual commonality, a commonality that transcends whatever divisions stand in its way. In some cases, this transcendence could be ideological, in the sense of recognizing that some forms of human difference, such as color or gender, are differences *within* a common humanity. (Leave aside for the moment the problem of a false universalism that takes one color or one gender as the standard for what counts as human; even leave aside for the moment the fact that any ethical-political universalism may very well include this false moment as a matter of necessity.) However, class divisions cannot be transcended in this way.

This, incidentally, is why "classism" is not as helpful a term as "racism" or "sexism." A world without sexism is not necessarily a world without sexual difference (though surely it is a world where this—or these—difference[s] is understood differently, and most likely it is a world where sexual difference is understood in a nonessentialist way). Likewise, *ceteris paribus*, with race and racism (though, indeed, the case against essentialism is perhaps even stronger here, as it is part of racist ideology to accept the categories of "race" handed down from European political modernity, even from the great Immanuel Kant himself, and, unfortunately, even to some extent from the great Karl Marx as well; see Eze, ed., *Racism and the Enlightenment*). Social classes, however, do exist, and changing opinions about them will not in itself transcend class divisions. Furthermore, the basis of normativity in Marx is surely the recognition that the division between classes that own and control the means of production and the rest of humanity that, for its daily bread, must seek an accommodation with these owners (and not always find it), does exist, and that there is no justification for this division in the modern world of socialized production, and that in the future either humanity will overcome this division or, quite likely, cease to exist altogether. Well, I have given a slight twist to this last bit—Marx only thought the first part, that humanity would keep struggling, through twists and turns, and through defeats and reversals, but eventually an "integrated society"—to borrow Levine's term, and note its similarity to Sartre's term, "integral humanity"—will win through; it is the imperialist mode of production that has added the second part, since the time of Marx.

Solidarity and Interest

However, the question arises as to whether real solidarity, which holds a hoped-for and struggled-for integral humanity as its norm, and which must be built on a global scale on the basis of a deep internationalism, can arise out of the "general interest that is to be discovered." Here I want to place pressure not on the concept of "general," which certainly ought to be interrogated in the same terms that we would apply to the universal or universalism, but instead on the notion of *interest*. Interest in both Rousseau and Marx plays the role of a "bridge," both conceptually and practically. How do I transcend my competitive drive when it is directed against my neighbor, in the case that my neighbor is also not an owner of the basic means of production, and even when it might be tempting to exploit some difference in race, gender, sexuality (or age, religion, or even the way someone looks, and on and on into every seemingly big or ridiculously little thing that divides people) for some small personal advantage for myself? For Marx, demythologizing Rousseau's general will, it is a matter of seeing one very basic commonality, namely that neither I nor my neighbor, nor almost all of the other people around me, nor almost all of the other people in the world, are the owners of the means for perpetuating life, and therefore we are all, in a substantive and not merely metaphorical sense, enslaved to the social systems where a small minority controls these means.

From a Kantian perspective, this bridging concept helps explain the situation in which we need to think about what ought to be done (and what people are up against), but what ought to be done is not a matter of any particular person's interest. Indeed, interest is just as useful for explaining why people do not come together, and my main concern here is understanding how this is especially the case when the world is not only subject to class division but also to forms of this division that are exceedingly lopsided, especially as regards relations among nations and peoples. If what ought to be done is not a matter of the interest of any particular person, neither is it, following what Marx said about classes as "aggregates" of persons and not as "supra-personal" identities, a matter of "collective interest." The matter of ethics is autonomous for Kant in this sense: to consider what is right is first of all to consider what is right, and to attempt to fulfill this consideration, regardless of my interest, your interest, anyone's interest—come hell or high water.

"Empty Formalism"

Despite this, surely there is a subject of ethics, of any ethical consideration, and despite Kant's limitations on this score (which especially go to the categories of race and gender), we can grant that this subject is humanity. Here pressure comes back upon the abstract and seemingly purely formal character of Kant's universalism—even if we leave aside considerations of "rational beings" in general (God, angels, conscious life on other planets), it is in fact highly significant that Kant introduced this last category, and even apart from the manner in which Kant would represent universalism and humanism in a race- and gender-slanted way, we might also inquire into what a "person" comes to as mere abstraction. This same critique has been applied to John Rawls's famous thought experiment, of the person behind the veil of ignorance—the question arises as to what sort of "person" this could be, a person with no "situation" (to use Sartre's term), no "sensuous existence" (Marx), none of the connections to other people and other creatures and the rest of the world that in fact are not "optional" aspects of the formation of anything that could be recognized as a person. (Or, it might be said, of any*one* who could be recognized as a person and not as a mere thing or automaton.) These issues (and Habermas's ideal of "transparency" can also be added to the discussion) should of course be explored in detail, and one sees in communitarian and feminist critiques of Rawls, or in critical race theory perspectives on the enlightenment, models for how this exploration can be carried forward.

Disagreement with the charge of "empty formalism" against Kant, therefore, does not mean that we do not need to understand the real flesh that has to find a way to live on those bones. For one thing, to be blunt about it, class division itself is the reason why the moral obligation to transcend, in practice, such division, is not going to happen simply because we are able to conceive of such an obligation. In the third part of this book I attempt to set out some of the issues as regards the "flesh" (indeed, I begin with a discussion of the ethically unjustifiable human practice of eating the flesh of creatures that have feelings and that can experience cruelty). However, there is also a way in which at least some "particularist" and even "substantive" critiques of univeralism, as necessary and justified as they are, throw out the baby with the bathwater. Certainly it can be argued that Rawls's notion of an "overlapping consensus" falls prey to the circularity of all universalisms: the citizen recognizes him- or herself in the consensus in the case that he or she was already formed as a person by the consensus to begin with. What Gramsci called "second nature" (and Marx called "false consciousness") is really the first and only "nature" that humans can know—we are formed in social collectives, and the sense that something essential in the organization of these collectives is oppressive issues from contradictions in the form of organization itself. And yet there is more than this to the bare fact that the formulation of universalisms is possible. It may be that the "baby/bathwater" image is not sufficient to capture what may be more than simply the "bad underside" of any universalism;

however, we should not allow this bad side of universalism to blind us to the good side and what its possibility may tell us.

A similar story can be told regarding Donald Davidson's argument about conceptual schemes. In the famous essay, "On the Very Idea of a Conceptual Scheme," Davidson argues that "speakers of different languages may share a conceptual scheme provided there is a way of translating one language into another" (184), while "a form of activity that cannot be interpreted *as language in our language* is not speech behaviour" and cannot be recognized (as a matter of epistemology) as such (185–86, my emphasis, and it should be added that Davidson is open to a wide range of activities that can count as "language-use behaviour"). Critics have objected to Davidson's arguments on grounds similar to communitarian and feminist objections to Rawls's arguments about the Original Position and the overlapping consensus: that in neither case is there sufficient recognition of difference, singularity, particularity, the other. While I am sympathetic to the motivation of these criticisms, I am not sure that they take into full account the epistemological thrust of Rawls's and Davidson's argument, namely, that between human persons a large background of shared assumptions (many, perhaps most, of which it would be exceedingly tedious to state explicitly) must be in place for differences to appear, and it is against this background that the meaning and significance of these differences—whether they are the subject of conversation or even violent struggle—appear. (In using the term "human persons" here, I want to set aside, at least for the time being, the question of understanding nonhuman animals or possible persons from other planets, though Davidson does in fact address both categories—as does Kant.)

Limits of Universalism

One of the strengths of Rawls's argument about "overlapping consensus" is that it recognizes the universalisms of diverse cultures as a human achievement. Now, to speak of "universalisms," in the plural, is to at least invite the charge of some kind of contradiction, so we might simply back up a little and say that Rawls's conception recognizes that there are impulses toward universalism in many different human cultures. Perhaps every one of these universalisms has its underside, its hidden ethnocentric and/or androcentric agenda. Kant's perspective, which is carried forward by Marx, is that humanity has entered a time of one world that we all could share in such a way as to encourage mutual flourishing, and that is a good thing. As Sankar Muthu writes in *Enlightenment against Empire*:

In recognition of the heightened discovery, travel, and imperial activity of his century, Kant believed that a discussion of justice at only the domestic and interstate levels could not fully capture the newly emerging *ethical problems* [my emphasis—BM] of the modern age. Although his discussion in *Toward Perpetual Peace* of ancient trade routes—such as those that connected Europe to Central Asia, India, and China—exemplify his understanding of the extensive history of commercial relations and activity between Europe and the non-European world, Kant also believed that the world of his day had become integrated to a degree that went far beyond transnational relationships of the past. One can plausibly describe this aspect of Kant's thought, then, as an early attempt to grapple with the globalization of economic, political, and hence moral ties. Kant suggests that since the "community of nations of the earth has now gone so far that a violation of right on one place of the earth is felt in all, the idea of a cosmopolitan right is no fantastic and exaggerated way of representing right." In formulating this new ethico-political category, Kant stresses that it rests not upon a preposterous and idealistic view of the international community, but rather responds to the actual global relationships that make the idea of cosmopolitan right a moral necessity. (189; inset quotation is from Kant's "Toward Perpetual Peace")

As Muthu notes, "Kant contemptuously labels . . . rationalizations of European imperialism as 'Jesuitism'" (188); we might compare the analysis that led Kant to this term to Derrida's discussion, in an essay on religion, of "globalatinization." ("Faith and Knowledge," in Derrida and Vattimo, *Religion*.) Significantly, this is first raised in the context of an analysis of an argument from Kant in *Religion within the Limits of Reason Alone*, where Derrida takes up Kant's notion of a "reflecting faith" that "favors good will beyond all knowledge" (10). I cannot do justice to this analysis here, but I want to underline this notion of a good will that not only exceeds knowledge but that can also "organize" or "orient" the pursuit of knowledge—for this notion returns in the work of contemporary philosophers of Kantian inspiration. In the conclusion, I return to the epistemological questions involved in this "good will beyond all knowledge" in relation to the problem of "religion," broadly construed.

In discussing problems of interpretation and translation, for instance, Davidson argues for what he called the "principle of charity." Interpretation depends on the assumption that most of what the speaker (language user) believes to be true is indeed true, and therefore that both the interpreter and the interpreted largely ("massively") agree in their beliefs. Davidson sometimes calls the "principle of charity" a "policy."

I propose that we take the fact that speakers of a language hold a sentence to be true (under observed circumstances) as prima-facie evidence that the sentence is true under those circumstances. . . .

Not all the evidence can be expected to point the same way. There will be differences from speaker to speaker, and from time to time for the same speaker, with respect to the circumstances under which a sentence is held true. The general policy, however, is to choose truth conditions that do as well as possible in making speakers hold sentences true when (according to the theory and the theory builder's view of the facts) those sentences are true. This is the general policy, to be modified in a host of obvious ways. Speakers can be allowed to differ more often and more radically with respect to some sentences than others, and there is no reason not to take into account the observed or inferred individual differences that may be thought to have caused anomalies (as seen by the theory).

. . . of course the fact that a theory does not make speakers universal hold-ers of truths is not an inadequacy of the theory; the aim is not the absurd one of making disagreement and error disappear. *The point is rather that widespread agreement is the only possible background against which disputes and mistakes can be interpreted.* Making sense of the utterances and behaviour of others, even their most aberrant behaviour [to "us"?], requires us to find a great deal of rea-son and truth in them. To see too much unreason on the part of others is sim-ply to undermine our ability to understand what it is they are so unreasonable about. If the vast amount of agreement on plain matters that is assumed in communication escapes notice, it's because the shared truths are too many and too dull to bear mentioning. What we want to talk about is what's new, sur-prising, or disputed. ("Belief and the Basis of Meaning," in *Inquiries into Truth and Interpretation*, 152–53; my emphasis)

My insertion of the editorial question in this last paragraph, "to 'us'?" was intended to be rhetorical, of course; the answer is "yes, to us, to the inter-preters." In Davidson's view, there is no other way. If I go out on a pro-ject of interpretation, even a project of "radical interpretation" (interpretation "from scratch," so to speak, which is Davidson's way of modeling Quine's thought experiments in the anthropology of an "alien" culture), I have to start with what I know and I have to assume that most of what I know (or think I know) is true. Otherwise there is no "here" from which to get "there."

However, I also have to start with the assumption that most of what the other person (or other culture or society) thinks she knows to be true is indeed true. (Remember that most of these truths, for either myself—the "home theory"—or the other, are "too many and too dull to bear mentioning" for the most part—though at least some truths of this sort do become relevant in radical translation, where I and the other are attempt-ing to trade terms for basic features of the world around us—"Es schneit" for "It is snowing," and so on.) Two questions immediately come to mind in light of Davidson's scheme and in light of the foregoing discussion of imperialism: (1) How do we know who or what counts as a "person," or as some entity that can be understood as an interlocutor? (2) What is the ontological status of the "here" from which "I" engage in interpretation, and perhaps especially *radical interpretation*—where "I" am doing something with a foreign culture, presumably attempting to understand it, but perhaps I am really up to something else, or perhaps I only want to "understand" that culture for the sake of some other, possibly malicious, motivation?

Principles of Charity

Over the years there have been objections to Davidson's use of the term "charity." As an alternative, Davidson proposed the "principle of rational accommodation," and others proposed the "principle of humanity" (see Grandy, "Reference, Meaning, and Belief"). This last proposal is interesting, in that it both partakes of a Kantian universalism and yet, like that universalism, is not entirely clear on who will count as "human." In other words, the proposal is at least a little question-begging. But then, the same problem arises in the case of what counts as "rational." Here we see how this argument encompasses not only certain key concepts in Rawls's and Davidson's work, but in Habermas's as well, especially his notion of the "ideal speech situation," where the day (socially and politically speaking) should be carried by the "unforced force of reason." Each of these proposals brings forward and elaborates on Kant's ethical-political universalism, and each of them has the shortcomings of this universalism. My larger argument in this book is that, despite this shortfall or underside of universalism, the possibilities for our world are greater and better when people are able to form regulative ideals.

In this light, there is something in particular to be said for Davidson's original term, "charity." Not to be obtuse, but it would be worthwhile to pursue, in a very "analytical" way, the difference between a Kantian regulative ideal, and what Derrida, in *Specters of Marx*, calls a "promise." What Davidson's charity implies, even if this theme is largely unexplored in his own work, is that the intermotivated problematics of truth, interpretation, meaning, understanding, and belief involve an irreducible element of what might simply be called "good will." (A whole other discussion could be had here regarding the role this good will plays in the models of anthropology one finds in Quine and Davidson.) To understand you, I have to *want* to understand you, and I have to be open to you. I have to take my analytic apparatus, so to speak, and tilt it at least a little bit in your direction. Perhaps this is again the difference between an indifferent, positivistic "knowledge," and what really might be understanding. (Obviously, this has been known for a long, long time, as captured in the old saying, "There is none so blind as he who will not see," or in drawing a distinction between hearing and *actually* listening.) What Kant shows in his arguments not only on ethics, but also on epistemology and intersubjectivity, is that responsibility is something that we not only have, but also something that we fundamentally *are*. We are constituted, as speakers, writers, and responders of the biologically human type, by the ability to respond—indeed, to the extent that we lose or reject this ability, we become less recognizably human. This is another reason why, in the example about the Nazi (who is about to throw the baby into the oven), a "discursive gap" opens up—not only is it a matter of the content of any conceivable argument concerning this action (the "what" and the "why"), but there is also the problem of the interlocutor: *who* is there to hear the claims of the mother? Ethically speaking, there is "no one home," and in Kant's scheme, this absence affects the larger fields of personhood and rationality. (These themes ought to be applied in the field of artificial intelligence, as regards the conceptions of knowledge and rationality generally operative in this field.) What Derrida argues (especially in *The Other Heading*, though this might be taken as preparatory to the argument about the "promise" in *Specters of Marx*) is that the notion of responsibility as constitutive needs a basic refinement, which he calls "responsibility to responsibility." Yes, responsibility is constitutive, but there has to be that moment when a commitment to this responsibility, which might also be called a commitment to a common humanity, is formed. (Perhaps "formed" is not the right word; perhaps it is that a "call" is "answered," at least in the sense that there is a response to the call.) Rational accommodation must indeed be led by and grounded in "charity." Davidson offered the term "rational accommodation" in part to respond to the criticism that "charity" sounds both condescending and optional. On the first criticism, perhaps "good will" is helpful, because the point is that, to interpret, one has to want to understand and to be open to the possibility that the other is saying something. This last bit is itself a response on the second point: *if* one aims to understand, then "charity" is not optional, it is itself constitutive of the activity of interpretation.

Many philosophers are not so charitable when it comes to applying Davidson's principle even in their own field, hence the dismissal of parts of philosophy as "not making any sense" and therefore not really being philosophy to begin with. This hangover from positivism still runs through a good deal of analytic philosophy, and, in perhaps a slightly different way, through Marxism (some of which is done in the style of analytic philosophy). Charity is often lacking when there are large disparities in power. There are many situations in which this occurs, especially situations that revolve around the familiar nodal points of class, race, gender, sexuality, differences in ages, generations, or for that matter physical size. The context that I want to stress here, where universalism and charity face tremendous obstacles and often fail (but do they fail to the point that we should abandon these values in disgust?), is imperialism, which binds to itself and exploits all of the other differences just named, even if these differences also have their own dynamics (which must be understood in their own right in order to be "resolved" or "transcended" in a just way), and that has created a tremendous global lopsidedness in power and wealth.

Lopsidedness

Lopsidedness (again, a term and related thesis that I am borrowing from Bob Avakian and Raymond Lotta, even if I am giving it a somewhat different spin) warps our senses of universalism and good will. It is in such a lopsided world, with the United States in a seemingly indisputable position at the top, that Vietnam does not begin to appear as a moral question to the citizens of the nation that visited horrible destruction on a Third World country on the other side of the world, a country that had never done anything to the people of the United States. This lopsidedness combines with the spoils of imperialism to allow for the formation of a society where people identify political values, especially "freedom," with participation in consumerism.

In such jaded, imperialist societies, a very large part of the population simply does not give a damn about ethical-political universalism, to be blunt about it. Imperialism, especially imperialism in a time of extreme lopsidedness, creates complicities to the point of making many people into outright jerks, callous "moral retards" who are simply not able to see the appeal of an argument such as Rawls's construct of the original position behind the veil of ignorance. No, instead, the United States, especially, has adopted what might be called a "roll the dice" attitude toward the original position—"yes, there might be a disadvantage if I come out as an African-American or as a woman, in a society where there is racial and gender discrimination, but, hey, that's the chance one takes." Now, there are mitigating factors here, of course: a callous sense of "that's just the way that cookie crumbles" is also intermixed with a sense that there is little one can do about the general social set-up, especially when considered in global terms, and it is also the case that even many in the middle classes in imperialist countries do not have a sense of long-term security and thus are caught up in their own narrow struggles to hold things together. Even so, the moral rot and callousness of imperialism, instantiated especially in a sense of entitlement, is a real thing and not merely ephemeral. The attitude of imperialist entitlement takes on a life of its own and shapes people down to something like the core. This entitlement also shapes the ways in which people respond when imperialism runs up against limits.

Aristotle

It is on this point especially that a debate between the Kantian currents that I have been presenting and the neo-Aristotelian (or sometimes neo-Thomist) arguments of Alasdair MacIntyre and others ought to be staged. On behalf of the latter it could certainly be argued that there has to be a basis in character-formation for universalist claims to have any purchase, and that the way that advanced capitalism undermines the appeal of ethical-political universalism is to create nasty, callous, purely self-seeking characters (which, in Aristotelian terms, is no kind of character at all). This is why, incidentally, it is not merely an exercise in *ad hominem* rhetoric to point to the basic moral incapacity of figures such as Richard Nixon, Ronald Reagan, George H. W. Bush, J. Danforth Quayle, Dick Cheney, and George W. Bush—they are exemplars and emblems of imperialist "morality," and indeed it is a topsy-turvy world when instead Bill Clinton's sexual escapades can be held out as true moral depravity. What needs to be examined instead is the way that Clinton also did his best for the imperialist system.

Loss of Moral Sense

To shift frames slightly, I am sure that every philosophy instructor who has taught courses on ethics, especially business ethics, has reached moments of absolute frustration with students who seem either to have no moral sense or perhaps to have buried that moral sense under the supposed practicalities of "real life." Early in my time as a professor at DePaul University, the chair of my department apparently thought it would be funny to send the Marxist down to the Loop campus (in the heart of downtown Chicago, where DePaul has its very large Commerce School) to teach business ethics. One day, in examining some issues in international business, I introduced a case that involved two hundred young girls who had burned to death in a factory fire in Thailand. The girls were mostly in the range of twelve- to fifteen-years of age, and the doors to the factory were locked to prevent any of the girls from taking unauthorized breaks (including bathroom breaks). The factory produced toys for a well-known American toy manufacturer. I reached my point of absolute frustration when a student said, regarding the fire and the deaths of these girls (whose conditions of work were little different from outright slavery), "that's just the way the cookie crumbles." What can be said in response to such a statement? It just doesn't seem a matter of words traded for other words, or of a discursive space, an argument. There are also limits to what we teachers are supposed to say to students, even students who exemplify a lack of moral sense to the point where, by all rights, they should be set aside from the group and not be allowed to interact with other human beings. In the case I am describing, the student spoke his words with a grin, which I interpreted as representing the proud, "pragmatic," and triumphant spirit of American capitalism. To challenge such an attitude with, "How would you feel if you, or your child, was in a similar situation?" is only to invite trivialities and cliches—"roll the dice," "I'll take my chances." (I would bet that every instructor who has taught courses in ethics, especially business ethics, has had similar experiences.)

The formation of persons in such a way, in the image of imperialist moral rot and entitlement, is absolutely a social phenomenon. These things create complicities, to the point of rendering people into callous jerks, but these people themselves are not the source of the social dynamics that make them jerks. Those formed in the image of imperialism (which includes millions and millions of people who have experienced at least some of the privileges associated with the relatively high standard of living in imperialist countries, and I certainly include myself in this category) are responsible for who and what they (we) are, and yet taking responsibility for the way the world is configured does not mean first of all engaging in rituals of self-flagellation, but instead grappling with the system and fighting it, overturning it, creating a system that does not treat people as mere things.

Reactivation

The larger question is, What is it that could call such a society "back" to the project of a global community of mutual flourishing? What is it that could reactivate (if that is the term, if there is still some repository—the "human reserve"—that can be reactivated) the broad fellow-feeling that can be called the characterogical basis for ethical-political universalism, the categorical imperative (in its diverse formulations, including Marx's "fourth formulation"), the problematics of the original position, the veil of ignorance, and overlapping consensus, what might be called the "open and inviting" side of the ideal speech situation, the principle of charity, responsibility to responsibility, and ultimately the promise of human emancipation? My argument, which I will resume in a moment, is that Marxism's central, "materialist" category of *interest* will not serve fully to call imperialism to account (or to call imperialism fully to account, both formulations apply). Some of my arguments here do indeed have some affinity with the "spiritual failure of the Left" discussion that is experiencing a revival as of this writing (see, for example, Jim Wallis, *God's Politics: Why the Right Gets It Wrong and the Left Doesn't Get It*, and *The Soul of Politics: Beyond*

"Religious Right" and "Secular Left"). If imperialism can only be called to account in the case that "the ethical" plays a key role, then this in itself speaks to the materiality of the ethical.

My argument depends on the idea that history is also a real thing, and that history is "in us," and in the social institutions that we inhabit and that form us. It has been the case for at least some decades that capitalism has its own response to the debts incurred in history, and this is not only to ignore or forestall the debts (certainly capitalism does that, right down to the way that history textbooks are written; this is just as much, if not more, true in Western Europe and Japan as in the United States), but also to render history into bunk. I am trying to read Marx and at least some currents in Marxism as being about a redemptive scheme in history and not only a structural analysis of political economy where human subjects have no ontological status that is fundamentally different from any other element in the picture (so that people are simply among the billiard balls of causality). But perhaps there is no history, or, if there ever was history, "history is in danger of dying in the world of nonhistory" (as Sartre put it in *Notebooks for an Ethics*, and it is worth reflecting on the fact that he wrote these words in the late 1940s). I will return to this question in the conclusion, but it is important to understand in the present context that the idea of Ethical Marxism depends on the recognition that the real, material situation that Marxism (or radical social theory and practice, however conceived) is up against is historical, not simply empirical in the sense of the "present challenges" that people face and to which they may or may not feel compelled to respond. To wax both Sartrean and Derridean, there is a *thickness* to history that involves not only "speaking with the ghosts" of the past (who still live with us now, even if we have not yet learned to live with them), but also responding to the call of a possible future, of what Sartre calls "integral humanity."

Past–Present–Future

Everything that has ever made up the world, including the people we have loved and admired and the people we did not love or admire and the people we never knew and the people who were brutally "disappeared," and everything else, still exists, but in the past. The existence of the past is tenuous, you say, and that is certainly correct—but the existence of the past is hardly more tenuous than the existence of the present or future. So perhaps we should not believe in any of it at all, and refuse to place any stock in it, either in a Buddhist or gnostic way (the material world is not real, and belief in such a world is itself the source of suffering; I hasten to add that a Buddhism that affirms the Bodhisattva idea does not view things this way), or in a Nietzschean way (recalling the first paragraph of "On Truth and Lie in an Extra-Moral Sense," and the fate of the "clever animals" who "invented knowledge" in what turned out to be "the haughtiest and most mendacious minute of 'world history'—yet only a minute"), or in the brute way proposed by Henry Ford, namely, that "history is bunk." Certainly there is a point to the fairly abstract philosophical question of the onto-epistemological status of human history, but almost as surely there is the likelihood that any perspective on this question will be colored by, perhaps thoroughly founded in, where the philosophical interlocutor stands in history. At the very least, it can be said that it is very convenient for some to claim that history is bunk, and the way of either the cynic (Nietzsche, or at least many who claim to pursue his thought) or the ascetic (a certain kind of Buddhism and Eastern religious practice more generally) can certainly seem appealing in the face of the overwhelming tragedy of human history and what appears to be an indifferent cosmos. But it is precisely our own human ability not to be indifferent to history (especially when history forces itself upon us) that makes history a peculiar onto-epistemological problem, a hermeneutic sort of problem, because we are constitutive of the phenomenon that we are attempting to study.

Marx said that all history is the history of class struggle (before the emergence of classes humanity is in a state of prehistory, and part of the picture here is that Marx sees the emergence of classes and the emergence of writing as co-terminous, an argument taken up by Jacques Derrida in *Of Grammatology*). Sartre's great question in the first volume of the *Critique of Dialectical Reason* is, "Is history intelligible?" If history can be understood, *what* exactly is "there" to examine and understand? In Sartre's scheme, in the absence of a god who is telling a cosmic story (that somehow passes through our little planet), history has to have an internal intelligibility, if indeed it has any intelligibility at all. As Sartre suggests in his remarks on atheism at the end of his lecture, "Existentialism Is a Humanism," even if God did exist, that would not be a solution to "the problem of man for man himself." In other words, if the intelligibility of *human* history is only to be found in a source that is absolutely nonhuman (and indeed ultimately unintelligible to finite beings), then this could never be an intelligibility "for us." (Think of the blithe and often cruel— if perhaps unintentionally so—statement often heard from religious believers of a certain type, "I think everything happens for a reason," in the case where what they mean is that God has some reason that is unintelligible to mere humans. Then what is the point of calling this "reason" as opposed to "unreason"?) One might say that, from the perspectives of Marx and Sartre, history and meaning, and therefore any meaning that history might have, are intimately, perhaps absolutely, bound up with struggle. However, it is significant that Marx did not worry very much about the "meaning" of history, or of "life," and it is unclear whether he thought these problems simply took care of themselves or that instead they are what Carnap called "pseudo-problems in philosophy" ("problems" admitting not of solution but instead dissolution). If the latter, then surely any thematization of the ethical relation would go the same way and also be subject to dissolution by the acids of positivism. In coining this expression I am referring to the phrase, "the acids of modernity," which are the chemicals of secularism and modern disenchantment.

Meaning and Struggle

The problem is, if there is no meaning to our struggle, why engage in it? If struggle is merely reactive, a way that the logic of modes of production speaks through human social relations, then there is no *real* role for truly human *engagement*. (I see Sartre's "Cartesianism" in this context as a reaction to the crude, merely reactive, mechanical materialism of the French Communist Party in the 1930s and 1940s and ever after; France is fascinating for having produced some of the most creative unofficial Marxism and probably the absolutely most uncreative, mechanical, and dogmatic official Marxism.) We will just do what we do, the same way that billiard balls do what they do when struck at such and such an angle at such and such a speed on such and such a surface. The history of human beings as billiard balls is indeed bunk. However, I have tried to stress from the start that there is another track in Marx, not only the track where Marx railed against the existing system for its injustice, but also the track where Marx talked about humanity becoming the subject rather than the mere object of history. I would like to go the next step and ask if there really can be a sense of history, or a subject matter for ethics, if "nothing really matters."

Sartre's existential insight is that, if history is not lit up, so to speak, from some cosmic (or at least external) perspective, then it will not be lit up at all except through our own human and finite efforts; it is in this context that Sartre conceives the project, humanity pro-jecting itself into the future—and this, in Sartre's view, can only be a future of "integral human-ity," where history will have become "one." For Sartre, Marxism as Marx left it defines the broad parameters of this project, and yet it does not rise sufficiently from the abstract to the concrete (to borrow one of Marx's own phrases). Thus, in his book-length preface to the *Critique of Dialectical Reason*, Sartre proposes existentialism as a "parasitical growth" within the horizons of Marxism:

Existentialism, like Marxism, addresses itself to experience in order to discover there concrete syntheses; it can conceive of these syntheses only within a moving, dialectical totalization which is nothing else but history or—from the strictly cultural point of view which we have adopted here—"philosophy becoming the world." [If I am not mistaken, this is a phrase from Marx's famous "conversion letter" to his father, announcing his conversion to Hegelianism.] For us, truth is something which becomes, it *has* and *will have* become. It is a totalization which is forever being totalized. Particular facts do not signify anything; they are neither true nor false so long as they are not related, through the mediation of various partial totalities, to the totalization in process. (30–31)

Our historical task, at the heart of this polyvalent world, is to bring closer the moment when History will have *only one meaning*, when it will tend to be dissolved in the concrete people who will make it in common. (90, gendered term modified)

Sartre in taking up the issue of historical totalization, has been accused of adding to a philosophy of totalitarianism (and then his "support" for the Soviet Union in the time of Stalin comes into play), when it can certainly be argued that his aim, at least on the theoretical level (and whether or not he succeeded) was just the opposite.

The totalizing investigation has given way to a Scholasticism of the totality. The heuristic principle—"to search for the whole in its parts"—has become the terroristic practice of "liquidating the particularity." (*Search*, 28)

. . . an already lived History *resists* any a priori schematism. We shall understand that even this History, made and known—incident by incident—must be for us the object of a complete experience. . . . Existentialism, then, can only affirm the specificity of the historical *event*; it seeks to restore to the event its function and its multiple dimensions. (*Search*, 123–24)

Another way to sum up Sartre's arguments is that if meaning is not in the particulars, then the meaning that only arises at the level of some whole (keeping in mind that, for Sartre, the whole is never finished and is always a projection—this is part of what places Sartre on the side of the "permanence of the revolution" and the "infinite task" of ethics) is indeed totalitarian.

The Tragic Dimension

One reason to raise these questions at the intersection of meta-ethics and the philosophy of history is that it seems to me a deeply ethical question to ask what possible good might come of the suffering and death of people who in no way deserved their fate. Is there a way to ask this question without going quickly, dismissively, and blithely past the tragic dimension of human life and history? (As an antidote to this sort of blithe dismissiveness, I find the work of David Krell especially powerful, for instance, in his earlier work, *Intimations of Mortality*, and in what he has said will be his last properly philosophical book, *The Tragic Absolute*.) Is there a way to ask what good may come without falling into a merely utilitarian framework? Certainly the lives of the people of Vietnam did not matter to the people of the United States for the most part (though we could establish a hierarchy of the not-mattering, from the workings of the social system itself, to the ruling class, to the administrative apparatus, to the technical apparatus, to the military apparatus, and ultimately to the broad masses); does it become a nearly theological question to wonder if there is some other level of reality where people and their lives matter? It is not hard to see why Marx avoided such questions (because they are extraordinarily difficult, and because pursuit of them leads to further difficulties, including what might be called the fatal distraction of imagined consolation). However, if the question of meaning has no answer, especially if it has no answer in materialist terms—well, to be blunt about it, isn't that the whole ball game right there? If there really is no meaning, and therefore no intelligibility to human struggle and history, then what is the point? Sartre, having come through the acids of existentialism and having dispensed some of those acids himself, is attempting to address this quandary with his theory of "totalization without a totalizer." Among other things, this is Sartre's response to the worry that "only a god can save us now" (as Heidegger put it). However, unlike Marx, Sartre does not argue that the outcome of this totalization is inevitable. Indeed, Marx's inevitability is too much a "totalizer" in Sartre's view, too much a "god." This god, to repeat with a slight spin, itself cancels the meaning that is made by conscious historical agents who struggle with and within history.

Certainly Marx is clear on the totalizing historical process in the time of capitalism and even colonialism: it is a process of immense brutality. It is also a process of the reduction of all qualities to quantity, signified by the "M" in the logic of commodity production, "M-C-M'." Historical struggle beyond capitalism, at least, is a process of once again bringing "mere" quantity under the domain of quality. The problem is that, for Marx, the development of capitalism plays a crucial, historical role, without which there cannot be communism. In the words of the *Manifesto*, "the bourgeoisie is the most revolutionary class in history." The capitalists bring about revolutions in production that are completely unimaginable in previous epochs. These revolutions create the productive and material basis for the "shared abundance" that is communism. Part of what is interesting in this last formulation is that, while in Marx's view, the productivity of capitalism creates the material basis for communism to be an "ethical society," this abundance of material goods and its creation through a process of commodity production is not in and of itself an "ethical basis" for the transition to communism. The aspect of the struggle to overcome capitalism that has to do with justice and the aim of creating a good society remains subordinate and epiphenomenal. My argument in this book is that, if there are not at least key moments when these terms are explicitly thematized and pursued in their own right, then this struggle cannot be carried through. The question remains how this thematization and motivation can be understood within an historical materialist framework, but my hope is that it can, and that the work of philosophers such as Davidson and Derrida to show "how meaning works," which help us to "materialize the signifier" (Derrida's expression, said in response to an interview with Marxists in *Positions*), contribute to this effort.

Part of what this "much thickened" and (I hope) philosophically vibrant historical materialism would show, however, is the real, material situation that Marxism (or any philosophy or movement that aims at the creation of a postcapitalist society) is up against, where the notion of "interest" is simply not sufficient for the creation of a good society. This notion is not even adequate in a purely "causal" sense, as a mechanism. Ultimately, people have to want to create a good society, or else they won't. We will return to this question and its relation to interest as Marx conceived it.

Experience

Thomas Flynn, in his monumental study of Sartre and Foucault (*Sartre, Foucault, and Historical Reason*), maintains that Sartre "in his own way was doubtless a philosopher of experience" (5). A fruitful comparison might be made between Marx's analytic of social practices and those philosophers who have concentrated on the idea of human experience. (Foucault, with his attempt to "consider the very historicity of forms of experience," [Preface to *The History of Sexuality*, vol. 2; cited in Flynn, 4], provides a useful bridge.) Surely it could be argued that Marxism needs some of this philosophy of experience to put some flesh on the bones of an analytics of practices (with practices of production at the core), even while it can also be argued, I think rightly, that Marx's framework offers an important corrective to narrow forms of empiricism, subjectivism, and claims of first-person authority. If Sartre was indeed a philosopher of experience ("of a sort," at least), it might also be interesting to draw some connections between his work and the work of two

American philosophers not often compared to Sartre, namely, Ralph Waldo Emerson and William James. The former was a prime inspiration for at least one current of existentialism: when traveling, it was quite often Emerson's *Essays* that Nietzsche would carry along for reading material. James clearly has a way of connecting history, belief, commitment, and hope in a way that foreshadows Sartre, though what I am primarily interested in here is whether James's matrix of concepts might also recommend itself to Marxism, in particular the Ethical Marxism that I am attempting to formulate here. In this respect let us consider some wonderfully written passages from *The Will to Believe*, from the section titled, "Is Life Worth Living?"

> If you surrender to the nightmare view [of the world] and crown the evil edifice by your own suicide, you have indeed made a picture totally black. Pessimism, completed by your act, is true beyond a doubt, so far as your world goes. Your mistrust of life has removed whatever worth your own enduring existence might have given to it; and now, throughout the whole sphere of possible influence of that existence, the mistrust has proved itself to have divining power. But suppose, on the other hand, that instead of giving way to the nightmare view you cling to it that this world is not the *ultimatum*. [I assume that James means by this the "ultimate reality."] Suppose you find yourself a very well-spring, as Wordsworth says, of –
>
> > "Zeal, and the virtue to exist by faith
> > As soldiers live by courage; as, by strength
> > Of heart, the sailor fights with roaring seas."
>
> Suppose, however thickly evils crowd upon you, that your unconquerable subjectivity proves to be their match, and that you find a more wonderful joy than any passive pleasure can bring in trusting ever in the larger whole. Have you not now made life worth living on these terms? What sort of a thing would life really be, with your qualities ready for a tussle with it, if it only brought fair weather and gave these higher faculties of yours no scope? *Please remember that optimism and pessimism are definitions of the world*, and that our own reactions on the world small as they are in bulk, are integral parts of the whole thing, and necessarily help to determine the definition [my emphasis]. They may even be the decisive elements in determining the definition.
>
> . . . This life *is* worth living, we can say, *since it is what we make it, from the moral point of view* [emphasis in original]; and we are determined to make it from that point of view, so far as we have anything to do with it, a success.
>
> Now, in this description of faiths that verify themselves, I have assumed that our faith in an invisible order is what inspires those efforts and that patience which make this visible order good for moral men. Our faith in the seen world's goodness (goodness now meaning fitness for successful moral and religious life) has verified itself by leaning on our faith in the unseen world. But will our faith in the unseen world similarly verify itself? Who knows?

> Once more it is a case of *maybe*; and once more maybes are the essence of the situation. I confess that I do not see why the very existence of an invisible world may not in part depend on the personal response which any one of us may make to the religious appeal. *God himself, in short, may draw vital strength and increase of very being from our fidelity.* [my emph.] For my own part, I do not know what the sweat and blood and tragedy of this life mean, if they mean anything short of this. *If this life be not a real fight* [my emph.], in which something is eternally gained for the universe by success, it is no better than a game of private theatricals from which one may withdraw at will. But it [this life] *feels* like a real fight,—as if there were something really wild in the universe which we, with all our idealities and faithfulness, are needed to redeem; and first of all to redeem our own hearts from atheisms and fears. For such a *half-wild, half-saved* [my emphasis] universe our nature is adapted. (60–61)

Certainly the more orthodox form of Marxism as well as many others will have all sorts of issues with what James says here, especially the very strong insistence on subjectivity at the one end, and the trappings of religion (theism and the unseen world) at the other. However, there is an analytic of possibility and truth here that suggests itself and does its work quite apart from outright subjectivism and an "objectivistic," Platonic (or gnostic) conception of an unseen world that is the "truly real" world. (Note also that it is common for Marxists to accuse Kant and Sartre of subjectivism as well, without giving much attention to the analytical framework in which each discusses subjectivity.) To simplify quite a bit (for clearly one could spend many hours with this passage), the truth of the hoped-for, redeemed world is inseparable from commitment, struggle, and even optimism—and what might even be called the moral duty of optimism. The redeemed world will not be achieved without these elements, and the "mattering" of this struggle issues from the matrix of these elements, not forgetting for a moment, of course, our "fallen" world and "the way that it is" and all that the struggle for a radically better world (or, quite possibly, any future for humanity at all) is up against.

Materiality and Praxis

Without going much further with issues in the philosophy of history or historiography (in terms of the basic issues I am raising here, especially as they relate to Sartre, Flynn's study is definitive; see especially "History as Fact and as Value" in vol. 1, and "Ethics and History: Authentic vs Effective History" in vol. 2), it can at least be asserted that any possible, future, *redeemed* world will issue from both the in-itself and the for-itself, from both the "brute materiality" of the existing world and the matrix of meaning, belief, intention, hope, optimism, and *praxis* of human beings.

Or else this will not happen. Victory is not inevitable, though my view is that either we change this world in fundamental ways, or else there will be no livable world for human beings in the future—either a "human future" or no future for humans. But there is another way in which victory definitely will not occur, and that is in the case that "brute materiality" is really all there is. Orthodox trends in Marxism have often gone overboard in reminding us of this "fact." The result of such an orientation is a Marxism that is every bit as good at "that's the way the cookie crumbles" historiography as any capitalist-minded person who recommends that we "grow up" and accept the "facts of life." In the history of Marxist-led struggle, these facts of life lead to the dead end of eggs and omelets, and Sartre's comment that what we see with Stalin is "Marxism purely as a theory of power" is not wide of the mark.

It is tempting to say that "historical inevitability," except perhaps as sheer, audacious, braggadocio ("We *will* win! Nothing can stop us!"), is every bit as theological as any scheme of pre-ordained end-time eschatology accepted by fundamentalists. Kant also, in his "Idea for a Universal History," indulged in the hope that "if we examine *the play of the human will's freedom in the large*, we can discover its course to conform to rules"; "what strikes us as complicated and unpredictable in the single individual may in the history of the entire species be discovered to be the steady progress and slow development of its original capacities" (*Perpetual Peace and Other Essays*, 15). This is a proposal for a "science of history" in broad contours, not unlike what Marx gives us. Marx aims to be a great deal more systematic, especially specifying the Aristotelian concept, "capacities" (Kant, like Marx, is invoking species being), and he writes at the time when, in his view, a class (the international proletariat) has emerged that can and must carry ethical-political universalism forward without limit (specifically without the limits of the bourgeoisie, who can provide the "equality" and "freedom" of the marketplace at best (and quite often not even that). Such a scheme presented as inevitability is either theology or strategic audacity; it is only in such a scheme as *possibility*, however, that the history and possible future of humanity actually matters. This is not a merely "sentimental" or existential point: in the scheme of inevitability the horrors visited upon the people of Vietnam (and upon the millions kidnapped from Africa, and upon the Jews in the Holocaust, and on and on) are just the way the cookie crumbles in the gears of the history machine. We are back into the problem of theodicy discussed in part 1—in which case "redemption" is not redemption, this life is not a "real fight" (James), there are no actual people who actually matter involved in history, but only the god of historical inevitability's "terroristic practice" of "liquidating the particularity" (Sartre), and the "theory" of such a "totalizing investigation" comes to the dead end (truly dead) of a "Scholasticism of the totality" (again Sartre).

Of Future Humanity

Toward the end of "Idea for a Universal History" (in the eighth of his nine theses), Kant writes that "human nature is so constituted as to be incapable of indifference toward even the most distant epoch through which our species must go, if only it can be expected with certainty" (37). This last part, "if only [the most distant epoch through which our species must go] can be expected with certainty," is strange, in a way, when placed in the context of what would seem to be Kant's greater "concern for the future" than Marx's. It isn't that Marx is not concerned for the future, of course (indeed, it could be said that everything in Marx is subordinated to the idea of a different future for humankind), but the role that this concern plays in what Marx allows himself of a philosophical framework seems deeply buried, to say the least. Indeed, to bring forward such concern as part of a philosophical framework, and, for that matter, to allow philosophy too much of a role in social theory, would be to cross the line from "scientific" to "utopian" socialism at least in the view of Engels, and probably Marx as well. However, given the intermotivation of Kant's three questions, and the placement of the question of hope at least on a par with the questions of ethics and epistemology, what is strange—even if completely understandable—is the focus on "certainty." For it has long been understood in philosophy, especially in philosophical theology going back to the earliest years of Christianity and even before, that certainty about the course of human events places limitations on both real human agency (which is, after all, the cornerstone of Kant's ethics) and on the possibility of God's meaningful concern for the struggles and fate of actual human beings. (In brief, how could God have concern for the outcome of events that are foreordained or at least known in advance? In the case of God it comes to the same thing. What is perhaps more interesting is the political role played by the "argument," sometimes heard from theists, that what is contradictory to mere humans is not necessarily so to God. I will return to this issue in the conclusion; however, just so there is no misunderstanding, I do not take this argument to be in itself a part of fascism, but the ability to "swallow contradictions" and theologize government actions and policies that to all outward appearances are awful *is* an integral part of the machinery of postmodern capitalism and fascism.) With regard to Kant's formulation, isn't it precisely the other way around (as Slavoj Žižek likes to say)—isn't the basis of our concern for the future precisely in the fact that we cannot know with certainty all of the twists and turns humanity may have to traverse on the way to either the kingdom of ends or oblivion?

Perhaps our hope ought to be that someday there will be people living in a fundamentally better society, who will remember that there were people in the fallen times who engaged in the real fight as best they understood it. In this respect, the "laws of history," as both Kant and Marx understood them, ought to be instead understood as "laws of possibility," ways of theorizing where the openings might occur in the existing society that would allow for something different and better to arise. In Marxism this investigation into possibility has been known as crisis theory; the argument is that people (the broad masses) will not look for a different way of organizing life unless the existing social form is coming apart. Lenin specified two conditions that demonstrate the emergence of a full-blown social crisis: the ruling class cannot rule in the same way that it had been doing previously, and the people cannot live the same way they had been living. In broad outline I accept this view of things, and I accept Marx's perspective on the basic mechanisms of capital that lead to crisis. In the age of imperialism, capital has created numerous ways of displacing crisis, these displacements running the gambit from the very crude (simply squeezing more out of people in the Third World) to the very sophisticated (the immense culture of distraction that Adorno referred to as a "spell," and that renders even the bourgeois notion of citizenship completely insubstantial and therefore meaningless). The problem is not the soundness of Marx's basic approach to political economy (quite apart from quibbling about numbers); capital gets itself into messes both big and small, and people are always hurt as a result. Furthermore, the capitalist notion of "externalities," where some costs are simply dumped into the river (or the ground, the atmosphere, or the oceans) and forgotten, has pretty much run its course. (See James O'Connor, *Natural Causes: Essays in Ecological Marxism*, especially part 2, "Capitalism and Nature.") My aim is not to make light of the systematic work that ought to be done in political economy and in ecology: the day of reckoning for capitalism will come, but it is important to grapple with the "laws of possibility" in order to see how the crisis will unfold and therefore where the strategic openings may occur. In addition to this strategic sense, however, and the theoretical work and leadership that goes with it, is the question of *what vision* can galvanize the popular understanding that the existing form of society needs to be overthrown and a new form of society needs to be created. This "vision thing" is not an optional add-on, and the argument of this book is that this vision has to have the question of the ethical relation at its core.

Vision and Orthodoxy

In recognition of this need, we have seen two broad trends in Marxism. These trends can be categorized simply, but in both practice and theory they are very complicated. One trend, which I would say has predominated within Marxism, has been to "dig in" with an orthodox reading of Marx's analytical tools, and therefore to eschew any talk that goes beyond the material interest of a particular social class that is situated in a particular historical way. One interesting thing about this trend, which I would call "economism" (though I am expanding on Lenin's conception, hopefully deepening the conception), is that it focuses almost exclusively on the better-off, unionized workers of the advanced capitalist countries. It is not that I do not have sympathy for these workers; moreover, these workers in more recent decades are fewer in number in any case, owing to the homogenizing force of imperialist globalization. However, these workers hardly fit under the description that Marx and Engels gave of the proletariat at the conclusion of the *Communist Manifesto*, a class that has nothing to lose but its chains. Furthermore, for this section of the working class there have been many *generations* of participation in the material culture of imperialism (in the case of the United States, superpower imperialism). Not only can this many-decades long, many-leveled experience of complicity not be shuffled off very easily, but it is also part of a history that I take to be a real thing, a history that has to be accounted for. A structural analysis of the class configurations of the working class under imperialism and in the imperialist countries (and here, perhaps, there is a case for an "American exceptionalism," at least in the sense of a specific analysis of the configuration of the working class in the imperialist hyperpower) is needed. It may be that such an analysis would show that the better-off part of the working class, the part that has "bought into" an imperialist compact for several generations, and that has a standard of living comparable to that of (at least parts of) the middle classes, ought to be understood within the framework of the "broad masses" or "the people" who need to be won over by the proletariat in the course of making its revolution. In any case, the "dig in," economist trend can be characterized by its insistence on interest as the prime motivating category of social classes, its stubborn refusal to recognize the reconfiguration of classes in imperialism, and hence its tendency to not only eschew moral categories, but also to engage in opportunism for strategic reasons. Probably the most frequently employed example of this opportunism is to use the language of "democracy" with "the workers," because the workers are not ready to hear about socialism (much less communism). Only a little further down this road is the problem of patriotism—especially the problem of patriotism in an imperialist country, to say nothing of an imperialist superpower.

Without presuming to give an adequate treatment of the subject of patriotism at this point, we might ask how much patriotism (in whatever country) will fit within a real commitment to internationalism. In the case of the United States, I would say, none whatsoever. There is simply too much of a contradiction between the social system of the United States, and its interests, and its machinery for organizing people to get behind its interests, on the one side, and a different future for humankind, possibly any future at all, to justify hoisting the American flag. This does not mean that there cannot be alliances with people who see things differently, people who believe in something like a different promise of America, or a defense of certain aspects of constitutional citizenship at a time when these things are very much under attack (as they are at the time of this writing), but even such alliances, if they are not shaped by an ethic of internationalism and a commitment to a transformed world, will find themselves pulled into the terms of the existing system. I will say a little more on this subject in the second section of part 3, where I take up the issue of place, as there is a longstanding connection between the idea of a "country" and the idea of "the land that I love." However, it might also be said that many of the right-wing super-patriots of recent decades can hardly be said to love "the land"—indeed, it appears that, often in the name of God, they despise the land.

The other broad trend in Marxism takes history to be a real thing. Recall Sartre's argument that the existence of God would not solve "the problem of humanity for humanity." In a similar vein, we can say that the problem *of* history is a problem *for* history, and then ask what it means to take this problem seriously. Thus there has been another trend in Marxism, which one way or another manages to rethematize issues raised by Kant— sometimes explicitly, as in the extensive literature on Marx and Kant/Marx and ethics/Marx and justice, and sometimes even while hoping not to traffic with Kant (or with the component of "German philosophy"—as Engels put it—in Marxism) at all, even while raising issues and questions that come straight out of Kant's philosophy.

Analytically, we can keep these trends separate and distinct; in practice there is some overlap. On the economist side, there remains some motivation that might be called "ethical"—people who are attracted to the economist trends (whether they be "orthodox Marxist" of the sort that came out of the Moscow-oriented Communist Parties, or the Trotskyist currents and splinters) are motivated by the desire to fight capitalism, believing it to be a bad social system that ought to be superceded. They are not motivated first of all by the desire to become a "revisionist bourgeoisie," except perhaps in the case of the top leadership of the most powerful and dogmatic parties (examples here would be the Communist Party of France and some Third World parties, such as the one in Haiti). At the same time, however, the irony is that economism is also based on a false analysis of the class situation under imperialism, and this false analysis is both motivated by and the source of much opportunism (of the sort that tells better-off workers in the imperialist countries that they could be even more better-off in a socialist system), and it means a denial that capitalism has indeed mutated into a global, imperialist system. Historically, the roots of this opportunism and denial have to do with both Western European revisionism (specifically, Karl Kautsky's rejection of internationalism as the First World War loomed, arguing that it was in the interest of the working class in the Western European countries to support "their bourgeoisies" and "their countries" when the social systems of these countries went into the kinds of crises that lead to war), and the fact that Lenin's rethinking of Marxism in light of the emergence of the imperialist world-system (or, at least, the level of integration of this system that occurred in the final decade of the nineteenth century and the first decade of the twentieth) did not, in practice, fully come together in a new synthesis. This may seem like an old and obsolete debate, but it has plenty of relevance, I think, to both the world of imperialism today, and to the idea of a new synthesis called Ethical Marxism.

Classes under Imperialism

Despite their argument that the working class is a single, international class, which ultimately must create a new social system for the entire world, Marx and Engels also tended to see class struggle as taking place on a country-by-country basis. They also tended to see Western Europe as the forward edge of the struggle for socialism, precisely because capitalism and bourgeois society had developed to its most advanced state there. Now, Lenin's analysis of the transformation of capitalism into imperialism does not address the cultural and ideological issues that also arise in the twentieth century, that have to do with the dynamics within capitalism that occur when capitalism stays around for a long time after having made what Marx thought were its main historical contributions, and this is where some integration of the political economy of imperialism and the kind of cultural critique one finds in theorists such as Adorno (well, especially Adorno) is needed. However, what Lenin began to grasp—and what was never fully consolidated in his thinking and was then increasingly lost in the years after his death—was that, with the transformation into imperialism, capitalism's contradictions operate more fully on the global scale, and then there are important ramifications for the question of classes and class struggle.

We have already discussed the way that class bifurcations unfold under imperialism, and the sorts of complicities that are created with parts of the working class in imperialist countries. Against Kautsky's Eurocentric economism (so narrowly tied to the notion of material interests of the working class that Kautsky asked Lenin whether he could *guarantee* that a revolution in Germany would not bring down the standard of living), Lenin formulated the idea of "revolutionary defeatism." When an imperialist country is in crisis, the bourgeoisie will of course attempt to rally the broad masses around the national banner. This rallying cry assumes its most acute form when the imperialist nations are drawn into war (by the internal workings of their own imperialist system, not by some external factor—though of course each imperialist nation declares that the factors are external), and of course Lenin and others in 1912 were looking at the possibility of war on a scale hitherto unknown. (In the 1890s Engels had written quite presciently about the elements that were coming into place for a "general European war.") Revolutionary defeatism is the argument that you don't help "your" ruling class when they are in crisis, you seize the opportunity to overthrow them. This is internationalism in practice, not falling for the idea that internationalism is a fine idea in theory, but, when the chips are down, one has to support his or her "own" country. (So that, in the final analysis—the final analysis as far as U.S. imperialism is concerned, that is—it may have been a "mistake" to have carried the Vietnam War as far as it was taken, but, as for the Vietnamese people, they are after all Vietnamese and not Americans.) The capitalist class of the United States has done such a superb job of manipulating this sentiment that it is very difficult to even raise the "fine idea" of internationalism; unfortunately, this notion that there is no higher reality, at least when one really gets down to what stand one will take, than "one's own" nation-state, is not only the province of right-wing thinkers, as one can see in Richard Rorty's *Achieving Our Country* (for example; the book is part of a series called "Leftist Thought in Twentieth-Century America"). Lenin established the beginnings of what might be called an "ethic of internationalism," and it is a testimony to how poorly this ethic took root in Marxism that in many imperialist countries, if one looks for the real internationalists, one will hardly find a one among the groups that call themselves "Marxist," but instead among anarchists and activists who claim a religious inspiration (most notably, radical Christians). This is a sad comment on the pull toward economism and the reductivism of material interest in much of what calls itself Marxism. The important exception is the Maoists, but note that there are only a few Maoist organizations in the first world—the majority are found in the Third World.

Why call Lenin's perspective an "ethic"? In part because it goes against the grain of the existing society, and it does this on the basis of principle—yes, a principle based in a material dynamic in the world, but not based in a narrow conception of interest. Many Marxists like to quibble over the definition of interest, and it is worth noting that even those Marxists whose theory and activism are oriented more toward what I would call a principled, ethical direction, still feel they have to cling to the notion of interest. Clearly they worry that, without at least some notion of interest, they will come unstuck from materialism. However, then the notion is stretched out so far—for example, in the 500-year perspective of Mao (and, significantly,

Ronald Aronson also raises this figure, though in terms of radical theory and activism that is "after Marxism")—that it is hard to see why it ought to be called "interest" any more. In fact, I would go with Kant and call it "concern" (and then it is also interesting that he employs the expression, "incapacity for indifference," especially given the Aristotelian thrust of much of his argument in "Idea for a Universal History"), and perhaps each of us has some "interest" in a future humanity that in one way or another "carries us forward." Then we encounter the questions of mortality that are raised by Freud, Heidegger, and others—but that seem of little interest to Marx. In his works outlining the idea of revolutionary defeatism, Lenin said that the reaction of the working class to this idea would not first of all be congenial; quoting Plato's *Republic* (without mentioning it by name), he said that the first inclination of most workers would be to tear the defeatist activists "limb from limb." This would especially be the case for those workers who are integrated into (what Lenin called) the "labor aristocracy," the union leaders and better-off workers whose horizon of class struggle was completely defined by the wage system and had no place for the abolishment of this system. My larger point is that Lenin was completely on the right track, but that one crucial element needed to be added to his argument: better-off workers and the better-off broad masses in imperialist countries need to not only transcend their narrow conception of interests, they need to transcend the whole social scheme in which they have been allocated a stake in the fate of the imperialist social system. This may mean not only transcending narrow interests, but even "overthrowing" their own interests—because imperialism creates even in the working class (or at least a significant section of it) an interest in the superexploitation and extreme oppression of workers and peasants in the Third World.

Interests under Imperialism

Of course, theorists and activists have to grapple with and attempt to understand the interests of the different classes and even different parts of classes, for two reasons. First, even in the imperialist countries there are people who indeed do not have a stake in the existing set-up, and these people are more like the "real proletarians" described by Marx. Recall the scenarios of Soviet invasion that were on view in the 1980s (during the Reagan period), lousy, stupid movies such as *Red Dawn* and (the made-for-TV movie) *America*. Ignoring the unlikelihood of an invasion/occupation of the territory of the United States by the Soviet Union (instead, both the United States and the Soviet Union were contending to dominate other parts of the world, especially the Third World), the message of these films was that the American "way of life" had to be defended. Well, there are strata of society, even in the imperialist hyperpower, whose material standard of living is nothing to write home about. (Certainly it can also be said that there are many millions in the United States who, though they live at a "high"—or at least not very low—material standard, their "way of life" has little to recommend it, even to these people themselves.) In the United States (as well as in most Western European countries), this "real proletariat" is racially very diverse, and indeed has a preponderance of non-white people (just as, earlier, the working class in the United States had many "whites" who still were not "really" white—people of Irish and Italian descent, for example, Elvis Presley; however, I do not accept the argument, heard in some quarters, that there are *no* proletarians in the United States who are white), which also speaks to the need for an ethic of internationalism. It is quite likely that the real proletariat is made up of more girls and women than boys and men, which speaks to the need for an ethic of anti-patriarchy. The concept of class in global terms in an imperialist world is a complicated thing, undoubtedly; its complexity does not mean that we can dispense with it, in the case that Marx is still right that we cannot understand and change the world without grappling with this concept in all its complexity.

Second, this investigation is necessary for understanding where the contradictions of the system may become most acute—for example, when the people who are sent as cannon fodder in an imperialist war come quite predominantly from the working class. Certainly this is not just one example among others. Warfare is an expression of social relations, and global lopsidedness is also expressed in the fact that, even if a soldier of working-class origin in the U.S. armed forces can be sacrificed without George W. Bush and his class feeling at all troubled, still the "kill ratio" is completely skewed. Even so, openings do occur when the contradictions of imperialism are acute, and one of these that relates to classes and interests is that people do tend to wake up at certain moments and ask why they or their relatives or friends are being sent to kill, maim, destroy, and die.

However, and this is simply a form of my main argument regarding Marxism and the matter of ethics, an analysis that must include an element of calculation (in this case, calculation of class interests) cannot end there. Otherwise, one is left with questions such as the following: Are your interests being met, or are they not being met, by this present imperialist invasion of a Third World country? If your interests are not being met, what can we do to better meet your interests? The point is that the first question, even when answered in the negative, allows for the legitimacy of an answer in the affirmative. In other words, the question itself is legitimated, when the first order of business is not the interest of an individual or even a substantial part of a class (keep in mind that, for Marx, classes are aggregates of individuals, not some mysterious entities that exist over and above the individuals that make them up), but instead the legitimacy, or lack thereof, of the military action and the polity that undertakes it. To put it simply, an Ethical Marxism would engage in "class calculus" (for it is indeed far more complicated than simple arithmetic) in order to see the openings for the thematization of questions of right and wrong, in such a way that some good in the world might actually be done.

Qualitative Developments in Marxism

Lenin's theory and leadership, set against economism, moved in this direction—in what Gramsci called "a revolution against capital." Gramsci meant not only the capitalist system, but also the dogmatically conceived, "received wisdom" of Marx's *Capital*. To develop Marxism in a new epoch also means to fundamentally reforge Marx's conceptions, which also leads to qualitative breaks. (It also means asking if some elements of Marx's perspective were simply wrong to begin with.) "Leninism" achieved a new synthesis to the extent that it played the leading role in finding and widening the opening that allowed the Bolshevik Revolution to break through the imperialist system. However, the "ethical" component of Lenin's transformation of Marxism was never fully articulated, and, after the death of Lenin, this component receded dramatically. It would be silly to presume to present even an overview of the Stalin period here—this is a very complicated question that should not be dealt with in a brisk or piecemeal fashion. Even while I would argue that Trotsky was also no Leninist (especially because he rejected Lenin's analysis of imperialism and classes under imperialism, as do all strains of Trotskyism today), I am still willing to accept that Trotsky could hardly have done a worse job of leading the Soviet Union than Stalin did. (However, in an essay on Sartre's theory of the Stalin period, I argue that Trotsky would never have become the leader of the Communist Party of the Soviet Union even if Stalin had never been born; see Martin, *The Radical Project*, 15–35.) Now, this may seem like no great admission to someone who would argue that *nothing* could have been worse than Stalin. "What if?" history is always dangerous territory, to be sure (it's fun, of course, but probably not a good basis for social theory); however, I would go so far as to say that even during the Stalin period there was at least a certain "interruption" in the "forward march" of imperialism (and this interruption included not only the Soviet Union, but also eventually China and other anticolonial revolutions, the opening for which owed at least a little to the existence of the Soviet Union), and that imperialism uninterrupted would indeed have come to something far worse. I also do not accept the commonly propagated view that the Stalin period was an unmitigated disaster in every way; certainly Europeans who think the defeat of Nazism was a good thing know that they owe a considerable debt to the Soviet people—a people now abolished and increasingly erased from history. Penultimately, let me add that the Soviet Union represented an attempt at something unprecedented in history. The fear that the representatives of imperialism have regarding this attempt, and the motivation for the propaganda of "unmitigated disaster," is not that it "failed," but that others will try to learn from the experience and do better in the future.

Stalin and the Ethical Turn

Ultimately, I would argue that Stalin (and the Stalin period) is the main impetus behind the revival of the concatenation of issues regarding Marx and ethics/justice/Kant. Admittedly, Stalin could be extraordinarily hamfisted in his understanding of Marxist categories to begin with, and we cannot and should not avoid the question of how "socialist leadership" got to the place that it did with Stalin (or with the Soviet system). To say the least, the tendencies within materialism and even "scientific" investigation (actually, "scientific" with or without the scare quotes), to be mechanical and dogmatic about material causality, and to apply this mechanical thinking to human beings as if they are *things*, these assumed an acute form in Stalin's leadership. In this sort of context, at least, it can be said that Marxists are sometimes the last people to figure certain things out. (For some provocative observations on this point, especially regarding the role of Stalin and the Soviet Union in WWII, see Bob Avakian, *Conquer the World?* 22–24.) To put it bluntly and naively, we can and ought to ask why Stalin never seemed to wonder (at least not in a way that found its way into print) if something about the way socialism was going in the Soviet Union might smell bad. This line of inquiry can be taken down to what appears to be a simple and straightforward contradiction, that the struggle for communism presents humanity with the loftiest of goals, the creation of a global community of mutual flourishing, and though this struggle will undoubtedly go through twists and turns and reversals and failures and mistakes and even severe foul-ups, still there have to be points where there is a thinking about right and wrong.

Perhaps Marx thought that the transition to communism would take place in a short enough period that these worries would take care of themselves. In his essay on the Paris Commune (*The Civil War in France*), Marx did say that the proletariat would have to go through seventy-five years of struggles, civil wars, advances, and reversals in order to make itself fit to rule. I think he was wrong about the "take care of itself" aspect (if that is what he thought) in any case—*ethical questions do not take care of them-*

selves. But, for what it is worth, and this is not a happy fact by any means, he was wrong about the seventy-five years too (we are going on twice that figure since Marx wrote this).

Perhaps there was something in Stalin's character that made him numb to what might be called simple ethical concerns. A more fruitful line of inquiry would be to look into the scientific character of Marxism and ask how this scientific "objectivity" can also be numb to ethical concerns—and then how leadership comes forward that is expressive of this numbness. Lenin did raise some questions about the character of Stalin (breaking off "personal relations" after Stalin had been rude toward his wife, Nadezhda Krupskaya). And yet these questions cannot be separated from the fact that the real work of revolution requires that leaders (and not only leaders, of course) steel themselves in various ways and at various times. Certainly it is the case that an absolutely rigid Kantianism that cannot accept any compromise in the pursuit of laudable goals probably does become an empty formalism, even if it is also right to worry about slippery slopes into tyranny and oppression. In the case of Stalin, that last clause is the understatement of the year. Everyone who has studied the *Groundwork* feels the overwhelming *fraughtness* of Kant's world, that there is a heavy ethical decision to make every way one may turn, and that one is going to generally make the wrong decision because the moral value of the decision depends on having a purely good will. This fraught state of being—the feeling that any movement will lead to calamity—encourages paralysis, which is the real problem of empty formalism.

(Algebra could be called an empty formalism too, but it is good for a lot of things. In the world of mathematicians, it might be noted, there is a longstanding distrust between the algebraicists and the geometers, and this might be compared to the differences between Kant and Hegel.)

Ironically, the ideal revolutionary is completely self-sacrificing, and though Stalin had a number of character flaws, lack of dedication was not one of them. Indeed, it is not hard to imagine an argument that Stalin was "too Kantian" in his dogged dogmatism. For Kant, a rule is a rule—lying is wrong, even if one is lying to a murderer who is seeking a victim. Perhaps Kant does need to come into the real world of hard choices and competing ethical demands a bit more, even while we are still entitled to ask if the "science of society" might adjust its science in order to understand ethical questions as part of the human reality that it hopes to study.

There is a missing step here. For any systematic attempt to study human reality, especially if the aim is to attempt to change that reality for the better, we have to remember two things: (1) human beings are not billiard balls or even the psychologists' rats, but are indeed the sorts of creatures for whom subjectivity, meaning, belief, intention, values, and hope are real; (2) we who are making this study are human too, and though it is not necessarily wrong to apply the social scientist's perspective that "what is subjective for you can be studied objectively by an other," there is a problem when this perspective is made "objective" by a denial or forgetting of humanity. Stalin in some respects forgot to be human. (This too is a complicated question; for instance, as Montefiore's book makes clear, Stalin could be a loving and even doting father.) It would be too easy to attribute this forgetting to character flaws.

Analysis of the Stalin Period

In the second volume of the *Critique of Dialectical Reason*, Sartre does allow that the character of the leaders of a revolution is indeed an important issue, but he does not take this to be the central issue. Instead Sartre's focus is what he calls the "deviation" and "detour" within Marxism that Stalin represented, and then he argues that this deviation was not simply an expression of Stalin's character, but instead was necessitated by the actual incarnation of the revolution. This problem of incarnation, which creates a contradiction for the revolution—in so much as the revolution is not limited to simply the formation of a new nation-state, but is supposed to be part of an unfolding global and international*ist* process—goes to the heart of the ethical issue that is at stake between Kant and Marx. The problem of incarnation goes to the concatenated issues of fraughtness and paralysis, the complexity of competing obligations, and the forgetting of humanity. With Stalin the character of Marxism is indeed at stake.

Sartre sets out the problems of incarnation and "detour":

> the Revolution, incarnated in the center of the world as a long-term praxis defined by definite material circumstances, could not itself develop without engendering—by its actual course, albeit in contradiction with its leaders' project—the impotence of foreign proletariats. In this sense, *it can be said that* [the revolution's] *incarnation was in direct contradiction with its universalization.* (*Critique of Dialectical Reason*, 105, my emphasis)

> It was necessary to choose between disintegration and *deviation* of the Revolution. Deviation also means detour: Stalin was the man of that detour. "Hold on! Produce! Later generations will go back to principles." And this was right, except that he did not see how in this very way he was producing generations which contained within them—as the inert materiality of the circumstances to be transcended—the deviation that had produced them and that they interiorized. (*Critique of Dialectical Reason*, 129)

Bob Avakian offers a gloss on the first issue (he isn't responding to Sartre per se) that is helpful:

there is a problem, a contradiction, that has to be grasped deeply and in an all-around way. The world, including the situation of the proletariat, really is different when the proletariat seizes, and particularly if it holds power in one or a few countries.

. . . I was in one discussion with someone who pointed out, "Well, the position of the prolerariat is that it has nothing to lose but its chains, but if it has a country, does it have nothing to lose but its chains?" There is a problem to think about, and to think that there's no contradiction between a proletariat that has state power [on the one hand] and the advance of the world revolution [on the other] means that you can only incorrectly handle what is a very profound and, at times, extremely acute and potentially antagonistic contradiction. (*Conquer the World?* 17)

A contradiction cannot conceivably be "handled correctly," of course, when it is not even recognized as such. Thus we find ourselves at Sartre's second point, the deviation is interiorized, never recognized as deviation or detour, but as simply the way things need to be done. Add to this Sartre's striking claim regarding this need, "And this was right."

Four consequences issued from this interiorization of the deviation, two directly practical, two in the ideological/theoretical realm that had practical—and bad—effects (to say the least). These consequences are deeply interrelated and could be given in any order (the order they are given in here, therefore, should not be taken as some sort of ranking). First, within the Soviet Union itself, when things did not go the way the leadership had hoped, in the field of production and elsewhere, the immediate conclusion drawn was that "an enemy is at work here." In addition to the terrible harm that was done to innocent individuals, the application of this perspective just made everything worse, with disastrous consequences. Second, the inability to recognize the contradiction that arises when the proletariat no longer has nothing to lose but its chains, but now has a country (in a very tenuous way, perhaps, but in this case also a country that is one-sixth of the earth's land mass), led to the subordination of international struggle to the national defense of the Soviet Union. This is an even more difficult contradiction, because it was not wrong at every point for this subordination to occur. However, when this subordination reached the point where, to give probably the most important example, the revolution in Spain was completely undermined (leading to four decades of fascist rule), it might be said that this interiorization had taken a qualitative leap (though, unfortunately, neither the first nor the last). We can see here the connection between the first and second consequences, too, in that Soviet advisors in Spain spent as much time, if not more, fighting "Trotskyites" and anarchists as they did Franco's forces. Third, tendencies toward linearity were confirmed by the application of a linear perspective, thus leading to more linearity. Fourth, and similarly, the expediency that may have been "right" under certain conditions (referring again here to Sartre's argument), was elevated to the level of principle, or was made into the trump card against all principles, these being deferred into an indefinite future.

It has long been argued that any analysis of the Stalin period, or of the Bolshevik Revolution itself for that matter, has to deal with the fact that the revolution was "incarnated" in a "backward" country, with a relatively small working class, a peasantry that comprised about eighty-five percent of the population, and both of these classes largely illiterate. Although processes of capital accumulation were well underway by the 1890s, the social relations in Russia were still largely feudal or at least semi-feudal. Certainly the prevailing religious order (Eastern Orthodoxy) was tenaciously medieval. (As Mao noted, Stalin's formative years—in Georgia, not Russia—were spent in an Orthodox seminary.) Although the western capitals of Russia, Moscow and Petersburg (Petrograd, later Leningrad), were advanced in culture, producing writers such as Tolstoy and Dostoevsky, and composers such as Glinka and Rimsky-Korsakov, the vast eastern and southern regions of Russia were Asian and Muslim. Indeed, there have been influential arguments to the effect that the Stalin period represented a form of the "Asiatic mode of production" (in Western Europe and the United States this argument was joined with the totalitarianism theses of Hannah Arendt and, later, the students of Leo Strauss, to advance the argument that there was no internal basis of change in the Soviet Union, and therefore it could only be changed by external force). Although I do not accept these arguments (though I also do not reject every part of them), there is no denying that the conditions for socialist revolution in Russia were quite different from those imagined by Marx and Engels. For some, economic backwardness and the lack of an advanced culture and advanced degree of secularism such as found in western Europe are *the* central facts about the Bolshevik Revolution and the Stalin period. Contributing to the linear and expedient ideologies that later became dogmatically consolidated with Stalin was Lenin's perspective that, though Russia lacked advanced levels of industry, culture (including basic literacy), and secularism, the revolution had to come first and then these things could be acquired. Well, to quote Sartre yet again, "And this was right"— but again there is an interiorization of contradictions that needed to be thematized as such. To this needs to be added the fact that "advanced" everything in Western Europe was based on exploitation of the working class and, increasingly, colonialism and imperialism. As Walter Benjamin put it, every artifact of civilization is also an artifact of barbarism.

It has to be insisted once again that none of what I am saying here is meant to be an adequate analysis of the Stalin period. This goes for the "backwardness" question as well. However, this last question should not be passed over without adding a crucial qualifier, one that will take us back to the question of ethics. Certainly economic backwardness presents a specific form of the contradiction involved in the incarnation of the revolution (as well as more straightforward difficulties, such as economic policies that must prioritize food over literacy). However, it would be wrong to think that it is only with a backward country that there would be a contradiction of incarnation. The more "advanced" countries have the contradiction that a socialist revolution would acquire advanced means of production and tremendous wealth that is based on the pillage of the Third World. Furthermore, the proletariat that acquires these things is the *international* proletariat; it has to acquire (through, as Marx put it at the conclusion of *Capital*, vol.1, expropriating the expropriators) this wealth for the sake of and for the advancement of itself as an international class and indeed for all of humanity. If instead that part of the proletariat (and especially its leadership, which is, as Mao argued, where these contradictions become most acute) simply constitutes itself as a "national" class that has "come into money" (as they say), that is the end of the revolution, and indeed the leadership of this class will simply be reconsituted by the workings of capital into a new imperialist class.

Contradictions of Incarnation

There are very difficult contradictions involved in the incarnation of the revolution, in other words, which might be characterized broadly as having to do with the particular things that need to be done such that a program of ethical-political universalism does not remain absolutely abstract and therefore empty. Socialist revolution must mediate the Scylla and Charybdis of "ethical" (or "principled") paralysis, on the one side, and the demands of the concatenation of necessity and expediency on the other, and the revolution cannot do this simply through either debate about principle or recourse to a worked-out blueprint.

However, it can also be argued that the abandonment of principles altogether (or the postponement of attention to principles to a never-to-arrive future) is in fact the abandonment of socialism, for the following reason. Marx argued that the modern world sees society dividing into two great camps, the bourgeoisie and the proletariat. There are complications in this picture, in that there is no single "bourgeoisie," but instead the different bourgeoisies of different nation-states. These nation-states represent a way that the world is carved up, a set of boundaries that must be overcome but that have to be taken account of in the present. Furthermore, there are many people who are neither bourgeois nor proletarian in origin, and yet who do not form a single "middle class," either. (Indeed, the "middle" strata of the world are fantastically diverse, but often have significant overlap with the working class.) We have also discussed some ways in which imperialism divides and otherwise affects the working class. Nevertheless, Marx's point was that the future of humankind will lie with one of the two great camps: either the bourgeois form of social organization, namely capitalism, which depends on the exploitation of labor power and the accumulation of surplus value to organize society, or a form of social organization that (in a thoroughly Kantian formulation from Marx) takes "human power" as its own end. (The formulation comes from *Capital*, vol. 3; in MER, 441.) "Human power becoming its own end," however, does not issue in a worked-out blueprint either for a new society or for the one and only road to the future society. Furthermore, to establish the *basis* for human power to increasingly become its own end, in the overthrow of the bourgeoisie of a particular nation-state, and the seizure of power by the proletariat, the *negation* of the economic system of capitalism must be carried through, but this negation cannot simply be a mirror-image or reaction-formation. Furthermore, "overthrowing" and "seizing" are military operations, and here the dialectic of struggle has a tendency toward the most reductivistic, not for any gratuitous reason, but because force must be met by force. This reductivism will tend to spread through the new society, and again we are reminded of Sartre's claim that Stalin represents Marxism as a pure theory of power.

Sea Change

The question of an "Ethical Marxism" might be posed just this simply: What could do the job of replacing the elements of capitalism in every social sphere (military, economic, political, cultural, even "personal")? There has to be a reaction to the existing capitalist elements; certainly their reality has to be recognized in order to be changed. And indeed, because of the deep-seatedness of this reality (and not only in five-hundred years of capitalism, but in thousands of years of the idea that society can only be organized by exploiting and dominating ruling classes, and the idea that the basis for such classes is a "natural" social hierarchy), there are many things that will have to be changed gradually, and that cannot be changed "overnight." Let us take a few simple examples having to do with patriarchy (and the way that patriarchy is incorporated within and used by imperialism). On the one hand, some of the ways that women are exploited and oppressed in capitalist society can be changed immediately—they ought to be changed immediately and they will have to be changed immediately. For example, advertising that uses women's bodies to sell products can, ought to, and will have to be eliminated immediately. (This is obviously not a very hard example, since advertising itself will be rendered superfluous in a noncapitalist context—if not necessarily all of the creative skills involved in advertising, some of which could be deployed for other purposes.) On the other hand, the overcoming of patriarchy will involve a sea change in sensibilities, and though much can be done (ought to be done, will have to be done) to encourage this sea change, it will take time for this change to fully set in. Attitudes cannot be changed simply by telling people what attitudes they ought to have. Indeed, here it is worth remembering Marx's argument that there is commodity fetishism because there is commodity production. There are patriarchal attitudes because there are patriarchal social relations. Of course, the attitudes reinforce the social relations, and the attitudes can persist for some time even when the social relations have been substantially changed (to create economic independence for women, to begin with). And, in fact, the attitudes, if not challenged, but instead left to "take care of themselves," can play a role in recreating patriarchal social relations. To return to my larger point, then, an Ethical Marxism would be one that reserves a central place for principles—and I would say that Kant was very much on the right track as to what sorts of principles are needed.

It is common for (at least) one kind of Marxism to protest that such an emphasis represents a kind of philosophical "backtracking." Probably the most reductivistic version of this Marxism would say that it is the same with philosophy as it is with both science and the succession of the modes of production: it is an historically retrograde maneuver to recapitulate that which has already been accomplished and superceded. (Thus the practice—as opposed to the history—of physics does not need to go back to Newton; capitalism cannot *really* go back to feudalism, even if it might take up some of the trappings of feudalism; and so on. Here there is an aspect of the Stalin question that could also be explored further, with the idea of the "red tsar"; but we will have to leave this for another day.) Significantly, the argument can be made that in certain respects Marx never caught up with Kant, not only in terms of ethics, but perhaps first of all in terms of epistemology. Thus the refusal to "go back to Kant" (for one thing, to do a little more philosophical homework, before chucking philosophy into the waste bin) results instead in a return to Hobbes, power-without-principle, reaction formations, and the *modus vivendi* that cannot afford the luxury of ethical questions. (In an earlier book I called this "prudential Marxism"; see *Humanism and its aftermath*, 29–46.) However, at least two major questions are raised by the idea of a forward march of ideas and culture in step with the progressive development of the mode of production.

First is what might be called the ecological-ethical question of the sustainability of industrial production, and the need to rethink agrarianism in the ways suggested by Wes Jackson, Wendell Berry, and others. Our species has to find a solution to the "progressive" spoiling of the nest, regardless of what this means to the teleology of forms of production. The erosion of topsoil may not seem like a very "avant" issue to those convinced of the idiocy of rural life (and it is typical of urbanophiles to imagine some easy technofix—which in fact is not in the offing), but in fact this is an issue of world-historic significance.

Second, there is the greatly significant de-industrialization of the United States and the countries of Western Europe. The transfer of millions of manufacturing jobs, and now even many high-tech jobs, to the Third World (which itself represents a transformation of this latter category), certainly goes to the issue of the internationalization of the economy that begins even in the early stages of capitalism, takes significant leaps with the emergence of colonialism and imperialism, and what we more recently call "globalization." I would argue that the latter remains a chapter in the development of imperialism, because it is a matter of the basic direction of the flow of wealth, but surely the "outsourcing" of jobs is a significant and qualitative development. Lenin emphasized the role of finance capital in imperialism, and certainly that role cannot be de-emphasized now, and yet two contemporary features of at least some "advanced-capitalist" economies ought to be noted: (1) that the previous connection between "advanced" and "industrial" has been significantly sundered; (2) that the military aspect of imperialism is heightened. "Advanced capitalist" powers that depend on resources from elsewhere for a very significant part, perhaps even the greater part, of their wealth generation, and perhaps even for the basic needs of their populations, have to have ways of controlling these resources, and this is ultimately a military question. In his outline theory of imperialism Lenin was already pointing in this direction, but the intertwining of force and economy has reached a point that neither he nor Marx likely could have imagined. One measure of this is that the U.S. defense economy, not only of the armed forces, but of all the police agencies that hold the American social system together, represent a planned economy on a scale that is far beyond what would be needed for socialism. Of course, this is a capitalist, not socialist, planned economy, planned for the purpose of continued wealth accumulation for the U.S. ruling class.

To put the point more straightforwardly: if the source of energy that makes the economy run is not found within the national borders of that economy, then there has to be a way to control that energy source, and this way will be military in the last resort. In our time we are experiencing a military-economic global reconfiguration in the wake of the breakdown of the previous system of global bifurcation by the United States and the Soviet Union. This is a reconfiguration in the international, globalized mode of production. The classical terms presented by Marx have to be reconfigured accordingly.

It is indeed one of the ironies of the recent reconfigurations in the imperialist world order that the imperialist countries are not able to solve basic economic problems within their national borders. In some sense, Marx saw socialism as the "icing on the cake" of the economic development that was being achieved in Western Europe in his time, and thus he did not think of a country such as China as "ripe" for socialist revolution. Eurocentrists can scoff at what has to be one of the greatest achievements of the twentieth century: by the late 1960s China had finally solved its food problem, though perhaps this achievement hardly registers from a Eurocentric perspective. But now the irony is that the imperialist countries themselves must use economic and military domination of other countries to deal with their own food issues, and this is an issue analytically distinct from, even if interrelated with, the unsustainable (and grotesque and ethically horrible) food production practices (which cannot legitimately be called agriculture) that predominate especially in the United States.

In fact, there are two more questions that need to be raised in this argument about ethics.

Culture and Economy

Marx argued that the level of culture in a society cannot be more advanced than the "material level" of society generally, and within this latter category the mode of production is the "beating heart," as it were. Now, Marx recognized that such a view runs into problems when it comes to certain artifacts of culture that seem to have persistent appeal and that would be hard to surpass: the dramas of Aeschylus and Shakespeare were among these artifacts for Marx. The whole idea of "progress" in the arts is very difficult. (Of the many sources that can be sited in this discussion, Terry Eagleton's remarks are especially interesting; see *Walter Benjamin, or Towards a Revolutionary Criticism*, 114–30, and *Literary Theory*, 1–14.) At the one end, there seems to be an "unsurpassability" to great art (in light of which questions such as, "Who is the better composer, Bach or Beethoven?" just seem silly); at the other end, the question of what counts as "art" in the first place is deeply, materially embedded within particular cultural configurations. (Bach's Suites for Cello were originally written as exercises for the composer's students, and really did not come into their own "as art" until centuries later, when they were taken up by Pablo Casals; the latter's interpretation of the Suites, in turn, were inflected with a deep romanticism that would have been completely foreign to the composer.) Despite all this, we might agree with Marx's basic argument about "material level" of society, and "cultural level"—the latter "level" crucially including such matters as philosophy and ethics—if we are careful, very,

very careful, to not fall into the reductivisms of simplistic reflection theory (the idea that the different realms of culture mechanically "reflect" the level attained by the mode of production). The alternative would be to say that even defining the "material" or "cultural" "levels" of a given society is such a complex matter, to say nothing of showing the relationship between these levels, that it would be better to abandon materialism on this point (at least) altogether. This would be a mistake. For one thing, there are large swaths of culture that quite clearly represent the imperialist system and its contradictions. More significantly for our present discussion is that an ethical-political universalism that is not understood within its material context is indeed in danger of becoming both an empty formalism and, on the practical level, mere moralizing. To make our principles material, however, is not mere philosophical backtracking. Indeed, it can be argued that this "materializing of the idea" (to borrow an expression from Derrida with a slight twist) is a path that Kant was already following and which resulted in the cosmopolitan, internationalist, and anti-imperialist perspective of his final period.

Basic Contradiction of Capitalism

The fourth question has to do with how Marx understood the basic contradiction of the capitalist epoch. Marx characterized this contradiction as that between socialized production and private appropriation of wealth (the exchange value that is created in the production process). Marx characterizes this contradiction as being in historical motion, from the early days of commodity production and the beginnings of a money economy, through, crucially, the commodification of labor power, to, ultimately, the point where capitalism encounters crises of overproductivity. The contradiction becomes acute in the oft-repeated scenario of "poor people dying in a rich man's war." Essentially, everyone is expected to stand up and defend a production process and attendant set of social relations that is absolutely socialized (except in the case of the "ownership" function, which is rendered superfluous by the socialization of production, which includes the production of the managerial strata), even while the material gains of military action are channeled almost exclusively to the ruling class. (Sometimes this channeling is so crude as to be laughable, as in the outright war profiteering of the Bush family during the Gulf War and of Vice President Dick Cheney and Halliburton during the Iraq War.) Almost, but not absolutely: imperialism spreads a few crumbs from the table, along with jingoistic calls to "serve your country" and other inducements of an ideological nature (e.g., a way out of a dead-end situation, or to "become a man"), in order to forge armies that somehow remain this side of the question, "Why are we fighting, killing, and dying for these people and this system?" The acute form of the contradiction expresses the everyday form that is obscured by commodity fetishism (and by millennia of the ideology of "natural hierarchy"), the simple truth that a complex society requires everyone's efforts to keep going.

The ruling class risks the thematization of this truth when it sends the poor to fight its wars—again, its wars against people who have never done anything to the people of the United States. For this thematization to become revolutionary, however, there has to be a moment of moral recognition in addition to the analysis of capitalism's economic contradictions. The contradiction between socialized production and private appropriation can be expressed as a moral imperative: if "it takes a society" to make a society, then the form of appropriation itself *ought* to be social.

This imperative would seem to apply to all societies where the form of production is sufficiently socialized—which is arguably all societies. (The transition from ape to human is itself already bound up with the evolution of the opposable thumb and the attendant greater facility with tools.) However, capitalism, and especially imperialism, binds all people into a single set of production relations, and, Marx demonstrated (and actually Hegel before him), it makes for itself a place for the poor and unemployed. In other words, there is a social function within capitalism that is played by the poor and unemployed, as a "reserve army of labor." Thus there is a socialization of the labor process even in the case of those who are kept apart from actual production (the point of this function, within capitalism, is to exert pressure on those who are employed—this is our old friend, the iron law of wages). A society of socialized appropriation (which, to emphasize the point despite the redundancy I would call a truly "social society") would have no need of aggressive, offensive, imperialist war, and would indeed be fully aware that such wars are morally wrong. What we need in our own society is the understanding that the basis of the morally wrong wars that have been conducted by the imperialist countries is what might be called an "antisocial society." The argument for Ethical Marxism in a nutshell is that the creation of a "social society" has to issue both from a political-economic analysis and a moral recognition of what is morally wrong about the antisocial form of society. The difference between these two recognitions, the former "scientific," the latter "ethical," is that the ethical has to be acted upon in order to be what it is. Without ethical commitment and the praxis that makes such commitment real, a systematic analysis of society in itself does not lead to any particular form of life or struggle, especially given that (1) there is a necessary separation between the locus of theoretical analysis (first of all among intellectuals who are in a position to carry out such an analysis) and the people at the bottom of society who will be the leading agents of social change; (2) systematic analysis using Marx's basic categories can no longer be taken to demonstrate the inevitability of a better form of society; instead, this kind of analysis can show that capitalism will not escape the explosive nature of its basic contradictions, and it can help us understand in a strategic and tactical sense the places where pressure might effectively be applied and where openings toward a new society might occur.

However, even in the latter case there has to be an awareness that the contradictions of capitalist society can open up in all kinds of unexpected ways, and there is no pure science for predicting the forms that openings to a different future might take. This is where Derrida's problematics of teleology, eschatology, invention, and the new are very important, as seen in *Specters of Marx*, and in many other writings (for instance, his essay on Paul de Man, "Psyche: Inventions of the Other"). The future itself can be understood as a force that intervenes in history "from a certain outside," and the connection of present-day humanity to this possible future is at least as much a matter of ethical commitment, especially to what I call the value of "ongoingness," as it is a matter of a systematic analysis of capitalism and its contradictions. This is, as I have said repeatedly, not at all a reason not to engage in such theoretical analysis—indeed, on the contrary: we have to understand the world if we are to have a chance of changing it.

Autonomy of the Ethical

But we also have to talk about why it is *right* and *good* to change society, and why the present form of society is ethically bankrupt and indeed evil. Imperialism has done a fantastic job for capitalism, in opening every kind of gap among people, creating what might be called, after Sartre, "hyper-serialization." At the same time, it has concentrated the "great camp" of the proletariat in the Third World, and in parts of the Third World that are found in the first world. The ethical gap is expressed in the United States in, for instance, young people who weigh the question of joining the armed forces in terms of the "cool uniforms" and "getting their lives straightened out," and possibly in terms of getting hurt or killed, with a dash of service to country thrown in at least for appearances' sake, but with no thought whatsoever as to lives dominated and destroyed by U.S. invasions. To respond to this line of thought simply in terms of some "deeper" or "real" interest with which such a young person needs to get in touch is itself immoral. Of course there is a deeper level of analysis needed here, which goes to the immorality of the system and its attendant methods for recruiting youth from dead-end sectors of society (such sectors including educational institutions functioning at sub-minimal levels, and thus the youths are often subliterate). The ethical questions here need to be addressed in their own right. Napalm is unforgiveable; now a new generation of incendiary weapons (basically "improved napalm") is being used in the Iraq War (see Colin Brown, "Firebombing Fallujah: Bush Officials Lied to Britain About U.S. Use of Napalm in Iraq"). As I have said before, whether it is the young people going to Vietnam or to Iraq or to whatever far-flung or nearby place that the United States attempts to dominate, of course these young people are responsible for the choices that they are making. Indeed, they especially will be held accountable by the populations of the lands dominated by imperialism, who will resist this domination. But so are we "at home" accountable for what we allow to happen "in our name," and for the advantages that we have in the world that are based on plunder and domination. And ultimately we have to look to the source of the horror, the imperialist system.

Theoretically and practically speaking, this means that "ethics," the question of the possibility of ethical relations, has to be granted at least a certain autonomy. "Let the ontological chips fall where they may," it could be said. However, this approach is at the same time what I would call the very essence of a "materialism of practices," which, for Marx, forms the basis for any ontological investigation that is in the more strictly philosophical realm. The irony is that Marx is overly *philosophical* in his concentration on an ontology of necessity, while there is only ethics when there is contingency and possibility.

PART 3

Sites, Ramifications: Animals, Places, Mao

Domains of the Ethical Marxist Project

The project of an Ethical Marxism has very wide scope, and the project works on at least four levels as regards theory (and perhaps in even more domains as regards practice). First there is the broad effort to recast Marxism in ethical terms, which I have argued requires an intermotivation and intercirculation of Marxian and Kantian themes. A major difficulty in this broad effort is in both recognizing the previous efforts that have been made in this direction, under the heading of Kantian ethical socialism and various offshoots and tendrils issuing and emanating from this heading (from Hermann Cohen and the other original formulators of this idea, to diverse figures such as Martin Buber, Otto Neurath, Jürgen Habermas, and the ideas of John Rawls as found in the work of the "left Rawlsians" such as Thomas Pogge, Norman Daniels, and Amy Gutmann), *and at the same time* not yielding to the generally reformist (and "revisionist"— "revising" Marxism so as to retain aspects of its outward form but to remove its revolutionary orientation) slant or drift of much of this thought. The orientation I have proffered here is one in which we have many ethical obligations, but the most pressing and central obligation is to do what we can to advance the radical overturning of the imperialist system and to organize a form of life that does not depend on exploitation, oppression, and domination.

Second, and dialectically related to this first effort, is the ongoing need to take our Marxist theory and indeed our "Marxist activities" beyond the utilitarian economism of "interests." This has proven to be an extremely difficult task, in part because it is too easily accomplished in theory and devilishly difficult to accomplish in practice. In theory it is a matter of demonstrating, again and again, the necessity and the power of that which is excluded by economism: the ethical and the possibility of ethical relations; indeed, "the political," in the sense of the notion of a true polis, a political community, which is not unrelated to Derrida's notion of "democracy to come"); the future and even the past—an open future and an open past, as set against a utilitarian, monological "present-ism"; and everything that might go under the related headings of vision, *eudaimonia*, utopia, redemption, and indeed communism. Well, perhaps these demonstrations, such as seen in a variety of venues from Ernst Bloch's *The Principle of Hope* to the post-*Postmodernism* writings of Fredric Jameson (*The Seeds of Time, A Singular Modernity*, and *Archaeologies of the Future*, a book about science fiction and utopia), to contemporary utopian novels such as *The Dispossessed* by Ursula Le Guin and *Woman on the Edge of Time* by Marge Piercy (and novels that portray a distinctively postmodern, post-political dystopia, such as *Neuromancer* by William Gibson, as well as novels that have much to teach us about the concepts of redemption and

185

community, such as many of the novels of Orson Scott Card), to the expressions found in many other fields of art (and, controversially, I would say religion—a topic to which I will return in the conclusion), are not so simple and easy after all. They walk a fine line between expressing a vision of the future (either a redeemed future of mutual flourishing, or a cautionary tale of what can happen when humanity fails to achieve decisive steps in the direction of redemption—the sad thing about *Neuromancer* and its sequels being that it is very much coming true before our very eyes) and being the kind of *mere* utopian fantasy that acts as mere escape and palliative.

It turns out, however, that writing a book that is set against economism, or creating a work of art that resists the overwhelming utilitarian thrust of global capitalism is easy when compared with the difficulty of transcending economism in practice, in the attempt to organize effective resistance to the existing order—to borrow Marcuse's term, a "great refusal." In practice, there cannot help but be a dialectical intertwining of economism and opportunism, and the temptation toward the latter is often overwhelming, at least in an imperialist country, and most of all in the imperialist hyperpower. Consider: even in imperialist countries, and let us again focus on the United States as the archetype and lynchpin, most people spend most of their time dealing with issues of personal economic security and a stable existence—just as do people everywhere else. To be sure, there are broad swaths of the populations of North America, Western Europe, and Japan that have a relatively stable lifestyle at a level of material comfort that is all out of proportion to the opposite and *unequal* levels of material discomfort experienced by broad swaths of the masses in the countries dominated by imperialism. (These are, again, not coincidentally the countries with histories of being plundered and dominated by colonialism.) It would be easy to simply say "to hell with the people of the imperialist countries, especially the people of the United States," and go off on a rant about their stupid junk cultures and idiotically extravagant lifestyles (especially everything oriented toward gas-guzzling motor vehicles) for the sake of which the rest of the world is supposed to suffer. It is also tempting to rant against the utter stupidity and moral vapidness of the imperialist set-up, especially when imperialist countries are on aggressive global campaigns to reconfigure the globe and when the United States is proclaiming a *theology* of its supremacy. Furthermore, though it is all too easy to take the path of the purely "to hell with them" rant (recognizing that "them" includes some of "us," and most certainly your author), this is still better than the other easy path, that of opportunism, which most often takes the form of attempting to construct a commonality of interests between the broad masses of the "mainstream" populations in the imperialist countries (the definition of which will have an ethnic or racial component) and the broad masses in countries plundered and dominated by imperialism.

And yet it is still the case that even in the United States there are not only many poor people and even many more who, despite being relatively well off (certainly in global terms) are for the most part trying to just hang on. Indeed, their sense of their lives is that they are simply hanging on for the ride, playing the hand they have been dealt—"just like most people everywhere," it could be said. Most of the time, even people in imperialist countries in general have neither the luxury nor the necessity of questioning their basic economic, social, political, or cultural circumstances. In Marx's perspective, people do not question their circumstances (in general, broadly, deeply) except when motivated by material interests. Interests are experienced differently in different strata of society (indeed, for Marx, this differentiated experience is integral to the concept of class); for there to be a larger change in society, however, there has to be a more general *crisis*, indeed a crisis felt by all sectors of society. In Lenin's memorable description, the crisis has to be such that people cannot any longer live in the ways in which they have been living, and the ruling class cannot any longer rule in the ways in which it has been ruling. The Marxist perspective is that, short of an actual deep crisis in the social system, people do not (again— generally, broadly, deeply) go into motion against the existing order. People do not set themselves against the existing order simply because it is an unjust order. The dialectical correlative to this last point, which ought to be insisted upon, is that the existing order cannot be overturned in "normal times," times of "normal functioning." This is not to say that people ought not to protest injustice and to organize for a time when the system does indeed go into crisis. It is a crucial point, and also a "Leninist" point, that change will not come without these "anticipations," even if these anticipations will not, of themselves alone, bring about change. Furthermore, practicalities aside, people ought to speak out and otherwise do what they can to challenge an unjust order and its unjust actions.

The Hardest Nut to Crack

This, however, is the point at which imperialism complicates things. Or, perhaps it ought to be said, this is where U.S. imperialism in particular is so vexing. There have been two major crises of the imperialist system thus far. To be absolutely trite about it, these crises were not pretty; indeed they resulted in the greatest horrors thus far known to humankind. We call these crises the two World Wars. The horrors of the World Wars go beyond the wars themselves, but the wars themselves went very far into horror, and anyone who wants to put a pretty face on capitalism ought to have to answer for this. If we look at the world around us now, where at the moment there is a single superpower, and where others of the traditional imperialist powers, such as Great Britain, France, Germany, Japan, and Russia are in the "second rank," and where the United Kingdom and France have for a time been in what might be called the "over-the-hill gang," the process by which some imperialist powers receded to this status was not some pacifistic retirement party. Neither do these powers simply accept this status, and there are emerging players on the world stage (especially China and India) that are gearing up for global contention. The imperialist world system works through exploitation and domination; when the existing circuits of capital are no longer served by existing national boundaries, then these boundaries are redrawn through military action. There can be no doubt what another world war could mean for our planet, and, even in the case where the main contenders in such a war are, to speculate, China and India, it is the imperialist system as a "world-system" that will drive things in this direction—and those global powers that are the most ravenous (first among them the United States) are the driving force of this dynamic.

The previous crises of the imperialist system also represented openings, and out of these openings came the revolutions in Russia and China (and many other revolts against colonialism that, despite the fact that they did not ultimately succeed in overturning neocolonial domination, still caused the imperialist countries to address the ways they went about the business of dominating the Third World). Despite everything, and against distortions and outright lies, these revolutions represented fundamental advances against and beyond the imperialist system. (I will return to this question directly in the third section below.) Be that as it may, these revolutions are long past, something of a closed chapter, and, in any case, the imperialism and postmodern capitalism of the United States barely resembles the imperialism of Czarist Russia, to say nothing of China when it was dominated by colonialism, imperialism, and semi-feudal social relations. Despite this, there are lessons of struggle and transformation that ought to be brought forward (both positive and "negative" lessons, of course). And yet the fact is that U.S. imperialism has yet to experience a crisis that would rock the system to its very foundations. Indeed, the last deep systemic crisis occurred before the era of imperialism *proper* (in the systemic sense of capitalism as a comprehensive, global mode of production): the Civil War of 1861–1865. This is not to say that the Great Depression and the period from the rise of the Civil Rights movement and then everything we associate with the sixties did not shake the foundations. Indeed, with the right kind of understanding and leadership the upheavals of these periods might have gone a good deal further. But it might also be said that U.S. imperialism has done a splendid job, on the whole, of learning the lessons of the sixties, especially. My larger point, apart from the particularities of history, struggle, and strategy "since 1968" (or whenever) is that U.S. imperialism—or, the world imperialist system, but with the United States as its lynchpin—remains both the context of our largest ethical questions (and indeed itself the largest ethical question, the United States as "ethical problem"), and the toughest nut to crack.

Is there a kind of historical dialectic here, one that Kant would have been quite ready to recognize? The hardest thing turns out also to be that which is the most pressing ethical concern, and vice-versa. The most pressing ethical concern is the hardest thing not only to accomplish, but even to thematize, even to begin to get people to grapple with. Thus, on the one hand, the trivializations of much academic discourse on "ethics," and, at the level of structural analysis of the world system, the sense that ethics has nothing to do with the "real workings" of . . . "things," or "power."

Certainly there are ways in which power and "things" work, and there are subtleties here that go far beyond "billiard-ball causality." Even while these workings have to be studied and understood and grappled with from a strategic perspective, it is precisely the reduction to causal "thingness" that is the essence of economism, or, to put the point the other way around, it is the complete setting aside of any role for consideration of the thing that *ought* to be done, in some matrix of pure causality and interest, that is the essence of economism. Lenin saw this, in his critique of economism, and yet, out of the orthodox Marxist refusal of the ethical, did not thematize the point this way. As Steven Lukes argued forcefully in *Marxism and Morality* (and others as well, such as Norman Geras, in *Discourses of Extremity*), this refusal has had consequences, indeed dire consequences. I would say that, while this limitation does not cancel the real achievements of the Russian and Chinese revolutions (in their actual socialist periods), overcoming this limitation is absolutely essential for any future Marxist project. Overcoming this limitation is absolutely essential for any future Marxism, for that matter, but I take the first overcoming as more important, as this has to do with the future of our world, and not just the future of a particular radical social theory.

In this part, I will carry these first two levels of inquiry, regarding the ethical reconfiguration of Marxism and the deep-going critique of economism, into a third level and a fourth level, concerning quite specific "sites" of ethical inquiry, and the history of Marxism as applied in specific revolutions, respectively. Under the third heading, I have chosen two issues that have hitherto received little attention in a Marxist context, namely the question of ("nonhuman") animals and the question of place. Each is a worthy question in its own right (and there are areas of interrelation between the questions), but I also choose them precisely because Marxism has been resistant to them. I take this resistance to be demonstrative of Marxism's resistance to the ethical "as such" and Marxism's tendency, an inherent tendency I would argue, toward economism. Indeed, on this latter point, the difficulty is that Marxism (or simply the thought of Karl Marx, to be direct about this) entails a critique of reification, and yet Marxism, especially when it becomes only a structural "science" of the causality of things and interests (where interests are conceived as something like the forces and directions of bodily motion—and, again, it is not that we should not study these questions) seems itself to reify. In practice, especially in the practice of Stalin in the leadership of the Soviet Union, but not only there, this orientation has had, again, dire consequences. The willingness to use people, or, even more deeply, to understand persons under the category of what Heidegger called the "standing reserve," has at the very least alienated many people who might otherwise have been eager to get involved in the effort to change society. Among those who have maintained their enthusiasm, but rejected Marxism (even if retaining aspects of Marx's analysis of capital), there is an anarchist trajectory that runs from Emma Goldman's "If I can't dance, I don't want to be in your revolution" (and she might well have placed "revolution" in scare quotes) to the critique of "state philosophy" in contemporary, post-Foucault and post-Deleuze anarchists such as Antonio Negri, Michael Hardt, and Todd May. The anarchist critique of Marxism (especially its more recent, theoretically-sophisticated manifestation in the work of the figures just mentioned, for instance in books such as *The Political Theory of Poststructuralist Anarchism*, by Todd May, and, for that matter, in the "primitivist," "anti-civilization" arguments of John Zerzan) cannot be treated adequately here, but two of its persistent questions certainly ought to be thematized: Can Marxism be fixed, such that it overcomes the tendencies that I described under the heading of the first two levels (the resistance to ethics, and the tendency toward economism and utilitarianism), and, Even if Marxism could be fixed, why would we bother with this reparative work at this late stage?

Crisis and Conjuncture

Marx argued that crisis is an inherent part of capitalism, and Lenin and others provide arguments for what the crisis tendencies of capital mean in the era of imperialism. I have argued, in a post-Marxist vein, that crises in capitalism and imperialism represent possibilities and openings rather than absolute necessities and inevitabilities. (I accept that crisis is inevitable in capitalism, but not that the outcome of crisis will "ultimately and inevitably" be communism, for the sad fact is that the outcome in our contemporary world may instead be the outright destruction of humanity.)

Rather than call this line of reasoning "post-Marxist," I aim instead for a "postinevitablist" Marxism that is reconfigured in terms of ethical themes. And yet I accept the validity of the challenges offered by at least some of the recent anarchists (even if I do not accept their alternative proposals) regarding some of the basic problems of Marxism, and I accept Ronald Aronson's challenge regarding the question why such a reconfigured Marxism ought to even be called "Marxism" anymore, though what the thing is called is hardly the most pressing issue. However, I think that I am retaining and attempting to carry forward enough of the analysis of Marx, and, for that matter, the analyses and practices of Lenin and Mao, that it seems right to associate what I am doing with Marxism and even with "Marxism-Leninism-Maoism," or simply "Maoism."

Lenin's term for the way that the contradictions of capitalism come to a head is "conjuncture." In the era of imperialism, the conjuncture is a point of both global crisis and global opportunity. (Here one might be mindful of the poet Friedrich Hölderlin's dialectical formulation, "Where the danger is greatest, there the saving power is greatest also.") Such a focal point, Lenin argues, is a rare moment, when years and even decades are compressed into a matter of days.

> It is not so *often* that history places this form of struggle on the order of the day, but then its significance is felt for decades to come. *Days* on which *such* method of struggle can and must be employed are equal to *scores of years* of other historical epochs. (V. I. Lenin, "The Collapse of the Second International," cited in Lenny Wolff, *The Science of Revolution*, 175; italics in original)

Such moments, Lenin argues, must be seized—and in these moments the form of life changes. "Normal times" are suspended; there is an opening. An opening for what? Neither the exact form of the opening nor what arises to transform the situation can be predicted with certainty or even with great confidence. Indeed, on the latter score, the "what arises" will either be irruptively new and different, or it will simply be something already in the order of the day, in the established order.

However, it can be said, in a Marxist and Leninist spirit, that both the anticipation of this irruption—the preparation for seizing "the opportunity for advance that *presents itself*" (Lenny Wolff's formulation, 175; my italics)—and the irruption itself must speak in the language of ethical-political universalism.

The complication is that the irruption *itself* establishes the truth of the new, emergent form of ethical-political universalism, or at least the *form* of this universalism. To understand this rather large topic, we must study the idea of the conjuncture—the idea of an irruptive sea change—especially in light of the relationship between ethics and ontology. For the moment, let us simply mention that two thinkers who are very helpful in thinking through these problems are Louis Althusser (see especially *Machiavelli and Us*, 5–32) and Alain Badiou (see especially *Ethics: An Essay on the Understanding of Evil*, 40–61). (There is also a debate to be had here between the different conceptions of the "event" in Derrida and Badiou; again, however, this is simply to announce yet another project that will have to be pursued elsewhere.) The notion of conjuncture maps well enough onto Thomas Kuhn's well-known distinction between "normal science" and "revolutionary science," the latter being a situation where there is a change not only in the theory regarding some particular domain, but even a change in the root terms and language used to understand the *world*. We say, for instance, that Einstein's world, and the world "after Einstein" is a different world from Isaac Newton's. Without worrying at the moment how *incommensurable* such "different" worlds are (I accept, for the most part, Davidson's argument in "On the Very Idea of a Conceptual Scheme," where the issue is presented as one of translatability and where a radical failure in translation would at the same time represent an inability to see that there is a "language" there to be translated in the first place), my main interest here concerns the status of ethics before the conjuncture, the sea change, or radical break, which is to say ethics in "normal times," but specifically the "normal times" of imperialism.

"Normal Times"

After all, it is in such normal times that we must do what we can to make people ready for that which "presents itself," for the day which must be seized. This means, however, taking account of who these people are—in their tremendous diversity, of course—as "ordinary people" in "ordinary times," but where the "ordinary times" here is the ordinary functioning of imperialism before the deep crisis and the conjuncture that may develop. The point is that we who live in and have grown up in imperialist countries are ourselves subjects formed by imperialism—we are imperialist subjects—and this form of subject-formation extends into most strata of society. It is not wrong, from a strategic standpoint and as a matter of political economy, to map the different interests at work in these strata, and to show that perhaps the majority of people even in the imperialist strongholds (even in the United States) have no long-term or "deeper" interest in the imperialist system. (I do question, however, the efficacy of the term "deeper" in a postmodern society where depthlessness and superficiality are powerfully active cultural principles—as represented quite well, and I do not mean this as a joke even if there is a funny side to it, by politicians of extraordinary vapidity such as Ronald Reagan, J. Danforth Quayle, and George W. Bush. This is a *systemic* question, and not just a matter of taking potshots at easy targets.) It is also not wrong to recognize that, *on one side of things*, we are talking about "ordinary people" who are simply trying to go about their lives, many of them, possibly most, simply caught up in the difficulties of day-to-day life. "Someone else in the same situation would be trying to do the same thing," we might say. But there is another side of things: as a matter of political economy, the spoils of imperialism (even if these are only "crumbs from the table," relatively speaking) are spread over a great deal of imperialist society, and not to address the ways in which subjects are not only "fed" (with material goods) but also formed psychologically (even if formed in an increasingly depthless way) in explicitly ethical terms, in terms of what we ought to do (or even what we ought to try to do) and what we ought to care about in this grossly unequal and unjust world, will mean giving in to economistic notions and strategies of interest. That would be wrong, ethically, and it is also the case that we will never change the world that way, because capitalism cannot be beat at its own game.

"Ethical Leadership"

Revolutionary leadership, therefore, must be *ethical* leadership, which means no kow-towing to the many temptations of economism under imperialism, which, simply to be direct about it, will largely take the form of attempting to convince people that they are not doing as well as they think they are under imperialism, and they will do much better (materially) in a socialist system. That is both unethical and opportunistic. Yes, of course people who are truly in desperate straits even in an imperialist country such as the United States will be materially better-off in a postcapitalist society, and it is not wrong to say this. Here we are talking about a class that more approximates what Marx meant by the proletariat. But, even here, to say nothing of the broad masses in an imperialist society, where the proletariat is a minority, the leadership must be "ethical" leadership, which is to say aimed toward the values of a good society as opposed to the present, *evil* society. Imperialism vastly complicates class struggle, perhaps most of all within an imperialist society itself—which means not only an imperialist economy but everything else that issues from the class hegemony of the imperialists, including the larger culture and the organization of the means of violence in the police, the "justice system" more generally, and the armed forces. More work in political economy is needed for understanding what imperialism has meant for the working class globally and in the imperialist countries themselves. This will mean, among other things, understanding better the gender and ethnic compositions of different divisions of the working class in different countries. Philosophically, it means transcending the language of interest, especially where that language plays into economism. This does not mean not mapping interests and understanding what interests there are in different sectors of society, but it does mean understanding the basic Kantian point that, in a general sense (which of course means in a necessarily messy, variegated, and contradictory struggle), the logic of interest in itself will not lead to the good, it is only through the thematization of the good itself that a better form of society will come about.

Lenin and Mao, I would argue, understood this point in a general kind of way, even while Lenin, like Marx, resisted the language of ethics per se. Lenin's critique of economism comes into full force especially in his exemplary internationalism, even while, it has to be said, Lenin at times endorsed a brutal expediency that cannot be separated from the resistance to ethical language. (There is also the peculiar fact that, when Lenin and others attempting to address issues in a Leninist or Maoist vein do take up ethical discourse in a self-conscious and explicit way, this is often in connection with practices of sexuality, where the essence of "proletarian morality" seems to be focused on "sexual morality"; Bob Avakian and I discuss this issue in our book, *Marxism and the Call of the Future*, esp. 238–62.) Mao did not seem to have as much resistance to this language, and of course many of his popular formulations have a distinctively "categorical imperative" ring to them—probably most of all the famous statement, "Marxism consists in thousands of truths, but they all come down to one thing: It is right to rebel against reactionaries." Perhaps Mao's ethical slant (or at least the "discursively" ethical slant of his arguments and concentrated formulations) came from two sources: (1) his distance—formatively, geographically, intellectually—from the European centers of Marxist orthodoxy; (2) his understanding that a socialist alternative to Stalin had to be formed. In neither case, however, did this understanding or experience reach the point of systematic integration. Even though Maoism, especially when fully understood as carrying forward the contributions of Marx *and Lenin*, represents a new stage in the analysis of imperialism, and therefore a new stage of Marxism, there still remains much to do in integrating the various parts of this new Marxism—a task made complicated by two facts: First, there is the need not only to bring the Maoist project into greater systematic focus, there is the even more pressing need to transcend this project, in the form of a new synthesis, in our contemporary world. Second, there is always the problem, with revolutionary Marxism, of flying by the seat of one's pants in a world that has to be addressed in practice as well as theory, a world that is constantly changing and posing new challenges—and thus our theoretical practices cannot always "set the stage" (the dramatic activity of *theoria*) so neatly, there is a tendency toward fragmentary and episodic "bursts" of theoretical discourse. Even so, this discourse needs to be more integrated and systematic. The question then arises, around what pivotal point should the integration occur, and my answer to this question should be quite obvious by now: the ethical.

We will explore Maoism (and Lenin and Stalin) further in section 3 below. Now let us turn to two questions that are important to the project of a Marxism cutting its teeth on ethical discourse. My aim is, rather than exhaustively to investigate these questions, merely to put them on the table—something that has not yet been done in Marxism—preparatory to putting the questions on an agenda.

1. The "Animal Question"

There are not only many "animal" *questions*, plural, but there are even many animal questions for Marxism. Only two of these questions will be raised here, but each is raised in recognition of the fact that Marxism has been resistant to any and all animal questions, even while Marxism is deeply implicated in asserting the animality of humanity. Indeed, one might ask if Marxism is even possible without Darwin (perhaps especially given that Marxism today cannot help but get involved in the defense of Darwin and of biological evolution more generally). My first question involves the difficulties that philosophy and "reason" generally have with the animal question, here narrowed to the specific issue of vegetarianism, and what we might learn from these difficulties. My second question is related to what I ultimately find to be the reason for these difficulties, namely an inquiry into the systematicity of carnivorism, especially in the age of industrial food production.

a. Vegetarianism and the Limits of Philosophy

Philosophy, What Is It Really Good For?

What does philosophy amount to? What are the connections between philosophy and the world of actual ethical decisions? These are questions that have been posed throughout the whole history of Western philosophy, from Plato to Marx, with the latter perhaps raising it in the most direct terms in his famous Eleventh Thesis on Feuerbach. Marx scoffed at vegetarianism and those who advocated for the ethical treatment of animals. Though one might connect his attitude toward animal questions with the usual "arguments" that one hears against vegetarianism (that "people are more important than animals," etc.), surely there is an intersection here of

Marx's attitude with his general perspective that the entire discourse of ethics is nothing but a distraction. A fruitful line of inquiry might compare Marx's rejection of ethics with Nietzsche's, as both are concerned with the machinations of power and hierarchy (morality for Nietzsche necessarily being "slave morality," which must be opposed by the irruptive transvaluation of all values—an argument not *necessarily* at odds with at least some kind of Marxist perspective). Perhaps Marx had more in common with Kant's claim, which is hard to square with the latter's deontology, that even a race of devils could create a good society if the constitution were written in the right way. (In "Ethics and the force of history" I argue that Kant was not being a very good Kantian when he made this essentially Hobbesian argument; see my *Politics in the impasse*, 105–21.) For Marx, and, I would argue, for Kant as well, there is a way in which the fundamental ethical questions are subsumed under the question of how society is constituted— which is to say that each carries forward Aristotle's argument that the possibilities of the good person, the good life, and the good society are deeply interconnected. This is a very large question of the relationship between ethics and political philosophy, a question that hovers over this entire book. Here I would like to pursue what would at first appear to be a much narrower question: Why is it the case that not all philosophers are vegetarians? It will turn out that the question is not so narrow after all, and that the pursuit of it is quite helpful for thinking about the place of ethics in Marxism, and the relationship between ethical discourse and political philosophy.

In a Nietzschean vein, some philosophers have raised the worry that vegetarianism, especially if it takes a "philosophical" form, which is to say that it is motivated by ethical concerns, is an opening to moralizing and self-righteousness. The latter is, *above all*, to be avoided. Indeed, in some versions of this claim, it would be worse to proselytize for ethical vegetarianism than it would be to remain within the system of carnivorism. ("Carnivorism" may not be the most apt term—on the other hand, it sounds right—but there is more to the animal question than whether or not a particular individual eats animals; there is a fully global system at work that is based on such subsystems as the "meat factory" and the distribution channels for meat and meat by-products.) I reject this Nietzschean claim at root because I do not accept Nietzsche's conception of power (not that it is not insightful), and, more superficially, because it seems unlikely that persons advancing moral claims (yes, perhaps sometimes inauthentically or hypocritically, or as masks for agendas of power, but still) are truly one of the real dangers in the world today.

The arguments for vegetarianism are powerful. The arguments against vegetarianism are weak, and they cannot be made powerful by the way they are formulated. Therefore, either philosophers should all be vegetarians, or there is some intrinsic limitation within philosophy such that it fails on some important points to move even those who are (one would think) most concerned with it. (Both of these things could be the case, of course.)

Life is more complicated than that, some would say, and I accept that, but this complexity is simply a restatement of the second disjunct just given. In some crucial way, philosophy seems to fail—or, is it instead that philosophers fail to be philosophical? Whether the failure of some philosophers to be vegetarians speaks to a larger failure of philosophy itself is undoubtedly a difficult question, and I should not leave it as given that there is more here than the fact that not all philosophers live up to the calling of good philosophical thinking, and drawing the requisite conclusions for living, at all times. However, there is at least a part of this question that hinges on the problem of what philosophy is. If it is simply a matter of philosophers sometimes failing to be philosophical (of living up to the demands of the better argument), then we can rest with the notion that philosophy is something like the pure operation of reason, or perhaps this combined with the most objective descriptions of phenomena of which we are capable. Another model of philosophy might take the philosophical activity as not unrelated to purified rationalism and neutral empiricism as regulative ideals, but also see philosophy as deeply embedded in history, social relations, and life practices. In this model, these factors also crucially shape the terms and language in which we form and pursue philosophical questions. In a fascinating essay that gave impetus to the project of analytical feminism (feminist theory that applies the approach of analytic philosophy), Merrill Hintikka asks how language itself could be sexist. In a similar vein, we might ask if language could be carnivorist—and, if so, how so. Fortunately, the argument I offer from this point on does not depend on resolving this exceedingly difficult question.

Vegetarianism and "Arguments"

One complexity is that arguments against vegetarianism rarely even rise to the level of what would ordinarily be taken to be arguments—especially by those who are in the business of arguments—and often what is put forward as an argument against vegetarianism is downright stupid. "Got to have those steaks!" a good friend, a philosopher of otherwise tremendous sophistication (and not a Nietzschean), once said to me as an explanation for why he is not a vegetarian. However, this sort of case, where what is being given is the description of a drive or a desire, not even presuming to be a statement on the level of ethical discourse, might actually be preferable to what some people put forward as "arguments" (I will turn to some of these shortly). Then, however—turning to programmatic concerns about philosophy and its limits—one still has to wonder why the level of cruelty represented at the family dinner table, described by Peter Singer in his famous "Down on the Family Farm" essay, does not rise to the level of ethical consideration. What sort of society and culture underlies what seems so deep in the consciousness as to be down there close to what R. G. Collingwood called "absolute presuppositions" (in this case, the presupposition of what Derrida calls "carno-phallogocentrism"—which, however, is not "absolute," in the sense that we can thematize at least part of the issue), such that *even many philosophers*, if I can put it that way, are quite insensitive to the moral dimensions of the system of carnivorism?

A "Won" Argument

My thoughts on the inadequacy/outright ridiculousness of antivegetarian arguments were recently reinspired by reading Colin McGinn's review of the second edition of Peter Singer's *Animal Liberation*. (This was republished in McGinn's *Minds and Bodies*, 207–14.) McGinn does a nice job (from a vegetarian perspective) of restating most of the silly things one hears, so I will quote from him just to show the discursive state into which some philosophers devolve. McGinn doesn't mince his words and his preliminary formulaic statement is worth quoting, since it encapsulates a big part of the argument that I am trying to make here:

> our treatment of animals, in every department, is deeply and systematically immoral. Becoming a vegetarian is only the most minimal ethical response to the magnitude of the evil. What is needed is a complete revolution in the way that we deal with other species. Do not expect, then, to find me in any way "balanced" on the question: this is not really an issue on which there are two sides. It's a won argument, as far as I'm concerned—in principle if not in practice. (207)

A similarity might be noted, as regards issues of truth, politics, and power, between the "won argument" that McGinn is referring to here, and the way that biological evolution is also a won argument "in principle if not in practice." (I return to this complex of problems in the conclusion.) It would seem that neither issue—vegetarianism or evolution—speaks so well of the "force of reason," and then we are reminded of what Marx said about intellectual debates between capitalism and communism, that it is not debate that will decide the issue. I'm also mindful of the old adage in chess, that there is nothing so hard to win as a won game.

The cast of McGinn's claims, which I respect for their stridency as much as for their content, are taken here as bedrock—what I am interested in is instead the meaning for philosophy that there is a "won argument" out there that seems to be little recognized. (And this seems to go as much or more for those in the academic field of ethics.) McGinn says that, if he had written the words I just quoted

> twenty years ago [in the late 1970s], I would have been accused either of shocking moral arrogance or of mild insanity. Even now I am sure that I shall be charged with exaggeration and hysterical extremism. Extrapolating from the changes of moral outlook that have occurred in the last two decades, however, I predict that 2010 will most likely see me accused of euphemistic soft-pedaling. Why wasn't I more scorchingly critical of the countless animal abuses that scar the moral record of *Homo sapiens*? Why did I hold back from pressing the historical parallels with more widely conceded forms of violent oppression? Where was my moral rage? The reason, future reader, is that an air of moderation is prudent when your audience still thinks that eating the dead bodies of intensively reared animals is quite okay morally, really not such a bad thing at all. You have to sound as if you take this to be a matter for serious moral debate, even when you know very well that the opposition doesn't have an ethical leg to stand on. (208)

Let us note that statements such as the final one in the passage just quoted, that "the opposition doesn't have an ethical leg to stand on," are often cited by this opposition as evidence for a far-greater offense than meat-eating, namely self-righteousness or moral self-satisfaction. It is worth noting that, when this critique is posed from a Nietzschean perspective, the aim seems to be to debunk ethics, not to restate Kant's argument about heterogeneous motives (that is, doing something for some other reason than its being the right thing to do).

McGinn also presents a highly quotable, compact description of the scene that every vegetarian knows from being in the company of carnivores for a group dinner. I've been tempted to write my own account of such a scene, which I often encounter when dining at philosophy conferences, which I would title, "I'm sure you can get a salad." (I also cannot help recalling the philosopher who is well known in continental philosophy and philosophy of religion asking me across the dinner table why I am a vegetarian while himself eating veal. There is something philosophically instructive about this kind of scene—with which every vegetarian is well familiar.) However, to be fair, it seems quite likely that the percentage of vegetarians in philosophy is higher than in other fields, so the point is not that philosophers are less sensitive on this issue than other people. Instead, I am attempting to pose as problems the fact that (1) not all, in fact not even most, philosophers are vegetarians, and (2) that philosophers often give as "arguments" against vegetarianism the same sort of silly and insensitive stuff that one hears from anyone else. The point, however, is not to impugn the moral integrity of philosophers, per se, each of whom in his or her life, including his or her "dietary life," is an individual human being going through life a day at a time and dealing with daily problems, including the problem of what to eat. There is a parallel here to the problem of "ordinary life" in "ordinary times" *in an imperialist society,* namely that our lives in such a society are formed from the ground up by the imperialist organization of society, and this "marks every atom of our being" (to use one of Derrida's expressions, to which I will return in the conclusion). What could mark us more in our daily lives than our dietary practices? A very large part of the animal question in our era is what has been "normalized" and made "ordinary" in food production. Just as with the imperialist shape of society more generally, our dietary practices are formative and carry with them values and intentions, and yet all of this (the formative qualities of the practices, values, and intentions) are damnably hard to thematize, and especially to thematize as a matter of ethics and responsibility. Philosophers, as individual human beings who face the daily grind for the most part just like anyone else does (or perhaps it is anyone else in the middle classes, but this is a complex issue), are subject to the same pressures of the normal and ordinary. Instead, if anything is impugned, it is the scope of philosophy itself, the real world that reason runs up against and often has difficulty penetrating. I would like to think that good philosophizing would make every philosopher into a vegetarian. Perhaps this line of thought is simply a subordinate part of the wish that the philosophical study of ethics would make people ethical (a wish about which Kant was skeptical). Clearly, the *is/ought* gap marks a difference between the questions "What can I know?" on the one side, and "What ought I to do?" and "What may I hope?" on the other. (Kant differs with Plato here, on the question of knowledge and virtue, and this opens the way toward the notion of radical evil.) Again, the reason for saying this is that the argument for vegetarianism is a "won argument," and yet that *in itself* (or perhaps "by itself") does not make even philosophers into vegetarians, even when good arguments are supposedly their very *raison d'être.*

Typical Claims

Just for the sake of good form, let us rehearse the sorts of things that people offer as "arguments" against vegetarianism, or at least in justification of eating animals. I will do this even though I completely agree with what McGinn says about balance—indeed, it is offensive to be "balanced" on this issue in roughly the same way that it would be to offer "equal time" to racism or the defense of slavery or the defense of misogyny and patriarchy or Holocaust revisionism. And yet one of the arguments for meat eating is that we cannot place the arguments against it in the same sort of category as an ethical issue involving human beings. Let us begin here with the standard list: (1) eating animals is justified because human beings are more important than animals; (2) (the related but slightly different claim that) no justification for eating animals is required, because human beings are more important than animals; (3) human beings, as rational animals (or as *zoon politikon*), are the sorts of beings who have and can claim rights, nonhuman animals are not; (4) human beings are carnivores by nature, as a result of biological evolution; (5) human beings are carnivores by their God-given nature, as the crown of creation and those to whom dominion over nature has been given; (6) many other animals, including many other mammals, eat other animals, and human beings are animals too; (7) human beings are at the top of the food chain; (8) other meat-eating animals would eat human beings, given the chance; (9) human beings have souls, other animals do not; (10) human beings have consciousness, other animals do not; (11) other animals either do not experience pain, or do not experience pain in the way that human beings experience pain; (12) other animals are not future-oriented in the way that human beings are; (13) human beings need protein and other nutrients that can only be obtained from animals; (14) women, especially, need nutrients that can only be obtained from animals—and thus vegetarian and animal rights arguments are part of a patriarchal ideology or even strategy (this last claim represents a recent twist to the argument, as put forward by Kathryn Paxton George in *Animal, Vegetable, or Woman?*); (15) finally, and this one is perhaps even less of an argument than the others, eating animals is justified because it is just the case that life is cruel.

My aim here is not to attempt a systematic refutation of these claims, though a few things ought to be said. The systematic refutation is developed at length in works such as Peter Singer's *Animal Liberation*, Tom Regan's *The Case for Animal Rights*, Carol J. Adams's *The Sexual Politics of Meat*, Michael Allen Fox's *Deep Vegetarianism*, and H. Peter Steeves's anthology, *Animal Others*. If anything, I would hope that the flimsiness of these typical claims would stand out. I appreciate the work that Singer and Regan and others have done, but I also think the case against the antivegetarian arguments is presented quite well in the "Lisa the Vegetarian" episode of *The Simpsons* (the satirical television series that consistently proves itself brilliant in the critique of American society).

However, let us say a few things in response to the list given above. If there is no baseline agreement that inflicting pain, suffering, and cruelty upon innocent creatures without some sufficient and overriding justification is wrong, then probably there is no "human," characterological basis for the discourse of ethics to get started in the first place. This is to return to themes presented at the very beginning of this book: if a person does not have the baseline sense that to rip a baby from its mother's arms and throw this child into an oven is bad, if a person does not have the baseline sense that to enslave other human beings is bad, then there is no basis for engaging this person in discourse regarding right and wrong. As with Jeffrey Dahmer (to pick a very easy example), this person has become, through whatever process, fundamentally separated from humanity. The solution to this inhumanity is not argument or discourse. (The tragic paradox is that the solution also cannot be to engage in inhumanity toward the inhuman; perhaps there is no good solution to the problem, even apart from the problematic humanistic discourse employed here.) To give as a justification that "*life* is simply cruel" is not a response to ethical arguments, but instead a negation. It is the sort of thing that, on one level, deserves no response, at least not to its "argument" (or its argumentative claim), and yet, as a *pathology* this sort of thing does require response, and there is an important sense in which this pathology connects most deeply to the animal question and the dinner table.

The Importance of Being Human

Often the claim that humans are more important than other animals is instead expressed in words such as, "What I care about is people." In either case, even granting the idea that humans are more important (whatever that means), it is hard to see how this concern for humanity is fulfilled by the grotesque cruelty toward other animals that is integral to the industrial food production system. It is also hard to see how this kind of claim does not then issue in a hierarchy of importance among humans, even on the matter of basic human rights, and we might note that three ways in which people are abased are represented in the interrelated terms of demasculinization, infantilization, and animalization. The root problem is in the assumption that it is wrong to treat a human "like an animal," but it is all right to treat an animal "like an animal," where there are no moral limits. Yes, people do object to the cruel treatment of animals when taken in some "singular" way—the abuse of pet cats and dogs being the obvious example. Certainly, there is something to be learned from this "singularity" of the pet, or the pet who is understood to be a "member of the family" and who gets to be a "who"—even a "she" or "he"—rather than an "it." Perhaps the larger lesson, however, concerns the millions and millions of "food animals" who do not get to be singularities, even within their own species and otherwise natural (nonfood industry) environs. This is why it does not hurt to remind some people that their beloved cat or dog or bunny rabbit is dinner in some cultures. Kant, while apparently no vegetarian (though looking at the few drawings of him, it is hard to believe he ate anything) or specific defender of animal rights, did recognize that the way people treat animals is emblematic of the way people treat each other. Kant lived, of course, before the time of industrial food production.

Carnivores

The idea that humans are evolved as carnivores rests on shaky ground. Certainly it is the case that we are physiologically equipped for eating animal flesh; physiologically, we are omnivores. The ability to adapt to different conditions is a great survival mechanism, to be sure, and it seems quite likely that the human capacity and propensity for eating meat developed during the last ice age (roughly thirty-five thousand years ago), when vegetable nutrition was scarce. However, two things can be said about humans as carnivores. First, we humans, as conscious and communicative creatures with many abilities, can do all sorts of things, including have interpersonal discussion about what we *ought* to do. We can murder people, we can physically and psychologically abuse people—heck, we can even eat the flesh of people. It is also the case that the capacities we have that allow us to do these things also allow us to do many other things. For that matter, it can be added that other animals do not generally use their capacities wantonly or rapaciously. Of course, the fact that very few people, especially in the imperialist countries, deal with their "food animals" directly, or even as whole animals, but instead as packaged bits of meat (which, as Carol J. Adams demonstrates, has its pornographic, fetishistic, and misogynistic sides), adds a further complication, one that is analogous at least on some levels with imperialist "action at a distance." None of the complexities, however, obviate the basic point that we humans can decide, in light of ethical considerations, what to do with our capacities.

Second, while it is obviously true that humans have at least some minimum capacity for eating meat, this in itself does not make our species "true carnivores." We humans can also *not* eat meat, and there are whole cultures in which meat is not eaten, and this cannot be said for species that are truly carnivorous and cannot survive without eating meat. There are many mammals that eat meat, including the aforementioned cats and dogs (but not the rabbits), but the specific branch of the mammal class to which the species *Homo sapiens* belongs is the primate order, and all of the other primates are vegetarian. It is sometimes pointed out, as some sort of "argument," that one sign of humanity's evolutionarily preprogrammed carnivorism is that we have two sets of incisors in our mouths (teeth, that is) that are called "canines," and these are for ripping through animal flesh. This nomenclature is itself representative of carnivorist ideology. (It is also one of those ironic places where the antivegetarian is willing to say that we are like some other animal—in this case dogs—in some respect, but we remain "higher" and "more important.") Monkeys also have "canines," and if you have ever seen a monkey eat an apple, it is clear enough what they are for. (I propose that we henceforth call these human teeth our "monkey teeth"!) Lastly, comparing the procurement (hunting or scavenging), eating, and digestive practices of true carnivores to the practices (in those same domains) of humans shows clearly that humans are not true carnivores. Besides the obvious fact that no other animal cooks meat, there are other facts that should be just as obvious but are somehow overlooked by antivegetarian polemicists. Most carnivores will eat the whole animal, including the intestines, bowels, and anus. Some carnivorous animals that come upon, say, a dead squirrel, will eat everything there, including the maggots. True carnivores have much shorter digestive tracts, because it is not good purely from a health standpoint to have animal flesh in the system for a long time, and there are many human health problems related to having animal flesh in the system for long periods. All of this is of course apart from what is done to animals in the industrial food production system to render them for consumption, which contributes greatly to the many health maladies associated with meat-eating in recent decades.

Respect for Antivegetarians

A little story might illustrate something about these last two points (about humans as carnivores, from either the ethical and physiological standpoints) and their relation to my larger point, about the limits of philosophy. In the spring of 2001 I presented some of the arguments that make up this part of the present book at a session of the Central Division meeting of the American Philosophical Association. During the discussion period of the session, a fellow philosopher identified himself as a professor at an agricultural university in the Netherlands, and introduced his comments by saying that people in Northern Europe and people working at agricultural schools were having a terrible time dealing with the outbreak of foot-and-mouth disease in cows. Optimistically, I thought this fellow's next remark would be something to the effect of this being a good time to become a vegetarian. Alas, no; instead, I was taken to task for not sympathizing with the difficulties faced by meat eaters and for not respecting antivegetarian arguments. I reiterated that my point was that in fact there *are no* antivegetarian arguments, only flimsy rhetorical strategies and willfully accepted justifications for something that people want to do and have been conditioned to do, and that my main aim was to ask why philosophy has such a hard time dealing with this flimsiness and willfulness, especially on a matter of such importance. (My suspicion, not voiced then, is that it is precisely because of the importance of the matter that philosophy has a difficult time with it, or at least many philosophers do.) Later that evening, at the conference reception, this same fellow approached me and again upbraided me for not showing respect for antivegetarian arguments. I could have pointed out to him that he has a vested interest in the food-animal industry, given his employment by an "agricultural" institution. Instead, I finally relented and said, all right, give me an example of such an argument. He said that, for instance, a certain philosopher points out that a cat will eat a bird. (It's true, I've seen it happen.) Having had a long day and feeling rather punchy, I shot back, "Yes, and a dog will take a crap in your yard, what lesson do you draw from that?" We had reached the point of the discursive gap and each simply turned around and walked away. However, though I recognize that the gap existed for my erstwhile interlocutor as well, what needs thematization is that it is right that the gap opened up, the gap would have been there even if I had not responded somewhat rudely and testily. In other words, what does it mean to argue with something that should not be afforded the respect of a philosophical argument, the sort of thing where, yes, if an "ordinary person" had said it, I would have been more than willing to work through the issues. My *best* reaction to a fellow philosopher, however, would have been along the lines of "*come on*" or "*please.*" Recognizing, though, that every person I am seeking to communicate with here may not be a professional philosopher, let us review: (1) a human being is able to ask certain kinds of ethical questions that a cat apparently cannot (and yet, again, cats do not hunt birds rapaciously or set up vast "food-bird" production facilities); (2) cats are indeed true carnivores by their evolution and physiology; humans are not. These points would surely resonate with anyone who cares about arguments, as opposed to slim ideological justifications—except that, here again, we are up against the difference between knowledge and caring (about what ought to be done, about what may be hoped for).

Rights

Justifications for carnivorism that lead through the discourse of rights are on difficult ground as well. At the most general level, even if it can be said that animals do not have rights, this is not the end of the question. A tree may also not have rights, but that in itself does not justify harming it or cutting it down. The same could be said for a mountain or a river. Perhaps this is not a problem from the perspective of "everything not prohibited is permitted," but surely there is more to a thorough consideration of ethics than this. Furthermore, it is not as if the case for human rights is philosophically airtight, either, and the supposed justifications for denying rights to animals (that they are not the sorts of beings that make a claim for rights, or have consciousness or language or souls) rebound upon certain categories of humans too (babies and young children, the mentally disabled, people in the advanced stages of senility or Alzheimer's disease—and for that matter why not include the many people who seem to be the complete products of the soulless system of commodity production?). It is mean, cruel, ugly, and grotesque what is done to animals in the system of industrial food production, and this treatment surely cannot be justified simply because there is a question whether or not a human philosophical construct applies to animals. (On the other side of the coin, I do not mean to imply that rights are not important and real; but that is a different conversation.) There is an interesting connection here, perhaps difficult to see at first, between rights-based justifications for meat-eating and our old friend, "might makes right." Suppose we say that the question of whether or not animals have rights is a philosophical "blind corner." In ordinary cases of blind corners, whether or not one goes around them with hesitation, slowly, or quickly and quite possibly recklessly, may depend on what sort of vehicle one has. The pedestrian or bicyclist may be more careful, because he or she is more vulnerable. The driver of the big truck or SUV may just charge right through, figuring that he or she will be protected from the possible consequences.

Realistically, human beings are no longer in the food chain. There are philosophical and religious traditions recommending vegetarianism and the just treatment of animals (in other words, the treatment of animals according to a standard of justice, and not just according to human preferences) going back to Pythagoras and beyond (the ancient debate in the West and its relation to contemporary discussions is traced in fascinating detail by Richard Sorabji in *Animal Minds and Human Morals*), when more of a case could be made that humans were part of the food chain and where there might have been more of a basis for saying "they eat us and we eat them." I still do not think the argument works, hence the debate going back thousands of years. However, there is also an historical turning point to be marked, and that is the passage into the preponderance of industrial food production. In the era of such production, there is no food chain with other animals (and plants) of which humans are a part. It can be added that it was not only Heidegger (in a way that was historically insensitive, to be sure, but not inaccurate) who said that "mechanized agriculture equals mechanized death," but also Isaac Bashevis Singer who said, "For the animals, it is an eternal Treblinka." (Charles Patterson has written an important book on this comparison, basing his title on Singer's statement: *Eternal Treblinka: Our Treatment of Animals and the Holocaust.*) The more recent grotesque atrocities that have to be added to this equation are the massive cattle and hog lots of recent decades, with tens and even hundreds of thousands of cows and pigs crammed close together, standing in their own excrement. To this can be added the more recent "innovation" of fish and shrimp "farms" in the middle of deserts and other places far from the oceans, where these creatures swim in a chemical soup and, again, in their own excrement. Meanwhile, the actual oceans are largely fished out, and the industrial "fishing" methods (which are to fishing what industrial food production is to agriculture) that are employed these days are akin to strip mining, destroying underwater habitats wholesale. None of this has anything to do with some archaic notion of the "food chain."

Future Orientation

While it is likely true that nonhuman animals do not have, and cannot have, a sense of future-orientation the way that human beings potentially can, why would we make of this fact a justification for cruelty? It may be true that, for the most part (with some possible exceptions), nonhuman animals cannot be understood under the category of Heidegger's "being toward death." In the same vein, it is unlikely that it can be said of most nonhuman animals what Heidegger says of the human being, that she or he is the sort of creature for whom death is an issue. (Even though I agree with Heidegger on this point, a great deal hinges on what is meant by an "issue," and we might wonder what it means that human beings can be acculturated such that the unjustifiable and grotesque slaughter of untold millions of animals is *not* an issue.) On the other hand, it seems clear enough, and no anthropomorphism is needed to make the case, that most animals in the prime of their lives do not want to die, and they will do what they can to avoid death. Pigs have the misfortune of having skin that is very similar to human skin, and for this reason all sorts of noxious products are tested on pigs. One of the products tested on pigs was napalm. I once saw some film of such a test, and the screams of these pigs will remain with me for the rest of my life. This is not a matter of comparing this grotesque horror to some other grotesque horror that has been done to a human being—though it is significant that the horror done to the pigs was for the purpose of inflicting horrors on human beings. What would be the point of such a comparison? What would be the point of arguing that the horror is greater when the victim is a human being, even if the point might be granted? The sort of person who would dismiss my concerns here (as trivial, as mere sentimentalism, or as somehow not respecting the difference between animals and humans and not affording sufficient importance to the latter) is not the sort of person who will ultimately play a positive role in transforming human society in a good way. Perhaps more work is necessary in order to make claims such as these into systematic philosophy (to say nothing of "scientific" Marxism).

There is a bridge here, on at least two levels, to the arguments I will put forward in the next section. One level, obviously important for a Marxist analysis, is the way in which the mode of food production and the mode of (daily) bodily reproduction is integral to the mode of production more generally. When we think of the latter, there is a tendency to think of metal and concrete and smoke billowing out of smokestacks. But of course the production and transport of food is a very big part of production, and, in the modern world, it involves a good deal of the metal, concrete, and smoke (perhaps the latter most of all in transport). A second level, perhaps one that fits readily enough into the base/superstructure distinction, but that also shapes the elements of that distinction, has to do with the relationship between culture and psychology. At the very least it is a bizarre, even if "normal" and "ordinary," psychology that holds that a person can show how much they care about human beings by participating in systemic cruelty to animals. Here, clearly, some animal solidarity is called for. There is a longstanding association in many human cultures between eating meat and happiness, as evidenced in the idea of *carnival*— the root of the word, of course, is *carne*, Latin for "flesh." The meat industry plays on these associations in advertising, in ways that are sometimes subtle (perhaps more subtle than understood by the people who design the advertisements) and sometimes quite direct and even crude. The origins of carnival, or the "meat time," however, are in prehistory, when the main practice of food acquisition was gathering, mainly by women, and when male hunting parties would be away from the village for weeks at a time. When these groups of hunters returned to the village with their prey there would be a festival. However, the mainstay of these villages was the vegetable matter that was gathered, and thus the entrenched term, "hunting and gathering," is itself representative of carnivorist ideology and patriarchy. This lifestyle and dietary practice has very little in common with contemporary practices.

Souls

Is there a connection between future-orientation and an essential and intellectually thematized concern with mortality, on the one side, and the having of a soul, on the other? The irony here, at least as regards Christianity (and perhaps Judaism and Islam as well), is that, if there is a connection, then the soul really is a "human" thing, it arises in a specifically human context and is an emergent property of humanity. In other words, there is no necessary role for God in this stage of "ensoulment."

Otherwise, in the Christian scenario, it seems just as likely that other animals have souls. Add to this that Adam and Eve did not eat animals in the Garden of Eden; indeed, the Bible says that Adam and Eve (and God, for that matter) communed with the animals. Furthermore, when food is supplied from heaven, as with the Israelites in the desert, this "manna" is clearly not animal flesh. In the Abrahamic and many other traditions, the eating of meat is associated with the fall from grace. Finally, as in a number of domains, we might ask why "dominion" has come to mean, in some interpretations, something cruel, rapacious, ruinous, and so on, rather than something like caring stewardship. Of course, many (nonfundamentalist) Christians do have this view of things, and there is a growing literature that develops this perspective as regards the animal question. (See, for example, Richard A. Young, *Is God a Vegetarian? Christianity, Vegetarianism, and Animal Rights*, and Andrew Linzey, *Animal Theology*, where there is a proposal for "liberation theology for animals" as well as for "vegetarianism as a biblical ideal.") There is a kind of Christianity, unfortunately, in which "God so hates the world," and where the believers take it as their duty to hate the world and everything in it as well. After all, we are born in sin in this world, and we can hardly turn around without sinning further—what a miserable place. Here is a contrary thought. One way we ought to empathize with other animals is to understand that our human lives matter no more than theirs if there is some cosmic scheme of "mattering." (I return to this problem of materialism and mattering—that is, meaning—in the conclusion, specifically in the context of the longstanding relationship between religion and ethics.) Perhaps obsessive carnivorism is a kind of manic denial of this condition of not mattering (and on more than one level). There seems to be a deep human resentment toward the innocence of animals.

Meaning

Experimental, post-Christian religious thinker Don Cupitt claims, in books such as *The Way to Happiness*, that we would do well to emulate the animals and plants in our perspective on meaning, which is to say that we ought to give up the desire for any larger meaning and live as best and brightly as we can, in the moment. (Cupitt is much influenced by Buddhism in this perspective.) In *Emptiness and Brightness*, Cupitt argues that the only point to life is to burn brightly until we burn out, and then, "that's it," there is nothing more, and none of "it" (or "it all"—Cupitt has based an entire theory on a kind of Wittgensteinian reading of common terms—"everyday speech" and "ordinary language"; see Leaves, esp. 91–100) means anything, at least in some larger scheme. (Cupitt in his later works changes his identification from "post-Christian" to "empty radical humanist," and is even comfortable with the term "nihilism.") Though I find much of Cupitt's work insightful and provocative (and refreshingly direct), I wonder if it is constitutive of the human form of being that we cling tenaciously to the idea that there is some meaning to existence, and that, if the meaning is not to be discovered, then it will have to be made. Cupitt is a postmodern thinker in that he recommends not only giving up on some cosmic scheme of meaning (his work, and the "Sea of Faith Network" which he has inspired, represents one pole of a fascinating bifurcation in contemporary Anglican and Roman Catholic Christianity, the other pole being the reassertion of logocentrism in the "Radical Orthodoxy" trend—John Milbank, Catherine Pickstock, and others), but also there seems to be no place for "the future," as a philosophical category, in his work.

What is humanity, however, without the future? (Recall the passages I quoted from William James in part 2, concerning optimism and pessimism as definitions of the world.) I would say that humanity without the future is what capitalism progressively imposes upon humanity, beginning with the idea that our world (and the living beings in it, including people) consists in things that exist to be commodified, traveling through the idea that history is bunk, and culminating in a postmodern stage where everything is collapsed into the intentionally superficial "now." To be fair to Cupitt, though in fact he does embrace the free market as an aspect of open, public communication, he also understands the now under the heading of radical contingency rather than as an absolute. (On Cupitt and the market, see *Philosophy's Own Religion*, for example, p. 7; another postmodern post-Christian thinker who has become quite keen on the market and on what might be called the nihilist reading of contingency is Mark C. Taylor; see *Confidence Games: Money and Markets in a World Without Redemption*. The subtitle makes the vital connection, even if it is one that is difficult to swallow for right-wing fundamentalists—or for Marxists who believe that the transformation of the world must in some sense be redemptive. By contrast, the Radical Orthodoxy thinkers are quite critical of capitalism, and see it as of a piece with secularism; see, for instance, Catherine Pickstock, "Capitalism or Secularism? Search for the Culprit"; John Milbank, *Theology and Social Theory*, 27–45, 177–203, and 380–434; and Graham Ward, *Cities of God*.) On the other hand, Slavoj Žižek has helpfully—I think—pointed out the affinity between postmodern capitalism and a certain Buddhism, at least of a sort that is attractive to some Western intellectuals and middle-class, New-Age seekers. (See Žižek, "From Western Marxism to Western Buddhism.") History drops out; is there a redemptive sense of history that remains from Judaism and Christianity that might still have a positive contribution to make in the transformation of the world?

I raise these points regarding the place of animals in Christianity (especially) not only as a response to the particular things some self-identified Christians say. The same *Marxist* theodicy that subsumes human singularity under History or that forgets about persons in the name of "The People" would hardly have a place for animals—and it would hardly have a place for anything that deserves to be called ethics, either. A Christianity that is unable to thematize and embrace as an ethical issue the idea that the immense cruelty done to animals in modern industrial food production is horribly wrong is an awful Christianity—some would say not a very Christian Christianity. There are even some in the Christian fundamentalist camp who say that vegetarianism and a concern for animal flourishing is itself anti-Christian, indeed "satanic" and evil. I think it is time to take the gloves off regarding this sort of thing, and perhaps especially so for others who call themselves Christian—it is no longer a matter of hoping for one big, Christian tent where the fundamentalist and the "liberal" Christian can get along. (In other words, liberals—Christian or otherwise—need to think more deeply about what calls itself "conservative" in the post–September 11 world.) The kind of Christianity that calls vegetarianism "satanic" *is itself evil*, it is promoting a terrible evil. I am interested in what we can learn about good and evil from this example, but, again, I am especially interested in what a Marxist perspective can learn.

Resistance to Animals/Ethics

If anything, Marxism has a harder time making a self-critique of this sort than Christianity does—because Marxism resists both ethics and the animal question, and it is at this point that the ethics of the animal other appears to be the very essence of ethics. As David Wood puts it, in an essay on deconstruction and humanism,

> The question of the other animal is an exemplary case of responsibility . . . , even if for that reason it may seem too good. It is an exemplary case because once we have seen through our self-serving, anthropocentric thinking about other animals, we are and should be left wholly disarmed, ill-equipped to calculate our proper response. It is exemplary because the other animal is the Other *par excellence*, the being who or which exceeds my concepts, my grasp, etc. ("*Comment ne pas manger*," 32)

It would not be a stretch to say that it is from animals that we humans learn ethics, or learn something crucial about what ethics really is, and by this last I mean *real* ethics as a resistance to mere utilitarianism and calculation based on interests. This is very, very important, in itself and for the project I have proposed in this book, because there are plenty of inter-preters of Marx and Marxism who argue precisely that the Marxist project is all about a certain kind of class calculation. Clearly I disagree with this perspective on all kinds of grounds. One of these grounds is that capital-ism is the calculating machine *par excellence*, and that any attempt to beat this form of calculation—which has reification at its core, and this aspect has special relevance to the animal question—at its own game is doomed either to failure or to mere reinvention of capitalism, even if it is called instead "socialism" or what-have-you. This does not mean there is not a place for calculation (for instance, even in the sense of cost accounting under socialism, though this must be radically transformed in the transition to communism and the transcendence of commodity production) in the struggle to change the world. To take a simple example, to carry forward a just struggle involves strategy, and one part of strategy is a measurement of the forces that are arrayed on the battlefield (whether literal or in some broader sense)—in other words, tactics. But, at the end of the day, if cal-culation is "all that it was all about," and winning means no more than that "our side" beat "their side," then there may be winning and victory, but this is not justice.

A great deal of the first part of Derrida's *Specters of Marx* is taken up with this question, and the elided words in the passage quoted above refer to responsibility "in Derrida's sense." In setting out this responsibility as regards animals, which is a responsibility we learn from animals or "the case of animals" (or the "animal question"), Wood demonstrates the Kantian cast of Derrida's thinking, and the Kantian cast of something that needs to be learned—by Marxism, or by whomever is open to learning something about ethics and responsibility, but my argument in this book is that while we need Marxism, more than ever we need a Marxism that has been recast in ethical terms. The following passage from "*Comment ne pas manger*" demonstrates the conceptual difficulties of an ethics that exceeds calculation.

> There is a place for argument, proof, and demonstration in philosophy. I have insisted on its critical function. . . . But I have also suggested that what this crit-ical function opens onto are more or less motivated *possibilities of response*. As far as our relations to other animals are concerned, nothing is prescribed. Or if there is a prescription—thou shalt not kill—we are not obliged to listen. Or if we are obliged to listen to this prescription, this proscription, we do not have to respond. And if we do have to respond, nothing determines how we respond. (33)

The problem is that responsibility is in its very nature underdetermined, for, if how we respond is already fully determined, this would be simply the mechanical calculation of "more or less motivated possibilities of response," but not actual responsibility, not an actual response. And yet there is no ethics, either, if this underdetermination results in mere skepticism, quietism, or frustration (which is not to say that the matter of the ethical is not continually frustrating, as is the matter of the political). One could say, in the spirit of Kant's opening sentence of the *Groundwork* (only the good will is good without qualification), that it is in the striving to do good that the *matter* of ethics is concentrated. However, as in the case of the understanding, striving cannot be understood without its object. Otherwise, the good will does not get us beyond an empty formalism (one version of which is a purely ideal scheme "in the heart," so to speak, concerning which God will either reward or punish each of us). Although Kant did not address directly the problem of the materiality of ethics or the ontology that is presumed by his arguments about ethics (the "ontological commitments" of his language, to use Quine's helpful term), he pointed the way toward at least a certain materialist conception with his arguments about intersubjectivity, intentionality, and objectivity.

Rational Animals

In my view, and as I have indicated previously, these arguments, as part of a materialist approach to philosophy, ethics, and history, are brought into post–linguistic turn focus in the work of Donald Davidson. In that respect it would be valuable to mention Davidson's perspective on nonhuman animals, where he argues (in the well-known essays, "Thought and Talk" and "Rational Animals") that consciousness is intimately related to language; nonhuman animals, not possessing language (or being possessed by language, as the case may be), do not have consciousness. (Davidson's main aim is to show what language and consciousness are for human beings, it should be added, and only secondarily to say something about nonhuman animals.) However, Davidson argues that, if anything, the conclusion to be drawn is that humans should give even more consideration to nonhuman animals; in this respect he cites Jeremy Bentham's well-known claim that the relevant question is not whether animals can think, but instead that they can feel. I do not mean this to be the end of a discussion on animal thought and consciousness, but instead only to underscore the basic point, that the immense cruelty done to animals in the current food-production system and through human participation in that system is a great wrong that calls us to ethical action. Furthermore, and to repeat, the animal question gives us the very model of such a call.

"Life Is Cruel"

Lastly, as regards the kinds of things that are typically said in defense of carnivorism, let us turn to what ought to be thought of as the last refuge of scoundrels, the claim that it is simply the case that "life is cruel." Though this is a claim that is rarely presented as some sort of developed, philosophical (or ethical) argument, it is in fact absolutely bedrock, for the dinner table in the modern, economically-advantaged world is not only the scene of unspeakable cruelty (as Peter Singer argued in the first sentence of "Down on the Family Farm"), it is indeed a *school* of cruelty. The carnivorist dinner table is a place for inculcating the lesson that life is cruel and that a young person, as she or he matures, will have to accept this tragic fact. Indeed, learning (or "learning") that meat is "real food for real people" ("it's what's for dinner," and so on, and I could easily imagine a deconstructive analysis of the way that the copula is casually folded into a double contraction, subtly and powerfully hiding what precisely is the *is* of the animals that are consumed) is perhaps the most normal aspect of social normalization in the modern consumer society. Carnivorist normalization has it all, from the most tangible involvement with the body, to the deepest recesses of the mind. (This normalization goes to the subconscious mind and to the unconscious—in this latter case, demonstrated quite simply by the association of meat and the carnal, "carnal pleasures," and so on; investigation into these matters would be part of a larger discussion of carnivorism and the limits of reason.) In 2005, the Mexican government presented to the United Nations a resolution for the commendation of Mexican food on UNESCO's list of the "Masterpieces of the Oral and Intangible Heritage of Humanity" (as reported in Inter Press News Service, NPR, and elsewhere). Just to be clear, Mexican food was proposed under the category of the intangible, not the oral. Perhaps it is because I like Mexican food that the idea of its intangibility strikes me. There is a tradition in Western philosophy, certainly, that takes vision to be the sense most connected to reason, so that clarity and distinctness, to use Descartes's standards for example, are understood on a visual model (the inner light is our guide). Eating, of course, involves more than the sense of taste, much more, and yet to situate the work of the eyes at the center of a model that then takes the work of the tongue as on the periphery of epistemology is part and parcel of a model that can understand food as intangible.

One could go further here, I suppose, and examine what is excluded from Plato's realm of the forms, for example, dirt and excrement. This latter pair, however, "make the world go 'round," as they say. Furthermore, nutritive topsoil is in fact largely made of excrement—from ants and worms. Here perhaps we are a little closer to the grounds of our being, pun intended, and therefore of reason—or "Reason" and its exclusions and marginalizations. I will return to these grounds in the section on the question of place, and in part I am just having a little fun here. After all, what could be *more tangible* than the set of practices associated with what we put in our mouths and process through our bodies? In the case of meat-eating, what could be more tangible and more *intimate* than the body-to-body relationship, from the animal body to the human body, that is involved in every instance of meat consumption?

Animal Embodiment

This "involvement" is the ground of both reason and deconstruction—or certainly one of the grounds or perhaps the very model of what we might understand to be the ground. In this most intimate of relationships, of (human) body to (animal) body, so much is done to obscure the animal body. The work of deconstruction is to show that certain normalizations are based upon a double work of obscurantism, first of that which is made obscure (a process that quite often involves reification, a rendering into mere "thingness"), and then a cover-up of this cover-up itself. Certainly it can be argued that there is an even deeper movement, that which normalizes the idea that there are "things" to begin with, and an analysis of this movement would help us to both thematize the real stuff of ethics and to understand the basis for the reductive tendencies in Marxist materialism. Even Derrida, in the working out of his own philosophy, had a blind spot with regard to vegetarianism, and the question might be whether this blindness carries over into deconstruction itself. David Wood explores the issue:

> A carnivorous diet, it is true, is only the most visible and violent front of our undeclared war on the creatures with whom we share the planet. Although Derrida may seem to be bringing deconstruction down to earth when he says, for example, that "deconstruction is justice," this formulation actually reinforces the separation between deconstruction and any particular concrete practice. Deconstruction is a practice of vigilance and cannot, as such, become some sort of ethical seal of approval. Why then am I tempted to declare, in the face of Derrida's sidestep on this issue, that "vegetarianism is deconstruction"? Vegetarianism, like any progressive position, can become a finite symbolic substitute for an unlimited and undelimitable responsibility—the renegotiation of our Being-toward-other-animals. But it can also spearhead a powerful, practical, multidimensional transformation of our broader political engagement. Derrida's ambivalence toward vegetarianism seems to rest on the restricted, cautious assessment of its significance; one which would allow vegetarians to buy good conscience on the cheap. But Derrida does not thereby avoid entanglement in the paradoxes of "good conscience." For the avoidance of that

widening path of resistance to violence that is vegetarianism could end up preserving—against the temptations of progressive political engagement—the
kind of good conscience that too closely resembles a "beautiful soul." (32)

We are once again troubled here by a classical philosophical theme, understood under the various headings of "knowledge and virtue" (Plato and
Aristotle), "empty formalism" (Kant and Hegel), "theory and practice"
(Marx), and "good conscience" (Nietzsche). Does the person who resists
the duty not to eat animals (because the practice of eating animals is cruel)
simply not know what he or she is doing? While I would not want to join
the rush to throw out Plato and Aristotle on this point (as many reductive
Marxists and other reductivists would tend to do), Marx does contribute
an important reorientation on the matter of what "knowledge" is, exactly.
We might pursue some of the larger implications of an orientation toward
practice, whereby it might be held that the "truth" of a material practice is
always on the lower part of Plato's divided line (never rising above the level
of mere opinion). In the most extreme versions of this "truth-orientation,"
neither the ethical nor the political has anything to do with real knowledge.

In Marx there is an inversion, already seen dramatically in the famous
"conversion letter" that Marx wrote at the age of nineteen to his father:
"From the idealism which, by the way, I had compared and nourished with
the idealism of Kant and Fichte, I arrived at the point of seeking the idea
in reality itself. If previously the gods had dwelt above the earth, now they
became its center" (MER, 7). We can fill out the basics of this inversion
with formulations concerning "the rise from the abstract to the concrete,"
and so on. For the purposes of the present discussion, however, we need
go no further than two recognitions: (1) that, where practices of cruelty
are concerned, there is no separating theory and practice; (2) any philosophy, whether that of Plato or Kant or Derrida, and I daresay even Marx,
can be turned into an empty formalism, especially when the difficulties of
changing practices and institutions run very deep. To take Wood's argument one step further, we do not even have to get into the "unlimited and
undelimitable" in order to show that the efforts of individual vegetarians
hardly amount to a drop in the bucket against the quantitative enormity of
the meat production and consumption system. This quantitative aspect has
to be underscored, even without denying either Wood's claim that vegetarianism "can also spearhead a powerful, practical, multidimensional
transformation of our broader political engagement," or the things we
ought to do because they are right (or the things we ought not to do
because they are wrong), regardless of what anyone else does. All of us,
vegetarian or not, *live* in a system of carnivorism, and in that sense we participate in the carnivorist system, even if in some small way we do not participate in it if we are vegetarians. The problem of the "finite symbolic

substitute" exists throughout every arena of ethical and/or political endeavor—especially in the case of the ethical when this is confined to the "merely interpersonal," the field where individuals are treated with respect (to the extent possible given other social parameters) but the social system in which persons are rendered "contemptible" (to use Marx's word) is never addressed. And yet it might be formulated as a principle that each of us *must* take the step that *can* be taken, even given the limitations of a particular step at a particular time in a particular situation, but also in respect of those limitations and the larger systemic issues that must ultimately be confronted.

Perhaps the most brutal normalization of the reduction to mere thingness is encapsulated in the last refuge of justification for intimate harm and oppression: life is cruel. Not to recognize this "reality," at least in the final analysis, can be the very definition of unreasonableness. An examination of the "reasonable" and the "unreasonable" does not, perhaps, take us to the commanding philosophical heights of Reason and the Abyss (or Heidegger's *Abgrund*), but these categories do help us understand processes of normalization and acculturation. Colin McGinn remarks upon Peter Singer's observation that children are often sensitive to the matter of what the food on the plate actually is. McGinn writes of a postcarnivorist future, where the narrow horizon of speciesist right will have been crossed (these last words are my pithy adaptation from Marx's "Critique of the Gotha Programme"); significantly, he connects this crossing with the possibility of overcoming other forms of oppression. Indeed, the intertwining of themes in the final paragraphs of his essay is what I am attempting to give a more systematic treatment to here.

> Old habits and powerful vested interests will thus eventually succumb to moral common sense, and one of humankind's greatest tyrannies will collapse like so many others before. As a bonus, there will be enough food to feed the world's hungry, once plant protein is no longer wasted on fattening unnecessary food animals for the better-off. The deepest form of exploitation and institutionalized death in human history will have been eradicated, making other forms of oppression psychologically harder to bring about, because less built into our daily lives.
>
> I suppose such a rosy future is not impossible, though in my experience we shouldn't bank on ordinary civilized adults to bring it about: we need to appeal to the natural moral instincts of the preindoctrinated. As Peter Singer remarks, children very frequently express their horror at the origin of their dinner and wish to become vegetarian; it can take a lot of adult cajoling or worse to wean them off their sound moral standpoint. Children are the natural friends of animals, and paying them more respect might be the best way to get animals liberated. Put more practically: animal activists should work to ensure that the facts of animal life under human dominion are taught in schools and made

generally available to the young. Put speciesism on the curriculum. To parents I say: do you really want your children to blame you for keeping them in the dark about all the rotten things we do to animals? Wouldn't you prefer to be able to boast to your grandchildren that you were in the vanguard when animals were given their freedom? (*Minds and Bodies*, 214)

I agree with each of the assertions made here, as well as with the general way that McGinn has shown the intermotivation of his themes—with perhaps the proviso that, exploring this intermotivation to the next step brings us up against the carnivorist *system*. That is, our ideological blindness that, in the final resort, comes to a justification of brutality, cruelty, and the most grotesque reification in the name of *reality itself* being cruel, is rooted in a comprehensive social system that works on every level of human experience, from the economic to the ideological, even integrated into gender, race, and class relations. McGinn points in this direction when he highlights the basis on which the human oppression of other humans is psychologically tenable—even if the oppression of animals is not the only basis. Surely, even on a superficial level it does not hurt to point out that the standard moral intuition that it is wrong to treat a human being "like an animal" accepts the notion that it is all right to treat a nonhuman animal "like an animal." For many children there comes a point when this distinction is questioned at the dinner table, when a child realizes that she or he is eating the leg of a chicken (this seems to do it for many children, because a chicken leg or wing more clearly looks like what it actually is) or the haunch of a cow or pig. Not recognizing this distinction brings down every resource of "reasonability" and every other emotional resource ("cajoling or worse"), so a child signals his or her reasonableness by "taking the pill"—eating the meat that your parents worked hard to provide for you. At one and the same time one signals one's willingness to be reasonable and one's desire to "grow up" and be "mature," by recognizing a basic fact of life, that life is essentially cruel.

Ideological Machinery of Carnivorism

However, carnivorist reasoning could not work on all of these levels and on such a vast scale if there were not a carnivorist system. Even without yet establishing more clearly what it means that carnivorism *is* a system, it can be seen that this system has no hesitation about going directly into action when anyone attempts to take McGinn's advice and takes even the most simple and innocent steps to inform children about alternatives to meat-based diets. A simple story illustrates this point. Carus Publishing Company, the parent company of Open Court (the publisher of the book that you have before you), also publishes a children's magazine, *Muse*. In its March 1997 issue the magazine published an article about young people who are either vegetarians or who at least have questions about eating animals. While the story did contain elements of animal rights and vegetarian advocacy, it also said that each person has to think about this issue for themselves. Specifically, in answer to the question, "Is meat eating right or wrong?" the conclusion offered was, "We can't give you the answer; you have to decide for yourselves." Certainly the story demonstrated well that there are alternatives to eating meat, and it gave some basic descriptions of the cruelties of the factory farm system and the ethical problem of "unnecessary pain." The article offered a model for critical thinking about issues that are for most part taken for granted in our society. Of course the meat industry could not allow this small effort to pass. In the form of the National Cattlemen's Association (the cover of the magazine featured a photograph of a cow above the words "Please don't eat me!"), and in part because the magazine had an arrangement with the Smithsonian Institution, the meat industry was able to pressure the magazine to present the views of meat-eating young people in a subsequent issue. As is so often the case, the demand was for "balance," as if American society is not permeated with inducements toward meat-eating.

(There is an analogy here to the imperialist empire in which every corner, nook, and cranny of the globe figures into "national security." One outstanding example, in my opinion, is the case of New Zealand in the mid-1980s, during the Reagan period, which did not want to allow U.S. naval ships carrying nuclear weapons to come into their ports. Suddenly, New Zealand's unwillingness to follow every edict and instruction from the United States became a "vital" national-security matter.)

What is going on in the world, in society, in the minds of people, with "reason" itself, when the final resting place of rationality as maturity and reasonableness is the recognition that life is, in the end, cruel? Can a Kantian argument on this point go much further than the recognition that "out of timber so crooked as that from which man is made nothing straight can be carved"? Such an argument is not far from being narrowly circular (though perhaps not every "circular" argument is bad, if the "circle" is big enough): life is cruel, human nature is fundamentally flawed—everything goes to some harsh reality. It is hard to imagine Kant wanting to stay with such claims in the end. For one thing, consider his claim, which seems to run in the entirely opposite direction, that "even a race of devils could form a good society if the constitution is written properly." This famous line, from "Toward Perpetual Peace," indicates that a decent social order can indeed be carved from the crooked wood of human subjects. It seems to me that Marx carries forward this line of thought from "Perpetual Peace" and other of Kant's historical essays, that the shaping of "reason" to serve cruel ends is a social, institutional, and systemic phenomenon, not simply the proper result of a coldly analytical reading of reality. (Recall that Marx argues that Hobbes's characterization regarding life in the "state of nature"—that it is "solitary, poor, nasty, brutish, and short"—is instead a reflection of Hobbes's own society.) We might also argue, in a Sartrean spirit that perhaps goes more deeply to something in the core of Kant's thinking than Kant himself always does, that even a cruel reality would not excuse intentional or negligent cruelty on the part of any particular human person. Every young person can see the inadequacy of the appeal to the notion that "life isn't always fair" when used as a justification or excuse on the part of the person who him- or herself is being unfair. The same can be said about cruelty. Surely it can never be enough, in the face of grotesque cruelty and injustice, to take recourse to mere ontology: that's the way things are. We need to be both Marxist and Kantian on this matter. A Marxist would say: we can say a good deal more about the social relations that present us with this supposed ontology. (An analogy can be made to "natural disasters" that are in fact thoroughly social.) A Kantian would say: the way things are is not necessarily how they ought to be.

Ontology, Necessity, Anomaly

Recall the concluding claim of part 2: "Theoretically and practically speaking, this means that 'ethics,' the question of the possibility of ethical relations, has to be granted at least a certain autonomy. 'Let the ontological chips fall where they may,' it could be said. However, this approach is at the same time what I would call the very essence of a 'materialism of practices,' which, for Marx, forms the basis for any ontological investigation that is in the more strictly philosophical realm. The irony is that Marx is overly *philosophical* in his concentration on an ontology of necessity, while there is only ethics when there is contingency and possibility." The ethico-ontological problem is one of conceiving of a materialist ontology that has space (this last term can be taken quite literally) for real human agency, which might be characterized as the meeting place of real intentions (in the sense of intentions that are not causally predetermined) and real actions (in the sense of human movements that are the outcomes of intentions). In other words there has to be a space for what we might call, following Davidson (with a slight twist) the *human anomaly*. Of course, there continues to be a vigorous debate as to whether the proper recognition of this space leads to ontological dualism. (For example, see not only the responses to Davidson by Jaegwon Kim, as well as Kim's work more generally, but also Derrida's response to Levinas, the former's well-known essay, "Violence and Metaphysics." Also see Hilary Putnam, *Ethics without Ontology*, which deals with Davidson, Derrida, Levinas, and Kant.) Is it instead the case that there is just so much more of the starry heavens (and everything else, recalling Carl Sagan's charming remark in the *Cosmos* series, that is made out of "star stuff"—this includes the complex chemicals in our human bodies and brains) than the "moral law within" that a *brute materialism* of pure mechanism *absolutely overwhelms* any and all anomalies—of meaning, interpretation, consciousness, caring, the ethical, humanity. This absolute, "in the end," serves as a kind of cosmic reminder that, "life is cruel"—though even this goes too far: "in the end," life is meaningless, nonexistent. So why care about creatures (including humans) who can experience cruelty?

Let us, for now at any rate, not get too caught up in reminders of human finitude. While such reminders are, I think, important at every level of human activity (and every level of philosophical activity), it can also be said that we are not yet "at the end," and the ethical imperative is that we who can do something good, something to make our society better, something to save our world from destruction by ourselves (for it is not the gods or some cosmic machinery of necessity that has placed humanity in its present predicament), have an obligation to do what we can in the time and space that we have and in which we find ourselves. (Obviously I am trying to cover all bases here!) However, it can be said for the moment that what Kant, James, and Sartre demonstrated phenomenologically is the structure of commitment that is necessary for there to be any sense of the starry heavens (which themselves cannot be explained in terms of purely mechanical causality) or anything else that seems to be a purely "given" reality that works according to laws of pure necessity. (Quine and Davidson work in the same direction, though from a different—and crucial—angle, as it were, in terms of problems of language, meaning, and interpretation.) None of this trumps the possibility of "objectivity"—that lousy word for the lovely fact that we live in a common world and the world has seen fit to share a bit of itself with us. Yes, yes, I know that this last bit hardly sounds "objective," indeed it sounds "religious" and/or Heideggerian.

Ethics and Finitude

Indeed, in a contrary motion, it could be said that it is absolutely unclear what obligation would mean except under the conditions of dwelling in finitude. That is not only the problem with God, but also with at least certain notions of political sovereignty, that there are no limits and no finite creature can say what obligations apply to either God or the "true sovereign." (For a commoner to pay compliments to the emperor is an insult.) Indeed, these two—God and sovereignty—come together in various ways, and not only in the form of emperor-gods or the divine right of kings.

Witness the god-like "sovereignty" claimed by the United States in the post–September 11, 2001 world, replete with theological groundings for the unlimited sovereignty of the U.S. and an explicit doctrine of limited sovereignty for every other nation-state. (This is to say nothing of a president "elected" by God.) In *Rogues*, Derrida argues that such an outcome is inherent in the very notion of sovereignty. (I am mindful here also of the chapter on God and the good in Murdoch's *The Sovereignty of Good*.) Again one can see a basis for resentment against other animals, in that they remind us, in their finitude (it might even be said in their acceptance of finitude, which might even be called a *graceful* acceptance, for even the fiercest lion does not expect to live forever), and in our own human-animal nature, that none of us is in fact God.

I wonder if cyclists who ride on country roads may feel, as I do, an intensified connection with some of our fellow creatures as a result of seeing their dead or dying bodies in the road. (In my part of the U.S. this includes possums, skunks, rabbits, turtles, snakes, deer, cats, and dogs.) Perhaps for some cyclists there is an intensification of resentment as well, and both resentment and empathy are mixed up with the fact that most of these animals have been run over by cars and other motor vehicles and any cyclist who hopes to live to ride on another day has to be mindful of this possibility as well—and essentially for the same reason that animals get run over, namely that of which motorists are not mindful. To paraphrase Marx, and without being overly deterministic about it, there is something to the idea that the mode of transportation shapes consciousness.

While it may be that the sense of "dwelling" (of which Heidegger writes, most directly in "Living, Dwelling, Thinking," but even on a broader view that may not accept all of Heidegger's analysis of the term) that is amenable to human contemplation is not congenial to other animals, there is at least a case to be made for dwelling in finitude *with* our fellow finite creatures (even if "full" *Mitsein* requires *Dasein*). And yet clearly there is not only a set of longstanding traditions (though perhaps most of all the "Western" monotheistic traditions) which asserts a brutal "dominion" over other animals (and "nature"), which arguably forms the model for all other assertions of sovereignty, there is in the last two hundred years, especially, a vast economy that is dependent upon the *unconditional* (therefore "theological") right of humans to visit the most insane and grotesque cruelties upon millions and millions of animals. A good deal of *Rogues*, a relatively short book, concerns the relationship between sovereignty and unconditionality, and it is significant that Derrida deals with the animal question: one model for the "rogue" is the animal that cannot be expected to obey human laws and conventions, so the rogue is a "dirty dog," and so on (see *Rogues*, 69, 93). It is also significant that Derrida subtitled his study "Two Essays on Reason."

Animals/Justice

Perhaps the train of thought pursued here depends on various conflations, and some would recommend a bit of scientific sorting. For instance, a little ways back I let slip what might in fact be a conflation (perhaps several), by the insertion of the term, "injustice." Is cruelty toward animals an "injustice"? How about systematically organized cruelty? Is there a quantitative dimension to this question? Is there a quantitative dimension to the difference between the individual who does something cruel to an individual animal, and the sort of machinery required for "billions and billions" to be "served"? Is there a qualitative difference between cruelty, which surely has to be recognized in the case of any creature that can experience cruelty, on whatever level of consciousness or nerve sensitivity, and "injustice," which might be said to more properly apply to human interpersonal, social, and social-systemic relations? These are not insignificant questions, as they go to the matter of what justice is, exactly.

Biology

It is a commonplace to think that such questions can be sorted in a purely "scientific" way, which almost always requires the marking of some essential human/nonhuman animal difference. Just to pull an illustrative example out of the air, allow me to cite a passage from the novel by Gregory Benford, *The Sunborn*. Benford, one of the major science-fiction writers of the contemporary period, is also a working physicist (a professor of physics at the University of California at Irvine); his novels are very good, both for the elements that make any novel of any genre good (character development, absorbing story, quality of writing) and for the rigorous yet speculative ways that Benford deals with scientific hypotheses. (It is the latter that is generally taken to define the genre of "hard SF," but it is the quality of the former elements that make for the possibility of a hard SF novel that is actually good.) Like science-fiction and utopian novelists in general, Benford reflects the existing culture in various ways; like many such writers, especially in science fiction, Benford reflects the idea that the horizon for any possible future human society is capitalism (though, to his credit, he also reflects the contradiction between the scientist who is motivated by the desire to know and the "entrepreneur"—usually some plucky billionaire out of the Heinlein mold—whose interest in scientific discoveries is overwhelmingly commercial). The passage below concerns the exploration of Mars and the question of food sources for the explorers.

Julia tried to forget the whole hour with Praknor [a corporate space-program administrator], which had seemed like a day, by tending to the rabbits. She fed them, petted them, and tried not to think.

In the last two decades [on Mars] they had mined ice, inflated high-tech greenhouses, and grown crops, and were never in danger of lean diets. But sending meat 100 million kilometers was pricey, so early on they asked for rabbits. The vegetarian movement had continued to grow Earthside, so there were demonstrations, some violent, against shipping rabbits or any other living, high-protein source.

In reply [mission co-leader and husband of Julia] Viktor made a video showing how much grunt work they did in a day, with his voice-over saying, "Hard labor needs solid food."

It worked. Omaha Steaks won the bidding to ship big canisters of beef and the fish Julia preferred to Mars, at their expense. Axelrod [the CEO in charge of the Mars mission] actually made a profit on the deal. The rabbits mated avidly, leaping about, giving them both pets and a long-term meat source.

Julia saw no contradiction between caring for the animals and later slaughtering them, but then, she was a biologist. That wasn't a lot different from being a farmer. And while she had longed for a cat as a pet, she knew the price in meat to feed it. (37–38)

These are characters in a novel, not a philosopher or social theorist presenting an argument, but the text is of a piece with many similar jabs at vegetarianism (and the defense of animals against cruelty more generally). It is not a stretch to assert that Benford is making such a jab.

There is much to consider here as regards "reason," perhaps most of all the most simple sentence in the passage: "It worked." This two-word sentence, with what appears to be the most basic of nouns and what can count, from the perspective of the narrow pragmatism that prevails in capitalist society, as the most powerful of verbs, is a dramatic example of what can be called (after Peter Sloterdijk) "cynical reason." "It" is everything that the author can take for granted about his readership. After all, what does it mean to "convince" the vast majority of the population, who are meat-eaters, that it is all right for a handful of other people to eat meat? Furthermore, "it" is everything that *reason*, in an instrumentalist society, can take for granted about Benford and most other writers.

Still, might one not pause for a moment over the question of the transplantation of the social systems from our planet to another planet, especially into a situation that has to be, by its nature, cooperative rather than competitive and aggressive? To say that animal food sources were shipped sixty-two million miles "at a profit"—so this last makes "it" especially all right—shows the conflation of two social systems of the modern world, capitalism and carnivorism. But these two systems are already conflated in the myth that must be accepted by every reasonable person, that of the absolute necessity of high protein, which itself is a concoction of the profit-based meat industry. There is a bumper sticker I've seen now and then, its words playing at the boundary between irony and cynicism: EARTH FIRST!—WE'LL SCREW UP THE OTHER PLANETS LATER! There is a utopian side to much science fiction in that it at least projects the existence of humanity (or some sort of humanity) into the future. (Fredric Jameson examines this "desire called utopia and other science fictions" in great detail in his *Archaeologies of the Future*; I find this investigation very important both for the fact that it takes the literary possibilities of science fiction seriously—I have attempted to make similar arguments for the musical possibilities of rock music—and for the fact that the book represents a further exploration of the postmodern turn in capitalism, a subject to which we will return in the conclusion.) There is, however, another side to much science fiction that is not exactly dystopian (that is there, too), but that might better be characterized by a more homely word: it is just *sad* to think that all of the ridiculous *crap* that is already destroying our planet would be carried into space and to other planets. (It is undoubtedly significant that the most important novels about the human colonization of Mars, *Red Mars, Green Mars,* and *Blue Mars,* were written by a former graduate student of Jameson's, Kim Stanley Robinson. Among many other achievements, these novels brilliantly explore Georges Bataille's notion of an economy of the gift.) As of this writing, there is talk at NASA of a "manned" mission to Mars by 2050; there is plenty of utopian significance to this idea, in that the presently percolating contradictions of the imperialist system make any long-term prospects for human projects unlikely. We might also consider the projects of scientific exploration and utopian speculation in terms of Kant's questions about hope and ethics, and why the latter must take priority.

There is an echo in the passage, intentional or not, of the extra bit at the end of Michael Moore's film, *Roger and Me,* titled "Pets or Meat." Not that Moore's take on the animal question seems very good; indeed, he seems to reflect the standard form of *workerist* realism, to which Benford's character Viktor is appealing as well, that "hard labor needs solid food." The latter can only mean meat, apparently. However, Benford's passage, and perhaps Moore's "addendum," capture quite well something that is heard quite often, the "animal lover" (almost always the dog or cat lover) who "sees no contradiction" between supposedly "loving animals" and killing them for food. At least two things are at work here. First, there is the question of what counts as a contradiction in the terms of carno-logocentrism and carnivorist reasonableness. To say that a person, with a particular point of view, "sees no contradiction" is not conclusive evidence that there is no contradiction. There are also ways in which contradictions become sublimated, and work themselves out in other forms, just to be a little Freudian for a moment. A lot of what might be called "brutal ideological work" goes into rendering soldiers of imperialist armies such that they can continue to love their families and friends and yet participate in massacres of quite similar people in other lands, without "seeing a contradiction." To do some of the terrible things we do as people, we have to shove certain concerns deep down into ourselves, and then we see, by and by, the return of the repressed in various forms, often very destructive forms. (The wake of the Vietnam War saw and still sees a good deal of this, and I believe that the wake of the current wave of "post-9/11" wars—which however have been configured to be never-ending—will be even worse as regards this question.) But it is probably the case that, concerning animals, carnivorist reason is able to swallow the contradiction—for surely it really is a contradiction to participate in a system of grotesque cruelty against animals and then to say that one loves animals—in a way that keeps it "externalized." (Clearly, a good deal more could be said here as regards the functioning of ideology; on this question I find the most perceptive thinker to be Slavoj Žižek, in works ranging from *The Sublime Object of Ideology* to *On Belief*.) Second, the reasonableness of Benford's character Julia in "seeing no contradiction" is dependent on the fact that her interaction with the rabbits on Mars is undoubtedly and vastly more humane than the human/"food animal" interaction on Earth, and yet (1) the production of meat on Mars remains a subset of overall human rendering of animals into meat (this is seen most directly in the Omaha Steaks—which is a real company—connection, and therefore in the idea that the shipment of "food animals" and meat to Mars can be done at a profit) and, (2) this more humane treatment of the Mars rabbits, therefore, serves as a legitimating ideology for carnivorism in general.

Scenarios of Meat Consumption

Unfortunately, the movement between these last two points is not only a matter of some future scenario. There is an argument, which is either sophisticated or sophistical or both, made even by some proponents of sustainable agriculture and humane treatment of animals, that allows for the human consumption of meat under certain very specific circumstances. This scenario is not addressed in the passage quoted from Benford (or in the rest of *The Sunborn*), but it is implicit, the assumption being that a person tending animals in a caring way and then consuming them as meat, has no connection to the horrors of the meat-production industry. Sometimes the fact that Native Americans consume meat (in certain contexts and with rituals of gratitude) is invoked as support for this position. This argument has been heard from different quarters, among them Alexander Cockburn (who explains at the end of his otherwise excellent introduction to Sue

Coe's *Dead Meat* that he is not in fact a vegetarian, but that he only eats the meat of animals that have been raised in a humane way on his neighbor's farm), from proponents of "resacralizing" our relationship to the animals that we eat, and some of the proponents of the "new agrarianism," such as Wendell Berry and Wes Jackson and the folks at the Land Institute. There is a deep connection among the problems of agriculture and the places of inhabitation for humans and other animals. Certainly, it has to be accepted that there are crucial differences in the different phases of human carnivorous activity, and that the global, industrial food-animal production system of the last one hundred years is a (disastrous, insane) leap beyond anything that ever came before. But such is indeed the system that exists now, and even apart from what may or may not be justified about animal consumption prior to the existence of this system (which, however, and just to be clear, I do not accept as justified), there is no way to be "differently involved" in meat consumption in the contemporary world without in fact (1) participating in the general system by which animals are rendered into meat; (2) thereby serving the function of legitimating carnivorist reason.

Techno-scientific Pragmatism

Lastly, as regards the particulars of the Benford passage, there is what might be called the *coup de grâce* of legitimating ideologies, an authoritarian and what might be called a "techno-scientific" gesture without the subtlety of the "it" (or the "it worked"), namely, "but then, she was a biologist." This simple, seemingly innocent phrase works on numerous levels, including that of cynical reason but not only that. The cynical element leads one to bypass critical thinking, by simply absorbing the phrase under the heading of "I don't know what that means, exactly, but it must mean something." If one does not remain stuck in this mode (which is further aided by the fact that one is reading a novel and therefore one wants to continue with a certain narrative flow), and instead one thinks about the phrase a bit more, the difficulty is then in seeing why one should accept the inferential force of the "but then." What is it that the biologist knows that bridges the gap between "caring for the animals and later slaughtering them"? If one is a biologist, does one see something that nonbiologists may not see, namely that in fact there is no "gap" wherefrom a contradiction might arise? Is it a matter of simply "seeing how life works, scientifically speaking," and therefore being able to take a coldly analytical view of material processes? If that is the idea of what it means to say that, "but then, there is a science of organic matter called biology," it would seem we could just as well say, "but then, Mengele was a doctor." I am not claiming that the Julia character (much less Benford) is something like a "Nazi doctor"; on the other hand, there is a relationship, and it works through the positivistic conception of science and the world.

I will return to this question in the conclusion, but the point I want to underscore is that the "but then" provides a concentrated example of the idea that science can deal with ethical questions by playing its trump card, "knowledge." Marxism, in theory and practice, has often taken recourse to this trump card. As with Julia here, who presumably *knows*, as a biologist, some difference between humans and animals that allows for the care/slaughtering conjunction (some difference that a nonbiologist would not see as readily), the Marxist "science" has itself been on shaky grounds, further complicating the issue of the ethical questions that are trumped by this science.

To sum up, there are two points to consider. First, if ethical questions are not granted at least "a certain autonomy," they will be subsumed in a way such that they are effectively obliterated. Second, good science has to find a way to be both audacious and humble to avoid hubris. Of course, good science does precisely this, because it holds fast to its own self-critical function. However, the pursuit of knowledge never occurs in a vacuum; science ensconced under the profit imperative and under imperatives such as carnivorist reason cannot help but be warped, and so again we see the cynical side of the "but then." The lesson for Marxism is that science can also be ensconced as a "state ideology" (and this can happen even in the case where there is not yet an actual state, as in the case of a vanguard party that is a kind of "embryonic state"), and of course state ideology can proceed with a confident and unquestioned carnivorist perspective, and it will play a large role in what counts as knowledge, and will undermine the self-critical function.

Benford is an interesting and creative writer, especially when it comes to making speculative extrapolations in physics and sometimes their moral implications. (In *Cosm*, for example, Benford deals with the accidental creation of a universe in a particle-collision experiment, and with the question of what moral responsibility the creator has for this universe; in *Eater*, as well as in *The Sunborn*, Benford deals with forms of life that are made of electromagnetic fields—if they *are* forms of life, and the question might be where the limits of a "science of life," which is perhaps "biology" but perhaps more than biology, lie.) None of the foregoing is meant primarily as a moral or aesthetic critique of Benford, but instead as a demonstration of the wiles of carnivorist reason. These wiles are such that many people are very creative and thoughtful in one way or another, but carnivorist reason does its work underneath it all, hardly noticed— though it is significant that Benford felt it necessary to at least mention "the vegetarian movement." Clearly there is some awareness of the significance of extending the system of carnivorism into a place where it has not existed previously.

The character Viktor might have also put in a word for the idea that hard work deserves decent wages. This would seem to be a whole other area of inquiry; however, to pursue the chain of necessary associations between hard work and "solid food" (which is also cynical in that it plays on typical carnivorist assumptions about how difficult it would be to eat tofu), on the one hand, and hard work and decent wages, on the other, both lead us in the direction of systemic matters. (Why is there not *good* work for all? For whom and for what does one work? Why is there a system of employers and wages in the first place?) One of my aims in this book has been to grapple with the difficult problem of showing how the question of the moral status of social systems (and even of social classes) has to "sit alongside" (an intentionally waffling expression) the reality of actual ethical decisions and orientations that are taken by individuals. In other words, to be simplistic about it, to say that certain practices (that are morally questionable, at the least) are "systemic" in character is not meant to let anyone off the hook. No, we are all "on the hook."

How Is Nonvegetarian Philosophy Possible?

To return, then, to the way in which I initially framed the question of vegetarianism and reason: Are nonvegetarian philosophers (and others who claim to be able to think critically) either unintelligent, deficient in the business of thinking in some respect, or extraordinarily insensitive? Perhaps a few are each or both of these things, but this could hardly be the totality of the matter. Thus we turn, finally, to the social-systemic dimensions of the animal question.

b. Carnivorism Is a System

Principles and Complexity

How could anyone, in *good conscience*, reject (what McGinn called) a "won argument"? Perhaps there is more than one strategy at work in such a rejection. In chess, for instance, there is what is called a "won position," but the player in a won position does not automatically win. (As the hallowed saying in chess goes, there is nothing so hard to win as a won position.) Then the recourse is to the idea that "the case is complicated." Well, yes, this could be said, this can always be said, in the sense that it seems that people take the case to be complicated—even while, as a systemic matter, they do not investigate the complex workings of the carnivorist system or the capitalist system with which carnivorism in our time is co-implicated. The same might be said for co-implication in a patriarchal system, or a sex-gender system, and then it is not hard to see how fantastically complex and intertwined the systems of exploitation, oppression, domination, and cruelty are in the world today. And yet, in each case, is there not at least "one simple thing" that ought to be taken into account? Exploitation is wrong. Treating girls and women as lesser persons than boys and men, or as not really persons deserving of fundamental respect, is wrong. Needless cruelty toward animals that are capable of experiencing cruelty is wrong. No complexity, however real and even fantastical, should stand in the way of recognizing these simple truths.

What is the relationship between the "simple truths" and the complexities? Marx is very helpful on the epistemological aspect of this question, and therefore on the way that either ontological or ethical issues have to come to terms with the existence of social systems that consist in relations of production and social relations more generally. In setting up ontology and ethics as being on either side of epistemology, and yet in also putting them together, as at least two sides of the same coin, I am mindful of the Kantian cast of Sartre's sense of the human being as not simply possessing freedom and responsibility, but instead as being defined "all the way down" by freedom and responsibility.

Then the argument in Marxism has to do with either proposing that Marx simply takes this Kantian view of ontological freedom for granted, just as he may take it that it goes without saying that exploitation is morally wrong, or else he at least implicitly—and, certainly it can be shown that he sometimes does this explicitly, in his rejection of ethical discourse—rejects this view, and instead is working from a more Hobbesian-Spinozan perspective on material forces. In the former case, it is a matter of then arguing that what is implicit needs to be made explicit and fleshed out and better taken account of. This describes the whole project of the present book. In the latter case, which certainly represents a "valid" interpretation of Marx, there are two main paths which have been taken in the last few decades, either the methodologically individualist form of analytical Marxism (as formulated by Jon Elster, John Roemer, David Schweickart, among others) or the "New Spinoza" Marxism of Althusser, Negri, Balibar, and others. (There are some interesting connections—for example, Elster was a student of Althusser; some of these connections are helpfully pursued in Andrew Levine, *A Future for Marxism? Althusser, the Analytical Turn, and the Revival of Socialist Theory.*) In general, these new Hobbesians and new Spinozans argue that their perspective is the truly materialist one, and that not only Kantian but also "German idealist" (mainly Hegelian) arguments in general veer into philosophical idealism. (This train of thought begins with Althusser's essay, "The Only Materialist Tradition, Part 1: Spinoza," in *The New Spinoza*, ed. Warren Montag and Ted Stolze.) This is a large and difficult discussion, to be sure, but I remain guided by Lenin's assertion, "better a good idealist than a bad materialist," and would argue that a materialism that does justice to consciousness, language, meaning, and interpretation, which is to say certain fundamental dimensions of what it means to be human (hence the debate over humanism—there is more to it than just the proposal of "objectivity" and the "scientific" critique of the notion that "man is the measure of all things"), as well as to those other places in material interaction where strict causality breaks down (domains covered by quantum mechanics), rather than making these phenomena merely epiphenomenal, has to struggle for precedence. It is a difficult and frankly strange question for materialism itself that the materialism we need is not the one that we *necessarily* have.

Even if there are ways in which Marx's arguments are open to abuse through oversimplification and reductionism (most often in recourse to some form of "one to one" correspondence theory), there is also real explanatory force to the way that Marx sets general parameters for thinking and ideas (good or bad, right or wrong) and consciousness in terms of the mode of production, and social relations more generally, and in the contradictions found in these. (Simply consider Marx's crucial argument that there is commodity *fetishism* because there is commodity *production*; e.g., in *Capital*, vol. 1, in MER, 323; or consider Marx's arguments regarding the "production of ideas" in *The German Ideology*, e.g., MER, 154–55, 163–75.) There is no need for a one-to-one reduction or for the elimination of the sorts of dynamic synergies in which "theory can become a material force" in order to argue that there would be no movement of thought without material movement in general. However, it is also the case that only if the world is *not* such that everything is determined by strict causality that the group of what might be called "humanistic phenomena"—consciousness, language, meaning, interpretation, and our concern for justice and beauty (and I would say truth as well, but this would not be the truth of a reductivist ontology or epistemology)—really count for anything other than merely epiphenomenal effluvia. If these phenomena/concepts do really count for anything, then there have to be ways in which they can work at least semi-autonomously and have (or be a part of) real effects on the material world and the material organization of life. (I do not mean to claim that every "new Spinozan, post-Althusserian, *real* materialist" denies this—there are many vital contributions from this trend of thought, at any rate—but there is a tendency in this structuralism to ascribe to what Foucault calls his own "happy positivism.") Simply to complete the picture (and to repeat), I take Davidson's anomalous monism argument, which is based on Kant's argument concerning intention and causality in the *Groundwork*, to provide the basic model of this "semi-autonomy."

This semi-autonomy, which is at least a bit of *real* autonomy in a world where there are indeed causal chains ("we are spirits in the material world," to quote Gordon Summers, but we are also spirits *of* and *from* the material world), this *anomaly*, is also what Derrida calls a "dangerous supplement," the element that appears marginal and purely parasitic (and it really is such), but that, when taken account of and seized upon, changes the nature of the game. (Perhaps this is the pawn on the seventh rank; it is still a pawn, it is not yet a queen, but the opposing side must reconfigure significantly in order to deal with this little guy.) In the conclusion I will return to the question of what this anomaly "amounts to" (to employ a locution from both Derrida and Badiou, it is a question of "counting"). After all, there is an argument, sometimes called "nihilism" but also a certain "realism," that brute, causal materiality is so quantitatively vast when compared with the human phenomena (or even "spirit," in some sense), that the qualities of the latter count for almost nothing—indeed, effectively nothing. But this is one of the places where there is a politics of mortality (and *immortality*), "life against death" we might say (except that death is not "nothing"), and where we ought to see the affinities of (at least a certain) Marxism with at least a certain lineage within Judaism and Christianity: *let's keep going*, let's go toward life more abundant, let us see what we can make of humanity. That a social system like capitalism, which reduces all qualities to quantities (as Marx puts it in *Capital*, MER, 311) and only values living labor that can be congealed as dead labor (that is, as a commodity with a price), arose at all is really sick and twisted. This is a social system *against life* and against any long-term prospects for humankind—and the problem is that there comes a day when the long-term becomes the short-term, and that day has arrived. It can be said, again, that this is also a system against "life/death," to use Derrida's term from *The Gift of Death*, and therefore it is a system against death, even, and therefore we anomalous humans have to carry forward, in an ongoing and qualitatively transformative way, the struggle against the rendering of human death into meaninglessness.

The Workings of a Social System

This capitalist system, having become imperialist and postmodern in the last century and decades, *is* sick, but it is also a *social* system. It is a mode of production and a consequent way of organizing life, even if it is also a way of organizing obliteration and meaninglessness. In some parts of the world, and through successive stages and qualitative leaps, capitalism arises as an answer to the exhaustion of feudalism. ("No social order ever perishes before all of the productive forces for which there is room in it have developed"; *A Contribution to the Critique of Political Economy*, in MER, 5.) Then capitalism goes on to take over the world. It would be ahistorical to say that capitalism is a cure (for feudalism) that is worse than the disease, but again we have to recognize what Marx didn't recognize, that capitalism could destroy humanity altogether. This is sick and horrible, but it happens precisely because capitalism is a social system, based in commodity production and the private ownership of the means of production, and a ruling class that "is compelled, merely in order to carry through its aims, to represent its interest as the common interest of all the members of society, that is, expressed in ideal form: it has to give its ideas the form of universality, and represent them as the only rational, universally valid ones" (*German Ideology*, in MER, 174). Of course, we have come some distance from the rise of the classical bourgeois classes (in different, emergent, modern nation-states), to the point where the class system is exceedingly complex and the existence of capitalist ruling classes is obscured by a good deal more than "universalist" ideologies.

Ethical arguments need to come to terms with historical contexts, but not to the point where they lose the ability to tell right from wrong. A simple example will illustrate, and this example has the virtue of dealing with private property in the means of production and the existence of social systems. One of Jean-Jacques Rousseau's famous claims in the *Discourse on the Origin of Inequality* is that the first person who put a fence around some land and claimed it as his own was engaged in a great scam. The example is also chosen because of Kant's great admiration for Rousseau. To be fair and more precise, Rousseau said, "The first man who, having enclosed a piece of ground, bethought himself of saying 'This is mine' and found people simple enough to believe him, was the real founder of civil society" (44). The "scam" aspect would seem to lie in the finding of "simple" people, people not intellectually sophisticated enough to realize that there is something fishy about the claim to own something as necessary for the collective good as is land. Why is land any different from air or water in this regard? Under imperialism, we increasingly find that there is no difference, at least in that the air and water are progressively brought under the logic of the commodity as well. Notice the connection between Rousseau's claim and what Marx called the "dirty little secret of capitalist exploitation." In Marx's scenario, the capitalist is not pulling a scam, he is just innocently purchasing the inputs of production—among them, labor power. In the world of Rousseau's thinking, the laborers hired by the capitalist would either have to be "simple," or else they would be saying, "Why would we work for you, rather than for ourselves? And who are *you*, in any case, to be controlling the possibilities and conditions under which we toil? Why should any part of the fruits of our labor go to you, when we are the creators of this value?" There have been many times and places where such questions have been asked, and it is a sign of how far this historical process has traveled that such questions are not heard very much now, so far-flung and obscured has the process of value creation become. This happens, to be sure, in the same upside-down world where Americans somehow think that the people of Vietnam had attacked the United States.

The ideology of capitalism, intermixed with colonialism, ideologies of race hierarchy, ideologies of gender hierarchy, and the transition of capitalism into a fully global mode of production—imperialism—has become, by now, lodged very deep in people, formative of every aspect of subjectivity. Hence, the *necessary* role for radical cultural critique, especially down pathways opened by Adorno and Freud (and, I would say, even if seemingly in a very different register, by Husserl and Heidegger, especially in that they pursue the critique of the culture of scientism and in that Heidegger, especially, does not take modern, "urban ideology" for granted). It is important to mark this role here, because otherwise these forms of cultural critique are not taken up at length in the present study.

Deep Presuppositions

To return to the previous line of thought, *carnivorism* not only runs very deep in subjectivity formation, it runs so deep that it comes close to assuming the character of an absolute presupposition (to borrow Collingwood's term again), a presupposition that runs so deep that it is very difficult to place it on the agenda of social theory and political philosophy. The idea is, instead, that this question must remain in a domain of "ethics," to the extent that it can be considered at all; indeed, a very special kind of "care," in the form of a very special combination of ignorance, mean-spiritedness, obfuscating, and outright silly "arguments," and whatever else is necessary to get the job done must be employed in order to insure that the animal question remains *sequestered* in the domain of "ethics."

Before there could be a "scam" of the fence, that first fence had to be erected. Or is it, instead, that before that first fence was erected, there already had to be people who had become "simple" in such a way that the claim, "this is mine," is believable? In our conversations on this question, of what I was calling the absurdity of owning things that would seem to be the common inheritance of humankind and our fellow creatures, such as land or sunlight, Bob Avakian recognized the "inspiration" (my word) that can come from Rousseau's claim about the origins of private property. However, on the other hand, Avakian had this criticism of my line of thought:

The thing with Rousseau is, on one level, that's true [about the normative force of his claim], but it's not exactly . . . it's also ahistorical. It's not exactly the way things evolved or how they have evolved, that somebody just put up a fence. In one sense it is—there was a certain point at which early communal societies broke apart and other forms which began to have class differentiation and private property did emerge. But it isn't just that somebody said, "I'm going to put up a fence"; because if that had been the only problem, then other people would have said, "no you're not"—and that would have been the end of it. So [there was] something historically evolved that was going on. (*Marxism and the Call of the Future*, 31)

Avakian is right, of course, and in Marx's thought this historical evolution has to do with what he called the "cell form" of what later emerged as capitalist society, namely the commodity (from the very first pages of *Capital*; see MER, 295) and the deepening of the division between mental and manual labor. If we grant that there are other systems working in tandem with the class system, even if not fully separable from the class system (or the latter from them, however), we might ask after their cell forms and their sedimented presuppositions as well.

Sexual and Species Difference

For instance, Marx and Engels maintain that the class system was itself erected upon a "natural" difference in humanity, that of the sexes. Sexual difference, for them, is predicated upon separate and different biological roles in reproduction. Upon this difference, which Marx and Engels take to be "natural" and therefore in some sense unquestionable, is erected what Engels calls the "world-historic defeat of women as a class" and therefore the first class of enslaved persons (Engels, *The Origin of the Family, Private Property, and the State*; in MER, see 734–41). Engels developed this train of thought in terms of the anthropological studies of his time (especially building on the work of an American anthropologist, Lewis H. Morgan, who proposed a "matrilineal theory of the origins of human society"—see Tucker's introduction in MER, 734), a reading of ancient (primarily Greek) dramatic and mythological literature that seems to bear traces of the prehistoric overturning of "mother right" (for instance, in the Medusa myth, where a revered, creative goddess is turned into a hideous hater of men), and what might be called a certain amount of speculation regarding the "state of nature." Whatever the problems with his methodology, or whatever the ways in which subsequent anthropological study may have altered the picture, it seems to me that Engels did something quite brilliant, and that the far greater part of it is not the essentialism that has been rightly criticized by feminist philosophers from

Simone de Beauvoir to Judith Butler (and some who propose that Marxist-Feminism represents a "bad marriage") but instead the demonstration that oppression and domination (in the form of patriarchy) is in fact *not* natural, but that there are certain material circumstances in which it arises.

However, my point is that these material circumstances have to be prepared by a dialectic that affords some strong role to ideology, even if the determination "in the last instance" is material. Of course, we have to be careful about importing anachronistic concepts into prehistoric, communal societies, such that we see an overturning of a relatively modern notion of "respect for persons." (After all, Marxism itself is fairly weak on the concept of the person, even if it proceeds on the basis of assumptions about this concept.) Still, a threshold had to be crossed which allowed one half of a population (male) to understand the other half of the population (female) as objects of domination. I am only trying to emphasize that this distinction—male/female—has its own ideological and political elements, at *any* stage of human development, and cannot be reduced simply to biology or "nature." Indeed, this is where the hallmark of reductionism, the "one-to-one" correspondence, especially runs aground on the attempt to read the true gender of a person directly from the presence or absence—*lack*, as Freud said—of a particular sex organ. Even the idea that there are "sex organs" that exist, straightforwardly, in a kind of "particularity," is ideological—as demonstrated by such important works as Luce Irigaray's *This Sex Which Is Not One* and Judith Butler's *Gender Trouble*. Indeed, in Irigaray's argument that the subordination of women is not only a key ingredient in the emergence of commodity production, but that, in fact, women then become not only the first class of slaves, but even the first commodities (and certainly the first people to be commodified), we also see the origins of ideology itself. (See *This Sex*, 192.)

Significantly, in a series of remarks from *Origin of the Family*, Engels repeats Marx's terminology from *Capital* about finding the "cellular form" of a social system. Of course, these remarks are very important for understanding the roots of patriarchy, but what I will argue is that they also prepare the way for considering the idea that carnivorism is a system. The passages come from a section of *Origin* in which Engels is describing the "domestication" of women in ancient Greek society.

> In Euripides, the wife is described as *oikurema*, a thing for housekeeping (the word is in the neutral gender), and apart from the business of bearing children, she was nothing more to the Athenian than the chief housemaid. The husband had his gymnastic exercises, his public affairs, from which the wife was excluded; in addition, he often had female slaves at his disposal and, in the heyday of Athens, extensive prostitution, which was viewed with favour by the state, to say the least. It was precisely on the basis of this prostitution that the

sole outstanding Greek women developed, who by their *esprit* and artistic taste towered as much above the general level of ancient womanhood as the Spartiate women did by virtue of their character. That one had first to become a *hetaera* [literally one of the "flute girls," but the connotation is "whore"; in French this remains one of the words for prostitute] in order to become a woman is the strongest indictment of the Athenian family. (in MER, 738)

A page further on, Engels writes,

monogamy does not by any means make its appearance in history as the reconciliation of man and woman, still less as the highest form of such a reconciliation. On the contrary, it appears as the subjection of one sex by the other, as the proclamation of a conflict between the sexes entirely unknown hitherto in prehistoric times. In an old unpublished manuscript, the work of Marx and myself in 1846 [the reference is to *The German Ideology*], I find the following: "The first division of labour is that between man and woman for child breeding." And today I can add. The first class antagonism which appears in history coincides with the development of the antagonism between man and woman in monogamian marriage, and the first class oppression with that of the female sex by the male. Monogamy was a great historical advance, but at the same time it inaugurated, along with slavery and private wealth, that epoch, lasting until today, in which every advance is likewise a relative regression, in which the well-being and development of the one group are attained by the misery and repression of the other. (in MER, 739)

Though it may seem an incidental point, it goes to the very heart of the argument advanced in the present book that "monogamy was a great historical advance" is true, in a classical Marxist sense, in the same way that it is true to say that "slavery was a great historical advance." (The reference is to slavery in the first societies based on class antagonism, not "New World slavery," which Marx analyzes under the category of "primitive capitalist accumulation"; see, e.g., the section in *Capital*, vol. 1, "The Secret of Primitive Accumulation," MER, 431–34; and the highly amusing remark in *Grundrisse*, on "the free blacks of Jamaica," in MER, 250.)

Commodity and Moral Logics

In either case of domination, surely the "moral sensibilities," such as they are, ought to be stirred. And yet in Marx and Engels it cannot be said that the stirring of the moral sensibilities enters into the equation, and this is for two reasons. First, while moral categories have little or no standing *as such* in the philosophy of Marx and Engels (which is not to say that they do not employ moral rhetoric, as has been noted), it could be said that such categories especially have no standing in the analysis of social *systems*.

The argument is that such categories are not helpful to the understanding of how such systems actually function. The "advance"/"regression" dialectic of societies based on antagonism is indeed a matter for an equation or calculation, not moral sensibilities. It seems to me that there are good, *scientific* reasons for not rejecting this approach. "Ethics" does indeed become an empty formalism if the normative and prescriptive has no basis in the descriptive. (Perhaps, in order to sidestep the metaphysics of description and truth, at least for the moment, we could speak of "the descriptive as best as it can be carried out by those who want to understand the world," but with the proviso that there is a fundamental relationship between understanding the world and changing the world.) Second, however, there is inescapable normative content to the term "advance." That patriarchal institutions (such as the first forms of monogamy) and slavery could be considered under this heading, of an "advance," raises the question, An advance toward what? I argued in part 1 that this rubric opens up problems of theodicy (or, at the least, flirting with a kind of teleology that appears to be quite "metaphysical," to use this last term in the pejorative sense that Marx preferred) and a kind of historical division where "political progress" takes such precedence over "moral progress" that the latter can somehow go straight to hell, so to speak, even while the former is supposedly taking us closer to heaven. This dichotomy becomes especially severe when history makes what Marx and Engels take to be its greatest "advance," into the capitalist epoch.

Marx and Engels are almost certainly right that the material ground for this oppression is the linked developments of the division of labor, a social surplus about which decisions for its disposal must be made, the first forms of exchange economy (and therefore commodity production), and the first forms of class society. These are elements of a reconstitution of a social system. (For, Marx reminds us, there is never not a social system, in that, at any stage of human development, people enter into definite relations of production, and, from these relations proceed the other three "alls"— social relations generally, legal relations, and ideas predicated upon these relations.) That there are material conditions for the crossing of an ideological threshold, however, does not mean that ideas as such, once they are "in the mix," as it were, do not play a material role of their own. That anyone could do something that is racist or sexist is enabled by both the material circumstances where some are held in subordinate positions and by the ideologies that formulate this subordination or take it for granted. This is not quite a chicken or egg question, in that it seems right, as Marx and Engels have it, that humans at whatever stage, including in their initial divergence from apes, find themselves in material circumstances and indeed *always already* (to use a Derridean term) in forms of life that are based around the material production and reproduction of life.

While these terms can be interrogated further, and there may be ways in which these terms have a "metaphysical" dimension, it does not seem as if anything especially metaphysical or reductionistic is needed to take these material circumstances as a starting place. In some sense, the difficulty comes when essentialistic constructions, such as "nature," are placed on such (seemingly basic, seemingly innocent) descriptions. What has to be avoided at all costs is anything that smells of the "it worked" as it is deployed in an argument such as the one I quoted from Benford's novel, *The Sunborn*. (The novel and the quoted passage are not "arguments," but there is an embedded argument in the passage: "hard labor needs solid food.") Putting Engels's *Origin* together with Marx's *Capital* (specifically the "Preface to the First German Edition," in MER, 294–98), it could be said that the commodity is the cell-form of capital, and the subordination of women is the cell-form of the commodity.

One could argue that, for both Marx and Engels, part of what it means for there to be a given social system is that there is a prefiguration of the system in a "cell-form," and this cell-form can be seen in a threshold that is crossed by humankind. Althusser's term for this, which he develops on the basis of Machiavelli and Lenin (in *Machiavelli and Us*), is "conjuncture." For Engels, and I do not think that Marx would have disagreed with him, there was a conjuncture, in prehistory, where the seeds of patriarchy, private property, commodity production, and even the state (as the enforcer of the foregoing, through ideology, legal arrangements, and, ultimately and when necessary, violence), and eventually capitalism were planted, in a single go. This turning point does not occur everywhere at once or even everywhere period, and indeed part of Engels's investigation is to explore contemporary cultures where the patriarchal-commodity turn does not seem to have occurred. These explorations, even despite certain methodological and historical-anthropological issues that need to be raised, stand as a testament to Engels's willingness to resist regulative notions of "human nature" and deterministic schemes—and this latter, especially, is not always Engels's strong suit (as seen most of all in his account of German Idealism, *Ludwig Feuerbach and the End of Classical German Philosophy*). However, as Engels notes, this turning point occurs on a certain material ground, which Engels calls "natural": again, "The first division of labour is that between man and woman for child breeding."

That it is in some sense undecidable whether Engels is pointing to a natural difference, out of which a social distinction was made, or whether the making of the social distinction is at one and the same time the making of the "natural" difference, does not cancel two basic points that are central to historical materialism: there was a turning point, beyond which at least a part of humanity was on a different course, and there was a material basis for this turning point. This turning point, which I am presently calling the patriarchal-commodity turn, had world-historic consequences, as Engels said. We do not have to overlay this turn with a deterministic, teleological scheme in order to see the connection between the time of this turn and our present-day society.

There are other ways to understand the turn where the connection is less clear. For Marx, part of the "cell-form" perspective is the idea that a line can be drawn from the first appearance of the commodity to the far-flung development of commodity production in industrial capitalism. Commodity production has developed through qualitative leaps since the time of Marx, though different trends in Marxism dispute the meaning and significance of these developments. If the cell-form thesis is right, then two consequences follow. First, we should be able to continue to draw a line from the initial appearances of commodity production to even these most far-flung developments. Second, the overcoming of commodity production must overcome not only its present forms, but also must, at least "in some sense" (as they say, and I realize this is also a device for waffling), restore our precommodified humanity. Another way to put this, to borrow from debates in French Marxism in the 1950s and after, is that the diachronic dimension cannot be dismissed in the name of the synchronic, the historical cannot be dismissed in the name of the structural. (This is as far as I will go with this debate here, but again we are on the terrain of Sartre and Althusser, and Kant and the "new Spinoza.") To go with the former terms in each of these formulations—the diachronic and historical—is to pursue a redemptive Marxism. One way to understand the latter idea is in terms of Kant's prioritization of ethics over hope. Even with this prioritization, it can be argued that there is no ethics without hope; there is no good without the temporal dimension. However, to return to the main line of argument, which is intended to show what it means for there to be a system, the connection between the first commodity forms and the development of the commodity in modern times is complicated when the seemingly innocent and even innocuous term, "market," is brought into the picture.

From the moment that there is production for exchange and not only for direct use (at least by some collectivity of human beings, if not by each and every individual per se—this is a subsistence economy we are talking about), there is a market. People have to work out a fair exchange, which comes to be the "market value" of commodities traded. At a later point in this process, the market becomes the name for the place where there is trade, the village center. Although in producing products for exchange it can be said that the producers are alienated from the fruits of their own labor, it is hard to see how the forms of market exchange that involve something like the village center, and that work primarily through barter, are especially damaging to some fundamental humanness. Indeed, it can be argued that such exchange opens up dimensions of human civility. The attempt to recover not only the market in this form, but also these dimensions of civility, informs the efforts of market socialists such as David Schweickart (see for example *Against Capitalism*). Insomuch as the initial stages of socialism cannot be based on some sort of immediate and absolute abolition of commodity production—and I am mindful here of Adorno's argument about the "absolute change" that in fact has the effect of even more forcefully inscribing one into the logic of the same; Derrida makes a similar argument in "The Ends of Man"—I see Schweickart's efforts as very important both for dealing with the complex mathematical and epistemological questions of the global market raised by critics of socialism such as Friedrich Hayek and Ludwig von Mises, as well as for modeling the political economy of socialism. But I also have two fundamental differences with this work (not that I am doing any kind of justice to Schweickart's arguments here), which in fact are two sides of the same coin. First, market socialism (as a complete program) represents a capitulation to an economistic model, in which economic interests are taken as the final cause of human action. Needless to say, proponents of such a model are not simply philistines, they hold that this conception of human motivation is the true and right conception—and they have plenty from Marx to build upon in this regard. Second—the other side of the coin, such a model also follows classical Marxism in subordinating the ethical demand to the point where it is effectively obliterated.

Economism

Raymond Lotta, in his provocative and valuable afterword to the English translation of what is generally called the *Shanghai Textbook on Political Economy* (the main title of the translation is *Maoist Economics*) calls for a socialism that is "visionary and viable." It is worth thinking about the dialectical relationship of these two terms. The "visionary" without the "viable" is clearly a mere utopianism in the bad sense—it is the ethical demand rendered into empty formalism. But what is the viable without the visionary? Proponents of economistic forms of Marxism would say it is just fine; it is exactly what is needed. My argument is that such a version of classical Marxism cannot begin to address the ethical gap that is opened up by imperialism, a gap that is qualitative—as Lenin argued—and not merely quantitative, a deep wound in humanity that in some respects can never be fully healed. Our Kantian work, our infinite work that was already well described by Rabbi Akiba in the second century and the notion of *tikkun* (to heal, restore, and transform the world—see Fackenheim's *Tikkun*) is to *try*, and this vision of an endless work, a permanence of the revolution, is itself necessary for any socialist revolution that will be viable. The Maoist argument here is in fact not only visionary, it is also deeply practical: the revolution that gets stuck in a particular stage, and that makes a principle out of getting stuck, will turn into its opposite, it will see the restoration of capitalism. This was Mao's analysis of the dynamics of the Soviet Union from the 1930s to the early 1960s. (This analysis finds a significant parallel in Sartre, *Critique of Dialectical Reason*, vol. 2—see especially part 1, ch. 5, "Are Social Struggles Intelligible? (A Historical Study of Soviet Society)"; also see "Dictatorship 'for' the proletariat: Sartre's theory of the Stalin period," in my *The Radical Project: Sartrean Investigations*, 15–33; Bob Avakian extends Mao's analysis, significantly and even qualitatively, in *Conquer the World?*) Unfortunately, Mao's analysis of the dynamics of capitalist restoration was proven accurate in the case of the People's Republic of China, as well.

An indispensable part of the ethical vision that must inform a viable socialism is internationalism. A very informative chapter on this question is the trajectory of the Second International after the death of Marx, especially as regards the leadership of Eduard Bernstein and Karl Kautsky. (In *Conquer the World?* Avakian also provocatively analyzes Engels's role in the transition of the Second International into complete reformism, Eurocentrism, and even simply German nationalism—even if Engels did not go all the way down these roads himself.) The most ironic part of this trajectory is Bernstein's turn to Kant precisely as a way of turning away from revolutionary struggle and toward reformism, the result of which was a Eurocentric pacifism that helped clear the way for the most horrendous violence of German nationalism and of imperialism more generally. (This may seem more than a little harsh; the point is that pacifism can sometimes underwrite very dangerous illusions.) We might also consider the supposed viability, which is intentionally the most narrow and antivisionary viability, in the section of the antiwar movement in the United States since the Gulf War that embraces the slogan, "Support Our Troops!" Though a simple, mechanical causality ought to be avoided here, there is a sense in which it is precisely the avoidance of an internationalist vision in the embrace of such a slogan that undermines the antiwar movement's viability.

Undoubtedly, the dialectic of vision and viability, especially as something that has to guide practice and that has to address real-world contradictions and not just be an academic exercise, is an extraordinarily difficult matter. This can be seen perhaps most of all in the Stalin period, where vision was progressively (or regressively, as it were) subordinated to viability—and not to what might have at least been a more visionary sense of the viability of a socialist country as a base for world revolution, but instead to a nationalist view of the viability of the Soviet Union (or even simply Russia). The practical necessities that were confronted by Stalin and the

Soviet leadership, however, cannot be reduced—as they often are in theories of "Stalinism" or "totalitarianism"—to no more than a lack of vision or even moral fiber on Stalin's part. There were such shortcomings in the case of Stalin, but there were also real contradictions in the world that had to be dealt with and that conditioned the dialectic of vision and viability and shaped the sort of leadership that rose to the top of the Bolshevik Party.

We will return to these issues; my aim in this discussion of markets and economism has been two-fold: first, to mark the differences between early forms of the market and historical but precapitalist forms of the market, on the one side, and capitalist markets, especially imperialist ones on the other; second, to mark the process by which the world becomes no more than a set of objects.

As a materialist, Marx is perhaps even more aware than Hegel of the way that the Owl of Minerva only takes flight at dusk: no one could have observed the early forms of the market, the division of labor, and commodity production and predicted the dazzling global markets of the 1850s, the 1950s, or the period of "globalization." Neither can it simply be said that the first elements of the market, the division of labor, commodity production, and, indeed, patriarchy and the first forms of slavery, were predestined to take over the world. (It might be argued that, if there was such predestination, then this would indeed be evidence for a more hard-wired conception of human nature.) Still, there is with Marx's conception of the "cell-form" the notion that the first forms of commodity production let the cat out of the bag and there is little or no chance of putting the cat back into the bag. A dialectic has been set in motion and, in Marx's social theory, this dialectic has to play itself out, ultimately in the resolution of the contradiction of socialized production and privatized accumulation.

Markets and Division of Labor

One important element of Marx's conception that market socialism abandons, as not viable, is the idea of overcoming the division of labor. But it is this division (including the gendered elements of it that come down to the present) that links early markets to global markets. Although this theme could be developed at greater length, something else could be said about this linkage. On the one side, early forms of the market should not be idealized or romanticized. The early form of the market is not simply a sort of communitarian agrarian democracy in the Jeffersonian mold, unless perhaps it is, in the sense that involved both slavery and patriarchal domination. (It is not my intention here to dismiss what can be learned from

Jefferson's vision, especially as set out in Richard K. Matthews, *TheRadical Politics of Thomas Jefferson.*) On the other side, in the contemporary world, the division of labor has become so internationalized and globalized that the economic viability of even the imperialist powers, and even the imperialist hyperpower (the United States) is progressively undermined, in the sense that these countries have become unable to sustain themselves on the basis of their own national territory (much less on the basis of their own ecological bio-regions). This same process of economic undermining, significantly, also undermines the very idea of these countries as actual "places," and, again quite significantly, therefore also as places where other animals can live (and other forms of life for that matter). By "live" I do not include the type of existence possible in the massive "feed lots" that contain tens and even hundreds of thousands of cows or pigs, and that themselves are not only the scenes of terrible cruelty to our fellow, feeling creatures, but that are also a multifaceted ecological blight and challenge to basic sustainability.

When I call these cows and pigs our "fellow, feeling creatures," I not only intend to invoke the idea that we should empathize with them as fellow sentient beings (of course we should), but also to convey that, if we do not experience fellow-feeling for cows and pigs, we are not likely to feel this for other people or our earthly habitat, either. To understand this point requires seeing certain connections to be sure, for example, that being an "animal lover" requires more than just loving one's cat or dog, or that the giant cattle and hog feedlots are environmentally disastrous.

The imperialist market system maintains not only a dependency of the Third World on the first, ultimately in terms of propped-up comprador regimes, but also a dependency of the imperialist powers on Third World countries for energy, food, and basic materials. This means that the Third World will *necessarily* be dominated by the first world, with military force when things come to this, as long as we live in a world where imperialist social relations prevail.

Reification

Clearly, Marx and Engels understand the emergence of commodity production as a threshold in human history. Indeed, this threshold occurs in prehistory and creates the basis for not only history but also for writing (at first as records of ownership and debts) and therefore for the writing of history (which itself might be understood as the "real" transition from prehistory to history; Derrida's *Of Grammatology* still contains many insights on this point that remain to be developed in a more explicitly political language, in my opinion). We might think further about the ethical import of the idea of the threshold and the related notion of the conjuncture. What is the nature of the line that has been crossed, and what is the meaning of the crossing of the line? There is a sense in which, when objects, phenomena, processes, *things* are brought under the purview of the market and commodity production, well, this is the process through which things really become "things." This is reification. That language—or at least European languages—becomes redundant here, so that we have to speak of "a thing being treated as a thing," or as a "mere thing," would seem itself a guide to how deeply reification runs in us, how "natural" it has become, at least in some forms. If we take one essential part of Marxism to be a critique of reification and the culture of commodification, which is developed in more explicitly Marxist language in the work of figures such as Georg Lukacs, Walter Benjamin, Theodor Adorno, Ernst Bloch, and Herbert Marcuse, we ought to acknowledge that our critique is enabled in other ways, or perhaps at a deeper level, by Heidegger's arguments about "the thing." As regards the threshold, this will turn out to be a very significant point in what follows. At least as regards ethical questions, once there is reification, which begins *at least* at the moment when there is production for exchange rather than direct use (but perhaps reification begins before this moment), there is the sense of the threshold as the point when all bets are off: If you will do this, what will you *not* do? If you will cross this line, which line will you *not* cross?

For Marx, however, the crossing of the threshold into commodity production is not yet the crossing of the threshold into capitalism, and it is this latter crossing, significantly, that opens the way to a culture of commodification and reification. Another way to characterize this latter culture is that it is one in which the idea that everything is merely a thing, with a price, and where money will ultimately determine everything that goes on in society and the world, has come to seem completely "natural." What is the threshold whose crossing opens up this new epoch? For Marx, this threshold is the crossing into the commodification of labor power. This is the point when it can truly be said that "all bets are off," and that a line has been crossed beyond which there are no longer any limits to the oppressions and horrors that can be visited upon people and the other creatures of the earth, and even the earth itself. (The extension of these horrors to "space" and to the moon, Mars, and further out is only inhibited in capitalism by whatever technological barriers are yet to be crossed.) Recall once again the famous lines from the *Manifesto*:

> The bourgeoisie, wherever it has got the upper hand, has put an end to all feudal, patriarchal, idyllic relations. It has pitilessly torn asunder the motley feudal ties that bound man to his "natural superiors," and has left remaining no other nexus between man and man than naked self-interest, than callous "cash pay-

ment." It has drowned the most heavenly ecstasies of religious fervor, of chivalrous enthusiasm, of philistine sentimentalism, in the icy water of egotistical calculation. It has resolved personal worth into exchange value, and in place of the numberless indefeasible chartered freedoms, has set up that single, unconscionable freedom—Free Trade. In one word, for exploitation, veiled by religious and political illusions, it has substituted naked, shameless, direct, brutal exploitation.

The bourgeoisie has stripped of its halo every occupation hitherto honoured and looked up to with reverent awe. It has converted the physician, the lawyer, the priest, the poet, the man of science, into its paid wage-labourers.

The bourgeoisie has torn away from the family its sentimental veil, and has reduced the family relation to a mere money relation. (in MER, 475–76.)

The later stages of this process can be understood as imperialism—where the social relations of capital are operative on a global scale and with increasing global integration, in a way that produces qualitative effects— and "postmodern capitalism," where the culture of the "mere money relation" has set in so deeply that people, at least in the first world, understand themselves primarily (and, after awhile, only) as consumers.

Consciousness and Commodification

In such a lifeworld, so fully colonized by the commodity system (to borrow terms from Habermas), it is exceedingly difficult for any higher vision of human freedom or flourishing to gain any traction. Though it may be argued, in line with Marxist crisis theories of times past, that this state of false consciousness lasts only as long as the flow of consumer goods and services is not dramatically impeded, this fully commodified consciousness has an exceedingly powerful effect (to say the least) on what people can imagine in terms of alternatives to the present system, even in the case of a deep crisis. This is Lenin's argument about the pull of spontaneity in *What Is to Be Done?*, itself an extension of Marx's dominant ideology thesis (a qualitative extension, however). In postmodern capitalism, we are up against more than the "spontaneous" pull toward ("back toward") the entrenched ways of acting and thinking, however; postmodern capitalism is a massive, organized failure of the imagination.

And yet there remains the connection to the "cell form," from the first commodities to this present form of life where commodities define every feature of human life, and where this is both good and necessary—for "there is no alternative."

This last is called the "TINA thesis," and there is plenty of historical and cultural exploration to be done regarding the relationship of this thesis to the closure of the first stage of socialism, the revolutions in Russia and

China and their eventual defeat by capitalism. Capital is not just wealth or property, it is a social relationship and a social process whereby living labor power is rendered into a thing, quality is rendered into quantity. The pull of this process is very strong, even to the point where it can eat away at the attempt to create a postcapitalist society and bring forth new capitalists; in the case of the Soviet Union and the People's Republic of China, when the time was right, these new capitalists seized political power and restored capitalism. Mao analyzed this process on one level, a very crucial level, having to do with the continuance of commodity production and class struggle in socialist society. We will turn to this analysis in due course. There is another level of analysis, however, that goes to the larger question of how the process of reification can have such a powerful pull, a process whereby that which is dynamic and qualitative and living can be rendered *inert*, a mere thing that corresponds to some number, some quantity of dollars and cents or whatever currency is the measure of the brutal cash nexus.

In using the term "inert," I am appealing to Sartre's term, "practico-inert." Sartre's terms from the *Critique of Dialectical Reason* are often a bit hard to pin down; roughly speaking, the practico-inert is the overwhelming "thingness" of things, which continually exerts its pull on not only individual human persons, but on our social formations and institutions as well. Indeed, a social "institution" in Sartre's theory is that which has had the life squeezed out of it. While Sartre and other proponents of the permanence of the revolution may be weak on the question of what sort of institutions actually do need to be created and articulated in a postcapitalist society (this is where the critiques of Arendt, Habermas, and the left-Rawlsians gain their purchase), the argument is that institutions have to serve living, developing, and contradictory processes, and not the other way around. (One of the themes that brings Sartre and Mao together is the idea that socialism is not a stable social form, it is riven with contradictions; however, there is obviously a great deal more to be said on the problem of the form of sovereignty that applies to the socialist state, and the meaning of the "rule of law" under socialism.) Capitalism is a form of society where reification enters a qualitatively new phase, where there are no limits to what can be made into a mere thing. Indeed, the most dramatic truth of imperialism and postmodern capitalism is that an addition can be made to the list Marx and Engels make in the manifesto of those things and relationships that must submit to "callous cash payment": the further and continuing existence of the world itself, or at least our human world.

Relations and Representations

Capitalists do what they do as representatives of capitalist relations of production and social relations more generally. Marx was right to argue that it is these relations that should be the primary focus of analysis. If anything, the defeat of socialism in Russia and China underscores this point: even after the old capitalist class has been expropriated, the remainders of capitalist social relations (which *must* remain for a time in socialist society, because commodity production and the wage system and the inherited division of labor and their ideological correlates cannot be abolished in one fell swoop, or even in a short period of time; in fact, there is a sense in which socialist revolution is what finally opens the door to radical reform, though Mao argued that there are also moments where this reform must give way to further revolution) and the preponderance of these relations globally will call forth new representatives. Mao argued, and it seems clear that history has borne this out, that these relations will especially call forth new representatives at the point where the levers of power are exercised (the existence of such levers is itself a major but unavoidable contradiction of socialist society), which is within institutions of the state, the party, and the military. All of this needs to be analyzed systematically and scientifically apart from ethical categories. And yet, at the same time, it has to be said that the imperialist classes of the world are made up of people who will put the existence of humanity and the earth on the line for the sake of their power and wealth, and this makes them the most morally reprehensible people in all history. Capitalism can regenerate itself even in the absence of particular capitalist classes, because capitalism is fundamentally a process and not first of all the essence of some particular human beings. Capitalism cannot be overthrown, however, without the overthrow of capitalist classes, and my point is that these classes, in moral terms, certainly deserve to be overthrown. Again there is a basic connection: the same roulette wheel that the capitalists are willing to spin, which might determine whether any given worker might have a job tomorrow, is the same wheel on which the fate of the world may come to depend.

Thresholds

Let us again remember to keep in mind the two thresholds under consideration here: the crossing into commodity production and the crossing into capital (the commodification of labor power). Now let us consider the possible extension of the first threshold backwards in time, and the extension of the second threshold forwards in time. In the case of the crossing into commodity production, we now have passed through many phases since the first appearances of a significant money economy and a system of wage labor. Marx wrote in a time when industrial production had become the dominant economic form in Western Europe. This economic form was greatly intertwined with and conditioned the forms of colonialism practiced in this period, from the late-eighteenth through the nineteenth century, but Marx did not concentrate very much on the political economy of this, and he certainly did not employ ethical terms as effective or substantial in any systematic way when describing the colonial plunder and exploitation of Asia, Africa, and Latin America (and even parts of Europe itself, such as Ireland) by the "great powers" of Western Europe. Now, it is also true that the development of industrial capitalism in Western Europe was also the development, at the same time and in the same process, of the proletarian class, and the exploitation of this class was thoroughly ugly and brutal—let us make no mistake about that. Yet, even here, while Marx does use moralistic language in describing the conditions under which the proletarians of Europe labored (in *Capital*, vol. 1, there is the famous description of the woman in the weaving industry), it is primarily the contradictions of capital that he is examining, and the mechanisms by which capital will be undone and the expropriators will be expropriated.

Let us mention three important aspects of the ethical and political-economic dimensions of colonialism before moving forward. First, it is worth noting that arguably the three most contentious "great powers" of Europe at the time when industrial capital and colonial domination were becoming thoroughly intertwined, namely, England, France, and Germany, are also the lands named by Engels as the "sources" of Marxism as "scientific socialism." In *Socialism: Utopian and Scientific*, Engels names as the sources of scientific socialism "German philosophy, French socialism, and English political economy." (To be clear, the philosophy was German idealism, the socialism was French syndicalism and other forms of utopian experimentation, and the political economy was more Scottish than English.) That this can be no coincidence is worth further reflection. Second, a greater sense of the cultural dimensions of colonialism and emergent imperialism might be gained by comparing the two great "island empires," England and Japan. Of course, both countries have a good deal to do with the colonization of East and Southeast Asia (and the Pacific islands). Lastly, any work in the political economy of colonialism has to come to terms with one basic fact as regards the rise of industrial capitalism. In the heartlands of industrial capitalism, a situation was created such that newly "free laborers" (in other words, peasants driven off the land) went into the marketplace seeking work. The workers had to go to the market, in other words. In colonialist ventures, the colonizers went in boats to the places where the people and "resources" were to be found, the colonizers took the market out into the world. Now, in both cases, the market was formed in such a way as to carry out exchange in unequal terms. However, in the emerging capitalist powers of Europe, these terms were set in a process that had at least some "organic" structure to it—not ignoring the role played by the brutal disenfranchisement of the peasants, in such episodes as the "Highland Clearances" (see Richards, *The Highland Clearances*)—but the new relations of production grew and developed within the shell of the old, feudal relations. This was Marx's classic scenario of social transformation driven by contradiction in the mode of production. (Again, to say that the transformation in this scenario occurs "organically" is not to say that it was a pleasant experience for the people who were transformed from peasants into proletarians—on the contrary.) In colonialism, the capitalist mode of production arrives first of all through military domination: first of all the new machines of war rather than the new machines of production. Again, Marx tends to assimilate this domination to the category of primitive accumulation, which eventually gives way to "advanced" accumulation (that is, the ordinary exploitation of labor power in a capitalist economy) because the primitive form is ultimately inefficient.

A World of Things

In other words, the world of commodity production is topsy-turvy from start to finish (though it is unfortunately not finished), as it were. The first forms of commodity production initiate humanity into a world of *things*. The emergence of capitalism places the reification of humanity on a purely calculative basis, and from there all human relationships are brought under the brutal cash nexus. The people who actually engage in the creative transformation of nature through their labor are the last in line to be able to make a livelihood from this work, and the explanations for what ought to be taken to be an utterly bizarre state of affairs become second nature even to the working people themselves. ("Bloody great race of people, the Romans!"—as that one poor sod in the dungeon in Monty Python's *Life of Brian* put it.) Often the ones toward the end of the line don't make it. Colonialism transplants a new set of social relations seemingly "out of nowhere," but this is no worry in the "object world." In imperialism, the disaster that had previously come across the water in boats is now dropped from the sky by aircraft (or missiles). Finally, a significant section of the "working class" in the imperialist countries has only the most tenuous relationship to actual production, and this is to say nothing of the many millions who are part of some nearly indefinable "middle class" (including philosophy professors). The world that Marx already described in the 1840s as "upside-down" has only become more so in the interval.

The cell-form of a world that is upside-down is the commodity. However, and now to return more directly to the animal question, it would not seem entirely necessary to identify "cell-forms," thresholds, or conjunctures in order to show how commodity production works in the present day as a fully articulated social system, and the same can be said for carnivorism. Carnivorism would already be a system if we lived in a society in which the main way of obtaining meat were through hunting—a person would have to know how to hunt, and also *why* to hunt; there would have to be a sense of not only who the hunters are, but also how and why to produce new hunters. (There would have to be a parallel system with cooking, and this is where the idea of the first division of labor as "natural" immediately looks odd.) But, of course, the present food-production system is a million miles away from a food system based on hunting. This present system is at least a large subsystem of the overall system of production, and the system of rendering animals into meat is at least a large subsystem of the overall food-production system. However, I would maintain that carnivorism is more than a subsystem, it is a system in its own right, and furthermore, it is the "heart" of the present system of commodity production.

System (s)

On the idea that carnivorism is a system in its own right, two points are essential. First, to see the systematicity of the carnivorist system, one need only look at the many dimensions of food-animal production, from the actual, individual animals (who have little to no individuality in the system, except perhaps as units, though this is how things work in commodity production, everything has to be understood as a quantifiable unit), to the dinner table, and even to the many health problems that are generated by the human consumption of meat (and even to the efforts expended on explaining away these issues); even here, only some elements of production and consumption, narrowly construed, have been mentioned. Transportation is a large sector of the system of production, and the forms of transportation associated with food-animal production and consumption are themselves a large part of the transportation sector. Additionally, much land is devoted to this form of production, and this is not only the land that is required for the animals to stand somewhere, but also the even greater acreage that is required for the production of crops for the sole purpose of feeding these animals. There is a great deal of water required for producing these crops. And so on—other scholars have provided the numbers that quantify what is involved in industrial food-animal production (a useful guide on this issue, with ample sources, is Fox, *Deep Vegetarianism*, 84–95; Fox cites some very scary figures, for example, on what he calls the "hamburgerization of the forests"). None of this happens by accident; all of these dimensions are part of an ever-more integrated system.

Then there is the very large ideological part of the production and consumption process, which itself has many dimensions that are related to one another, but that are also disparate, and where some are quite formal and others are quite informal, while others are somewhere in-between. For instance, to repeat a formulation employed in previous parts of this book, television advertisements do not make themselves, everything about them has to be guided in a formal way. And yet, even in the most extravagantly produced advertisement there are currents flowing from the subconscious and unconscious mind. Somewhere in between are, for example, religious inducements to eat meat—we tend to only think of religious prohibitions, the "thou shalt nots" that dominate the sense of religion that many have, and to focus less on the ways in which religion can be a subtle system of ideological enablement. Of course, such enablement is stated in a formal and authoritarian way (nothing could be more authoritarian than to invoke the supposed author of existence) when a challenge is posed: "God has given humanity dominion over the animals." Ordinarily, without an insistent challenge, the religious inducement to eat meat simply bypasses the notion that there could ever be any question of doing otherwise.

In the last two hundred years, the different dimensions of the industrial food-animal production system became globally integrated and took a qualitative leap. This leap occurred in the context of the overall development of industrial production and capitalism. The outcome is a vast global network and massive subsystem, the essential glue for which remains the human consumption of animals as food. If it is right to speak, as I have done, of the materialist trinity of food, shelter, and clothing (a trinity that is, after all, quite important in the Jesus movement: "When I was hungry, did you feed me?" and so on), then surely food is the head of this trinity. Certainly there is the temptation to once again refer to a "natural" distinction: the human stomach needs food, so perhaps the original division is between the eater and the eaten? Such a distinction, as somehow "originary," plays nicely into analyses of power that sidestep human evaluative activity—as not "realistic" in either a narrowly political or a larger ontological sense. Such analyses sidestep also the way in which humanity is formed through an initiation into a world of things, and here again one can see the connection with the "happy positivism" in some of these analyses: it is difficult to understand cruelty as simply the quantity of a bound variable.

Cost Accounting

On the other hand, it is not difficult to understand vast numbers of hamburgers sold as quantities of a bound variable. (The language I am playing with is from Quine, where he defines existence—the famous formula is, "to be is to be the quantity of a bound variable"; see "On What There Is.") After all, this is simply a matter of cost accounting in a particular sector of capitalism, but without the cost in animal suffering figuring into the accounts. Some readers may recall one of the many brilliant strips in the *Calvin and Hobbes* series, where a smiling Calvin asks his mom if hamburgers are made out of people from Hamburg; his mother finds that idea disgusting and tells Calvin that hamburgers are made from cows, at which point Calvin becomes physically repulsed by what he is eating. One can imagine a Seinfeld-esque bit on hamburgers (to parallel the bit on Ovalteen): "What's the deal with hamburgers? They aren't made of ham, though perhaps they are meant to be served to German city-dwellers." (Ba-dum-dum.) Both economically and ideologically (and in a way where the former connects with the latter in what would seem to be a compelling example of base and superstructure), the insistent beat of the hamburger business might be taken as the organizing center of the contemporary carnivorist system.

"I Am Man"/"Eat This Meat"

In this connection I want to enter the realm of "popular culture," not only into the realm of television, but into the most ephemeral district of these realms, that of the television commercial. I want to take up a particular commercial, which some readers may not have seen and which others may have forgotten. I am referring to the "I am man"/"Eat this meat" commercial for Burger King that was shown widely in the spring of 2006, especially during sporting events (for example, it was shown over and over again during the NBA playoffs). This commercial can stand as something like a masterpiece of what I would call a conjunction of *manic* carnivorism and *manic* patriarchy. It is a truly stunning work, achieving a level of reactionary ugliness previously unknown in this medium. The commercial's two most manic elements are (1) that, in a space of thirty seconds, the commercial manages to depict numerous scenes, and these scenes themselves are complex and variegated; (2) that all of these scenes continually build into a triumphant and virulent mob action. There is so much going on in this commercial that an entire book could be written about it, and I am not saying this facetiously. Allow me to reconstruct some of the elements, as best I remember them.

The commercial opens with a scene of individual rebellion. A strapping young buck of a man, white, perhaps late twenties in age, a five-o'clock shadow, dressed in jeans and a colored T-shirt "like a worker," is seated at an outdoor cafe, with a fashionable female companion, a plate of artfully arranged *haute cuisine* in front of him. The young man rejects this food (as

I recall, the plate contained a single shrimp and some sprigs of different vegetables), and seemingly the outdoor cafe and his companion as well. He forthrightly stands up from the table and begins to sing what turns out to be a parody of Helen Reddy's feminist anthem from the early 1970s, "I Am Woman." The emphasis on the male subjects of the commercial being *working class* continues throughout. Furthermore, in setting the initial scene as a rejection of *haute cuisine* the commercial does at least three things—and this is a great example of how brilliant this commercial is in compressing so much ideology into such a small space. First, the commercial plays on standard prejudices about "the French," prejudices that have been played up, expanded, and reinforced in the time since the United States has launched its post–September 2001 invasions of Afghanistan and Iraq. (One of the ringleaders of this effort, the horrible Bill O'Reilly of the Fox News Channel, has called the French "cheese-eating surrender monkeys," as if to again assert the manliness of eating meat.) Meat-eating then becomes a way of asserting Americanness. Second, there is an identification of this "French," *haute-cuisine* cafe fare not only with femininity, but also with being a pansy and a wimp, a *shrimpy* wimp. Lastly, and perhaps most subtly, there is the reinforcement of a proud stupidity, either as an ignorance of what the French actually eat or as a willful refusal, wrapped in some sense of what it supposedly means to be from the working class, to examine one's beliefs and prejudices. While cheese is not meat, the dairy industry is in many ways the worst part of the food-animal production system. Furthermore, while a shrimp is not a cow, commercial "fishing" has been fantastically ruinous to aquatic habitats, now to the point of basic unsustainability.

From this initial act of rebellion against what is labeled, in the song parody, as "chick food," a convergence upon a Burger King store develops. Masses of men. of different colors but again coded as working class, enter the Burger King and leave with the product that the company is promoting with this commercial, the Texas Double Whopper (!). In the space of a few seconds there is a kind of long march to the culminating scene, with numbers growing, voices raised ever louder in the "I am Man" anthem, banners unfurled from office-building windows with the inspired slogan, "Eat This Meat" (one of the lines in the song parody is, "I will eat this meat"), and guys doing various idiot-guy things such as smashing cans against their foreheads. Again I would call these "Three Stooges"–like bits a reinforcement of proud stupidity, and this is not at all unconnected to the specific forms that stupidity takes in an imperialist country, where ignorance (especially of the rest of the world and what it is like to live under conditions of imperialist domination and super-exploitation) is thematized as a good thing. Of course, there is nothing subtle about the demand to "eat this meat," but it does work on a number of levels, not all of them controllable by the shapers of the discourse that is this commercial. Most likely there is an inescapably homoerotic element to any male mob. Certainly there are elements of not only male bonding, but also even homoerotic male bondage in the gathering mob scene. In the final scenes of the commercial, the mob coalesces into a unilinear march (as in a political demonstration or a military seizure of territory), across a bridge. The crossing of a bridge is a symbolically charged act; in this case it is the crossing of a threshold into a brave new manhood, one that defines itself against the feminine—or, one might say, "the feminine" understood as prissy, emasculating, and French.

Halfway across the bridge, the mob appears to be confronted by a threat: one of those ubiquitous (in the white suburbs of the U.S., at any rate) forest-green minivans, heading straight for them! This van is the symbol of the soccer mom. There is yet another play on gender and class going on here, as the soccer mom is a figure of the suburban middle class. At the last second, however, the van skids and turns sidelong to the mob. Lo and behold, another working-class (coded) male emerges, liberated from his feminine role. He tosses away the keys to the vehicle, and joins the rest of the mob in lifting the van and pushing it over the side of the bridge. The van crashes into the back of an enormous dump truck. This truck, in turn, is being pulled by a biker-dude type, who pulls the truck with a chain that is harnessed to his back. The "carrot" that is leading him on is the Texas Double Whopper, held in a shovel by a scantily-clad blond woman.

Naturally you have to see and hear this to get the full force of it. But why discuss at all what will undoubtedly seem a relic of the distant past within a few months, given the politics and culture of speed and the jump-cut aesthetic that the commercial itself employs to dazzling effect? Because the "I am man"/"Eat this meat" commercial captures so perfectly so many elements of carnivorism in itself, and the interconnections between carnivorism and the other systems that are operative in contemporary society. One connection between the carnivorist system and the threshold of carnivorism that humanity crossed thousands of years ago is the way that a supposedly essential relation has to be stressed and reinforced: you are *man*, you will eat this meat. Carnivorism goes far beyond fast-food hamburgers, and yet these hamburgers are, economically speaking, the vital core of carnivorism today. Indeed, in our "McWorld," these hamburgers are the vital core of commodity production and cultural commodification.

Pervasiveness

If we take two major players in the present world economy, McDonalds and Wal-Mart, as emblematic of the way things work in the world today, we might draw a line between the present functioning of systems and the cell-form of which Marx wrote. On the one hand, it is not hard to pick on companies such as these since we increasingly live in a world that is completely shaped by them. On the other hand, attacking such companies, as gratifying as it may be, misses the point in at least one important respect. These companies are just doing what enterprises in capitalism do. It should be noted, however, that there are qualitative transformations occurring in the very nature of the market that are associated with the huge market share in retail that is enjoyed by Wal-Mart; these transformations have to do with the notion of "monopsony," a situation where "a firm captures the ability to dictate price to its suppliers, because the suppliers have no real choice other than to deal with that buyer." (See Barry C. Lynn, "Breaking the Chain: The Antitrust Case against Wal-Mart.") Indeed, the ingeniousness of the Burger King commercial is driven, in the first and last instances, not by carnivorist or patriarchal ideology, but by the need to compete with McDonalds for a share of the fast-food hamburger market.

We need a fully developed "ice-age Marxism" (in other words, one that takes the carnivorist turn as a conjuncture in the Althusserian sense), to demonstrate at greater depth the connection between the human fall into carnivorism and its ramifications for the ethical community of the future. My aim here has been to go far enough that we might draw some conclusions as regards the possibility of an Ethical Marxism; I want to conclude this section, therefore, with the following set of observations.

First Observation

If Marxism is ready, in a new synthesis, to accept that ethical questions are real questions, then the animal question provides a paradigm case of an ethical question that is not easily assimilated to a purely utilitarian or interest-driven framework, at least not such a framework that is anthropocentric.

Second Observation

For the individual, at least, part of what it means to recognize an ethical question as real is to examine one's own life and practices. (I have noted with interest a certain difference in the attitudes of my nonvegetarian friends toward my vegetarianism. Some of my friends, for the most part my friends who are intellectuals, do not joke with me about "trying meat," or ask questions such as "don't you think you would like it?" because they know that I hold a position on this question that has, at least in my view, an ethical basis. Whereas my friends who are not intellectuals tend to sidestep confronting the ethical question, so that, if they start to talk about how great some meat was that they had at a recent meal, or if they start to suggest that we eat at a restaurant where there are few nonmeat options, and then they remember that I am a vegetarian, they will say something along the lines of, "oh, I forgot, you don't like meat." In some sense they transfer the ethical to the aesthetic.)

On another plane, it is worth noting that there are certain bastions of environmental study—philosophy departments specializing in environmental ethics or institutes where ecology or sustainable agriculture is studied—where most of the people involved are not vegetarians and the treatment of animals is not a very big question. When I have engaged these folks on this question, in a generally nonconfrontational way, the tendency on their part has been to say that more systematic work needs to be done to prove the case (that eating animals is wrong). Now, while I do not take the foregoing analysis as having absolutely, decisively proven that carnivorism is a system, I have gone far enough. The proof is that, if I had done the same amount and type of analysis to show that New World slavery was a system, no one would dispute it. But that is because no one reading these words is contemplating a reintroduction of the slave system. No one reading these words, I think it is safe to say, owns a slave and is in some sort of quandary about whether or not to free this slave. In other words, the argument regarding carnivorism as a system (where I have tried to show the avenues that need to be pursued further) interpenetrates the argument regarding vegetarianism and the limits of reason because, frankly, some people would rather keep talking endlessly about such issues as whether the category of rights applies to animals, and so on, than stop eating meat.

"Reason" and philosophy just become obfuscations for an ethical question that one does not want to confront, because confronting the question would mean a change in the way one lives one's life, and that can be hard. However, having followed a vegetarian diet for over twenty years now, I do not think it is as hard as some people imagine it would be. It seems more the case that thinking of giving up meat as being monumentally hard is one of the mental barriers that some people erect, and of course there is a system out there working overtime to help them erect those barriers.

Furthermore, regardless of the arguments that concern the eating of animals in the centuries and millennia leading up to the emergence of the industrial food-animal production system (arguments put forward by figures from Pythagoras to Porphyry and beyond), I do not know how anyone could look at the contemporary global system of animal food production, from the gigantic feed lots to the slaughterhouses to the global distribution networks to the advertising, and not see that it is a very messed-up system. But in fact I do know how this works. Just take one ele-

ment in this system, the gigantic feed lots for cows and pigs that have pro-
liferated in the last few decades, where there may be as many as two hundred *thousand* cows or pigs crammed in together, shoulder to shoulder,
standing knee-deep in their own excrement, and in some cases fed ground-
up carcasses of other cows and pigs. How can anyone look upon such a
scene and remain insensitive to the immense suffering involved? I can think
of two ways in which this insensitivity is held in place. First, I am reminded
again of the scene in Claude Lanzman's film, *Shoah* (mentioned in part 2),
where the retired train engineer reminisces happily about driving trainloads
of Jews to Auschwitz. Others worked happily and contentedly in that apparatus of genocide as well. What happens in human psychology that allows
people to view suffering this way, as something that is not a problem for
them? A large and difficult question, but whatever is happening in human
psychology in these cases, no one is going to say that it is something good.
Second, the insensitivity is held in place if the alternative is confronting
some central life practice and changing it. Again there is an interesting psychological question, perhaps one that can be traced to the ethos of a postmodern capitalist society, where there is a kind of pervasive alienation from
alienation itself. Some of the advertisements for meat such as the ones I
mentioned might provide useful material for studying this phenomenon.

Perhaps I will have to eat my words in the case of asserting that no one
is going to say that it is something good that people can become so deeply
insensitive to suffering. The U.S. military, especially the Army and the
Marines, in the decades since the Second World War, has gone to enormous lengths to overcome what has been, historically, a strong aversion to
killing people in wars. As Jeff Tietz writes, a study of American soldiers in
WWII showed that seventy-five percent "failed to shoot back when fired
upon." The U.S. Army launched a program to "free the rifleman's mind
with respect to the nature of targets." The basic strategy was to draw a distinct difference between "us" and "them," using the tools of racism and
national chauvinism to define "them," and the "responsibility to deliver
[one's] comrades from danger" and to "Protect your buddy!" on the "us"
side. "The value of applied psychology soon became apparent: The firing
rate during the Korean War rose to nearly sixty percent. In Vietnam it was
ninety percent, and in the first Gulf War it reached ninety-eight percent. In
Iraq, the number of soldiers who fail to fire is thought to be statistically
insignificant" (quotations from Tietz, "The Killing Factory," 54–55).
Tietz goes on to explain in detail what it takes to turn a human being into
a "killing machine" for the U.S. armed forces, a system called "Total
Control," "a carefully crafted hell that hard-wires kids for combat" (54).

It could be argued that an even greater system of "total control" is in
place to ensure that the minds of young people are "freed" from moral
considerations when it comes to the nature of what is on the plate at the

dinner table. The animal question is not only a model for the reality of ethical questions; *it is also a model for the avoidance of the reality of ethical questions.*

Third Observation

Why not understand a system such as "Total Control" as an extreme outcome of the system of reification, a system that begins with the thingification and commodification of animals? In lands that are colonized and otherwise dominated by imperialist powers, the local populations are treated as if they are not of the same species as the personnel of the dominating powers, but instead are "animals." Furthermore, the imperialist domination of countries and the mechanisms that put meat on the table also have in common elements of psychological and physical distance—out of sight, out of mind. Still further, these distances shape what kinds of things appear to thought and therefore become "worthy" of philosophical treatment—and what kinds of things do not.

These considerations also bear on the ways in which ethical questions are avoided. However, we might ask whether these strategies of avoidance are the strategies whereby Marxism has tended to avoid both the animal question and ethical questions (as real) in general. With Marxism, is it not instead the other way around, that the animal question does not appear as a real ethical question (much less as the model for such questions), because ethical questions themselves do not appear as real in Marxism, but only as epiphenomenal? The ethical critique of reification, expressed well enough by the second formulation of the categorical imperative (to treat persons as ends, and never as means only), even if taken in a purely (human) speciesist way, is still open to some sympathy for our nonhuman fellow creatures. Kant expressed this straightforwardly and powerfully: "If man is not to stifle his human feelings, he must practice kindness toward animals; for he who is cruel to animals becomes hard also in his dealings with man. We can judge the heart of a man by his treatment of animals" (*Lectures on Ethics*, 212–13). There remain problems even with this formulation, certainly, and what Kant says here is part and parcel of his view that we have only "indirect duties" toward animals. However, even indirect duties are at least real moral obligations; a Marxism that takes ethical questions in general to be, at most, epiphenomenal, can only see reification as a mechanism. When this mechanism is applied to animals and to the rest of nature, well, that is just what humans do, *naturally.* In Marx's scenario, this mechanism leads, after millennia of doing its ugly work, to the happy result of a good society. But we can no longer believe in this inevitability, and we have to begin to take stock of this positivistic strategy of avoidance of ethical

questions. Such a strategy participates in a more general strategy of objectification that has set up a tremendous amount of *bad karma* for
humankind (case in point: ruined land and water). The question is whether
Marxism can be made to jump tracks and get with a program of redemption rather than the program of subordinating ethical questions into
nonexistence, even while hanging on to some of the important analytical
tools of revolutionary Marxism.

Fourth Observation

The concerns I raise in this section of the book could be linked to the concerns of the book as a whole by noting that one could find one's way
toward Marxism through a concern for animals (even if this path is not that
well traveled). Now apparently it is hard for Marxists to see how or why to
go the other way—though I am trying to show the way. If one wants to
explore how it could become a normal thing to eat animals, one would
look at the conditions under which human carnivorism first occurred, and
the myth-structure that explained this transition/transgression. At some
point in this transition, there must have been a moment when a fundamental distinction between animals and humans began to be made, as
regards cruelty and some sort of basic standing in the world, and here we
can see the roots of reification, at least regarding sentient creatures with
central nervous systems. (No complex understanding of anatomy would be
required to see that many animals, especially the ones that humans eat, can
feel pain and experience cruelty, that they will avoid pain and death, that
they are trying to continue with life.) We can see the beginnings of commodity production. Far more obvious is the fact that the modern food-animal production system is a vast system of commodity production. But
again, the harder path is to travel the other way, and this again is a demonstration of Marxism's tendency not to understand ethical questions as real.

Fifth Observation

My fifth observation concerns how the "good conscience" problem—if it
is a problem—in vegetarianism and other forms of effective concern for
animal welfare might be compared to the problem of so-called "humorless
feminism." On the one side, it is not hard to imagine why many people,
if they are concerned for the situation and welfare of women in this world,
would find it hard to smile. Indeed, even in the realm of humor itself, there
is so much misogyny that it kind of boggles the mind, how deep this stuff
runs. In recent years, too, since the heyday of the Women's Movement of

the 1960s and after, it is enormously distressing to see how sexism and misogyny have reentered "popular culture," perhaps most concentrated in the casual way that many people will use the word "bitch," which seems to me to be the gender equivalent of a racist epithet. (The latter have gained a new currency, too, helped along by someone's notion of empowerment that seems more connected to the "empowerment" of bling and the thug life than anything that has a chance of being liberatory.) On the other side, I don't know that we're going to make it in this world without a sense of humor; it could even be that, if we lose this sense, we lose everything. "Good conscience" seems like the other side of this humorlessness. Is there anything wrong with feeling good about helping our fellow creatures in the ways that we can? Kant tells us that there is something wrong if we are helping these creatures for the sake of feeling good. However, if one really gets involved in trying to help these creatures, especially in a way that goes to the systemic cruelties and destructions that are committed against millions of animals, there is not going to be that much about which to feel good. We have to fight the good fight without feeling smug about it or about ourselves; we have to have a sense of justice without feeling superior about it (and without announcing to others, "I have a sense of justice," as if these others do not, even though in fact they may not). Why do we need to do these things? Because we will poison the good fight by making it about the wrong things. This seems to me to be an adequate interpretation of Kant's argument about the difference between the pursuit of the good and the pursuit of happiness.

Sixth Observation

What is the relationship between human liberation and animal liberation? Would it be possible to achieve one without the other? It is commonly argued that a communist society would be one where gender and race inequality have been overcome, and there can be no socialist (transitional) society that does not have this work of overcoming as an integral element. (While Marxism has often been deficient in thematizing these questions as such, let us at least take it as given that there can no communism that maintains gender or race subordination.) There is then the additional argument that neither gender nor race equality can make fundamental progress as long as capitalism defines the basic structure of society, as capitalism has intertwined these inequalities with itself and has every interest in deepening these inequalities. This is right, I think, even if it is at the same time laudable and right that people take up the questions of gender and race inequality and oppression in their own right; indeed, communists need to do this too.

Are there parallels to be drawn, however, with the situation of animals? While I would like to think that a liberated human society would not and could not be one where the systemic horrors of the vast food-animal production system in the current imperialist world order continue to exist, it is more difficult to make the argument in a systematic, social-theoretical way. What, however, is a liberated human society? We can more readily see how it could not be a society where there is domination of people because of race or gender, because people of different colors or genders are human beings; indeed, they are the greater part of humanity. One aim of this discussion has been to downplay the differences between animals and humans with respect to the question of cruelty (and ways of short-circuiting the forms of *eudaimonea* that are appropriate to each species), but I am not saying that "animals are people too." It is not so much a matter of "minding the borders" (to borrow a theme from H. Peter Steeves), as it is a matter of thinking that not everyone has to be a "people" in order to be pretty cool, and that cats ought to be able to be cats, rabbits ought to be able to be rabbits, spiders ought to be able to be spiders, and so on.

Regardless of whether or not the term "ethical community" would exhaustively describe everything that might be theorized under the term "communism," at least as understood in a scientific rather than utopian sense by Marx and Engels, surely communist society would be, at least in part, an ethical community. And regardless of whether human obligations to animals are direct or indirect in the sense in which Kant made this distinction, there are ethical obligations toward animals. How could something that would be deserving of the name of ethical community carry forward the food-animal production system of the contemporary world, or anything at all like this present system? How could such a future society be a "liberated" society?

There is also the sense in which, for each liberation to be what it is, there has to be a separation, and this does go to Kant's argument about indirect duties to animals. We are left with a paradox: an ethical human community cannot be one that treats animals in the way they are treated in the present society, and thus, for the sake of the possibility of an ethical community of humanity, animals must be liberated from their present state of human subjection; however, in order for the question of this subjection to truly be an ethical question, it would seem that the animal question has to be an ethical question in its own right. Furthermore, it is only in recognizing that there are autonomous, real ethical questions that liberation movements can advance toward ethical community. And yet certainly another connection between imperialism and the animal question is that we should fear for the future of many species if the imperialist system keeps going the way it is going. Some biologists argue that we are already at the beginning of a big "die off" (*Deep Vegetarianism* once again provides many sources; see 88–95). Further philosophical work needs to be done on this paradox (or bundle of paradoxes), and yet it would already be a tremendous advance for Marxism, in the case that Marxism ought to be a philosophy of liberation (otherwise, what good is it?), to have these problems on the table, and for there to be a commitment in theory and practice to get somewhere with them.

Can human liberation movements go forward without addressing animal liberation, without making animal liberation a part of their program? At least two things can be said that go to systemic concerns, even if these things are also in a sense evasive. They are evasive in that I do not think that it can be decisively argued that Marxism must advocate either vegetarianism or animal liberationism in order to make a contribution to human liberation, nor do I think it can be decisively argued that one has to be a vegetarian in order to be a "real" revolutionary communist. However, there are at least two arguments that run in the other direction.

First, a liberatory Marxism will still be fundamentally interested in the mode of production, but one can no longer be focused, systematically and scientifically on this question without also being concerned with questions of ecology, agriculture, and place. (More on this in the next section.) Therefore, simply the environmental devastation that is associated with the food-animal production system, and the diversion of tremendous agricultural and other "resources" (especially water) to the maintenance of this system has to be a central concern for anyone who hopes to see any kind of future.

Second, I do not know what it would mean for someone to claim to be a revolutionary communist, and to believe that we are hoping and struggling for a future global community of mutual flourishing (and, yes, the mode of production that is appropriate to such a community), but who also takes a callous attitude toward the suffering of animals. Following what Kant said about the way that such an attitude (and participation in practices that reflect this attitude, though of course Kant knew nothing of how grotesque and vast these practices would become) leads to a hardening of a person's heart toward humanity, we are entitled to argue that systemic cruelty toward animals, and, for that matter, personal cruelty toward animals, are part of a general culture of cruelty. I argued earlier in this section that initiation and integration into carnivorism is a kind of schooling in this culture and in the acceptance of this general culture of cruelty as normal.

Can a person be a revolutionary communist or otherwise be committed to a better future for humankind, and yet not be a "good person"? It is common for people to avoid larger political struggles precisely with the declaration, "I just want to try to be a good person." Aristotle already had it right when he said that this is not how being a "good person" works. A human *person*, living in sensuous reality, and especially in the reality of a social system based in exploitation and reification, cannot help but have contradictions. Indeed, that was one of the problems that Kant thematized, how do we make a good society out of deeply flawed people such as ourselves. Perhaps the most difficult form of the contradiction is that it is very difficult to struggle against the horrible systems that prevail in the world today without hardening one's heart at least to some extent, and humanity finds itself at times in a situation where it must devote more of its energies to struggling *against* the present than to struggling *for* the future. This can make a person sick at heart. Once the process of hardening sets in, it is difficult to contain it. The crux of the matter cannot be whether this or that person, who claims to be a part of the movement for human liberation, is a vegetarian, and this tells us something interesting. In a sense, this perspective is humanist and speciesist, because it is right to say, on the other hand, that such a person *cannot* be a misogynist or racist and be a true fighter for liberation.

Again, I would say that we are left with a quandary, if not a paradox. However, it could be said, at the least, that it can no longer be acceptable that someone could be a fighter for human liberation who at the same time has a callous or even simply indifferent perspective on either animals or nature more generally. Perhaps it was at least understandable that for a fairly long period Marxism partook of the thoroughly entrenched Western ideologies of "man against nature" and "conquering nature" and various "tooth and claw" scenarios. However, as applied in practice, in the Soviet Union and China, these ideologies were environmentally ruinous (and they also tended to hold up the availability of meat on the dinner table as an important standard of material progress). Perhaps these policies were no more ruinous as applied in the Soviet Union and China than they were in the industrial revolutions of the Western countries, but surely that is not good enough—even while Russia and China came to socialism with basic, indeed very deep, deficiencies in basic production, including in the production of food. (Regarding the preoccupation in China with damming rivers, we might make a comparison with the United States; see the excellent book by Donald Worster, *Rivers of Empire.*) In China, at least, there was a more developed perspective on agriculture, during the Mao period, as reflected in the *Shanghai Textbook on Political Economy*. The factors that necessitated this policy, however, did not lead to a decisive break with the "conquering nature" mode of development. The planetary ecology as a whole can no longer take this kind of "development" (or will not be able to take much more of it), and the great irony today is that China may very well become the lynchpin of global disaster—even while, to use Maoist language, the United States remains the "main force" of this gathering crisis.

Just staying with Marxism as a philosophy that still has a decisive contribution to make to creating a radically better society—albeit in a patched-up, reconfigured, and updated form that will not, and should not, be especially congenial to certain orthodoxies of the past—I would say that we can no longer afford Marxisms that are not ecological (and ecology is also concerned with biodiversity) or that partake of, rather than decisively break with, the capitalist, colonialist, and imperialist culture of cruelty (which then includes the animal questions we have already discussed). Perhaps this means that Marxism can get no further than Kant did on the animal question: ethical obligations to animals are indirect duties. Even so, indirect duties are duties all the same.

If it turns out that Marx and Kant have to come to the same point, and in somewhat the same way, on a significant question, this should open up an interesting avenue for a larger comparison. Without letting go of the injunction, which, for the purposes of the present book I am more interested in directing toward Marxism, that indirect obligations are still real obligations, there is something that is critical of both Kant and Marx on this point that needs to be said, and the question is whether this criticism goes to their personal limitations and historical situations or to their frameworks. Kant and Marx, of course, did not see the industrial food-production system of the twentieth century. Anyone who takes an honest look at this system, especially the part that deals with animals, from the massive feed lots to the slaughterhouse to the forms of packaging, distribution, and sales, to advertising and other ways that the ethical questions involved in the food-animal system are trivialized in various media will see, or should see, that this is a bad system. It is a system that is doing horrible things to our fellow creatures, and a person can only get around this by some combination of maintaining a willful ignorance and incorporating a certain amount of callousness in his or her world view.

On my long bike rides in the countryside of Kansas, I sometimes take roads that pass by the large cattle lots, including one near the western Kansas town of Ulysses that contains over 180,000 cows (it is the second-largest such lot in the world). The smell is unreal; to use a favorite Southern expression, it would gag a maggot. It makes me wish that everyone who eats these poor creatures would have to live out there with them. I would like to think that anyone with any moral sensitivity whatsoever would, upon experiencing this scene, be immediately convinced that it is a horrendous thing. I would like to think that, upon realizing this, any morally sensitive person would recognize that our obligations to the creatures who are rendered through this system go beyond indirect duty. But perhaps moral sensitivity is overcome by nasal sensitivity, and one hopes to simply get away as quickly as possible and forget about it, and have a nice steak or hamburger for dinner. This is where, again, it seems that the ignorance and callousness to which the great majority is acculturated, and toward which the great majority does not have the wherewithal to resist, has to be a *systemic* thing—which does not, however, cancel the responsibilities that we have toward our fellow creatures.

Harking back to my fifth observation, on this matter of personal responsibility, it is not a question of having a "good conscience" about being a vegetarian; there isn't much to feel good about here.

Whether Kant and Marx, in looking at the feedlot, would adjust their perspectives is not something that can be known. Perhaps it does not matter, but it does matter what can be done with their philosophies in light of the industrial food-animal production system.

The willful ignorance/callousness combination, in the case of the carnivorist system, has many parallels to the same combination that is at work in the imperialist system. These systems are intertwined and they reinforce one another. It may even be that one cannot be opposed and transcended, ultimately, without opposing and transcending the other.

Seventh Observation

Finally, if carnivorism is a system, are there contradictions in this system? This question can be addressed on three levels.

First, we might consider Marx's use of the notion of contradiction in the largest frame that Marx gives us, in terms of the cell-form and the future. The connection between the two is that the future must represent a resolution to the difficulty into which humankind fell in the distant past. The difficulty, the fall into alienation, is the emergence of the commodity form and the process of commodification. If this emergence passes through the commodification of women, then the transcendence of patriarchy is an integral part of humankind's transition into another kind of society. If the emergence of commodification is fundamentally bound up with the reification of animals (so deeply that it is difficult even for theorists of reification to grasp that there is a problem), then the transition into another kind of society, one not based on reification, entails the transcendence of this cruel, alienating, and objectifying relationship. This means that the redemptive and "tikkun" (healing, reparative) elements of social transformation are not sentimental, optional add-ons.

Second, there are indeed structural contradictions involved with the industrial food-animal production system, and even if the recognition of these returns us to the area of indirect duties, they should still be understood. Most likely the most important among these contradictions are (1) that this system leads to and is a part of widespread environmental devastation, which undermines the basic sustainability of the global ecosystem (and this occurs on numerous levels, from pollution and global warming to the qualitative disruption of biodiversity—the bee needs the flower, and the flower needs the bee; if one is undermined, so is the other), and (2) imperialist food production, especially the food-animal system, produces bad food that makes people unhealthy and sick. *Fast Food Nation* by Eric Schlosser, and the film *Supersize Me*, by Morgan Spurlock, and other popular works have helped to highlight this. Of course literally *billions* of people do not need a book or a film to know that there is a lot of bad food out there, and that it is doing bad things to their bodies. I raise this in part because, when I have discussed the animal question in some Marxist circles, especially activist circles, I am often asked about the supposed case where the only thing for the basic masses to eat, with the hope of getting some protein, is meat, because a system of production (and to some extent a system of normativity) that is beyond their control has made things this way. Speaking only of the United States here, the fast-food capital, it is indeed the case that it is hard to get *affordable*, decent, healthy food in many places. This is true in the urban centers, as well as in many less urban areas. There are financial and ideological barriers that people have to overcome, in the midst of daily lives where this question would be very hard to prioritize. And yet the question ought to be prioritized, because the junk that the basic masses are encouraged to eat is destroying them. It is no accident that the popular urban fast-food chains make every use of a very low-level cultural populism, as if Mickey D. and his buddies are your best and hippest friends. Behind the scenes they are fighting each other for every dollar, and the long-term health of ordinary people with low incomes is not their concern. There are activists, such as the great Richie Havens and hip-hop artist KRS-ONE, who have addressed this issue specifically. It is an uphill battle, but in one way it is not unlike every other big issue that confronts the world today: namely that, for the basic masses it is always an uphill battle for them to back up from the struggle just to hold body and soul together on a daily basis, and to aim their sights at the major challenges that confront the world—including the future existence of the world and humanity itself. There is an important way in which the uphill battle concerning food is different from many other uphill battles; food is a day-to-day concern, and the fact that the best the food-production system in the richest country in the world can do for millions of people is to provide choices that are literally sickening makes food both a daily and a long-term issue.

This *contradiction*—which is a good term for food, which is supposed to sustain a person, but where it also progressively undermines a person's long-term viability—is not unrelated to the basic contradiction of capitalism, namely, the contradiction between socialized production and private accumulation. Food production is the most essential aspect of any society;

as Engels said in his graveside eulogy, Marx's great discovery as a philosopher is that people have to eat. (Somehow philosophers had missed this over the millennia up to that point, and, after Marx, most philosophers started missing it again.) I often tell students in my courses on Marx that a good deal of Marx's analysis of capitalism can be unfolded simply through pursuing the question of why certain groups of people who do very essential work, such as garbage collectors, do not rule the world. Why is essential work not *valued* essentially, and why is it not transformed into good work? Why are we not able to care, collectively, about the quality of food and the conditions under which it is produced? The answer, in a word, is capitalism—the way that society is presently organized. On the food question alone, is it not clear that the world is upside-down?

Third, when Marx talked about the contradictions of the capitalist system, he did not discuss the difference between right and wrong as a "contradiction." Perhaps on this point he was right to avoid this language; the language of right and wrong seems like too blunt an instrument to address the unfolding of historical and social processes. The simplest example, given no better airing than in the *Manifesto* itself, is that capitalism is not only not *wrong*, but also for its time it is radically *right*. Capitalism only becomes wrong when capitalism itself has created the conditions for its *Aufhebung*, its overcoming, sublation, transcendence. Capitalism is right in its time and wrong when its time has passed. What it means, in Marx's view, for a social system's time to have passed is that it has developed all of the "productive forces for which there is room in it" ("Marx on the History of His Opinions," in MER, 5). For Marx, this means that any social system will reach a limit where it can no longer bring about qualitative developments in production. At least in the case of capitalism, it seems he was not exactly right about this. What we might say instead, then, is that it is not only a matter of the point at which another social system becomes *necessary* (in order to most effectively employ the means of production that have been created—in recent years this discussion has come to center around the role that cybernetic technology plays in production and different labor processes; on this point, see *Cutting Edge: Technology, Information, Capitalism, and Social Revolution*, ed. Jim Davis, et al.), but instead the point when a better system becomes *possible*. In either case, of Marx's necessitarian scheme, or some form of what Bob Avakian and I came to call, in our book of conversations, "postinevitablist Marxism," there is an irreducible element of normativity involved. Whether this element is truly a sufficient basis for the creation of a larger ethical discourse, which is able to talk about right and wrong in a substantive way, has been debated for many decades by now. If we are able to derive this larger discourse from a Marxist framework, it has to be understood forthrightly that this philosophical move would occur *despite* Marx, quite likely even against Marx. But part of my reason for bringing Kant into the conversation is that, if it is only possible to talk about right and wrong and good and evil by speaking in another register, then let us not shrink from speaking in this other register. We will also want to know how this other register fits with the core of Marx's arguments, because we need his language too.

If being stuck in a certain register prevents us from seeing that the way animals are treated in this world of carnivorism and industrial food-animal production is a hugely significant and very *real* ethical issue, then we had better address this problem. The cruel, horrible, grotesque way that many, many of our fellow creatures on this planet are treated is just wrong.

2. Agriculture and the Question of Place (an Appreciation of Wendell Berry and Wes Jackson in the Context of Marxism)

It became increasingly difficult to locate them in any particular place; they were gone, that was all. To be nowhere or not to be at all isn't very different.

—Simone de Beauvoir, *The Mandarins*

One of the things that Marx's philosophy makes clear is that all of humanity lives in a place called Earth. We all live on this planet where, first of all through broad processes that can be called "economic" (in shorthand, for the moment), and then through other processes that are driven by economics, we live an increasingly interconnected life—"together," but not together. We humans have a collective life in this place, on this planet, because capitalism, colonialism, and imperialism have organized vast collectivities, but these are not consciously collective collectivities. There are a number of reasons for this, but one reason I would like to propose is that, when capitalism makes the whole Earth a "place" where humanity lives, it creates at the same time a fundamental "placelessness." Everywhere on our planet becomes *the* place, while, increasingly, nowhere is *a* place. Among the processes by which this occurs are:

- the movements of peasants off the land, a process that continues today, such that now, for the first time in history, half of the world's population lives in cities;

- the separation of the working people from the means of production, such that only a relative handful of people can feel some sense of security in their location, their "locatedness" (to coin an infelicitous term)—Marx and Engels spoke to this issue in saying that "the workers have no country" (and they do not yet have a world, either; "they have a world to win");

- in the United States, where there used to be a substantial class of family farmers, there has been what Wendell Berry calls "the unsettling of America," thanks to the rise of agribusiness;

- there is the destruction of what has traditionally given at least many parts of the world the character of being "a place," namely the flora and fauna ("biodiversity");

- and there are the forms of homogenization typical of imperialist globalization, which gives us the McWorld.

(My favorite joke about globalization goes as follows: "I went into a Starbucks, and I had to use the men's room, and there was a Starbucks in there." This goes nicely with comedian Lewis Black's claim that he had found the end of the world, in Houston, Texas, on a street where he had stopped in at a Starbucks; coming out of it, he realized that there was another Starbucks directly across the street.) One "big place," where there are fewer and fewer actual *places*, is no place at all.

The dynamic that drives the process of rendering the world placeless can be specified simply enough, even if there is more to be understood about what gives people a sense of place, and also what makes people feel "placeless." Indeed, this dynamic goes very directly to this latter case, especially when people are rendered placeless by not having the resources to obtain at least a little bit of shelter. In other words, our old friend, the brutal cash nexus, carries forward a process of rendering places into property, into real estate.

One World, Many Places

But, what is "place," or "a place," and why does this matter?

To back up slightly, it was not Marx who first of all gave us the notion of the earth as a place. Certainly Kant played a fundamental role in establishing this notion, not only in being the first philosopher to systematically address the subject of international relations, but also in the fact that he lectured frequently on geography. Schelling and Hegel gave us philosophies of world history (I can only mention in passing that there is some very perceptive material on Schelling's *The Ages of the World* in David Farrell Krell, *The Tragic Absolute*, esp. 104–48, and Slavoj Žižek, *The Indivisible Remainder*, 35–39). Certainly a greater, broadening sense of the world was helped along by those thinkers and investigators in early Western modernity who grappled with the fact that the European Christian tradition is not the only religious tradition. (Among these can be counted Leibniz; see Franklin Perkins, *Leibniz and China: A Commerce of Light*.) It might be said, given fundamentalist currents in the United States and elsewhere in the world today that these thinkers grappled with not only the fact but also the significance, something today's fundamentalists are at pains *not* to do. A certain parallel might be drawn, one that is indicative of the fundamentalist refusal to exist in the world that is planet Earth. In the matter of religion, we might ask: If Christianity is the only true religion, who and what were these other characters, such as Gautama the Buddha? Was he an agent of Satan? How is it that Buddha came to have thousands and millions of followers, in lands that had not even heard of Jesus of Nazareth (not that Jesus was a Christian either) until quite recently? Similarly, in the matter of science, if fundamentalist Christian creationism ("creation science," "intelligent design") is right, then what was Darwin all about? What was he doing that was different from any other scientist who is investigating one part or another of our material world using methods of empirical investigation and hypothesis and theory formation? Was Darwin also an agent of Satan, unlike other scientists who discovered or helped to explain things that are not seen as being in conflict with a supposedly biblical world view? (I return to these questions and their relation to ethical questions in the conclusion.) What we might say in the case of Marx is that instead of introducing the idea of the earth as humanity's place, he provided a certain "cement" for the notion, such that it would be very difficult to go back to anything else, perhaps analogous to the way that it would be very difficult if not impossible to go back to an earth-centric notion of the cosmos. We cannot refuse to recognize that we live on planet Earth after Marx, or after the things that he recognized about the way that the capitalist mode of production was creating an increasingly interconnected world. Just to put the idea in epistemological terms, and borrowing an example from Davidson (from "On the Very Idea of a Conceptual Scheme"), it could very well be that the ancient Israelites were right in believing that the world was destroyed by a great flood in an earlier time—it depends on what is meant by "the world." The example is relevant: once Marx provides the cement for the idea that humanity lives in a *place* called Earth, there is the basis for asking one of the fundamental ethical questions of our time. That is, if the earth is the place humanity lives, how can people in just one part of the earth do things that will mess up the whole planet for everyone?

Such a question demonstrates the positive side of Marx's contribution, and it would be silly for us to let go of it. If this planet is the home of humanity, and of countless other species, and if, without this planet, humanity will not only not have a home, but will not exist at all, then, certainly, let us not mess up the whole planet. And, if there are forces that are working to mess up the planet altogether, let us do what we can to stop them, and to transform situations so that our planet is sustainable. One would think this much does not even need saying, and yet, in one of those upside-down realities that Marx excelled at analyzing, it is both a bizarre and at the same time normal and everyday fact that there are forces arrayed against the ecological sustainability of the earth. Indeed, most of us humans participate on a daily basis and on myriad levels in processes that undermine sustainability. This also barely needs saying. However, my aim here is not to go very far with an encounter between Marxism and eco-logical concerns; this encounter has been pursued in detail and with great insight elsewhere, perhaps most of all in the work of James O'Connor (see *Natural Causes: Essays in Ecological Marxism*; O'Connor is also the co-founder and editor of *Capitalism, Nature, Socialism: A Journal of Socialist Ecology*). Instead, my aim in this section is to lay the ground for offering yet another corrective to Marx and most of what calls itself Marxism, and to demonstrate that the question of place is an ethical concern that should be incorporated into Marxism.

It is an extraordinary thing to even attempt to imagine what has to underlie, historically, philosophically, scientifically, the attempt to connect all the dots and to understand planet Earth as "a place." Though this task is forced upon us more and more (by "geo-politics," by financial institu-tions such as the World Bank and the World Trade Organization, by global warming, and the role that each of these phenomena plays in structuring the lives of every person—and the animals and trees and rhizomes and rivers and so on—on the planet), it is not clear that we radically finite, mor-tal humans are entirely up to the task. We can certainly screw things up through hubris in this endeavor, and this is where I return to Wendell Berry's example of topsoil (that we are good at using it up, but we do not know how to make any more of it, and the future of humanity depends on topsoil) and his and Wes Jackson's argument for an "ignorance-based world view." Be that as it may, let us not abandon too quickly Marx's con-tribution on this point: global consciousness is indeed forced upon us; if being determines consciousness, then global being necessitates global con-sciousness.

Global and Local

However, there is not much room in Marx for the "be that as it may" part, and this is the part where, if one is not able to stand somewhere, then one is not able to stand anywhere. Wendell Berry gave the famous formulation of this point when he said, "If you do not know where you are, you do not know who you are"; he also offered a prohibition against giving one's location as simply "planet Earth" with a critique of the popular 1970s slogan, "Think Globally, Act Locally." Berry argued that the very idea of "thinking globally" is a problem; indeed, the very idea that one could understand what it might mean to think globally and that one would want to do so are problems. Berry argues that the only real thinking is "in place" and that we only do damage to the earth in presuming that we might "think" it.

If Berry is on to something here, and I think he is, this does not mean that we should go so far as to accept the idea that there is no need for global thinking and global activism. There are global problems that will require global solutions. Still, according to Berry, at least some of these big problems are actually the result of thinking too "big" in the first place, and that they are best addressed by a climbdown from this kind of thinking. While the solution may be to split the difference with Marx, there is some distance to go in understanding the value of "local" places (such as they exist anymore, or such as there is the possibility of returning to a sense of such places) before an equitable split may occur.

In this proposal to split the difference, we can take a page from Sartre once again, though we will take Sartre's approach in a direction that did not seem a concern for him. In *Search for a Method*, Sartre proposes that the big, totalizing "system" (in this case, of Hegel and Marx) requires a reassertion of the existential particular and singular, or else the system will have an overwhelming tendency to not only totalize, but to proclaim itself the transcendental totalizer—in other words, God. A "thinking" of the planet Earth that is unaware of the earth that is here, or there, or somewhere, or that subsumes the particularities of this earth into a big concept and thereby obliterates the particularities, has the character of the sort of cosmic, theological thinking in which finite beings do not count for much. It is undeniable that Marxism has gone down this path more than a few times, in theory and practice, thus Sartre's corrective. Ignoring the likely incoherencies of the idea (because human beings would seem to have projects in a way that other animals, or trees or rivers or mountains, do not), we might propose a kind of ecological existentialism as a corrective to overly ambitious and often hubristic "global thinking."

Now, Wendell Berry and Wes Jackson do not tend to talk this way, with the exception that both focus on human finitude and the problem of hubris. What interests them more directly are the problems of the land, agriculture, and community. Together they are credited with inspiring a "new agrarianism," with Berry playing the role of the farmer-philosopher, poet, and novelist, and with Jackson, the scientist-philosopher, founding and leading an institute dedicated to the scientific study of sustainable agriculture.

Marxism and Agriculture

There is not only no real analysis of agriculture in Marx, there is a basic resistance to carrying out such an analysis. This resistance may seem strange in the case of the thinker who discovered that people have to eat, and it *is* strange, but it is also an artifact of what I call (mimicking an early work by Marx and Engels), "the urban ideology." Engels wrote a book on the peasant war in Germany (of 1525), an important and interesting book that prefigures some aspects of peasant struggles in the twentieth century (and, in its portrayal of Thomas Muenzer, an inspiration to liberation theology), but about agriculture per se there is nothing. Marx of course dealt with the peasants as a class, though primarily in Europe (where there was a significant peasant class—or classes—well into the twentieth century), but agriculture itself is subsumed under very general schemes such as the human transition from gathering and hunting into forms of cultivation and animal husbandry, and later into the general scheme of the feudal mode of production. There is not anything very specific to say about agriculture; instead there is the infamous comment, from *The German Ideology*, about "the idiocy of rural life" (in MER, 178). Apparently, knowing how to grow the food that feeds humanity is part of this idiocy, or, at least it does not count as real knowledge. Marx did not find the phenomenon of the American yeoman farmer worthy of study, either; neither he nor Engels, in studying utopian or syndicalist movements, concerned themselves much (beyond a stray comment or two, some of them derogatory, such as Marx's only known comment on the Latter-day Saints, referring to something as "making about as much sense as Joseph Smith's golden bible") with the agrarian-communitarian movements of nineteenth-century North America, even though these movements were clearly a reaction to the imposition of money economies and the development of industrial production. But that is the point: for Marx, all you need to know about agriculture is that it represents an outmoded form of production. Even in formulating the dramatic theses, again in *The German Ideology*, that "The greatest division of material and mental labour is the separation of town and country," and "The abolition of the antagonism between town and country is one of the first conditions of communal life," there is no particular attention paid to the question of where the food is going to come from. Even in the *Critique of the Gotha Programme*, where Marx goes as far as he ever did in describing a future society, one gets the sense that the paradigm of work is in a factory. (A very interesting book that takes Marx's "town/country" theses as a starting point is *The Limits of the City* by Murray Bookchin.) Marx perpetuated an urban ideology that is so influential that, even today, the question of agriculture has no place in the work of many political philosophers or social theorists. Indeed, it would not even occur to them to consider this question, and here there is a parallel with the nonstatus of the animal question in Marx and in Marxism. Of course, there are direct connections between the animal question and the questions of place and agriculture (one strange connection being that the animal question is often just as much in the realm of the "unthought" for the latter pair as it is in other areas of social theory): animals need places too, and indeed it would seem that biodiversity (of plants and animals) is a key part of the definition of "place."

Great historical irony, then: when the first countrywide socialist revolution took place in Russia in 1917, it occurred in a place where the peasants were in the vast majority, and where industrial production was relatively nascent.

(To this another irony can be added: the first seizure of power by the proletariat, as Marx understood it, was not in a country, but rather in a city. This is the case of the Paris Commune of 1871. The Commune only lasted a few weeks, and it was essentially starved into submission by a military blockade. And yet no analysis of food or agricultural questions by Marx issues from this experience. Mao, on the basis of a quite different experience in an even more predominantly agricultural society, finally takes up these questions as such—not in a merely, and crushingly, pragmatic way as Stalin did—and in "The Ten Great Relationships" and elsewhere demonstrates how one basis for capitalist restoration in a country where there has been a socialist revolution is an unbalanced and inequitable relationship with the countryside. Mao also stresses the knowledge that is in the countryside, not only as regards agriculture and food, but also in other matters such as medicine.)

Marx had in fact been in communication, in the last years of his life, with populist revolutionaries in Russia, who were studying Marx and wondering if there was some way to go more directly from communal village to socialism, without the full-blown development of capitalism in between. Here, at least, the "agrarian" question is raised. The documents from this communication as well as supporting materials are presented in *Late Marx and the Russian Road: Marx and "The Peripheries of Capitalism,"* edited by Teodor Shanin. This is fascinating material that bears much further study, especially on the questions of land, agriculture, and place. The inquiry that Vera Zasulich wrote to Marx is interesting on many levels. Zasulich (1849–1919) was a member of a kind of anarcho-populist group called the "Black Repartition." Jonathan Sanders writes in a biographical sketch of Zasulich, "In 1878 she shot the St. Petersburg governor Trepov for flogging a prisoner. In a great political trial she was acquitted" (178). Aleksandr Il'ich Ulianov, the elder brother of V. I. Lenin, was a member of a similar group (of what in Russia were called *Narodniki*, radical populists); in 1887 he was arrested for his part in a plot to assassinate the Tsar, and he was executed the same year. Three years after shooting the Petersburg governor, Zasulich wrote to Marx:

> Honoured Citizen,
>
> You are not unaware that your *Capital* enjoys great popularity in Russia. Although the edition has been confiscated, the few remaining copies are read and re-read by the mass of more or less educated people in our country; serious men are studying it. What you probably do not realise is the role which your capital plays in our discussions on the agrarian question in Russia and our rural commune. You know better than anyone how urgent this question is in Russia. You know what Chernyshevskii thought of it. . . . in my view, it is a life-and-death question above all for our socialist party. In one way or another even the personal fate of our revolutionary socialists depends on your answer to the question. For there are only two possibilities. Either the rural commune, freed of exorbitant tax demands, payment to the nobility and arbitrary administration, is capable of developing in a socialist direction, that is, gradually organising its production and distribution on a collectivist basis. In that case, the revolutionary socialist must devote all his strength to the liberation and development of the commune.
>
> If, however, the commune is destined to perish, all that remains for the socialist, as such, is more or less ill-founded calculations as to how many decades it will take for the Russian peasant's land to pass into the hands of the bourgeoisie, and how many centuries it will take for capitalism in Russia to reach something like the level of development already attained in Western Europe. Their task will then be to conduct propaganda solely among the urban workers, while these workers will be continually drowned in the peasant mass which, following the dissolution of the commune, will be thrown on to the streets of the large towns in search of a wage.
>
> Nowadays, we often hear it said that the rural commune is an archaic form condemned to perish by history, scientific socialism and, in short, everything above debate. Those who preach such a view call themselves your disciples *par excellence*: "Marksists". [This is meant as a conflation of Marxist and market.] Their strongest argument is often: "Marx said so."
>
> "But how do you derive that from *Capital*?" others object. "He does not discuss the agrarian question, and says nothing about Russia." (Shanin, 98–99)

As Shanin observes, Marx took this inquiry very, very seriously, writing four drafts of a response; "The drafts are testimony of puzzlement but also of a growing consciousness of and the first approach to a new major problem" (14).

Sense Certainty and Place Empathy

Significantly, the first three drafts of a response to Zasulich are a good deal longer and more detailed than the letter that was finally sent (in the same year that Marx received the original inquiry). In these drafts we see Marx grappling with the issue of *land* more than before, though not with the question of agriculture per se—which is also to say not with the question of food. One could imagine that, in this context, to raise the question of "place" would seem nonsensical or, at best, merely sentimental. Perhaps this is something of a sentimental question, but that judgment, even if right, should not be the end of it. What Marx does say is quite important, as it goes to the question of "historical inevitability." In his actual reply to Zasulich, Marx claims that "my so-called theory has been misunderstood" by the "Marksists":

> In analysing the genesis of capitalist production, I said:

> At the heart of the capitalist system is a complete separation of . . . the producer from the means of production . . . *the expropriation of the agricultural producer* is the basis of the whole process. Only in England has it been accomplished in a radical manner. . . . *But all the other countries of Western Europe* are following the same course. (*Capital,* French edition, 315) [italics and ellipses in original]

> The "historical inevitability" of this course is therefore *expressly* restricted to *the countries of Western Europe.* The reason for this restriction is indicated in Ch. XXXII: "*Private property,* founded upon personal labor . . . is supplanted by *capitalist private property,* which rests on exploitation of the labour of others, on wage-labour." (Shanin, 124)

Now, Marx goes on to say that things could turn out quite differently in Russia, because peasant property in Russia is already collective and communal rather than private. However, we might note that Marx's response does open up a difficulty as regards the question of place. Either Marx gives us the earth as a place, which, however, will develop as Western Europe has—this is the basis on which we might "know" the earth, that it is not yet like Western Europe, but eventually it will be. This is the "Marksist" view, it could be said. Or, what Marx really gives us instead of the earth is Western Europe, and he has not really thought very much about dynamics of place and society elsewhere. Does Marx, following Hegel, lose sense-certainty from his system, his so-called theory—and does Marx thereby also lose what might be called "place-empathy"?

This difficulty is well known. To oversimplify greatly: hence the modifications of Marx by Lenin and Mao. These modifications are not simply add-ons, but require qualitative breaks with certain aspects of the previous "so-called theory." The important thing about these modifications is that they were forced by a dual imperative: to consider, on the one hand, specificities of particular parts of the world, and, on the other hand, to grasp better the idea that the new revolutions, the revolutions of the *interna-*

tional proletariat, are part of a global process. But, there was an important shift in the time from Marx to Lenin, where qualitative developments in capitalism had bound the world more tightly under a single mode of production.

Emphasis on Mechanization

Lenin interpreted this development of capitalism into imperialism as meaning that the proposals of Zasulich and others (that Russia might develop a form of socialism based on the peasant village, which would allow Russia to bypass the course of capitalist development typical of Western Europe) were off the table, overtaken by events. It was not until the Bolsheviks formed a socialist government, and then of necessity had to have an agricultural policy, that they finally developed a perspective on agriculture—by incorporating the policy of the Social Revolutionary Party (which had developed as a party representing the peasantry) wholesale. Although the Soviet Union was established as the "democratic dictatorship of the workers and peasants," a formula to which some took exception in the name of "classical Marxism" (Trotsky being the most outstanding example), the former embarrassment—or what should have been an embarrassment within Marxism, its failure to grapple with agriculture as such rather than to entertain fantasies of eventual food factories—carried over into a crude approach to the peasants as a class. Mao, himself of peasant background, characterized this approach as, "You want the cow to give milk, but you don't want to feed the cow." There was a marked tendency to focus almost exclusively on the mechanization of agriculture and, under Stalin, to squeeze the peasants on the one hand, and to buy into bogus "science" (that is, Lysenko) on the other. Anything to keep the idea that the future of society is industrial production, which after all was not something Stalin just dreamed up—and to never have to appreciate the land or take it seriously. This was even the case in the revolutionary slogan that brought workers, peasants, and soldiers together on the eve of the revolution, "Land, Bread, and Peace." The "land" part referred to "land to the tiller," the expropriation of the big landlords and the sharing out of the land to the peasants. "Bread" was for the hungry workers—but then, where does bread come from?

The issues of land, agriculture, place, and, for that matter, the city and urbanization, can be taken as analytically distinct, but in practice they are deeply interconnected. The orthodox Marxist perspective on agriculture up through the Stalin period was of a piece with the idea that there are no "places" that have their own integrity that ought to be attended to before they are radically remade. The projection of this view into our day would hold that the corporate agribusiness set-up has it right as regards agriculture, just wrong on the matter of ownership and management. This is all fine from the standpoint of the urban ideology, in which food magically appears in the grocery store and, as for what it takes to get it there, we don't want to know about it. I do not want to go so far as to say that cities are not places too, but I would be inclined to argue that an analysis of place that does not begin with dirt and the land and the flora and fauna that are natural to an area, and topology, and the sources of water, and the interconnections of all of these elements with the possibilities for sustainable human habitation (which, first of all, is habitation that is not ruinous to these elements) is deeply misguided. We need not go so far as to say that cities are not places, but, on the other hand, no one will dispute that the cities of the McWorld, as further homogenized by the present wave of imperialist globalization, are becoming less like real places every day. This development still proceeds *from* the city, *as it always has*—from city to city, and from the city to the countryside on the basis of the demands of the city, but now we see a shift from quantity to quality, such that the sense of place is being lost altogether, and agricultural and ecological sustainability are being lost at the same time and indeed in a way that is fundamentally connected to what might be called the new and perhaps final wave of placelessness.

The City in Thought

Many theorists, including some whose focus is the fate of the city in this time of globalization (see, for example, Marc Auge, *Non-Places: Introduction to an Anthropology of Supermodernity*), have thematized these issues, but it is the new agrarians, led by Berry and Jackson, who are demonstrating the connections between place, agriculture, and ecology—and, conversely, the connections between placelessness, the city, and extractive economy. It is worth mentioning that some of the harshest arguments I have had in academia have come from raising questions about the city as a social form. Indeed, even to say that there might be something to be learned from the countryside is already viewed as going too far—according to my interlocutors to say something good about the countryside, or to point out that the countryside is where the food comes from, is already taken as a criticism of the city. Premise number one of the urban ideology is that the city must not be criticized, and it yields what I call "the unthinking city." In the mix of what gets lost in this unthinking, along with the problems of where the food is going to come from and what it takes to get it, is the division of labor that makes possible being an urban intellectual. The city is not so exciting with culture and thought if one is

an undocumented busboy for most of one's life. What is especially interesting in the dynamics of urban unthought is that the counterattack against
the criticism of the city very quickly becomes personal in nature—something about not knowing how to enjoy the city. The logic of this unthinking is something like, "eat, drink, and be merry, for tomorrow we die." In
the meantime, other parts of the planet are dying for the sake of the merriment, and as in the Tony Soprano household—one does not want to
inquire too deeply into what is paying for all of this excitement. But the
merriment will indeed come to an end, perhaps catastrophically, precisely
because we are not addressing the interconnected questions of place and
placelessness, sustainable agriculture and industrial/extractive economy,
and the city and the countryside.

Homecoming

In *Becoming Native to This Place*, Jackson writes of the need for a new generation of (what he calls) "homecomers." This does not necessarily mean
people going back to where they came from (even if such a place exists any
more, and for many people, it does not), but instead those who will *become*
native in doing the work necessary to fulfill "the need for each community
to be coherent" (100). The roots of this coherence, in Jackson's view, are
in sustainable agriculture. The focus on "each community" means eschewing "grand solutions," which are "inherently anti-native because they are
unable to vary across the varied mosaic of our ecosystems" (100). This
work will require science, and historical learning, and culture, and even a
new role for what Jackson, in a passage I find especially provocative, calls
accounting:

> An extractive economic system to a large degree is a derivative of our percep-
> tions and values. But it also controls our behavior. We have to loosen its hard
> grip on us, finger by finger. I am hopeful that a new economic system can
> emerge from the homecomer's effort—as a derivative of right livelihood rather
> than of purposeful design. It will result from our becoming better ecological
> accountants at the community level. If we must as a future necessity recycle
> essentially all materials and run on sunlight [note here that Jackson and Berry
> often discuss agriculture as the primary form of solar power], then our future
> will depend on accounting as the most important and interesting discipline.
> Because accountants are students of boundaries, we are talking about educat-
> ing a generation of students who will know how to set up the books for their
> ecological community accounting, to use three-dimensional spreadsheets. But
> classroom work alone won't do. They will need a lifetime of field experience
> besides, and the sacrifices they must make, by our modern standards, will be
> huge. They won't be regarded as heroic, at least not in the short run.

> Nevertheless, that will be their real work. Despite the daily decency of the women in the Matfield Greens [Jackson is using the name of a particular farming community in southeast Kansas to refer to farming communities in general], decency could not stand up against the economic imperialism that swiftly and ruthlessly plowed them and their communities under. (99–100)

Notice a particular point of resonance here with an argument central to the present book: we need a systematic radical social theory that has an ethical heart, but ethics by itself does not have what it takes to be ethical—which should not give us license to eliminate this ethical heart, either.

Two further points need to be made as regards the science of boundaries. Both Jackson and Berry speak often of (1) the "imperialism" of extractive industrial economy (just to be clear, an extractive economy is one that takes material out of nature such that it cannot be put back into nature except in a poisonous form: polluted rivers and oceans, a polluted atmosphere, and landfills are emblematic of such an economy) and (2) the city's relationship to the countryside. Neither speaks enough of imperialism in Lenin's sense of the term, and this shows both the strength and the weakness of their approach. On the one hand, they resist the grand scheme; it is the grand scheme that is the problem. That is correct; the grand scheme is the problem, but what this means is that the grand scheme has to be addressed. It cannot simply be side-stepped by making a proposal for the small scheme. The grand scheme cannot be wished away, nor will it be absent from the few small schemes that might get set up. The expand-or-die structure of capital will not leave these experiments alone; one way or another it will reabsorb such experiments if they are indeed experiments, in other words if they are indeed in one way or another outside of or resistant to the dictatorship of M-C-M′. This is where Berry and Jackson need to "split the difference" with Marx, a point to which we will return in a moment.

Even so, let us not abandon what is good here. The second point, the other side of the boundary, has precisely to do with the sorts of radical accounting that might be done based on the guidelines we might still find in nature. On the level of the grand scheme, in fact, it might be getting easier to find these guidelines, but only because the extractive economic systems on our planet are crossing lines—trip wires, as it were—and the "feedback" (or "blowback") is quite possibly on the verge of becoming utterly disastrous. This is most evident on the question of global warming, with melting icecaps, glaciers, and icebergs being the most dramatic result at present, but with rising rates of skin cancer for humans, and a qualitative diminishment of biodiversity waiting in the wings, perhaps to make their appearance quite soon. What is increasingly more difficult, precisely because of the effects of the grand scheme of environmental destruction, is to find what Kirkpatrick Sale and others call the "bioregion." Significantly, Sale titled his book about "the bioregional vision," *Dwellers in the Land*. One way to find a bioregion is to look for a river and the area around it. This is a key to finding an area where agriculture can be practiced in a way that does not undermine sustainability. To take a negative example, a region that does not have its own source of water is one where a city should not be built—much less a large city, such as Phoenix, Arizona. This is one of Berry's favorite examples of a city with no ecological basis, or, we could say, with an anti-ecological basis. Phoenix and Las Vegas are great examples of the heroic masculinist ideology of "diverting mighty rivers," and "bending nature to man's will." (Again, see Donald Worster, *Rivers of Empire*, as well as his *Nature's Economy*.) Simple enough: to find a bioregion, start by looking at rivers—or conversely, if it is clear that the only way to make a place habitable for a human gathering of much size is to divert a river (or build a pipeline to it), then that is not a bioregion, at least not for humans. Leave it to the fragile ecology of the lizards and cactuses. In *The German Ideology*, Marx did in fact remark upon the industrial pollution of rivers, to the point where all of the fish die—but he seems to be making a point about nature and essence (see MER, 168). Clearly, the particularities of the bioregion do not exist in Marx's grand scheme. We might investigate more thoroughly how much this omission owes to the nature of grand schemes, and how much of it owes to a narrow conception of interest (and perhaps even to a narrow conception of humanism). Surely each plays its role.

Conversation with Nature

Berry also makes a proposal for a "natural" setting of guidelines, one that also goes to the question of place:

> an agriculture using nature, including human nature, as its measure would approach the world in the manner of a conversationalist. It would not impose its vision and its demands upon a world that it conceives as a stockpile of raw material, inert and indifferent to any use that may be made of it. It would not proceed directly or soon to some supposedly ideal state of things. It *would* proceed directly and soon to serious thought about our condition and our predicament. On all farms, *farmers would undertake to know responsibly where they are* [my emph.—BM] and to "consult the genius of the place." They would ask what nature would be doing there if no one were farming there. They would ask what nature would permit them to do there, and what they could do there with the least harm to the place and to their natural and human neighbors. And they would ask what nature would *help* them to do there. And, after each asking, knowing that nature will respond, they would attend carefully to her

response. The use of the place would necessarily change, and the response of the place to that use would necessarily change the user. The conversation itself would thus assume a kind of creaturely life, *binding the place and its inhabitants together* [my emph.—BM], changing and growing to no end, no final accomplishment, that can be conceived or foreseen. (*What Are People For?* 208–9)

When Berry uses the term "farmer," he of course means a *real* farmer, not a technological-industrial agent of agribusiness. Contained in this notion of a real farmer is already the responsibility of which Berry writes, a responsibility to know where she or he is, which means not only having a sense of place in general, but also engaging with a particular place. This is an appreciation that is not that of the tourist, but rather one that comes from getting one's hands into the dirt. Is there a larger model of responsibility here? After all, the urban ideologist will say, "yeah, that's great, you farmers go ahead and do that, whatever . . . it doesn't have anything to do with me, and I don't want it to have anything to do with me." We will return to this scene in the next section, the contempt that the urban ideologist has for the farmer, in what might seem to be a rather different context, namely that of the Cultural Revolution in China. The urban ideologist in fact does not want to be entirely left out of this scenario—this person does in fact have something to do with the farmer, but purely in an instrumental way—the farmer is the source of food. But the urban ideologist hardly wants to know even that much, much less think about it.

My proposal runs the other way: that what it means to farm responsibly tells us something about responsibility more generally. Why, or how? If we want to talk about responsibility, then we also need to talk about the question toward whom or what we are responding, or toward whom or what we ought to respond.

Recall the lines I quoted from Gregory Benford's novel, *The Sunborn*: "Julia saw no contradiction between caring for the animals and later slaughtering them, but then, she was a biologist. That wasn't a lot different from being a farmer." In light of the foregoing, let us mark this one crucial difference: it is built into the very idea of the farmer that the farmer cares about the land and the plants and creatures that live on the land. Good farming, at least, is not possible without this element of care, which includes the openness necessary for being a good conversationalist. I am sure, of course, that many, probably most, who are attracted to the biological sciences feel reverence, concern, and love for the diverse life-forms of our planet. These feelings, however, are not an essential part of the objectivity of biological study, and, indeed, it can be argued that scientific objectivity requires such feelings to be bracketed. (Let us set aside for the moment the epistemological problems involved in such an "objectivity.")

Furthermore, many of the institutional settings in which biology is practiced require a form of bracketing that fundamentally crushes and cancels
ethical concern for the fauna and flora of our planet. This is what would be
expected from the capitalist context of such institutions; unfortunately
objectivistic Marxism does no better. So, at least in these contexts there is
not a fundamental contradiction between the practices of the biological
sciences, which can find an understanding of life by hurting life-forms, dis-
secting them, tearing them apart, killing them, and capitalism or some
other (supposedly more advanced) form of objectivism. It could be argued
that this is biology, but not "good biology"—I think it is indeed necessary
to make such an argument. However, the contradiction seems to run
deeper in the case of farming. If farming pursues such a scientistic, objectivistic course, bracketing or otherwise eschewing ethical concern and conversational openness, it eventually ceases to be farming at all, and we see
this in the case of the brutal transition from the traditional farm to
agribusiness/industrial food production. When this transition has been
completed and all ethical concern for the land and creatures who live
within the natural systems of the land is set aside, then a great wrong will
have been perpetrated and the nest will become increasingly spoiled, ultimately to the point of unsustainability.

Significantly, the upshot of this scenario is that good, ethical, empathetic farming is *objectively* an integral part of a sustainable future for the
human species. There is, therefore, a deep contradiction between this kind
of farming, and industrial food production that is guided by what is also an
objective criteria, profit, the logic of M-C-M′, but this capitalist objectivity cares nothing for the longer-range prospects of humanity or anything
else. Indeed, capitalism makes a philistine view of these prospects a proud
part of its ideology: "In the long run, we're all dead." Capitalism goes further, actually, and so do other forms of objectivism; to use Sartrean language again, we might say that, for capitalism, every thing and any thing
is always already dead, already rendered inert.

The Categorial Imperative to Farm

We might overlay the foregoing onto another distinction that could be
made between the biologist and the farmer, what I would like to call "the
categorical imperative to farm." Of course, by "farm" is meant to farm in
the way that Berry and Jackson advocate, in a conversational, empathetic,
"natural systems" way. (The idea of "natural systems agriculture" has especially been developed by Jackson; see, for example, "A Search for the
Unifying Concept for Sustainable Agriculture"). Naturally we would hope
for a world that would go on with biological investigations (good ones,

though), just as we hope for a world that will continue with aesthetic experimentation—humanity does not live on bread alone, and so on. Neither does humanity live, or have culture and science, without bread, and therefore what is interesting is the level of urbancentric contempt that exists on the supposedly "cultured" side of the supposed culture/agriculture divide. The more significant point is that there is a sense in which there is nothing else that is enough like being a farmer to replace what good farming does; hence, there is a categorical imperative to farm, at least in the sense that humanity has to ensure that good farming is given pride of place within any society.

The other side of the coin is that a good deal can be told and foretold about a society that instead breeds ignorance of and even contempt for good farming. Perhaps a categorical imperative of good farming does not mean that everyone has to be a farmer, but it is also significant that, in an urbancentric culture that is contemptuous of agriculture, there are many urbancentric intellectuals for whom there could be no worse fate—indeed, even the idea of visiting a farm seems horrifying to some. This is not an exaggeration, and it turns out to be a nontrivial point on many counts, among them the Western view and reception of views concerning the Cultural Revolution in China, which had the greatest impact in the countryside.

Sometimes farming is referred to as "living on the land." In giving us some good models of life on the land, good farming also provides a core perspective on what it might mean to have a sense of place. We might ask what it would mean to bring places under Berry's conversational model.

Consider the alternative to the conversational model, as Berry understands it:

> Industrial agriculture, built according to the single standard of productivity, has dealt with nature, including human nature, in the manner of a monologist or an orator. It has not asked for anything, or waited to hear any response. It has told nature what it wanted, and in various clever ways has taken what it wanted. And since it proposed no limit on its wants, exhaustion has been its inevitable and foreseeable result. This, clearly, is a dictatorial or totalitarian form of behavior, and it is as totalitarian in its use of people as it is in its use of nature. Its connections to the world and to humans and the other creatures become more and more abstract, as its economy, its authority, and its power become more and more centralized. (*What Are People For?* 208)

Here again there is an opening toward a kind of ecological existentialism, perhaps building on certain affinities between Emerson and William James, on the one side, and Kierkegaard and Sartre on the other. We would also want to engage with Hannah Arendt's theory of totalitarianism, on the one side noting her own arguments about a monological discourse being integral to totalitarianism, while on the other side noting that Arendt was

as urbancentric as they come. She was hardly alone in this among intellectuals, but she was also a student of one of the best-known anti-urbancen-
tric intellectuals of the twentieth century, Martin Heidegger.

Left and Right

I only raise this at this juncture because it might be interesting to study the
way that Heidegger's left-minded students tended to be the urbancentrists
(I'm thinking especially of Herbert Marcuse), while at least some of his
students who took up the "peasant" and dwelling themes tend to be more
right-wing. (A valuable collection that deals with these issues in terms of
ecological questions is *Heidegger and the Earth*, edited by Ladelle
McWhorter.) Until recent decades there was at least the appearance that
this is how the categories of the "political spectrum" fell out, with a supposed alignment between conservatism and the land. But perhaps all of
these categories ought to be reconsidered, and it is also the case that the
emergence of neo-conservatism cancels this alignment (to the extent that
it existed at all). Your typical neo-conservative is someone such as Dick
Cheney, who had "better things to do" than to go to Vietnam, but who
now rides in a truck to shoot small birds and then instead shoots his fellow
ruling-class buddy in the face.

More to the point for present purposes (if only Cheney and the like
were simply comic characters instead of sinister power-players in a far-
ranging attempt to reforge U.S. global hegemony), we might ask how
Marxism went from being the party of industrial production (though collectivized, and I mean this as a good thing) to being the party of the general technofix—and this as an unthinking solution to the problem of
food. In this same basket we must place the notion of science (a Marxist
science of revolution first of all, but also science generally) as somehow
being omniscient, which fits well with Berry's formulation, "it has not
asked for anything, or waited to hear any response." The "it" in Berry's
formulation, "industrial agriculture, built according to the single standard of production," has no *questions*, and therefore it has no need of listening and learning, and thus it becomes very skeptical and suspicious of
philosophy—and unfortunately all of this can be said of some longstanding core trends within Marxism. This has to be said in a certain shame-
faced way, in that the institutions of philosophical practice are largely
attached to the urbancentric perspective. Socrates and Plato are often
cited as proponents of such a perspective, conveniently forgetting that
the ideal "city" in the *Republic* has five thousand people in it and a minimal division of labor—but I suppose that, if you can make it there, you
can make it anywhere.

The Weight of Urbanism

Certainly, however, to these ideological issues has to be added the sheer *weight* of actual cities and actual institutions and practices of industrial agriculture—and the deep and weighty interconnections of the two, for the former simply could not exist without the latter. Looming in the background is also the very difficult question of the human population, something that Marxism and left-wing politics in general has not wanted to touch other than to denounce those who do raise the issue as opening the door to eugenics or Malthusian measures. That good farming is necessary to the future of humanity does not in itself mean that everyone has to be a farmer; likewise, the fact that the human population of planet Earth hovered around ten million for many centuries does not mean that this should be the population now. But both give us something to think about, and it would be a bad idea to simply dismiss either of these points. I could easily see a good Kantian-universalist argument, and a good Marxist argument about overcoming the division of labor, that would say that everyone ought to at least participate in farming and not just take it for granted that other people will take care of one's need for food.

Abundance

One definition of communism is "shared abundance." The latter half of the definition captures Marx's understanding of what capitalism contributes to the historical process. As with the population question, there is a tendency in Marxism to avoid what in ecology is called the "carrying capacity" question, or to figure that this can also simply be the object of a technofix. Now, today, it seems one would have to be completely deluded to accept such an idea, but this is where Marxism's tendency to cul-de-sac thinking can underwrite such a delusion, aided and abetted by a failure to appreciate the particular places on Earth—the earth of Earth—and therefore a failure to appreciate the forms of ecological despoilment that are caused by and quite possibly necessary for producing "abundance," at least under some definition, for six billion and more people. There is much to be said about the alignment of abundance and needs (as abundance is meant as a response, in communism, to the needs of each person). There is also a way in which, however, abundance is a way around ethical questions, in that Marx seems to believe in a Hobbesian world where, if the things that will meet needs are scarce, then people will fight over these things, and some people will be made subordinate to others; some will be made expendable outright. For Marx, the only way to overcome this state of affairs is to have production at a level where there is so much need-meeting stuff around (and recognizing, with Marx, that "capitalism makes people rich in needs") that there is no need for any fighting. The process that gets humanity to this point is also one where we break free of capitalism's structural insatiability. My aim here is not in any way to detract from this idea as a good thing. But nowhere in all this did Marx think it important to talk about the quality of the ground that people would be standing upon as they sorted out these other things. Suppose we were to take better-off working-class people in the United States as the standard of abundance. Then either the earth would not have the carrying capacity to provide this standard of abundance for the world's billions, or this standard would only be possible on a technofixed, "paved planet." If such a thing is sustainable (which is very doubtful), it would not only be a really crummy place, it would not even be a place at all.

Go with Beauty

Perhaps this is where ethics most of all needs an aesthetic sense; the other side of the Navajo saying, "go with beauty," might be something like, "do not make the earth ugly." Unfortunately, it is a little too late for this idea, but we might henceforth try to act according to this idea. Heidegger spoke of motorized food production as equaling motorized death. We all know the problematic context in which he said this, but perhaps it is time to move on from this context and look at our motorized world. In using motors to transform the earth and to move about the earth, it is very difficult to gain an appreciation for the places where we are, and in this same movement we are no longer in these places, and soon enough these places do not exist any longer. In at least certain circumstances in at least certain parts of the world, a car is a necessity, because there are certain needs that have to be met in our advanced capitalist societies. These needs can be met in other ways, and some of these needs are thoroughly and almost transparently artificial, but here again there is the weight of the existing system, right down to the existing buildings and roads and everything in what is called the "built environment" that will not be easily changed. Indeed, capitalism excels in pushing us deeper and deeper into problems, to the point where it just seems that "this is the world" and there is no other, so a person had better learn to work within these parameters. It is from this perspective that reading Berry (for example, when he says in *Home Economics* that it would be better to farm with horses rather than tractors) just seems unreal. Berry discusses David Kline, an Amish "Good Farmer of the Old School," who mentions in his book, *Great Possessions*, that, because horses don't have headlights, he and his fellow farmers don't work after the sun goes down. Now what is unreal? Somehow, "reality" is whipping past places at high speeds, on roads that have already gone a great distance in making a place far less a place, and after a while we have no idea what we are missing.

Stewardship

Berry offers a certain defense of private property, mainly having to do with the family farm. As a result, Berry is sometimes cited as being on the side of private property. (See "Private Property and the Common Wealth," in *Another Turn of the Crank*, 46–63.) However, his notion of property is completely intertwined with the stewardship model, which has nothing in common with ownership relations in modern capitalist, imperialist societies. Instead, Berry's model shows the intertwining of the notions of good farming, care for the earth, and appreciation of place, as we see in the following passage:

> The idea of the family farm . . . is conformable in every way to the idea of good farming—that is, farming that does not destroy either farmland or farm people. The two ideas may, in fact, be inseparable. If family farming and good farming are as nearly synonymous as I suspect they are, that is because of a law that is well understood, still, by most farmers but that has been ignored in the colleges, offices, and corporations of agriculture for thirty-five or forty years. The law reads something like this: Land that is in human use must be lovingly used; it requires intimate knowledge, attention, and care.
>
> The practical meaning of this law (to borrow an insight from Wes Jackson) is that there is a ratio between eyes and acres, between farm size and farm hands, that is correct. We know that this law is unrelenting—that, for example, one of the meanings of our current high rates of soil erosion is that we do not have enough farmers; we have enough farmers to use the land but not enough to use it and protect it at the same time. ("A Defense of the Family Farm," 163; in *Home Economics*)

Now, certainly there are some issues here that any critic of the current systems of power would want to jump on, and jump on these issues critics have.

Agriculture and Patriarchy

One of the best-known disputes concerned Berry's essay, "Why I Am Not Going to Buy a Computer" (in *What Are People For?* 170–77). That essay and the one entitled "Feminism, the Body, and the Machine" (178–96) deal with some of the gender issues that surround a defense of the family in the family farm. Significantly, it does not seem that Berry initially intended to enter this territory; instead, he accidentally backed into it when he said, "My wife types my work on a Royal standard typewriter bought new in 1956 and as good now as it was then" (170). One of the respondents to the essay wrote, sarcastically, "Wendell Berry provides writers enslaved by the computer with a handy alternative: Wife—a low-tech energy-saving device. Drop a pile of handwritten notes on Wife and you get back a finished manuscript, edited while it was typed. What computer can do that?" (The responses and Berry's reply are printed with the essay, 173–77). Berry's failure to mention his wife's name (Tanya Berry) in this context, much less to have her name listed on the covers of his books of essays as the editor, is, I think, a concentrated expression of the difficulties of the kind of "local communitarianism" Berry advocates, with its attachment to family, place, and general skepticism toward technology. It could be said that there are competing claims of justice, and that, in responding to some of these claims, Berry appears to have made things worse for other claims. Urbancentric critics of Berry and other "new agrarians" simply use such apparent contradictions to dismiss any of the claims Berry makes for agriculture or place (and now let us add "locality" to this list). But these claims do not appear in the urbancentric perspective to begin with. That is why such a perspective, which is necessarily intertwined with a fetish for technology, is a kind of road to nowhere, even when part of an emancipatory agenda (such as Marxism or feminism).

Patriarchy is a big thing; it is everywhere in the world; it insinuates itself on many levels of human life; and it has been around for thousands of years. Berry has a skepticism toward big problems, for what seems like a quite legitimate reason: the big problems seem to demand big solutions, and big solutions tend to be monological, "one size fits all," not sensitive to particularities, and even totalitarian. I think Berry is right about these tendencies, and yet this cannot be the end of the discussion. Patriarchy is not only a big thing, but also it is a big hurdle that humanity has to get past if we are ever to have a just and decent society. A synthesis is needed, though I say this with some trepidation. The question of place may set a standard for us, for it is certainly a "small" problem, or "a problem of the small," so to speak—which might also be to say a problem of the "appropriate unit," as defined with terms such as the "eyes/acres ratio" and the bioregion—but it is also a big problem: places are disappearing everywhere, the causes of this disappearance are global, and, when this disappearance is absolute, then the earth will no longer be a place, either.

Sustainable Agriculture as Baseline

Synthesis can be a form of splitting the difference, something I recommended we look into in the case of Berry and Marx. Clearly, however, in order not to make our methodology monological and totalitarian, we need also to respect at least certain differences and have a practical hesitancy about "combining two into one," to use a Maoist expression. Synthesis for Marxism might simply mean having a mind big enough to learn from both Berry and Derrida, for instance. Synthesis might mean the creation of a theoretical and practical space where certain important and pressing needs can be appreciated and acted upon, without too quickly rushing to see how they connect at every instance. At the same time, Berry and Jackson give us a kind of baseline to consider, and strangely there is a kind of Marxist, and even Hegelian, logic to this baseline. First, we have to recognize that there is a sense in which ecology trumps everything, at least in the sense that humanity has to exist in places and these places have to have long-range sustainability. Perhaps there is not only one way for this to happen, and certainly all of the interconnections that are involved in sustainability are susceptible to being treated in a merely utilitarian, instrumentalist, or calculative manner. However, there are limits; there are breaking points in local ecologies and in the global ecology, and humanity has come up against many of these in the case of the former, and it is now coming up against at least one (but more likely several) of these limits in the case of the global ecology. Happily, however, and this is the Hegelian part, the inseparable notions of good farming and care for place can also ground or be understood as closely connected to other notions such as *good work* and therefore to some extent even justice.

City Dwelling

Interestingly, this scheme has a central place for basic forms of production, especially the production of food, what I have called the most important member of the materialist trinity. It also demonstrates a connection between good farming and good work. As Marxist as this seems, it is also interesting that Marx, with his urbancentrist, industrialist orientation, just does not seem interested in a scheme such as this. Marx may have some good reasons for his orientation, though it is interesting to consider the relationship between the French word "bourgeois" and the German word "Burgher." The latter is usually translated into English as "city-dweller," and it is not an exaggeration to say that Marx had *burgherlische* hopes for the proletariat. Perhaps it has to be said again that all of these hopes were not bad, necessarily, and that there are some "city-values" to which Marx gave little or no consideration but that we would certainly want as part of any future society, primarily those values that have recently gone under the headings of diversity and multiculturalism. (To further explore the question of the city from a Marxist perspective, see especially the work of Manuel Castells, David Harvey, and Ira Katznelson. For a feminist perspective that is critical of communitarianism and that defends the city, see the work of Iris Marion Young. And finally, Berry takes another look at questions of gender and sex in *Sex, Economy, Freedom & Community*.) We worry that the countryside will not be a place for human difference, even while the life of the city, especially the metropolis, depends on monocultures and other reductions of difference (the temptation is to call these differences "natural," but we do have to delve far into this question to see what is lost in the industrial food production system) in the countryside. In considering the idea of the *Burgher*, we are right to see the associations among "city" and "citizen" and "civic" (Murray Bookchin also wrote an interesting book on this question, *Urbanization without Cities: The Rise and Decline of Citizenship*.) *Perhaps* we can have better cities and a better countryside, something that integrates the best of both worlds, but this is not something to be blithe about, in part because the baseline for such an integration or combination is something with which urbancentrists will always have difficulty until they give up their urbancentrism, namely sustainable farming. In other words, how much industry and urbanization can we afford, on the assumption that we think of humanity as an ongoing project? The answer is, as much of these things as is commensurate with sustainable agriculture. If we go further than this, and explore the link between good farming and the ideal of good work, which cannot exclude, I think, notions of equitable work that provides everyone who engages in it a decent standard of living (and it can be shown, I think, that good farming sets this sort of standard, because good farming cannot base itself on the "single standard of productivity," and especially not upon the "productivity" of a monetary profit that circulates in an economic system that is unstuck from such problems as humanity being able to feed itself), then perhaps we can afford only less industry and urbanization in the long run.

In order to bring these issues to the forefront, a better sense of the interconnections among the questions of place, agriculture, and ecology, and the animal question is needed. This is where I find Berry a little wanting, and where I want to split the difference. In *New Roots for Agriculture*, Jackson writes:

> In the earliest writings we find that the prophet and scholar alike have lamented the loss of soils and have warned people of the consequences of their wasteful ways. It seems that we have forever talked about land stewardship and the need for a land ethic, and all the while soil destruction continues, in many places at an accelerated pace. Is it possible that we simply lack enough stretch in our ethical potential to evolve a set of values capable of promoting a sustainable agriculture? (13)

The answer to this last question is, unfortunately, yes, but the real problem goes back to the root concerns of the present book. We need an analysis of social structures and their contradictions (carried out in the general spirit of Marx) in order for the possible context in which "ethics" might do its work can appear.

Natural Neighborhoods and Big Ideas

Both Jackson and Berry often speak to the large, systemic issues, but then, in a recoil against large solutions, and an affirmation of E. F. Schumacher's famous slogan, "small is beautiful" (or the corollary offered by designer/design theorist Victor Papanek, "nothing big works"), tend ultimately to settle on the local level as the only locus of meaningful change, though sometimes they also advocate working on a national level and talk about "our country" and the United States. This dynamic can be seen in the following passages from "Word and Flesh" by Berry:

> In his essay on Kipling, George Orwell wrote: "All left-wing parties in the highly industrialized countries are at bottom a sham, because they make it their business to fight against something which they do not really wish to destroy. They have internationalist aims, and at the same time they struggle to keep up a standard of life with which those aims are incompatible. We all live by robbing Asiatic coolies, and those of us who are "enlightened" all maintain that those coolies ought to be set free; but our standard of living, and hence our "enlightenment," demands that the robbery shall continue.
>
> This statement of Orwell's is clearly applicable to our situation now; all we need to do is change a few nouns. The religion and the environmentalism of the highly industrialized countries are at bottom a sham, because they make it their business to fight against something that they do not really wish to destroy. We all live by robbing nature, but our standard of living demands that the robbery shall continue. (*What Are People For?* 200–201)

> For a long time, then, the minds that have most influenced our town [Berry is referring to his actual hometown, Port Royal, Kentucky] have not been *of* the town and so have not tried even to perceive, much less to honor, the good possibilities that are there. They have not wondered on what terms a good and conversing life might be lived there. In this my community is not unique but is like almost every other neighborhood in our country and in the "developed" world.
>
> The question that *must* be addressed, therefore, is not how to care for the planet, but how to care for each of the planet's millions of human and natural neighborhoods, each of its millions of small pieces and parcels of land, each one of which is in some precious way different from all the others. Our understandable wish to preserve the planet must somehow be reduced to the scale of our competence—that is, to the wish to preserve all of its humble households and neighborhoods. (*What Are People For?* 200)

Berry is right; this world will not survive, or at least humanity will not, if we do not begin to care for and restore places, and there is necessarily a one-by-one aspect to this care and restoration.

Furthermore, Berry is right to resist the "big idea" if it is only a way of avoiding the sham that follows upon the standard of living of many in the "developed" world. Berry asserts:

> We must achieve the character and acquire the skills to live much poorer than we do. We must waste less. We must do more for ourselves and each other. It is either that or continue merely to think and talk about changes that we are inviting catastrophe to make. (*What Are People For?* 201)

It would be the easiest thing in the world, and a kind of bad utopianism of the sort Marx rightly criticized, to avoid dealing with this sham by invoking a "universal" solution, especially one that presumes that the standard of living enjoyed by relatively well-off people in the first world can be made global. At the same time we have to address the terms of the question, what "standard of living" really means in the context of gross inequality and exploitation. But this is where the big ideas are unavoidable, and where one big idea has to be opposed by another one: namely, imperialism has to be opposed by internationalism. This latter cannot be simply a lovely idea about universal love and fellowship (though I think that we need this idea, and such basic ideas as goodwill toward and fellow-feeling with people; this is to say, in a Derridean vein, that we need the politics of friendship and not just a Hobbesian politics of identifying the enemy); internationalism must manifest itself in practice to really be what it is. This means, among other things, that internationalism must manifest itself in anti-imperialism; it must confront imperialism in its global actuality; it must work to overturn imperialism. The stakes in the world today are such that this is an either/or: *either* internationalism will succeed in overturning imperialism, and set society on a different basis that does not involve people competing against each other to generate power and profits for a relative handful, and to the detriment of the basic sustainability of the global ecosystem, *or* the imperialist world-system will continue down the path of this destruction and destroy the world outright.

How does this either/or stand with Berry, Jackson, or anyone who sees the need to attend to the singularity of places, "the millions of small pieces and parcels of land"? A typical Marxist answer, which has tended to proceed from the very notions I just set out regarding imperialism and internationalism, is that we cannot at this time afford the luxury of these particulars. In this context, Berry's refusal of the big idea would seem to yield a politics of disengagement; I suppose that we could ask whether Berry has the ecological equivalent of Marcuse's "great refusal." There is a structural problem here, one that Marx did not see, and neither did Lenin, Stalin, or Trotsky; it might be said that, of necessity, Mao saw the problem, though in a quite difference context. The problem is that, for the sake of the "universal," we have to have farms; for the sake of the long-term health of the universal, we have to have good farms. And real farms, especially good farms, cannot be manufactured in a system of industrial mass production. Berry and Jackson are operating on the basis of a structural either/or as well: to invoke William Blake, either the restoration of the green and pleasant land, or the predominance of the dark, satanic mills will completely undermine ecological sustainability—and that will be that.

Different Tasks and Paths

If this much is right, then it would appear that humanity is faced with different, distinct tasks. These tasks may be related, and even have a common basis in confronting the destruction brought by capitalism and imperialism, but they are not related in a simple, one-to-one way. This is the sort of thing that Marxism has such a hard time with, even though the need to work on many semi-distinct levels is undeniable. Historically, this problem of one-to-one reductionism has arisen repeatedly where the "role" of intellectuals and artists is concerned, but perhaps this is again a reflection of urbancentrism, because what I am trying to place on the table is the "role" of good farmers and the question of particular places, neither of which is served by a cookie-cutter logic. In the name of materialism, Marxism tends to force these distinct levels into a reductive scheme. With Hegel's reductive idealism, sense-certainty drops out—we cannot be sure about any particular thing (or process or phenomenon) in the world. With Marx, and this is rather bizarre when one thinks about it, the land and places and food (or where it comes from) drop out. Assuming that we still need Marxism to help us understand and change the world we had better find a type in which this is not the case. Let us consider two examples of splitting the difference that might help us work out the methodology of such a Marxism.

First, I made a reference earlier to the funny idea of a Marxism that could be in conversation with both Wendell Berry and Jacques Derrida. What makes this funny is that it is hard to imagine these two having much to say to each other. I thought of this pair because of an essay, an "open letter" in fact, that was published in a book about Berry as a poet, novelist, and prose stylist. The letter is from Judith Weismann, a professor of English (at Syracuse University at the time of the letter, 1991, while Berry was teaching English at the University of Kentucky). Weismann is troubled by the trends in literary criticism from New Criticism to deconstruction; she writes to Berry, "The last fifty years of literary criticism have been an attack on wholeness, a denial that it could possibly matter" (Paul Merchant, ed., *Wendell Berry*, 54). In particular, Weismann is concerned with Paul de Man and Louis Althusser and their followers. Speaking of the Khmer Rouge, Weismann asks, "Would it be too bold to remind people that Pol Pot got his training under self-styled Marxists like Althusser in France?" (55) Whoa! I'm not too sure who these other "self-styled" Marxists are who are *like* Althusser, and certainly it would be interesting to know which one of them had Pol Pot as a student. Weismann reveals how little she understands about both politics and theory with her final paragraph:

> It does not look as if your way [supposedly "wholeness"] will ever win, but who knows? Last year who would have believed that we would live to see Alexander Dubcek return in triumph? We may never have a moral springtime, but if capitalism ever has a human face, the face will look like yours. (Merchant, *Wendell Berry*, 58)

Capitalism is indeed the product of humans, and certainly human faces are placed on it, but it is also important to show how capitalism can never have a truly human face. There are ways in which someone such as Paul de Man, in his analysis of organicism, is demonstrating, through a kind of ideology critique, how an absolutist notion of property unravels in its own terms. The stewardship model is also a critique of an absolutist conception of property; as it is fleshed out in terms of the ideal and practices of good farming, it is also a critique of capitalist notions of productivity. This latter critique is important, because it might be argued on the basis of Locke's theory of property that one is entitled to land as long as one uses it productively, but capitalism seems fine with the idea of using land and people until they are used up, and the only measures of speed and intensity of use are simply what is commensurate with the maximum rate of profit. The larger point is that both are valuable forms of critique and we need both; we need all of the good instruments of critique we can get our hands on, and this is the case even if some are better than others. We must "not cease from mortal fight," to wax Blakean one more time.

Second, and closer to the interests of Berry and Jackson, there is the problem of understanding what we might be defending if we are not first of all pursuing internationalism. There is perhaps a sense of "our country" with which one could be in sympathy without supporting patriotism, exactly, especially if this sense has most of all to do with "this land that I love." But we have to be careful about this sort of thing; a lot of us have a long way to go toward understanding what this land is all about, in its diversity of terrains and places, and what it would mean to love it and care for it. One has to be skeptical about this notion especially in the midst of a population as geographically impaired as is that of the United States. On the other hand, this issue is also complicated in a time when the ruling administration has little use for the constitution of the polity, and indeed where the constitution is effectively in abeyance. Perhaps things will have changed within a few years of the publication of this book, but what seems more likely is that what Dick Cheney and John Ashcroft called, soon after September 11, 2001, the "new normality," will continue for some time. So, all of this is complicated, but I think the writer J. B. Priestley (1894–1984) gives us a useful way of understanding the terms on either side of what I am calling "splitting the difference," in an essay called "Wrong Ism."

> We are still backing the wrong ism. Almost all our money goes on the middle one, nationalism, the rotten meat between two healthy slices of bread. We need regionalism to give us roots and that very depth of feeling which nationalism unjustly and greedily claims for itself. We need internationalism to save the world and to broaden and heighten our civilisation. While regional man enriches the lives that international man is already working to keep secure and healthy, national man, drunk with power, demands our loyalty, money, and applause, and poisons the very air with his dangerous nonsense. (*Essays of Five Decades*, 257)

We might quibble with Priestley's formulation here or there—in particular, from the perspective of good farming, we also need regionalism to save the world. But the most helpful aspect of Priestley's argument is that he gives us a good sense of why we need both regionalism and internationalism; and though we may work on how these two notions interrelate and align with one another, the point is that one cannot be sacrificed to the other.

Circumventing the System

From either side, regionalism (which will stand readily enough for the care of actual, singular places, even if we would want to sharpen the notion in terms of the kinds of particularities and localities to which Jackson and Berry are attentive) or internationalism (which, again, can become merely conceptual or sentimental if it is not fleshed out in terms of practical anti-imperialism), not sacrificing either notion to the other is a vital necessity, not simply a conceptual problem. From the one side, good farming is up against capitalism, which is to say imperialism. Good farms are disappearing, and at some point good farms will effectively disappear altogether. As Berry documents in *The Unsettling of America* and elsewhere, each generation sees a significant decline in the number of family farms, and the point when quantity (as in very little) will become quality (no more good farming) is quite likely not very far off. From the other side, even if it is the case that we will not get back to increasing the amount of good farming—and this has to happen if the question of place is also to be addressed—until society has moved beyond capitalism and imperialism, there still has to be farming in the meantime. Indeed, Berry caused a bit of a controversy in 1991 with an essay praising the artistry of tobacco farmers, for it seems that tobacco growing "requires an intensity of care and a refinement of skill" that cannot yet be replaced by mechanization (54). When this "skill set," to use the contemporary jargon, is lost altogether, and can no longer be passed down to a new generation, Berry argues, we will be at the point of catastrophe. However, we see at the conclusion of this essay—"The Problem of Tobacco"—as we do with so many of Berry's essays, the pro-posal of the "local" solution, the small thing that seems to set itself against the big thing that needs to be done. The second half of "The Problem of Tobacco" is an imaginary dialogue about farming and local sources of pro-duce. At the close of the dialogue, Berry is suggesting ways of circum-venting industrial agriculture, and he describes these means as if they are the basis of a movement that could make substantial change in society. Let us join the dialogue at the end:

> . . . "A local food economy, in short, implies higher prices for farmers and lower costs to consumers."
>
> "And you think the government doesn't see this but the people do?"
>
> "Some people see it now. And more are going to see it, for it is going to become easier to see. And those who see it don't have to wait for the govern-ment to see it before they do something."
>
> "But what can they do?"
>
> "They can start buying produce from local farmers."
>
> "As individuals?"
>
> "As individuals, if necessary. But groups can do it, too, and can do it more effectively—conservation organizations, consumer groups, churches, local mer-chants, whoever is concerned. The government's approval is not necessary. In fact, the process has already begun. Scattered across the country, there are farmers who are selling produce directly to urban consumers. There have been consumer cooperatives for this sort of dealing for a good many years. Local merchants sometimes stock local produce. If churches and conservation orga-nizations—the two groups with most reason to be concerned—would get involved, much more could be accomplished. But everything that is done demonstrates a possibility and suggests more that might be done. That is the way it will grow."
>
> "What are you talking about—some kind of revolution?"
>
> "Not 'revolution.' I'm talking about economic secession—just quietly forming the means of withdrawal, not only from the tobacco economy but from the entire economy of exploitative land use that is ruining both the coun-tryside and the country communities. The principle of this new economy

would simply be good use—the possibility, often demonstrated, that land and people can be used without being destroyed. And this new economy would understand, first of all, that the ruin of farmers solves *no* problem and makes many." (*Sex, Economy, Freedom & Community*, 67–68)

Now, as nice as all this sounds, surely Berry must have some sense of the limitations of this vision. In fact, I almost have to wonder if his proposal is meant to evoke in the reader a sense of unreality as regards what can be accomplished under the existing social parameters. I had a similar feeling about an earlier essay of Berry's, "Property, Patriotism, and National Defense" (*Home Economics*, 98–111). There he makes three proposals concerning national defense: (1) that there be a general term of national defense that everyone has to serve, without exception; (2) that the term be served by people who have reached the age of thirty, so that the draftees will be citizens who have already experienced some years of an independent, adult life; (3) that there be no profits to be made from the production of weapons, or from war generally. These would be laudable principles to be followed by a society that would be worth defending, and perhaps that is why, even though these principles could conceivably be enacted within the parameters of the U.S. Constitution, we can be quite sure that such proposals will *never* be enacted in the imperialist United States. There is not a snowball's chance in hell that such principles would be enacted in the U.S., even if, in some sense, these are proposals for *reform*. And thus the principles call out the basic injustice of the system.

There is an element of this sort of thing in Berry's proposal for cooperative circumvention of the existing food economy, but I think there is also an element of unreality in Berry's own thinking, and the problem is simply that Berry does not want to cross the line where something big has to happen for the sake of some of the "small" and local things to happen. If anything, Berry's notion is especially unreal in light of recent decades, where even neighborhood cafes and pubs (in cities, at least) have become units in the corporate chain. For a great history of cooperative circumvention, we might go to the religious and other communitarian movements of the first half of the nineteenth century in North America, which were very much a response to what Joseph Smith called the emergent society of "bankers, lawyers, and businessmen." This was the period when, in the U.S. Northeast, it became possible to lose the farm because of factors having nothing to do with hard work and good farming practices, but instead with financial manipulations of the land-ownership system. With one significant exception, these communitarian movements were undermined, assimilated, or crushed outright. The exception is the Latter-day Saints, who probably faced more persecution than anyone, but who also dealt with one of the big questions that Berry hopes to simply circumvent, namely that of the state. In their cooperative farming ventures in Missouri and Illinois, it is hard to imagine that the Mormons were doing much different from what Thomas Jefferson envisioned as an agrarian democracy (then and still today the basic unit of LDS organization is the ward), but in the case of both states the Saints came up against competitive economies that could not allow the success of their cooperative system. (In the case of Missouri the fact that the Mormons farmed without slave labor—the LDS opposed slavery—was a central issue.) Ultimately, the LDS were driven out of Missouri, their leader was assassinated, they were driven out of their highly successful city state (Nauvoo, Illinois, which I would argue was a kind of "Paris Commune on the Mississippi" twenty-five years before the Paris experiment that so excited Marx and Engels—and, unlike the Paris Commune, Nauvoo was set up on a specifically agrarian basis), and the majority of Saints began the rugged exodus to the Great Salt Lake Basin and points west, led by Brigham Young. An alternative economic system, if it comes up against the existing system (perhaps first of all by taking profits out of the existing system), will be dealt with by the existing system. Quiet circumvention (of course, Joseph Smith was not exactly quiet) will never get very far, it will come up against the interests of capitalism—and those interests have a state, they have state power, financial institutions, police, jails, and an army.

(There are many resources for further exploration of this question as regards LDS history, but I would especially recommend: Kenneth S. Winn, *Exiles in a Land of Liberty: Mormons in America, 1830–1846*; and Robert Bruce Flanders, *Nauvoo: Kingdom on the Mississippi*.)

Another way to put it is that, if the quiet circumvention of food cooperatives was a true economic secession, it would not be allowed; historically there are plenty of examples to draw on where, again, such attempts at secession, are destroyed through either assimilation or harsher measures. Marx dealt with this issue thoroughly in his analysis of Pierre-Joseph Proudhon's Labor Federation and Labor Bank, in *The Poverty of Philosophy*—and it was not that Marx somehow wanted these syndicalist institutions to fail just so that he could make a point. One very significant thing about Brigham Young is that he opposed the entrance of mining interests into Utah, because he advocated an agrarian basis for the economy and opposed an extractive economy. One might ask, quite innocently, why these folks could not have their territory without other people coming in and digging it up. (At the time the Mormons went out to the Utah Territory, incidentally, it was technically a part of Mexico.) Likewise, why can't some folks have an informal food economy that supports good farmers and provides better food than the general run of bad food out there? They *can* have this (community supported agriculture, farmers markets, and similar arrangements), within a certain margin, and until some way is discovered to make more of a profit from this sector, or until it appears that this margin constitutes some sort of threat to the existing system—and then push will come to shove. (Push came to shove in the case of mining rights in Utah, obviously.) And, frankly, if push does not come to shove, then this means that the existing system is able to continue to operate just fine with this little "boutique foods" margin on the side.

Agrarianism and the Animal Question

Significantly, too, both Berry and Jackson have a blind spot on the animal question, and this is very important for two reasons. First, a tremendous amount of the bad farming—industrial farming—that is done in the world (including in the United States) is done for the sake of fattening cows, pigs, and chickens. The now-standard practices of food-animal production are both horribly cruel *and* environmentally disastrous (Jackson and Berry would not deny this). Second, if you really want an example of where economic secession, even when done quietly and cooperatively and circumventing the state will come up against the existing food system, try advocating for vegetarianism and animal rights in general.

The point, though, is not to berate these attempts to set up alternative food systems, even if they have their limitations. Such alternatives may very well foreshadow the future, as well as play a positive role in showing what we are really up against. A comparison might be made with the women's alternative health care movement that came out of the Women's Liberation Movement of the 1960s and 1970s; the comparison, though, might show a parallel of both strengths and limitations. At the same time, certainly there is also a limitation of revolutionary strategy that focuses almost exclusively on the state. In Lenin's version, which I will discuss more in the next section, there is a kind of monological orientation, the notion that, if we do not aim for the jugular, we are really not aiming for anything at all. As I mentioned earlier, the problem that has often been associated with this strategic orientation is that of the "role" of intellectuals and artists, especially when it is recognized that one component of revolutionary change is the emergence of a lively, oppositional culture and intellectual ferment. The Leninist current, in the past, has tended to instrumentalize this culture—it is "useful" on the way to revolution, but after the revolution we won't need it anymore. Another manifestation of this orientation is the idea that "without state power we are nothing." (This was a slogan of the Communist Party of Peru, the Maoist organization often referred to as the "Shining Path.") Perhaps this idea even has the larger share of truth, but there are two ways in which this idea is misleading. First, the attempts of people to create alternatives that circumvent the existing structures are not "nothing." In particular, the efforts of Jackson and the other geneticists, biologists, and plant breeders at the Land Institute to study the science of sustainable, "natural systems" agriculture is not only not "nothing," but could also become the key to everything, and this can be said without exaggeration or hyperbole. Second, there has been the tendency in practice, again "after the revolution," to flip this slogan over, to go from "nothing" to "omnipotence"—"with state power we are everything." The Stalin period gives us every reason to be wary of this sort of thing, and it is probably the main reason why there has to be a way of articulating the ethical with Marxism—or else it would probably be better not to have Marxism any more. We do not need any more Marxist statism that ends up being "here comes the new boss, same as the old boss," or worse.

My intent in this section has been to open up many issues that will require further investigation. Here is a series of theses that I think ought to be developed more fully.

1. If the problems of good farming, land, food, and place are to be solved, they will have to be confronted *both* piecemeal and in the arena of the state. If the state is an imperialist state, driven by the commodity logic of capitalism, and prepared to defend and extend this logic with all of the instruments at its disposal, then these problems cannot ultimately be solved without the overturning of this state. "Quiet" economic circumvention by itself will just be a way of watching the world go to hell in a hand basket.

2. This does not mean, however, that in the meantime it is not a good thing to create experiments and foreshadowings of an alternative food economy. This is not only a good thing in itself; it is part of the road to the future.

3. In this future, however, cooperatives will have to exist in a kind of "grid," at least until the ethos of competitive self-destruction is transcended. This grid is something like the revolutionary state. Even so, care for the land and for actual places means that everything that can be done locally (or in a "local way") *ought* to be done locally; everything that cannot be done locally but that still needs to be done ought to be continually under scrutiny. For instance, if there are forms of production that cannot be carried out in a given locale, then there should be a broadly participatory way of talking about whether these forms should be carried out at all. Alternatively, if there are certain locales that are, on the whole, dependent upon nonlocal production, which cannot be made dependent upon sustainable local production, then a transition away from that locale must be made.

4. People cannot go without air or water or food. In some sense, people can live without land, but this is deceptive. When there is no more productive land, there will be no more people. But this question does not

seem to be what Marx and Engels were addressing in saying that "the workers of the world have no country." And yet it is a fact that most of the people in the world do not live on and *with* the land, in a caring relationship; this has made capitalism, as it has developed through successive stages, both deeply alienating and unsustainable economically and ecologically. In commodity production, in Marx's scheme, people become unstuck from the creative processes that allow them to sustain themselves and "make something of themselves." Marx's thesis that all history is the history of class struggle needs to be brought more fully into contact with his (parallel? alternative?) thesis that history can be understood as the transition from the countryside to the city. Perhaps there can be different kinds of cities, a better kind of city that is not in conflict with good farming. Our present cities *require* bad farming, which is really not farming at all. Our present cities *require* that there be fewer and fewer places in the world. This sort of city is emblematic of a humanity that is unstuck from the world. (This does not mean that everything about the great cities of the world today is bad; that isn't the point.)

Someday, perhaps in the not-too-distant future, there will be so few places that the workers of the world will have neither a country nor a world to win. We need to think about the struggle of the dispossessed as crucially involved with becoming *both* native to places, in their tremendous plurality and singularity, *and* native to this whole earth.

3. Maoism and Beyond: The Next Synthesis

. . . there are not only difficulties but also great dangers. The people who so viciously rule the world oppress and exploit people in the most ruthless and murderous way. These are not just words that get thrown around; those are words that hardly capture the reality of the suffering that people are put through—totally unnecessarily—under the domination of this system and the way it twists and distorts the relations among people and turns people either into instruments to be used for the amassing of wealth on the part of a relative handful, or else just to be thrown onto the scrap heap like so much useless material. And there is the crushing of human potential and spirit that goes along with that. None of that has lessened. The need to do away with all that— and, from a strategic point, the basis that exists to do away with all that—hasn't been eliminated, or even lessened, despite these setbacks and even real defeats.

When I reflect on all this, I think of a conversation I had with a friend when I was a teenager. He was a little older than me, and he was going to medical school. One day I asked him what he wanted to do when he got out of medical school, what kind of medicine he was going to practice. He answered that he wasn't going to practice a particular kind of medicine, he was going to go into cancer research because he wanted to help find a cure for cancer—he believed that was not only very important but was also possible, and he wanted to make whatever contribution he could to that.

It has been many decades since that time, and while some advances have been made in treating cancer, it's still a scourge. It hasn't yet been eliminated. A cure, to put it that way, hasn't been found. But that person has been working in this field all these years, and I would never say that his efforts have been wasted just because cancer is still here. The need to eliminate cancer, or find a cure for it, if you will, is as great as ever. And, if you take a scientific approach to disease, you know that it is within the realm of possibility to find the means to eliminate this scourge on humanity and that it is worth persevering in that effort.

The same applies to the question of uprooting, overturning, and abolishing these horrendous relations of exploitation, oppression, and plunder on which this system is based and on which it thrives . . .

—Bob Avakian, *From Ike to Mao and Beyond*

If, on the most important questions of human survival humanity can only move ahead through revolution, then we need revolution. And, if this is the case, then we also need revolutionaries. It is in this light that I want to conclude this part of the book by discussing Maoism and the Maoists, the Marxist revolutionary current of recent decades.

A Provocative Opera

Some readers may be familiar with John Adams's opera, *Nixon in China*, a fine and important work, with brilliant music that demonstrates that minimalism has tremendous capacity for subtlety and sophistication, and a libretto filled with fascinating historical allusions and ironies. (For instance, the librettist, Alice Goodman, has the Nixon character singing lines that are famously associated with Mao, such as "Seize the day, seize the hour!") While in the final stages of completing the present book, I had the enormous pleasure of witnessing an astounding performance of *Nixon in China* by the Chicago Opera Theater. In his pre-performance lecture, the conductor, Maestro Alexander Platt, described a number of scenes from the opera. Act two, scene two of *Nixon in China* actually features—in a kind of inset scene—a scene from another opera, namely *Red Detachment of Women*. This is a work that was developed during the Cultural

Revolution, in the mode of developing in a revolutionary way the traditional form known as Peking Opera—hence, "Revolutionary Peking Opera." A series of "model works" were developed, under the leadership of Jiang Qing ("Madame Mao," as she is known in *Nixon in China* and elsewhere), with the aim of bringing forward some of the aesthetic achievements of Chinese culture, but also of imbuing these forms with revolutionary content. (Among the other works in this vein were *The White-Haired Girl, Taking Tiger Mountain by Strategy,* and *The Red Lantern*; see Lois Wheeler Snow, *China on Stage.*) One very significant aspect of these works was the featuring of women in strong and rebellious roles, as well as ballet sequences featuring women, this latter as a response to the legacy of foot-binding. Maestro Platt described the scene from *The Red Detachment of Women* where a woman is nearly beaten to death by a landlord and his lackeys. This was met by a wave of titters from the audience—not everyone, of course, and probably not the majority, but a significant part. Perhaps Platt encouraged this response to some extent in the tone of his description, which seemed to me to have an undercurrent of cynicism. More likely the response was underwritten more by the idea that these depictions of torture and oppression of women must surely be exaggerated, especially if Jiang Qing had anything to do with it.

Later, Maestro Platt described a part of act three, where Mao and Jiang Qing are reminiscing about "the good old days of the revolution when they lived in caves in the mountains" (this is how Platt put it). Again titters. Those Chinese and their revolution—how funny and quaint, how crazy; we saw what it led to. As if these folks had any idea whatsoever what they were tittering about. I think the tittering was a cultural expression having to do with a more general lack of any sense of what history or struggle really is in the population of the imperialist superpower.

Another issue that Maestro Platt addressed in his lecture was the aim the composer and librettist had of making this a heroic opera, and of making the principal characters each heroic in his or her own way. (There are six principal characters: Richard Nixon, Patricia Nixon, Mao Zedong, Jiang Qing, Henry Kissinger, and Chou En-lai; however, there is also a fascinating role for a nonsinging or -speaking actor, an old peasant woman, who moves through the ensemble or sometimes lurks in the margins for much of the opera.) Platt said that if there was any "buffo" character (a buffoonish character, and Platt said that every opera needs a buffo character) in the opera, it was Henry Kissinger. During the performance of the opera itself I thought about this, and about the idea of Richard Nixon as somehow heroic, and as being in a kind of "heroic symmetry" with Mao Zedong. The audience for the lecture seemed quite willing to accept this, though the idea of this symmetry may not have been Adams's intention (in fact, my impression from the performance was that, if anything, Nixon was the buffo character). Maestro Platt pointed out that Nixon's trip to China was "before we knew about Watergate," as if it is in the latter episode that we see that Nixon was actually not a good guy. As usual, the crimes committed in Vietnam and Southeast Asia are so far down the memory hole as to be effectively erased from the history that Americans know.

That Nixon could be understood as being in a kind of symmetry of heroism with Mao seems bizarre, ridiculous, and stupid to me. (Again, it is not clear that this was the aim of either Adams or Goodman, though certainly there were various symmetries at work.) In discussing Mao and the Chinese Revolution, the primary focus should not be on the heroism of *any* particular leader, but instead on the heroism of the Chinese people in their many millions. The cult of the person aside (not that I am dismissing this as an issue), this is where Mao himself placed the emphasis. The idea of a comparison in terms of heroism reminds me of the sorts of symmetries that are mainly constructed by right-wingers "for balance." I am thinking of the situation where a university invites a well-known left-wing figure to speak, so then a certain audience goes nuts for the idea of inviting some fascistic right-wing figure. For instance, in 2004, Utah Valley State College invited Michael Moore to speak, and the president of the school and a coterie of "conservatives" demanded that radio and television talking head Sean Hannity be invited "for balance." (An excellent documentary was made about this whole scene, *This Divided State.*) If nothing else, it can be said about this "symmetry" that, on the one side, regardless of what one thinks of Michael Moore's politics, he is a filmmaker who is making films, and these films have been recognized with some of the highest awards for filmmakers; on the other side, who is Sean Hannity (or Bill O'Reilly or Ann Coulter), other than a loud-mouthed reactionary? What do they really have to show for themselves? Why should anyone *care* what they say any more than anyone should care about the latest prepackaged pop junk in music or movies?

Perhaps more to the point, Mao was the leader of an immense revolution, indeed a revolution that was necessarily made up of several revolutions. If we care about changing the world, I think we have to ask about the basis for those revolutions, why they were needed and possible in the first place, and what Mao tried to do in leading them. My view is that the course of the Chinese Revolution, from the 1920s through the country-wide seizure of power in 1949, until the defeat of socialism and the restoration of capitalism in 1976, was a momentous struggle that accomplished many great things. Just to mention one of these things—because it simply seems unreal; it was a huge struggle in China just to reach the point where all the people would have enough to eat. Indeed, there were plenty of setbacks and mistakes in this struggle, but this immense effort was finally successful by the 1960s. On the other side, just to complete the thought about any possible symmetry of heroism, what was Nixon doing about hunger? Well, in taking the war in Southeast Asia into Cambodia, Nixon and Kissinger and the United States destroyed the agricultural base of that entire country, setting up the desperate situation of the Khmer Rouge (who were predominantly Khmer nationalist in their orientation, and indeed radically national-chauvinist against the Vietnamese, rather than "rouge"). Unfortunately, to disturb the idea of this symmetry, and to speak to the culture of tittering and cynicism, is an uphill battle in our postmodern society. In a way it is a strange battle, too, in that there seems to be no end to the anti-Mao current, even though the kind of revolutionary leadership that Mao tried to provide in China was decisively turned back decades ago. As a general cultural trend of our postmodern society, I would say this is a manifestation of the "TINA thesis" ("there is no alternative") once again.

If it is argued that the Chinese Revolution represented a momentous struggle that accomplished many great things, is it merely a form of utilitarianism to also argue that the problems, mistakes, and sometimes even momentous bad things have to be considered in this context? Is it merely utilitarianism to say that some of the limitations of the Chinese Revolution have to be considered in the context of how bad things were in China before the Revolution?

Kant and Violence

Kant struggled with the French Revolution; he had to make circumnavigations in his own thought to find a justification for it. He had argued that the violent overthrow of a monarch or other head of state was never justified, even in the case of unjust or illegitimate dominion, because violence instrumentalizes. To get around this argument in the case of Louis XVI, Kant argued that the monarch "had not been overthrown by force but had *voluntarily* abdicated 'to extricate himself from the embarrassment of large state debts'" (Allen Wood, *Kant*, 176; the quotation from Kant is from *Metaphysics of Morals*). One might wonder if, at a slightly later stage of the revolution, the king's neck had voluntarily let go of the king's head, remarkably at the same moment that the guillotine's blade fell. Rather than taking Kant's circumnavigation as mere hypocrisy and falling back to the position that the second formulation of the categorical imperative, especially, means that any violent revolt of the masses is necessarily an instrumentalization of the existing regime and those who defend it, instead we might think of better ways in which Kant's enthusiasm for the French Revolution could issue from his ethical-political universalism and, yes, his opposition to any "ethics" that is merely calculative. Surely it is universally right to rebel against and work to overturn reaction and unjust, illegitimate dominion—or at least it is surely right that such a thing can be proposed? At the same time, even if rebellion and revolution are both needed and not only justified, but also fundamentally *just*, this does not mean that everything that is done in the pursuit of fundamental social change is justified. If we apply a sense of ethical-political universalism to the former, what we might call the "revolution in general," we have to apply this sense to the latter, the particulars, as well, and we have to do this in such a way that the end result is not simply a utilitarian calculation on the question whether the good outweighs the bad.

Having said this, however, I would contend that the common observation in recent years that somehow it "might have been better" if the Chinese Revolution, or the Soviet Revolution before that, had never happened is an artifact of tremendous ignorance regarding what those societies were like before their respective revolutions.

Before moving on, it ought to be said that the relationship between these arguments, which need to be gone into deeply, and the actual performance of an orchestral conductor in a particular opera is, to say the least, tenuous; to the extent of my competence in judging such things, Alexander Platt gave a brilliant performance. Of course I mean this as (an attempt at) a coy comment on politics and aesthetics.

In the Shadow of the Sixties

As a young person I was greatly affected and influenced by the sixties. As I mentioned in the preface, the combination of the upheavals of the 1960s and their aftermath and a radical sense of Christianity ultimately led me to explore Marxism and its various activist currents. Except for certain meager attempts to connect with the counterculture (bell bottoms, long hair, Jefferson Airplane), I was too young to participate in the upheavals and, in that sense, I was not in a position to be a true sixties person. I was fourteen years old in 1970, though a few years later, I did come close enough to the draft to have angry arguments with my father about it. In my last two years of high school I attended a remarkable church, of the United Methodist denomination, that was led by two ministers who advocated liberation theology and who were militant opponents of the Vietnam War. At that time I hoped to become a Methodist minister myself (until I was about sixteen I was a member of the Presbyterian church), but that church and my aspirations came apart because of the struggle over the war.

During this time I was vaguely aware of the Chinese Revolution and the Cultural Revolution. Because I grew up in Miami, Florida, what I heard about more was the Cuban Revolution and the ongoing situation in

Cuba and its relationship to the Soviet Union. The global role of the latter in those times was a very important question, and literally millions and millions of people went around and around on it. One question that loomed large was, If the Soviet Union really was socialist and/or revolutionary, why was it against China? When Mao Zedong died in 1976 it was clear to me that something heavy had happened (*Time* magazine eulogized Mao with a sentence that went something like, "a lifelong rebel with a fierce love for humankind," if you can imagine that), but I was very unclear on what this something was, exactly. It took some time for me to realize that there were Maoist currents in other parts of the world besides China. I think I became aware of this because of Sartre's essay, "The Maoists of France."

The Maoist current in France in the aftermath of May 1968 was a mixed bag; at least parts of it were not really Maoist in that they were not really Leninist—and Mao and his thought were certainly Leninist. In fact, some of the erstwhile Maoists of that period explicitly rejected Leninism, and in particular the idea of the vanguard party. In his essay, Sartre also seemed to take this line; among three characteristics he attributed to the Maoists was the quality of "spontaneity." What is a more accurate description of Maoism, as Mao understood it, is what might be called a refinement of Lenin's notion of democratic centralism, which Mao called the "mass line," a systematized concentration by the party of the practices, ideas, impulses, and yearnings that come from the masses, and that have to be returned to the masses in a concentrated form such that these things can be wielded as weapons in the struggle to transform society. Certainly, however, this characterization of the mass line as "spontaneity," and much in the French Maoist currents that rejected (at least some) of Lenin's contributions, has to be understood against the background of the thoroughly *establishment* Communist Party of France, a party that played a key role in reining in the rebellion of 1968. This party, it is widely agreed, was the most thoroughly "Stalinized" and dogmatic of the western-European, Moscow-oriented Communist parties; although this party played a key role in the French Resistance, it was never, in my opinion, revolutionary. In any case, it is not hard to see how, against the background of this dogmatism, rigidity, and sometimes outright political backwardness (on the question of French colonialism in Algeria, especially), Sartre would emphasize the value of spontaneity.

The other two characteristics that Sartre attributed to the Maoists were, significantly, "violence" and "morality." By "violence," Sartre meant that the Maoists sought to place the question of the overthrow of the state back on the political agenda—to overthrow capitalism the state must be overthrown, and this cannot be accomplished by peaceful means. Of course Maoists everywhere took up Mao's slogan, "Political power flows from the barrel of a gun." This slogan has been much maligned, and generally presented in a backwards way. What Mao meant first of all is that the political power of the existing, capitalist-imperialist, order is ultimately backed up by guns; to defeat this power, it will be necessary for guns to be wielded by the revolutionary masses. It will take revolutionary war to defeat what amounts to a never-ending reactionary imposition of structural and more "direct" (military, police) violence upon the masses. The capitalist ruling classes will never surrender to a peaceful challenge; indeed, the real problem is that they are so willing to use every possible weapon at their disposal to maintain their rule that the danger is that they will destroy the world outright rather than give up power.

Unavoidable Contradictions

One of Mao's contributions was to recognize that the forms of struggle that are necessary for defeating imperialism entail contradictions, first and foremost the contradiction that our aim is a society where the basic direction of society is not determined by force. That it is *necessary* to struggle through rather than "around" this contradiction does not make it any less of a contradiction. Clearly this is something that Stalin, and even Lenin to some extent, tended to sweep under the carpet. However, to use Freudian language, there is always a return of the repressed. This is an especially difficult problem when the imperialists are willing to up the ante in every way that is technologically possible, creating and using weapons, from napalm to nukes, that the revolutionary masses and its leadership should *never* use. There are other ways of *using* weapons than "firing" them off outright— one can "point" them, continually threaten with them, and it is for this reason that I would argue that the imperialist ruling classes of this planet, first and foremost among them the ruling class of the United States, are the most hateful scumbags in history. How can there be the slightest room for doubt that, for the sake of the present and future of humankind (and, even in a sense of the past of humankind, the very "historical existence" of humankind), these ruling classes have to be overthrown? And yet, if the form in which this revolution occurs comes to *match* or *compete with* the stark immorality (which also takes the form of amorality) of the imperialist ruling classes, then, to use the future anterior tense, this will not have been a revolution.

So, lastly, Sartre placed in the foreground the moral impulse that drove the French Maoists, and again this can be set over against the "cold" political economic calculations of the Parti Communist France (PCF), which were of course a pure capitulation to reformist economism. Components of this moral impulse that Sartre discussed were internationalism, anti-imperialism, anti-economism, and what in that time came to be called "Third Worldism." Economistic "Marxists" of the PCF or Trotskyist sort jumped on this *Tiers Mondialism* as a deviation from an orientation toward the working class. However, on the one side, it was clear that their conception of the working class had little in common with the idea of the proletariat as a class that has nothing to lose but its chains, and, on the other, that the rejection of "Third Worldism" was, at least in significant part, a way of not confronting the transformation of capitalism in the twentieth century into an imperialist system. Certainly it could be said that the economist Marxists are faithful to the Eurocentric side of Marx, and in fact in recent years these currents often appeal to and call for a return to "classical Marxism," but what issues from this orientation might be called "imperialist workerism." In this orientation, and it cannot be denied that there is an affinity with one significant side of Marx here, the struggles of the Third World (or the countries that have a history of being colonized and dominated by imperialism) are at best a sideshow to the main driving force of history, which is the class struggle of the working classes in the countries where there is "advanced capitalism." (This last term is placed in scare quotes because the political economy of economistic Marxism uses the idea of "advanced capitalism" as a substitute for confronting the transformation of "classical, industrial" capitalism into imperialism.)

Imperialism and the Working Class

My argument in the present book has been that this substitution is a way around the admittedly difficult problem of imperialism's creation of divisions in the international working class and longstanding complicities of the better-off workers in the imperialist countries with imperialism itself. Furthermore, my argument is that we need both a deeper investigation into the political economy of imperialism (which would include investigation into the networks of these complicities and, in more recent decades, the ways in which cultural postmodernism affects this political economy) as well as a primary focus on the ethical gaps (and indeed aporias) that open up with the development of capitalism, and especially with colonialism in the era of capitalism, and with imperialism.

Much of the foregoing is at least implicit, and often explicit, in Sartre's understanding of Maoism, and it is the basis for his affinity with the French Maoists. There is an intermotivation of these concepts, not only spontaneity, morality, and violence, but also internationalism, anti-imperialism, and Third-Worldism. In addition to working with the current of French Maoism (the Gauche Proletarienne, which also attracted the attention of Michel Foucault, Gilles Deleuze, and other leading Parisian intellectuals),

Sartre also examined the experience of socialism in the Soviet Union, especially during the Stalin period, and he was personally and intellectually involved in the experience of militant opposition to French colonialism. While Sartre's friends in the Gauche Proletarienne maintained that he would have done well to have studied the writings of Mao more systematically, it could also be said that these young Maoists would have done even better to have studied the *Critique of Dialectical Reason* and *Search for a Method*. (However, note that the second volume of the *Critique*, which contains all of the material on the Soviet Union and Stalin, was not finished in Sartre's lifetime and therefore was not available to the post-1968 militants.) In many respects Sartre, who opened "The Maoists of France" by declaring "I am not a Maoist," was a better Maoist than the members of the Gauche Proletarian.

I cannot do justice to the history of French Maoism here, but let me add that the other current of Maoism in France in the 1970s and 1980s was the Union des Communistes de France marxiste-leniniste, which had among its leading members and thinkers Alain Badiou. As the reader will see, this current upheld Leninism. (A collection of articles on Badiou and the Cultural Revolution has been assembled in the journal *Positions: East Asia Cultures Critique* 13, no. 3, 2005. As a side note, it has been interesting to see how Badiou's recent reception into the circles of continental philosophy in the English-speaking world—he is of the generation of Derrida and Foucault, but only in the 1990s and since have his works been widely translated into English—has involved a certain amount of squeamishness and circumnavigation about and around his engagements with Maoism and the Cultural Revolution.)

As is well known, Sartre's conception of revolutionary violence is especially connected with the anticolonial struggle and his interaction with Frantz Fanon and the revolution in Algeria. In recent years, Hannah Arendt is often cited on the question of violence. She directed her arguments especially toward Sartre. We will return to this subject.

Engaging with Bob Avakian

I included in the foregoing some comments regarding my own path toward Maoism in part to show where one might find oneself if one is attempting to assemble certain elements for the revolutionary transformation of society—again, internationalism, anti-imperialism, anti-economism, a recognition of the crucial role of the ethical impulse, a recognition that the imperialist system will use every means of violence (and much else, of course) to keep itself empowered, and a recognition that there is a learning curve to radical change, which means building upon historical experience.

My own engagement with Maoism, in a more direct way, goes back about twenty-five years as of this writing, to the early 1980s; this is an engagement, to be more specific, with the Revolutionary Communist Party, U.S.A., and its chairman, Bob Avakian. This interaction led, in the spring of 2002, to a series of structured discussions with Avakian, which were published as *Marxism and the Call of the Future: Conversations on Ethics, History, and Politics* (Open Court, 2005). One of our mutual aims with the book was to place it in a more general intellectual-political milieu. What follows draws on the introduction to that book (with significant revisions).

The world needs revolution; therefore, the world needs revolutionaries; when there is a revolutionary current, one ought to support it and engage with it. In a Kantian spirit, I want to work with the people who are trying to do the things that need to be done. It isn't that the Maoists are the only people doing these things, but it does appear to me that they are the main ones who are actively and explicitly working for revolution. Whatever disagreements I may have with them over a whole range of questions, I place these disagreements in that context. Because readers of this book may worry about my attempt to associate a theory of Ethical Marxism with a current of activist, vanguard Marxism that runs through the Bolshevik Revolution and the Stalin period, and the Chinese Revolution and the Cultural Revolution and the subsequent development of Maoism, I will discuss my key historical events, in particular the Stalin era and the Cultural Revolution.

Marxism and Mao

Marxism, especially as interpreted and developed by Mao Zedong, offers a perspective on what it means to do philosophy: philosophy (and other work of a theoretical nature) develops in the context of attempting to understand the world in order to change it. Now, such a perspective should not be construed narrowly or reductively. We have to allow for the idea that many intellectuals do not hold this perspective and yet all the same at least some of them contribute to our understanding of the world—this is perhaps most of all the case in fields such as the natural sciences and fields where there is a good deal of abstract thinking, such as mathematics or philosophy. Perhaps a defining feature of what Sartre called "engaged" intellectual work is that it intends not only a system (to use Kant's language, it has an orientation toward holism and integration), but also a future. Certainly, there have been more than a few swollen-headed philosophers who believed that they had set things down once and for all. Occasionally this attitude has infected Marxism as well. And yet, as Derrida argued in *Specters of Marx* (as quoted earlier on this point), Marx was quite clear concerning the "intrinsically irreducible historicity" of his work, the need to take account of the "effects of rupture and restructuration."

Lenin

In this light it can be proposed that Lenin enriched our understanding of both Marxism and the world. This is the case on a number of points, but two in particular that are very important in the present context are the questions of imperialism and the revolutionary party. Lenin argued that the world changed in qualitative ways even in the decades between the death of Marx (1883) and the years leading up to the First World War. The transition was from the "classical" period of industrialization described by Marx and Engels, to a world where class positions are replicated on a global scale, in the form of what we would now call "advanced" capitalist countries, which play the global role of the bourgeoisie, and the so-called "developing" countries, which are more in the position of the proletariat. The capitalists from the dominating countries, global imperialists who remain rooted in nation-states and who do not form a single class (as evidenced by the conflicts between them), assimilate the colonialist enterprise to these new structures, in which capitalism becomes the dominant mode of production not only in the majority of countries (and certainly in all of the most powerful countries), taken one by one, but indeed, and profoundly, in the world as a whole.

Further investigation ought to be done into the extent to which this process was already advancing in Marx's day, as well as Marx's understanding of colonialism. There may have been a basis for Marx to have seen the development of imperialism if he had not been hampered by Eurocentric blinders. However, Lenin definitely took the measure of this qualitative development of capitalism (whether it was indeed "the highest stage of capitalism" is another question, another hundred years on) and its implications for the class struggle, such that it is right to speak of a qualitative development of Marxism, in other words, Leninism.

It is often said that Lenin's theory of the revolutionary party speaks to something called "the organizational question." I think it is less often understood that *What Is to Be Done?* is arguably even more about the question of epistemology. Marx said, "the workers have to emancipate themselves, no one else can do it for them." He was really speaking (in the vein, I would argue, of what Kant called "autonomy"—understanding that the basis of the law is within oneself—but then, "one's self" is constituted intersubjectively, in the matrix of social relations) of the only kind of emancipation there is, really, since "freedom imposed by another" would be an oxymoron. One of the steps in this emancipation is for the subjects of emancipation to know themselves, to achieve a class consciousness of the reality of their own position in the world, vis-à-vis the mode of production (broadly and structurally speaking, including legal and ownership relations, channels for disseminating the ideology of these relations, the larger culture, and so on). This truth will not by itself set people free, but it is a necessary step on the road to freedom. But the workings of capitalism obscure this understanding, and capitalism has done a fine job, since the time of Marx, of getting into the "consciousness business." People try, in various ways, to penetrate this "false consciousness," and one of Lenin's most profound and controversial arguments (such that there are many who call themselves Marxists who have a difficult time accepting it) is that the proletariat's consciousness of itself and its historic role (as Marx put it, "to liberate itself and all humankind") will mostly come to it from "outside" of itself. This is largely because most real proletarians (people at the bottom of society who really do have nothing to lose but their chains) do not have the "leisure of the theory class" (as I once heard it put, in a clever play on Thorstein Veblen's book title). Anyone from this theory class who would hope to hold a mirror up to social relations and the proletariat's situation within them, with the aim of creating critical emancipatory theory, has to become a "class traitor" to the bourgeoisie; given the milieu from which most intellectuals come, such an intellectual has to make a leap beyond her- or himself. But Marx had already shown (in a way that ought also to be controversial, because I'm not sure that most Marxist activists or intellectuals have really come to grips with the point) that this is the case for proletarians as well—they also have to make a leap in consciousness.

Perhaps Lenin saw this need even more clearly in light of the development of imperialism, where the whole question of classes and the mechanisms of exploitation and domination become vastly more complicated. One of the most difficult examples of this complexity is the complicities and even institutional ties (often through labor movements and unions themselves) that imperialism creates, especially in the imperialist countries themselves, such that the working class in a given country needs to understand itself not only in relation to the capitalist ruling class of that country, but also in terms of the way the world is organized internationally and the role played in the global economy by (what Lenin called) superexploitation in the dominated ("imperialized") countries. In order to forge this understanding, and make it available as a sharpened instrument to the proletariat, there is the need for parties of revolutionary communism. These parties must, in turn, sink roots among the masses and enable the masses to turn their understanding into activism—always with an eye toward the prize, toward the overturning of the imperialist system.

This is simply "Leninism 101," but my point here is that a new dynamic opens up with regard to philosophy and theory. With the revolutionary party, philosophy and theory are intimately tied to the practical issues of understanding the world in order to change it. The practical issues give a certain focus, let us say, to the theoretical work. In engaging in dialogues with Avakian, I engaged not only with him as a person and thinker, who has a history and a "context," as we all do, but also with the context of a particular organization—the Revolutionary Communist Party, U.S.A.—and its history.

Herein lies a contradiction—in fact, two contradictions.

Theory and Activism

The aforementioned "focus" cuts two ways. There is a certain power to the way that theory is done in the context of an organization whose primary work is activism. There is a distinction in philosophy that goes back to Aristotle, between the *via activa* and the *via contemplativa*, the life of action and the life of contemplation, respectively. Much of the history of Western philosophy is concerned with getting thought away from the life of action, by sequestering the philosophical priesthood in monasteries or universities (consider those black robes worn at convocation and commencement). There is an assumption at work in such sequestration, that good thinking will not come from the world, but instead comes from "the sky" or perhaps from the inner workings of especially bright minds. Now, there is something that this methodology of thought speaks to, namely that a certain amount of peace and quiet is necessary for a person to gather some thoughts and integrate them. Think of Marx in the reading room of the British Museum. This could be said to be Lenin's point about the "outside," as well.

The question is whether the aim of such moments "outside" the buzz and hum of life is to become like the most abstract "god"—"thought thinking itself"—or to, in Plato's famous scenario, go back inside the cave and tell people what you saw. Interestingly, Lenin uses this image as well, and he says that the people in the cave may not be pleased to hear what the philosopher has to say; indeed, their first reaction may be to tear the philosopher limb from limb. Significantly, Lenin refers to the cave analogy in discussing what he calls "revolutionary defeatism," the idea that, in crises and wars of imperialism, the party and the people must work for the defeat of "their own" ruling class. What is perhaps more significant is that such an understanding could perhaps only come through the forging of revolutionary leadership. So perhaps the issue of an orientation toward action versus an orientation toward contemplation comes down to what counts as "knowledge," and what are the things that are worth knowing. For there has always been another tradition in philosophy, one that does not see itself as completely apart from the materiality of human life, one that understands that a human being is not simply a "mind" with a bothersome and ultimately ephemeral body attached, but that the human form of being is intrinsically a form of embodiment.

Philosophical-Political Tendencies

Now, this distinction between these two traditions does not play out as simply as some have supposed—I am especially thinking of Engels in his *Feuerbach and the End of Classical German Philosophy*. There it is said that there are two kinds of philosophy, idealist and materialist, and it is more or less taken for granted that the politically progressive philosophers are the materialists and vice versa. Interpreters differ, however, even over the question of whether Aristotle was ultimately oriented toward the *via contemplativa* or the *via activa*. For Marx, and this is one of a number of areas where Engels (although I resist the trend to set him aside from Marxism or to blame only him—and never Marx—for every instance of reductivism within Marxism) just didn't seem to "get it," materialism is not first of all a matter of some (in reality, quasi-theological) allegiance to an ontology (a theory about what sorts of substances there are in or underlying the world), but instead the material of what Marx called, in the famous "Theses on Feuerbach," sensuous human practices. We learn from practices. Our practices ultimately take place in the context of the forms in which human life is produced, perpetuated, and reproduced. These forms, at least beyond tribal societies that are not based on class division (even here, however, there is the question of a gendered division of labor, and what might be called the "mode of reproduction," which in human societies is never just "biology," as well as relations with other tribes—and, I would say, relations with nonhuman animals insomuch as this relationship becomes part of production and reproduction), depend on divisions of labor, especially between mental and manual labor, and on a division between those who own and control the means of production and those who do not.

Marx argued that there is a structural dependency between our future as a species and the overcoming of the basic division of labor and therefore the collectivization of production. Those who are dispossessed learn about the basic injustice of a system characterized by socialized production, on the one hand, and privatized accumulation of wealth and power, on the other, through their practices—of trying to live their lives, of trying to hold body and soul together, of resisting the worst brutalities that issue from this contradiction, in "fighting the power," so to speak, and ultimately in taking the system on and overcoming it through revolution. In the midst of this practice ideas about the sorts of things that philosophy has traditionally discussed—the true, the good, and the beautiful, and so on—are forged. For these ideas to become concentrated and integrated, and for these ideas to then become a part of the struggle to make a world that actually has a future, and hopefully someday a world where people can flourish together, some things have to "get organized"—there need to be ways that theoretical work can be carried out, and there needs to be organization itself, but organization that is oriented toward the idea that understanding the world and what to do about it comes from the practices of oppressed people in their struggle to overcome oppression.

Methodology and Engagement

If I were to take a "neutral" position (that in fact I do not hold), it would seem to me that there is much to be said for this orientation as a methodology of philosophy; there is a prima facie case for it. For one thing, it would seem clear that, in a very general way, such an orientation opens philosophy to what might be called the ordinarily observed richness of human life, experience, and practice. It could also be argued that the ideal of "thought thinking itself," as indeed with some monastic and/or theological orientations, not only does not open thought to this richness, but also denies that human experience (and the experience of being human) offers much of any significance. In Western philosophy as it is practiced in academia we see this tendency in both continental (for instance, Heidegger was right to critique the "chatter" of everyday life, and yet there are moments when he seems to argue that all involvement with the materiality of life, and therefore with questions of economics, politics, or even survival, is merely chatter) and analytic (especially of the more scientistic or what I would call "microproblem" sort, the latter mainly having to do with careers, pedigrees, and cleverness) trends.

However, and here we finally arrive at the first contradiction, not only are most philosophers and social theorists (broadly speaking, working in numerous disciplines) not so cloistered these days, but it is also the case that parties of the Leninist type can themselves become insulated and insular. The trick is for those outside such organizations, but who are sympathetic with the aims of fighting imperialism, standing up for internationalism, taking the side of the oppressed, saving the world, and creating a new society, to understand that there is a good argument for the kind of focus that such an organization has, and that much can be learned through the pursuit of philosophy and theory as "secondary" to the more basic aims of such an organization. This understanding means nothing, however, if there is not another "trick" at work, from within such organizations themselves, which is an openness to ideas and theoretical work that are generated in a social process, like all ideas and theories, but that do not come directly through the work of the party. I have the aforementioned sympathy, and Avakian has the aforementioned openness, and this made our conversations not only possible, but also productive.

The second contradiction that hovers behind my conversations with Avakian is related to the first. I agree with the Leninist argument that there will not be a revolution without a revolutionary party. The party itself represents the contradictions in society, especially the division of labor, but there is no way around that. If there really could be a purely messianic intervention from beyond that immediately made of our planet the beautiful world that it is capable of being, I don't know how any of us could not wish for it. Lacking the basis for believing in such a thing, a road to the future must be found and forged, and revolutionary organization is an essential part of this effort. In the early 1980s, in the midst of what appeared to be a drive toward nuclear war and therefore the nuclear annihilation of humanity on the part of the two imperialist superpowers, I gravitated toward the Revolutionary Communist Party. There are many organizations out there that claim inspiration from Marx. All of them, including the RCP, are relatively small. What matters to me is not the size of the organization, however, but what it stands for. What attracted me to the RCP was their anti-imperialism and internationalism, and the fact that they did not balk at talking about and organizing for actual revolution. On the latter point, too, their aim was to build on the previous experience of revolution, especially in the Soviet Union and China. Their view, forged in the development and founding of the party in the mid-1970s (significantly, at the point when the 60s, understood in a political sense, was turning into the anti-60s, which continues to this day), was that Mao Zedong led the forging of a new phase of Marxism, and so they speak of "Marxism-Leninism-Maoism," or, for short, just Maoism. I do not necessarily agree with every position ever held by the party, but that isn't the point. There have even been some relatively sharp disagreements. However, I believe that the only real solution to the basic problems confronting humankind is a revolution that will take us beyond the present way that society is organized, and therefore I want to work with the people who are doing what they can about this. The contradiction is that I believe in the need for the party, and I support it, and yet I do not belong to it. That is also part of the context of the conversations that became *Marxism and the Call of the Future*.

Phases of Revolution

We might speak of three phases of the Soviet and Chinese Revolutions: the period of organization, but before the revolutionary seizure of power; the period of socialism, when the proletariat held power (with various contradictions and difficulties, of course—these being a substantial topic in *Marxism and the Call of the Future*); and the loss of proletarian power and the restoration of capitalism. Significantly, we have to speak of an additional phase in the Chinese Revolution, namely the Cultural Revolution. From the first page of our conversations it is clear Avakian and I share the view that these experiences of revolution from the past are connected to the possibilities of the future.

When I first entered graduate school, I had just spent two years reading a bunch of radical thinkers who had not been part of my undergraduate education—not only Marx, Lenin, and Mao, but also Proudhon, Bakunin, Trotsky, Goldman, Kollontai, Dubois, Malcolm X, Che, Fanon, Gramsci, Sartre, Beauvoir, Foucault, Dunayevskaya, the Redstockings Collective, and many more. (Whoever presumed to critique and bang away at the capitalist system, as well as the systems of patriarchy and white supremacy, I had wanted to know what they had to say.) In my first university course on Marxism, taught by a professor who considered himself a Marxist, I learned a good deal, but it blew my mind to find out that there were whole trends of Marxism in the academy, especially in philosophy and sociology, that essentially had no interest in the experience of the Soviet Union or China. It isn't that the folks who are exploring the thought of Sartre or Althusser or Adorno or even Habermas aren't coming up with some good stuff—they are (and certainly Sartre and Althusser have to be set apart from a good bit of what is called "Western Marxism," because they were indeed looking at the Soviet and Chinese experiences, and at the experience of anticolonial revolution). But I still do not know how it is anything other than Eurocentrism not to try to learn from these experiences and make them part of Marxism. There is a lot of good Marxist and otherwise radical thought that is done in the context of the academy, but there is also a sense in which purely academic Marxism is not really faithful to what Marxism is really all about.

Undoubtedly there was some McCarthyism hovering over work in Marxist theory in the academy, too, resulting in at least a certain amount of self-censorship as regards thinking dangerous thoughts or at least saying anything about them, and certainly there were cases of outright repression too. Since the overturning of socialism in China (and, of course, the collapse of the Soviet Union, which is a different kind of story) we have now had three decades of capitalist triumphalism, one dimension of which is the continuously repeated bleat that no alternative to capital-ism is possible, and that every attempt to construct an alternative, espe-cially in the Soviet Union and China, was a dismal failure and worse. Indeed, we are under what Slavoj Žižek calls a *Denkverboten*, a prohibi-tion on thought—do not even think for a moment that there is any alter-native, and there is no need to explore any of the historical experience of the attempt to construct an alternative. All you need to know is that socialism in the Soviet Union and China was an unending horror, and that Lenin and Mao were evil monsters. If anyone asks you about these things, you'll know what to say.

Restoration of Capitalism

The Maoist view, just to be clear, is that the Bolshevik Revolution of 1917 initiated socialism in the Soviet Union, and the ascendancy of Khrushchev signaled the decisive end of socialism and the consolidation of a new, cap-italist ruling class in 1956. Obviously, there is a great deal to examine in the intervening years, especially in the Stalin period. The Maoist view is that the strategy of surrounding the cities from the countryside, and the whole strategy of "people's war," as developed by Mao, led to the coun-trywide seizure of power in China in 1949, and that this experience con-stituted a fundamental contribution to Marxism. The Chinese Revolution was decisively overturned in 1976, after ten years of struggle to create a "revolution in the revolution."

This Great Proletarian Cultural Revolution had as its primary objective to transform the superstructure of Chinese society—Mao argued that, with the achievement of a socialist economic base, class struggle does not end, but instead even intensifies in the political and cultural sectors of society (for instance, in the university system, which had remained very elitist). Mao argued that, under socialism, "capitalist roaders" will attempt to gain control of levers of power, especially within the communist party itself—because socialism is not a "settled society," it is still filled with contradic-tions (especially forms of the division of labor, including the difference between leaders and led). The Cultural Revolution achieved many great things (more on this in a moment), one of which was to show graphically what it means to say that capitalism can be restored from within socialist society (and not just by "external" forces, or "hirelings" of such forces, as Stalin thought). Unfortunately, this lesson was learned the hard way when capitalists seized power in China shortly after Mao's death in 1976, and today we once again have a China that is a vast sweatshop for the advanced capitalist world.

Good Riddance to All That

Marxism and the Call of the Future takes these experiences of revolution as background, but not dogmatically or uncritically. I don't think one has to be a Maoist or even a Marxist to appreciate the need for grappling with the experiences of revolution in the Soviet Union and China (as well as the wide variety of topics Avakian and I consider that are less directly connected to this experience).

Critique of Stalin

Mao was also deeply critical of Stalin—for instance, in the *Critique of Soviet Economics*, in the discussion of Stalin's book, *Economic Problems of Socialism in the U.S.S.R.*, at one point Mao writes of one of Stalin's formulations, "with friends like these, who needs enemies?" Mao gave the famous "70-30" assessment, that Stalin's leadership was seventy percent good and thirty percent bad. Some have questioned whether this kind of formula is very critical, though I do not know that Mao meant it to be— he had a knack for compressing basic ideas into simple statements, sometimes expressed quite poetically. But, just to be provocative, suppose the figure were reversed, and everything that happened in the Soviet Union during the Stalin period was seventy percent bad, and only thirty percent good. I would think that, even if the assessment was "30-70," I would still want to try to understand what happened with the proletarian revolution in the Soviet Union, so that some lessons could be learned. Indeed, I think that has to happen, because revolution is a global process, and it has a "learning curve," so to speak. One of the shared commitments of our book is that, regardless of the problems that socialism has encountered, none of them make capitalism somehow workable as the long-term future of humankind.

The reader who does not share our perspective, and who has heard all kinds of things about these Marxist revolutions, is entitled to a bit more. Without presuming to give anything like a developed account, it is worth taking a moment to reflect on some aspects of the Soviet and Chinese experiences. Some of the material that follows is drawn from a project undertaken by the RCP, especially under the leadership of political economist Raymond Lotta, called "Setting the Record Straight" (the entire series of articles can be found in the *Revolution* newspaper, online at revcom.us). My aim here is not to paint a rosy picture simply to counterbalance the unendingly bleak picture painted by imperialists and even some honest critics. There were indeed many aspects of the revolutionary experience in Russia and China that were problematic or worse. But was this the whole story? I do not believe so, but I also would pose this issue in stark terms, at least as a hypothesis. It may be that "hitherto existing socialism" will turn out to be a very primitive form of what humanity is capable; certainly, this will be true and it will have to be true, in some sense. My hypothesis, however, is that, if the experience of socialism in the twentieth century truly had nothing good going for it, then let us say goodbye to Marxism, in whatever form or variation—but also, and this is the stark part, let us say goodbye to any future for humanity. The hypothesis comprehends the idea that these two things—a future for the radical critique of capitalism and the creation of alternatives, and the future of humankind—are that closely and dialectically related. However, the hypothesis goes even further: that, if Marxism has nothing to show for itself other than horrors and new forms of oppression, one hundred fifty years on from the *Communist Manifesto*, then let us move on to something else altogether. And yet, it has to be said that, for all that I do believe that the Soviet and Chinese experiences were in fact more positive than negative, it is also the case that each has important shortcomings (again, to say the least), and therefore there are significant respects in which we must move on from Marxism, and even from Leninism, and even from Maoism.

The Soviet Experience

The Soviet Union was created by an unprecedented mass uprising, led by Lenin and the Bolshevik Party. The initial military event of the October Revolution was the storming of the czar's Winter Palace in Petersburg, but the revolution spread over a very large area through two years and more of civil war. Seventeen countries, including the United States, put together an army of intervention to attempt to aid the "white" forces (the forces that were fighting for the restoration of the czar). The German army in the First World War had already devastated Russia. Despite this, or in large measure because of this, people rallied to the new system. "Economic growth" can be a dubious measure as presented in capitalist countries (for instance, phenomena such as home invasion and rising divorce rates contribute to economic growth, as people buy burglar alarms and move into separate domiciles), but the Soviet economy was a great achievement, despite all of its twists and turns and contradictions. Although the perspective from which some in Russia today march in demonstrations with placards of Stalin is problematic, to say the least (generally the perspective is nationalistic, not that of an internationalist communist), still there is something to a slogan heard in recent years: "Stalin took a wrecked country and made it into a superpower; Gorbachev and Yeltsin took a superpower and made it into a wrecked country." In the first years of the revolution priority was given to the overcoming of national and ethnic inequalities and to fighting the oppression of women. On this latter point, abortion was legalized, the right to divorce was recognized, and equal rights and equal pay became public policy and law. Women in the new republics of Central Asia cast off the veil after many generations. The Soviet Union eradicated illiteracy and vastly expanded educational opportunities for people from the working class and peasantry. During the Stalin period, a modern industrial base and a collectivized system of agriculture were established.

The Stalin period was a time of intense contradictions. It has to be admitted forthrightly that many of these were not dealt with correctly. But this is too easy to do if one does not try to gain an appreciation for the real problems and threats that the Soviet Union faced, and the fact that the building of socialism on the scale of the U.S.S.R. was absolutely unprecedented. If you study documents from the Communist Party of the Soviet Union from the late 1920s, you will see that there is an overwhelming feeling that invasion from the west could come at any moment. Stalin thought that the Soviet Union had to accomplish an industrial and military revolution of the sort that took many decades and even centuries in countries such as Germany, England, and the United States—*but in ten years.* When the invasion did come, Germany threw most of its military might against the Soviet Union. Twenty-three million people were lost in the war; to gain a perspective on the scale of the destruction, the number of Soviet civilian and military deaths during the siege of Leningrad was greater than the combined losses of the British, French, and Americans for the entire war. Despite what we learn about D-day and the landing at Normandy, the real turning point of the Second World War was the Battle of Stalingrad— a battle that still bears study for the concentration of contradictions we see there, for the military strategies applied, and as one of the most important examples of an historical watershed. In large part, the United States used nuclear weapons not to defeat Japan, which was largely defeated already, but to send a message to the Soviet Union about who was top dog in the world. The message was sent in other ways, too, for instance, by American political and military leaders (most famously General George S. Patton) who called for the continuation of the Second World War, with the U.S. armed forces marching into the Soviet Union.

Marxism in the midst of all this increasingly became a "fortress" and "siege" mentality, a process "helped along" by Stalin's tendencies toward dogmatism and reductivism. Significantly, Mao attributed some of this to Stalin's background as a seminary student. At the same time, I again think it is too easy to simply think that Stalin was a dullard or intellectual lightweight and that this explains his tendency to be ham-fisted about the contradictions of socialist society. Actually reading Stalin's works, the remarkable thing is that, though many of his ideas and inclinations appear wrong-headed in hindsight, there is a certain logic to them that seems almost inescapable when understood "from the inside." One reason for this, and what is really more significant, is that many of Stalin's dogmas were simply "orthodox Marxism" for the time, and the real failure was to learn from experience and to trust the masses. Many innocent people were victimized because of this failure, and throughout the Stalin period the political and cultural atmosphere of the Soviet Union grew increasingly rigid and oppressive. People became cynical and passive, such that, when Khrushchev and his cronies took over the CPSU in the mid-1950s, and used it to restore capitalism in the Soviet Union, there was only token resistance. The legacy of this cynicism and then capitalist restoration under the cover of a reformed "socialism" remains very much with us today.

The Chinese Revolutionary Experience

China at the time of the Bolshevik Revolution (and for a long time before that, of course) was a country divided up by foreign "interests" in the urban and coastal areas, and by warlords in the interior. Politicians and capitalists in Japan, Germany, France, England, and the United States talked openly about the cheap labor and resources in China, stating their colonialist ambitions without compunction. Japan, especially, believed it had a kind of "natural right" to dominate and exploit China (and much of the rest of east and southeast Asia), a "right" that the United States hoped to take over—indeed, this is the origin of the "War in the Pacific," not Pearl Harbor. (This is why U.S. politicians and diplomats would ask "Who lost China?" after the 1949 revolution, as though it was theirs to lose.) Undoubtedly there would have been resistance to foreign domination in China apart from the October Revolution; however, as Mao said, the ideas of Marx and Lenin became known and popular in China because of the establishment of the Soviet Union.

China also had to find its own way to revolution, however. Indeed, it had to find a way to a number of revolutions: for national liberation, against colonialism, against a comprador capitalist class that facilitated the domination of China by foreign powers, for radical agrarian reform, against many centuries and even millennia of the severe subordination of women, against the subordination of minority nationalities, and even against a pervasive ideology that held that all advanced thinking came from the West. Social relations in general remained feudalistic, or at least semi-feudal. Poverty was widespread and dire. There were areas of China where people not only had no shoes, they literally had no clothes and walked around naked. China in the first part of the twentieth century was light years away from the sort of society that Marx thought would be ripe for socialist revolution and socialist construction. As far away from such things as Russia was at the time of the First World War, China was much further away in the orthodox Marxist conception.

Lenin had to make a leap to conceptualize the possibility of socialism in Russia. In his thesis about the weakest link in the imperialist chain, I would say that Lenin gravitated toward the view that dynamic social evolution is driven from the margins rather than the center of society. He had to break with the linear, Eurocentric view that saw socialism as emerging first of all in the most "advanced" capitalist countries (especially Germany, France, or England). At the same time, Lenin demonstrated an exemplary internationalism, seeing the class dynamics that were driving Russian society in global context and thereby developing his theory of "conjuncture." Simply put, a conjuncture is a time in which the contradictions of capitalism on a global scale (what Lenin means by the imperialist system) are bound very tightly, "cast on the scales of history for resolution," as Lenin put it. It has become commonplace to say that the Bolshevik Revolution occurred "prematurely." However, revolutionary situations are rare in history, and the masses will not take advantage of these situations without the leadership of the party. Surely those who speak of the immaturity of Russia in 1917 would have to acknowledge the ripeness for revolution of Western Europe before and during the First World War. There were no Leninist parties there, however, to lead people through this window of opportunity; indeed, most of the socialist movement in Western Europe either threw away their internationalism the moment it might have meant something, and instead joined in with their own ruling classes for the defense of "their" countries, or, in a few cases, slogans of pacifism were raised, helping the powers that be ensure that the masses of Europe, and even more the masses of the colonized countries, were condemned to more decades of systemic (and often openly brutal) violence.

This would be one of several places where a longer discussion of the question of violence could be opened, but I do not want to bury this discussion in the midst of another discussion. But I am, of course, aware that the question of violence hovers over all of this "other" discussion. My aim is not to shunt this question away, but instead to give it a certain autonomy.

Lenin argued that our era is that of imperialism and proletarian revolution, and he saw two great streams of revolution coming together: socialist in the advanced countries, and national liberation in the dominated countries. Mao made a further leap in understanding by arguing that only socialism could save China and other countries that were dominated by foreign powers. National liberation would never occur under the leadership of a rising bourgeoisie, he argued, because it is in the nature of capitalism not to carry liberation for the popular masses (in a country such as

China this would include the proletariat, the peasantry, and the relatively meager middle classes) through to actual independence, but instead to sell out to much richer and more powerful foreign capitalists at the earliest opportunity. The sorts of alliances that Mao believed were necessary to really liberate China (he even saw a role for what he called the "national bourgeoisie," that part of the capitalist class that was not beholding to foreign capital, not a comprador class or positioning itself to become such) were riddled with contradictions, as were, for that matter, the alliances necessary to create the Soviet Union. It really is an idealist fantasy, however, to think that any revolution could be made without working through contradictions. (Indeed, there are some contradictions involved in making a revolution in advanced capitalist countries, to say nothing of the imperialist hyperpower, that are, if anything, much deeper and far more difficult than those faced in Russia and China.) Further, Mao argued that a socialist revolution must create a self-reliant economy; especially it must be able to feed, shelter, and clothe its people, because, in a country where these are real issues, there will otherwise be a tremendous temptation to cut deals with foreign powers. These deals can be inroads to renewed foreign domination—this is essentially the Maoist view of what happened in the case of Cuba (and it is significant, in that light, that Soviet patronage has now been replaced with a tourism economy, which not only undermines independence, but also brings with it such other Third World problems as sex tourism).

"Food, shelter, clothing"—this is what I like to call the "trinity" of materialism. But that sounds so simple and is indeed an oversimplification. Quite possibly most people in a country such as the U.S. can hardly begin to imagine the levels of deprivation that were common in China before the revolution. Undoubtedly all kinds of mistakes were made during Mao's leadership, but why is it that we hear about the sort of thing one sees in a film such as *The Red Violin* (a musician is attacked because he specializes in Western music), but we do not hear that by 1970 China had solved the problem of adequately feeding its population? Does that justify attacks on Beethoven and all who admire his music? I feel like saying, "get real!"— and I certainly admire (even revere) Beethoven. We are talking about a country that had two wars fought against it by the British (at the time, 1839–1842 and 1856–1860, the predominant military power in the world) to ensure that tens of millions of people remained opium addicts (by 1949 these addicts totaled almost 90 million). Before the revolution, China had a vast criminal underground. The situation of women was especially dire—footbinding, arranged marriages, child brides, prostitution, and the killing of female babies in the countryside were all very common. To say the least, the Chinese Revolution faced an extraordinary uphill struggle, and yet only a revolution could address these issues.

In the ten years after the 1949 seizure of power, land reform and cancellation of peasant debt was carried out on a scale never before seen in world history. In 1950 a new Marriage Law established marriage by mutual consent and the right of divorce. Infanticide and the sale of children were outlawed. It is true, of course, that making a law does not by itself make good things happen. There was a protracted struggle to establish gender equality in the countryside, and practices such as infanticide were largely eradicated by 1970. Significantly, this practice, as well as international adoption, has returned since the restoration of capitalism in 1976. Indeed, what we see of China's new "freedom" and "prosperity" is almost entirely concentrated in a few urban centers—and even then we see the things that glitter and not that which is on the side streets and in the shadows. Take a visit to almost any large discount store, which may as well add the words "Chinese Sweatshop Distribution Network" to its sign, and imagine what kind of freedom and prosperity are enjoyed by the masses of workers who produce the products sold there.

In 1949, about fifteen percent of Chinese people were literate; in one generation this figure soared to over eighty percent.

Maoist China did what the United States has never done, it established a system of universal health care. Unlike in the United States, the health care system was guided by principles of cooperation and egalitarianism, and Western and traditional practices were synthesized with the aim of treating the whole body and the whole person, in the context of the social and environmental factors that lead to health problems. One of my favorite chapters in the history of the Chinese Revolution is that of the "barefoot doctors," the 1.3 million peasants who were trained in basic medicine, who walked from village to village, not only helping other peasants with their problems, but helping the peasants to understand and treat their problems. Since 1976 this system has been destroyed.

We continually hear nowadays about the supposed endemic violence of the Chinese Revolution, but somehow we hear nothing about the fact that between 1949 and 1975 life expectancy in China went from about thirty-two years to sixty-five years. In the early 1970s, infant mortality rates in Shanghai were lower than in New York City. Does this not indicate a profound reduction in the violence of everyday life?

Our perspective on these favorable statistics, which are not in themselves controversial, and the way that people focus their attention on some things and not others, is bound up with horizons of expectation and senses of entitlement. If, in the imperialist West, we can ordinarily expect to live more than seventy years, then perhaps the doubling of lifespan in remote China will not mean very much. Maybe it is a little bit like if someone told you they finally got indoor plumbing. Indeed, in the material cited above, I am simply relying on the sources used by the Setting the Record Straight

Project. It is instead a matter of a shift in emphasis and a shift in how the Mao era is interpreted. To hold the "unending atrocity" view, however, it is necessary to forget any of the achievements of the Chinese Revolution.

The Cultural Revolution

The struggle of the Cultural Revolution, which was to deepen the basis of socialism and to prevent the restoration of capitalism, sometimes devolved into a certain amount of chaos, in which undoubtedly some people were treated unfairly or worse. This was a class struggle, but one in which Mao and the other revolutionaries repeatedly called on people not to resort to violence or to get into a mode of settling scores. The class of capitalist roaders, as Mao called them, especially those in the Communist Party of China who were basing themselves on the class contradictions that continue to exist in socialist society and on the possibility, as we have seen, of making deals with foreign capital, had every interest in fomenting chaos and violence, to show that socialism does not work. For instance, they had every interest in sabotaging factory committees that were breaking down the division of labor between management and workers on the shop floor—and now they have restored capitalist methods of management in the factories, and also created a new class of millionaires and even billionaires.

The Cultural Revolution as it affected universities is of special interest to intellectuals. In considering this issue, it is important to attempt to gain some sense of the real context. Just as it is very difficult for people in the West to understand as a felt reality the levels of deprivation that were common in China before 1949, it may be difficult for intellectuals in the West to grasp how much the few universities that existed in China by 1949 were the provinces of the elite. This goes back to the kinds of alliances that made the revolution of 1949 possible in the first place, and also to the way that, for at least the first ten years or more of the revolution, reforming the university system was not a major priority. In the United States, the university and college system is on the whole quite plebeian, not only compared to a place such as China before the Cultural Revolution, but even compared to countries such as Germany, France, and England before the 1960s and '70s (and still today to some extent). A large percentage of people in the U.S., even from the working class, attend some sort of college. In China at the time of the revolution, basic literacy and even providing grammar school for most people were the priorities. Some of the academic elite in China figured that, since their fields had not been touched very much by the revolution from 1949 until the mid-1960s, life would go on more or less in the same way. Some of them took their elite status for granted, and when their privileges and autocratic teaching methods were criticized, they reacted with a sense of entitlement about the lifestyle to which they had become accustomed.

The situation in the early years of the Soviet Union has some similarities. There, in some cases, aristocratic and bourgeois families that had lived in large houses with many rooms were told that they had to move into one half of the house, so that a working-class family that had previously lived in a hovel or had been homeless could move into the other half. This is the sort of situation where we see the class basis of a sense of entitlement. Couldn't those aristocratic families have said, "You know, we have lived in luxury for many years, we were very lucky to have had that level of opulence, and to be able to acquire some of the things that go with great wealth, such as a sense of culture. But, after all, the basis of the wealth of any society is the actual work that people do, and these people have done that work, and we haven't, so they could at least have half of this house, which is ridiculously large for a single family in any case"? But, gee, rich people rarely seem to say anything like that! No, they are outraged, about what has been *stolen* from them and how their lives have been shattered.

Granted, though, there are particularities to the intellectual milieu that are not accounted for by this analogy. And any revolutionary movement on any kind of scale, but especially a very large scale, is going to lose track of some particularities, period. A legitimate struggle will sometimes have aspects that fall short of or even go against the ideal. We all know the old discussion about "after the revolution . . . ," where it is very tempting to wonder what we would do if we encountered a certain previous landlord or employer or even college professor. Of course, it would be wrong to use the revolution to simply settle scores. Imagine what the temptation would be if you never had the old professor, because the old professor's idea about you is that you should be out in the countryside your whole life growing rice and other crops for food, and you do not need even basic literacy for that, much less advanced study in the humanities or sciences.

The temptation to settle scores is related to what might be called the problematic side of egalitarianism, leveling, which was severely criticized by Marx. Surely there were some, perhaps driven by resentment (though often understandable resentment), who took egalitarianism to the point of mere leveling, especially when it came to the elite university system. Being an intellectual myself, and generally having grand plans for writing projects for many years to come, I can be very protective of how my time gets organized. To really carry through with intellectual work, one has to pursue it as a calling, a vocation, a life project. To have that life project disrupted can be traumatic, perhaps in a way that would be very difficult to comprehend for someone who has never conceived of a life project in that way. And yet there is also a class dimension, generally, to who gets to even consider having life projects, and who is brought up to think he or she is entitled to have a vocation, and the assumption of an elite educational system (which, again, is somewhat different, for the most part, from much of what is done in most colleges and universities in the United States—though not without significant exceptions) is that the masses of workers and peasants are not the sorts of people who should or ever could have life projects. "Trauma" comes from the Greek word for "cut" or "break" (as in a break in the skin); the traumatization of the elite academic *cloister* could actually have a salutary intellectual effect.

Now, having said all this, the fact is that the decade of the Cultural Revolution was one in which the educational system was broadened considerably. For instance, in the countryside, middle school enrollment went from fifteen million to fifty-eight million. For this to happen, teachers were needed in the countryside; some professors did not want to go there, but many embraced the idea of breaking down the divisions between city and countryside, schooled and unschooled, privileged and dispossessed. Many found that the peasants had a thing or two to teach them.

Critique of Twentieth-century Revolutionary Experience

I have tried to present an alternative to the story that is often told about the Stalin period and especially the Cultural Revolution, an alternative that needs to be set out at greater depth and in greater length. In the years since the passing of Mao, there has seemed to be an almost endless stream of attacks on the Chinese Revolution and especially the Cultural Revolution. If anything, these attacks have intensified in the last ten years. It would be wrong, I think, to see these attacks as *only* based upon reactionary falsehoods. As Avakian has emphasized in recent years, not only have there been atrocities in the history of socialist revolution—to the point where, as Avakian puts it, revolutionary communists *ought* to cringe and recoil—but we will not go forward with either Marxist theory or practice if we do not confront these atrocities. There are many episodes in the history of the revolutions in Russia and China that are problematic and deserving of critical scrutiny, but that are not atrocities; however, I use this latter term because it is claimed in many recent monographs and memoirs that these revolutions were nothing but atrocities from beginning to end. (Some examples of books making such claims would include *Mao: The Unknown Story* by Jung Chang and Jon Halliday; *Life and Death in Shanghai* by Nien Chang; and *Red Azalea* by Anchee Min.) This is not true, even while, in fact, there have been atrocities; it is necessary to ask if there is a way of understanding revolution and atrocity, even in the case where the positive aspects of the former are not canceled by the latter (in the real cases, of course), that is not merely utilitarian, calculative, or instrumentalizing. It is telling that it is almost always the case that these condemnations are not accompanied by any attempt to understand why these revolutions occurred in the first place. Despite what I said about the real need to recognize the real shortcomings, difficulties, defeats, and even atrocities of the Russian and Chinese revolutions, it is hard not to think that the volume and prominence of the atrocity books and memoirs is connected to the need for imperialism, especially American imperialism, to promote the idea that there is no alternative to the existing social system. One might ask, too, if there is such a concern in the United States, at least in certain quarters, about atrocities committed in Asia, why we (in the U.S.) are not being flooded with memoirs by people who were burned by napalm in Vietnam, and who saw others around them burned to death.

Let us take a moment for one of the many examples that could be cited: *Humanity: A Moral History of the Twentieth Century* by Jonathan Glover. This book has been much praised, and is recommended by two prominent philosophers, Martha Nussbaum and Peter Singer. Glover is not a reactionary who can be dismissed as such. Indeed, his critique of Marxist instrumentalism is not so different from what I have offered in the present book. *Humanity* has many interesting references to Kant, including one that takes stock of twentieth-century skepticism about the existence of the moral law (and argues that "those of us who hope for an international order based on something other than force must hope that there is some middle way between Kant and Hobbes," 231), and another mentioning that Kant was on a list of philosophical works drawn up at Stalin's request, so that he could pursue his supposed interest in philosophy; about this list, however, Stalin purportedly said, "Who uses all this rubbish in practice?" (310). Furthermore, Glover puts front and center many difficult facts, especially about the Stalin period, that should not be dismissed. In particular he presents some rather damning statements from Lenin and Stalin regarding intellectuals and philosophy; we will return to this issue. At the same time, one has to wonder at Glover's own sense of philosophy when he says, "Some have seen Heidegger as a major thinker" (372). You think? Glover has a chapter of about fifteen pages entitled "Mao's Utopian Project" that is a compendium of disasters. It has exactly one small paragraph toward the beginning that says anything positive at all, and even that in a backhanded way.

Many thought a planned socialist economy might eliminate poverty. Mao and his colleagues were widely trusted. In the two-year retreat in the mid-1930s known as the Long March, the Communist army and its leaders had shown great strength in the face of daunting obstacles and had refused to exploit the people along their route. Now the communists were in power, they set out to raise standards of health and literacy. They improved the status of women, ending child marriages and the practice of binding women's feet. There were reasons to see the new government as both determined and idealistic. (283–84)

But never mind—in the very next sentence Glover has returned to the only real theme of the chapter, "Mao's utopian project" as unending catastrophe and disaster. Glover says nothing in his book directly about capitalism, colonialism, or capitalist imperialism. The Soviet polity led by Stalin made many of its mistakes out of a paranoid, siege mentality, and that mentality itself was largely a mistake, but it was not a mistake that occurred outside of any global context. Because of the way that capitalist-imperialist ruling classes generally administer their polities, with a certain democratic facade and with "market freedom," I suppose it is less appealing to speak of the "utopian project of Henry Kissinger, Milton Friedman, and Augusto Pinochet." While Glover does indeed deal with the atrocities committed by the United States in Vietnam (there is a short chapter on the My Lai Massacre), it is very clear that he does not understand these atrocities as fundamentally connected to a polity, or to the "utopian project of Kennedy, Johnson, Nixon, Kissinger, and McNamara."

An Alternative Account

Returning to the idea that there is no alternative for the future, there is also not even an alternative account of the past—so don't look for one, don't even think about it. As one last, small attempt to counter this idea, consider this interview with a participant in the Cultural Revolution, Wang Zheng, who provides not only an alternative account, but also a perspective on why we have so few such accounts and so many of the atrocity accounts. Wang Zheng is a professor of women's studies at the University of Michigan, and an editor and contributor to a collection of memoirs titled, *Some of Us: Chinese Women Growing Up in the Mao Era*. Professor Wang is not a revolutionary communist or even a Marxist; she is a radical feminist who has coined the provocative and interesting term "state feminism" to describe the gender policies of Maoist China. In the interview, Wang says that she is sure there were (what she calls) persecution disasters, but, at the least, there are other stories to be told, too. Lastly, as regards these other stories, and the perspective from which they are told, Wang says that she "would never condone any violence." This, of course, separates her from revolutionary communism, even if perhaps the word "condone" does not capture how communists ought to view the question of violence, either. Furthermore, though I am making a conjecture concerning Wang's position, the wholesale critique of violence is common in contemporary feminism, one aspect of the critique being that violence is a fundamentally "masculinist" phenomenon. As the reader will see when I take up Sartre's defense of violence (and Hannah Arendt's critique of it), I do not believe this view should be dismissed out of hand—far from it. Nevertheless, Wang presents a perspective on the Chinese Revolution and Cultural Revolution that is rarely heard:

> I would never condone any violence. However . . . a revolution to achieve an egalitarian society did involve some drastic measures, like land reform to con- fiscate landowners' land, to redistribute among all the landless people. So, if you go to interview the landlord, their children, they would tell you that the landlord's land had been confiscated, the landlord had been executed—if you hear that story, of course, they are full of hatred. But if you go to interview the landless class and they got land from the communists, you will hear a very dif- ferent story. So that's why it's important to have a fuller picture of what's going on. The relationship of the poor peasants to the communist revolution is drastically different. But those poor peasants cannot write their memoirs in English. That's why you have never heard a peasant talking. Or even those peasants' children who can write English—their writing can never be promoted in this country [the United States] because the people who control the pub- lishing market, they will not promote these kinds of stories. ("We had a dream that the world can be better than today," in *Revolution* newspaper, no. 59, Sept. 3, 2006; online at revcom.us.)

Wang's further reflections on the kinds of stories that can be told present a perspective that is *never* heard in the mainstream media, publishing world, or even intellectual world (I quote the interviewer's questions as well).

> **SRS:** There are many memoirs being written by people who lived in China dur- ing the socialist years, or "the Mao era" (1949–1976), especially about the Cultural Revolution decade. What compelled the writing of *Some of Us?*

> **Wang Zheng:** This book is collective memoirs by nine authors, all from the People's Republic of China. We were all graduate students in this country [the U.S.], and then most of us got teaching positions here. The motiva- tion to do this is that we were amazed by many memoirs published by the Chinese diaspora, people from China. Those memoirs that were promoted or that achieved the most market success were the ones depicting Mao's era in China as the "dark age": terrible, nothing but persecution and dictator- ship and killings, all the horror stories, just a one-sided voice.
>
> Even though I cannot say they are telling lies, a lot of the stuff is fic- tional. Like Anchee Min's *Red Azalea*, which was widely used here, even in universities. She claimed it's autobiographical when she was in the U.S. But when she went back to China, among all her friends and relatives, all the people who knew her, lived there in that setting, when people asked her about this book, she said it's fiction. So that's one point.

That type of autobiography achieves the most market success due to the politics of publication in this country. What kind of books are they promoting in this country? You see that pattern there. They play into this Cold War mentality, still in the U.S., in the West, that capitalist countries are wonderful lands of freedom, socialist countries are terrible, Communist China, red China was awful, like hell. So they are telling all these horror stories to you. Those books always have the widest circulation, always receive a lot of media attention.

My point is not that persecution disasters did not happen. Our point, I just want to say, is that China is so big, with a population of one billion. We have different social groups, and different social groups experience even the same historical period differently. As Chinese, when we read those memoirs, we don't share a lot of their experiences. Whatever their experiences, even if it's true, it's not our experience.

I found out in my peer group of all these Chinese women that we shared the same sentiment towards those memoirs. So we wanted to do something. At least we can raise our voices. If they're telling their stories . . . what about our stories and our experiences? But our experiences didn't get told. So we feel, especially I myself as a historian, that the important thing is not to vindicate anybody; rather, it is to present a complicated picture of history.

Also if you look at who wrote all this "condemnation literature," they are usually people from elite classes. You really don't hear the voices of workers, peasant class, those who are in the lower classes, the bottom of society. How did those people experience Mao's China, or Communist China?

The Communist Party was very complicated, with different factions with different visions of China, different visions of socialism even. People had different visions in the Communist Party. In those years, there were all kinds of people involved in different things and the policies proposed by different people within the Party had different effects.

It was an extremely complicated situation. But in this country, what you hear is just one single voice, condemnation—how the people from the elite classes suffered during those years. That's a terrible distortion of the larger picture if you believe that's the truth, the only truth.

SRS: Why did this "condemnation literature" get such play?

Wang Zheng: There was a mass movement to produce victim narratives in the late 1970s and early 1980s in China, a line that was later largely transported to the West along with those Chinese who found an especially lucrative market in the capitalist "land of freedom" to claim the status of "victims" emerging in the post-Mao era.

"Thoroughly negate the Cultural Revolution" was a scheme by Deng Xiaoping to pave the way for his dismantling of socialism while consolidating political power. It was a way to whitewash or shift attention from his and his associates' crimes.

After Deng Xiaoping's call to thoroughly negate the Cultural Revolution, being a victim of the Cultural Revolution was a hot status symbol in China. Chinese intellectuals jumped on this bandwagon to produce narratives of victims. This was sanctioned by Deng Xiaoping, and helped him clear the ideological ground for staging neo-liberalism and social Darwinism to accompany the rise of a capitalist market economy. In the process, they have retrieved their power and privileges that had been reduced in the Mao era, especially in the Cultural Revolution. Those who dare to deviate from the design of the new architect Deng Xiaoping have been excluded from the privileges enjoyed by the new elite if not punished with imprisonment.

In this interview Wang expresses many rarely heard views, including this one: "Many scholars think that Jung Chang's new book" (*Mao: The Unknown Story*, co-authored with Jon Halliday—this is the "atrocity narrative" of the moment, at the time of this writing) "and their story of Mao is a piece of shit . . . These scholars do research, study history and documents, and they know this book cannot be held against academic standards." I find Wang's words tremendously refreshing, especially given the number of books that take the opposite position. However, let us at least visit a moment in the interview that goes more to the heart of something that happened during the Cultural Revolution.

> **SRS:** I want to talk about the mass movement of urban youth like you that were sent to the countryside. That's one of the things being attacked.

> **Wang Zheng:** Yes, yes. There are a lot of debates in terms of why Mao and the Party did that in terms of motivations. Even today, I don't think it's wrong to ask the urban educated youth to make a contribution to the poor areas even though we may not have to use that kind of drastic measure. Still I think it is necessary for educated people to go to the poor places, to contribute their knowledge to develop those areas.
>
> Even though I was sent to the countryside, I never shed a tear all those years when I was on the farm. If you read all those memoirs talking about how terrible it was for "sent down girls," like in *Wild Swans* for example, where she [Jung Chang] talks about her "sent down" experience, her countryside experience . . . oh, she felt so wronged. Because she was from this high Communist cadre official family—how can she be sent to work on the farm like a peasant? She just couldn't work as a peasant. It's horrible! When I read that part, I was so offended by her sense of entitlement, her sense of being elite, how can she do that kind of work? So when her parents went through the back door and got her out of the countryside, oh, she was so elated. And even to the time when she was writing, she never reflected on that privilege.
>
> Why couldn't you be a peasant where some 90 percent of Chinese were peasants at the time? On what ground could you not work as a farmer? Do

you have a crown on your head? I just don't see it. If you read all those condemnations, they are all complaining, saying that we are urban people, we are educated, my parents are professors or high officials and I had all these talents, now I have to work as a peasant. What is wrong with that? You can contribute your talents to the peasants, to the rural community. I still don't know what is wrong with that.

There is a politics and epistemology of personal experience, and a politics of this epistemology. Most often, in the kinds of "victim narratives" that Wang cites, this "I was there, don't tell me about my own experience" epistemology is used to make any alternative account of the Chinese Revolution and Cultural Revolution a nonstarter. We could go a long way in discussing epistemology and the politics of knowledge as they relate to this interview with Wang, looking also at the venue of its publication (a revolutionary communist newspaper) and therefore the relationship between publication and what is out there in some public forum to be known in the first place.

Intellectual Life

To return briefly to the issue of intellectuals, intellectual life, and intellectual institutions, perhaps a reminder is needed that the elite universities of China, which had not been substantially challenged in their elitism from 1949 until the Cultural Revolution started in 1966, were staffed entirely by males (as professors)—unless of course one considers the janitorial staff. This is one of the places where the question of violence, or force at least, hovers. Was it always, or even often, the best use of educated persons, in a society that needed education, to send them to the countryside? Was this the best way to deal with the inherited division of labor, in a society that had as a long-range goal to overcome this division but that also had the contradictory need in the short-term to expand this division at least in some fields? One thing that needs to be underlined, to return to an Aristotelian-Marxist spirit invoked much earlier in this text, is that the division of labor is itself a form of violence. This is especially true with the fundamental form of the division of labor, that between mental and manual labor. This division is the violent imposition of a conception, corresponding to a social formation and a mode of production, of what any given individual can be. It is not an exaggeration to say that many of the professors of the elite universities were not only comfortable with this imposition, at least as it affected them, but had indeed been formed by institutions inherited from traditional Chinese elitist educational culture.

One of the main guiding ideas of the Cultural Revolution was to challenge these divisions and forms of entitlement (that run very deep, into what Pierre Bourdieu calls "habitus"). There was a mass debate during the Cultural Revolution about this question, and about the idea of the "red expert." New institutions, such as the "three-in-one combinations" (in which experts, workers and peasants, and soldiers came together to share knowledge and work on problems) arose. Sometimes drastic measures were employed; tempers flared; people who wanted to hold on to their supposed entitlements dug in or attempted to sabotage the process; some people were targeted unfairly; some people used the situation to settle scores, and so on. Let us take it for granted that the formation of a society of well-rounded people who are not divided into a few "minds" and many "bodies" is itself a laudable goal; indeed, this could be the very definition of eudaimonea or even communism. The question becomes one of the types of counterforce that can be *justifiably* applied to breaking down the force of the division of labor. The opening to the justifiable forms may also open the door to some unjustifiable forms. Of course, there will be those who will say that counterforce is never justified, that it is in its very nature unethical. Proponents of this position should realize that they have to go all the way with it, to cases in which force will only be stopped by counterforce. In the given example, there was a need for the sharing of basic literacy and numerical skills, and it was thought that it was up to the urban educated students and professors to share their knowledge, especially in the rural areas of China. Some people did not want to take part in this work in the countryside and saw it as a horror—a horror not because many millions would be in poor, rural areas all of their lives, but *because they* (the educated elite) would have to disrupt their privileged lives for a period of time. (As an aside, a tradition of scholars at the University of Beijing was to grow their fingernails very long as a sign that these were not fingers meant for manual work.)

An analogy might be offered that perhaps has its limitations, but that seems fundamentally apt. In the United States, in the South but not only there, there was a system of racially segregated schools that persisted into the 1970s. Many of the constituents of the all-white schools, students and even more their parents, did not want "their" schools to be integrated, and they were willing to defend "their" turf with force. Should the response to this system of racist entitlement, in the case that force had to be met by at least some amount of counterforce, have been to say that it would have been better to have left things the way they were, and that either force (even the force of counterforce) is never justified, or that counterforce cannot be applied if it might lead to a more general chaos or violence? Certainly the struggle to integrate the public school systems in the United States opened up some more general chaos, and it might be argued that not only did this struggle need to go much further, but so did the chaos.

Bad Things

Even if it is the case that atrocity and other bad things (that do not sink to the level of outright atrocity) were not the norm of China in the Mao period (or of the Soviet Union in the Stalin period, though I would argue that there was an enormous difference between Stalin and Mao), and even if it is important to establish this, to set the record straight, over against the "unending atrocity" version, is it not still the case that there is something like a "quantitative issue," that atrocities and bad things not only occurred, but they occurred all too often, and in a way that goes to the polity that was led by Mao and the Chinese revolutionary communists and to the conception of Marxism they had? On this latter point, too, we have to consider that, whatever the revolutionaries were trying to do, or supposedly trying to do, there are differences between ideals and reality that need to be understood. Again, there is a quantitative dimension. How big were the gaps between ideals and reality, and how often did these gaps open up?

Economic Growth

One of the ironies and, obviously, unintended consequences of the Cultural Revolution is that it in some ways opened the way for the economic growth and "modernization" of China that has occurred in the post-Mao era. Here is how China scholar Lee Feigon puts it in his book, *Mao: A Reinterpretation*, in a chapter titled, "The Cultural Revolution Revisited":

> Nothing has damaged Mao's image as much as his role in initiating the Cultural Revolution, yet few of Mao's actions deserve as much praise. From today's perspective it is hard to understand why many still condemn a movement that not only battled corruption and streamlined bureaucracy but also strengthened the economy and promoted artistic and educational reform. Far from being the wasted decade, as it is usually called, the movement inaugurated a period of cultural and economic growth which set the stage for the celebrated transformation of China's financial system that has been much ballyhooed since Mao's death. The decade dominated by the Cultural Revolution left an enduring legacy of social justice, feminist ideals, and even democratic principles which today still resonate with many Chinese. (139)

Perhaps this is all the more reason that the post-Mao leadership in China, the capitalist roaders who came to power and restored capitalism, want to separate themselves from the Cultural Revolution and from Mao himself, other than as some sort of "father of the country" type monument.

To state the obvious once again, the difference in the standard of "economic growth" during the Cultural Revolution and after it is that, in the former case this growth was considered in terms of the general welfare, while since the close of the Mao era "growth" is understood in neo-liberal terms, as an increase in the bottom line, apart from concern for the general welfare and, in fact, generally set against this welfare. Asian and Asian-American studies scholar Peter Kwong describes in detail the real world dynamic of the "market reforms":

> China started its economic reforms by abolishing the people's communes. Suddenly, without the collectives, the peasants had to privately purchase seed, fertilizer and water rights, and to pay higher taxes to support a large cadre of local party officials. But the prices of farm products were kept low, forcing many to work as migrant workers in the cities. Others followed when their land was seized for urban and industrial development. Once in the cities, they were given neither residential status nor legal rights and protection, but they were nevertheless expected to be gainfully employed. Otherwise, under the "custody and repatriation" laws, beggars, vagrants and those with no employment were repatriated back to their villages, held at detention centers, or even used as forced labor. The Chinese version of the English "enclosure" process created approximately 150 million impoverished migrants who had to sell their labor cheaply in order to survive. . . .
>
> The secret of China's economic miracle is its browbeaten working class. The picture of China's Gilded Age of inequality is not pretty. On the average, the yearly income of a Chinese peasant in 2003 was $317. The monthly wages of factory workers ranged between $62 and $100—only marginally higher than in 1993, even as China's economy grew by almost 10 percent annually during the same period. On the other side of the social spectrum is the increasingly wealthy urban middle class that is emerging on the coattails of the coterie of the super-rich. In 2006 Shanghai held a "millionaire fair," featuring displays of jewelry priced at $25 million, and a diamond-studded dog leash valued at $61,000. (Peter Kwong, "The Chinese Face of Neo-Liberalism," 1–2)

So, the irony, as Žižek and others have pointed out, is that there is now underway in China an unprecedented wave of proletarianization.

After Maoism?

What I have said here barely scratches the surface; readers will undoubtedly want to investigate these issues in far greater depth. Mao said, speaking of his youth, "First we were revolutionaries, and as a result we became Marxists." That captures very well what I am trying to capture with the idea of Ethical Marxism: first we see that there is something very wrong about the way society is set up, and as a result we look for a systematic understanding of society that will allow us to move forward and try to make things right. I will say about Maoism the same thing I said about Marxism in the conclusion of part 1 during my discussion of Aronson's arguments for decisively placing ourselves "after Marxism": as with Marxism, some of Maoism might have been wrong from the start, some of it may have been more than wrong as it was applied in practice, some of it may have become outmoded and overtaken by developments in the world (including the restoration of capitalism in China and the role that China is now playing in the world), but *enough* of Maoism either was or is right that it ought to be carried forward and built upon. The primary focus in this effort, however, has to be understanding the world as it is now, and asking ourselves what has to be done to make the fundamental changes that will allow humanity to have a future—and again I would underscore the dialectical, historical materialist argument that the choice in our time seems to be between a better future (a future that is on the road to the global community of mutual flourishing) and no future for humankind.

There is, however, a pressing need not only to "build upon" the previous experience of proletarian revolution and socialism (I place the term in scare quotes because it is matter of building upon not only the positive experiences, but also the negative experiences, though "building negatively," as it were), but also and even more so to surpass this experience. For, it might be argued that, regardless of whether the previous experiences of Marxist-inspired revolution were predominantly good or bad, they are in some sense a closed chapter, and it is not *immediately* clear anymore what they have to do with the present and future.

This is indeed a difficult problem, for at least two reasons. Avakian once wrote an article entitled "The End of a Stage—The Beginning of a New Stage" (*Revolution* magazine, Fall 1990) in which he describes a stage in which there were socialist countries in the world, the period from 1917 to 1976, with a brief period in the middle when there was even a "socialist camp," albeit riddled with contradictions. (In *Conquer the World?* Avakian argues that, apart from the U.S.S.R. itself, the Warsaw Pact countries were never socialist, as there were never proletarian revolutions in those countries. This goes as well for those "socialist" countries that emerged as Soviet client states in the period after capitalism was restored: Cuba, North Korea, Ethiopia, South Yemen, etc.) We are now in a stage where our "models," so to speak, are in the past, even as the goal is not to go back to the past (we could not do that even if we wanted to) but to create a different future.

The second factor that has to be struggled over concerns the new things in the world that have developed in the most recent thirty years or so. (It is interesting that this coincides with the end of the first wave of

proletarian revolutions, and my guess is that this is not a mere coincidence.) There are new factors of production (developments in cybernetics, transport, materials science), new levels of concentration and
dissemination of the culture industry, new configurations of class, and the
general acceleration of life (one author calls it "turbo-capitalism"). Because
of the end of the earlier stage of socialism, and the collapse of the Soviet
bloc, there is an immense grab for power and resources underway, which
is a good deal of the dynamic that is driving U.S. aggression in the present
period. Even if the argument is that the basic outline of the imperialist
world system still underlies all of these new phenomena, there are, nevertheless, developments that are not simply quantitative add-ons to what
already existed—there are transformations going on in the world that are
real, even if certain underlying contradictions remain essentially the same
(again, socialized production and privatized accumulation, the division of
labor, the division between imperialist and dominated countries). A
"Marxist orthodoxy" that goes blithely past these developments will ossify
into a mere "belief system" that has little to do with changing the world.

There is yet a third reason why we might ask what the past experience
of revolution has to do with the future, one that has to do with the basic
idea of proletarian revolution as conceived by Marx. Above I referred—
without actually using the word—to the "unfolding" of history. It might
be argued that however much credence Marx would invest in this idea
depends on the depth of his commitment to Hegel. There is no need for
a heavy and thick, somewhat theological, sense of capital-H "History" if
the mechanism of social change in our period can better be described in
terms taken from political economy, not philosophy. In such terms, what
matters most is that the contradictions of capitalism call forth the
"gravediggers" of the system, as Marx put it, and that this process is an
integral part of the workings of capitalism. Other ways of coming at this
question, of something law-like at work in society, range from what might
be called Aristotle's teleological humanism (that there is a sense of what it
would mean to flourish inherent in the human species—and every other
species or even "nonliving thing," for that matter—and that people strive
toward that possibility of flourishing) to Mao's view that, "where there is
oppression, there is resistance." Marx, who was influenced at least a little
by Aristotle on this point, held that the specific form of capitalist exploitation increasingly brings forward the agents of its ultimate overturning—a
class that eventually is global in scope, as capital increasingly is, but that is
also, unlike the different capitalist classes that are rooted in different
nation-states, a single, international class. This is, of course, the international proletariat. The argument about past revolutionary experiences con-
tends that the proletariat undertook these revolutions as part of a global
process. The process is not necessarily continuous, or at least it contains

significant discontinuities. The process contains advances as well as set-backs. Mao said, "the road is tortuous" (though the outlook is bright); to use a more recent metaphor, we might say that the "learning curve" for revolution is very steep. But why, now, believe that there is any "process" (or "road," etc.) any more, if there ever was one? Why believe this especially now, when there are no socialist countries in the world, when capitalism is exulting in triumphalism (indeed, when we live in a strange time of monopolarism, with the United States as the "hyperpower"), when new factors of production and culture are reshaping society in ways that seem unprecedented and quite foreign to at least some of the economic and social phenomena that Marx analyzed?

No Retreat to Orthodoxy

To say the least, all of these factors militate against the recreation of or retreat to a Marxist orthodoxy of any sort, including a "Maoist orthodoxy." This goes as well for any call to return to "classical Marxism," an easy way out in the face of the twists and turns of the twentieth century. Instead, these factors call for both a recognition of what is actually unfolding in the world, and for creative thought and theorizing. One achievement of my dialogues with Avakian , in my view, was simply that a number of questions were brought to the table, such as the "animal question," issues of secularism (and even the old philosophical question of "the meaning of life"), and issues involved in sexuality. Indeed, on this last score, I was especially pleased that Avakian and I were able to explore some problems in the way that the Revolutionary Communist Party had previously understood homosexuality, an issue that had been difficult and problematic (to say the least) for people working in and around the organization. Beyond the particularities of this specific question, the previous stand that had been taken (and that has been definitively overturned in recent years) was a good example of the kind of cul-de-sac thinking in which Marxists sometimes find themselves stuck. On some level, such thinking can be a testimony to a style of inquiry that wants primarily to do something about the awful state of the world. And yet, a thinking that erects barricades will soon enough not be engaged, other than with dogmatism and mental ossification.

The give and take of the conversations shows the opposite of such ossification—we raise questions and attempt to find some answers, or at least arrive at some terms of agreement, but more than that we try to open things up and grapple with difficult issues with respect to their actual complexity. Still, the question might be raised, what is the relationship between Ethical Marxism, as I have conceived it in the present book, and Maoism and the "new synthesis" as conceived and practiced by Avakian and the

Revolutionary Communist Party? I would like to think, despite some of the substantial disagreements we might have, that the aim in both cases is to find a resistance to orthodoxy that all the same retains an orientation toward radical social transformation, a Marxism that is theoretically lively and adventurous and (which ought to go without saying) not merely academic.

A New Synthesis

Since the publication of *Marxism and the Call of the Future*, people have asked me about some of the areas where there was more disagreement than agreement in the conversations. This catches me up a bit short, because I do think there is not only the question, which is fair enough, but also the perspective from which the question is raised—some people are only interested in getting an argument going, or engaging in some sort of sectarian divisiveness. It is of course right to try to answer the question forthrightly, but there is something that I want to place front and center as the context of this answer: Avakian and the RCP have worked determinedly for many years for the radical transformation of society, and after all this time they have not given up. Furthermore, I think there is something here more than mere doggedness or stubbornness (though there is something to be said for these things), and something other than commitment, namely, a material basis for believing that there is a point to carrying on with revolutionary struggle. This may be a "marginal" struggle—in some sense, it is marginal because it is a struggle of the *marginalized*. It is a struggle that has gone through twists and turns and setbacks, including some self-imposed setbacks. (Indeed, I do sometimes wonder if the RCP can live down its previous—but longstanding—line on homosexuality, a line that hurt the organization itself in the end.) I have tried to argue that the *material* basis for change includes the felt need for change and the commitment to work for change, and that these elements affect our understanding of historical materialism. One of the disagreements that Avakian and I have is over "religion" (I place the term in scare quotes because it is often unclear what people mean by the term, and often people discuss "religion" as if they are talking about the same thing, when they are not). Avakian says that we should stop believing in things that don't exist, and instead apply our conscious activism to changing *this* world. There is a sense in which I agree with that, but I would also want to point out that the future we hope to achieve also does not exist, and that our faith in the possibility of this future can never be fully underwritten by a "scientific" theory of society. Three other areas where we did not come to agreement concerned the animal question, the value of Kant's philosophy, and the role and understanding of truth. On at least the latter pair of issues, however, I would say that our conversations themselves represented at least something of an agreement, in that we agreed that there is a conversation to be had—and let it be said that that is not nothing.

In recent years, Avakian has been speaking of a "new synthesis," going "beyond Mao." This synthesis is still coming together, at least in my opinion, and it will be interesting to see how a more systematic integration of its elements develops. The new synthesis is emerging in documents such as "The New Situation and the Great Challenges" (which responds directly to the events of September 11, 2001 and their aftermath), "Dictatorship and Democracy, and the Socialist Transition to Communism," "The Basis, The Goals, and the Methods of the Communist Revolution," "A Radically New Kind of State, A Radically Different and Far Greater Vision of Freedom," "On Epistemology: On Knowing and Changing the World," "A Leap of Faith and a Leap to Rational Knowledge: Two Very Different Kinds of Leaps, Two Radically Different Worldviews and Methods," and the book, *Observations on Art and Culture, Science and Philosophy*. (The documents, apart from the book, are online at revcom.us.) Clearly, this period of productivity and rethinking Maoism is not unrelated to September 11, 2001 and its aftermath, especially the attempt by the U.S. ruling class, or at least dominant elements within this class, to reforge American global hegemony and to implement a far-Right agenda that has at least some elements of fascism.

In an article titled "Bob Avakian Reenvisions Socialism," Raymond Lotta sets out some of the key elements of the new synthesis (*Revolution* newspaper, June 4, 2006), three in particular: (1) the importance of intellectual ferment; (2) a reemphasis on truth and a scientific perspective, drawing lessons from the Lysenko affair; and (3) an affirmation of the role of dissent and people's rights in socialist society. Among the other, related, themes in these recent documents from Avakian are the rethinking of questions of sovereignty even in the midst of reemphasizing the necessity for state power, the roles of spirituality, myth, and romanticism, the reiteration and extension of Mao's idea that "Marxism embraces but does not replace" the knowledge that is generated in "different disciplines and fields of inquiry and struggle" (*Observations*, 113), and the idea that Marxism (at whatever stage) as a science does not signal "the end of philosophy" (see *Observations*, 65–67).

These are ideas that not only did not receive the qualitative development that was needed in the previous history of the international communist movement (ICM) and in the revolutions in Russia and China, but indeed these are ideas that were largely disparaged by Marx and Lenin (though, significantly, to a lesser extent by Mao). These ideas were developed in other domains of Marxism, and in what might be called radical and progressive philosophy and social theory more generally, but, for various reasons, the door between the international communist movement and these domains was locked from both sides. Perhaps not all of the reasons for this mutual disappreciation were bad, there were in fact reasons for revolutionary communists to be suspicious of Western intellectuals, and there were *very* good reasons for progressive and radical intellectuals to be wary—to say the least—of the purity of (supposedly) Marxist theory as practiced by the leading figures of the ICM. This purity—which meant, among other things, never venturing outside of an extremely narrow canon for a theoretical anchor, is inseparable from a violent reductivism that can be, in its "materialist" form, *even worse* than that of theological fundamentalisms. Indeed, there is little difference between these fundamentalisms, at a certain stage reductivism in Marxism passes over into theology, and not in a good way, either—in other words, lacking any commitment to the ethical (or the ethical-political, and therefore to the political, to the notion of the just society) as such. Obviously, I am once again thinking of Stalin—even while, also once again, not wanting to buy into the view that socialist construction in the Soviet Union during the Stalin period was nothing but endless horror—and yet again it can be said that Stalin and his period is the main impetus to the need for a theory of Ethical Marxism.

The possible unity of these diverse ideas, all of which I see as standing against the history of reductivism in the ICM, and all of which—let it be said—I think are moving in the right direction, in a "new synthesis," is a developing and "gathering" sort of thing. A good deal more systematic work needs to be done to put it all together. Naturally, a philosopher and social theorist such as myself, who is not in the party, and who is a professor in a university, thinks of the *big book* that needs to be written—like the one I have written here. But there is a tendency for intellectuals in our society, which generally means people who are connected to academic institutions in one way or another, not to really understand the specific circumstances of working in revolutionary theory in the midst of leading a revolutionary movement. (I do not claim to fully understand these circumstances either.) Theory in the academic context often lacks certain things that we in the theory class wish were there, even while there are also elements of this kind of revolutionary theory (which perhaps ought to be called "revolutionary movement theory," so that we might better grasp the specificity of this activity) that are not much appreciated by some intellectuals who are too locked up in academia and its peculiar world.

Perils of Stupidification

For instance, in a gesture that is somewhat typical of this world (though, admittedly, not exactly from this world), science fiction writer Ken

MacLeod criticized American stupidity in his blog, saying, "French Maoism gave us Sartre and Althusser[;] American Maoism gave us Klonsky and Avakian" ("The Early Days of a Better Nation," at kenmacleod .blogspot.com, entry for March 23, 2003). MacLeod was mostly responding to the American-led Iraq War, and I find it hard not to sympathize with his frustration with America and "Americans." Our interpretations of the source of this "stupidity" are different, however. I attribute it to successive campaigns of stupidification, not unrelated to actual machinations of the ruling class, shaped in a particular, post-60s way, but also not unrelated to Neil Postman's notion of "amusing ourselves to death" and Mark Crispin Miller's notion of "big brother is you, watching" (on the former, see the book of that title; on the latter, see *Boxed In: The Culture of TV*). Returning to themes from part 1 of the present book, perhaps most of all I attribute the success of the campaigns of stupidification to the fact that it is very difficult to face what it means to be a beneficiary of the plunder carried out in the name of America, and chief among the strategies for coping with this is a kind of moral vacuity, one that both leads to and feeds from mental vacuity in general. (For instance, in right-wing Christian fundamentalism this moral vacuity expresses itself in terms of a "God" whose "moral concerns" concern activities or even "comportments" such as homosexuality that, even if they were somehow morally wrong—and, of course, they are not—would not even begin to make it on to the map of the truly grievous wrongs that are perpetrated in this world, especially by the American imperialism that is the real "religion" of these fundamentalists.) It is hard for Americans to look upon what might be called their own moral nakedness, and so they dress themselves up in a variety of ways that do not stand up to much scrutiny.

Indeed, on this score, we might simply extend what I think is a very powerful example from Avakian, one that ends with literal nakedness:

> If you don't believe this is an imperialist system, if you don't see how the seal of parasitism is set on this whole society by imperialism, go home to your closet and throw out every piece of clothing except those made in the United States—which, in reality, means every piece of clothing that is made under conditions of not "normal" but *extreme* exploitation, including exploitation of little children, all throughout the world. Throw all those out and keep only the ones that aren't made that way—and see if you can go out your front door. See if you will have anything to wear. All you have to do is look at the labels on your clothes to see what kind of system this is—to see a reflection of the fact that it is an international system of exploitation, with the most extreme forms of exploitation, including of children, throughout the Third World. ("The Basis, the Goals, and the Methods of the Communist Revolution," revcom.us, 20–21)

Even so, without a stitch, many Americans go boldly forth into the world as if they were dressed in the finest garments and with the intellectual finery of such brilliant minds as Bill O'Reilly, Sean Hannity, and Ann Coulter.

However, MacLeod's explanation for this stupid state of affairs is something I often hear from left-wing commentators in the U.K., namely the lack of a major "labor" or social-democratic party. As MacLeod writes, "This particular distribution curve has a long tail at the low end. Why?"

> Not because Americans are more stupid than anyone else, but because *there is no American party of the Left*." . . . . "This means that the American Right can indulge in lying and character assassination with almost as much impunity as if it dominated a one-party state. And it means that the American Left either buries itself in the Democratic Party, where it's treated as an embarrassment, or spins its wheels with a complete lack of social tradition (in academia or in tiny irrelevant sects) and embarrasses itself.

Now, it seems to me that all of the reasons that I gave for the success of stupidification apply to the U.K. as well, at least in general but with perhaps some significant variation, and that the existence of the Labour Party has not stood in the way of the efforts of the British ruling class to continue to carry forward an imperialist agenda, even if this agenda is now in a subordinate role to the United States.

In certain sectors of the Left, perhaps most of all the Trotskyist Left (with which MacLeod has some sympathy in the U.K.), there is a good deal of emphasis on continuity, and on the "authentic Marxist tradition" and an affirmation (or reaffirmation) of "classical Marxism." One of the reasons that Maoists reject these terms is that an affirmation of "classical Marxism" is a denial of the qualitative changes that occurred in the world in the twentieth century, especially imperialism. But in addition to this, and partly because of these qualitative developments (which led Mao to argue for not only the possibility but also the necessity of socialist revolution in China, and again the irony is that the kind and level of capitalism that exists in China today would not have been possible within the circuit of economic and social development that existed in China up until 1949), Maoists tend to stress discontinuity and development from the margins rather than the center. This also means that Maoists attempt to be rigorously internationalist and perhaps especially non-Eurocentric, and this ought to be counterposed to social-democratic parties, organizations of the economistic Left, and even the U.S. Democratic Party, whose outmost leftward limit, in the end, is perhaps a different distribution formula for the spoils of imperialism and neocolonialism. Be that as it may, I do not want to entirely deny that there may be some significance to the fact that there is not even what might be called a "loyal opposition" in the United States, not anymore, if there ever was—the Democratic Party is all loyal and no real opposition.

In going beyond Marx, Lenin had to not only extend some of Marx's arguments, he had to qualitatively break with some of them—and Lenin really did have to do this, because "classical" capitalism had changed, qualitatively. And the same with Mao and now with Avakian.

Michael Klonsky was the leader of one of several parties in the United States that called themselves "Maoist" in the 1970s, none of which other than the RCP exist today (or at least, as with the Progressive Labor Party, they do not exist as parties that call themselves Maoist). Klonsky's group, the Communist Party, Marxist-Leninist (CPML), supported the counter-revolutionary coup in China carried out by Deng Xiaoping, and the "four modernizations," which only the most hard-headed would deny was and is a program for capitalist restoration. Initially, the new regime in China gave the CPML the nod as the official Maoist group in the U.S., but within a few years it became clear that what the new regime needed was not these erstwhile "Maoist" organizations (even if they were neither revolutionary nor communist, and therefore not really Maoist either), but instead direct dealings with other capitalist ruling classes in the world. I do not know how anyone with even a passing familiarity with the writings and work of Avakian and the RCP could make a comparison with Klonsky, the CPML, or any of those other groups that either never were much oriented toward revolution (all of the other "Maoist" groups in the U.S. that came out of the 1960s were very economistic and "workerist," and this in fact was a trend within the RCP in the mid- and late-1970s as well, a trend that was struggled over and overcome). That part of MacLeod's remark is simply intemperate and inaccurate.

All right, but what about Sartre and Althusser? The situation is a bit too complicated to say that "French Maoism gave us Sartre and Althusser," and, more to the point, neither Sartre nor Althusser were attempting to lead a proletarian revolutionary movement. The question might be whether we ought to add to the foregoing, "which is something altogether different from writing systematic works of philosophy." The fact is that neither MacLeod (who is not a philosopher), nor myself (who am trying to be a philosopher), is attempting to lead such a movement, either, and therefore we might not have as good a feel for the role of philosophy (or "theory," more broadly) in such a movement as does someone who is—whether this is Lenin, Mao, or Avakian.

Proposed Distinction: Philosophical Marxism and Revolutionary Movement Theory

Having said this, I want to once again make a proposal of the "split the difference" sort, or at least to look at two sides of the question, and pose this as a criticism of the ICM. One side of the difference contains another proposal that I think ought to stand in its own right. Suppose that instead of speaking of Western Marxism as a trend in philosophy that is counter-posed to the post-Marx Marxism of Lenin, Stalin, and Mao, we instead speak of a tradition of *philosophical Marxism*, that runs from the early works of Marx and Engels, up through Kautsky, Lenin, Lukacs, Adorno, Benjamin, Sartre, Marcuse, Althusser, among many, many others, and that remains an important philosophical trend today in the work of thinkers who are engaging with themes in Marx and Marxism, from Derrida and Deleuze to Slavoj Žižek, Alain Badiou, and Judith Butler. I will say with-out hesitation that this is a *great trend*. I want to separate with at least that last momentary *period* (I mean the grammatical dot) this declaration from what I want to say next, namely that this trend from Lukacs to Badiou and beyond, despite being a great trend, has seemingly not meant a damned thing to the leaders of the ICM, unless it has meant something negative, something to be denounced, dismissed, negated. Certainly there is noth-ing to be learned, and the tendency has been to put a one-word label on the philosopher/philosophy in question and get him/her/it out of the conversation: most often "idealism," but also "bourgeois," "petty-bour-geois," "individualism," or "nihilism" and thereby to have "handled" the "problem."

Marx—the "revolutionary philosopher"—had already set the pattern for these dismissals, but Lenin—the "philosophical revolutionary"—really raised the stakes on the "intellectual question." "The intellectuals, the lack-eys of capital, who think they're the brains of the nation. In fact, they're not its brains, they're its shit," Lenin apparently said in a Central Committee meeting. This is reported in Glover's *Humanity* (278), and rather than waste time questioning the authenticity of the statement (Glover takes it from the biography of Lenin by Dmitri Volkogonov), it would be better to grant that Lenin was indeed given to saying these sorts of things, and to analyze the consequences of this perspective. I have heard it said by Alexander Cockburn and others that Marx says somewhere, "When the train of history goes round a bend, all of the intellectuals fall off." Yes, probably, or perhaps most of them do fall off of this train—as probably do many physicists, for example, when the "train of physics" goes round a bend. Among the intellectuals who sometimes fell off of the train were Marx and Engels themselves. But so what? One can easily see such a formula, which is far from being entirely false, as mainly being used as a license for the most philistine anti-intellectualism. The stakes of such a line of thought (that, unfortunately, contained a large kernel of thoughtlessness) were raised qualitatively and even immeasurably after the October Revolution, when this perspective "achieved state power" and effectively became the policy of a state.

Let's take this thumbnail sketch of the intellectual question in the International Communist Movement a little further by considering Stalin. In the following, Glover quotes Stalin at length:

> Did philosophers question the attack on objective truth? The answer is understandable but sad. Like nearly everyone else, they did not speak out because they were afraid. They had a special problem because Stalin, in his irascible way, was interested in philosophy. He wrote a chapter on "Dialectical Materialism" in *The History of the CPSU: Short Course.* The person whose philosophical views had most influence was Stalin himself.
>
> Stalin asked his assistant to assemble a library of books for him and he put philosophy first on the list of subjects to be included. He then appointed the philosopher Jan Sten to be his tutor. Sten must have thought that he had a chance of influence not given to any philosopher since Aristotle taught Alexander the Great. He drew up a programme to teach Stalin about Kant, Hegel, Fichte, Schelling, Feuerbach, Plekhanov, Kautsky, and F. H. Bradley. In the tutorials, Stalin sometimes asked questions like "What's all this got to do with the class struggle?" or "Who uses all this rubbish in practice?"
>
> Despite his impatience, Stalin persevered with the subject enough to think of himself as a philosopher. In 1930 he gave a philosophical lecture to an institute of philosophers, which is summarized in the minutes: "We have to turn upside down and dig over the whole pile of manure that has accumulated in philosophy and the natural sciences. Everything written by the Deborin group has to be smashed. Sten and Karev can be chucked out. Sten boasts a lot, but he's just a pupil of Karev's. Sten is a desperate sluggard. All he can do is talk. Karev's got a swelled head and struts about like an inflated bladder. In my view, Deborin is a hopeless case, but he should remain as an editor of the journal so we'll have someone to beat. The editorial board will have two fronts, but we'll have the majority."
>
> After this philosophy lecture there were questions. Unsurprisingly, they were undemanding. One was, "What should the Institute concentrate on in the area of philosophy?" Stalin replied: "To beat, that is the main issue. To beat on all sides and where there hasn't been any beating before. The Deborinites regard Hegel as an icon. Plekhanov has to be unmasked. He always looked down on Lenin. Even Engels was not right about everything. There is a place in his commentary on the Erfurt Programme about growing into socialism. Bukharin tried to use it. It wouldn't be a bad thing if we could implicate Engels somewhere in Bukharin's writings." It would be a nightmare for any philosophy tutor to give tutorials to Stalin. And a tutor might be depressed at being described as a desperate sluggard by the most famous person he had taught.

But things got worse. Jan Sten was later described as a lickspittle of Trotsky and executed. (*Humanity*, 279–80)

Speaking of objective truth, the foregoing seems a good example of a situation where disagreeing with the perspective from which Glover presents his case (certainly both Avakian and I would disagree with this perspective) would simply be a way of sidestepping the most important questions. It would completely miss the point to say, "Glover says so and so about Stalin, but Glover is an anticommunist."

That being said, it is easy to get fed up with Glover's gloss on complex events. For instance, Glover says that in the aftermath of the Great Leap Forward the "new regime" (with Liu Shaoqi as head of state) "allowed people to wear different clothes instead of the uniform Mao suits" (287). This is another case in which it could be said that a commentator who is presuming to care about the Chinese people is instead only piling on claims that have already been proven false in order to advance an agenda that has little to do with caring about the Chinese people. People in China, including Mao himself, wore the "Mao suits" as a great advance over a society where many millions had only rags for their "clothes," and sometimes not even that. Again, this goes to the fact that China still had, for some years after the countrywide seizure of power in 1949, hundreds of years of poverty and deprivations to address, in the most basic areas of food, shelter, and clothing. The achievements should not make us blind to the shortcomings, but neither should the shortcomings make us blind to the achievements. On this point, Glover's account promotes a slanderous ignorance.

Be that as it may, this new emphasis on intellectual ferment, and on objective truth, and especially on the objective truth of how intellectuals have been treated in the societies where Marxism, or some version of Marxism, has guided state power, has to not only build on the negative experience of the past (and this seems to be one of those points on which perhaps most of the experience is negative, and where what is negative about this experience has spread to other areas of life) but also bring about a reversal of this experience.

Just as the tradition of what I will now persist in calling "philosophical Marxism" is a great trend, the larger philosophical projects of not only the West, but also diverse cultures, should be seen as the intellectual inheritance of humankind. Plato and Aristotle were not first of all intellectual operatives of an oppressive ruling class. For Stalin, but perhaps even for Marx, Engels, and Lenin, intellectual ferment was not a good thing. An argument could be made that for Mao the opposite was true. Avakian argues that intellectual ferment is indeed a good thing, but he also argues for a reemphasis on science. What worries me is that it was especially the emphasis on science that, for Marx, was the reason that "the end of classical German philosophy" (to use Engels's phrase, and where "end" could also be understood as "culmination"), meant that there was little need for much more philosophy. Now, it is also the case that Avakian has proffered the formula, "Marxism is a science, it is not the 'end of philosophy'," but this idea could stand to be spelled out in a bit more detail. Let us come back to this question. However, let us not leave the discussion of intellectual life in the context of the Stalin period in particular, and of Marxism as an orthodox, "state philosophy" in general, without addressing the ethical question that demands a response. It is not only the case that nothing good whatsoever came out of the way philosophers were treated in the Soviet Union during the Stalin period, but the full measure of this fact needs to be taken. Furthermore, the way philosophers were treated in this instance affected the whole society, not just the relatively small sector of philosophers or other intellectuals (especially those in the humanities and the arts). The message from Stalin was clear, and not only to the hapless Jan Sten: no one can tell me anything. Beyond these things, however, the core ethical matter of this historical episode is that it is *wrong* to persecute and execute people for proposing ideas that are different from those of the state ideology.

For almost all readers, I am sure this is not to say anything too penetrating or startling (though it remains significant that something like this has to be said at all), but the difficulty is in asking what it means to go in the opposite direction, toward what is right, in the context of socialism and state power. In the early 1980s, Avakian began to rethink the history of the ICM, especially in the aftermath of the overturning of socialism (and Maoism) in China, and one thing he argued in works from that period (including his essay on the hundredth anniversary of the death of Karl Marx, *For a Harvest of Dragons*, 1983) was that Marxism in the Soviet Union became more and more a "state religion" (especially during the time when socialism had been overturned, but the USSR still claimed to be socialist—in the Stalin period, too, there were significant elements of this phenomenon). The development of Avakian's thought in that period laid the ground for even more qualitative developments in the period after September 11, 2001. Moving in a new direction with regard to the "intellectual question" means drawing conclusions about the very idea of a "state philosophy." This applies not only in the case of a new revolution, but also in the case of the party, which in important ways prefigures proletarian state power. This last point also shows, at least in part, where there are interconnections among the themes that have been put forward as central to the "new synthesis."

Engaging with Jacques Derrida

In developing these issues further, let us turn now to the other side of the question, and here I would like to frame the difference as that between "philosophical Marxism" (and even "radical philosophy" in general and even simply philosophy in general) on the one side, and (what I propose to call) "revolutionary movement theory," on the other. In the *Observations* book, Avakian has a short chapter with the funny title, "Epistemology: The Derridas and the Communists," in which he makes these comments:

> With regard to philosophers like Derrida, and others in other fields (unfortunately, Derrida is no longer alive, but speaking about him as representative of larger groups of people), it is not that we shouldn't struggle to win these people to communism. But two things: First, there are always going to be people—or, for a long time there will be people—who are *not* going to be communists. That is just an objective reality. So, then, the question is: what about them? Can they contribute anything, do we recognize that they can make contributions? Are they not going to learn important things about reality? For example, can people who are religious who study the history of the Bible teach us anything? Yes. It is not that we shouldn't struggle to win people like this to communism. And then, when we do get to communism, it will be a different dynamic: There will be different schools of thought which will all probably be "post-communist" schools of dialectical materialism. (*Observations*, 107)

> . . . What about them—not just "how can we use them" in the practical struggle, but what about them in terms of how we are going to be able to approach and learn from and assimilate what they come up with even while they are not, or not consistently, applying the communist outlook and methodology?
>
> It struck me—it was over a period of time that it struck me, not one day like a bolt of lightning—that you have all these people in all these spheres whom we now seek to learn from to help us understand reality. It just struck me: Well, why would you think that would stop at some point—when you seize state power or something? Why would you think that would no longer be the case? It didn't make sense to me, epistemologically, that all of a sudden it would no longer be the case that these people could investigate reality and teach us something. Even though we have to apply the dialectical materialist outlook and method to really get the deepest understanding of reality, that doesn't mean that they might not teach us a great deal without applying that outlook (or without applying it consistently and systematically). There is a unity of opposites in that case, too. (*Observations*, 108–9)

> . . . And yes, under socialism, like under capitalism, there are constraints. Somebody is setting the parameters (the framework and the boundaries or limits). Here is the point: Yes, there are always parameters and somebody is always setting them. And, in this connection, there are a couple of questions:

According to what principles? And are there rules to the game—in a relative sense—or is this all arbitrary? There have to be rules to the game that everybody has to adhere to, even though that may be a moving thing that changes, and not something static and forever the same. That is why you have rules and laws and Constitutions, including in socialist society—so people can know what the hell the rules of the game are. How do things get decided and by whom? And through what procedures and institutions do they get decided and implemented? And what and who is accountable to what and whom? Those are things that in socialist society you will still have to have. If there are no institutions and instrumentalities like that, then it is just "the party and the masses" and it can be very arbitrary. That was the problem with Lenin's thing about no laws, about dictatorship being unrestricted rule, and specifically rule unrestricted by laws.

Then who is exercising this dictatorship [of the proletariat] and how do the masses know what the rules are? . . . If they don't know what the rules are, how can they be relatively at ease? How can they actually contribute to socialist society and the advance to communism? And how can you actually struggle with people in a good way and toward a good end? . . .

The old answer we would have given, 25 years ago or more, would have been: "Somebody is always setting the rules, somebody is setting the parameters, so don't get too upset. We're better than the bourgeoisie. End of discussion." But there is more to be said and excavated [from the history of the ICM] about that too. Even while it is true—both things are true: Somebody *will* be setting the rules and the parameters, and we *are* better than the bourgeoisie. But we won't remain better than the bourgeoisie if that is all we say, and all we think, about it. That is the trick right there. (*Observations*, 109–11)

Note that these formulations represent a reversal of Marx, Lenin, and Stalin on certain points, and a qualitative extension of positions held by Mao. I also think they represent a step in the right direction.

Having said this, I want to address certain particulars here, beginning with Jacques Derrida. I realize that Avakian is more interested in the general point, essentially about intellectuals who are not communists or dialectical materialists in the senses in which Avakian understands these terms. However, it is not helpful to speak of "philosophers *like* Derrida," any more than it would help to speak of "composers like Beethoven." First, we lose the singularity of the person in formulations such as these. We had better attend to this question in the wake of Stalin, and to the factors involved with Stalin, both "personal" (that's the irony) and "systemic-political." Jonathan Glover claims that neither Stalin nor Mao had any friends; it is not hard to imagine this being the case with someone who is in a certain position of leadership in a movement that is attempting to work big changes in the world, and we have to appreciate the fact that we need such leaders. Lo and behold, however: Derrida has written a great deal on the politics of friendship. Second, a formulation such as "philosophers like Derrida" glosses over his specific works and ideas, for instance, about the aforementioned politics of friendship or about the issue of sovereignty, another topic from Avakian's article. Lastly, by using "Derrida" as example Avakian gets mixed up in a whole discourse of "postmodern philosophy" (or sometimes "poststructuralism") that is not very helpful for understanding the work of any of the figures who are usually, and carelessly, lopped under this heading.

Unlike Michel Foucault, who addressed the question of the role of the intellectual in some detail and who was specifically responding to the model (or models) presented by Sartre, Derrida did not speak very directly to this issue—though this avoidance of specific definitions of intellectual work and its "role in society" can itself be understood as a response to Sartre. However, in practice, both Derrida and Foucault often appeared to do what *engaged* intellectuals do. Perhaps the more interesting question is how we understand what the intellectual is doing when she or he is doing the more specific intellectual work of framing and studying specific questions.

There are already different schools of "dialectical materialism," and these differ as to what matter is and what the "laws" or principles or even the movements of the observed phenomena are. So while it is great that Avakian is very careful to negate the "how can we use them" idea (which is inscribed in a history that runs from Marx's view of most intellectuals as essentially useless—they fall off the train when anything significant happens in society—to Lenin's very bad—indeed execrable—term, "useful idiots"), and it is, further, a very good step when Avakian speaks instead of learning from these intellectuals, there is in the end the assumption that the "real" communists have a deeper understanding of reality or at least a better way of getting to this understanding. I think Avakian does make this assumption. We have to be very careful about this. Perhaps it would help to make a provisional distinction between two different kinds of theory: philosophical Marxism, radical philosophy, and philosophy and "theory" (systematic investigation) more generally on the one side, and "revolutionary movement theory" on the other. Stalin made this assumption about dialectical materialism and his "mastery" of it, which then was mixed up with not only state power, but also power that understood itself to be "unconditionally sovereign." I won't join in the chorus that is all too ready to explain things in terms of Stalin's supposed "mediocrity" or intellectual dullness; indeed, a more fruitful line of inquiry is to take a position toward theoretical questions that is fallibilistic and yet not skeptical, but where, on the other side, this fallibilism does not undercut the radical project of changing society. Perhaps this is another version of the "trick" that Avakian refers to at the end of the essay, or perhaps his formulation ought to be considered this way.

In addition, the assumption of necessarily having the most penetrating version of dialectical materialism (or, it might be said, whatever is the most penetrating instrument of explanation—but, of course, this again raises the question of whether Marxism is a "science" for which dialectical materialism is the methodology of its description) has underwritten the tendency to limit which questions appear as such. This is a prescription for positivist reductionism, for instance, with questions of meaning and language—on which questions Derrida has a great deal to teach us, I would argue; at the very least it ought to be recognized that he put these questions on the table in a way that is resistant to positivistic reduction, which is also to say on the table for a *materialist* theory of language and meaning.

Like Avakian, Derrida spoke in the aftermath of September 11, 2001 on the issue of sovereignty, and indeed both of them are speaking on the issue of unconditionality (or what is called "unlimited sovereignty," which necessarily has as a corollary limited or conditional sovereignty for every other power other than the one that claims unconditionality). For Avakian, this occurs in the context of reconsidering Lenin's claims about unconditionality, but for both Avakian and Derrida the analysis of the idea of sovereignty occurs against the backdrop of the unprecedented claim of sovereignty and hegemony being put forward—and not just in the realm of ideas or ideology, but ultimately through the weapons of *world destruction*—by the United States in the post-9/11 period. The ideological pillars of this claim are, on the one side, a neo-conservative philosophy inspired by Leo Strauss, and a theology of the divine mission of America embraced by right-wing Christian fundamentalists, on the other. Behind or underlying them both, however, is an imperialist ruling class that is less interested in the specific ideologies for their philosophical value or coherence than in the strategic deployment of these ideologies for the purposes of reforging global hegemony. In Derrida's analysis of this interpenetration (where he examines, for example, the role of the Security Council in making the United Nations fundamentally an instrument of the "great powers"—first of all the United States, but also France) in *Rogues*, there is much to learn—so much that I want to raise the following provocative question: Not only, "what if the Derridas were communists," but also, what if at least some of the communists took the time to study deconstruction and ask how they might learn from it (and yes, apply it)?

"Embrace, Not Replace"

Significantly, *Rogues*, one of the last books that Derrida published in his lifetime, is subtitled "Two Essays on Reason." While we are questioning the notion of unconditional sovereignty in politics and statecraft, we might also question the claim of unconditional sovereignty of Marxism or dialectical materialism in science and philosophy, and especially *in* science and *therefore* philosophy. This is where Mao's formula is very important, that "Marxism embraces but does not replace" the results of inquiry in different disciplines, and it is significant that the next chapter in *Observations* is on this very formula (112–30). To speak in Kantian terms, this embracing could be understood as intending a synthesis, and even being predicated upon a possible synthesis, at least as a kind of regulative ideal. However, if things are taken too quickly or too forcefully in this direction, the embracing aspect of the formula could overpower the "does not replace" part. Avakian argues that error "in one direction or the other (or one and then the other, or some combination of them)" is a danger.

> You can forget the "embraces" part and get lost in a particular sphere and think that our basic principles have nothing to do with this, or that this has nothing to do with our strategic objectives. You can fall into tailing spontaneity, tailing the masses, pragmatism, losing sight of the relation between the particular and the universal—that is, between a particular arena of activity or struggle and our ultimate goal of achieving communism, and between learning about one particular sphere and increasing the store of knowledge of humanity as a whole. So you can forget the "embraces" aspect and forget the universal in that sense.
>
> On the other hand . . . you can lose sight of the particular, the "does not replace" aspect. That's what Mao means with "does not replace": he means you can't just have Marxist principles in a general or abstract sense. You have to apply them. You have to apply them in a living way, and you have to learn from others in the course of applying them. . . . (*Observations*, 117–18)

Significantly, when Avakian speaks of the different spheres of inquiry and activity that Marxism embraces but does not replace, he expands the number of spheres significantly beyond Mao, especially into the areas of culture, art, and the humanities. In this case, however, while we might keep in mind, at least as a regulative ideal, that all of these spheres are ultimately a part of the same world that we humans are attempting to live in, there are also qualitative differences in these spheres and we must be wary of a synthetic "embrace" that crushes the life out of these spheres—and here to say the "life" is also to say the "difference," in a normative sense.

Here I have some questions regarding Alain Badiou's rethinking of Platonism and set-theory mathematics as ontology (in *Being and Event*, *Briefings on Existence*, and *Logics of Worlds*), questions that I would pose from the perspective of a Sartrean concern with incarnation and a Derridean concern with difference, questions that I would then turn back toward the possible methodologies of embracement and the notion of "objective truth." However, this discussion must wait for another day.

The project of "embrace but not replace" might be further helped, I propose, by making a distinction such as that between philosophical Marxism and revolutionary movement theory.

One way to come at this is to recognize that Avakian cannot spend all of his time reading Derrida. It may be that the distinction I am proposing is at least somewhat parasitic on the so-called "scholar/theorist" distinction. To paraphrase what Derrida says of Marx (in *Specters of Marx*), to read Derrida is also to read a few others. As someone on the "theorist" side of the distinction, I am not able to spend all my time reading Derrida and all of the others (which more or less turns out to be most of the Western philosophical and much of the Western literary canons) either; of course, it doesn't help that Derrida tended, for some years, to put out work faster than anyone could read it. That is why I depend on the scholars and appreciate the work they do. We could stand a little more mutual appreciation in the intellectual world: I am not sure that Avakian appreciates the scholars enough (though I am not saying that he doesn't read widely). I am also quite sure that the scholars often do not appreciate the theorists very much. As a revolutionary movement theorist, Avakian continually sifts through the history of the ICM, studies the current state of society (which involves not only reading the work of more empirically oriented figures such as urban sociologist Mike Davis, critical race theorist David Roediger, and Jared Diamond, but also novels and memoirs that paint a vivid picture of life in the different strata of society, as well as reports that come up through the party, from activists who are "in the field," so to speak), studies the works of the main figures in what might be called the ICM "canon" (Marx, Engels, Lenin, Stalin, and Mao), studies work in political economy especially (and plays a leading role in the furtherance of the work of political economists in the party, such as Raymond Lotta), studies the work and activities of reactionaries who are trying to hold the existing society together and provide an ideology for it (figures such as Pat Buchanan and George Soros), and, lastly and perhaps most tangentially, engages with philosophical Marxism and political philosophy and other work in philosophy and theory more generally.

Avakian ought to be taken seriously because revolution ought to be taken seriously, and the latter ought to be taken seriously if we truly recognize what a grotesque thing the capitalist-imperialist organization of the world is, and what a lovely world humanity is capable of creating in its stead—and the necessity for humanity to live up to this potential if there is going to be any world at all in the future. I question how Avakian approaches the work of revolutionary movement theory in some instances though. In the case of the two "canons" of Marxism, I think it is a problem that he deals with issues in art and aesthetics by returning to Mao's *Lectures at the Yenan Forum on Literature and Art* again and again (even though I recognize that these lectures themselves represent a contribution to revolutionary movement theory), but does not pay any attention to the important work on aesthetics that has been done in the canon of philosophical Marxism, from Lukacs and Adorno to Jameson and Badiou. It would be wrong to take this limitation as an invitation to dismiss what is important about revolutionary movement theory and what it *is* trying to do, as opposed to what it is not necessarily trying to do and perhaps ought not try to do.

The Marxist Philosophical Canon

I aim to provoke: the ICM philosophical canon does not inspire or excite me very much "as philosophy"—I mean the works of not only Engels, Lenin, and Stalin, but also Mao and Marx, for the most part. One of the paradoxes of Marxism is that Marx by himself is not so interesting or exciting, but we can also observe that theorists who attempt to do "political things" with thinkers such as Derrida apart from a grounding in Marxism often end up going in superficial, naive, or just plain silly directions. On the other hand, if you want to take a subject such as ethics seriously, and attribute some substance to questions of right and wrong, good and evil (and I am aware of having elided the differences between these two pairs in this investigation), you are not going to get very far with just Marx.

Furthermore, if one were to take the canon of philosophical Marxism, from Lukacs's *History and Class Consciousness* to Derrida's *Specters of Marx* and beyond, and interpolate the more directly philosophically oriented works from the ICM canon, such as Engels's *Feuerbach and the End of Classical German Philosophy*, Lenin's *Materialism and Empirio-Criticism* and the *Philosophical Notebooks*, Stalin's *Dialectical and Historical Materialism* and *Marxism and Problems of Linguistics*, and Mao's *Five Essays on Philosophy*, these works of "ICM philosophy" do not look like much from a certain vantage point. From a perspective that is not "merely academic," it is hard to argue, for example, that Stalin's essay on the philosophy of language is important work in that field. From another angle, however, this work *is* important because it represents a concentration of experience and an attempt to apply that experience to changing the world.

Having made this distinction, I find Avakian inspirational because he is serious about leading a revolution and has applied himself for many years to the extraordinarily difficult task of making revolution in the "advanced-capitalist," imperialist, postmodern superpower-cum-hyperpower—perhaps an impossible task (but, as Derrida says, that does not mean that we do not have to try to do it). Certainly there are some criticisms that ought to be made, including the ones I raised in *Marxism and the Call of the Future*.

Fundamentally, however, I think the criticism comes from one of two places. One is a place where revolution is considered not impossible, but instead not desirable. This is a place where there is a good deal of illusion about the present social system and the supposed possibilities for substantial reform. These "possibilities" are instead, in my view, their own kind of impossibility—which does not mean that many proposed reforms should not be supported, especially if these proposals have real roots in mass discontent and are not simply the career strategies of establishment politicians. The other place is that of a bad or "mere" or perhaps naive utopianism, that wishes for or is somehow convinced of an easier and simpler path to a post-capitalist society, without working through the contradictions of either the party or the state. While there is a good utopianism that ought to be affirmed, what has become, in contrast to the "There Is No Alternative" thesis, the "utopia" of "another world is possible," it might be the hallmark of bad utopianism to want a movement without contradictions that works without contradictions toward a world without contradictions.

Marginal Maoism

In his memoir, *From Ike to Mao and Beyond*, Avakian writes, "Sports has been a big part of my life since I was very, very young" (and by this he means five-years old; see p. 11). Avakian often uses sports analogies, and is a keen observer of what might be called the "dialectic of sport" as well as the culture of sports. A sports analogy occurs to me in the matter of the marginality and supposed irrelevance of Avakian and the RCP, namely the sports contest where one side is losing the game for most of the contest, and yet, in the end, and after a key transition, that side wins. A chess analogy is apt as well; take the case where to all appearances one side is losing or has seemingly lost, but in the end that side wins because of two factors: an unseen weakness in the structure of the other side, and a strategy on the winning side that exploits this weakness. These phenomena cannot be taken simply as a formula for success, but they are emblematic of how revolutions actually develop. Even so, more analysis is needed of the ways in which revoutionaries are sometimes self-marginalizing and of what might be called the "new factors of marginalization" typical of our postmodern society.

Needed: Big Book?

Now, a great deal more could be said about the new synthesis, the work of Avakian and the Revolutionary Communist Party, and its relationship to the trend of philosophical Marxism and to the kinds of arguments I am putting forward in this book. I wish that the "big book" presenting a systematic working out of the new synthesis would be written, though there are some lengthy documents that develop the synthesis, such as "A Radically New Kind of State, A Radically Different and Far Greater Vision of Freedom" (henceforth "Radically New"). In *Marxism and the Call of the Future*, Avakian and I discuss the problem of ethics and the philosophy of Kant at length and in some detail. Avakian has continued to speak and write on these subjects, generally in a way that is not very affirmative of Kant. One irony of this is that, in the new synthesis, Avakian affirms as part of the new vision of socialism what he calls the "John Stuart Mill principle," "about how people should be able to hear arguments from their ardent advocates" and not only from those who are hostile to the arguments ("Radically New," 46). In framing this principle, Avakian writes:

> in fact Mill did not insist on and apply a principle of unrestricted liberty in some universal and absolute sense—he didn't think it applied to workers on strike; he didn't think it applied to people in "backward countries" who, as he saw it, were not yet ready to govern themselves, and he implemented that by being an official in the East India Company, a major instrumentality of colonial depredation and ravaging in Asia and other places. But, nonetheless, leaving those contradictions aside here, there is a point that Mill is raising. . . . ("Radically New," 46)

What I am interested in here is this willingness to bring forward Mill but not Kant. The problem, as I see it, is that Mill shares a certain affinity with one side of Marx, but this is the side of Marx (and indeed a side of Mill) that ought not to be affirmed. There is the utilitarian side of Marx and there is the ethical-political universalist side. What many critics of Mill's utilitarianism have pointed out for a long time (even in Mill's own day, and the formulation of what is called "rule utilitarianism," in contrast to "act utilitarianism" is meant as a response to these critics) is that in order to work utilitarianism needs to incorporate normative principles that look more Kantian. Case in point, Mill argues that utilitarianism can only operate in a society that already has a certain level of culture and maturity—and he excludes India and other "backward" countries from consideration of the greatest happiness for the greatest number on this basis. (The argument parallels Locke's claim, in the *Second Treatise of Government*, that people have to understand what it means to have a claim to rights, effectively they have to have a theory of rights, in order to be treated as if they have rights. On this basis Locke "implemented" his own participation in the slave trade.) The other side of this is that, for neither Mill nor Marx is there any *substance* to the moral conversation; it is instead a matter of utilities and interests. This affinity intersects with what is perhaps a larger affinity between Mill and Marx, namely that both claimed that their work could proceed on a "purely empirical basis," as Marx put it in *The German*

Ideology and elsewhere. But then there are some troubling normativities that have to be hidden or denied. Here I am proposing a Marxism in which there is substance and reality and truth to ethical matters. It seems that Avakian is somewhat sympathetic to this idea, though it is clear that he is wary of some of the philosophical implications of this "substance."

Another way to put this is that the "John Stuart Mill principle" could easily be considered a corollary of the second formulation of the categorical imperative. Then we would be talking about ways in which we might not always be able to live up to the regulative ideals of ethical-political universalism, ways in which we might have to compromise in order to achieve some greater end, but without saying that, because the principle cannot always be implemented perfectly or consistently (nor did Kant expect such in this world; that is why ethics, like revolution in Mao's perspective, sets tasks without end), "so much for the principle." This leaves us in the position of being able to look upon the "implementation" of a purely utility- or interest-driven colonialist and/or imperialist venture without being able to say that it is morally wrong in and of itself.

Before finally turning to the question of violence, then, let us ask if the elements of the new synthesis could go forward not only in the context of a renewed commitment to objective truth, but also on the basis of an independent moment that is the ethical moment, where right and wrong and good and evil are real questions and not simply ancillary to some other kind of calculation. What should we do, according to a reflection on what it is right to do? We cannot always immediately enact what we understand to be the highest good, but we should be mindful of avoiding not only mere expedience but that which, philosophically, places us on the road to expedience. This includes a "materialist" reductivism (or a reductivist materialism) that has no substantial place for the ethical demand as real or true. The difference between materialism (I mean *good* materialism) and idealism in philosophy might be understood as follows: with materialist philosophy there is always more to do and more to learn (and in this sense it resists "metaphysics"), while idealism proceeds from the self-conception that, when it is finally "done right," there will be nothing left to do. Note the parallel that can be drawn to an ethics that sets an infinite task and a finished ontology that cannot help but underwrite intellectual and social ossification.

Forging Ahead, but also Retrieving

For the new synthesis, then, there is primarily the necessity of going forward, but there is also an element that is necessarily restorative (taking up Mill on a particular point could be seen as a nod in this direction; certainly I affirm "the John Stuart Mill principle"—that particular one at any rate), that addresses shortcomings and even disasters and atrocities, and that retrieves some things that were incorrectly set aside. These would be "things"—figures, texts, ideas, practices—that are not only in the past, but that are still calling from the future as well. This combined retrieval/openness to the call of the future is necessary for a new synthesis that is visionary, and vice versa. Progress in revolutionary movement theory is primarily oriented toward theoretical work that is done in the context of (a) struggle and the attempt to give leadership to struggle, (b) context of exposure of the system, and (c) the formulation of a program for revolutionary change and the revolutionary seizure and exercise of power.

Revolutionary Violence

Let us turn to the question of violence and its possible justification in the context of both the revolutionary seizure of power and the exercise of state power. Certainly it could be argued that, if no violence of any type or form is ethically justifiable, then revolutionary violence is also not capable of receiving ethical justification. However, I want to start at the other end of the question and ask if at least *some* revolutionary violence is justifiable. There are three points I would like to set out at the beginning of this discussion. First, even if some revolutionary violence is justifiable, this should not open the door to the idea that all of it is. Second, even if some revolutionary violence is justifiable, this should not open the door to the justification of violence more generally. If this door should not be opened, however, that may tell us something about the character of the revolutionary violence that might be justified. It is also the case that there is a category of violence that is not revolutionary, what is sometimes called "violence in everyday life," some of which is not justifiable but is all the same understandable. We know why it happens, and in some cases this is because of some prior violence. If we care about diminishing violence, especially violence that cannot be justified, then we know it is not enough to just point the finger of ethical superiority at the perpetrators of this understandable violence, we have to get at the root of the violence. Third, then, the hypothesis is placed on the table that there is at least some violence in revolutionary struggle and even in the revolutionary exercise of power that, while it cannot (and should not) be justified, is of this "understandable" sort and, at least up to a point, this understandable violence does not *completely* undermine the revolutionary character of the struggle.

Clearly it is absolutely necessary to respond to the question of violence without simply "finessing" the matter. However, it is important that we understand what the question really is, what it is really about, and the context in which it is situated. I am going to work through these issues in a coldly analytical way—recognizing that in this discussion there is often more heat than light. Please keep in mind, as well, that this particular discussion of violence is meant specifically as a coda to the discussion of Maoism, and also is situated in the larger context of formulating the theory that I have called Ethical Marxism.

There is a tendency to think that a certain kind of pacifist perspective is a kind of ethical baseline, against which any other perspective on violence, for instance, a perspective that argues that some revolutionary violence is justifiable and at least understandable (in a special sense), must be measured.

Instrumentalization

We can add to this the Kantian perspective, which sees violence as a particularly harsh and concentrated form of instrumentalization. However, the place of violence in Kant's philosophy is not so clear; it does not seem as if his perspective is simply pacifist. For one thing, when the second formulation of the categorical imperative demands that persons not be treated as means but instead as ends in themselves, this imperative includes respecting the person that I am, as well. In other words, it does not appear that Kant rules out self-defense. For another thing, we might take a lesson from Kant's defense of the French Revolution, even though he had to dance around his own philosophy in order to justify his enthusiasm. Despite this, certainly it has to be admitted that Kant did not accept the idea of a right to revolution; I do accept this idea, but there are at least a couple of ways in which Kant should have accepted it, too. This is an important point in the present context (which I defined earlier as a discussion of Maoism in the midst of a discussion of the idea of Ethical Marxism), because I do take Kant's philosophy as a kind of baseline (at least in the sense that I cannot see making any major argument in philosophy in the modern period without checking in with Kant to see what he says about it), while I also reject the "pacifist baseline."

Perhaps most important of the general reasons for rejecting the "pacifist baseline" is that, providing a false perspective on the real situation as regards violence, pacifism (as a complete philosophy, not as a strategy of nonviolent resistance which is sometimes appropriate) very often has the effect of allowing (in a supposedly "innocent" way) the violence to increase.

Sidesteps of Pacifism

There are three, interrelated ways in which pacifism fundamentally sidesteps the real question of violence; the important thing is that, from the other side of the question, as it were, these are the problems of violence that revolutionary violence seeks to address, at least in principle, and yet in the real world of violence and not simply in the realm of thought. This difference between pacifism and revolutionary violence gets to the root of the issue, that violence may exist in some "primordial, metaphysical" way (as suggested by Derrida, for example, in "Violence and Metaphysics," his essay on Levinas), which, however, can also be taken as simply the metaphysical correlate to the idea that "peace" exists in this way (I am not claiming that Derrida says this), but the violence that tears bodies and minds apart has to be dealt with in a way that is itself embodied, and which does not conceptually sidestep the forms of violence that are a felt reality for human bodies and minds. Understanding the ways that pacificism sidesteps the real questions of this felt reality will also give us a sense of the ways in which some revolutionary violence is justified.

Let us consider these three ways in which pacifism sidesteps the real question. One of the achievements of "the sixties," building on the experience of the Civil Rights movement of the period from the end of the Second World War into the mid-1960s, was to place the issue of systemic violence on the table. First and foremost, this is the idea that social structures that are based on exploitation, domination, and oppression, and these in ever-expanding ways, are inherently violent because they are inherently based on the instrumentalizing of persons. One might even say that the political-economic mechanism by which capitalism functions is the express violation of the second formulation of the categorical imperative. Societies that function under this instrumentalizing imperative are necessarily rife with more obvious forms of violence, perhaps best encapsulated in the police, with their guns (and judges with their jails, and so on) that are aimed at serving and protecting, in the final analysis, this imperative. This is not only what happens "in the end," as in "when it really comes down to it," but also *as* the end, as the directing telos of the police function in a society based on exploitation. Another way to put this point about systemic violence is that reification is violence, it is a violent operation when a person (and I would say any feeling creature, any creature capable of suffering) is rendered into a mere thing.

There was a reason, in other words, why people who experienced the dynamics of the sixties started referring to "the injustice system."

Second, and relatedly, a world that is enclosed by capitalism, an imperialist world, gives us a world that is an environment of violence, and thus it becomes a false dichotomy to speak as if the "choice" is simply between violence and no violence. As long as a system based on exploitation and reification exists, and is predominant in the world, the world will be a violent environment. The terms of this dichotomy make no distinction, for instance, between the violent rebellion of the oppressed who can't take any more, on the one side, and either the violent—systemic or more direct—oppression of the people, or what Lenin called wars between (or among) the slaveholders. The consequences of not making this distinction are morally bad. By not addressing violence in a real as opposed to philosophically-abstract way, the basis for actually changing this violent world is undercut.

The real dichotomy is the one between (a) this systemic and "rife, enclosing" violence and (b) what it will take to stop the violence and transform the situation into one in which violence is less definitive of the basic terms of life. Pacifism does not do this, either in philosophy or in felt reality, and neither can it really claim to be so innocent ("don't blame them, they wouldn't hurt a fly") in all of this. The difficulty, instead, is that of going down the other path, of revolutionary violence, but without opening the door—again, either conceptually or in felt reality, in the ways that bodies are torn apart—to an even more general violence. That has been exceedingly hard.

Lenin on Pacifism and Violence

Lenin wrote the pamphlet "Socialism and War" in the summer of 1915, in the midst of the First World War and in preparation for the Zimmerwald Conference, which was a gathering of socialist parties to address perspectives and strategies regarding the war. Here and elsewhere Lenin proposed the strategy of "revolutionary defeatism," for socialists in each imperialist country to turn the aggressive imperialist war against each respective "fatherland" and bourgeois ruling class thereof, into revolutionary civil war with the aim of the socialist revolutionary seizure of power. Some participants at the conference, most notably the standard-bearer of Marxist orthodoxy in that period, Karl Kautsky, threw out internationalism altogether and instead opted for "defense" of the German fatherland. (Kautsky was the leader of the German Social-Democratic Party, which had representatives in the German parliament, and who voted for the war, so this was not merely a "conceptual" support being offered by a marginalized figure.) Other participants in the conference called for a position of "pacifism." (Some of these also proposed the slogan, clearly meant as a refutation of Lenin's revolutionary defeatism, "neither victory nor defeat.") Some of the passages from the opening pages of this pamphlet address the issues that I am pursuing here, especially the consequences of not making certain distinctions.

> The epoch of 1789–1871 [from the French Revolution to the Paris Commune] left deep traces and revolutionary memories. Before feudalism,

absolutism and alien oppression were overthrown, the development of the proletarian struggle for Socialism was out of the question. When speaking of the legitimacy of "defensive" war in relation to the wars of *such* an epoch, Socialists always had in mind precisely these objects, which amounted to revolution against medievalism and serfdom. By "defensive" war Socialists always meant a "*just*" war in this sense. . . . Only in this sense have Socialists regarded, and now regard, wars "for the defense of the fatherland," or "defensive" wars, as legitimate, progressive, and just. For example, if tomorrow, Morocco were to declare war on France, India on England, Persia or China on Russia, and so forth, those would be "just," "defensive" wars, *irrespective* of who attacked first; and every Socialist would sympathize with the victory of the oppressed, dependent, unequal states against the oppressing, slave-owning, predatory "great" powers.

But picture to yourselves a slave-owner who owned 100 slaves warring against a slave-owner who owned 200 slaves for a more "just" distribution of slaves. Clearly the application of the term "defensive" war, or war "for the defense of the fatherland," in such a case would be historically false, and in practice would be sheer deception of the common people, of philistines, or ignorant people, by the astute slaveowners. (*Lenin on War and Peace: Three Articles*, 6–7)

When Lenin uses the expression, "*irrespective* of who attacked first," he should have placed this notion of "attacked first" in scare quotes as well, as the "attack" (and its supposed chronology) occurs in the environment of violence that is the imperialist world-system. And, to the term "historically false," Lenin might have added "morally wrong" and it is significant, and too bad, that he did not.

Let us go one further step and get a better sense of how Lenin develops this notion of the war between the slave-owners for a more equitable distribution of the slaves. The following is only a few lines further on, but in a separate section of the article titled, "The present war is an imperialist war." Part of my intention in quoting the passage, and even the title of the section, is to return us to the point that imperialism is the moral question of our time, and that imperialism and the struggle against imperialism, the struggle to move society beyond the imperialist world order, sets the ethical terms of our time.

Capitalism now finds the old national states, without the formation of which it could not have overthrown feudalism, too tight for it. Capitalism has developed concentration to such a degree that whole branches of industry have been seized by syndicates, trusts, and associations of capitalist billionaires, and almost the entire globe has been divided up among the "lords of capital," either in the form of colonies, or by enmeshing other countries in thousands of threads of financial exploitation. . . . capitalism has developed the forces of production to such a degree that humankind is faced with the alternative of going over to Socialism or of suffering years and even decades of armed struggle between the "great" powers for the artificial preservation of capitalism by means of colonies, monopolies, privileges and national oppression of every kind. (7–8)

Everything that Lenin has described here has gone so much further in the intervening years such that the basic terms he sets out seem almost old hat, indeed, too much so.

To begin with, the terms of things should be the just struggle of the oppressed against the oppressors, apart from making the question of violence or nonviolence primary or central. Then the question becomes how anyone could have ever become confused on this point, and I would offer three (and, as often, intertwined) reasons for this confusion. First, imperialism has deepened its hold on the world since the time of Lenin, in every area from the economy and ideology (including ideologies of "great power" national chauvinism as well as more cynical ideologies that simply take the social set-up as "the way things are") to the creation, threat, and sometimes use of weapons of mass destruction and world destruction. Second, though there has been a period of breakout from the imperialist system, and though I have argued that there were many aspects of this breakout (in other words, socialist revolutions in Russia and China) which were good, there were also aspects that, to say the least, ought not to be carried forward into the future. Even if these revolutions and the socialist construction that proceeded from them were mostly good, it also has to be admitted that socialism has been a mixed-bag, and this *is* confusing to people who are trying to tell the good guys from the bad guys—add to this that imperialism has every interest in spreading this confusion and makes stuff up to add to the confusion. Third, the postmodern turn in society has given us a world where it becomes even more difficult for people to get their moral bearings or even to form the idea that it is important to find such bearings. This last point perhaps relates more to ethos than ethics.

If pacifism does not address the situation that Lenin describes, because in important ways it does not really consider this situation, this also tells us something about the "realistic" alternative to pacifism. If the primary situation is of a world that is rife with violence, and where the slave has a right not to be a slave, and the oppressed person has a right not to be oppressed (I mean this without invoking a particular theory of rights at this point, more in the sense that it is right that the slave struggle to throw off his or her state of being a slave), then it is also right that the slave-owner be rendered no longer a slave-owner, and the oppressor no longer an oppressor. A number of things can be said about this, but I do not want to get too far ahead. The notion that I want to underline here is that the upshot of this perspective, if it is right, leads us to understand revolutionary violence as *primarily* defensive violence, where this notion and orientation must be at the core of revolutionary struggle. And, if this much is right, then we also have a sense of how to approach the problem of "understandable" violence when it occurs in the context of revolution.

Systemic Violence

A link between systemic violence and the idea of a capitalist and imperialist world that is enclosed in violence can be seen by looking at a particular aspect of the "injustice system," namely the prison system in the United States. This is a horrible, evil system by any measure, a severe embarrassment to industrialized countries (the problem being a culture that is unable to be embarrassed about sheer barbarism), and yet also, in the logic of imperialist society, a representation and concentration of the violence that permeates the larger system, where the racist as well as the class stratifications that permeate American society are also represented in a concentrated and intensified way. To take one example of this, not only is it the case that a person sentenced to prison in the United States will very likely be continually submitted to rape and gang-rape by other prisoners, but also this occurs to such an extent that, in American society as a whole, more boys and men are raped than girls and women. But the phenomena of prison rape and other aspects of the way the prison system operates in the United States, where people are abandoned to cruel fates, represent a concentration of the social relations predominant in imperialism.

Pacifists who are confronted with terms such as these (not only this prison example, but the basic model of slave/slave-owner, oppressed/oppressor) do not often reject these terms, and indeed start to back off from a more absolute pacifism and to qualify their positions. For example, one might consider one artist and two philosophers who are pacifists (or at least proponents of nonviolent resistance) of a Christian persuasion, but who, when confronted with real situations of oppressive violence, show sympathy for real resistance. Bruce Cockburn, the excellent songwriter, singer, and (bloody brilliant) guitarist wrote a song about his experience in Nicaragua during the Contra War, saying he "wished he had a rocket launcher." Ronald Santoni, a superb colleague in the North American Sartre Society, wrote a book on Sartre and violence, calling Sartre's position "curiously ambivalent" and especially criticizing Sartre's "inflammatory" statements on violence in his preface to Fanon's *Wretched of the Earth*. Yet Santoni was also in Nicaragua during the Contra War, and in a session on his book he expressed sentiments similar to Cockburn's, despite his own purported commitment to nonviolence (meeting of the North American Sartre Society, February 2005, San Francisco). In an interview in his book of conversations with contemporary continental philosophers, Richard Kearney resorts to the old chestnut: while proclaiming his commitment to pacifism, he sets out the scenario of the violent intruder who comes into his home, threatening to hurt his wife or children (*Debates in Continental Philosophy*, 244).

Floods of Violence

It would be wrong to use these examples as a wedge to open the flood-gates of revolutionary violence or violence more generally, but let me mention a particularity of Christian pacifism. Foremost is the role played in this version of pacifism by the afterlife and other aspects of classical Christian theology that can be interpreted to mean that nothing in this world really matters. In its worst form, this is "peace" without justice, and I would argue that this peace then becomes support for injustice and the violence that that entails—and pacifists ought to have to give an account on this point. It is hard to view the way Jesus dealt with the money changers in the temple, namely with a whip, as an expression of pacifism (when the context is developed, it appears more to be an insurrectionary act). Then there is Buddhist pacifism (which the "this world doesn't really matter" Christianity resembles in important ways), where self-defense is not justified because the self is an illusion. However, the workings of compassion and the Bodhisattva idea in Buddhism may also lead to the conclusion that, although *my* self is an illusion that I ought to work to transcend, I cannot simply sit idly by and assume that *your* self is an illusion, *for you*.

This recognition leads in an important direction (not that one actually needs Buddhism for this argument, and neither am I really following Buddhism on this point). Perhaps there could be an ethical imperative that would require me to sacrifice my life rather than to forcefully resist a violent attacker. (I do not actually believe this, but simply pose this as a hypothesis. I am also wary of sacrificial logics in general—clearly such a logic was at work especially in the Stalin period, and neither was the theological element lacking.) It is another thing, altogether, if I presume to make this decision for an other, and stand by while the slave is oppressed, dominated, bodily beaten down, or killed. If it is truly the case that the slave-owner, the oppressor, can only be stopped by removing him from power, and meeting that power with counter-power, then don't we have a responsibility in that regard?

A Pacifist, But . . .

This "I am a pacifist, but . . . if someone tries to attack my child" (or some other proviso) line of thought comes up quite often; I am not raising the example merely to be critical of Kearney or Santoni or anyone else, but instead to ask about the millions and millions of other children in this world, who are condemned to starvation, disease (including some such as diarrhea that would rarely if ever kill anyone in wealthy countries), abuse, super-exploitation, extreme poverty, and dead-end life, if that, by the social and production relations of imperialism. The Contras, speaking of another atrocity of imperialism that postmodern capitalism has done a good job of shoving so far down the memory hole that it is hardly retrievable, would engage in such military strategies as laying land mines on the paths leading to elementary schools. A good deal, certainly, could be said about land mines and the creation of an environment of violence, or violence *as* the environment. Taking a pacifist attitude toward those mines and the system that created this horrible Contra army goes beyond mere complicity with violence; it becomes a part of the network of violence itself.

One version of Christian pacifism, at least, is also demonstrative of the third form of pacifist sidestepping, namely a projection of humanity onto a future without contradiction, which then underwrites the notion that the anticipation of this world requires that we adopt a strategy of mollification toward present contradictions. The Maoist view is that there is no world without contradiction, and that the road to the future will require not only the resolution of certain contradictions but even the intensification of some contradictions, regardless of whether in our heart of hearts we really want this. The *resolution* of contradictions, for instance that between socialized production and private accumulation (which Marx names as the central contradiction of our epoch) requires a movement through contradictions, not around them. To take a simple example, though one that is appropriate for what we are really talking about here, I wish for a world where there is more love than hate. In the world as it is today, however, it is not possible to really love the oppressed without at least hating the system that holds these people in oppression. Frankly, I think we have to hate the ruling class and the political representatives of this system, too, though perhaps not uniformly or always in an absolutely "personal" way— (though some of these people, such as Dick Cheney and Donald Rumsfeld, are so thoroughly hateful, that it is not at all hard to hate them); I say this as someone who does not generally find it easy to hate people, and who would prefer not to have to hate people. I recognize that hate can just eat at a person's heart, and thereby undermine the capacity for love. But what does my love for the oppressed, and even for the far greater part of humanity, and for its possibility of creating a far better society, come to, if one also, evenhandedly, loves the oppressor? Let the oppressors give up their schemes of oppression and their positions in society that are dependent upon an oppressive system, *then* I'll try to love them. Mao discusses love and hate in similar terms in *Talks at the Yenan Forum on Literature and Art*.

Likewise, we have to work for a world where society encounters *better contradictions*, of the sort that do not require revolutionary violence for their resolution, which also means that revolutionary violence must conform, at least broadly, to this goal. The way to this society, however, does not lie in sidestepping the contradiction between exploiter and exploited, oppressor and oppressed, dominator and dominated, or wishing them away. This is the case even if, in a world enveloped by imperialist social relations, class divisions are very complicated and there are especially many complicities available to one (in reality, formative of subjects) in the imperialist countries. One of the complicities that ought to be most resisted is the sort of "innocent" pacifism that helps what Lenin called the "astute slave-owners." It is also the case that what Adorno called the autonomous artwork, which attempts to give a glimpse of the world "seen from the standpoint of redemption" (as he put it in *Aesthetic Theory*), can inspire us to work toward a better world. But such work becomes "merely utopian" if it lacks the element of negativity, in other words if it is taken as a utopia in which we can loll around for relief from the ugliness of the existing world. Radical negativity is the central value for Adorno (and arguably for Sartre and Mao as well, though their perspectives on negativity are different); without it, no work of art is even momentarily autonomous. The utopia of the autonomous artwork is not that of mere escape or catharsis, it cannot be simply a bit of prettification.

To say that strategies for sidestepping the problem of violence are not adequate responses to our world of systemic violence is not yet to provide everything that ought to be required for a justification for *some* revolutionary violence. The qualifier, "some," is meant as an alternative to any opening that might be seen as going in the direction of violence without limit, even in the supposed name of revolution. The argument here runs parallel to previous arguments about sovereignty and unconditionality, and indeed there is a practical intersection between the arguments on the question of state power.

Let us take a moment, then, to gain more specificity on a number of questions relating to revolutionary violence and its justification.

Present Contradictions and a Different World

In this world of systematic, generalized violence, the contradiction between violence and the absence of violence has to be understood as the contradiction between a social system that is predicated on violence and a social system that has as its ultimate goal a society that is not so predicated.

At the least, the question of revolutionary violence can be divided into two segments, before the revolution and after the seizure of state power.

Before the revolution, as a revolutionary movement builds, it is much clearer that violence is defensive. Revolutionary leaders and organizations can only channel the rebelliousness that is there, no one goes into violent revolt against the existing system simply because a revolutionary leadership calls for it. This channeling is a good thing, from the standpoint of violence, as it serves to aim the rebellion at the proper targets. Thus the leadership and organization serve to underscore the defensive nature of violent rebellion. In 1992, in the wake of the verdict in the first "Rodney King trial" (for those who do not remember, Rodney King was not on trial, but rather several police officers who helped to beat King to within an inch of his life), there was a spontaneous outpouring of rage by African-Americans and others in Los Angeles (the epicenter of the rebellion) and elsewhere. ("Some things I learned in Berkeley" discusses my own experience in the midst of the rebellion in the Bay Area; see *Politics in the impasse*, 231–43.) This outpouring is a good example for the present discussion, because it contained all of the elements we need to address in a discussion of violence. The rebellion was justified. There were elements of the rebellion that went beyond a purely defensive response to the systemic violence that was encapsulated in the beating of Rodney King and the not guilty verdict in the trial of the police officers, but these elements were, in the category of what I am calling "understandable." Perhaps foremost among these elements were the attacks on small businesses owned by Asians in the predominantly African-American area of South Central Los Angeles. There was also the brutal beating of a white truck driver, Reginald Denny, who happened to be in the wrong intersection at the wrong time.

Let us keep in mind that the violence of this rebellion pales in scale when compared to both the ordinary systemic violence that is necessary for the operation of American imperialism and the more direct violence that erupts at regular intervals from this system; indeed, the L.A. rebellion occurred in the shadow of the Gulf War. This military action by the United States was in some ways less a war and more a high-tech massacre from the sky. Estimates vary, but some argue that between 150 and 200 thousand were killed by the United States in the Gulf War (for example, Beth Daponte, a demographer for the Commerce Department during the war, estimated the total at 158 thousand; see post-gazette.com, Feb. 16, 2003). This does not include the hundreds of thousands, perhaps up to a million, who were killed by the sanctions applied in the aftermath of the war. Leaders of the American bourgeoisie such as J. Danforth Quayle openly gloated about the "kill ratio" in the war. Casualties on the American side were so low that American soldiers in that period were actually safer in Iraq than they would have been in the United States. (In other words, the likelihood of dying from an accident or other non–war related incident was greater back in the U.S. than it was in the actual theater of war.) How many were killed by the rebellious masses in the Los Angeles rebellion (which spread to other cities as well)? Apparently none. Some people were beat up, but most of the "destruction" that came from the rebellion was in the category of "property crime," which of course the capitalist ruling class hates most of all because it affects what is most important to them. Reginald Denny himself, at the trial of the young men who had beaten him, expressed understanding for the rebellion and the frustrations of people living in the midst of systemic racism.

The Necessity of Rebellion

I am setting out the context because what is perhaps most difficult for some people to understand is that the rebellion—including the violent aspects of it—was not simply justifiable and understandable, it was also *necessary.* Yes, there were bad things that happened *in* the rebellion (though *in* the rebellion, the other side—the establishment—was fighting, too; they did not sit idly by and watch the thing unfold, and indeed the police and National Guard carried out the largest mass arrest in the history of the United States). There were even senseless things that happened, but oppressed humanity, and therefore "society" or "the world" would have been *far worse off* if this rebellion had not occurred. For the nonoccurrence of rebellion would have added weight to the seal of approval that the not guilty verdict had already placed on the idea that systemic racist violence can be enacted in the most brutal forms with impunity, in other words, unconditionally. The rebellion asserted some conditions that absolutely had to be asserted, and it would have been *tragic* if there had been no rebellion.

Perhaps this is a matter of weighing tragedy *in* the rebellion (just as there will always be tragedy in the dynamic of resistance, rebellion, revolution) in the context of the tragedy of the nonoccurrence of the rebellion and the tragedy of ongoing systemic violence. What does not figure into the discussion, except in the most abstract fantasy, is "peace" or pacifism—though it is significant that it was the police and the powers-that-be, with president George H. W. Bush in the lead, who took up slogans such as "increase the peace" and "be good in the 'hood." (as if the Bush clan knows anything about a 'hood). People supporting the rebellion instead raised the slogan, "no peace without justice." This is right, and it gets at the fact that an unjust peace is one where in fact there is not peace, there is systemic violence.

Leadership and Tragedy

The additional tragedy, then (obviously I am playing on the idea that there is no avoiding tragedy, and that it would be wrong to downplay tragedy; this includes the tragic aspects of the things that have to be done in order to overcome the imperialist system) is that revolutionary leadership was not in a position to take the rebellion further. As a matter of fact, somewhat spontaneously, the L.A. rebellion did in fact target government buildings, but the media tended to downplay this and to instead play up the attacks on Asian-owned convenience stores and acts of looting. The way to achieve a less violent society, a society that is not predicated on the violence of exploitation, a society that is not permeated with violence, is through a rebellion that turns into revolutionary struggle. However, even without this focus, it can be said that the response to the state declaration of the nonexistence of African-Americans as people who count for something in the world was not only just, it carved out some space where systemic racist violence could not operate as usual, at least for a while.

Let us consider two points by way of transition to the matter of revolutionary seizure of power and the operation of revolutionary state power.

Animals and Violence

First, let us return for a moment to the animal question. Rarely is violence against an animal justified. Much of the violence perpetrated against animals is in some sense "understandable," because there is a connection to a real human need, namely to eat and have food nourishment. However, this comprehension occurs in a frame that radically shapes perceptions. The more it becomes abundantly clear that people do not need to eat animals for nourishment, the less understandable and comprehensible this practice becomes, though the situation is very complex for the reasons explored earlier (both the way that carnivorism is interwoven with "reason" and human thought more generally, and the larger parameters in which carnivorism is a system). Already it is the case that, in some circles at least, and even in certain populations, to eat animals is not merely hard to understand, it is incomprehensible. Furthermore, to close the circle on justification and comprehension, violence against animals has much in common with (human, social) systemic violence—namely, the way animals are rendered into food in the industrial system, as opposed to more direct encounters between individual humans and individual animals (as in hunting). Carnivorist, systemic violence against animals lacks broad justification. At the same time, this violence is so vastly present in the "understandable" form that it could not even be a "candidate" for justification.

The quantitative question is not the totality of the question, but it is not inconsiderable, either. Three conclusions might be drawn. First, at the level of a certain quantity, even if not strictly or absolutely quantifiable, "understandable" violence passes over into a violence that cannot be justified; instead it passes into the violence that should be rendered incomprehensible. Second, the foregoing argument makes it clear (or more clear, at least) that, while *rebellion* is most often spurred by a specific, direct outrage, *revolution* is in general directed against a social form organized on the basis of systemic violence, and this tells us something about the role of leadership in moving from rebellion to revolution. Third, and the other side of this last coin, as it were, a proletarian revolutionary society, unlike a bourgeois society even in its revolutionary phase (as it is rising to overcome feudal social relations), cannot be *predicated upon* systemic violence, of whatever sort—I contend that there is no "proletarian" systemic violence, nor is there any systemic violence that will serve the proletariat's mission of liberating itself and all humankind. This is important because the revolutionary proletarian state will in fact have to engage in some forms of coercion, primarily in relation to the bourgeoisie and attempts to restore capitalism. Again, however, this cannot be systemic violence, and, if this violence were to go too far out of certain bounds and quantitative parameters, to the point of assuming the character of "unconditional sovereignty," this would be a strong indication that the revolutionary character of the new state has been seriously compromised, if not undermined altogether. As with many parts of the present study, the Stalin period is very much present in this discussion.

Before and After the Seizure of Power

Second, and this is a point that needs stating even though it may be obvious, there are many ways in which it is "easier" for revolutionaries to hold to (even if not in a fully conscious way) an "ethical Marxist" perspective on the way to the revolutionary seizure of power, than it is to maintain that perspective after the revolution. This ought to tell us something about the relationship between justice and power. Perhaps Sartre's comment that Stalin shows us what Marxism means as a mere or even "pure" theory of power is best illustrated by Stalin's remark, made in the midst of the Second World War, "How many divisions has the pope?" Obviously, the context in which Stalin said this was one where the question of power, and of holding on to state power, was in the forefront. (Then again, perhaps this is not so obvious anymore, and it strains comprehension to imagine the circumstances of the sieges of Leningrad and Stalingrad.) At the same time, Stalin's dismissal of the moral authority of the leader of the Roman

Catholic Church was conditioned by the fact the pope had not in fact used his moral authority to oppose fascism and Nazism. Even so, the result was to collapse justice into a mere question of power. This has had disastrous results. Significantly, this collapse is wrong in a comprehensive way: ethically, politically, epistemologically, ontologically.

After the revolutionary seizure of power, the defensive character of revolutionary violence is not entirely eclipsed, but surely the situation is changed significantly. There is at least one set of issues that bridges the before and after (the revolutionary seizure of power) periods. There are revolutionary struggles that have to be fought. This is "the good fight," but it stands in an ambiguous relationship to "the good." The oppressed, in fighting the oppressor, faces a problem that is not a problem for the oppressor, namely the contradictory character of revolutionary violence. The contradiction is in fighting the fight that has to be fought, as a good fight, without embracing violence as good. On another level, the contradiction is that revolutionary violence is sometimes necessary and sometimes good, but not always both. On yet another level, the contradiction is that revolutionary violence is sometimes good (if it is indeed both revolutionary and necessary), but it can be an opening toward the embracing of violent solutions to problems in general.

Mao made a significant step toward recognizing this contradiction in "On the Correct Handling of Contradictions among the People," not only in the way that he set out the contradiction, but also in the way he emphasized that there is a contradiction that has to be worked through—something that was not part of Stalin's interpretation of Marxism, and possibly not even Lenin's or Marx's. Still, this argument needs to be taken further. This is one of the points on which we have to surpass Mao.

On the most *fundamental* level, the contradiction is that, after the revolutionary seizure of power, there would have to be people who exercise power in a coercive and directly violent form, in particular an army and even some form of police. To take the former example, that of the need for revolutionary armed forces for the defense of the new revolutionary polity, the contradiction manifests itself in the fact that it would be very difficult to have soldiers who are not committed to their work. It is fortunate that the armies of imperialist countries, and first of all the United States, have to go to extraordinary lengths to generate the mentality that allows soldiers to shoot at actual human beings who can be seen up close. This is one reason for the heavy reliance on air power in the various interventions that have occurred since the Vietnam War. No army that has a liberatory aim can employ the racist, misogynist, and animalizing strategies that are common with imperialist armies. While it is true that a revolutionary proletarian force will fight for good things, by definition, it is also true that, once the gun is taken out, it is hard to put it away; even more to the point, revolutionary soldiers cannot be taught or implored to hate their guns.

Perhaps things are different in the case of police and weapons. Still, it is no accident that "police" and "polis" share a common root. If the revolutionary party has to be a place for grappling with contradictions and carrying forward the revolutionary struggle, we might say that the party has to foreshadow not only the overturning of the imperialist state and the creation of a proletarian state, but also the polis, and, what has not yet existed and perhaps what strains the imagination (and what *should* strain the imagination), the "polis without police." I would call this latter *communism*, the global community of mutual flourishing.

Perhaps it is not possible to organize an army and some form of police on the basis of a "tragic necessity"—it is unclear what this would even mean. Indeed, the idea is suspect in a number of ways, but perhaps the way that should be placed in the foreground here has to do with the fact that military and police forces are social *institutions*. In a revolutionary society, these forces would be institutionalized instruments of violence, somehow not forgetting that these forces are made up of *people*, and the problem would be to have an institutional instrument that is not at the same time a new form of systemic violence. There are many dimensions to this question, and it could be worked out in a number of domains. Let us consider the connection between Hannah Arendt's focus on institutions and her critique of Sartre's justification of violence in his preface to Franz Fanon's *The Wretched of the Earth*.

Loving One's Enemies

I remarked somewhat flippantly that I would try to love the oppressors after they had stopped being oppressors. It will always be an insult to the people to try to love reactionaries on the order of Dick Cheney and the like. The point is more that the new society cannot be based upon mere vengeance, nor can it emerge from such. Yes, the new society has to be *against* the *ancien régime*, but even more it has to be *for* the future and future possibilities. Thus far, this orientation has involved some very difficult contradictions, even disastrous and fatal contradictions in the case of the Stalin period—though it can also be said that Stalin was *against* so many things—though sometimes by necessity—that there was not much left for him to be *for*. It could be said that the dialectic of negativity is essential, but it is also in danger of becoming purely reactive without the notion of the underdetermined, redeemed future. The latter can become either a "mere utopianism" that is unrelated to the real problems facing humankind and actual solutions or, at worst, a sacrificial logic in which concrete, singular human beings in the present come not to matter. The dialectic of negation and the (shall we say) necessarily open dialectic of redemption have to work together; the bridging principle is, in my view, the ethical impulse.

Unfortunately, Sartre's justification of anticolonialist violence also has a sacrificial logic to it, and it has the additional "pagan" element (which was also taken up into the mainstream of Christianity) of a masculinist notion of self-formation and nation-formation. This is the case even if much of what Sartre says about violence is not only right, but also the sort of view that needs to be put forth in current debates. Here then is the part that still needs reiterating:

> Laying claim to and denying the human condition at the same time: the contradiction is explosive. For that matter, it does explode, you know as well as I do; and we are living at the moment when the match is put to the fuse. . . . It is the moment of the boomerang; it is the third phase of violence, it comes back on us, it strikes us, and we do not realize any more than we did the other times that it is we who have launched it. The "liberals" are stupefied; they admit that we were not polite enough to the natives. . . . The Left at home is embarrassed; they know the true situation of the natives, the merciless oppression they are submitted to; they do not condemn their revolt, knowing full well that we have done everything to provoke it. But, all the same, they think to themselves, there *are* limits; these guerillas should be bent on showing that they are chivalrous; that would be the best way of showing they are human beings. Sometimes the Left scolds them . . . "You're going too far; we won't support you any more." The natives don't give a damn about their support; for all the good it does them they might as well stuff it up their backsides. (22–23)

> Try to understand this at any rate: if violence began this very evening and if exploitation and oppression had never existed on the earth, perhaps the slogans of non-violence might end the quarrel. But if the whole regime, even your non-violent ideas, are conditioned by a thousand-year-old oppression, your passivity serves only to place you in the ranks of the oppressors. (25)

Unfortunately, it is much harder to adapt these arguments to struggle within the imperialist countries; indeed, it is very hard to form a notion of "the people" in such countries. Revolution in "advanced" imperialist countries (as opposed to the Russia of Lenin's time, the "weakest link" in the imperialist chain) remains an uncharted course. Of course Sartre's arguments apply more clearly to a world, such as ours and despite arguments found in the influential *Empire* (Antonio Negri and Michael Hardt), where national liberation of the oppressed countries remains a task of the proletariat. The demand that invaders and occupiers "get out of our country" ("Yankee go home," and so on) is not available to those of us who live in the imperialist countries, despite the appeal of a slogan such as "U.S. out of North America," which is at least clever and funny.

Fanon, Sartre, Arendt

Arendt, in responding directly to what Sartre wrote in his preface to Fanon, seems once again to subordinate the problem of colonialism to the question of violence, if the former problem can be understood to exist at all in her work. Even so, some of what she says about Sartre's "glorification of violence, which "goes . . . farther than Fanon himself" is aimed at a very important point, namely the deep associations of a sovereign subjectivity and a sovereign violence, both without ethical limit.

In *On Violence*, Arendt insists that Sartre makes statements in the preface that "Marx never could have written." In particular, Arendt is concerned with two formulations of Sartre's, both of which have to do with subject formation. Arendt argues that "Sartre is unaware of his basic disagreement with Marx on the question of violence, especially when he states that 'irrepressible violence . . . is man recreating himself,' that it is through 'mad fury' that 'the wretched of the earth' can 'become men'" (12). Similarly, Arendt argues that Sartre's claim that "To shoot down a European is to kill two birds with one stone . . . there remains a dead man and a free man" is "a sentence Marx never could have written" (13). It is interesting how much Arendt relies on Marx in her critique of Sartre; indeed, she sets Marx against any attempt to talk about the Third World as a subject for liberation or a basis for liberatory politics—she says that "The Third World is not a reality but an ideology." This is tantamount to saying that colonialism and imperialism are not realities (even if there are subtleties of Arendt's argument having to do with social classes and the idea of a supposed "unity" of "natives of all underdeveloped countries," that supplants the idea of the international proletariat, that we cannot pursue here; see 21), and unfortunately there is a basis in "classical Marxism" for making this point. What might be said of Marx is that he does not take the full measure of what it means to have a world where colonialism has been fully assimilated to capitalism, and where the dominant mode of production operates on a global scale. What is more important is that Marx does not find the wherewithal to make a moral condemnation of colonialism. Apart from using Marx to criticize Sartre, Arendt mainly castigates Marx as a purveyor of illusions and delusions.

However, to give Arendt her due, even as a Sartrean I have to wonder at the way that Sartre sometimes does almost seem to make anticolonial violence a kind of royal road to the identity formation of the colonized subject. Furthermore, there is in Sartre a valorization of the cathartic element in violence, and specifically in killing the enemy, that seems quite masculinist to me. Whether Arendt has in her framework the analytical tools to critique this masculinism per se is another question, for it seems that the primary form of her critique of violence is that it cannot rise to the level of "the political." Although I do not accept the distinction between "the social" and "the political" as Arendt sets it out (where questions of production and economics also do not rise to the level of the political), there is a lesson to be learned here that would apply after a revolution especially. Namely, if the new state is formed *primarily* as a representation of this cathartic violence, then that will lead very quickly to the undermining of the revolution—for such violence will have achieved sovereignty without condition. If this was not understood very well in previous revolutions, and therefore too much violence became "all too understandable," this can no longer and never again be the case. And yet this is not an easy or abstract problem, for the fact is that imperialism accepts no limit on the violence that it is willing to employ, up to and including the destruction of the world itself.

A more extended analysis of Sartre and Arendt on the question of violence would also engage with Arendt's crucial category of "natality" and contrast her analysis of what it means for the new to emerge with Sartre's "mad fury" by which "men recreate themselves." (On this question, see Peg Birmingham, *Hannah Arendt and Human Rights*, especially ch. 1.)

Contribution of Norman Geras

Without invoking the actual term or referring to Sartre, in his *Discourses of Extremity* Norman Geras brings the "mad fury" question into sharp focus. Significantly, he uses as a test case the struggle against the Apartheid regime in South Africa, "chosen to exemplify these issues precisely because of the overwhelming justice of the revolutionary cause" (44). Geras discusses the use of what was called the "necklace," where a burning tire was placed around the torso of a supposed collaborator, and other cases where violence against supposed enemies of the struggle was especially sadistic and torturous. After presenting an especially graphic example (44), Geras remarks that he "anticipates two types of counsel: one, of historical realism; the other, to speak not of what does not concern you." These two responses do not strictly replicate what Sartre says in the preface, but they are closely related and perhaps capture well enough what he was after. What I appreciate about Geras's response to these "two types of counsel" is that they retain the sense of justification while not accepting the glorification of violence. Geras writes,

> In any historically, or sociologically—or just "humanly"—informed perspective, there must be an acknowledgement of some limits to the proper reach of moral discourse itself. To let an extreme case illustrate this: if a group of slaves or of prisoners in a concentration camp should, having the opportunity, suddenly get the better of a vicious overseer or guard and brutally slaughter him, it would not be apt to say they had gone too far or to reflect critically on the notion of "cruel or unusual" punishments. *In extremis*, moral judgement fails. More generally, the violence of oppressors tends to breed violence among those they oppress. Their brutalities are brutalizing. A political or social order that must be overthrown by revolution will have generated, not only amongst its defenders but also with some of its victims, impulses of moral criminality and murderousness. An altogether morally "clean" revolutionary struggle is probably rare, therefore, if it is conceivable. (44–45)

To repeat, I think this captures everything Sartre needed to say, with perhaps one exception, namely the critique of what might be called the pacifism of the colonizer. Is it this latter element that opens the door to the element of glorification? I am thinking of the angry righteousness that arises when one tells the invader or occupier to "get the hell out of *my* country" (or *my* house), and "take your advice about how I should struggle against your domination and shove it up your backside."

Nevertheless, Geras proposes ethical principles regarding "legitimate modes of attack" (43). This last term, "attack," is important for two reasons. First, while mad fury and even the roots of revolution in rebellion begin in a defensive mode, for a revolution to succeed there must be a decisive moment when the offensive is taken. Second, while the revolutionary state retains something of the "self-defensive" character to it (especially as it is born into an overwhelmingly hostile world, a world still dominated by imperialist social relations), any new state that has any hope of survival must be able to act as well as react. What makes the principles proposed by Geras specifically "ethical" is that they propose a "clearer reason for ruling out . . . cruel methods of killing, the deliberate infliction and aggravation of pain, as in torture, than if we say these contradict the ends of liberation." What is important about this route is that going the other direction, of only talking about what will undermine the struggle, cuts us off from being able to say that some things are just wrong. (Even while not invoking or discussing Kant, Geras's arguments are an important response to the utilitarian perspective of Steven Lukes's *Marxism and Morality* in particular; see Geras, 31–34.) Then, of course, if we cannot say this, there is nothing that cannot under some context be justified—and this undermines the struggle. Finally, here is Geras's outline of these principles and a little of the discussion of them; the reader will note that these principles are derived, first of all, from the tradition of "just war" theory:

Just as only the combatants of the other side may be attacked, because they are the ones making war on you, so too they may be "stopped", killed, because that puts an end to the threat they have been to you or their contribution to it. Extreme and purposeful cruelty, beyond what is necessarily involved in any act of killing or wounding, is wrong because it is more than their activities can justify—as it were defensively—on your own part. Unless, that is, it is allowed that the ethics of socialism may embody, as a component, some fairly terrible theory of retributive punishment. I assume without argument here that they may not.

A slow, painful death by burning [such as happens with the "necklace"], consequently, lies beyond the limits of what is morally defensible in the light of an ethic of just revolutionary struggle. Likewise, killing an old woman by forcing her to drink the bottle of detergent or cooking oil she has bought in defiance of a shop boycott. . . . *Jus ad bellum* is in itself no guarantee of *just in bello*. The justice of the cause does not make good, cannot transmute, moral atrocities committed in its name. (43–44)

One would have to be skeptical of such principles if they were enunciated by the colonizer, or by someone who has been shaped by the life possibilities and entitlements of a colonialist, imperialist society. We do not need any "two wrongs don't make a right" claptrap from the perpetrators or beneficiaries of the first wrong, and it is very important that Sartre includes himself in at least the category of the beneficiaries and possibly even the perpetrators (after all, the famous formulation is, "we are all murderers"). And yet the proper rejection of such claptrap will have instead achieved the opposite of this rejection if it results in the dismissal of the ethical altogether.

To return to the nonpacifist comrade Jesus for a moment, it might be recalled that he is reported to have said that, if anyone would harm a child, a millstone should be tied around that person's neck and that person should be thrown into the sea. An entire social theory could be unfolded from that idea alone, on the provision that we emphasize what quickly goes past many of our students and also Richard Rorty's postmodern bourgeois liberalism, namely that there is a social system. It is the present social system that needs casting out. Unfortunately, this means fighting the people who defend the system, and many of these are people "just like you and me" in many respects. It should be easy, one might think, to say, "people, we need a new social system," especially since it is likely that most people would agree (they know very well that something is rotten in the State of Denmark), but this turns out to be very hard. Perhaps it is the case that revolutionary leadership—the party—has to say this during the times when it is hard, and to stand fast upon this position even while not becoming simply dogmatic or inflexible, in order to play its role in bringing the new system into being once this becomes "easy," in the sense that the need for the new society becomes abundantly clear and abundantly *pressing*, because the *ancien régime* is falling apart of its own accord and has reached a tipping point. Thus the party has to be an "ethical beacon," and this *central activity* of the party must not be eclipsed in the formation of the new state, indeed it must come to the fore. This is all the more the case *precisely because* there has never been the least indication that the imperialist system will "go quietly."

Can there be a revolution without an unleashing of the "mad fury"? Quite possibly not. We can study further the so-called "peaceful transitions," perhaps most of all the Velvet Revolution in former Czechoslovakia, to see where the previously existing forms of systemic violence simply acquired a new "shell" and administrative class (for all that the Soviet-backed regimes deserved to fall). At the same time, the factors that lead to a mad fury in the first place do not come first of all from revolutionary leadership, nor does, primarily, the moment when this mad fury boils over into violence of the sort described by Geras. To accept "realistically," however, that it is not likely to be a revolution without "a certain amount" of the sort of violence that attempts to assert its unconditional sovereignty, is very different from accepting such violence as justified, legitimate, or normative. Indeed, it is precisely because the imperialist classes of this world do take their systemic violence as normative, and, in our postmodern world, increasingly set aside any sense of legitimacy or the ethical imagination, that revolutionary leadership and the revolution itself have to plot the opposite course, that of being an ethical beacon.

The Last Straw

In past revolutionary experience, the contradictions of society have tended to manifest themselves indirectly, or at least such that the last straw that brings people into the streets, that is exemplary of a general crisis where people cannot live in the old way anymore and the existing system is constrained from providing any new answers, may appear to be something relatively small. The 1905 revolution in Russia (which failed, ultimately, but from which Lenin and others took many lessons) was called forth by a million oppressions, but its immediate spark was a moment in a strike by the people who set type in printing presses. Previously, they had been paid for setting letters, but not punctuation marks, and now they wanted to be paid for this. Government repression of the strike led to many other workers coming into the streets, and a general uprising spiraled from there. A revolution for the apostrophe! The fire next time may come from some equally "far-fetched" source—quite possibly from the effects of capitalism's war on our very planet, which is manifesting itself in rising rates of skin cancer, "dead zones" in oceans and seas, soil erosion, a preponderance of excrement and junk, the severity of the obesity/starvation contradiction, the pandemic of HIV/AIDS, the (related) writing-off of much of sub-Saharan Africa from the supposed advance of "global prosperity," and wars of aggression to control energy resources—framed as a "clash of civilizations."

Indeed, this energy question is just one major point on which the system of imperialist markets cannot resolve its own difficulties except through force and oppression. Beyond this issue (which, however, along with related ecological questions, could be the tipping point of the imperialist system), undoubtedly the reader knows the list (which is far longer than the one just given) of horrors as well as I do. In the final analysis, the main assumption lying behind my conversations with Avakian, apart from interpretations of past experience, is that the horrors are systemic and therefore must be dealt with on that level. People, it's bad—we need a new society.

A Theory of Justice

How much does Ethical Marxism depend on Maoism, and vice versa? Certainly there are crucial points on the theoretical plane where the two perspectives part company or at least cannot be brought into full agreement, and yet I resist the impulse to drive a wedge. It is the most ethical thing to support the revolution, and therefore to support the revolutionaries (and join them, of course). Ethical Marxism is a philosophical theory of justice that attempts to show us clearly that we need to overturn the existing society and create new forms of society that are transitional to the global community of mutual flourishing. This theory has its utopian side, but it is not exactly utopian, because it aims to incorporate scientific and political economic investigation to help us understand where the openings are. The theory aims to subordinate strategic thinking to the ethical perspective, but not to eliminate strategic thinking, because to do so would render the ethical dimension into a mere formalism and therefore not capable of helping us do the overwhelmingly ethical things that need to be done.

As regards my distinction between "philosophical Marxism" and "revolutionary movement theory," which is also meant to be helpful in terms of communication across the very division that it sets up, my own perspective could certainly be understood as existing in limbo. In attempting to respond on many fronts and speak in different discourses, perhaps no one will be left very pleased. On the whole, revolutionary movement theory has done a better job—not that it has done a good job—of learning from philosophy and theory more broadly than the other way around—but perhaps that is as it should be, since this theory has the aim of the overthrow of the existing society and the achievement of revolutionary state power. A real, radical contribution to the ethical would go to the root of the unethical, instrumentalized, reified, commodified relations among people, and thus would join in with this aim.

Conclusion

Ongoingness: The Ethics of Liberation and the Liberation of the Ethical

Codes, conspiracies, prophecies, encryptions: in all these ways, a civilization in which everyday life seems increasingly directionless compensates for a lack of sense with an excess of it. Frenetic overinterpretation makes up for a general hemorrhage of meaning. The more crassly materialist modern life becomes, the more it gives rise to pseudo-spiritual clap-trap. As social life grows increasingly two-dimensional, it grabs for some spurious sort of depth. The more ruthlessly rationalized the society, the more desperately irrational its members. Capitalism is at once far too rational, trusting in nothing that it cannot weigh and measure, and far too little as well, accumulating wealth as an end in itself. It is shot through with myth and pinned together by collective fictions. No rational animal would spend ten minutes with a junk-bond trader.

—TERRY EAGLETON, "The Enlightenment is Dead!
 Long live the Enlightenment!"

Capitalism robs life of any larger significance. What Marx calls the "Moses and the prophets" of capitalism—"accumulate, accumulate, accumulate"—is not foreign to capitalism's understanding of itself. And yet Marx praised the clarity that capitalism, when combined with secularism, provides: for Marx, the melting of everything solid into air is on the whole a positive thing. It is a painful thing for humanity as well, to be sure, and yet it is one of the necessary birth pangs of a new society.

Meaning and Mattering

We humans would like to think that our lives matter. Certainly it could be argued that such a disposition is definitive of what it means to be human, even if the recognition of this disposition, or perhaps it ought to be called this *yearning*, is largely absent from Marx's view. Marx certainly dealt with

389

matters of life and death, but he did not seem much attracted to mortality as a philosophical or theoretical issue. This avoidance might remain one step short of outright positivism, in that Marx did not explicitly declare mortality to be a "pseudo-problem in philosophy" (as had Carnap and Neurath in their manifestos of logical empiricism), nor did he have to confront the possibility that humanity could come to an abrupt end. However, it is not a far stretch to imagine Marx as sympathetic to the "pseudo-problem" charge, at least on this question. Here the negation of ethics in twentieth-century philosophy (in parts of it, that is) is again relevant. Significantly, Otto Neurath proposed a de-Hegelized Marx, in his *Wissenschaftliche Weltauffassung, Sozialismus und Logischer Empirismus.* Even while relegating ethics to the realm of nonphilosophy (which, from their perspective, meant the realm of that which is qualitatively underdetermined by scientific investigation), Carnap, Neurath, and other members of the Vienna Circle affirmed the synthetic approach of Kant (filling this approach out with quantification in logic and the problems of meaning and language—or perhaps more specifically with the problem of reference). Furthermore, the Vienna positivists affirmed the strategies of disenchantment of both Marx and Nietzsche (see the conclusion of Carnap's manifesto, "The Elimination of Metaphysics through Logical Analysis of Language"). What then remains is an empirical sociology of the workings of power, where any ethics that appeals to principles is just so much pseudo-philosophical fluff.

This "happy positivism" that was affirmed by Foucault, and that owes an intellectual debt to Althusser's analysis of ideology, finds its theoretical precursors not only in Marx, but also in Hobbes, Spinoza, and Nietzsche. Certainly this is a *clarifying* mode of disenchantment. For instance, it is an important clarification to show that the activities of gangs such as the Crips, Bloods, and Latin Kings represent economic rationality in the capitalist context no less than the activities of "legitimate" corporations. Furthermore, this mode of disenchantment (in shorthand, the demonstration that talk of principles operates within the circuits and machinations of power) shows exactly what the formulation of an Ethical Marxism is up against—namely, that if the workings of power (whether through economic relations or sexuality and the situating of bodies—Foucault's "biopower"—or the modes through which people are named and defined, as in Rorty's analysis) is all there is that is *real*, then ethics (ethical discourse, the subjects of ethics, and so on) is *unreal*. Quite arguably, that is what Marx thought. It is also arguable that even many of the attempts to "return to ethics," in the wake of disenchantment and the acids of modernity do not quite manage to make ethics a real subject with at least a degree of philosophical autonomy. By this last expression ("at least a degree of philosophical autonomy"), I mean a discourse that has to be explored in its own right, at least to some extent. There has to be an "ethical moment" in political discourse and struggle, or else it ought to be admitted forthrightly that there is no room for ethics in these arenas. (The disenchantments of Althusser and Foucault, among others—perhaps best described as the "New Hobbesians" and the "New Spinozans"—can at least be credited with this forthrightness; but I am not doing any of their arguments justice here.) Certainly the workings of power and other "real things" have to be taken into account, and my argument in this book has been that a Kantian perspective that does not take these things into account is indeed an empty formalism.

Modern Disenchantments

However, the modes of disenchantment did not arise to simply clarify the situation as regards the philosophical or "scientific" status of ethics. That such modes did arise, generally in step with the advance of the physical sciences (and mathematics and logic), was itself a displacement of not only ethical discourse, but of much else besides, especially all that goes under the very broad heading of "religion." The connection between ethics and religion has long been noted, not only in the ancient traditions, but also in light of the acids of modernity, as in Dostoevsky's famous line, "In the absence of God, everything is permitted." It can also be argued that, without an "ethical grounding" (or without a grounding for the metaphysics of morals), "politics" can only mean a set of tactical considerations concerning the machinations and mechanisms of power, and not a "thinking of the polis," particularly a thinking of the just polis, as in the tradition that runs from Plato and Aristotle, through such figures as Augustine, Aquinas, Locke, Jefferson, Rousseau, and Kant, and more recently Sartre, Habermas, Rawls, and Derrida (and arguably Arendt, though with important provisions regarding her anti-utopianism). This is a thinking of the "best possible," even of the impossible, in the sense of a *summum bonum* (highest good) that ought to be affirmed as a regulative ideal. One question I have attempted to raise in this book is the possibility of stitching or restitching Marx and Marxism into (or back into) this line of thinking. In some sense this is what Mao attempted to do, for which he was labeled "utopian" and "moralistic" (both in the context of a supposed "Stalinism" of socialism in conditions of material deprivation). Hobbesian, anti-utopian political arguments, on both the political right and the Arendtian and ostensibly Marxist left, have made much of the supposedly endless disaster that was Maoist China, in the context of which the quite palpable and enormous accomplishments of socialism there count for nothing. (Indeed, one would also have to think that Mao and the communists came along and wrecked what had been a wonderful society.) Thus we are left with another disenchantment, one that imperialist political formations have done everything to drive home. This has been called, in the years of triumphalism following the collapse of the (nonsocialist) Soviet Union, the "TINA" thesis—"there is no alternative." It is worth contemplating that this is what anti-utopianism and anti-"moralism" has come to.

If disenchantment and clarity go together, and if clarity is a good thing, and if these lead at best to a Marxism that is set against the idea of an Ethical Marxism, does this mean that an Ethical Marxism can be understood in the context of some form of "reenchantment" of the world? Perhaps this reenchantment could achieve its own form of clarity (I have aimed for clarity in this exposition, for example, especially in the discussion of what the United States did to the people of Vietnam, where the moral issue could not be clearer), but this would most likely not be a clarity of "cold," dispassionate reason. It was the possibility of such a form of "scientific" reason, and the status of truth under such a perspective, that both Marx and positivistic philosophers formulated their theoretical agendas. In this perspective, at least as understood by Marx, it is only a happy by-product that socialism and ultimately communism would be *good* for humanity (and expressions of the good that humans are capable of); instead, these social forms are *inevitable*—"communism is not an idea, it is the real movement of history"—these forms are simply what will occur in the objective unfolding of the material dialectic of history. Part of my argument here has been that, in the wake of inevitability (of its demise), but instead in the light of possibility (a Marxist "science"—systematic perspective—of the contradictions, fissures, and openings of the present society, using the tools of analysis developed by Marx and by others in a Marxist vein, from Lenin and Mao to Adorno and Sartre and beyond), the Kantian thesis is right: a significant part of humanity (a critical mass) has to *intend* to defeat the existing, evil form of society and it has to *intend* to create a better form of society, in order for a better form of society to come about. A society that came about from simply riding the waves of supposed inevitability would not be a better society. Indeed here we might apply once again Lenin's argument about the "spontaneous consciousness" of even the working class and the oppressed masses more generally; this consciousness will tend to remain within the ideological and political parameters set by the existing society (though sometimes with a "militant" or "radical" form, as for example with much that goes under the heading of "anarchism").

But this is not yet to answer the question. If we recognize some positive function for disenchantment, clarity, and what needs to be named forthrightly as secularism, and of course for the achievements of the physical sciences, all of which it would be exceedingly foolish to deny (such that the critique of scientism need not and should not become antiscientific, and the proposal of a "postsecular" perspective should avoid the silly attempt to simply restate the presecular), does an Ethical Marxism all the same require that the world be "enchanted"? To state the question negatively: If the world truly is disenchanted, and only subject to understanding by "cool reason" and "scientific objectivity," which will yield "cold truths" (which are then the *only* "liberating truths"), then would it not be the case that such a world really would have no use for a Marxism such as that proposed here, and indeed would find such a Marxism misleading as a matter of truth and reality and a dangerous and bad diversion as a matter of practice?

Facts and Values

The approaches of disenchantment and positivism (and in general the acids of modernity) are to deny the significance of certain questions if, from the perspective of science and logic, there are no answers to the questions. It was indeed a clarifying move on the part of the Vienna Circle to then propose that such "questions without answers" are not really questions in the first place; they are pseudo-questions, examples of what Wittgenstein called "language on holiday." The further proposal, stated most clearly in the manifestos of Rudolf Carnap and Moritz Schlick ("The elimination of metaphysics . . ." and "The turning point in philosophy," respectively— and it might be noted that, for his work in clarification and disenchantment Schlick was assassinated by a fascist student), is that it is only appropriate to assign truth values to statements of mathematics and logic, on the one side, and empirical inquiries that are subject to public confirmation, on the other. (In the latter case, such confirmation may require expert knowledge, as in the case of many inquiries of advanced science, but the point is that truth cannot be a matter of "irreproducible results.") Statements and positions that fall outside of such forms of inquiry, which for the positivists would include all statements of value (in ethics, politics, or aesthetics), cannot be assigned truth values (which is to say that they are neither true nor false, they are not matters of "truth" to begin with). It may seem easy to dismiss such a claim out of hand, but surely one should take at least a moment to consider the positivist argument's contribution to philosophical (and therefore perhaps even to ethical and political) clarity. If it is *true* that the earth does indeed revolve around the sun, as Copernicus established through empirical observation and mathematical calculation (observations and calculations that can be and have been confirmed), then it is *not true* that the sun and the rest of the cosmos revolves around the earth, as supposedly understood from the revealed word of God. Furthermore, if it is one truth that the earth revolves around the sun, then the question arises as to whether it is "another truth" that "Shakespeare is a great writer." Surely it seems absurd to deny that Shakespeare is a great writer (though, if you don't like the example, supply your own), but can this denial of the denial legitimately take the form of a logical double-negative ("it is not the case that Shakespeare is not a great writer")? Let us take it as given that Shakespeare is a great writer; is this a truth that can be set beside the truth about the earth revolving around the sun? The two statements, the one about Shakespeare and the other about the earth and sun, seem to be of quite different orders, different kinds. The "positivist clarification" is to argue that it would be best not to confuse the issue by applying truth values to both kinds. Thus it can be said that Shakespeare's writing is beautiful, arguably, but it is not possible to establish the truth of such an assertion in the way that we can establish that the earth revolves around the sun.

This conclusion sounds perfectly reasonable and quite fitting for our modern world where we can investigate empirical issues in a scientific way, and we can apply standards of logical reasoning to find which of our beliefs harbor contradictions (and which ones are, therefore, strictly speaking, "unbelievable"). However, there are important consequences of this clarification, and these consequences have been worked out in the tradition of which the Vienna Circle was a part, crucially by figures such as Quine, Davidson, Putnam, and Rorty (among many others). Furthermore, the consequences of a scientistic point of view have been very significantly addressed by Husserl, Heidegger, Gadamer, and many others, and neither should the work of feminist philosophy of science and Marxist philosophy of technology be neglected. In other words, I am not saying anything very original here—my contribution lies in my attempt to develop this issue as regards the idea of a Marxism that has the ethical moment at its core. The positivist clarification (which, again, I am arguing is fundamentally accepted by Marx) cannot and should not be so easily dismissed, either, in our present context of a postmodern capitalism that is seemingly moving into fascism (in the United States, at least). More on this context in a moment. However, let us state quite clearly what is perhaps the main upshot of the positivist clarification as regards the matter of ethics.

Values and Truth

To say that truth values apply to some kinds of statements and not to others is to valorize the former. To say it can be said of the statement "The earth revolves around the sun" that it is "true," and that it cannot be said of the statement "Shakespeare is a great writer" that it is "true" (or even, in a more waffling mode, "true exactly"—"well, speaking more precisely, that is not exactly true"; neither can the statement be said to be "false," though this aspect of the issue has a way of falling along the wayside), is to confer a kind of value on the former statement. It is to assert or at least aver that the former statement has to do with reality, while the latter statement does not. And, again, this is not an unreasonable proposal, for it is not very clear to what "reality" an appeal can be made in adjudicating the truth value of Shakespeare's status as a writer, or exactly what methodology should be applied in approaching the reality (would this simply be the reality of the words on the page, which is already an extraordinarily difficult reality to define, or would this investigation involve consideration of an author's intentions and psychological make-up, or the historical and political context?). Now, there are such questions in science, too—there is a sense in which the earth is just as much the center of everything as is, indeed, anywhere else where some conscious being is contemplating its place in the grand scheme of things. Furthermore, it has been well established by now that there is creativity in science and that scientists bring value-laden perspectives to their work. This is not the end of the positivist clarification, however; not only could textual analysis of the creation story found in the book of Genesis (actually, there are two stories, in the first two chapters of Genesis) never reveal the mechanisms of biological evolution (especially the mechanisms working at the microscopic level that reveal how visionary Charles Darwin truly was), the representation of this story as a *scientific explanation* (or as supportable by scientific explanation) stands not only against biological evolution in the sense that Darwin and his successors understood it, but also against every other branch of science as well (first of all geology), against scientific explanation, against science itself, and, here's the kicker, *therefore against truth*. No dogmatic fetishism of science, and no scientism, is necessary for making these claims, including the final claim about truth itself. It is not even necessary to hold that the truths of science (and mathematics and logic) are the only truths in order for it to be argued that a denial of these truths results in the denial of truth itself. The earth is not flat; it is the case that the earth revolves around the sun and not the other way around; and if these things are not true, then nothing is. Biological evolution is a more complex case, and it goes to many worries concerning "our place in the grand scheme of things." Certainly this is true regarding the heliocentric model (and our own wonderful sun is itself not the center of the cosmos, of course— indeed, it appears that there is no center, which is perhaps the largest expression of the general issue of "our place," at least along one plane of inquiry) as well, hence the censoring of Galileo and the execution of Giordano Bruno.

No matter who first set down the creation stories that come to us as the book of Genesis (Moses, the "J-source," etc.), one truth that can be set down with great certainty is that the aim was not to set out the results of a scientific investigation. Was there even any language in the culture of Moses that would pertain to the idea of a scientific investigation? It can safely be argued that whatever truth there is to the Genesis story (or the stories in other "religious" texts, which can instead be understood as founding texts for particular cultures, which themselves are often derived from the texts and stories of cultures that came before them), this truth is not of a "scientific" sort, it is not the result of scientific investigation (*neither can it be*). The positivist clarification, however, tells us that such "truth" is either not real or is of some lesser order. This clarification extends to the matter of ethics.

Ethics and Religion

Apart from the specific topic of "narrative ethics" (a branch of ethics that has emerged in recent years—see, for example, Newton, *Narrative Ethics*), it can be observed that one thing that ethics and religion have in common is "narrativity": both have to do with the unfolding of individual lives, of lives together in groupings of people (and other creatures), and ultimately of an unfolding story of humanity (under some conception, often severely flawed) and life in general. This is not just a matter of "ethics with or without God," or, it might be said that there is a way of understanding this question without immediately dealing with the conception of God held by any particular religious tradition. Indeed, the questions, concerns, and anxieties we have about our lives have to do with our finitude, not God's supposed omnipotence, omniscience, and infinity (notions that are truly nonsensical at any rate). In his book *The American Religion*, Harold Bloom argued that humans have religion because we die. Other creatures also die, of course, so it has to be added to Bloom's claim that we not only die, we think about death and live with an awareness of finitude. Heidegger argues that such a concern—what he called "being-towards-death"—is definitive of the human form of being. Two things that are common to many of the world religions—though significantly not all—and in particular to Western monotheisms are (1) a story that attempts to situate each of us in an unfolding drama that is larger than each individual life (or character) in the story, a story that informs, "fills," and makes sense of our lives; (2) the idea that the story continues beyond the life of any particular individual who is a character in the story, going toward a point of fulfillment, redemption, and transformation. These stories go beyond us, but they are also shaped by how we live now—thus the peculiar connection between the narrative of humanity and ethical-political codes that one finds in narrative religious texts, especially the Bhagavad-Gita and the Jewish and Christian holy books. As much as the priestly castes promote and depend on notions of theodicy, predetermination, and an omnipotent/omniscient god who is in contradiction with any meaningful sense of human agency, the actual narratives are themselves not "objective"—they have to do with stories that people themselves tell in the living of their lives under specific conditions, but under the twin imperatives of mortality and the possibility of redemption. This latter cannot be disassociated from the idea of a humanity that lives in a different way and that is not besieged with constant worries about the production of the necessities of life.

To be brief, there is a relationship between how we live now, what we do in the world, and the ongoingness of humanity. There is a relationship between changing how we live, collectively, and the possibility of an ongoing humanity. To borrow Emmanuel Chukwudi Eze's phrase, it is a matter of "achieving our humanity."

This language is both near and far from Marx. It is near in the heritage of German Idealism and in the way that the German Idealists related to a Christian framework of redemption in the context of modernity. It is near in that Marx aimed for a "sensuous" materialism, not one that is either abstract or mechanical. Certainly Marx has a central place in his philosophy for the fact that human beings are creatures with feelings. But it might also be argued that, by the time philosophy has given way to political economy in Marx's scheme, these feelings are not understood to be very complex. Perhaps the key transitional passage is the following one, from *The German Ideology*:

> [People] can be distinguished from animals by consciousness, by religion, or by anything else you like. They themselves begin to distinguish themselves from animals as soon as they begin to *produce* their means of subsistence, a step which is conditioned by their physical organization. By producing their means of subsistence [people] are indirectly producing their actual material life. (MER, 150)

Thus it could be said that, for Marx, the "story" of humanity is first of all a story of production and forms of production, and therefore the "human story" has its basis in the same compulsion that affects all organisms, the struggle to survive and to propagate the species, to go on. Other species, however, do not develop consciousness, religions, language, writing, folklore, and narratives that presume to situate individuals (to the extent that this term applies in particular species), subgroups of the species, the species altogether, and even the whole of observed reality into some sort of context that makes sense of the whole.

Organisms and Economies

It does not seem to me that Marx is wrong in his observation about what distinguishes humans from other animals. Every form of organism has to find a way to be a part of an economy, a way of acquiring the necessities for life and continuance of the particular species. Humans not only partic- ipate in economies that represent evolutionary and ecological niches, we produce our economies such as to create our own niches. Indeed, we do this in such a way as to throw the other niches out of balance, and in such a way as to create the basis for ecological disasters. Stories have been told that purport to justify this sort of behavior—indeed, it could be argued that Marx tells one such story, of heroic humanity conquering nature. This is a story of dominion as domination rather than stewardship. One might think, again given Dostoevsky's "everything is permitted" or Nietzsche's tale of the clever people whose star burned out, that in the absence of a "cosmic scorekeeper" there is no larger sense in which it matters what hap- pens to the species of the earth that have come and gone. Indeed, in the absence of such a scorekeeper, why would it matter if humanity comes and goes as the dinosaurs did?

In his provocative book, *Bad Marxism: Capitalism and Cultural Studies*, John Hutnyk emphasises the liberating aspect of contingency: "There is no reason to believe the hype that demonises, since there can be no recognition of some ultimate authority—a god—who would sit as chair of a council of evidence to sift through the files and punish us for getting things wrong" (192). At the same time, Hutnyk is critical of a Marxism that rests on a moral critique, pointing out the relationship between this critique and the religious perspective. (I should point out that "bad Marxism" is an ambiguous term in Hutnyk's argot; in the following pas- sage, however, he seems to mean "bad" in the sense of good.)

> A bad Marxism that valorised critique of everything as the ethic of the anti-cap- italism movement might avoid doom and impotency because it does not rest only on a moral critique. Insofar as what Hardt and Negri [authors of *Empire* and theorists of the "multititude"] offer (and [anthropologist James] Clifford, for that matter) remains a moral critique, it retains a residue of Christian salva- tion, a salvation for "everyone" (who chooses Christ), but salvation nonethe- less (some Christians were communal after all). The trouble with salvation is its reliance on a saviour who will not arrive, reliance on an outside power, an imag- inary god. A communist would not suffer this morality but would devise ways to achieve what is needed, not wait for its delivery from afar. (198)

Apart from the particulars of Hutnyk's critique of specific figures, the larger question is well framed here: Is there a necessary intertwining of reli- gious and ethical themes? Does an ethical critique of capitalism necessarily depend on "something external," an "outside power," a cosmic score-keeper? Does "human mattering" depend on these things as well—some foundation? In the absence of such a foundation, is human mattering a nonstarter?

Of Dinosaurs, Cephalopods, and the Human Interlude

For some decades it was not unusual to call an outmoded way of doing something a "dinosaur." The dinosaur was the symbol of inability to adapt. Of course, there were many different kinds of dinosaurs and, as we have become more aware of the time of the dinosaurs it has become harder to use the term pejoratively. Dinosaurs were around for millions of years, and their extinction was caused by an event that humans would, even now, have great difficulty surviving. Ironically, the mass extinction that marked the end of the Mesozoic era left us with substances that could quite likely play into a mass extinction that brings our own era (the Cenozoic) to an end, namely fossil fuels. In 2003, *The Future Is Wild*, a book about "how life on Earth may evolve over the next 200 million years," was produced by "a team of international scientists, based on biological and evolutionary principles" (the book was coordinated and illustrated by Dougal Dixon and John Adams). Was the book written with the intention of demonstrating the fragility of human existence on our planet?

> This book refers to the age of humans as the Human era. Our *brief existence*, which begins and ends in the latter half of the Cenozoic era, covers a short period of geological time, but has a devastating impact on the planet. The Human era ends a few thousand years from the present with a huge drop in temperature as the Ice Age reaches its peak. (21; emphasis added)

What is at least a little amusing, even if it is somewhat in the way of gallows humor, is that the authors give humanity a few thousand more years. Even I, something of a technology skeptic, would hope that humanity will find ways to cope with environmental changes (and to cope with the way that humanity causes the environment to change, which is at least as much a question of social relations as it is of technology). However, the seemingly innocent description of the Cenozoic era and its conclusion is interesting because it combines the flavor of Nietzsche's pithy comment about the "clever animals" ("After nature had drawn a few breaths the star grew cold, and the clever animals had to die"—from "On Truth and Lie in an Extra-Moral Sense"), with a "coldly scientific"—even if highly speculative—perspective on biological evolution. Thus the succeeding eras after the Human, what the authors call "Future time":

Few species survive the Ice age that led to the extinction of the humans, and successive mass extinctions in the future wipe out large numbers of land and marine species, including mammals, fish, and many birds. But evolution responds in surprising ways. Fish abandon the oceans and take to the air, while octopuses and squids become the dominant species on land. (21)

This last bit is quite a kicker, and surely the dinosaur ghosts are laughing at human smugness already. Looking 200 million years into the future, as the book does, we see a vastly different Earth:

The last of the land vertebrates died away in the mass extinction, 100 million years after humankind. An important evolutionary niche had been vacated, and it was filled by cephalopods—octopuses, cuttlefish, and squids.

To successfully colonize land, cephalopods had to improve their land-living adaptations. . . .

With such adaptations, a new group of land-living squid, called terrasquids, evolved. They branched into many forms, from small hunters to the biggest land animals of the time. The biggest of all is the megasquid.

Heavy as an elephant and almost as tall . . .

The megasquid is not terribly clever. It doesn't have to be. With plenty of food so readily available, an absence of predators and movement achieved by the simplest of processes ["eight legs, each as broad as a tree trunk, support the beast as it lumbers through the forest"], the brain of a megasquid is tiny. It weighs about one pound (about 400 grams)—a tiny fraction of its eight-ton bodyweight. Not all species of terrasquid are stupid, however. (149–50)

The authors go on to describe another branch of the terrasquid family:

Squibbons are the most agile of the terrasquids, having adapted their natural dexterity to a tree-dwelling existence. They swing through the branches *as gibbons* used to, but looping end-over-end in a continuous somersaulting action. Their eyes are set on muscular stalks, which stay with the body's center of gravity as they swing through the trees, always looking forward towards the next branch. With their *sharp vision and large brains*, they are able to navigate through the forest at speed. . . .

Squibbon society displays an intelligence closer to that of humans than anything that has evolved since the human era. While the ability to operate tools and act communally reflects an intelligence ideally suited to life in the Northern Forest, it may be that a changing environment will encourage the development of even greater sophistication. Perhaps a reasoning type of intelligence will evolve once again. (151; emphasis added)

And then, watch out!

Perhaps the Squibbons will then themselves only have a few thousand years. Then perhaps the megasquid won't look so "stupid" after all.

My reason for bringing the future squids into all of this is that Western and non-Western philosophy has dealt with the theme of contingency for hundreds, even thousands of years, but Darwin brings the point home with a force previously unknown. Galileo and others did their part, too, but somehow the force of disenchantment could be contained better until Darwin came along. This "somehow" can be mapped and explained; essentially this is the story of Western modernity. From Galileo to Darwin humanity finds itself on a path of perpetual displacement, the earth being displaced from the center of the universe, the human species displaced from being the crown of God's creation, and a path in front of us that may lead to the extinction of humanity without the achievement of "inevitable communism." Two hundred million years from now, give or take a few million, perhaps intelligent squids will finally establish a global community of mutual flourishing. Good luck to them, at least in some possible world.

There are at least two ironies in the "few thousand years" left to humanity in *The Future is Wild*. One is that, as I mentioned already, surely humanity by two or three thousand years from now will have long since achieved collective control over human destiny. However, this future has come to depend on not the next few thousand years, but in fact the next five, ten, twenty, fifty, and hundred years. This is the other irony. And let us hope the cephalopods make it that long too, especially the way things are going in the oceans these days—thanks to the nonexistence of conscious, collective human control over human destiny.

Contingency and Destiny

Is all talk of destiny ruled out by the recognition of contingency? Certainly Marx recognized the contingency that Darwin's perspective demonstrates as fact. And yet it might be argued that what distinguishes *historical* materialism from some other kinds of materialism is that it concerns creatures who wonder at the point of existence. Strangely, humans evolved with the capacity to "produce their means of subsistence," while other organisms acquire what they need to live and propagate their species out of instinct. Humans do not get very far on instinct alone; the extrapolation at the other end of the spectrum might be that humans best succeed when they act with the most informed understanding of the natural and social processes that they are involved in. (Indeed, this is part of the problem with Marx's formulation in *The German Ideology*—consciousness is thoroughly intermingled with the human ability/necessity for producing the means of subsistence; we have no choice but to consciously produce our means of subsistence, we are not able to do this instinctively.) This understanding would not preclude what Wes Jackson calls the "ignorance-based worldview": the recognition that there is a great deal that we do not know, and that, in our infinite cosmos, there will always be more that we do not know than that we do know (see Jackson, "Toward an Ignorance-Based Worldview"). Especially as regards the larger biosphere of which humanity is a part and which humanity did not create, the audacity of the modern, "scientific" approach has produced "knowledge" that has been exceedingly harmful and exceedingly ignorant. As Wendell Berry argues, we are very good, with our "scientific" methods of food production (which do not deserve the name "agriculture") at destroying topsoil, and we do not know how to make more of it (Berry remarks on this point in many places, including *Home Economics*, but also see "Farming and the Global Economy"). To this it can be added that language brings its own infinities, in terms of the making of meaning. And yet none of this cancels the basic Enlightenment proposition that things (generally) go better when we humans know what we are doing—even if we are swimming in a sea of cosmic contingency.

Of course, we humans can wonder at the point of existence all we want, but this does not mean that our question will be answered by "something larger," something outside of humanity. There is an infinite cosmos outside of humanity (which may be simply one universe "within" the infinite multiverse), but there is a paradox involved in any "answer" it gives to our queries on behalf of humanity, a paradox pointed out by existentialist philosophers. Sartre's formulation will suffice:

> Existentialism is not atheist in the sense that it would exhaust itself in demonstrations of the non-existence of God. It declares, rather, that even if God existed that would make no difference from its point of view. . . . the real problem is not that of His existence; what humanity needs is to find itself again and to understand that nothing can save humanity from itself, not even a valid proof for the existence of God. In this sense existentialism is optimistic. ("Existentialism Is a Humanism," 11; gendered terms modified)

Sartre's conclusion may seem strange. Certainly, other philosophers, existentialist or otherwise, taking the measure of contingency, have not necessarily found reasons for optimism, but instead for either "fear and trembling" or a "coldly scientific perspective" that tells us our questions about existence are not *real* questions. Surely, though, it is not outside the realm of social science to recognize that people have these questions, and are caught up in them, regardless of whether or not they are "real."

Evolution and Ethics

What Daniel Dennett calls "Darwin's dangerous idea" unleashed not only a scientific revolution in the understanding of the development of life on this planet (which, from a Darwinian perspective, one has to hesitate to call "our planet"), but also a spiritual crisis. Again, we could say that Darwin qualitatively deepened a spiritual crisis that had already begun in the preceeding three hundred years or so; or we could say that, after Darwin, it became that much more clear that Humpty Dumpty was not going to be put back together again. In this book I have been critical of a reductionistic Marxism, and I am critical of reductionism in general, though I have not really explained what I mean by "reductionism." There are those who argue—some happily, others critically—that any materialist perspective will necessarily be reductionistic. What I mean by a reductionistic materialism is one that is overly mechanical and that cannot allow for qualitative transformations and the appearance of the different, the new, and the unexpected. Clearly, Marx aimed for such a nonreductivist perspective when he argued for a *dialectical* materialism. Significantly, however, Marx never wrote at length about dialectical materialism *as such*, as a philosophy; philosophers and revolutionary leader-theoreticians, from Lenin to Lukacs and from Mao to Althusser, have pondered the meaning of what the latter called this "long philosophical silence." When Engels did write a short book on dialectical materialism as the outcome and *Aufhebung* of German Idealism (*Ludwig Feuerbach and the End of Classical German Philosophy*), he gave us a mechanical, reductivistic treatment that was especially antagonistic toward Kant. But it was Kant who set up the problem of the irreducibility of vocabularies (the causal and the value-driven) in such a way that any materialism that sought to describe the human form of life either has to make room for qualitative difference—albeit "materially based"—or has to declare that questions of value are merely epiphenomenal. Donald Davidson developed Kant's argument along more directly materialist lines (analytic philosophers quibble over the terms "materialism" and "physicalism," but that need not worry us here), to show that a materialist perspective does not rule out anomalies— pockets within the material world that, though they are the product of causal interactions, do not themselves follow strict causality. Humanity itself is one such anomaly, and Marx's description of the "human difference," that we make our own means of subsistence, cannot in fact be separated from other phenomena that make for the human form of being: language, meaning, valuation, consciousness and self-consciousness, a deep concern for finitude and mortality, and the attendant concern for "something more," life more abundant.

Dennett argues for a reductionism that is "bland," not "preposterous." Readers of Dennett's work are familiar with his argument for "cranes" rather than "skyhooks"—everything in our material world, including human evolution, consciousness, culture, Beethoven, and Garry Kasparov, and chess-playing computers (this is a favorite example of Dennett's) is built up from material, "nonmiraculous" sources. Here, then, is Dennett's brief for a nonpreposterous reductionism, along with some comments on the use of "reductionism" as a term of abuse:

> Those who yearn for skyhooks call those who eagerly settle for cranes "reductionists," and they can often make reductionism seem philistine and heartless, if not downright evil. But like most terms of abuse, "reductionism" has no fixed meaning. The central image is of somebody claiming that one science "reduces" to another: that chemistry reduces to physics, that biology reduces to chemistry, that the social sciences reduce to biology, for instance. The problem is that there are both bland readings and preposterous readings of any such claim. According to the bland readings, it is possible (and desirable) to *unify* chemistry and physics, biology and chemistry, and, yes, even the social sciences and biology. After all, societies are composed of human beings, who, as mammals, must fall under the principles of biology that cover all mammals. Mammals, in turn, are composed of molecules, which must obey the laws of chemistry, which in turn must answer to the regularities of the underlying physics. No sane scientist disputes this bland reading: the assembled Justices of the Supreme Court are as bound by the law of gravity as is any avalanche, because, they are, in the end, also a collection of physical objects. According to the preposterous readings, reductionists want to abandon the principles, theories, vocabulary, laws of the higher-level sciences, in favor of the lower-level terms. A reductionist dream, on this reading, might be to write "A Comparison of Keats and Shelley from the Molecular Point of View" or "The Role of Oxygen Atoms in Supply-Side Economics," or "Explaining the Decisions of the Rehnquist Court in Terms of Entropy Fluctuations." Probably nobody is a reductionist in the preposterous sense, and everybody should be a reductionist in the bland sense, so the "charge" of reductionism is too vague to merit a response. (*Darwin's Dangerous Idea*, 80–81)

> Darwin's dangerous idea is reductionism incarnate, promising to unite and explain just about everything in one magnificent vision. Its being the idea of an *algorithmic* process makes it all the more powerful, since the substrate neutrality it thereby possesses permits us to consider its application to just about everything. It is no respecter of material boundaries. It applies . . . even to itself. The most common fear about Darwin's idea is that it will not just explain but *explain away* the Minds and Purposes and Meanings that we all hold dear. People fear that once this universal acid has passed through the monuments we cherish, they will cease to exist, disolved in an unrecognizable and unloveable puddle of scientistic destruction. This cannot be a sound fear; a *proper* reductionistic explanation of these phenomena would leave them still standing but just demystified, unified, placed on more secure foundations. We might learn some surprising or even shocking things about these treasures, but unless our valuing these things was based all along on confusion or mistaken identity, how could increased understanding of them diminish their value in our eyes? (82)

Even while I agree with "bland reductionism" to a large extent, I wonder at the tone of some of Dennett's remarks. Is it *wrong* to "yearn for sky-hooks"? I mean this as something that could be a philosophical question because it seems to be a human question about mortality and finitude and not first of all about some complex and sometimes vexing scientific question such as the actual pathways of biological evolution. Why is it right to "eagerly settle" for cranes? Is it wrong for a materialist, someone who does not believe in God in any conventional Western-monotheistic or classical-theological sense, to all the same wish that such a God did exist? In the "dirty war" in Argentina that took place from 1976 to 1983, some political prisoners were taken out over the ocean in airplanes and helicopters and dropped into the ocean from a great height. Is it wrong to wish that there was "something," someone "ready to catch us, should we fall"? Well, yes, it might be wrong, especially if we succumb to the temptation to turn our wishes into horses. In "scientific" terms, the wish might be wrong if it keeps us from dealing with reality as it really is, a reality that includes a U.S.-backed regime in Argentina that did that horrible thing to those people. In Sartre's terms the wish is wrong because it opens the road toward moral and political abdication. I take those points as cautionary, and yet I still find myself wishing for something for those people for whom there is nothing. I mean the people who had little or nothing when they were alive, and then they were gone altogether.

The section title from *Darwin's Dangerous Idea* from which these passages were quoted is "Who's Afraid of Reductionism?" Even with the paradox of human meaning (that a "larger" scheme of meaning that undergirds human existence would thereby undermine "the problem of humanity for humanity," to put it in Sartrean terms), is there no sense in which one might mourn the death of God for at least a moment before "eagerly settling" for cranes? For the passing of God would also seem to mean the passing of a cosmic scheme of meaning, and therefore a humanity in perpetual free-fall. I am not saying that the human wish or hope for meaning is answered by something larger than humanity itself, I am only saying that there are certain schools of scientific thought (such as Dennett and Dawkins), philosophical or otherwise, that do not seem to appreciate the full scope of the cultural and spiritual crisis that attends the absence ("an absence that is felt as a presence," in Derrida's memorable phrase) of the "larger scheme." Is there any larger scheme of meaning in which the "story of humanity" (if it is a story, or even if it is many stories) is enveloped? For thousands of years, at least, a good portion of humanity (though, significantly, not all of humanity) has believed in such a "narrative substratum," and this belief and the stories people have told about this substratum and the human connection to it has constituted a good deal of what has been called "religion."

Meaning and Reference

Certainly, on some level, this question of existence (is there any "larger than humanity" scheme of meaning, does such a scheme *exist*?) is a problem of reference in the same way that the question of whether or not my car keys are in the place where I thought I left them is a problem of referential semantics. This is how the "purely scientific" perspective treats the problem. "Does God exist? No, we find no evidence of God's existence. We find no actual referent for the term 'God.' Next issue: Where did I leave my car keys?" Now, in fact, I do not believe there is a referent for the classical, heavily "Greek-ized" notion of an omnipotent, omniscient, omnibenevolent god. Perhaps, as some theologians have argued, it is not a matter of reference, or even of "existence" (but instead of "Being" or even "nonbeing"). However, at least as a matter of reference, the "omnis" do not make sense, and in this case the positivist clarification seems appropriate: the "omnis" are pseudo-concepts, and if they have some "meaning" that is beyond all human understanding, then, hey, what is that doing for me or my fellow, finite humans? (This matter is distinct, at least analytically, from the attempt—a necessary one, I think—to "press thought to the limits" and to attempt to transcend existing limits, a philosophical project that characterizes much of Derrida's work and that is explained well by Drucilla Cornell in *The Philosophy of the Limit*.)

Of the classical "omnis" (which were quite arguably *not* adhered to by the ancient Hebrews or the early Christians), it is omnibenevolence that is perhaps most in need of challenge and rejection, at least as a practical matter, for it seems to be this perverted notion of the good that motivates the upside-down moral values of fundamentalists. In Kant's ethical philosophy, one sign of the universality of the categorical imperative is its publicity— the way that the reasoning process that leads us to the imperative can be explained and embraced broadly. No such publicity attends the moral values of the fundamentalists; indeed, these are the people who are often heard to say that "everything happens for a reason" (almost always referring to a bad thing); however, don't ask them for the "reason" in any particular case, the "reason" is known to God (and is part of some larger plan). This is not "reason" for Kant (or Aristotle, for that matter). Furthermore, an actual ethical imperative that is amenable to the reasoning of finite beings would require us to struggle against many of the bad things for which God supposedly has a reason. "Omnibenevolence," as interpreted by humans, is a license to justify (at least through nonopposition) the most disgusting and horrible things and to vilify things that are either arguably (to finite reasoning) good or at most trivial (in the grand, yet radically finite, scheme of human affairs).

Meaning without Foundations

This, however, is not the end of the problem. There are two broad issues, at least, that remain. First, there are other important categories of inquiry that can be challenged in the same way that the god of classical, Western theology and his "omnis" can be challenged. Second, the flip side of the coin as it were, there is the problem of meaning and values of a species that finds itself in free-fall, without metaphysical foundations. This is also the problem of mortality: meaning and values are problems (at least in part) because of mortality (if we had forever or "eternity" certainly the nature of these problems would be radically different), and because of mortality we *might* wonder (and many do wonder, myself included, at any rate, even if a reasonable reductionism tells us that our fears are "not sound") what the point is—who cares what we do and why we do it, what the "meaning of it all" is, if life is over in the proverbial blink of the eye—in any case, and not just the life of any given individual, but quite possibly the life of the human species as well? What difference does any of it make?

Marx never talks this way. Analytic philosophers of a scientist bent do not talk this way. Dennett, significantly, makes a nod toward such issues, though he is often dismissive of the existentialist way of approaching them. It could be that Marx's tendency to not talk about these sorts of issues has not only its (strong, I think) positivist side, but also that he did not think about, because there was no reason for him to think about, the possibility that humanity might destroy itself altogether. (Neither did he think about mass extinction events such as those that occurred at the conclusions of the Paleozoic and Mesozoic eras, for the perfectly good reason that these things were not understood in his time.) Gary Shapiro once related to me a chance conversation that he had with a leading member of the Black Liberation Movement back in the heyday of the New Left. This person argued that the world would not be destroyed by nuclear war, because "communism is inevitable." It is conceivable that Marx could have thought something like this, in the case that he knew absolutely nothing of what nuclear war would be all about. (Marx also did not know that the end of the dinosaurs was most likely brought about by a meteor strike.) On the assumption that humanity has a good many more years still in front of it, perhaps Marx is right, that it is inevitable that humanity will get its collective act together, in the sense that this will happen one day, sooner or later. But we can no longer make this assumption, and indeed we have to take account of the possibilities for humankind's outright destruction in how we think about the possible futures for humankind.

There is a certain structure to this thinking, which might be called a thinking of contingency and in light of contingency. Indeed, there are different schools of what might be called "contingent" philosophy (which is either the same thing or very close to "postfoundational" philosophy), and without developing this theme at length, I think there is much to be learned from all of these schools. These schools might also learn a thing or two from each other, even if the day has not yet arrived (and perhaps never will arrive) when the whole project of "thinking in light of contingency" can come together.

When I say "this person *argued*" (that global nuclear war could not happen because communism is inevitable), I am attempting to be generous toward what might count as an argument—but the form of the claim is interesting, a meeting of *post hoc, ergo propter hoc* with the future anterior sense ("this will have been . . ."). Derrida argued, in an essay titled "No Apocalypse, Not Now," for what might be called the "nuclear theory of meaning": that the fundamental premise of all speech in our time is that a nuclear war has not yet occurred. In 1984, when Derrida wrote in the context of the nuclear "competition" between the United States and the Soviet Union, he discussed a "speed race" and its effect on the human experience of time and meaning:

> Whether it is the arms race or the orders given to start a war that is itself dominated by that economy of speed throughout all the zones of its technology, a gap of a few seconds may decide, irreversibly, the fate of what is still now and then called humanity—plus the fate of a few other species. [One assumes that Derrida was engaging in irony or sarcasm here.] . . . no single instant, no atom of our life (of our relation to the world and to being) is not marked today, directly or indirectly, by that speed race. (20)

I will turn more directly to this "speed race," which is characteristic of twentieth-century capitalism (that is, imperialism) and even more of the capitalism of recent decades (which I call postmodern) in a moment. What I would like to highlight here is what might be termed "the call of the future," a radically different future, and what is involved in listening to this call. Recall William James's argument that optimism and pessimism are "definitions of the world." If the radically better future world has no foundation in a scientifically discovered inevitability, as Marx had thought (or, to be provocative about it, as many, many generations of Jews and Christians had thought), then the epistemology of hope becomes a significant question, as do the existential questions of speed and world destruction that Derrida emphasizes. Every "atom of our life" is marked by the uncertain possibilities of the future, including the possibility that there will be no future, including the possibility that there *will have been* no call of the future in the case that there is no one to respond to this call.

Hope Now

This epistemology of hope, inseparable from the optimism of James and Sartre, inseparable from the messianic force (albeit "weak") that Benjamin and Bloch thematized and Derrida developed in *Specters of Marx*, is more known to us historically from a religious perspective than a scientific one. Certainly we can say the epistemology of hope ought to be characterized as a "broadly" religious perspective. Marx thought he could get rid of any need for such a perspective because the utopian hopes of humankind could be given a scientific foundation. Marx was not wrong to think that trying to understand society in a systematic way, based on empirical investigation, and looking at aggregate tendencies in terms of causal mechanisms would show us the general trends of history and the possibilities that are imminent to any given social present; he was not wrong to argue that capitalism depends on at least one "iron law," the iron law of wages; he was wrong, however, to claim that history has an inevitable outcome. Marx was wrong on this point both "scientifically" speaking, and morally speaking. For if the outcome is inevitable, then whether we are talking about God or History, humankind is just along for the ride.

Perhaps Marx meant inevitability in the same way that the Early Christians did, as a kind of audacious braggadocio: We *will* win! *Nothing* can stop us! That's fine, except that sometimes we are blinded to reality if we go too far with such a perspective, and then the oppressed will have a hard time formulating good strategies for struggle. *Secondarily*, such a perspective is not very "scientific," either. Strategic confidence should not lead to strategic boneheadedness and blindness. If anything, the confidence we really need is one that, while it cannot wholly or even very often fly in the face of science—though sometimes it does—holds central faith in the principles that exploitation, domination, and oppression are *wrong*, that we are ethically compelled to struggle against every form that these things take, and that another world is possible. Call this an "ethical confidence," even an ethical faith and an undetermined faith in the ethical. But perhaps we have to call this a *religious* confidence as well, for two reasons. First, the connection drawn between the "core faith," that exploitation, domination, and oppression are wrong, and "*that* another world is possible" (where "that" is a term that seems to do some work—but how, exactly?) is a connection more typically found under the heading of "religion," historically. It is not clear anymore—even if the matter seemed too clear to Marx—that the connection can be placed on a "fully sound" scientific basis. If this appraisal is correct, then surely we should revisit the passages in the early Marx where he writes of the fulfillment of religion. Second, the idea (or whatever it is) that another world is possible is itself necessarily underdetermined: many worlds are possible, and so is no world at all, at least no "human" world. I propose, then, that "ongoingness" is an indispensable conceptual bridge or bridging concept.

Otherwise, we have Althusser's famous formula, "history is a process without a subject," which is an accurate understanding of at least one major strain in Marx's thinking. Without being dismissive of Althusser or even this particular formula (Althusser's understanding of the subject is more complex than the formula would lead one to think), there is a sense in which, if "history is a process without a subject," then—What's the point?

Reductionism

Earlier, I raised two objections to reductionism without exploring them. I claimed that there are categories of inquiry that can be challenged in the same way that the god of the classical "omnis" can be challenged. My point in raising this issue is two-fold: on the one hand, if we are going to deconstruct God, let's not let something else take the place of God; on the other hand, if there truly is no God and also no "god-concept," in the sense of the unifying force or substrata, foundation, ground, necessity, or what have you, then an adequate account of the human condition (or at least the human condition for a significant part of humanity) and therefore an account of what people might conceivably and ought to care about is needed. Or else nihilism is true.

What are these "categories of inquiry"? To put it categorically and simplistically, any field of scientific or systematic inquiry becomes a "god" (or, to use Heidegger's term, "onto-theological") when it is taken to be absolutely complete and to be fully operating within the domain of necessity. It has to be added immediately that real science does not work this way, at least not when science is being true to itself, and neither could real science work this way: scientists are trying to understand a world that exists contingently, that has many contingencies within it, not to mention lots of slippery stuff in general, and where any systematization of facts is necessarily incomplete because there is always more, infinitely more. One could imagine a mathematician saying of physics what Rutherford said of every other science, that it is all stamp collecting. And yet we do not have to go beyond zero and one (themselves slippery concepts) before we are troubled by infinity (just put the one over the zero). The problem of meaning confronts the difficulty that what we have empirically are many different languages, for the overwhelming part translatable one into the other (I accept Davidson's argument that a nontranslatable language would not be recognizable as a language, as a candidate for translation, in the first place), but we do not seem to have "language as such" (what Walter Benjamin called the "Adamic language"; when God said, "Let there be light," what language was he speaking?) or, to use Quine's term, "meant entities." Neither does it work to argue, as Marx did, that language is simply "practical consciousness" (*German Ideology*, in MER, 158); it can be argued that it is just as much the case that consciousness is an expression of the materiality of language (other things are required, too—a brain of a certain type, a material world, other people with whom to communicate, daily bread to sustain the body, and so on; the argument is that language is a necessary if not sufficient condition for consciousness). Neither human consciousness nor human languages seem to need to be complete systems or to be hooked up to the cosmic Rosetta stone in order to do what they do. In fact, their working seems to require that they not be complete, and by "complete" I mean representable in a fully developed and noncontradictory algorithm.

This is an important question for Dennett; as he said, the unifying power of Darwin's vision lies in the notion of evolution as an algorithmic process. I think Marx would be pleased with this conception: Darwin showed that the development of organic matter and even the development of a form of conscious organic matter that produces its own means of subsistence is a subset of material processes in general. Marx aimed to add the processes of human social and cultural development to a universal science of all material processes. The algorithms that represent (or govern) material processes that occur in the different domains of the material world (the different fields of scientific investigation) are themselves related through algorithms: this is reductionism, though perhaps it is not so bland after all. At an even less bland level (heading into the theological realm, I would say) is the algorithm that governs the algorithms of *all* material processes. (One imagines that the speed of light, which Einstein labeled "C" for "constant," is in there somewhere.) But we cannot stop there: the algorithm governing everything in our material world must bow down before the algorithm that allows for the possibility of our universe (which in this description seem even less like *ours*, to be sure) and possibly for the possibility of other universes, perhaps an infinity of universes.

An Algorithm of Everything?

Perhaps there really is an ur-algorithm for all being or for the possibility of all being. It would be interesting to explore the connection between such an algorithmic conception of existence and theories of truth. Alain Badiou, one of a number of figures in recent years placing renewed emphasis on truth, recommends a return to Plato and especially to the idea that mathematics is ontology (and vice versa). (Badiou also reinstates the divided line, drawing a strong distinction between the eternal and the ephemeral.) In the wake of quantum mechanics it is quite commonplace for physicists to say that reality is statistical, even to the point that the multiverse (and therefore our own universe) is generated from variations in the vacuum flux, "a quantum fluctuation in which some virtual particles were created out of empty space." (For a layperson-accessible presentation of this quantum "something out of nothing" theory, see Richard Morris, *The Edges of Science*, 167–93; quotation from 174.) I believe in singing the praises of science, and even of truth, especially in the world today when both are embattled; to return to Dennett's initial comment about reductionism and "those who yearn for skyhooks," it seems to me that the scientific endeavor of searching for connections within different fields, and the pursuit of an ideal, unified scientific framework that demonstrates connections and interrelations among the fields (and that often leads to the emergence of new fields, such as molecular biology) is the very opposite of philistinism. But what about the question of "heart," or of "heartlessness"? Of course, many scientists are passionate about their work, perhaps most of all those involved in "pure research." (For example, in *A Brief History of Time*, Stephen Hawking gives an account of flared tempers regarding his proposal that "black holes ain't so black"—that black holes have radiation signatures; see 99–113.) Certainly the great scientific discoveries should and do inspire awe in both scientists and the rest of us, both at the discoveries themselves and at the ingenuity and creativity of the scientists.

It would seem that one does not have to get too worried, initially at least, about the ethical and political implications of the marvelous fact that we humans live in a world that we can come to understand, by and by and with a will to do so. For this is a marvelous fact and yet not a miracle: we evolved in this world, we are suited to it. Parts of this world are even suited to us, the parts where we evolved—as opposed to the vast regions of the cosmos that are not suited to life and certainly not to the kind of life that humans have. What separates us from these less congenial regions is a very thin skin of life-supporting elements, a skin that presently we are abusing at an alarming rate. At the same time, we also abuse a good deal of the life that is contained within this skin.

Parts of this earth, at least, are not "foreign" to us, and this is the basis on which we evolved here and therefore the material basis for our being able to understand, progressively, how the world around us works and to look ever more deeply and further out. There is a way to talk about ethics that is very abstract, and Kant excelled in this perhaps more than any other philosopher. The categorical imperative applies to "rational beings," whether these are humans on planet Earth or aliens on a planet circling the Dog Star. Kant's argument can be made a little less "cosmic" by the simple proposal that we are talking about ethics when we are talking about ethics (what is it right to do, what ought we to do), and when we are talking about something else (pleasure, happiness, instincts), well, then we are talking about something else. If ethics has any real substance as a discourse, then it at least has to have this kind of autonomy. Kant recognizes, however, that there is a connection between the discourse of right and wrong and the discourse of where humanity is heading (if anywhere) and the point of human life—if there is a point. This does not mean that the discourses link up at every moment; on the side of ethical discourse, the anti-consequentialist argument is that we have to try to do the right thing come what may. If human life and human history are truly pointless, however, then it is hard to see why questions of right and wrong matter. Put quite differently: How does "heart" come into the picture?

The Anomaly of Heart

The worry is that objectivity and the concern for truth, on the one side, and passionate commitment to a better world ("heart") can find themselves at odds, even if not necessarily in contradiction. Obviously, this worry is expressed quite strongly by many opponents of evolution, who reel and freak out at the notion that the world was not created so that we humans could be the crown of creation and the center of a cosmic drama. As I've argued throughout, theodicy can and ought to be rejected on ethical grounds (it glorifies a monstrous, hateful god and absolutely denigrates humanity in a way far beyond a contingent universe's "disinterest"); on ethical grounds we can and must reject the idea of any "caring presence" that is characterized by the "omnis." However, in this context, a word can also be said for truth and objectivity. If some version of creationism (such as "intelligent design") is true, then one upshot that the proponents of such perspectives (which are not "theories," in the scientific sense of a theory) have not dealt with is that their god is the perpetrator of an extraordinary fraud. If the species on our planet did not develop more or less the way that evolutionary theory says they did, this would be a fantastic blow to not only biology, but to the very idea of empirical investigation and even to the idea of trusting our senses at all. The god of the creationists is really what Descartes called an evil genius, and in His world we puny humans are all insane. Creationists do not want to deny that people can for the most part trust their senses, but they think that they can somehow contain distrust to one area of science. But this is where Dennett's reductionism shows its strength: Darwin's vision is "no respecter of material boundaries." This can be said of the scientific perspective generally, and the creationist ought to be asked what he or she thinks Darwin was doing that is different from empirical, scientific investigation more generally.

Trashing Science

Part of what separates creationism (or other theistically driven views of how the world is the way it is) from actual scientific investigation, a big part, is a difference in modality. Supposedly in either case there is a concern for truth. An interesting onto-epistemological problem (that cannot be pursued at length here) is that, even if creationism and science are working with different conceptions of truth, they are still in contradiction regarding their claims about the world. The sting of this contradiction for creationists and other theists (perhaps not all) is what Dennett called the fear that "the monuments we cherish" will be "dissolved in an unrecognizable and unlovable puddle of scientistic destruction" (*Darwin's Dangerous Idea*, 82). (I do not agree *entirely* with Dennett that "this cannot be a sound fear"; more on this in a moment.) Perhaps there is not destruction, but instead *deconstruction*, or what Derrida (in *Of Grammatology*) called *desedimentation*; an analysis that shows how something came to be and how a crucial part of its functioning is the concealment of its true workings (almost always there is an ethical-political dimension to this concealment). Still, in the present case, of biological evolution, there appears to be what can still be called a contradiction.

The following is from an account of the creationism controversy in Kansas by Stan Cox, a biologist there; the account concerns state school board hearings held in May 2005 to determine if evolution ought to be presented in science textbooks as "only a theory" and if "alternative accounts" of how the species and especially the human species came to be should be presented. At this time, the Kansas state school board was packed with neo-conservatives and fundamentalists, and it appeared that the "intelligent design" position had carried the day. Indeed, the hearings themselves were promoted by the Intelligent Design Network, based in Shawnee Mission, Kansas. As Cox writes, "'Intelligent Design' is a mutant form of creationism that attempts to mimic biological research."

> Kansas' scientific community boycotted the Topeka hearings, but a hardy group of its representatives, led by Kansas Citizens for Science [KCFS], was present outside the hearing room to rebut the weird science being presented inside. Several of the scientists were outraged at the claim by the hearing's organizer that to teach evolutionary theory is to teach atheism.
>
> A significant portion of the KCFS membership is made up of theistic evolutionists. Their position is compatible with that of the almost 5500 signers of the Clergy Letter Project, who "believe that the timeless truths of the Bible and the discoveries of modern science may comfortably coexist."
>
> But what theistic evolutionists don't say, and what the creationists fear, is this: Once you realize that the bewildering diversity of life on this planet has

evolved through natural processes, it's much, much easier to discard religious belief altogether.

If intelligent design is responsible for life on earth, then belief in a Supreme Being is mandatory. If life evolved through natural selection acting on naturally occurring variation, such a belief is entirely optional. This is why big slabs of the religious right are so obsessed with attacking evolutionary theory. ("Kreationism in Kansas," *Counterpunch*, July 26, 2005 [www.counter-punch.org])

Many similar arguments and accounts could be presented, but this one has the significant virtue of demonstrating the issue of modality. In fact, the contradiction between evolution and (whatever version of) creationism is softened here: as Cox allows, there are theists who find ways to accept evolution, and there are evolutionists who find ways to accept theism. However, the key point is that biological evolution provides a complete picture of speciation (many details remain to be worked out; indeed, there are still new species being discovered), and, in relation to this picture, the order-giving role of God is *entirely optional.* One is reminded of the response of a French Enlightenment philosopher to Napoleon Bonaparte when the latter asked why there was no mention of God in a treatise by the former; Pierre Simon LaPlace said, "Sir, I have no need of that hypothesis." An optional god is an unnecessary god—and what is God if He is not necessary?

Now, it is not *impossible* that there is a "god" (or group of gods) who operates at some level lower than the nonsensical "omnis." It is also the case that the "god-concept" is not so easily dispensed with (or sometimes not so easily ferreted out—a good deal of deconstruction, at least as practiced by Derrida and de Man, can be understood as dealing with precisely this question) in philosophy; perhaps an analogy could be drawn to mathematics and physics, where troubling infinities are sometimes generated. Surely Anselm was on to something (with the ontological argument), even if this was "only" the power that certain conceptual formulations can display. In the first case, of the "non-omni" god, this could be the "god of the possible," discussed by some recent theologians. (See, for instance, Gregory A. Boyd, *God of the Possible: A Biblical Introduction to the Open View of God.*) Creationists, in employing their "wedge strategy," to gain a foothold in science classrooms in public schools, are willing to play fast and loose with modalities and therefore in their own way soften what I previously called a contradiction. "Wedge strategy" is a term used by proponents of intelligent design themselves, for instance, in materials published by the Discovery Institute (a think tank for creationism). When Stan Cox asserts that intelligent design attempts to mimic biological research, the key point is that this mimicry is almost entirely at the level of discourse: intelligent design attempts to co-opt terminology from actual research, but presents very little research itself. Indeed, its main work is "philosophical," except that its philosophical position is motivated by a certain politics of truth; the main claim of creationism (presented as "creation science," especially in this recent manifestation as intelligent design) is that the world is simply too complicated to be explainable by science alone. Intelligent design presumes to use science itself to demonstrate this inexplicable complexity, but it really depends for its appeal on nonscientific factors: a politics of truth in the context of the casual relativism of postmodern society, a fear of the secular and what it might mean to live in a world without foundations (which, again, I am not as willing as Dennett to call an unsound fear), a certain concomitant "dumbing down" of some sectors of society, and, more recently, political power that is reforging institutions in the United States and that is connected with the ascendancy of the Christian Right within a larger tendency toward what looks like a new kind of fascism.

To return to the earlier point, then, and to draw together some thoughts about all of the topics just glossed (modality, foundations, the politics of truth, postmodern capitalism, dumbing down, and the fascistic slant of post-9/11 America), let us take the argument about evolution a few steps further. It is part of the politics of truth that the creationists and fundamentalists have been able to insert the word "theory" into the discourse, even while demonstrating minimal if any responsibility to what it means to have or propose hypotheses and to form theories in science. Intelligent design marches forward with a banner reading, "Now we're really cooking with our own science." In the context of science, of real scientific inquiry that is responsible to protocols of investigation and hypothesis- and theory-formation, something can be said about intelligent design in terms of modalities (and the larger point I will drive toward is the relationship between modality and truth): again, it is *not impossible* that there was some outside tinkering with the biological structures that allowed a species such as *Homo sapiens* to emerge. It is even not *impossible* that some external force set up the whole deal (all of biological evolution on our planet, or even the universe itself). It is not impossible; therefore, it is in some sense *possible*. (There are some good science fiction novels that play with this idea, such as *Calculating God* by Robert Sawyer and, as mentioned above, *Cosm* by Benford.) However, to work up to this as a scientific explanation would require the hypothesis of an exceedingly "inelegant universe" (to play on Brian Greene's title); that is, it would require a procedure of explanation that begins with outlandish proposals. Intelligent design, as a backdoor to creationism, wants to conceal those proposals—in part because the direct assumption of a supernatural force creating and structuring nature is an approach contrary to the methods of empirical investigation. Certainly this assumption responds to what I would call "real" and not unsound reasons why people want to believe in a supernatural, metaphysical foundation for the world, for humanity, and for our individual lives (though much of modern Christianity sets its priorities in an order that is the reverse of my listing), but there is also a level at which creationist "theories" depend on an ignorance that is systemically generated and disseminated. Intelligent design is a sham that depends both on getting a wedge into the many issues in biological evolution that remain to be investigated or need much more investigation (and surely there will be many surprises there; one can only hope that this poor Earth will give us the time to investigate species that are being destroyed by the imperialist system that is the real god of the Christian Right)—in theology and philosophy of religion this is called the "god of the gaps" idea—and on an assault on science generally. There are things in the world that are extraordinarily complicated; the genetic structure of even simple organisms is one of these things. We ought to be awed by the fact that Darwin developed the theory of natural selection without knowing about the existence of genes, and that genetic theory has, in turn, put flesh on the bones of natural selection. People can be intimidated by complexity and by scientific investigation, especially in a capitalist society that depends on and continually deepens and extends the division of labor. The "argument from complexity," however, assaults all science. *Gravity* is an enormously complicated phenomenon, and physicists do not yet have a full picture of how it works. Why not just say then that gravity cannot possibly be a completely natural phenomenon, and go over to a "theory" of "God-waves"? Perhaps the next step would be to propose a new mathematics based only on numbers that are mentioned in the Bible.

However, the idea of a sham (or even a scam) perpetrated upon science and upon ordinary people does not go far enough in explaining what people in the camp of what I would label "rationalist skepticism" (e.g., enthusiastic readers of magazines such as the *Skeptical Inquirer* and other venues for debunking pseudo-science) call the question of "why people believe weird things." There are at least four analytically distinct (albeit practically intertwined) levels on which the appeal of creationism and the "critique" of evolution needs to be understood: (1) the modality of scientific investigation; (2) the politics of truth; (3) the problem of "scientism," the idea that the only explanations of phenomena that stand a chance of being true are scientific explanations; (4) concern about foundations and the meaning of a world without (metaphysical) foundations.

In claiming intelligent design as a scientific proposal, creationists can only go so far toward the god of their version of Christianity. (Even then, they are most concerned with bolstering the "omnis," and not necessarily old Jehovah with his numerous questionable character traits.) Stanley Kubrick's *2001* presents a scheme whereby evolution was helped along, and let us say again, as regards modalities, it is not impossible that such a thing could have happened, even if extremely unlikely. Even the most inelegant and outrageous possibility of the involvement of monoliths (or the Easter Bunny, for that matter) in human evolution does raise an issue regarding what truth is, what truth is all about. Scientific truth has to do with the "judicious study of discernable reality." This was actually an expression used by an aide to George W. Bush, and it goes to the politics of truth, to which we will turn in a moment. Perhaps this is not all that scientific truth has to do with, and perhaps there are other domains where it is appropriate to use the word "truth," but I think it is fair to say that a conception of truth that is proper to both science and to human pursuits more generally, as finite creatures in a far-flung cosmos that is extraordinary and beautiful but that seems, on the best evidence and argumentation, not to be the result of conscious design, must necessarily be a *fallibilistic* conception. And that is not good enough for creationists, fundamentalists, and some others who are, shall we say, primarily motivated in a theological way. "True truth" for this bunch is absolute certainty, and it operates under the modality of necessity. We finite fallibilists, on the other hand, live with contingency and deal with truth under this modality. This does not mean acquiescing in relativism; indeed, some of the relativist forms of postmodernism and fundamentalist theism actually agree on the claim that truth is not to be found in this world. Indeed, this view of truth is at the core of the intelligent design proposal, in the idea that humans cannot investigate this world and come to an understanding of it in its own terms.

The Strength of Fallibilism

A scientific, yet fallibilistic, conception of truth may sound weak, but it is not. We might approach this issue in terms of a kind of holism and through a *via negativa*, as it were. The difficulties of explaining gravity aside, we might look at areas of inquiry that are more closely connected to evolution—and here we will see the force of Dennett's argument about algorithmic processes. If evolution is wrong in the way that "young-Earth creationists" (the view that the Earth is the age given by adding up the "begats" in the Bible, and the lifespans of those begat, from Adam to Jesus, plus a few days before the creation of Adam—roughly six thousand years) claim, then, among other things, carbon dating is wrong. If carbon dating is wrong, however, then physicists have been way off in their understanding of atomic structure. In other words, scientists could not be wrong about evolution, in its broad outlines, without being wrong about many other things too. Then we are back with Descartes's evil genius, who must be having a good laugh as we pitiful humans stumble about, erroneously thinking we know something. Apparently, we don't know anything. Intelligent design attempts to soften this contradiction by accepting other timelines than what the young-Earth view proposes, which seems merely wimpish. Why not just bite the bullet? The monoliths from *2001* are not going to cut it, ultimately, for the intelligent design crew, because that scenario opens onto inquiry into where the monoliths came from. Even if through mimicry of science, it is just that sort of inquiry that intelligent design forestalls; at least good old young-Earth creationism has the decency to make a frontal assault on science.

Evolution Wars

On this score, one can appreciate the sharpening of contradictions rather than their softening. The renewed "evolution wars" are of a piece with a renewed and far-ranging agenda of U.S. imperialism that was bubbling under the surface in the years after the collapse of the Soviet bloc (and that included the attempt to cut short the presidency of Bill Clinton), that came to a larger share of power within the administrative structure with the dubious election of George W. Bush, and that went into high gear with the trigger that was September 11, 2001. In a story on the evolution "controversy" (the real story is that the controversy is political, not scientific), *Time* magazine asked three scientists and a theologian if it is possible to believe in both God and evolution. Two of the scientists argued that there is no contradiction, that evolution is the mechanism by which God brought about humanity. I prefer the responses that meet the issue head-on. The first is from Albert Mohler, president of the Southern Baptist Theological Seminary:

> Given the human tendency toward inconsistency, there are people who will say they hold both positions. But you cannot coherently affirm the Christian truth claim and the dominant model of evolutionary theory at the same time.
>
> Personally, I am a young-Earth creationist. I believe the Bible is adequately clear about how God created the world, and its most natural reading points to a six-day creation that included not just the animal and plant species but the earth itself.
>
> . . . Evangelicals must absolutely affirm the special creation of humans in God's image, with no physical evolution from any nonhuman species. Just as important, the Bible clearly teaches that God is involved in every aspect and moment in the life of His creation and the universe. That rules out the image of a kind of divine watchmaker.
>
> I think it's interesting that many of evolution's most ardent academic defenders have moved away from the old claim that evolution is God's means to bring life into being in its various forms. More of them are now saying that

a truly informed belief in evolution entails a stance that the material world is all there is and that the natural must be explained in purely natural terms. They're saying that anyone who truly feels this way must exclude God from the story. I think their self-analysis is correct. I just couldn't disagree more with their premise. ("Evolution Wars," *Time* magazine, August 15, 2005, 35)

Such refreshing clarity! The scientist who supplies equally valuable clarity on the other side is Steven Pinker, psychologist and innovative investigator into the workings of language:

It's natural to think that living things must be the handiwork of a designer. But it was also natural to think that the sun went around the earth. Overcoming naive impressions to figure out how things really work is one of humanity's highest callings.

Our own bodies are riddled with quirks that no competent engineer would have planned but that disclose a history of trial-and-error tinkering: a retina installed backward, a seminal duct that hooks over the ureter like a garden hose snagged on a tree, goose bumps that uselessly try to warm us by fluffing up long-gone fur.

The moral design of nature is as bungled as its engineering design. What twisted sadist would have invented a parasite that blinds millions of people or a gene that covers babies with excruciating blisters? To adapt a Yiddish expression about God: If an intelligent designer lived on Earth, people would break his windows.

The theory of natural selection explains life as we find it, with all its quirks and tragedies. We can prove mathematically that it is capable of producing adaptive life forms and track it in computer simulations, lab experiments, and real ecosystems. It doesn't pretend to solve one mystery (the origin of complex life) by slipping in another (the origin of a complex designer). ("Evolution Wars," 35)

Let us take stock of the way a *contradiction* is framed by these two quotations; it seems that everything comes down to what Albert Mohler called "the premise"—"that the material world is all there is and that the natural must be explained in purely natural terms."

When I speak of the "contradiction," however, I do not mean a contradiction between "religion" and "science"—in fact, in a moment I am going to defend what I call a "broadly religious perspective," as necessary not for "grounding" meaning and morality, exactly, but as necessary for seeing that meaning and ethics are real and that we would not get very far in scientific investigations without them. What I mean by the "contradiction" is the power of different fields of scientific inquiry to help us to not only understand the world but also to live in the world, with biological evolution as an important example in not only scientific inquiry but also the larger fabric of society, as opposed to the way that some try to describe what it is we humans are doing on this planet, how we got here, and where we are going.

Belief in a Time of Science

One of the central issues here is the problem of belief in an age of scientific inquiry. Even if one is not committed to the idea that all and only those truths grounded in scientific inquiry are real truths (and I am not), it is another thing to believe—or try to believe—a claim that runs contrary to what has been well established by science. To take up one of Pinker's examples, what would it even mean for me to claim *in this day and age* to believe that the sun goes around the earth? We see again the role of holism in this discussion: as Copernicus demonstrated, the mathematical model of the motions of heavenly bodies that would be required by an Earth-centered universe (or even just the solar system, which would be instead the "Earth system" in this case) would be the very opposite of elegant, and indeed would be so impossibly inelegant as to only be possible in the case where a conscious, vastly powerful being controls these motions. Science contradicted this Earth-centered scheme, and a person can believe in the Earth-centered universe only by going against science. What would it even mean to go "against science" in this case? Perhaps this could mean one (or both) of two things: (1) a personal, psychological state of sheer inability to reckon with the world (which does afflict some people, sadly yet understandably), or (2) a social-political agenda of power that depends on fomenting and spreading ignorance. Observation and theoretical reasoning in the case of the sun and the earth are complicated affairs, even if, after the Copernican Revolution there is no going back to the view that the sun revolves around the earth. (Or, it might be said, there is no going back short of a fairly complete shattering of civilization.) Evolution is an even more difficult nut to crack, and yet to deny that the species on our planet are the result of biological evolution takes us back along the very same regression as a latter-day Earth-centered perspective would—toward denying that through a synthesis of observation and theoretical reasoning humanity can come to an understanding of how things work in our world.

The politics of truth comes to the fore, then, in that the question is not so much how the denial of such activity is possible—in terms of epistemology, the way that people come to hold beliefs—but instead *what* and *who* has an interest in promoting what really amounts to a kind of cynical skepticism or skeptical cynicism. (Actually, I think it is the latter, at least for creationists, because the key to their metaphysical scheme is that this world, and humanity, really counts for nothing, it really doesn't matter.) Of course, it is possible to disagree selectively with the results of scientific investigations; scientists themselves do this all the time, and this is how science itself advances. Taking an auto mechanic as a scientist of the car, he may have been wrong about the fuel injector being the problem, and it might turn out to be the electrical system. We can bemoan the hassle, but we had better also get on with getting the electrical system fixed if we want the car to run. What we don't do is reject the theory of the internal combustion engine altogether. What we don't do is say, "No one really understands how cars work—as evidenced by this recent failure of my mechanic to solve the problem on the first attempt—therefore there must be some mysterious force at work that is beyond human comprehension." (Too bad this mysterious force doesn't want to fix your car!) There are many, many aspects of the evolutionary picture that remain to be filled in—and many parts that may never be filled in (the millions of species of insects, for instance, or life-forms at the bottom of the oceans that have come and gone). However, if evolution as a whole is wrong, if the way the species came to be on our planet is radically different from the overall picture that evolution gives us, then radical skepticism is recommended—this hemorrhage in the larger body of scientific knowledge would not be containable. The real question then becomes why capitalism, especially in the form of a globally interwoven imperialist system, and recently guided to some extent by right-wing "Christian," antievolution forces, has brought about this hemorrhage. What does capitalism hope to gain by this strategy? Can this strategy be carried very far without causing the widespread hemorrhaging of capitalism itself?

We might pose the contradiction another way, and ask how "real Christianity"—something that I would identify as being closer to the better spirit of Christianity, a kind of radical Judaism that emphasizes ethical-political universalism, rebellion against systems of injustice, taking the side of the poor and the outcast, the formation of egalitarian communities, and the identification of justice with the integrity of bodily existence (all ideas that do not mean much to fundamentalists)—can abide capitalism.

Let us consider two points by way of summary.

Science and Interpretation

First, let us refocus on the question of Marxism and science. Science deals in probabilities, what is most likely the case. In some areas of research, what science holds to be true is not only so well established and therefore "extremely probable," such that it appears nearly impossible that the established perspective could be wrong, but it is also the case that, if the established perspective were to be found completely wrong, there would be a crisis not only in the particular field of study (for instance, evolution), not only in science generally, but even in the very nature of truth and knowledge. However, in the social sciences there is a good deal more room for probabilistic thinking. There is not only more room for interpretation (such that some speak of "interpretive" or "hermeneutic" social science), interpretation itself is one of the problems already built into the "object" of analysis. (The possibility that all science is in some sense "social" science is an important question, but not one that is essential for the line of argument I am pursuing here.) This view of social science is not unusual, though it is still resisted by an academic mainstream that is hung up on positivism and quantification (the "do the math" versions of sociology and political science, for instance, and the many psychology experiments that never get into the difficult problem of what the subject *understands* by what she or he is told by the experimenter; Donald Davidson critiques this approach in "Psychology as Philosophy"). The problem of interpretation is also resisted in positivist and reductivist forms of Marxism.

Now, if reductivism means showing connections, then reductivism seems like a good idea. However, among *what* are the connections being shown? In other words, in these last two sentences I intentionally avoided the obvious term—that connections are being demonstrated as among *things*. It is the very hallmark of reductivism in Marxism, at any rate, and in positivist social science generally, to treat human beings (to say nothing of other animals that would appear to have their own forms of *eudaimonea*, and at least to have feelings about these forms) as things, as things among all the other things among which connections can be shown. (Whether Dennett has this perspective is a question that will have to be addressed elsewhere.) The great irony is that Marx attempts on many levels to make the critique of reification—of the "thingification" of human beings—a matter of a science of society and not "only" or "merely" a matter of ethics or philosophy. For Ethical Marxism the question then becomes whether at least some elements of Marx's critique—for instance, the notion of the domination of living labor by "dead labor," or the "rising organic composition of capital"—can be recaptured in ethical terms; the larger question in which this activity would have to be situated is a matter of showing why this reformulation *ought* to be carried forward, and why this reformulation is necessary for both the liberation of ethics and the liberation of humankind.

Surely, if it can be shown that there is a natural process or phenomenon at work that spells the end of humankind, then even the most "inevitablist" Marxist would question the inevitability of communism. (I am thinking of some fantastically catastrophic circumstance, such as an unstoppable meteor or some strange imbalance in the sun. Incidentally, it has become common for people to think about the meteor scenario in the case of the earth—bad blockbuster movies are made about the subject—

but few have thought about the fact that, if a sufficiently large meteor were to hit the moon, the results could be equally disastrous.) What is worth pondering from the perspective I am putting forward in this book is that such an outcome (of the naturally-caused end of humankind) cannot be a matter of indifference for humankind. Who knows how such a scenario would actually play out, and I hope that we never have to find out, but somehow I do not see humankind going "gentle into that good night."

Most people care about the continued existence of humanity. Is this claim an observation, or is it simply a cliché? I would say it is a *truth*, possibly even the "core" of truth or the first truth or the beginning of truth or the way to/of truth. However, there are three exceptions to this claim that bear examination.

Concern for the Future, Exceptions To

There are people who have been convinced by what might be called "anti-life" religious systems that humanity as a whole is a wretched thing that is deserving of the worst that can come to it. Obviously, there is the irony that these folks identify themselves as "pro-life" on one particular issue (of denying reproductive rights); furthermore, these people have at times (such as the time of this writing) found influence in social systems. They care about at least a limited future, though it seems the aim is to hasten the day of the apocalyptic destruction of humankind. Certainly, there is a difference between the leadership of this current (which, in the United States, mainly consists of right-wing Christians), who are most likely more self-conscious about propounding a hateful world view in the service of American imperialism, and the rank-and-file of what really is a fascist movement. One lesson to be learned is that, when a current such as this obtains significant political power, there is a kind of *discursive break* in society—for, to return to the example introduced at the very beginning of this book, regarding what sort of *discourse* is possible concerning the matter of the Nazi who rips away the child from its mother's arms, in order to murder the child, it is exceedingly difficult to see what sort of discourse is possible with people who not only believe in the biblically literal apocalypse but are also (what's more the point) *thrilled* at the prospect. (I placed "biblically-literal" in scare quotes because it is also a nonsensical notion, in my view.) What kind of conversation is possible with someone who so hates humankind that he or she *welcomes* the sorts of unimaginably horrible and torturous destruction that will befall most people in this fundamentalist perspective on the end times?

Next there are people who may or may not care about the future of humankind, but what they do really care about is the future of their own narrowly defined segment of humanity. This theme can be parsed out in many ways. While it is quite common to worry about this form of narrowness under the heading of "tribalism," what concerns me most is the form this narrowness takes under imperialism, in other words imperialist nationalism. The imperialist nationalist citizen takes his or her nationality to be the one that matters not only the most, but in reality the only one that matters significantly. This perspective is exemplified by all of the colonialist and imperialist powers, whether it is seen in the actions of the British in India or the French or Belgians in much of Africa or the Japanese in China and Korea. Now we are confronted by the global example of the actions and comportment of the United States "in everywhere." Without entering into detailed discussion of the sense that *some* Americans have of being the most special of the special (so special that even other imperialist nationalisms hardly count), as well as the contradictions of this sense (for instance, the imperialist nationalisms of Japan and the greater and lesser European powers have an ethnic component that does not sit quite as easily with what can be said *officially* in the United States), it is not difficult to see how this perspective places whichever imperialist nationality ahead of the much greater part of humanity. The workings of political economy in an imperialist world-system are such that, when the gloves come off and the capitalist scramble for labor and materials assumes a more directly military form, the imperialist nationality is not only jingoistically projected as being ahead of or above the rest of humanity, it is increasingly at odds with the rest of humanity. Indeed, we are beginning to see such an acute form of this dynamic in the world since the George W. Bush administration was put into place that America truly is at odds with the rest of the world.

Lastly, and I would argue most significantly, the capitalist ruling classes do not care about the future of humankind. Neither do they care about the past or present of humankind, for that matter. Certainly, the ruling classes are made up of people, of members of our own species—and in fact it is a very bad idea to forget this, to ascribe the inhuman system and acts of the capitalists to something that is different from what human beings are doing. The system is alienating, and thereby dehumanizing, and certainly the actual people who are members of the ruling class become separated from any larger sense of humanity (for those born into the ruling class this process of separation begins even before birth). There are strong winds that blow the rest of us away from a larger sense of humanity "on the other side," as it were—we become not only alienated, but also sometimes cynical and despairing. This ideological wind is especially forceful in the imperialist countries, and the two groups I mentioned prior to turning to the ruling class are made up of people who have been blown by this wind into a basic cynicism and despair about humanity, and their ideological positions of "religious" or otherwise ossified imperialist nationalism are pillars of popular support for imperialism and, in the period of this writing, a global agenda of reforged imperialist domination.

However, my point here is that this remains a *human* problem, a problem of the sorts of people humans can be, and a problem that has to be traced to social systems that work through human interaction, albeit guided by a force that is alien to any larger sense of human eudaimonea. This alien character of the capitalist social system has reached the point in our time where not having a larger sense of humanity and its ongoingness and potential for mutual flourishment is not simply an "attitude problem." Instead, a systemic bifurcation has emerged whereby one is either on the side of one or another narrow agenda for a small part of humanity (some of these agendas representing a general hatred for humanity, as with much of right-wing Christian fundamentalism), or one is on the side of a future for humanity—*without which* there will have been no past or present.

The ruling classes certainly care (if that is the word) about the future of something, or rather some *things*, important for the continued existence of particular ruling classes. There is no single "international" ruling class, particular ruling classes remain profoundly rooted in particular nation-states— even if this picture is indeed complicated by the rise of corporate power and the tremendous mobility of capital that is one of the key elements of what I call "postmodern capitalism." One ramification of this aspect of capitalist political economy is that any given capitalist ruling class does not even care about the future of all of the other capitalist ruling classes, except in the context of calculated alliances, and often these ruling classes have entered into deadly conflicts with each other, with disastrous consequences for the rest of humanity. But it is only *things* that the ruling class cares about, and only the aspects of humanity that can be rendered into things. And, in fact, "care" is not the word, for this reifying orientation issues from the mechanisms of capitalist political economy. This is why, to return to themes introduced in part 1, Marx was right to focus on the mechanisms of capital, and the social form, rather than the "evil intentions" of the capitalists. On the other hand, these very mechanisms undercut care about the future of humanity (and the present and past, for that matter—and it is on the matter of concern for the past where many "honest conservatives" are deluded about capitalism, the social form where everything solid melts into air), and indeed generate the opposite of this care—whatever name might be given to this opposite, and perhaps there are many names.

Necessary but Underdetermined Commitment

Now, what is it we can learn from these exceptions to concern for the ongoingness of humanity? I would say again that it is something about the kind of commitment that is both necessary and underdetermined, and about the particularities of this commitment as expressed in care and love. To save humanity, we *have to* care about and love humanity and its future possibilities of flourishing. Indeed, to love humanity, one has to love its possibility of redemption—because, without this possibility, we might as well give it up right now. This is what the "exceptional cases" do, even the religious-apocalyptic ones, because for them it is not about the future of humanity. However, the paradox is that a love that is "enforced," that *has to* be taken on, is not exactly love, is it? This paradox goes to the problem of the *truth* of love. On this point Badiou has some important things to say from the standpoint of ontology, while Derrida's arguments concerning the politics of friendship are also important here. In a Kantian spirit (more akin to Derrida than Badiou, I think), I will not go any further here than to say that, despite this paradox—which is at the heart of the categorical imperative as well, because it offers a formula but, in its focus on intention, also depends on a commitment to the formula (or to ethical-political universalism broadly)—we have to *try* to love humanity and care about its future.

Proletarian Love of the Future

We have to strive and we have to do what we can; we have to also try to do what we perhaps cannot. And now to become directly Marxist about this again, it is the proletariat, as the international class that has nothing to lose but its chains, as the class that has the least to hang on to in the way that the world is presently set up, that is the most open to being *effectively seized* by this commitment. It is not only the proletariat, and indeed it may not always be first of all the proletariat, but, it is because there is a proletariat, and it is because the imperialist system works in such a way as to continually generate and replenish the proletariat (a coldly analytical way of describing a very ugly process), a class of people whose material underpinnings in the system are exceedingly tenuous, a class of people who live under the constant threat of being completely discarded, that there is a material basis for the *kind* of love of humanity's future possibilities that we can have today. In fact, it is on this question of the "kind of love" that a Marxist view of the future can be distinguished from utopianisms of the pre-industrial capitalist world. And yet, even if we can demonstrate the material basis on which commitment, love, and care are generated and needed (and one might say that Lenin's epistemological argument is that the proletariat is the material basis, but the actual *expression* of these qualities comes first of all from outside of the proletariat), there remains the sense in which these qualities, as with the ethical, have to be thematized as such, and thus have at least a kind of relative autonomy.

Significantly, Pinker closes his comments for the "Evolution Wars" article by discussing the desire that people have for meaning and a basis for morality. In my view, this is where he runs into problems.

> Many people who accept evolution still feel that a belief in God is necessary to give life meaning and to justify morality. But that is exactly backward. In practice, religion has given us stonings, inquisitions, and 9/11. Morality comes from a commitment to treat others as we wish to be treated, which follows from the realization that none of us is the sole occupant of the universe. Like physical evolution, it does not require a white-coated technician in the sky. (35)

In at least some religious perspectives, there is a co-implication of the problems of meaning and morality, and to this list I would also add mortality, which concept might be fleshed out in terms of the fact not only that we are animals, who, like other animals, only live for so long and then die, but also that we are capable of a radical sense of finitude and a sense of radical finitude. Let us mark one difference between scientific and religious perspectives (or at least a perspective that might be called religious) as being that a number of perspectives that think of themselves as scientific, such as scientific Marxism and various trends in analytic philosophy (with which I would associate Pinker and Dennett), are either not convinced of the connection or are not especially impressed by it; these perspectives do not take the religious perspective as demonstrating a profound insight in either seeing or asserting this connection.

For instance, on the question of meaning per se (apart from its implication in other questions), Pinker is very close to Dennett and both may be said to be engaged in what have lately been called "deflationary" strategies as regard meaning and consciousness. These strategies are significantly different from those philosophies that concentrate on the contingency of meaning and the meaning of contingency, though there might be a way in which the more straightforwardly philosophical approaches of Sartre, Derrida, and Davidson on this point come together with approaches such as Dennett's and Pinker's, rooted more in evolutionary biology, in the work of Richard Rorty. In the latter case, though, again there is more of an effort to grapple with the meaning of contingency and the question of what it means to study the ways in which consciousness and meaning are material phenomena. Rorty was a resolute secularist, and yet, in asking about these meanings, his work is quite different from the more scientifically oriented investigations of Dennett and Pinker. But then, Rorty, following Davidson, would also not have accepted that language is either purely algorithmic or for the most part (even if not "purely") instinctual.

Rorty then makes a move, however, in a kind of fidelity (ironically) to the spirit of Carnap and logical positivsm, where he separates discourse about which consensus can be built (with scientific discourse as the model of publicity) from ethical and aesthetic vision-making, the work of the "ironist," which is a "private" matter.

Algorithm of History

I bring up this debate to make the point that such a division would seem to be warranted in the case where there is no algorithm that definitively takes us to a particular future. Marx thought he had discovered such an algorithm, and it is worth noting once again that he was working from a philosophical trajectory that included not only Hegel, but also Kant. The "real movement" in history is the algorithm, working according to material contradiction, that takes us through the modes of production to communism. Certainly, Marx and Engels protested that the discovery of this algorithm did not amount to an historical determinism. However, given that Marx presumed to make his arguments under the heading of necessity, we need more of an explanation as to why his scheme is not deterministic. Perhaps there is only one necessity we need to swallow, or just a few at most: the fact that, at any stage of human development, people enter into particular relations of production and social relations more generally; that more efficient means of production will tend to replace less efficient means, and that the division of labor tends to follow this development; and, perhaps most important for how we might understand the contemporary world, the iron law of wages under capitalism. In other words, grant to Marx a handful of premises, which can be empirically studied and grounded, and the rest follows. The thing is, I do grant Marx these premises. The problem is, there are a few other premises that have to be granted as well, and this makes trouble for the way that "the rest" is supposed to "follow."

Contingency and the Future

To grossly oversimplify, the two major premises that have to be accounted for concern contingency and the future. One of the things I find fascinating and provocative about Rorty's arguments, especially in *Contingency, Irony, and Solidarity*, is that they represent an attempt to formulate a leftist alternative to Marxism, where contingency trumps necessity. Rorty does invoke Sartre here and there, as an ally in the attempt to forge a politics of contingency (even while joining the chorus that condemns Sartre's political commitments). Still, it could not be said that Rorty is the Marx of contingency. Antinecessitarianism (to use Roberto Unger's term) is taken so far with Rorty that there is no sense of there being a social *system* at all, or a mode of production; not only are there no "laws" of history, there are not even any historical, social, or economic tendencies. Taking the cultural relativism of the later Rawls (which holds that political liberalism can only speak to societies that have a certain historical and cultural background, basically already that of liberalism) one step further, into what Rorty calls a kind of "ethnocentrism," the critique of "postmodern bourgeois liberal" societies (the "lucky" North Atlantic democracies) extends only to bad policies that further greed or cruelty.

The problem is that Marx does not really recognize contingency; contingency is a marginal element, at best, in the grand sweep of things, and the grand sweep works, in Marx's view, in a law-like way. However, we should also be wary of simply flipping over into a sense of contingency that is just as overwhelming as a deterministic sense of necessity. For in neither case is there room for human possibility, for meaning, or for matters of life and death. One of the interesting aspects of Rorty's reformulated pragmatism is that it is not only at odds with Kant (*Contingency, Irony, and Solidarity* is rife with criticisms of Kant, especially for his "residual Platonism" and for the idea that we can read moral principles out of ourselves, out of our own human, rational constitutions; see especially 32–35), but it also does not have much room in it for William James. Kant looked for the relationship among knowledge, ethics, and hope. James demonstrated the relationship between commitment and knowledge. Neither looked at the future as determined, but rather as a realm of possibility where our commitments and actions would play a role in bringing about a redemption of the world. What I am proposing is an articulation of these contingent, underdetermined factors with Marx's discoveries regarding the tendencies in history and production, and in capitalism in particular. What is missing otherwise, in either Marx's secular necessitarian view, or in Rorty's secular antinecessitarian view, is a sense of a redeemed future that calls to us and that plays a real role in the possibility of its achievement.

Marx does of course speak of the proletariat as necessarily "taking its poetry from the future." Rorty does in fact speak constantly of "social hope," especially in a mode taken from John Dewey. But I imagine that the formulation I just gave, of the call of a redeemed future, would be far too metaphysical—which, at least on this point, is also a way of saying far too Kantian—for either Marx or Rorty. The problem might come down to seeing the relationship between the formulations of the categorical imperative, and, for simplicity's sake, let us say that it is a problem of seeing the relationship between the first and third formulations. The problem looks quite metaphysical, something akin to asking what the Christian "god" is when *it* is taken apart from its manifestation in three "persons." (I won't go any further with this vexing issue, at least not here!) What *is* the categorical imperative apart from its manifestation in the three formulations? (All right, one brief digression on the "blessed trinity": why is it always *three*? Why three persons of the trinity, why three formulations of the categorical imperative, why three parts of the soul in Plato, three moments of the dialectic in Hegel, and so on? Augustine attempted to show the necessity of the godhead's division into three persons—but then, it didn't bother him that he was doing metaphysics.) The problem, I think, can be put in Marxist terms, and we can avoid for the moment the ontological difficulties. If there is a background against which it makes sense to strive to enact the ethical-political universalism stated plainly in the first formulation, then it is in the ongoingness of the human project and in the possibilities of creating a society where people do not treat each other as mere things.

Stated a little differently, if there is a background against which it makes sense for Marx, through a kind of Kantian *via negativa*, to rail against the society where all human relationships (and, I will say it again, despite what is clearly a large dose of normative humanism in my approach, all relationships among creatures who are capable of experiencing cruelty) are reduced to the cash nexus, it must be the background of another world that is possible.

Otherwise, struggle is ultimately, merely reactive; "justice" is merely vengeance; and the world will not be transformed. Now, reactive struggle and justice-as-vengeance are not only possible as well, they are most often the more forceful "reality" in this world, and though there have been significant efforts to transform the world beyond the cash nexus, the fact is that "the harvest is past, the summer is ended, and we are not saved" (Jeremiah 8:20). There are moments when humanity raises its head above reaction and vengeance, and at least begins to bring about something new and liberated, but nowadays we seem especially stuck in the muck of a postmodern capitalist system that has as a key component the destruction of any larger scheme that would give meaning to struggle; this is, in the view I am offering here, an attack in the present against a redeemed future. Marxists and other leftists, as well as, significantly, conservatives (we could have a longer discussion about what this term means now), sometimes blame postmodernism for this assault on meaning, by which they mean certain philosophers, predominantly from France. Derrida is often singled out. But Derrida is in some ways a good Kantian philosopher in that he is simply interrogating the conditions for the possibility of meaning, and finding that meaning has an uphill battle to wage. For those scientific realists out there who do not like this finding, it might be said, "like it or lump it, this is the way things are."

Meaning and the Future

One of Derrida's most famous arguments is that meaning is always deferred. This does not mean that there are not bits of contingent and fragile meaning to be found in our present; instead, what his argument means is that meaning depends on the future. This is again the point about the idea that our every utterance and set of marks in the present is accompanied by the proposition that "a global nuclear war has not yet occurred." The cancellation of the future is a cancellation of present and past meaning. This can also be said for present-day trends that, if they run their course beyond a certain point, will also cancel the future: these trends render life meaningless in the present, *except* in the struggle against them.

There are material processes that can be modeled on algorithms. Indeed, this might be taken as a modern, scientific definition of what it means for something to be a material reality or process, that it can be modeled in this way. It is not hard to imagine that Marx would accept this definition, and I imagine that Dennett would too. (Dennett's appreciation of the power of the algorithm is demonstrated in pages 48–60 of *Darwin's Dangerous Idea*.) Badiou is aiming for an avowedly Platonic, mathematical materialism in terms of set theory, which would be a more central topic for consideration here if I were *primarily* concerned with ontology. My point throughout this investigation is that I am only *secondarily* concerned with ontology, precisely because, contrary to certain "realist" forms of Marxism, which depart from Marx significantly on this point, I think that ontology is a secondary pursuit—which is not to say that it is not important. Or, to put this in the terms I have used before, of course humankind needs all the science that it can get its hands on, but it needs this in the context of trying to create a good society.

Let us imagine that there are many pathways into the years to come, some of which end in the destruction of humankind, and one or a few of which lead to a transformed world that is sustainable and good. (I say "one or a few" because I do not want to insist that there is only one way for humankind to go forward. This kind of view has had very bad consequences as one way of understanding Lenin's argument about "line"—"we got here this way, therefore we *had* to get there this way, and thus every aspect of what we did to get here is confirmed as *true*, as *corresponding to reality* and to material necessity." On the other hand, I say "one or a few" because the path may indeed be rather narrow, if not at all straight.) Perhaps from the standpoint of some redeemed future it will be possible to specify the algorithm that connects our present to this future. This algorithm would then show how what appears to us as severely underdetermined now—our faith that it makes sense to go on with things now, because perhaps we will get to a better future—is instead just another component in the package that led to this future, a package that is also made up of the trends in history and society that Marx analyzed.

This picture only makes sense, however, from the standpoint of a retroactive conferral of necessity. Let us assume that no one can believe in such a thing anymore, or at least no one who has an appreciation for scientific investigation and a fallibilistic conception of truth, no one who is not a religious fundamentalist or pre-Einsteinian mechanical materialist. So that, yes, our future sisters and brothers will be able to say that we in the present had to have had faith and commitment and love and the aim of doing the right thing, or else we in the future would not be here to say these things, but this seems qualitatively different from specifying a formula that included these things in a more or less precise mix. It seems to me that this qualitative difference remains even though the story can be told of how things got from then to now. To return to themes from part 1, to tell this story only under the modality of necessity is to engage in theodicy, but the result of theodicy is not redeemed humanity but instead a cosmic drama in which humanity remains a mere object. Thus there has to be not only an ethics of liberation, but also a liberation of ethics itself from the algorithm or other descriptions of history as purely law-like in its motions.

Dodging the Bullet

We have a very good case for study on this question in the dissolution of the Soviet Union. The laws of historical necessity in this case would seem to have dictated in the 1980s that *either* the Soviet Union and the United States, in the pursuit of their respective imperialist agendas, would have come into open military confrontation that could have escalated into a large-scale nuclear exchange, *or* revolution in either or both countries would have short-circuited the imperialist agenda. The laws of historical necessity seem to dictate that capital does not back down, that of necessity it must press its advantage (again, this is the reality of opportunity cost, if you do not win, you lose), and if this means unleashing untold destruction, then so be it. Twice in the twentieth century this had happened already. But then, something else happened, something where the oft-heard quip, "didn't see that coming, did you?" applies quite broadly. No one was predicting that the outcome of the mounting tensions between the United States and the Soviet Union would be that the latter would stand down. And so, we live on for now, with certain new difficulties that are truly monstrous, but also with possibilities that would not exist, because humanity would not exist, if things had gone where they appeared determined to go in the 1980s. And, although it is not as if we cannot say anything about how the state of affairs came about that has allowed us some more time on this earth, there are elements of the whole scenario that are simply vexing, especially because things could have gone otherwise. Humanity dodged a bullet—this seems to be the explanation (that does not explain anything) on some level. We lucked out.

However, the world we find ourselves in now is one in which truth and meaning are under assault as never before. One side of this is the current assault on science, in the form of the attack on evolution, in the remaining imperialist superpower; another side is an assault on the idea of a qualitatively different future, of a society not based on exploitation, domination, and oppression. Each represents an assault that has to be fought and ultimately negated; each represents an embattled truth that, at some point, will either break through or will be destroyed altogether—and soon enough humanity as well. But what is the relation between these two truths? Again, side-stepping momentarily the metaphysics of the issue, I would say that the great human project of scientifically investigating the world and coming to understand its workings (including the workings of evolution) will at least practically have to be situated within the effort to transform the world into a global community of mutual flourishing—in a word, communism. I would propose, again given the secondary orientation on ontology, that this answers the metaphysical question, and it is the same answer that is given in terms of the first and third formulations of the categorical imperative.

Morality and Mortality

Let us return to Pinker's comment for a moment, so that I can insert the problem of mortality into what Pinker said about meaning and morality by making this problem a part of the problem of meaning, at least for the moment: we are concerned about the meaning of life in part because we come and we go and it is hard to see the point of it. For many of us, about the time we figure out a few things, our time is nearly over. Now, in his comments, Pinker does not stay with the question of meaning for very long, and so we would need to look at his works such as *The Language Instinct* to get the larger view. Let us note, too, that Dennett has chapters on meaning and morality, respectively, in *Darwin's Dangerous Idea*. There is nothing, however, in Dennett's book about mortality in the terms with which I am presenting it here, though there is a great deal on survival and reproduction. Without doing the least justice to what Pinker and Dennett do say on these subjects (and recognizing that Dennett has also written books on freedom and religion), however, let us take stock of the fact that they represent, at least in a certain sense, a paradigm of scientific and analytic thought in that the questions of meaning, morality, and mortality are not seen as interconnected, and the more (admittedly) Kierkegaardian or Heideggerian ways of characterizing mortality (as a sense of radical finitude) are nonstarters for this perspective. The more important point for our present discussion is that the same would seem to be true for most of what calls itself Marxism. But, again, for the moment let us just consider Pinker's comment about morality. Again the approach could be called deflationary, though what is interesting is that Pinker's formulation is closer to Kant than to Hobbes, and it is often in a kind of spontaneously Hobbesian direction that quick-and-easy ethical prescriptions tend to go—that is, ethics as mutual back-scratching.

Notice three things about what Pinker says, however, and remember that these comments are made in the context of a response to religion. First, there is at least a little Hobbesianism to the bit about the "realization that none of us is the sole occupant of the universe." In other words, we have to find a modus vivendi. Second, Pinker's other formulation is a version of the golden rule, and we might consider the way in which Kant is both trying to capture something from this ancient idea and the way that the categorical imperative goes significantly beyond the golden rule both in what it requires of us and in the metaphysical background that is assumed (in other words, why it is important to show the grounds for the metaphysics of morals). Third, there is a tone to his remarks that is worth noting. This tone is in the vein of "all you really need for morality is X, you don't need this other mumbo-jumbo." The "all" that is needed is not very much, seemingly just some common sense. Furthermore, not only is the other mumbo-jumbo not needed, we also do not need to show any connection between morality and this other stuff, especially in the case where this other stuff involves a bad engineer with questionable morals.

Basic Kant, Again

A little "commonsense Kant" is not the worst thing, I think, especially when it comes to ethical questions. Assuming that our aim is to do the right thing, it does not hurt to have little reminders in the form of questions such as, "What if everyone did that?" Even regarding the metaphysical framework that Kant supplies for ethical reasoning, it does not hurt to remind ourselves that we are concerned with ethics when we are concerned with ethics, and not with some other topic such as happiness, desire, or interests. (More sophisticated reflections on this point are provided in Karl Ameriks, "A Commonsense Kant?") However, the need for the framework and the connections that Kant forges reveals itself precisely on this question of not being the sole occupant of the universe. It is often assumed that a distinguishing difference between Kant and utilitarian or otherwise consequentialist theories of ethics is that the categorical imperative would apply to me even in the case where I really was the last and only person in the universe. Autonomy is not a form of solipsism, however. If I was the last human being on the planet (just to narrow the field of inquiry a bit), for what could I hope? If it were truly the case that all hope for humanity had been foreclosed, and that there is no future for humanity because there is no humanity for which there can be a future, then ethics, autonomy, hope, and the kingdom of ends can once again be seen to be interconnected, except now in the negative sense that they are all together in being nonstarters. Perhaps in my remaining days I can at least try to feel hope for my fellow (nonhuman) creatures, and that, someday perhaps 200 million years in the future, smart squid will make a better run at living in a just and sustainable way than did humanity. But this is a rather dismal picture, obviously, at the very least a kind of hope against hope.

Epistemology and a Religious Perspective

In the case that the third formulation, as the "culmination" of Kant's thinking on autonomy in the realm of ends—the ethical community—is indeed the background (which, unfortunately, Kant calls "certainly only an ideal"; *Groundwork*, 39) against which the first and second formulations make sense, then a certain comparison with Marx comes into the picture. In Kant, there is an essential connection between the ethical community and what he calls "true religion." Marx, too, in his early work, at least seems to speak of a true religion, or a religion that can and ought to come true. Significantly, he says these things in proximity to his "fourth formulation" of the categorical imperative. Perhaps just as significantly he gives his fourth formulation at the end of a paragraph that he begins by addressing the question of violence, providing the famous formula, "the arms of criticism cannot replace the criticism of arms. Material force can only be overthrown by material force; but theory itself becomes a material force when it has seized the masses" (MER, 60). At least two other things are significant about this text, the "Contribution to the Critique of Hegel's *Philosophy of Right*: Introduction." First, Marx remains in this text closer to the philosophy of history; in his later work it will appear that he has abandoned this field for political economy. Second, this text that speaks of "a total redemption of humanity" at the end, begins with the famous announcement that "the criticism of religion is the premise of all criticism." But what is "religion," exactly? Marx has some interesting things to say on the issue; certainly for Marx religion is more than and other than simply stonings, inquisitions, terrorist acts, or even opium. Apart from these interesting things—such as that religion is a theory of the world (but upside-down), that it is the cry of the oppressed, that it is a catalogue of humankind's suffering—however, I am not sure that Marx really grappled with the problem of the religious perspective as an epistemological question. Orthodox Marxism, if anything, has been even far less insightful on this issue: religion would never even get on the agenda as an epistemological issue, since, as the saying goes, Everything you know is wrong. That is, everything the religious person "knows," at least from a religious perspective, is wrong.

Difficult, vexing problem—I wish more Marxists would see it this way. In the case that a scientific perspective is committed to a correspondence epistemology, one could see how the religious perspective would be a false perspective altogether. From the standpoint of correspondence, many people who hold a religious perspective do in fact believe in things that simply are not real, and of course this is a problem. The species on our planet evolved biologically, there is no scientific basis for the "theory" of intelligent design. Neither will it do to make some sort of coherence of science and religion the basis for asserting claims that go against the best science that we have at any given time. Again, to put it in a formula, even if scientific truth is not all truth, and even if scientific truths are to be understood on a fallibilistic model, there is no negating at least big parts of science without negating truth in general. Allow me to add (in a way that is too quick and that also has the worrisome aspect of sounding as if I really know what I am talking about, when, to be sure, these issues demand a good deal more exploration, in the philosophy of science and elsewhere) that I do not think that scientific investigation is necessarily committed to a correspondence epistemology. I base this claim on the twin presuppositions that (1) correspondence theory does not really work, and (2) scientific investigation does work. However, the real issue that concerns me is the relationship between what can be discovered by scientific investigation, on the one side, and questions that at least have some dimension that does not appear to be a matter of scientific investigation, on the other.

In this latter category are the questions of ethics and the future. Marx thought that he could deal with these issues in a purely scientific way, but he was wrong. Marx thought that a scientific, materialist political economy would either generate a kind of ethics, but as an epiphenomenon, or demonstrate the basic unreality of the field. Marx thought that the logic of the modes of production, properly studied, would yield a pathway to a communist future, at least in broad outline (an algorithm, if you will). Marx was not completely wrong about these matters; indeed, he contributed much that was right. But he missed some crucial truths, because these are not exactly or entirely scientific truths and, therefore, he was in a crucial way wrong about ethics and wrong about the future.

Community

If one wants to study the question of community, and to be more empirical and experiential about the question, instead of being simply conceptual (as post-Rawlsian analytic political philosophers tend to be on what is
called in those circles the liberalism/communitarianism debate), then one
will come up against the fact that humanity's hitherto existing experience
with community (for better or worse, and admittedly often enough for
the worse) is bound up with religion—whatever that is. (Engels once
wrote in a letter that, if one wanted a sense of what the future communist
society would be like, it would be like the Shaker community in America,
"but without the religion." But *what is* "the religion"? One place to start
on this question would be to ask what the Shaker *community* could possibly have been without the religion.) Similarly, if one wants to study
humanity's hitherto existing experience with the idea that ethics and the
possibility of a (just to be all fuzzy about it) good future for humankind
are somehow fundamentally connected, then again one will come up
against the fact that humanity's experience with this connection is bound
up with religion. At least up to a point, indeed up until relatively recent
times, this connection was made without considering a role for scientific
investigation. Or, if something of science was included, it was from a heavily teleological perspective where science plays the role of providing evidence for the overarching design. There is a sense in which Marx is the
outcome of this process, one crucial juncture of which was Augustine's
modifications of Aristotle's four causes (another big topic for another
day!), but then the outcome was such that science replaced the two poles
of the original connection: what we ought to do now and humanity's
hope for an ethical community in the future. How all of these things
could be integrated into a coherent picture, or a picture that is as coherent as we can make it, but where the two "original poles" remain substantial and not merely epiphenomenal might very well be more a matter
of a kind of religious perspective and even of what Kant called the "New
Church." David Ray Griffin has some interesting proposals for a coherent
vision, in his books *The Two Great Truths* and *Religion without
Supernaturalism*, while James L. Marsh and Anne Fairchild Pomeroy pursue the connections between process theology and Marxism in *Process,
Praxis, and Transcendence* and *Marx and Whitehead*, respectively. (I think
that Joseph Smith and Brigham Young also had some interesting ideas
about community now and in the future, and they at least attempted to
cast these ideas in a materialist way.) The vexing aspects of this epistemological problem—how to hold these different truths together—should not
be ignored or dismissed.

Crushing Vexation

While the vexation should not sanction supernaturalism or any other kind of view that holds anything other than that humanity will have to liberate itself, neither should this vexation be dealt with by a crushing scientistic reductivism. I see this reductivism at work in formulations, which would suit most Marxists, such as the one offered by Pinker: "for morality we don't need the white-coated technician in the sky, all we need is the commonsense recognition of a pair of simple ideas." The recognition of the historical connection between religion and ethics is not accompanied by an appreciation for why this connection existed in the first place.

Early Christianity

In this respect, two pathways out of Early Christianity are instructive, plotted roughly in terms of orthodoxy and orthopraxy. (In actual practice, the difference in the paths is not always so great.) Regarding orthodoxy, a more nuanced, materialist reading of the reason why the connection between ethics and religion has been longstanding would reveal that there was a turning point in the early movement, where, through the machinations of power and the sense that the movement could only go so far in achieving the ethical community on this earth, the ethical-political teachings of Jesus were displaced into the nether-realm, subordinating and largely betraying these teachings in the name of an other-wordly, supernatural scheme. However, there has always been an underground and/or subordinate orthopraxy, even sometimes from within orthodoxy, that emphasizes what might be called the material side of taking up the cross. This orthopraxy has far more to do with the church, which from the early days was called the "body of Christ," as the messianic embodiment that continues the messianic work. This orthopraxy is itself an expression of what might be called a "root impulse" of Judaism. This is not merely a secularization to read the story this way. After all, the heart of Christianity is a human intervention into the order of the day, into time. The formation of the messianic embodiment—which gets into the problem of institutions and all of the Sartrean, *Critique of Dialectical Reason* problematics of the group-in-fusion, practico-inert, and so on—is aimed toward the New Earth, a time and place of the ethical community. In other words, there is a fundamental connection between the universalism of our ethics now, which can be broadened as our ethical-political stance and praxis, and the future—the hoped-for universal ethical community. This is what Kant captures in the relationship between the first and second formulations of the categorical imperative and the third formulation, even if there is a sense in which the logic of the relationship is obscure.

There is a sense in which the logic will remain obscure, but we can actually specify somewhat precisely why this is the case, and this specification will tell us something not only about the relationship between (the philosophies of) Kant and Marx, but also about how we have to understand our ethical-political praxis. To continue with the "Christian" scenario, it is still possible—despite everything—that humanity might transform this world into the global community of mutual flourishing. This possibility, and the fact that we are still here now to think about it, act upon it, and hope for it, is *grace*. But we have work to do, a great deal of work, perhaps even an *impossible* work and an infinite work. The obscurity of the logic is found in this is/ought gap, especially in the case where the "ought" requires of humanity the infinite and the impossible. *Some* of the logic is filled out by either Marx's scientific discoveries regarding the nature of capitalism or at least by his approach to problems in political economy and social theory. This approach helps us to understand not only what is, but also what is possible. This sort of methodology also helps us to understand strategically where our efforts might be best applied. (We should recall the discussion in part 3, section 3, about the contradictions of strategic thinking, the pull toward expediency and the tendency to set aside the ethical issues involved in violence.) However, there still remains an obscure part of the logic, and here again William James's argument about optimism and pessimism as "definitions of the world" is helpful. To use Rousseau's lovely expression, "The Golden Age is in us." The potential to make this world a "Kingdom of God" is in us, and so is the potential to make this world a wretched hell and to unmake the earth altogether. (This last reference is to the idea of the "unmaker" in Orson Scott Card's series, *The Tales of Alvin Maker*.) We humans are constituted by the ability to respond, but, in Derrida's formulation, there is still both the decision and the work of "responsibility to responsibility" that remains. (To my knowledge, this theme first appeared in Derrida's *The Other Heading*.) Lastly, to bring this point to a head, neither commitment, nor the future, nor communism is what they are without at least a measure of underdetermination. As overdetermined, all of these things are not what they are.

"Only an Ideal"

It is in respect of this point, too, that the question "What ought we to do?" takes precedence over "What may we hope?" If there is an equality or if the order is reversed, then the result is a kind of empty, formalistic utopianism. And yet, without hope, or too great a "scarcity of hope" (to borrow an expression from Martin Beck Matustik), the fiery spirit of the ethical is deprived of oxygen. This is where it was wrong of Kant to say that the ethical community is "certainly only an ideal." This is not only a matter of the material possibility of such a community, but also, crucially, a question of what role this ideal plays in our present attempts to take up our responsibility to responsibility, or to form an optimistic defintion of the world. The latter plays a crucial role in the former: without this ideal, we can be sure that the ethical community is deprived of any chance of realization.

Surely calling the ethical community "certainly only an ideal" is not very Kantian of Professor Immanuel Kant, unless perhaps I am feeling too much the sting of the "only." The notion of the "regulative ideal" plays a central epistemological role for Kant. What James shows in his argument about optimism and pessimism is perhaps no more than what Marx was after with his well-known formulations about the ways in which, under the right circumstances, theory can grip the masses, and theory can become a material force. The difference between James and Marx is that perhaps the latter thought the theory-materiality connection runs a little more smoothly, and is hooked up a bit more tightly, than it in fact is. Certainly the matter becomes greatly more complicated at the point where capitalism goes into ideological overdrive to make war on the idea of a different future. If we have to fight not only for the different future, but also to keep the idea of such a future alive, where this latter fight is indeed an ineliminable and irreducible part of the former struggle, then we must recognize the materiality of the regulative ideal. There is the danger of going overboard with this, into not only philosophical idealism, but also the formalistic utopianism that would empty out our present responsibilities. Strategically, I do not see this as a great danger today, in the face of the blithe and sometimes brutal anti-utopianism of postmodern capitalism. Instead I see a greater danger in the kind of "political realism" that completely eschews the visionary, the sense of a different future. Such "realism" is hopeless.

As a footnote to the discussion of the regulative ideal, I would like to make a proposal concerning Daniel Dennett's terminology of "cranes" and "skyhooks." In his view, there are only cranes, and anything that appears to be a skyhook is simply a crane with a base that is presently unseen. My proposal does not really disagree with this typology; it merely makes a little modification within Dennett's scheme. Perhaps there is something else out there, something more akin to a helicopter. From an onto-epistemological point of view, I appreciated the scene in the first *Superman* movie, where Lois Lane falls off of the Daily Planet skyscraper and Superman catches her about half-way down the building. Superman says something along the lines of, "Don't worry, Lois, I've got you." Lois responds, "You've got me? Who's got *you*?!" Well, the material basis for Superman's being able to catch Lois in mid-air is that he comes from the planet Krypton, and under a yellow sun he has great powers, including flight and super strength. Or, if you prefer, we could instead consider one of the advertising slogans for the film, "You'll believe a man can fly." In other words, the material basis for Christopher Reeve *seemingly* to be able to catch Margot Kidder in mid-air is cinematic special effects: smoke and mirrors and wires and harnesses. Do we say that the wires and harnesses are the "crane," while the smoke and mirrors are more like what we find with "religion"? To shift narratives, is nothing left after Toto pulls back the curtain? The wizard, after all, was all about hopes and dreams and the desire to find a place in this world. If his form of inspiration was not supernatural after all, if it was indeed entirely a human "construct," is this the end of the matter, or is there a kind of enchantment that remains or is even reinvented on the other side of secularism, science, and disenchantment? I will repeat something that I said in part 1: What the displacement of philosophy by political economy obscures is that the passage beyond this pure secularization of society requires the passage to a postsecular understanding of the world, and ultimately a postsecular society. Some of what appear to be skyhooks are actually cranes; I propose that some other things that appear to be skyhooks are more like helicopters. We humans put them up there, though it may be obscure to many of us how the helicopters made their way into the sky, or many of us may have forgotten that it was humans who put them up there, but once the helicopters are up there, they can play the role of gaining our attention, drawing us out, drawing us forward. Regulative ideals are a human creation, as is an argument such as Anselm's ontological argument for the existence of God—the most pure argument in the history of philosophy—and of course we should recognize such examples of reason as existing within the sphere of materiality and the things that human brains concoct. It is in the sphere of materiality that we hope for and dream about a transformed world, a global community of mutual flourishing. We make a project of this, and this ethical community is the most significant of human projects, it is the project that informs every other human project. And yet it is also "out there," like a helicopter or Superman, with seemingly nothing (or not enough) to hold it up; perhaps unlike a helicopter or Superman, this future requires our belief and commitment and committed action (praxis) to hold it up, to even give it a ghost of a chance of existing.

Zoology of Religion and Sacred Botany

In light of the foregoing, consider how Dennett brings his inquiry in *Darwin's Dangerous Idea* to a close:

What, then, of all the glories of our religious traditions? They should certainly be preserved, as should the languages, the art, the costumes, the rituals, the monuments. Zoos are now more and more being seen as second-class havens for endangered species, but at least they are havens, and what they preserve is irreplaceable. The same is true of complex memes and their phenotypic expressions.

. . . What may happen, one may well wonder, if religion is preserved in cultural zoos, in libraries, in concerts and demonstrations? It is happening: the tourists flock to watch Native American tribal dances, and for the onlookers it is folklore, a religious ceremony, certainly to be treated with respect, but also an example of a meme complex on the verge of extinction, at least in its strong, ambulatory phase; it has become an invalid, barely kept alive by its custodians. Does Darwin's dangerous idea give us anything in exchange for the ideas it calls into question?

In chapter 3 ["Universal Acid"], I quoted the physicist Paul Davies proclaiming that the reflective power of human minds can be no "trivial detail, no minor by-product of mindless purposeless forces," and suggested that being a by-product of mindless purposeless forces was no disqualification for importance. And I have argued that Darwin has shown us how, in fact, *everything* of importance is just such a product. Spinoza called his highest being God or Nature (*Deus sive Natura*), expressing a sort of pantheism. There have been many varieties of pantheism, but they usually lack a convincing *explanation* about just how God is distributed in the whole of nature. As we saw in chapter 7, Darwin offers us one: it is in the distribution of Design throughout nature, creating, in the Tree of Life, an utterly unique and irreplaceable creation, an actual pattern in the immeasurable reaches of Design Space that could never be exactly duplicated in its many details. What is design work? It is that wonderful wedding of chance and necessity, happening in a trillion places at once, at a trillion different levels. And what miracle caused it? None. It just happened to happen, in the fullness of time. You could even say, in a way, that the Tree of Life created itself. Not in a miraculous, instantaneous whoosh, but slowly, slowly, over billions of years.

Is this Tree of Life a God one could worship? Pray to? Fear? Probably not. But it *did* make the ivy twine and the sky so blue, so perhaps the song I love [the traditional song, "Tell Me Why"] tells a truth after all. The Tree of Life is neither perfect nor infinite in space or time, but it is actual, and if it is not Anselm's "Being greater than which nothing can be conceived," it is surely a being that is greater than anything any of us will ever conceive of in detail worthy of its detail. Is something sacred? Yes, say I with Nietzsche. I could not pray to it, but I can stand in affirmation of its magnificence. This world is sacred. (519–20)

Does the path Dennett travels in this remarkable passage amount to a kind of postsecular perspective? I would say so, even if I still do not see where Dennett, at least in *Darwin's Dangerous Idea*, appreciates the religious insight into the connection between the ethical ought and hope for the ethical community (and, in the present discussion, I am largely using

Dennett and Pinker as exemplary of the scientific perspective on this issue). If I cannot exactly pray to the Tree of Life, can I at least feel a sense of grace in the possibilities that it offers to me and my species and my fellow creatures? Can I be *thankful* to this Tree of Life? Can I be thankful to the extent that, again to cite Heidegger, there is fundamental thankfulness to all of my thinking, or even to *all* "true" thinking? ("Denken ist Danken.") Is this affirmation of the magnificence of this Tree, and the possibility that it offers for humanity to find itself and to make itself at home in this world in a nonantagonistic way, a kind of religious perspective? Can—and should—this perspective re-envelope our attempts, our necessary and righteous scientific attempts, to conceive of the details of the Tree of Life in a way worthy of its detail?

Philosophy of History and the Trace of Religion

Did Marx realize, perhaps reflecting on his earlier, more Hegelian phase, that a theoretical orientation that takes philosophy of history as its starting place or basis will always have a religious side, or at least retain a trace of the religious perspective? (In light of what Dennett says about pantheism and Spinoza, see Daniel Brudney, *Marx's Attempt to Leave Philosophy*, 58–71, on Feuerbach's critique of Christianity as also a critique of philosophy itself.) Did Marx then discover, starting with *The German Ideology* (the place of the famous "epistemological break," from the standpoint of "scientific socialism"), the "happy" fact (or strange coincidence) that everything previously found in scenarios of redemptive history (associated until this point with the Western monotheistic religions) can all be done instead with a scientific inquiry into modes of production and reactive mechanisms? Does this discovery then tell us that there is no need either for values or a vision of the future—or at least that these elements of the scenario are epiphenomenal?

Despite the achievements of socialism under this reactive, "scientific" mold—real achievements that should not be buried under what were also the real shortcomings and failures but also the real attacks and slanders— we can also see real limitations that go directly to this purely "scientific" scenario, and we can also see the way in which the languages of value and vision are continually smuggled in, though without ever being given their due. This smuggling operation is philosophically illicit and incoherent. It is also absolutely necessary, because there is no transformation of the world without values and vision. The upshot is *not* that values and vision should be artificially attached in a purely instrumental way to a Marxist science. The result of such an operation, repeated many times in revolutionary (or ostensibly revolutionary) movements, is that values and vision become themselves instrumentalized, treated as mere means, and this is a fundamental betrayal of what they really are. Significantly, the redemptive transformation of the world is betrayed in the process.

Instead, the upshot is that a new synthesis is needed in Marxist theory and practice, and this synthesis requires "biting the bullet" in terms of recognizing the substantiality of the languages of right and wrong, good and evil, and the future. This does not mean that we should not at the same time maintain a healthy skepticism and be on guard for mere moralism, merely utopian scenarios of the future (though here I see little danger in dreaming fiercely and wildly, especially in the realm of art), and leaps to the supernatural. Following Dennett, it is clear that there is no shortage of magnificence in this world to inspire our awe, appreciation, and affirmation. Significantly, this magnificence requires science for its appreciation, and the supernaturalist creation "science" types who would cancel this magnificence—and cancel humanity along with it—in the name of some loathesome exaltation of a nonsensical "supreme being" can . . . well, I was going to say they can go to hell directly, but I do not want to replicate their ugliness, even if dialectically. This world, in all its contingency and mind-boggling complexity (that real scientists have helped us to appreciate), has given our species a chance to make something of itself, and to make a beautiful world out of this presently-ugly one. It is a chance, not a guarantee. The recent machinations of postmodern capitalism are largely oriented toward removing even this sense of a chance. Biting the bullet means accepting that a commitment to a redemptive philosophy of history, though one under the heading of contingency rather than necessity, allows us to reach a stage where humanity can thematize ethical questions and ethical-political universalism as substantial. This philosophy of history allows the possibility for the achievement of the ethical (and even aesthetic) community. This much is integral to what remains of the philosophy of history in Marx: humanity has to come to a certain point to be able to see more of what is possible, even while what is seen as possible is also dependent upon having come to a particular point. However, biting the bullet here also means that there is an irreducibly religious dimension, as a matter of epistemology, to the commitment to history as redemptive. It is *not* simply a "happy fact" or "strange coincidence" that Marx's scientific scenario parallels the redemptive scenarios of Judaism and Christianity in important respects.

Embracing a Religious Perspective?

Therefore, should we not *embrace* this "religion"? Should we not even go to the point of looking for the ways in which existing religious institutions can contribute to the "New Church"?

There is an important and complex dialectic unfolding in the world today, centered around the question of religion. This dialectic needs to be grappled with, in a way that goes beyond a strategic consideration of the "positive role" that some religious people can play or are playing. It would be tempting to think of this dialectic in terms of reactionary religious people who are attempting to restore a presecular understanding, and progressive religious people who aim (whether they know it or not) for a postsecular understanding. There can be some truth to this, even if there is no more basis for restoring a presecular understanding than there is for restoring a feudal mode of production. Marx continues to help us with a question such as this, in texts such as *The Eighteenth Brumaire of Louis Bonaparte*, which has been taken as a seminal work for understanding the rise of fascism in the twentieth century. Reactionary leaders who are really more political than religious, such as Pat Robertson and Jerry Falwell, can use the language of presecular religion to draw together a certain social base for aggressive action by the imperialist bourgeoisie. It remains to be seen, however, whether they can pull off the trick of breaking a big part of science without breaking all of it. It also remains to be seen whether the program of patriarchal reentrenchment can truly succeed in chaining women once again to "*Kinder, Kuche, Kirche*" ("children, cooking, church," a Nazi slogan on the place of women in society). Certainly this form of "religion" is making some serious headway; the wreckage that has been caused in the public school system, for instance, will not be easily reversed or repaired. This "religion" however, is so much the mirror of the present situation of U.S. imperialism, that it is also important to see the way that it is shaped by not only a certain urgency, but even a certain desperation. This does not mean that the agendas and ploys of this "religion" will not succeed, unfortunately. But there is a real sense in which reactionary religion represents a kind of spasmodic "last gasp" of a belief-system that is increasingly hard to sustain.

Perhaps a concentrated example of this quality was the sad case of Terri Schiavo, a woman who had been brain dead since soon after she fell into a degenerative coma in 1990. (Indeed, parts of her brain became liquified, so she was beyond brain dead.) A struggle was waged by right-wing, essentially fascistic, religious and political forces to keep the body of Ms. Schiavo hooked up to a feeding tube. When Senator Tom DeLay visited Ms. Schiavo in 2005, after she had already been brain dead for fifteen years, he reported that he had found her "lucid." (For these and many other details see *Revolutionary Worker* newspaper, "Worlds in Collision: The Storm Over Terry Schiavo and the Raving Demands of the Christian Right.") DeLay has since resigned from the senate, as it has become quite apparent that at least one side of him is nothing more than a common criminal and thug, and not even an "honest criminal." For this sort of thing, the United States is a laughing stock to the rest of the world, but also a horrible fright and danger. There are relatively harmless nuts out there, and then there are people who have insane ideas and weapons of world destruction. The religious glue that holds this insane vision of U.S. global hegemony together for some people sits alongside of another social base, a necessary one for this social formation, of young people who join the military in search of "pussy and cigarettes" (as it was put it to me by one fellow who hoped to join the National Guard, though it turned out that he was unable to meet the minimal literacy requirement), or a "cool-looking uniform" (as it was put to me by a fellow who hoped to join the Marines, who finally got in after taking the literacy test a third time with a barely passing score). This social base includes an army that pours what the soldiers jokingly call "cocktail number four" on political prisoners at Guantanamo, a concoction made of semen, blood, urine, and excrement. Lawyers argue that Lindy England, one of the low-ranked torturers at Abu Ghraib, should not be convicted, because she is not capable of understanding complex verbal instructions. At a Fourth of July (2006) church service at Wichita mega-church Emmanuel Baptist, Pastor Terry Fox (one of the contemporary breed of Christian hate-mongers) said in his closing prayer that he and his congregation are thankful for the soldiers who are fighting in Iraq, to "defend our freedom." Referring to the 2500 *American* military personnel who had died in Iraq to that point in time, Fox said that many of them were Christians, and he and his congregation look forward to thanking them personally when they get to heaven. What about the many who were *not* Christian, Pastor Fox (which would be a large number according to your narrow definition of "Christian")? Are you not thankful to them, or will you go to hell to thank them? (Most of his sermon to that point was an attack on gay people and those who believe that gay people ought to have basic civil rights.) Church groups offered to send reading materials to soldiers in Iraq; a large number of the requests that came in were for *Hustler* and other pornographic magazines. And so it all comes together. How can anyone want to have anything to do with religion when the side of it making the most noise in contemporary American society is the side that is plainly and straightforwardly rendering people mean and stupid? Or does this kind of religion instead *attract* people who are already mean and stupid?

Perhaps the most important angle on religion is the fact that so much of it, in basically every tradition, is taken up with expressing a hardened and deep and theologized patriarchy. Yes, there are important countercurrents in some traditions (though, significantly, not all); while these countercurrents can be bases for empowerment and for reconsideration and rethinking of the liberatory potential of these traditions, they should not make us blind to what have been the main currents. While the Western monotheistic traditions certainly deserve much criticism and scorn on this issue, "Eastern" traditions should not be given a complete pass on this question.

Indeed, what is disturbing is the way that religion on the other side of the dialectic, or Christianity specifically, at any rate, is so hung up on being "nice" and tolerant, that it keeps progressive religious people from taking things as far as they ought to go. Theoretically, what is needed is more work on the underpinnings of the postsecular perspective, in part to demonstrate that progressive and radical religious people and seemingly nonreligious, "secular" progressives and revolutionaries share some understanding in terms of redemption and the transformation of this world and a possible future of ethical community. (As mentioned in part 3, of crucial importance here is the work of John Milbank and others in the Radical Orthodoxy movement who are making crucial contributions to the idea of postsecular thought.) One thing that demonstrates this shared perspective is that, in light of this perspective it is clear that fascistic fundamentalists do not really have a religious or nonsecular viewpoint after all. They worship U.S. imperialism, which requires a theological justification because it cannot be legitimated in any other way. The only future in their sights is the future of U.S. imperialism, which is no future for the greater part of humanity, and perhaps for all of humanity.

To be sure, it is especially difficult to press the case for a dialectic of religious perspectives in the time of this writing, a time when our postmodern capitalist society is manifesting at least some fascistic elements, because the dialectic is resulting in social polarization—which is a good thing, but that also means that the fascistic fundamentalist is not just some wacked-out Holocaust-denying professor of engineering you read about in the *Chronicle of Higher Education*, but quite likely some of your neighbors or the person you depend on to fix your bike. That is not a bad thing, either, in the sense that social transformation toward something better involves a period when society is ever-more intensely divided against itself; but this is not an easy thing.

Anomalous Materialism

There is a connection made in certain religious traditions, and in Kant's philosophy, between ethical thinking in the present (whatever present one finds oneself in) and a possible ethical community of the future. To make this connection is not to go "against science," and the possibility of the ethical community may be helped by science in a number of ways, but the connection itself does not depend on science, or at least not completely or entirely, at any rate. Many progressives, radicals, and revolutionaries (and many Marxists, obviously) would prefer not to deal with this issue, even while perhaps hoping to take unto themselves some element of the "spiritual" that is not "religious." This is completely understandable; one reason that I said some harshly negative things about one part of religion in the contemporary world (the part that is more akin to Pinker's view of religion) is that it is perfectly understandable why anyone who cares about making a better world would not want to get within a million miles of that religion stuff. I disagree with this perspective on a number of levels, but I understand it. However, I do not see any way around the epistemological problem, even if I also think that it does not lead us in the direction of the supernatural. To wax Davidsonian, this problem does not require that we reject materialism, but that we have an anomaly.

In discussing the religious perspective (which I am confining to this one point about ethics and the future), I have focused on Christianity. Certainly it was against the background of Christianity that Kant framed the ethics/future community connection. Christianity, of course, is a variegated set of institutions and discourses; it does not speak with a single voice any more than does its bible. The same can be said for other religious traditions, too, and the idea that might help us to sort them all out is again this sense of a connection between the possibility of ethics and the possibility of an ethical community.

In making such an investigation, we will be aided by Rawls's notions of reflective equilibrium and overlapping consensus, which are meant to be of Kantian inspiration, even if Rawls's sense of the "well-ordered society" is "neither a community nor an association" (these are all terms and expressions from the "later" Rawls, from *Political Liberalism*).

Kant, Marx, and the Future

Significantly, Allen Wood concludes his valuable introductory book, *Kant*, on the connection between religion and politics, demonstrating that Kant was concerned with this question to the end of his life.

> . . . Kant's philosophy of religion was grounded on the historical hope that there would be a convergence between religion and enlightened reason. All our reservations about it must be attributed to the sad fact that what he hoped for has simply failed to come to pass. But Kant's hopes for religion, however much they may have been disappointed, must be seen instead as the form taken for him by a hope that many of us still share—the hope for the gradual progress of the human species in history toward a realm of ends in which the divisions between people will be overcome and humanity will be united in a cosmopolitan moral community which respects the rights of everyone and unites the happiness of each with the happiness of all as a shared end of human striving. This

was the hope with which Kant ended his lectures on anthropology, the last major work published under his own name, and in this sense it may be called literally Kant's last word about the human condition. "In working against the [evil] propensity in [human nature] . . . our will is in general good, but the accomplishment of what we will is made more difficult by the fact that the attainment of the end can be expected not through the free agreement of *individuals*, but through the progressive organization of citizens of the earth into and toward the species as a system that is cosmopolitically combined." (186)

Fellow philosopher Patricia Huntington once used the charming expression, "a world for people"—which I immediately wrote down. I would say that our social future ought to be a world for people and for our fellow mortal creatures as well.

Wood, in his characterization, is perhaps bending Kant a little toward Marx. And certainly it is the case that we cannot make any ethical-political universalist sense of "the progressive organization of citizens of the earth" (which however remains a lovely expression) without confronting the ways that capitalism has so disenfranchised the great majority of these very "citizens," and murdered many of them outright. And yet we also cannot make sense of why we need to transcend capitalism and work in the direction of the "species as a system that is cosmopolitically combined" without this vision of the ethical community. So Marx can stand to bend a bit as well.

Going beyond but not negating his scientific contributions and methodology, could we consider Marx as more on the order of a prophet, as having a vision that is ultimately "religious," a vision called communism? By "prophet" I do not mean a predictor of the future, but instead as someone who attempts to listen to the call of the future, and to make clear to people that the future is indeed calling, and to try to show, in various ways—in Marx's case these would be ways that aim to be scientific and systematic—how this future is possible and how we might get there. Can Marx bend this way without breaking? Imagine Kant and Marx as prophets and, yes, philosophers and scientists also, in the New Church, the new "religion" of ongoingness, the future, and mutual flourishment. Surely any real revolutionary expresses this spirit—call it what you will. But what would be different about the revolution (and the revolutionary) if this spirit were embraced and affirmed?

Perhaps a real commitment to the ethical does not require this further elaboration. I simply put forth these last thoughts as a set of hypotheses that require investigation. It would be enough if my proposal for an Ethical Marxism is grappled with—a Marxism that recognizes that there are real ethical questions and that, indeed, the questions that ought to be most central to it are, at their core, ethical questions.

Bibliography

MER = *Marx-Engels Reader*, 2nd ed. Edited by Robert Tucker. New York: Norton, 1978.

Adams, Carol J. *The Sexual Politics of Meat: A Feminist-Vegetarian Critical Theory*. New York: Continuum, 1991.

Adorno, Theodor. *Aesthetic Theory*. Translated by C. Lenhardt. London: Routledge, 1984.

Alperovitz, Gar. *The Decision to Use the Atomic Bomb*. New York: Alfred A. Knopf, 1995.

Althusser, Louis. *Machiavelli and Us*. Translated by Gregory Benford. London: Verso, 1999.

———. "The Only Materialist Tradition." In *The New Spinoza*, edited by Warren Montag and Ted Stolz. Minneapolis: University of Minnesota Press, 1998.

Ameriks, Karl. "A Commonsense Kant?" *Proceedings and Addresses of The American Philosophical Association* 79, no. 2 (November 2005): 19–45.

Anscombe, G. E. M. "Modern Moral Philosophy." *Philosophy* 33, no. 124 (January 1958): 1–19.

Arendt, Hannah. *On Violence*. New York: Harcourt Brace & Company, 1970.

Aristotle. *The Politics*. Translated by Carnes Lord. Chicago: University of Chicago Press, 1984.

Aronson, Ronald. *After Marxism*. New York: Guilford Books, 1995.

Auge, Marc. *Non-Places: Introduction to an Anthropology of Supermodernity*. Translated by John Howe. London: Verso, 1995.

Avakian, Bob. "The Basis, the Goals, and the Methods of the Communist Revolution." *Revolution* [newspaper], Mar. 5–Apr. 16, 2006; http://www.revcom.us/avakian/ basis-goals-methods/index.html.

———. *Conquer the World?* Chicago: RCP Publications, 1981.

———. "Dictatorship and Democracy, and the Socialist Transition to Communism." *Revolution* [newspaper], Aug. 22 – Dec. 12, 2004; http://www.revcom.us/bob_avakian/new_speech/avakian_democracy_dictatorship_speech.htm.

———. "The End of a Stage—The Beginning of a New Stage." *Revolution* [magazine], Fall 1990.

———. *For a Harvest of Dragons*. Chicago: RCP Publications, 1983.

———. *From Ike to Mao and Beyond: My Journey from Mainstream America to Revolutionary Communist*. Chicago: Insight Press, 2005.

———. "A Leap of Faith and a Leap to Rational Knowledge: Two Very Different Kinds of Leaps, Two Radically Different Worldviews and Methods." *Revolution* [newspaper], Jul. 31, 2005; http://www.revcom.us/a/010/avakian-leap-faith-leap-rational.htm.

———. 'The New Situation and the Great Challenges. *Revolution* [newspaper], no. 36, Feb. 26, 2006; http://www.revcom.us/a/036/avakian-new-situation-great-challenges.htm.

———. *Observations on Art and Culture, Science and Philosophy*. Chicago: Insight Press, 2005.

———. "On Truth: On Knowing and Changing the World—A Discussion with Comrades on Epistemology." *Revolutionary Worker* [newspaper], no. 1262, Dec. 19, 2004; http://www.revcom.us/a/1262/avakian-epistemology.htm.

———. *Preaching from a Pulpit of Bones*. New York: Banner Press, 1999.

———. "A Radically New Kind of State, A Radically Different and Far Greater Vision of Freedom." *Revolution* [newspaper], Mar. 8, 2006; http://rwor.org/bob_avakian/view/index.htm.

Avakian, Bob, and Bill Martin. *Marxism and the Call of the Future: Conversations on Ethics, History, and Politics*. Chicago: Open Court, 2005.

Badiou, Alain. *Being and Event*. Translated by Oliver Feltham. London: Continuum, 2005.

———. *Briefings on Existence*. Translated by Norman Madarasz. Albany, NY: State University of New York Press, 2006.

———. *Ethics: An Essay on the Understanding of Evil*. Translated by Peter Hallward. London: Verso, 2001.

———. *Logics of Worlds*. Translated by Alberto Toscano. London: Continuum, 2008.

Barnes, Hazel E. "Sartre as Materialist." In *The Philosophy of Jean-Paul Sartre*. Edited by Paul Arthur Schilpp. Library of Living Philosophers, vol. 16. La Salle, IL: Open Court, 1981.

Benford, Gregory. *Cosm*. New York: Avon, 1999.

———. *Eater*. New York: Avon, 2001.

———. *The Sunborn*. New York: Warner Books, 2005.

Berry, Wendell. *Another Turn of the Crank*. New York: Counterpoint Press, 1996.

———. "A Defense of the Family Farm." In Berry, *Home Economics*.

———. "Farming and the Global Economy." In Berry, *Another Turn of the Crank*.

———. "Feminism, the Body, and the Machine." In Berry, *What Are People For?*

———. *Home Economics*. San Francisco: North Point Press, 1987.

———. "Private Property and the Common Wealth." In Berry, *Another Turn of the Crank*.

———. "The Problem of Tobacco." In Berry, *Sex, Economy, Freedom & Community*.

———. "Property, Patriotism, and National Defense." In Berry, *Home Economics*.

————. *What Are People For?* San Francisco: North Point Press, 1990.

————. *Sex, Economy, Freedom & Community.* New York: Pantheon, 1992.

————. *The Unsettling of America: Culture and Agriculture.* 3rd ed. (1st ed. 1977.) San Francisco: Sierra Club Books, 1996.

————. "Why I Am Not Going to Buy a Computer." In Berry, *What Are People For?*

Birmingham, Peg. *Hannah Arendt and Human Rights: The Predicament of Common Responsibility.* Bloomington: Indiana University Press, 2006.

Bloom, Harold. *The American Religion.* New York: Simon and Schuster, 1992.

Bookchin, Murray. *The Limits of the City.* Montreal: Black Rose Books, 1986.

————. *Urbanization without Cities: The Rise and Decline of Citizenship.* Montreal: Black Rose Books, 1992.

Boyd, Gregory A. *God of the Possible: A Biblical Introduction to the Open View of God.* Grand Rapids, MI: Baker Book House, 2000.

Brown, Colin. "Firebombing Fallujah: Bush Officials Lied to Britain about U.S. Use of Napalm in Iraq." *London Independent*; republished at the *Counterpunch* website [www.counterpunch.org], Jun. 17, 2005.

Brudney, Daniel. *Marx's Attempt to Leave Philosophy.* Cambridge, MA: Harvard University Press, 1998.

Card, Orson Scott. *Pastwatch: The Redemption of Christopher Columbus.* New York: Tor, 1996.

Carnap, Rudolf. "The Elimination of Metaphysics through Logical Analysis of Language." Translated by Max Black. In *Logical Positivism*, edited by A. J. Ayer. New York: Free Press, 1959.

Castells, Manuel. *The Urban Question: A Marxist Approach.* Translated by Alan Sheridan. Cambridge, MA.: MIT Press, 1980.

Chalier, Catherine. *What Ought I to Do? Morality in Kant and Levinas.* Translated by Jane Marie Todd. Ithaca, NY: Cornell University Press, 2002.

Chang, Jung and Jon Halliday. *Mao: The Unknown Story.* New York: Anchor Books, 2006.

Coe, Sue. *Dead Meat.* New York: Four Walls Eight Windows, 1995.

Cording, Robert. *Against Consolation.* Fort Lee, NJ: CavanKerry Press, 2002.

Cornell, Drucilla. *The Philosophy of the Limit.* London: Routledge, 1992.

Cotkin, George. *William James, Public Philosopher.* Urbana-Champaign: University of Illinois Press, 1994.

Cox, Stan. "Kreationism in Kansas." *Counterpunch*, July 26, 2005, www.counterpunch.org; http://www.counterpunch.org/cox07252005.html.

Cuppit, Don. *Emptiness and Brightness.* Santa Rosa, CA.: Polebridge Press, 2001.

————. *Philosophy's Own Religion.* London: SCM Press, 2000.

————. *The Way to Happiness.* Santa Rosa, CA.: Polebridge Press, 2005.

Davidson, Donald. "Belief and the Basis of Meaning." In Davidson, *Inquiries into Truth and Interpretation.*

————. *Essays on Actions and Events.* Oxford: Oxford University Press, 1980.

————. *Inquiries into Truth and Interpretation.* Oxford: Oxford University Press, 1984.

————. "On the Very Idea of a Conceptual Scheme." In Davidson, *Inquiries into Truth and Interpretation.*

———. "Rational Animals." In Ernest LePore and Brian McLaughlin, eds., *Actions and Events*. Oxford: Blackwell, 1985.

———. "Thought and Talk." In Davidson, *Inquiries into Truth and Interpretation*.

Davis, Jim, Thomas Hirschl, and Michael Stack, eds. *Cutting Edge: Technology, Information, Capitalism, and Social Revolution*. London: Verso Press, 1997.

De George, Richard T. *Business Ethics*. 3rd ed. New York: Macmillan, 1990.

Dennett. *Darwin's Dangerous Idea*. New York: Simon and Schuster, 1995.

Derrida, Jacques. "The Ends of Man." In Jacques Derrida, *Margins of Philosophy*. Translated by Alan Bass. Chicago: University of Chicago Press, 1985.

———. *The Gift of Death*. Translated by David Wills. Chicago: University of Chicago Press, 1995.

———. "No Apocalypse, Not Now (full speed ahead, seven missiles, seven missives)." Translated by Catherine Porter and Philip Lewis. *Diacritics* 14, no. 2 (Summer 1984): 20–31.

———. *Of Grammatology*. Translated by Gayatri Chakravorty Spivak. Baltimore: Johns Hopkins University Press, 1974.

———. *The Other Heading*. Translated by Pascale-Anne Brault and Michael B. Naas. Bloomington: Indiana University Press, 1992.

———. *Politics of Friendship*. Translated by George Collins. London: Verso, 1997.

———. *Positions*. Translated by Alan Bass. Chicago: University of Chicago Press, 1981.

———. "Psyche: Inventions of the Other." Translated by Catherine Porter. In Lindsay Waters and Wlad Godzich, eds., *Reading de Man Reading*. Minneapolis: University of Minnesota Press, 1989.

———. *Rogues: Two Essays on Reason*. Translated by Pascale-Anne Brault and Michael Naas. Stanford, CA.: Stanford University Press, 2005.

———. *Specters of Marx: The State of the Debt, the Work of Mourning, and the New International*. Translated by Peggy Kamuf. London: Routledge, 1994.

———. "Violence and Metaphysics." In *Writing and Difference*. Translated by Alan Bass. Chicago: University of Chicago Press, 1978.

Dixon, Dougal, and John Adams. *The Future Is Wild*. Richmond Hill, Ontario: Firefly Books, 2002.

Eagleton, Terry. "The Enlightenment is Dead! Long Live the Enlightenment!" *Harper's Magazine*, March 2005, 94.

———. *Literary Theory*. Minneapolis: University of Minnesota Press, 1983.

———. *Walter Benjamin, or Towards a Revolutionary Criticism*. London: Verso, 1981.

Elster, Jon. *Making Sense of Marx*. Cambridge: Cambridge University Press, 1985.

Engels, Frederick. *Ludwig Feuerbach and the End of Classical German Philosophy*. Peking: Foreign Languages Press, 1976.

———. *The Origin of the Family, Private Property, and the State*. Edited by Eleanor Burke Leacock. New York: International Publishers, 1972.

———. *The Peasant War in Germany*. 2nd ed. Translated by Moissaye J. Olgin. New York: International Publishers, 1966.

Everest, Larry. *Oil, Power, and Empire: Iraq and the U.S. Global Agenda*. Monroe, ME: Common Courage Press, 2004.

Eze, Emmanuel Chukwudi. *Achieving Our Humanity: The Idea of the Postracial Future*. New York: Routledge, 2001.

———, ed. *Racism and the Enlightenment: A Reader*. Oxford: Blackwell, 1999.

Fackenheim, Emil L. *Tikkun: Foundations of Post-Holocaust Jewish Thought*. New York: Schocken Books, 1982.

Feigon, Lee. *Mao: A Reinterpretation*. Chicago: Ivan R. Dee, 2002.

Flanders, Robert Bruce. *Nauvoo: Kingdom on the Mississippi*. Urbana: University of Illinois Press, 1975.

Flynn, Thomas R. *Sartre, Foucault, and Historical Reason*. Vol. 1: *Toward an Existentialist Theory of History*. Chicago: University of Chicago Press, 1997.

———. *Sartre, Foucault, and Historical Reason*. Vol. 2: *A Poststructuralist Mapping of History*. Chicago: University of Chicago Press, 2005.

Fox, Michael Allen. *Deep Vegetarianism*. Philadelphia: Temple University Press, 1999.

George, Kathryn Paxton. *Animal, Vegetable, or Woman?* Albany, NY: State University of New York Press, 2000.

Geras, Norman. *Discourses of Extremity: Radical Ethics and Post-Marxist Extravagances*. London: Verso, 1990.

Glover, Jonathan. *Humanity: A Moral History of the Twentieth Century*. New Haven: Yale University Press, 1999.

Gottlieb, Roger. *History and Subjectivity*. Atlantic Highlands, NJ: Humanities Press, 1987.

Grandy, Richard. "Reference, Meaning, and Belief." *Journal of Philosophy* 70, no. 14 (1973): 439–52.

Griffin, David Ray. *Reenchantment without Supernaturalism*. Ithaca, NY: Cornell University Press, 2001.

———. *The Two Great Truths*. Louisville, KY: Westminster John Knox Press, 2004.

Harvey, David. *The Condition of Postmodernity*. Oxford: Blackwell, 1989.

———. *Social Justice and the City*. London: Edward Arnold, 1973.

Hawking, Stephen. *A Brief History of Time*. Toronto: Bantam Books, 1988.

Heidegger, Martin. "Living, Dwelling, Thinking." In David Farrell Krell, ed., *Martin Heidegger: Basic Writings*. New York: Harper and Row, 1977.

Hintikka, Merrill B., and Hintikka, Jaakko. "How Can Language Be Sexist?" In Sandra Harding and Merrill B. Hintikka, eds., *Discovering Reality*. Dordrecht, Holland: D. Reidel, 1983.

Hutnyk, John. *Bad Marxism: Capitalism and Cultural Studies*. London: Pluto Press, 2004.

Irigaray, Luce. *This Sex Which Is Not One*. Translated by Catherine Porter with Carolyn Burke. Ithaca, NY: Cornell University Press, 1985.

Jackson, Wes. *Becoming Native to This Place*. Washington, D.C.: Counterpoint, 1994.

———. *New Roots for Agriculture*. 2nd ed. (1st ed. 1980.) Lincoln: University of Nebraska Press, 1985.

———. "A Search for the Unifying Concept for Sustainable Agriculture." In *Altars of Unhewn Stone: Science and the Earth*, 119–46. San Francisco: North Point Press, 1987.

———. "Toward an Ignorance-Based Worldview." *The Land Report*, no. 81 (Spring 2005): 14–16.

James, William. *The Will to Believe*. New York: Dover, 1956.

Jameson, Fredric. *Archaeologies of the Future*. London: Verso, 2005.

———. *Postmodernism, or, The Cultural Logic of Late Capitalism*. Durham, NC: Duke University Press, 1991.

———. *The Seeds of Time*. New York: Columbia University Press, 1994.

Kant, Immanuel. "The End of All Things." In *Perpetual Peace and Other Essays*, 93–105.

———. *Grounding for the Metaphysics of Morals*. 3rd ed. Translated by James W. Ellington. Indianapolis: Hackett Publishing, 1993.

———. "Idea for a Universal History with a Cosmopolitan Intent." In Kant, *Perpetual Peace and Other Essays*, 29–40.

———. *Lectures on Ethics*. Edited by Peter Heath and J. B. Schneewind. Translated by Peter Heath. Cambridge: Cambridge University Press, 1997.

———. *Perpetual Peace and Other Essays*. Translated by Ted Humphrey. Indianapolis: Hackett Publishing, 1983.

———. *Religion within the Bounds of Reason Alone*. New York: Harper, 1960.

———. "To Perpetual Peace: A Philosophical Sketch." In *Perpetual Peace and Other Essays*, 107–43.

Katznelson, Ira. *Marxism and the City*. Oxford: Oxford University Press, 1992.

Kearney, Richard. *Debates in Continental Philosophy: Conversations with Contemporary Thinkers*. New York: Fordham University Press, 2004.

Kim, Jaegwon. "Philosophy of Mind and Psychology." In *Donald Davidson*, edited by Kirk Ludwig. Cambridge: Cambridge University Press, 2003.

———. *Supervenience and Mind: Selected Philosophical Essays*. Cambridge: Cambridge University Press, 1999.

Kline, David. *Great Possessions: An Amish Farmer's Journal*. San Francisco: North Point Press, 1990.

Krell, David Farrell. *Intimations of Mortality: Time, Truth, and Finitude in Heidegger's Thinking of Being*. University Park: Pennsylvania State University Press, 1986.

———. *The Tragic Absolute: German Idealism and the Languishing of God*. Bloomington: Indiana University Press, 2005.

Kwong, Peter. "The Chinese Face of Neo-Liberalism." *Counterpunch* 13, no. 12 (Jun. 16, 2006): 1–3.

Lenin, V. I. *Imperialism*. In *Lenin Collected Works*, vol. 22. Moscow: Progress Publishers, 1977.

———. *Lenin on War and Peace: Three Articles*. Peking: Foreign Languages Press, 1970.

———. *Materialism and Empirio-Criticism*. Peking; Foreign Languages Press, 1972.

———. "Socialism and War." In *Lenin on War and Peace: Three Articles*. Peking: Foreign Languages Press, 1970.

———. *What Is to Be Done?* New York: International Publishers, 1969.

Levine, Andrew. *A Future for Marxism? Althusser, the Analytic Turn, and the Revival of ocialist Theory*. London: Pluto Press, 2003.

————. *The Politics of Autonomy: A Kantian Reading of Rousseau's Social Contract.* Amherst: University of Massachusetts Press, 1976.

Lévi-Strauss, Claude. *Tristes Tropiques.* Translated by John Weightman and Doreen Weightman. New York: Penguin, 1992.

Linzey, Andrew. *Animal Theology.* Urbana, IL: University of Illinois Press, 1995.

Locke, John. *Second Treatise of Government.* Edited by Richard Cox. Arlington Heights, IL: Harlan Davidson, 1982.

Lotta, Raymond, with Frank Shannon. *America in Decline.* Chicago: Banner Press, 1984.

Lotta, Raymond, ed. *Maoist Economics and the Revolutionary Road to Communism: The Shanghai Textbook.* New York: Banner Press, 1994.

Lukacs, Georg. *History and Class Consciousness.* Translated by Harvey Livingstone. Cambridge: MIT Press, 1972.

Lukes, Steven. *Marxism and Morality.* Oxford: Oxford University Press, 1985.

Lynn, Barry C. "Breaking the Chain: The Antitrust Case against Wal-Mart." *Harper's Magazine,* July 2006, 29–36.

MacLeod, Ken "The Early Days of a Better Nation." Entry for March 23, 2003, http://kenmacleod.blogspot.com/search?q=Avakian%2C+Klonsky.

Mao Tsetung. *Critique of Soviet Economics.* Translated by Moss Roberts. New York: Monthly Review Press, 1977.

————. *Five Essays on Philosophy.* Peking: Foreign Languages Press, 1977.

————. *Talks at the Yenan Forum on Literature and Art.* Peking: Foreign Languages Press, 1967.

————. "The Ten Great Relationships." In *Chairman Mao Talks to the People,* edited by Stuart Schram. New York: Pantheon, 1974.

Marcuse, Herbert. *One-Dimensional Man.* Boston: Beacon Press, 1964.

Marsh, James L. *Process, Praxis, and Transcendence.* Albany, NY: State University of New York Press, 1999.

Martin, Bill. "Ayn Rand and the Music of Rush: Rhapsodic Reflections." *Journal of Ayn Rand Studies* 5, no. 1 (Fall 2003): 189–213.

————. "Ethics and the force of history: three possibilities in Kantian political philosophy." In Martin, *Politics in the impasse.*

————. *Humanism and its aftermath.* Atlantic Highlands, NJ: Humanities Press, 1995

————. *Politics in the impasse: Explorations in postsecular social theory.* Albany: State University of New York Press, 1996.

————. *The Radical Project.* Lanham, MD: Rowman and Littlefield, 2000.

Marx, Karl. "Contribution to the Critique of Hegel's *Philosophy of Right.*" In Tucker, ed., MER, 16–25.

————. "Critique of the Gotha Programme." In Tucker, ed., MER, 525–41.

————. "Economic and Philosophic Manuscripts of 1844." In Tucker, ed., MER, 66–125.

————. *The German Ideology,* pt. 1. In Tucker, ed., MER, 146–200.

————. "Marx on the History of His Opinions." In Tucker, ed., MER, 3–6.

————. "To Make the World Philosophical." In Tucker, ed., MER, 9–11.

Marx, Karl, and Engels, Frederick. *Manifesto of the Communist Party.* In Tucker, ed., MER, 469–500.

Matthews, Richard K. *The Radical Politics of Thomas Jefferson.* Lawrence: University Press of Kansas, 1984.

May, Todd. *The Political Theory of Poststructuralist Anarchism.* University Park: Pennsylvania State University Press, 1994.

Mayer, Arno J. *Why Did the Heavens Not Darken?* London: Verso, 1990.

McGinn, Colin. *Minds and Bodies: Philosophers and Their Ideas.* Oxford: Oxford University Press, 1997.

McWhorter, Ladelle, ed. *Heidegger and the Earth.* Kirksville, MO.: Thomas Jefferson University Press, 1992.

Meikle, Scott. *Essentialism in the Thought of Karl Marx.* La Salle, IL: Open Court, 1985.

Merchant, Paul, ed. *Wendell Berry.* Lewiston, ID: Confluence Press, 1991.

Milbank, John. *Theology and Social Theory: Beyond Secular Reason.* Oxford, UK: Blackwell 1990.

Miller, Mark Crispin. *Boxed In: The Culture of TV.* Evanston, IL: Northwestern University Press, 1988.

Montefiore, Simon Sebag. *Stalin: Court of the Red Tsar.* New York: Alfred A. Knopf, 2004.

Morris, Richard. *The Edges of Science: Crossing the Boundary From Physics to Metaphysics.* New York: Prentice-Hall, 1990.

Murdoch, Iris. *The Sovereignty of Good.* London: Routledge and Kegan Paul, 1970.

Muthu, Sankar. *Enlightenment against Empire.* Princeton, NJ: Princeton University Press, 2003.

Negri, Antonio, and Michael Hardt. *Empire.* Cambridge: Harvard University Press, 2001. Neurath, Otto. *Wissenschaftliche Weltauffassung, Sozialismus und Logischer Empirismus.* Frankfurt: Suhrkamp, 1979.

Newton, Adam Zachary. *Narrative Ethics.* Cambridge, MA: Harvard University Press, 1995.

Nietzsche, Friedrich. "On Truth and Lie in an Extra-Moral Sense." In *The Portable Nietzsche,* edited by Walter Kaufmann. New York: Viking Press, 1968; 42–47.

O'Connor, James. *Natural Causes: Essays in Ecological Marxism.* Boulder, CO: Guilford Press, 1997.

Patterson, Charles. *Eternal Treblinka: Our Treatment of Animals and the Holocaust.* New York: Lantern Books, 2002.

Peffer, R. G. *Marxism, Morality, and Social Justice.* Princeton, NJ: Princeton University Press, 1990.

Perkins, Franklin. *Leibniz and China: A Commerce of Light.* Cambridge: Cambridge University Press, 2005.

Peukert, Helmut. *Science, Action, and Fundamental Theology: Toward a Theology of Communicative Action.* Translated by James Bohman. Cambridge: MIT Press, 1984.

Pickstock, Catherine. *After Writing: On the Liturgical Consummation of Philosophy.* Oxford, UK: Blackwell, 1998.

———. "Capitalism or Secularism? Search for the Culprit." *Telos,* no. 108 (Fall 1996); 165–68.

Pinker, Steven. *The Language Instinct.* New York: Morrow, 1994.

Pomeroy, Anne Fairchild. *Marx and Whitehead: Process, Dialectics, and the Critique of Capitalism*. Albany, NY: State University of New York Press, 2004.

Priestley, J. B. *Essays of Five Decades*. Edited by Susan Cooper. Boston: Little, Brown, and Company, 1949.

Putnam, Hilary. *Ethics without Ontology*. Cambridge, MA: Harvard University Press, 2004.

Quine, W. V. "On What There Is." In *From a Logical Point of View*. 2nd ed., rev. Cambridge, MA: Harvard University Press, 1980.

Rand, Ayn. *Atlas Shrugged*. New York: Random House, 1957.

———. *The Fountainhead*. New York: Scribner Classics, 2000 [1943].

Rawls, John. *Political Liberalism*. New York: Columbia University, 1993.

Regan, Tom. *The Case for Animal Rights*. Berkeley: University of California Press, 1983.

Revolutionary Worker newspaper. "Worlds in Collision: The Storm Over Terry Schiavo and the Raving Demands of the Christian Right." *Revolutionary Worker*, no.1273, April 3, 2005; online at RevCom.org.

Richards, Eric. *The Highland Clearances: People, Landlords and Rural Turmoil*. Edinburgh: Birlinn, 2000.

Rockmore, Tom. "Heidegger and Holocaust Revisionism." In *Martin Heidegger and the Holocaust*. Edited by Alan Milchman and Alan Rosenberg. Atlantic Highlands, NJ: Humanities Press, 1996; 113–26.

Roemer, John. *Free to Lose*. Cambridge: Harvard University Press, 1988.

Rorty, Richard. *Achieving Our Country: Leftist Thought in Twentieth-Century America*. Cambridge, MA: Harvard University Press, 1998.

———. *Contingency, Irony, and Solidarity*. Cambridge: Cambridge University Press, 1989.

Rousseau, Jean-Jacques. *Discourse on the Origin of Inequality*. Translated by Donald A. Cress. Indianapolis: Hackett, 1992.

Sale, Kirkpatrick. *Dwellers in the Land*. Athens: University of Georgia Press, 2000.

Sanders, Jonathan. "The Russian Scene: a biographical note." In Shanin, ed., *Late Marx and the Russian Road*, 172–78.

Santoni, Ronald E. *Sartre on Violence: Curiously Ambivalent*. University Park: Pennsylvania State University Press, 2003.

Sartre, Jean-Paul. *Colonialism and Neocolonialism*. Translated by Azzedine Haddour, Steve Brewer, and Terry McWilliams. London: Routledge, 2001.

———. *Critique of Dialectical Reason*. Vol. 1: *Theory of Practical Ensembles*. Translated by Alan Sheridan-Smith. London: Verso, 1976.

———. *Critique of Dialectical Reason*. Vol. 2: *The Intelligibility of History*. Edited by Arlette Elkaim-Sartre. Translated by Quintin Hoare. London: Verso, 1991.

———. "Existentialism Is a Humanism." In Walter Kaufman, ed., *Existentialism from Dostoevsky to Sartre*. New York: Meridian, 1975.

———. *Life/Situations*. Translated by Paul Auster and Lydia Davis. New York: Pantheon, 1977.

———. "Materialism and Revolution." In *Literary and Philosophical Essays*, edited and translated by Annette Michelson. New York: Criterion Books, 1955.

———. *Notebooks for an Ethics.* Translated by David Pellauer. Chicago: University of Chicago Press, 1992.

———. Preface to *The Wretched of the Earth* by Frantz Fanon. Translated by Richard Philcox. New York: Grove Press, 2005.

———. *Search for a Method.* 1960. Translated by Hazel E. Barnes. New York: Vintage, 1968.

Sawyer, Robert. *Calculating God.* New York: Tor, 2001.

Schlick, Moritz. "The Turning Point in Philosophy." Translated by David Rynin. In A. J. Ayer, ed., *Logical Positivism.* New York: Free Press, 1959.

Schlosser, Eric. *Fast Food Nation.* New York: Harper, 2005.

Shanin, Teodor, ed. *Late Marx and the Russian Road: Marx and "The Peripheries of Capitalism."* New York: Monthly Review Press, 1983.

Shibata, Yoko. "The Art of a Failed Economy." *J@pan Inc. Magazine,* Dec. 1999.

Singer, Peter. *Animal Liberation.* 2nd ed., rev. New York: Avon, 1990.

———. "Down on the Family Farm." In James P. Sterba, ed., *Earth Ethics.* New York: Macmillan, 1994.

Snow, Edgar. *Red Star Over China.* New York: Bantam Books, 1978.

Snow, Lois Wheeler. *China On Stage: An American Actress in the People's Republic.* New York: Vintage Books, 1973.

Solway, David. *Chess Pieces.* Montreal: McGill-Queen's University Press, 1999.

Sorabji, Richard. *Animal Minds and Human Morals: The Origins of the Western Debate.* Ithaca, NY: Cornell University Press, 1993.

Stalin, Joseph. *Dialectical and Historical Materialism.* New York: International Publishers, 1975.

———. *Marxism and Problems of Linguistics.* Peking: Foreign Languages Press, 1972.

Steeves, H. Peter, ed. *Animal Others: On Ethics, Ontology, and Animal Life.* Albany, NY: SUNY Press, 1999.

Taylor, Mark C. *Confidence Games: Money and Markets in a World without Redemption.* Chicago: University of Chicago Press, 2004.

Tietz, Jeff. "The Killing Factory." *Rolling Stone,* Apr. 20, 2006, 54–60, 76.

Tucker, Robert, ed. *Marx-Engels Reader.* [MER] 2nd ed. New York: Norton, 1978.

Vallette, Jim. "The Lawrence Summers World Bank Memo." *The Jackson Progressive,* May 13, 1999; online at http://www.jacksonprogressive.com/issues/summersmemo.html.

Van der Linden, Harry. *Kantian Ethics and Socialism.* Indianapolis: Hackett Publishing, 1988.

Volkogonov, Dmitri. *Stalin: Triumph and Tragedy.* Edited and translated by Harold Shukman. New York: Grove Press, 1991.

Wallis, Claudia, et. al. "Evolution Wars." *Time* [magazine], Aug. 15, 2005.

Wallis, Jim. *God's Politics: Why the Right Gets It Wrong and the Left Doesn't Get It.* San Francisco: HarperSanFrancisco, 2005.

———. *The Soul of Politics: Beyond "Religious Right" and "Secular Left."* San Diego: Harvest Books, 1995.

Wang, Zheng. "We Had a Dream That the World Can Be Better Than Today." *Revolution* [newspaper], no. 59, Sept. 3, 2006; online at revcom.us.

Ward, Graham. *Cities of God*. London: Routledge, 2000.

Weismann, Judith. "An Open Letter." In *Wendell Berry*, edited by Paul Merchant. Lewiston, ID: Confluence Press, 1991; 53–58.

West, Cornell. *The Ethical Dimensions of Marxist Thought*. New York: Monthly Review Press, 1991.

Winn, Kenneth H. *Exiles in a Land of Liberty: Mormons in America, 1830–1846*. Chapel Hill: University of North Carolina Press, 1989.

Wolff, Lenny. *The Science of Revolution: An Introduction*. Chicago: RCP Publications, 1983.

Wolff, Robert Paul. *Moneybags Must Be So Lucky: On the Literary Structure of Capital*. Amherst: University of Massachusetts Press, 1988.

Wood, Allen. *Kant*. Oxford: Blackwell, 2005.

Wood, David. "*Comment ne pas manger*: Deconstruction and humanism." In *Animal Others: On Ethics, Ontology, and Animal Life*, edited by H. Peter Steeves. Albany, NY: SUNY Press, 1999.

Worster, Donald. *Nature's Economy: A History of Ecological Ideas*. 2nd ed. Cambridge: Cambridge University Press, 1994.

———. *Rivers of Empire: Water, Aridity, and the Growth of the American West*. New York: Pantheon, 1985.

Wright, Evan. *Generation Kill*. New York: Penguin, 2005.

Young, Iris Marion. *Justice and the Politics of Difference*. Princeton, NJ: Princeton University Press, 1990.

Young, Richard A. *Is God a Vegetarian? Christianity, Vegetarianism, and Animal Rights*. Chicago: Open Court, 1998.

Zerzan, John. *Against Civilization*. Los Angeles: Feral House, 2005.

———. *Running on Emptiness: The Pathology of Civilization*. Los Angeles: Feral House, 2002.

Zhong, Xueping, Wang Zheng, and Bai Di, eds. *Some of Us: Chinese Women Growing Up in the Mao Era*. New Brunswick, NJ: Rutgers University Press, 2001.

Zimmerman, Michael E. *Heidegger's Confrontation with Modernity: Technology, Politics, Art*. Bloomington: Indiana University Press, 1990.

Zinn, Howard. *A People's History of the United States*. New York: Harper and Row, 1980.

Žižek, Slavoj. *Did Somebody Say Totalitarianism?* London: Verso, 2002.

———. "From Western Marxism to Western Buddhism." *Cabinet Magazine Online*, no. 2, (Spring 2001); http://www.cabinetmagazine.org/issues/2/ western.php.

———. *The Indivisible Remainder*. London: Verso, 1996.

———. *On Belief*. London: Routledge, 2001.

———. *The Sublime Object of Ideology*. London: Verso, 1989.

Index